# Economic Freedom of the World

# 2000 Annual Report

James Gwartney & Robert Lawson
*Florida State University* *Capital University*

with Dexter Samida
*The Fraser Institute*

Cover designed by Brian Creswick @ GoggleBox

Printed in Canada
ISBN 088975-202-8

**Canadian Cataloguing in Publication Data**

Gwartney, James D.
Economic Freedom of the World: 2000 Annual Report

ISSN 1482-471X

1. Economic history--1990- --Periodicals. 2. Economic indicators--Periodicals.
I. Fraser Institute (Vancouver, B.C.) II. Title

HB95.G93 330.9'005 C97-302072-5

# Table of Contents

# Acknowledgments

Given the nature and history of this project, we owe an enormous debt to many people. Without the assistance and guidance of both Mike Walker and Milton Friedman, this project would never have gotten off the ground. Mike organized the Fraser Institute/Liberty Fund conference series that provided the foundation for our measure of economic freedom. He also edited several of the conference volumes and provided both input and encouragement throughout. Milton Friedman's criticisms and suggested modifications shaped the research design of the project.

The institutes of the Economic Freedom Network provided invaluable support for this report. They helped verify information and supplied us with missing data. We look forward to a continuing working relationship with them.

We would also like to express our appreciation to the DeVoe L. Moore Center of Florida State University for providing the research and computer support that made the project feasible. Kathy Makinen and Harold White assisted with data gathering and calculations. Dexter Samida, Research Economist at The Fraser Institute did an excellent job of coordinating the design and publication of the book. Robert Copeland and Liwen Zhang assisted by checking data in the country tables. Peter Kloepping assisted by checking data and by performing a number of other tasks helpful to the completion of this volume. Thanks to Phaedra Kaptein-Russell for helping with the bibliography of articles that have used *Economic Freedom of the World.*

James Gwartney

Robert Lawson

# About the Authors

**James Gwartney** is a Professor of Economics at the DeVoe L. Moore Center, Florida State University. He is currently serving a two-year term as Chief Economist with the Joint Economic Committee (JEC) of the United States Congress. He has a doctoral degree in economics from the University of Washington. Along with Richard Stroup and Russell Sobel, he is the author of *Economics: Private and Public Choice* (Harcourt Brace). This text, now in its ninth edition, has been used by more than 1 million students during the last two decades. A member of the Mont Pelerin Society, Professor Gwartney taught at the Central European University in Prague, Czech Republic during 1993/1994. He has published in the leading journals of professional economics, including the *American Economic Review, Journal of Political Economy, Industrial and Labor Relations Review, Cato Journal,* and *Southern Economic Journal.*

Professor Gwartney has been involved in this project since the early 1990s. Most of his work on this publication was prior to his appointment to the JEC. The views expressed in this publication represent those of the authors. They do not necessarily represent those of the JEC, its Chairman, Vice-Chairman, or any member of the Committee.

**Robert Lawson** is an Associate Professor of Economics at Capital University in Columbus, Ohio; he taught previously at Shawnee State University. He earned his B.S. from the Honors Tutorial College at Ohio University in 1988 and his M.S. (1991) and Ph.D. (1992) from Florida State University. He has published articles in several journals, including *Public Choice*, the *Journal of Labor Research*, and the *Journal of Public Finance and Public Choice.* Professor Lawson has written extensively on public policy issues such as welfare reform, Medicaid, tax policy, and prevailing wage regulations. He also serves as the Director of Fiscal Policy Studies for the Buckeye Institute for Public Policy Solutions in Dayton, Ohio.

**Dexter Samida** is a Research Economist at The Fraser Institute. He majored in economics at the University of Saskatchewan, from which he received his B.Comm. (high honours) with Great Distinction in 1997. He obtained his M.A. in Economics from the University of Toronto in 1998. In the summer of 1997, he worked as an intern at The Fraser Institute, where he did research on taxation in Canada. He recently published *A Hand Out Instead of a Hand Up: Where Foreign Aid Fails* (Public Policy Sources 30, The Fraser Institute) and was co-author of *Provincial Economic Freedom in Canada 1981–1998* (Fraser Institute Critical Issues Bulletin). He has written articles on economic freedom and poverty, provincial economic freedom, foreign aid, international trade, and consumerism. Some of his work has appeared in national newspapers such as the *National Post*, as well as in regional papers, such as the *Vancouver Province.* Mr Samida is a native of rural Saskatchewan.

# About the Participating Institutes

## Co-publishers of *Economic Freedom of the World*

**ACER, Albania**
The Albanian Center for Economic Research is a public-policy institute that focuses on research and advocacy activities. In addition to providing policy makers and academics with applied economic research, it works to build public understanding of economic development issues. (E-mail: zefi@qske.tirana.al)

**African Research Center for Public Policy and Market Process, Kenya**
The African Research Center for Public Policy and Market Process, Kenya, is the first research centre founded in Africa by the African Educational Foundation for Public Policy and Market Process, an independent educational organization registered in the United States. The primary mission of the Center and the Foundation is to promote ideas about free markets and voluntary associations in Africa. The Center seeks to conduct research on all aspects of free markets, voluntary association, and individual liberty, and to disseminate the results to as wide an audience as possible. The Center also organizes seminars and conferences to examine issues related to liberty and enterprise in Africa. (E-mail: kimenyi@kippra.or.ke)

**Association for Liberal Thinking, Turkey**
The Association for Liberal Thinking is a non-profit, non-governmental organization seeking to introduce the liberal democratic tradition to the Turkish public. It engages in activities that promote the understanding and acceptance of ideas like liberty, justice, peace, human rights, equality, and tolerance. It encourages development of academic writing on liberal themes that will improve the ability of the Turkish people to assess contemporary domestic and international changes and attempts to find effective solutions to Turkey's problems within liberal thought. The Association for Liberal Thinking is not involved in day-to-day politics and has no direct links to any political party or movement. Instead, as an independent intellectual group, it aims to set and influence broader political agendas so as to contribute to the liberalization of Turkey in economics and politics. (E-mail: liberal@ada.net.tr)

**Association pour la Liberté Economique et le Progrès Social (ALEPS), France**
The objective of ALEPS is to promote the idea of free markets generating social progress. It connects French liberal intellectuals with the world scientific community. Thanks to its permanent contacts with various prestigious foreign institutes, in 1990 ALEPS published "Manifeste de l'Europe pour les Européens," signed by 600 faculties from 28 countries.

The economic collapse of central planning and the disappearance of totalitarian regimes in Eastern Europe has not solved all social problems. The post-socialist society remains to be set up. This requirement in Eastern Europe is also needed in Western countries, such as France, where 40 years of the welfare state have led to mass unemployment, fiscal oppression, a social security explosion, an increase in poverty and inequality, and a loss of moral virtues and spiritual values. ALEPS provides the political and intellectual push for this necessary revival.

**Cato Institute, United States of America**
Founded in 1977, the Cato Institute is a public policy research foundation dedicated to broadening the parameters of policy debate to allow consideration of more options consistent with the traditional American principles of limited government, individual liberty, free markets, and peace. To that end, the Institute strives to achieve greater involvement by the intelligent, concerned lay public in questions of policy and the proper role of government through an extensive program of publications and seminars. (E-mail: ivasquez@cato.org)

**Center for the Dissemination of Economic Knowledge (CEDICE), Venezuela**
CEDICE is a non-partisan, non-profit, private association dedicated to the dissemination, research, and promotion of philosophical, economic, political, and social thinking that focuses on individual initiative and activities conducive to a better understanding of the free market system and free and responsible societies. CEDICE carries out a variety of activities and programs to meet its objectives, including operating a library and bookstore, researching and writing the *Venezuela Today* series and other studies, conducting economic training for journalists, and offering special events and community programs. (E-mail: hfaria@newton.iesa.edu.ve)

**Center for the New Europe, Belgium**
The Center for the New Europe is a European research institute based in Brussels. It aims to promote the advancement of a market-oriented economy, personal liberty, and creativity and responsibility in an ordered society. CNE is founded on the belief that European integration can work only in a society led by a spirit of democratic capitalism. The Center focuses on developing policy alternatives; encouraging economic growth and deregulation; seeking new market-based solutions for social and environmental concerns; and promoting individual freedom, choice and responsibility.

**Center for Policy Research, Sri Lanka**
The Center for Policy Research (CPR) is a non-partisan advocacy and policy research institute dedicated to fostering democracy and promoting free enterprise. As part of its philosophy, CPR actively takes positions on critical policy reform issues and aggressively lobbies key decision-makers in the country. (E-mail: mmoragoda@eureka.lk)

**The Center for Research and Communication, Philippines**
The Center for Research and Communication (CRC), which started operations in 1967, conducts research and publishes works on domestic and international economic and political issues, focusing on the Asia-Pacific region. It provides fora for discussion and debate among academicians, businessmen, civil officials, and representatives of other sectors that help shape public opinion and chart the course of policies. CRC, which is the main research arm of the University of Asia and the Pacific in Metro Manila, Philippines, also currently serves as the Secretariat of the Asia Pacific Economic Cooperation (APEC) Business Advisory Council. (E-mail: hbasilio@info.com.ph)

**Centre for Civil Society, India**
The Centre for Civil Society is an independent, non-profit, research and educational organization devoted to improving the quality of life for all citizens of India by reviving and re-invigorating civil society. The focus on civil society enables one to work from both directions; it provides a “mortar” program of building or rebuilding the institutions of civil society and a “hammer” program of readjusting the size and scope of the political society. Both programs are equally critical and must be pursued simultaneously. Weeds of the political society must be uprooted and seeds of a civil society must be sown. The Centre was inaugurated on August 15, 1997, signifying the necessity of achieving economic, social, and cultural independence from the Indian state after attaining political independence from an alien state.

The Centre conducts Monthly Dialogues on topical issues to introduce classical liberal philosophy and market-based solutions into public debate. It has published *Agenda for Change*, a volume in 17 chapters that outlines policy reforms for the Indian government, Israel Kirzner's *How Markets Work*, and *Self-Regulation in the Civil Society*, edited by Ashok Desai. It organizes Liberty and Society seminars for college students and journalists. (Email: parth@ccsindia.org; website: www.siliconindia.com/civil)

**Centro de Investigacion y Estudios Legales (CITEL), Peru**
CITEL was organized in 1989. Its principal field is the economic analysis of law. To that end, it conducts research on different legal institutions, publishes books, and organizes seminars and colloquia. (E-mail: eghersi@computextos.com.pe)

**Centro de Investigaciones Académicas (CIVILIZAR), Colombia**
The Centro de Investigaciones Académicas is a private, non-profit economic and social research organization. Established in 1996, the Centro is affiliated with the Sergio Arboleda University of Bogata. It is dedicated to the scientific study of economic and social topics. It defends individual liberty, which it recognizes as a basic principle to guide programs of research and education. The Centro supports research and publishes studies on economic, social, and legal issues in order to promote Colombian economic growth and human development. (E-mail: usa5008@latino.net.co)

**Centro de Investigaciones Económicas Nacionales, Guatemala**
CIEN, the Center for Research on the National Economy, was established in Guatemala in 1982. It is a private, non-partisan, not-for-profit public policy institute, funded by the sale of its books and periodical publications, income from conferences and seminars, and the support it receives from its members and the public. The Center's program is devoted to the technical study of economic and social problems that need to be resolved to promote the stable development of the nation. Its members, staff, research associates and supporters share the principles of a social order of free and responsible individuals interacting through a market economy functioning within the rule of law. (E-mail: curizarh@cien.org.gt)

**Centro de Investigaciones sobre la Libre Empresa, A.C., Mexico**
The Centro de Investigaciones Sobre la Libre Empresa (CISLE) is a non-profit, educational and public policy organization founded in 1984. Its aim is to defend and promote the ideals of free trade and free enterprise in all areas of society, and it maintains that the fundamental source of well-being and the wealth of nations is a sound institutional order that guarantees competition, private ownership, and open markets. CISLE's activities are financed by a select group of generous donors. (E-mail: Ceninves@mail.infolatina.com.mx)

**Centrum im. Adama Smitha, Poland**
The Centrum im. Adama Smitha, Poland (the Adam Smith Research Centre) is a private, non-partisan, non-profit public-policy institute. It was founded in 1989 and was the first such institute in Poland and in Eastern Europe The ASRC is devoted to the furtherance of a free and fair market economy, participatory democracy, and virtuous society. Its activities in research and development, education, and publishing cover almost all important issues within the areas of economy and social life. The ASRC acts as a guardian of economic freedom in Poland. More than 50 experts are associated with the ASCR. (E-mail: adam.smith@adam-smith.pl; website: http://www.adam-smith.pl)

**The Edmund Burke Institute, Ireland**
The Edmund Burke Institute is a non-profit and non-political organization that believes that Ireland's political, academic, and cultural leaders have failed to draw the natural conclusions from the collapse of state

socialism and the growth of free-market ideas across the industrialized and developing world. It believes that these ideas are directly relevant to Ireland, and that hostility towards free markets and individual freedom needs to be challenged by an institution that promotes debate and discussion about the role of the state in our lives. (E-mail: Paul.MacDonnell@msc.ie; internet: www.his.com/~chyden/ebi)

**The Estonian Institute for Open Society Research**
The Estonian Institute for Open Society Research was established in 1993 as an independent non-profit public policy research institute. EIOSR's research and public communication programs focus on the key issues of Estonian social and political development: building a free-market economy and open civil society; enhancing social stability and integration of minority groups; and promoting Estonia's integration into European and world structures. EIOSR's first effort was the Estonian translation of Milton Friedman's book, *Capitalism and Freedom*, in early 1994. Current EIOSR projects include promoting the idea of philanthropy to local businesses and elaborating future scenarios concerning the integration of the Russian minority into Estonian society. (E-mail: volli@lin2.tpu.ee)

**The F.A. Hayek Foundation, Slovak Republic**
The F.A. Hayek Foundation is an independent, non-profit organization that brings together social scientists, business people, and policy makers to exchange their ideas on economic, social, political, and other issues. It provides practical reform proposals for the transition of economics, health, education, social welfare, retirement and legislative systems. The F.A. Hayek Foundation established a tradition that was virtually absent in Slovakia until 1989–the tradition of liberal thinking and its further cultivation in order to demonstrate market-economy solutions as alternatives to collectivist policies. The Foundation promotes the following liberal ideals: limited government, a free-market economy, and an open society based on the concept of individual choice and personal responsibility. (E-mail: oravec@cenezu.sk)

**The Fraser Institute, Canada**
The Fraser Institute is an independent Canadian economic and social research and educational organization. It has as its objective the redirection of public attention to the role of competitive markets in providing for the well-being of Canadians. Where markets work, the Institute's interest lies in trying to discover prospects for improvement. Where markets do not work, its interest lies in finding the reasons. Where competitive markets have been replaced by government control, the interest of the Institute lies in documenting objectively the nature of the improvement or deterioration resulting from government intervention. The work of the Institute is assisted by an Editorial Advisory Board of internationally renowned economists. The Fraser Institute is a national, federally chartered, non-profit organization financed by the sale of its publications and the tax-deductible contributions of its members. (Email: info@fraserinstitute.ca; website: www.fraserinstitute.ca)

**The Free Enterprise Commission, Panama**
The Free Enterprise Commission is a working group within the Panamanian Association of Executives (APEDE). APEDE is a non-partisan, non-profit association dedicated to the improvement of entrepreneurship, management, and the development of the individual in a free society. As such, APEDE invests a good part of its efforts in education and individual liberties. (E-mail: diabolo@pty.com)

**The Free Market Foundation of Southern Africa**
The Free Market Foundation of Southern Africa was established in 1975 to promote economic freedom. The FMF sponsors and conducts research, conferences, lectures, training programs and lobbying efforts in support of the free market. Its funding comes from membership subscriptions, project sponsorships, and income from sales and fees. (E-mail: fmf@jhb.lia.net)

**Fundación Economía y Desarrollo, Inc., Dominican Republic**
The Fundación Economía y Desarrollo, Inc. (FEyD) is a private non-profit organization dedicated to fostering the principles of competitive markets, private enterprise, strategies that promote economic development. To meet its objectives, FEyD has several regular publications in the most important newspapers in the country. It also produces a weekly television program called "Triálogo," a one-hour program that is broadcast three times a week, and elaborates numerous studies related to the performance of the Dominican economy and its sectors. (E-mail: feyd03@tricom.net)

**Fundacion Libertad, Democracia y Desarrollo, Bolivia**
The Fundacion Libertad, Democracia y Desarrollo (FULIDED), is a non-profit organization founded by a group of citizens interested in promoting democracy and freedom. The Foundation has the purpose of investigating, analyzing, and disseminating issues of national priority, keeping in mind that economic, political, and social topics are of great importance in strengthening the free market and private initiative, within the ideal of an open, pluralist, and honest society. Through seminars, debates, and publications, FULIDED seeks to create a climate of opinion reflecting Bolivia's participation in the global economy. (E-mail: fulided@cainco.org.bo)

**Gruppo Giovani Imprenditori and Centro Luigi Einaudi, Italy**
The Gruppo Giovani Imprenditori dell'Unione Industriale di Torino was founded in 1959. It is composed of 300 entrepreneurs and managers under the age of 40. A member of the Confederation of Italian Industry, it has always been on the forefront of the liberalization of the Italian economy.

Established in 1963, the Centro di Ricerca e Documentazione "Luigi Einaudi" is one of Italy's most influential independent think tanks. Its aim is to further free-market policies and personal freedom, to promote leaner government, and to enhance political pluralism. (E-mail: grusso@iol.it)

**Hong Kong Centre for Economic Research**
The Hong Kong Centre for Economic Research is an educational, charitable trust established in 1987 to promote public understanding of economic affairs and to develop alternative policy choices for government with the aim to promote the free market in Hong Kong. The Centre publishes and promotes authoritative research studies to achieve its goals. It is widely recognized as the leading free-market think-tank in Asia and has been influential in persuading public opinion and the government to liberalize telecommunications, open up air-cargo handling franchises, privatize public housing, adopt a fully funded provident scheme instead of a pay-as-you-go pension scheme, remove legally sanctioned, deposit interest-rate fixing among banks, adopt market mechanisms for protecting the environment, and other public-policy measures in Hong Kong. (E-mail: asiu@econ.hku.hk)

**Institute for Advanced Strategic and Political Studies, Israel**
The mission of the Institute for Advanced Strategic and Political Studies is the development of policies in economics, strategic studies, and politics, directed toward the understanding and realization of limited government in domestic affairs and the balance of power in strategic planning. The Institute's Division for Economic Policy Research (DEPR) produces *Policy Studies* in both English and Hebrew, while the Division for Research in Strategy and Politics produces one series of documents in strategic studies, and another series in politics. (E-mail: iaspsdc@aol.com)

**The Institute for Economic Freedom, Bahamas**
The Institute for Economic Freedom is an independent non-political, non-profit Bahamian institute that promotes economic growth, employment and entrepreneurial activity. It believes that this can best be achieved with a free market economy and a decent society–one that embraces the rule of law, the right

of private property, the free exchange of property and services, and the individual virtues of self-control, commitment, and good will. (E-mail: joanmt@bahamas.net.bs)

**Institute for Economy and Politics (IWIP), Austria**
IWIP is an affiliate institute of the Federation of Austrian Industry. Its duty is to give objective information to the general public about the economy, politics, and culture. It supports a social free market economy and protection of the environment. IWIP organizes meetings, workshops, symposiums, and lectures, and is editor of *Conturen*, a quarterly magazine aimed at the liberal and critical reader who is interested in diverse discussions about the economy, politics, and culture. (E-mail: e.bendl@iv-net.at)

**Institute for Market Economics, Bulgaria**
Established in 1993, IME is the first independent economic think tank in Bulgaria. It is a private, registered, non-profit corporation with a mission to elaborate and advocate market approaches to the problems Bulgaria is facing in its transition to a market economy, thus supporting market reforms. IME's objectives are to provide the following: independent assessment and analysis of the government's economic policies; a focal point for an exchange of views on market economics and relevant policy issues; and an internationally supported Bulgarian think-tank that is widely respected for its expertise. (E-mail: svetla@ime.bg)

**The Institute of Economic Affairs, England**
The IEA's mission is to improve public understanding of the foundations of a free and harmonious society by expounding and analyzing the role of markets in solving economic and social problems, and bringing the results of that work to the attention of those who influence thinking. The IEA achieves its mission by a high quality publishing program; conferences, seminars and lectures on a range of subjects; outreach to school and college students; brokering media introductions and appearances; and other related activities. Incorporated in 1955 by the late Sir Antony Fisher, the IEA is an educational charity, limited by guarantee. It is independent of any political party or group, and is financed by sales of publications, conference fees, and voluntary donations. (E-mail: editor@iea.org.uk)

**The Institute of Economic Affairs, Ghana**
The Institute of Economic Affairs (IEA) Ghana is an independent, non-governmental institution dedicated to the establishment and strengthening of a market economy and a democratic, free, and open society. The IEA was founded in October 1989. It considers improvements in the legal, social, and political institutions as necessary conditions for sustained economic growth and human development. The IEA supports research, and promotes and publishes studies on important economic socio-political and legal issues in order to enhance understanding of public policy. (E-mail: iea@ghana.com)

**Institute of Economic Analysis, Russia**
The Institute of Economic Analysis is a macroeconomic research institute designed to: analyze the current economic situation and policies; provide expert analysis of acts, programs, and current economic policy; consult Russian government bodies, enterprises, and organizations; prepare and publish scientific, research and methodological economic literature; and conduct seminars, conferences, and symposia on economic topics. The Institute is an independent, non-governmental, non-political, non-profit research centre that works closely with leading Russian and international research centres. Its research focuses on macroeconomic, budget, and social policy. (E-mail: ieamos@glasnet.ru)

**Institute of Economic Studies, Iceland**
The Institute of Economic Studies was founded in 1989. It operates within the Department of Economics in the Faculty of Economics and Business Administration at the University of Iceland. From the outset, the Institute has been active in carrying out applied research projects commissioned by a great

variety of private and public clients ranging from small Icelandic interest groups to the Nordic Investment Bank to the governments of Iceland, Denmark, and the Faroe Islands. More recently, funded by research grants, the Institute has put greater emphasis on large-scale applied research projects with substantial analytical content and economic research. (E-mail: tthh@rhi.hi.is)

**The Institute of Economics, Croatia**
The Institute of Economics, Zagreb, established in 1939, is a major scientific and research institution devoted to the study of economic processes and the application of contemporary achievements in economics. The Institute's objective is the economic and social advance of Croatia. Research encompasses both macro-economics and micro-economics, policy issues, including more specialized areas such as business economics; current economic trends, and policies; methods of economic analysis, development of human resources; spatial and regional economics, international economics and technological development, and investment project planning. The Institute engages researchers from both inside and outside the Institute, who work together on research projects. The Institute employs 40 full-time researchers, the majority of whom have completed specialized training courses in foreign countries. Results of the Institute's research activities are published in a considerable number of books, separate reports and studies, and in scientific journals. Close ties are maintained with various specialized international organizations and professional associations and with a number of institutes and universities. (E-mail: zbaletic@eizg.hr)

**Institute of Macroeconomic Analysis and Development, Slovenia**
The Institute of Macroeconomic Analysis and Development (IMAD) is a part of the Ministry of Economic Relations and Development. It plays the key analytical role in preparation of annual memoranda on economic policy and it coordinated the preparation of the Strategy of Economic Development of Slovenia and its Strategy for Accession to the European Union. Its activities also include current analyses of macroeconomic trends and of social, regional, and institutional development; simulations and evaluations of economic and developmental measures; development of methodological tools and information systems. In order to fulfill its tasks, the Institute has around 50 employees, two-thirds of whom are specialists. Its publications, *Slovenian Economic Mirror* and its Spring and Autumn Reports are translated into English and distributed to a large international audience. IMAD also publishes the international *Journal for Institutional Innovation, Development, and Transition* (IB Review) and organizes an annual conference on the general topic of Institutions in Transition. (E-mail: rotija.kmet@gov.si)

**Institute of Public Affairs, Australia**
Established in 1943, the IPA is Australia's oldest and largest private-sector think-tank. Its aim is to advance the interests of the Australian people. Those interests include prosperity and full employment, the rule of law, democratic freedoms, security from crime and invasion, high standards in education and family life. To identify and promote the best means of securing these values, the IPA undertakes research, organizes seminars, and publishes widely. (E-mail: ipa@ipa.org.au)

**Instituto Ecuatoriano de Economia Politica, Ecuador**
The Instituto Ecuatoriano de Economia Politica (IEEP) is a private, independent, non-profit institution. Its mission is to defend and promote the classical liberal ideals of individual liberty, free markets, limited government, property rights, and the rule of law. The IEEP achieves its mission through publications, seminars, and workshops that debate socio-economic and political issues. The IEEP's funding comes from voluntary donations, membership subscriptions, and income from sales of its publications. (E-mail: dampuero@ecua.net.ec)

**Instituto Liberal do Rio de Janiero, Brazil**
Instituto Liberal is a non-profit institution supported by donations and the sponsorship of private individuals and corporations. Its by-laws provide for a Board of Trustees as its supreme body, and forbid

any political or sectarian affiliations. Its principal objective is to *persuade Brazilian society of the advantages of a liberal order.* To attain this goal the institute publishes books, organizes seminars, and elaborates policy papers on subjects related to public policy. (E-mail: ilrj@gbl.com.br)

**Instituto Libertad y Desarrollo, Chile**
Libertad y Desarrollo is a private think-tank committed to free market ideas and devoted to research, study, and analysis of public policy issues inspired by political and economic freedom. Libertad y Desarrollo is wholly independent of any religious, political, financial, or governmental groups. (E-mail: ega@chilesat.net)

**Instituto para la Libertad y el Analisis de Politicas, Costa Rica**
The Institute for Liberty Public Policy Analysis (INLAP) is a non-profit, non-partisan organization, created to defend and promote all aspects of individual liberty through public-policy analysis and educational activities. Its specific objectives are (1) to increase awareness of the moral foundations of liberty and to promote liberty as an individual right without which it is impossible to achieve the highest levels of economic and human development and (2) to foster changes in social organization and public policies by influencing the thinking of policy makers, community leaders and citizens at large.

INLAP produces timely analyses of proposed laws, decrees, and regulations, and its specific recommendations provide insight and guidance for elected officials who seek to achieve the goals of greater individual liberty and creativity and a more productive economy. Detailed studies of public policies that have adverse moral or economic effects are published as study materials for academics and others interested in learning the effects of well-meaning but harmful public policies. These studies and recommendations are published in books and technical journals, as position papers and bulletins, as articles in newspapers and magazines, and via the Internet. (E-mail: riggo@attglobal.net)

**The Korea Center for Free Enterprise**
The Center for Free Enterprise (CFE) is a foundation committed to advancing guiding principles such as free enterprise, limited government, freedom and individual responsibilities, the rule of law and restraint of violence. The CFE was inaugurated as a non-profit, independent foundation funded by the members of the Federation of Korean Industries (FKI) on April 1, 1997, when woes over an economic crisis began seriously to plague Korean society. The CFE has concentrated its efforts on championing the principles of a free economy through books and reports on related ideas, philosophies, public policies, statistics and analyses. By holding occasional workshops and policy forums, the CFE has striven to put forward policy alternatives to proposed solutions for pending issues facing the Korean society. (E-mail: yooys@cfe.org)

**Liberales Institut, Germany**
The Liberales Institut (Liberty Institute) is the think-tank of the Friedrich-Naumann-Foundation. Based in Berlin and Königswinter, the Institute devotes itself to spreading classical liberal and free-market ideas through the publication of classical liberal literature, the analysis of current political trends, and the promotion of research. By organizing conferences and workshops, the Institute tries to stimulate an intellectual exchange among liberals around the world. (E-mail: LibInst@aol.com)

**Liberales Institut, Switzerland**
The Liberales Institut provides a platform where the basic values and concepts of a free society can be discussed and questioned. The Institute's aim is the establishment of free markets, not simply for the sake of having free markets but because they are the best way towards our real goals: openness, diversity, and autonomy. The Liberales Institut is not associated with any political party. Through publications, discussion fora, and seminars, the Institute seeks to foster the development and dissemination of classical liberal ideas. (E-mail: libinst@bluewin.ch)

**Liberální Institut, Czech Republic**

The Liberal Institute is an independent, non-profit organization for the development and application of liberal ideas and programs based on the principles of classical liberalism. The Liberal Institute's activities are based on the recognition of the following: each individual has inalienable rights, and the individual's life is valuable; the principle of voluntary action applies in all human activity; the institutions of private property, contract, and the rule of law are essential in the protection of human rights; self-regulating markets, free trade, and a clearly defined government sphere are crucial factors for the development of any society. The Liberal Institute is financed by funds realized from its various activities and by donations from individuals and private corporations. (E-mail: michal.uryc@libinst.cz)

**Lithuanian Free Market Institute, Lithuania**

The Lithuanian Free Market Institute (LFMI) is an independent, non-profit, organization founded in 1990 to promote the ideas of economic liberalism based on the principles of individual freedom and responsibility, free markets, and limited government. The LFMI's staff pursues this mission by exploring key issues of economic policy, developing conceptual reform packages, drafting and evaluating legislation, and submitting policy recommendations at the legislative and executive levels, and launching public educational campaigns. LFMI's activities also include sociological surveys, publications, conferences, workshops, and lectures. Since its inception, LFMI has addressed a variety of core issues confronting the economic reform process: it promoted the idea of a currency board and provided decisive input to the Law on Litas Credibility, led the creation of the legal and institutional framework for the securities market, and initiated the policy-making process on private pension insurance through pension funds. LFMI's recommendations were adopted in legislation on commercial banks, the Bank of Lithuania, privatization, credit unions, insurance, and foreign investment. LFMI influenced strongly the improvement of company and bankruptcy law. The Institute has also developed a conceptual proposal for tax and budget reform and proposals from LFMI were adopted in policy debates on income taxation, real estate tax, and inheritance and gift taxes. Recently, LFMI has initiated a business deregulation process. (E-mail: vaida@lrinka.lt)

**Making Our Economy Right (MOER), Bangladesh**

MOER champions free-market concepts and the freedom of the individual. MOER was founded in 1991, a period that saw the downfall of the communist empire across the globe as well as the fall of Bangladesh's own nine-year military dictatorship. Bangladesh is still a fully statist society where politicians promise jobs and economic development but are unaware that the function of the state and the government is merely to protect individual freedom, liberty, life, property, and the national geographic boundary. Today, in 1998, there are no dramatic changes towards free-market individualism in Bangladesh but MOER continues its work, writing in the national newspapers and translating free-market literature into Bangla. MOER solicits international support and cooperation in its efforts to liberalize Bangladesh's economy fully and thereby to democratize Bangladesh society. The use of the Internet has been tremendously helpful in our work and we are thankful for the support of the Atlas Economic Research Foundation. (E-mail: nizam@moer.org; website: http://www.atlas-fdn.org/moer)

**The New Zealand Business Roundtable**

The New Zealand Business Roundtable is an organization of chief executives of about 60 of New Zealand's largest business organizations. Its aim is to contribute to the development of sound public policies that reflect New Zealand's overall interests. It has been a prominent supporter of the country's economic liberalization reforms. (E-mail: 100405.1547@compuserve.com)

**Szazadveg Institute, Hungary**

The Szazadveg Institute is a non-profit organization performing political and economic research, advisory and training activities. This think-tank is independent of the government or any political parties and has been operating as a foundation since its establishment in 1990. Szazadveg endeavours to publish its research results in specific professional and academic areas to the public at large as well as to render professional services in order to support the preparation of decisions by economic institutions, political and civil organizations, political parties, and the government. (E-mail: stumpf@bsp.mtapti.hu)

**Timbro, Sweden**
Timbro is a Swedish free-enterprise think-tank. Its goal is to mould public opinion favourably toward free enterprise, a free economy, and a free society. Timbro publishes books, papers, reports, and the magazine *Smedjan.* It also arranges seminars and builds human networks. Founded in 1978, Timbro is owned by the Swedish Free Enterprise Foundation, which has as its principals a large number of Swedish companies and organizations. (E-mail: mattiasb@timbro.se)

**The Ukrainian Center for Independent Political Research**
The Ukrainian Center for Independent Political Research was established in early 1991 as a non-profit, non-partisan, and non-governmental research institution. Its purpose is to enhance the awareness of the Ukrainian people of democracy and to further the analytic research of Ukrainian domestic and international politics and security. The UCIPR is politically independent; it does not accept any funding from either the state or any political party. The UCIPR publishes books and research papers on Ukraine's domestic and foreign policy issues, economy in transition, security doctrine, relations with neighbouring states, the Crimean dilemma, inter-ethnic relations, and media freedom, and so on. The Center has hosted a number of national and international conferences and workshops on the above issues. (E-mail: kam@political.kiev.ua)

**D'Letzeburger Land, Luxembourg** (letzlan@pt.lu); **Fundación del Orden Social de la Libertad, Argentina** (E-mail: libertad@twoer.com.ar); **The Institute for Development of Economics and Finance, Indonesia** (E-mail: indef@indo.net.id); **Liberty Network (LINE), Denmark** (E-mail: psj@line.dk); and **Bureau d'Analyse d'Ingenierie et de Logiciels (BAILO), Ivory Coast** (e-mail: bailo@globeaccess.net)are also members of the Economic Freedom Network; descriptions of their activities will be included in the next issue of *Economic Freedom of the World.*

# Economic Freedom of the World

# 2000 Annual Report

# EXECUTIVE SUMMARY

- The index presented in this report represents a continuation of our efforts to develop an objective measure of economic freedom. Ratings are presented for 57 nations in 1970, 83 in 1975, 107 in 1980, 111 in 1985, 115 in 1990, 122 in 1995, and 123 in 1997. This is the first publication to present ratings for 1970. Although more recent data are available for some components, we present 1997 data mainly because the data for that year are virtually complete.

- The summary index is based on 23 components designed to identify the consistency of institutional arrangements and policies with economic freedom in seven major areas. The seven areas covered by the index are: (I) size of government, (II) economic structure and use of markets, (III) monetary policy and price stability, (IV) freedom to use alternative currencies, (V) legal structure and security of private ownership, (VI) freedom to trade with foreigners, and (VII) freedom of exchange in capital markets. Principal component analysis was used to combine the component ratings into area ratings and the area ratings into a summary rating. See Exhibit 1 for a list of the components that make up the index. Appendix 2 contains explanatory notes and data sources for all the components used in the calculation of the index.

- In 1997, the most recent year for which we had complete data, Hong Kong and Singapore shared the top ranking with an economic freedom rating of 9.4 on a scale of 10. New Zealand, the United States, and the United Kingdom were next on the list; these were the five freest economies in the world. Other countries ranking near the top of the list were Ireland, Canada, Australia, Netherlands, Luxembourg, and Switzerland.

- The least free economies in 1997 were (in order from the bottom of the list) Myanmar, Democratic Republic of Congo, Sierra Leone, Rwanda, Madagascar, Guinea-Bissau, Algeria, Burundi, Republic of Congo, Central African Republic, and Albania. See Exhibit 2 for the complete presentation of the summary ratings for 1997 ranked from highest to lowest. Exhibit 3 presents the summary ratings from 1970 to 1997 alphabetically. Appendix 1 reports the Area ratings for the period from 1970 to 1997.

- A number of Latin American countries have achieved dramatic improvements in both ratings and rankings during the 1990s. Peru, Nicaragua, Argentina, El Salvador, and Dominican Republic all improved their ratings by at least 2 points. The improvement in rankings was even more dramatic. For instance, Argentina went from 71st to 12th place.

- Among eastern European nations, Russia, Hungary and Poland have made measured improvements in economic freedom. The Czech Republic, however, has seen its rating stagnate since the mid-1990s.

- This report also presents several bar charts linking the economic freedom summary rating with various measures of economic and social welfare. For instance, Exhibit 4 shows that the nations in the top quintile of the ranking for economic freedom produce a per-capita income of over $18,000; those in the bottom quintile produce a per-capita income under $2000. Exhibit 7 shows a 20-year difference in life expectancy between the top and bottom quintiles. See Exhibits 4 through 8 for more details.

- Country Reports have been written for 65 countries. These reports present a bar chart with the country's summary economic-freedom rating and ranking, a bar chart with total government expenditures as a share of GDP, and a written summary of the country's economic freedom performance and prospects.

- Country Data Tables have been constructed that show, for years 1970, 1975, 1980, 1985, 1990, 1995, and 1997, the component ratings (and often also the raw data), the area ratings, and the summary ratings and rankings of all countries evaluated. These data are also available to researchers upon request or can be retrieved from the website www.freetheworld.com.

- Appendix 3 lists some of the many academic books, articles, and studies that have used the various editions of *Economic Freedom of the World* as source material.

# INTRODUCTION

*Economic Freedom of the World: 2000 Annual Report* is our latest, most detailed attempt to construct a useful indicator of economic freedom for the nations of the world. More than a decade ago, Michael Walker, the Executive Director of The Fraser Institute of Vancouver, British Columbia, and Nobel laureate Milton Friedman organized a series of conferences with the objective of clearly defining and measuring economic freedom. They were able to attract some of the world's leading economists including Gary Becker, Douglass North, Peter Bauer, and Assar Lindbeck to participate in the series and provide input for the study. These conferences eventually led to the publication of *Economic Freedom of the World: 1975–1995* (James Gwartney, Robert Lawson, and Walter Block, eds.) and the organization of the Economic Freedom Network, a collection of over 50 institutes in as many countries. Collectively these institutes assist in the production of each edition of *Economic Freedom of the World* and share our goal of developing the best possible measure of economic freedom. In 1997, we published *Economic Freedom of the World: 1997 Annual Report*, and last year *Economic Freedom of the World: 1998/1999 Interim Report.*[1]

In his foreword to *Economic Freedom of the World: 1975–1995*, Milton Friedman indicated that the indexes presented in that publication had brought the quest for an objective measure of economic freedom to a "temporary conclusion." Amplifying this statement, Professor Friedman indicated that subsequent studies would "surely make revised editions necessary, both to bring the indexes of economic freedom up-to-date and to incorporate the additional understanding that will be generated." The measures developed in this publication are indicative of this evolutionary process. They reflect improved knowledge about how to measure economic freedom and the development of a more complete data set for the achievement of that purpose. They represent movement to a new level.

The core ingredients of economic freedom are personal choice, protection of private property, and freedom of exchange. Individuals have economic freedom when: (a) their property acquired without the use of force, fraud, or theft is protected from physical invasions by others and (b) they are free to use, exchange, or give their property to another as long as their actions do not violate the identical rights of others. Like a compass, this concept of economic freedom has directed our work.

## METHODOLOGY OF THE INDEX

From the very beginning, our goal was the development of an objective measure of economic freedom rather than an index based on subjective assessments and "judgment calls." Therefore, the foundation of our index is a range of objective components that reflect the presence (or absence) of economic freedom. These components can be derived for a large number of countries from regularly published sources. This will make it possible both to calculate the index for earlier time periods and to update it regularly. We also wanted to combine the components into a summary index in a sound, objective manner. The measures presented in this report are an additional step in this direction. They are more comprehensive and based on more complete data than any prior measure of economic freedom; and they use value-free statistical procedures. Still, they are transparent. It is easy to see precisely how the various indexes are constructed, what data they reflect, and which factors produce rating differences across countries and time periods.

As Exhibit 1 illustrates, the index comprises 23 components designed to identify how consistent institutional arrangements and policies in seven major areas are with economic freedom. The seven areas covered by the index are: (I) size of government, (II) economic structure and use of markets, (III) monetary policy and price stability, (IV) freedom to use alternative currencies, (V) legal structure and security of private ownership, (VI) freedom to trade with foreigners, and (VII) freedom of exchange in capital markets.

Areas I and II are indicators of reliance on markets rather than the political process (large government expenditures, state-operated enterprises, price controls, and discriminatory taxes) to allocate resources and determine the distribution of income. Areas III and IV reflect the availability of sound money. Area V focuses on the legal security of property rights and the enforcement of contracts. Area VI indicates the consistency of policies with free trade. Area VII is a measure of the degree to which markets are used to allocate capital. Reliance on markets, sound money, legal protection of property rights, free trade, and market allocation of capital are important elements of economic freedom captured by the index. Of course, we recognize that economic freedom is heterogeneous and highly complex. No single statistic will be able to capture fully and accurately its many facets. However, the index outlined in Exhibit 1 does encompass key ingredients of the concept.

Our work on the measurement of economic freedom is an ongoing project. This publication represents an update and refinement of *Economic Freedom of the World: 1998/1999 Interim Report*, in which we altered the structure of the index and added (and in some cases deleted) components. We also changed the methodology for converting raw data to the zero-to-10 index ratings and for generating weights for the summary ratings to a more value-neutral procedure. The *1998/1999 Interim Report* was the subject of the annual meeting of the Economic Freedom Network in Manila, Philippines, in November 1998. We were able to listen to, and reflect upon, many comments made by the representatives of the participating institutes of the Economic Freedom Network and, as a result, several minor changes were made to this edition of *Economic Freedom of the World*.[2]

We had hoped–and, indeed, still hope–to add an area to this index that measures regulation of the labour market but we have not yet found satisfactory data available on a scale that is wide enough, both geographically and over time, to do so. We have, however, constructed this index back to 1970 to aid in the long-term study of economic freedom. Obviously, the data are less complete in the earlier years than the later years but, nevertheless, we believe this index can become a useful tool in analyzing the impact of economic freedom (or lack thereof) in the longer run.

There are 125 nations included in this study. However, as the result of incomplete data or other factors (e.g., the split up of Czechoslovakia), we were only able to derive summary ratings for 123 countries in 1997, 122 in 1995, 115 in 1990, 111 in 1985, 109 in 1980, 83 in 1975, and 57 in 1970. Data were assembled for each of the 23 components of the index. Since we wanted the ratings to be easily comparable across countries and time periods, they were placed on a scale from zero to 10. Higher ratings are indicative of institutions and policies more consistent with economic freedom.

How were the ratings derived? The ratings for 11 of the 23 components in the index reflect various categorical characteristics; those for the remaining 12 are based on continuous data. Countries with categorical characteristics more consistent with economic freedom are given higher ratings. For example, countries with few government enterprises are given higher ratings than those with widespread use of such enterprises. Similarly, countries where price controls are absent (or apply in only a few markets) are given higher ratings than countries where these controls are extensively applied.

Depending upon whether higher values are indicative of more or less economic freedom, alternative formulas are used to transform the 12 continuous variables into a zero-to-10 scale. When higher values are indicative of more economic freedom, the formula used to derive the zero-to-10

## Exhibit 1: Components of Index of Economic Freedom

| | | |
|---|---|---|
| **I** | **Size of Government: Consumption, Transfers, and Subsidies** | **[11.0%]** |
| | A General Government Consumption Expenditures as a Percent of Total Consumption | (50%) |
| | B Transfers and Subsidies as a Percent of GDP | (50%) |
| **II** | **Structure of the Economy and Use of Markets** (*Production and allocation via governmental and political mandates rather than private enterprises and markets*) | **[14.2%]** |
| | A Government Enterprises and Investment as a Share of the Economy | (32.7%) |
| | B Price Controls: Extent to which Businesses Are Free to Set Their Own Prices | (33.5%) |
| | C Top Marginal Tax Rate (*and income threshold at which it applies*) | (25.0%) |
| | D The Use of Conscripts to Obtain Military Personnel | (8.8%) |
| **III** | **Monetary Policy and Price Stability** (*Protection of money as a store of value and medium of exchange*) | **[9.2%]** |
| | A Average Annual Growth Rate of the Money Supply during the Last Five Years minus the Growth Rate of Real GDP during the Last Ten Years | (34.9%) |
| | B Standard Deviation of the Annual Inflation Rate during the Last Five Years | (32.6%) |
| | C Annual Inflation Rate during the Most Recent Year | (32.5%) |
| **IV** | **Freedom to Use Alternative Currencies** (*Freedom of access to alternative currencies*) | **[14.6%]** |
| | A Freedom of Citizens to Own Foreign Currency Bank Accounts Domestically and Abroad | (50%) |
| | B Difference between the Official Exchange Rate and the Black Market Rate | (50%) |
| **V** | **Legal Structure and Property Rights** (*Security of property rights and viability of contracts*) | **[16.6%]** |
| | A Legal Security of Private Ownership Rights (*Risk of confiscation*) | (34.5%) |
| | B Viability of Contracts (*Risk of contract repudiation by the government*) | (33.9%) |
| | C Rule of Law: Legal Institutions Supportive of the Principles of Rule of Law and Access to a Nondiscriminatory Judiciary | (31.7%) |
| **VI** | **International Exchange: Freedom to Trade with Foreigners** | **[17.1%]** |
| | A Taxes on International Trade | |
| | i Revenue from Taxes on International Trade as a Percent of Exports plus Imports | (23.3%) |
| | ii Mean Tariff Rate | (24.6%) |
| | iii Standard Deviation of Tariff Rates | (23.6%) |
| | B Non-tariff Regulatory Trade Barriers | |
| | i Percent of International Trade Covered by Non-tariff Trade Restraints | (19.4%) |
| | ii Actual Size of Trade Sector Compared to the Expected Size | (9.1%) |
| **VII** | **Freedom of Exchange in Capital and Financial Markets** | **[17.2%]** |
| | A Ownership of Banks: Percent of Deposits Held in Privately Owned Banks | (27.1%) |
| | B Extension of Credit: Percent of Credit Extended to Private Sector | (21.2%) |
| | C Interest Rate Controls and Regulations that Lead to Negative Interest Rates | (24.7%) |
| | D Restrictions on the Freedom of Citizens to Engage in Capital Transactions with Foreigners | (27.1%) |

Note: The numbers in parentheses, *e.g.* (27.1%), indicate the weights used to derive the area rating. The numbers in the brackets, *e.g.* **[17.2%]**, indicate the percentage weight allocated to each area when the summary rating was derived. These weights are derived by principal component analysis.[3]

ratings is: $(V_i - V_{min}) / (V_{max} - V_{min})$ multiplied by 10. $V_i$ is the country's actual value for the component, $V_{max}$ the maximum value for a country during the 1990 base year, and $V_{min}$ the minimum base-year value for the component. This formula is used to derive the ratings for all years. A country's rating will be close to 10 when its value for the component is near the base-year maximum. In contrast, the rating will be near zero when the observation for a country is near the base-year minimum. As the actual values exceed the base-year minimum by larger and larger amounts, ratings will rise from zero toward 10. Whenever the actual value for the component is equal to, or greater than, the base-year maximum, a rating of 10 is assigned. When the actual value is equal to, or less than, the base-year minimum, the rating is zero.

Often times, higher actual values are indicative of less economic freedom. Inflation and size of the transfer sector provide examples. Increases in these variables reflect reductions in economic freedom. When higher values for a component are indicative of less economic freedom, the formula used to derive the zero-to-10 ratings is: $(V_{max} - V_i) / (V_{max} - V_{min})$ multiplied by 10. This formula will assign higher ratings to countries with actual values closer to the base-year minimum. In some cases, component values of zero represent an ideal–a benchmark that should be required for a rating of 10. For example, a zero mean tariff rate and a zero rate of inflation (perfect price stability) are benchmark outcomes representing maximum economic freedom. When zero represents an ideal benchmark value, this value was included as $V_{min}$ in the formula even if no country actually achieved this ideal during the base year. In some cases where extreme component values are present (for example, a 10,000 percent rate of inflation), $V_{max}$ is constrained at a level clearly warranting a rating of zero even if this was not the maximum observed value during the base year. If this had not been done, extreme observations would have created such a large range that the ratings would have been concentrated near 10. The precise formula used to derive the zero-to-10 ratings for each component is presented in the section, Explanatory Notes and Data Sources, *pages 00 to 00*.

The procedures used to convert the continuous component values to the zero-to-10 ratings have two important characteristics. First, if all (or almost all) countries improve (or regress) with the passage of time, the ratings will reflect the change. Second, the distribution of the country ratings along the zero-to-10 scale reflects the distribution of the actual values among the countries.

Principal-component analysis was used to determine the weight given to each component in the construction of the area index. This procedure partitions the variance of a set of variables and uses it to determine the linear combination–the weights–of these variables that maximizes the variation of the newly constructed principal component. In effect, the newly constructed principal component–an area rating, for example–is the variable that most fully captures the variation of the underlying components. It is an objective method of combining a set of variables into a single variable that best reflects the original data. The procedure is particularly appropriate when several sub-components measure different elements of a principal component. This is precisely the case with our index. Economic theory is a road map indicating components that are likely to capture various elements of a broader area (a principal component). In turn, principal-component analysis indicates the permissibility of grouping components together and the weights most appropriate to combine a set of sub-components into a principal component. In Exhibit 1, the component weights derived by this procedure are shown in parentheses; e.g. (50%). The same procedure was also used to derive the weights for the area components in the construction of what we will refer to as the summary index. In Exhibit 1, the weights for each of the seven areas are shown in bold-face type and enclosed within brackets: e.g. **[11.0%]**.

# Economic Freedom of the World, 1970–1997 Ratings

Exhibit 2 shows the area and summary economic freedom ratings for 1997, sorted from highest to lowest.[4] Consistently high-ranking Hong Kong shares the title of freest economy this year with Singapore. Hong Kong has been the top-ranked economy in our study for almost every measurement period (except 1980 when it ranked second). The top five after Hong Kong and Singapore are New Zealand, the United States, and the United Kingdom. Other notable countries (ranks) are: Canada (7), Ireland (6), Chile (18), Japan (14), Sweden (25), South Korea (47), Czech Republic (51), Israel (66), China (75), and Russia (93). Myanmar (formerly Burma) ranks last with a rating of just 2.1

Exhibit 3 shows the summary ratings from 1970 to 1997 as well as the change in summary ratings in the 1990s where data are available. The economic freedom index suggests that economic freedom has been on the increase in almost all countries around the world in the 1990s.

For more information about specific countries please turn to the country report and country data-table sections of this volume. For selected countries, country reports have been written. These reports give a commentary on background information regarding the level of economic freedom in that country and, in some cases, prospects for future changes in economic freedom. The country data-tables contain the underlying component ratings used to calculate the summary ratings for all of the countries.

Appendix 1 shows the ratings for each of the seven areas that combine to form the overall summary ratings for the period from 1970 to 1997. Appendix 2 reports the details of each component's rating methodology and source. Appendix 3 is a listing of selected publications that have utilized the summary ratings from various editions of *Economic Freedom of the World.*

# EXHIBIT 2: ECONOMIC FREEDOM RATINGS, 1997/1998

| Country / Rank | Rating (0–10) | Country / Rank | Rating (0–10) |
|---|---|---|---|
| Hong Kong 1 | 9.4 | Egypt 62 | 6.6 |
| Singapore 1 | 9.4 | Lithuania 62 | 6.6 |
| New Zealand 3 | 9.1 | Turkey 62 | 6.6 |
| United States 4 | 9.0 | Israel 66 | 6.5 |
| United Kingdom 5 | 8.9 | Sri Lanka 66 | 6.5 |
| Ireland 6 | 8.7 | Ghana 68 | 6.4 |
| Australia 7 | 8.6 | Namibia 68 | 6.4 |
| Canada 7 | 8.6 | Barbados 70 | 6.3 |
| Luxembourg 9 | 8.5 | Belize 70 | 6.3 |
| Netherlands 9 | 8.5 | Malta 70 | 6.3 |
| Switzerland 9 | 8.5 | Slovenia 70 | 6.3 |
| Argentina 12 | 8.4 | Tunisia 70 | 6.3 |
| Denmark 12 | 8.4 | China 75 | 6.2 |
| Belgium 14 | 8.3 | Guyana 75 | 6.2 |
| El Salvador 14 | 8.3 | Haiti 75 | 6.2 |
| Japan 14 | 8.3 | Fiji 78 | 6.1 |
| Panama 14 | 8.3 | Jordan 78 | 6.1 |
| Chile 18 | 8.2 | Slovakia 78 | 6.1 |
| Finland 18 | 8.2 | Uganda 78 | 6.1 |
| Spain 18 | 8.2 | Morocco 82 | 6.0 |
| Thailand 18 | 8.2 | Poland 82 | 6.0 |
| Costa Rica 22 | 8.1 | Venezuela 82 | 6.0 |
| Germany 22 | 8.1 | Brazil 85 | 5.9 |
| Norway 22 | 8.1 | India 86 | 5.8 |
| Austria 25 | 8.0 | Cote d'Ivoire 87 | 5.7 |
| Bolivia 25 | 8.0 | Colombia 88 | 5.6 |
| France 25 | 8.0 | Pakistan 88 | 5.6 |
| Iceland 25 | 8.0 | Papua New Guinea 88 | 5.6 |
| Portugal 25 | 8.0 | Tanzania 88 | 5.6 |
| Sweden 25 | 8.0 | Zambia 92 | 5.5 |
| Bahrain 31 | 7.9 | Russia 93 | 5.4 |
| Italy 31 | 7.9 | Bangladesh 94 | 5.3 |
| Peru 31 | 7.9 | Bulgaria 94 | 5.3 |
| Philippines 31 | 7.9 | Nepal 94 | 5.3 |
| Mexico 35 | 7.7 | Cameroon 97 | 5.1 |
| Mauritius 36 | 7.6 | Gabon 97 | 5.1 |
| Oman 36 | 7.6 | Iran 99 | 5.0 |
| Paraguay 36 | 7.6 | Zimbabwe 99 | 5.0 |
| Kuwait 39 | 7.5 | Benin 101 | 4.9 |
| Malaysia 39 | 7.5 | Niger 102 | 4.8 |
| Trinidad & Tob. 39 | 7.5 | Croatia 103 | 4.7 |
| Greece 42 | 7.4 | Mali 103 | 4.7 |
| Guatemala 42 | 7.4 | Nigeria 103 | 4.7 |
| Hungary 42 | 7.4 | Senegal 103 | 4.7 |
| Jamaica 42 | 7.4 | Malawi 107 | 4.6 |
| Uruguay 42 | 7.4 | Romania 107 | 4.6 |
| South Africa 47 | 7.3 | Togo 107 | 4.6 |
| South Korea 47 | 7.3 | Chad 110 | 4.5 |
| Indonesia49 | 7.2 | Ukraine 110 | 4.5 |
| Unit. Arab Em. 49 | 7.2 | Syria 112 | 4.4 |
| Czech Rep. 51 | 7.1 | Albania 113 | 4.3 |
| Taiwan 51 | 7.1 | C. African Rep. 113 | 4.3 |
| Dominican Rep. 53 | 7.0 | Burundi 115 | 4.2 |
| Ecuador 53 | 7.0 | Congo, Rep. of 115 | 4.2 |
| Honduras 53 | 7.0 | Algeria 117 | 4.1 |
| Nicaragua 56 | 6.9 | Guinea-Bissau 118 | 4.0 |
| Cyprus 57 | 6.8 | Madagascar 119 | 3.9 |
| Estonia 57 | 6.8 | Rwanda 120 | 3.7 |
| Kenya 57 | 6.8 | Sierra Leone 121 | 3.2 |
| Bahamas 60 | 6.7 | Congo, Dem. R.122 | 3.1 |
| Latvia 60 | 6.7 | Myanmar 123 | 2.1 |
| Botswana 62 | 6.6 | Somalia | NR |

# Exhibit 3: Summary Economic Freedom Ratings, 1970 to 1997

| | 1970 | 1975 | 1980 | 1985 | 1990 | 1995 | 1997 | Change during 1990s |
|---|---|---|---|---|---|---|---|---|
| **Albania** | NR | NR | NR | NR | 2.9 | 5.0 | 4.3 | 1.3 |
| **Algeria** | NR | NR | 4.7 | 4.2 | 2.7 | 3.6 | 4.1 | 1.4 |
| **Argentina** | 6.6 | 3.2 | 4.8 | 3.8 | 4.9 | 7.9 | 8.4 | 3.5 |
| **Australia** | 8.1 | 6.9 | 7.4 | 7.8 | 8.1 | 8.6 | 8.6 | 0.5 |
| **Austria** | 7.2 | 6.2 | 6.8 | 6.9 | 7.6 | 7.8 | 8.0 | 0.3 |
| **Bahamas** | NR | 6.4 | 6.0 | 6.4 | 6.0 | 6.2 | 6.7 | 0.7 |
| **Bahrain** | NR | NR | 7.6 | 7.4 | 7.4 | 7.9 | 7.9 | 0.6 |
| **Bangladesh** | NR | 2.9 | 2.9 | 3.3 | 3.7 | 4.1 | 5.3 | 1.6 |
| **Barbados** | NR | 5.5 | 5.7 | 6.2 | 6.2 | 6.4 | 6.3 | 0.1 |
| **Belgium** | 9.3 | 7.8 | 8.0 | 8.1 | 8.1 | 8.2 | 8.3 | 0.3 |
| **Belize** | NR | NR | 5.5 | 5.1 | 5.3 | 6.1 | 6.3 | 1.0 |
| **Benin** | NR | 5.1 | 4.9 | 4.8 | 5.7 | 4.7 | 4.9 | -0.8 |
| **Bolivia** | NR | NR | 4.0 | 4.0 | 6.5 | 7.9 | 8.0 | 1.5 |
| **Botswana** | NR | 3.9 | 4.7 | 5.6 | 6.0 | 6.8 | 6.6 | 0.7 |
| **Brazil** | 5.6 | 4.5 | 4.1 | 3.2 | 4.4 | 5.4 | 5.9 | 1.5 |
| **Bulgaria** | NR | NR | NR | NR | 3.8 | 5.2 | 5.3 | 1.5 |
| **Burundi** | NR | 3.2 | 3.2 | 4.1 | 3.9 | 3.5 | 4.2 | 0.4 |
| **Cameroon** | NR | NR | 5.1 | 5.2 | 5.5 | 5.2 | 5.1 | -0.4 |
| **Canada** | 8.1 | 7.7 | 8.0 | 8.2 | 8.5 | 8.4 | 8.6 | 0.2 |
| **Central African Rep.** | NR | NR | 5.2 | 4.6 | 4.4 | 4.4 | 4.3 | -0.1 |
| **Chad** | NR | NR | NR | 5.2 | 5.2 | 5.1 | 4.5 | -0.6 |
| **Chile** | 3.7 | 3.7 | 5.9 | 6.0 | 7.4 | 8.2 | 8.2 | 0.8 |
| **China** | NR | NR | 3.5 | 4.4 | 4.2 | 5.6 | 6.2 | 2.0 |
| **Colombia** | 5.1 | 4.7 | 4.6 | 5.2 | 5.1 | 6.4 | 5.6 | 0.5 |
| **Congo, Dem. Rep.** | 4.6 | 3.2 | 2.7 | 3.7 | 3.2 | 3.2 | 3.1 | -0.1 |
| **Congo, Rep. of** | NR | NR | 5.1 | 4.4 | 4.4 | 4.8 | 4.2 | -0.2 |
| **Costa Rica** | 8.3 | 7.0 | 5.6 | 5.6 | 7.3 | 7.8 | 8.1 | 0.8 |
| **Cote d'Ivoire** | NR | NR | 4.9 | 5.4 | 4.9 | 5.2 | 5.7 | 0.8 |
| **Croatia** | NR | NR | NR | NR | NR | 4.3 | 4.7 | |
| **Cyprus** | NR | 6.3 | 5.8 | 5.8 | 5.9 | 6.6 | 6.8 | 0.8 |

| | 1970 | 1975 | 1980 | 1985 | 1990 | 1995 | 1997 | Change during 1990s |
|---|---|---|---|---|---|---|---|---|
| **Czech Rep.** | NR | NR | NR | NR | 3.9 | 6.8 | 7.1 | 3.3 |
| **Denmark** | 7.6 | 6.7 | 6.8 | 6.9 | 7.7 | 8.1 | 8.4 | 0.6 |
| **Dominican Rep.** | NR | 3.9 | 5.3 | 5.2 | 4.1 | 6.3 | 7.0 | 2.9 |
| **Ecuador** | 3.9 | 5.8 | 6.0 | 4.5 | 5.3 | 6.7 | 7.0 | 1.7 |
| **Egypt** | NR | 4.2 | 4.1 | 4.6 | 4.3 | 6.0 | 6.6 | 2.3 |
| **El Salvador** | NR | NR | 3.7 | 4.3 | 5.0 | 8.0 | 8.3 | 3.3 |
| **Estonia** | NR | NR | NR | NR | NR | 6.1 | 6.8 | |
| **Fiji** | NR | 5.0 | 5.3 | 5.4 | 5.7 | 6.1 | 6.1 | 0.4 |
| **Finland** | 8.1 | 6.7 | 7.1 | 7.4 | 7.7 | 8.1 | 8.2 | 0.5 |
| **France** | 7.3 | 6.3 | 6.3 | 6.4 | 7.8 | 8.1 | 8.0 | 0.2 |
| **Gabon** | NR | NR | 3.8 | 5.2 | 5.2 | 5.7 | 5.1 | -0.1 |
| **Germany** | 8.2 | 7.7 | 7.8 | 7.9 | 8.3 | 8.2 | 8.1 | -0.1 |
| **Ghana** | 3.3 | 2.5 | 2.1 | 2.6 | 4.8 | 6.1 | 6.4 | 1.5 |
| **Greece** | 6.3 | 5.8 | 5.7 | 5.2 | 6.1 | 6.8 | 7.4 | 1.3 |
| **Guatemala** | 6.4 | 7.3 | 6.5 | 5.6 | 6.5 | 7.7 | 7.4 | 0.9 |
| **Guinea-Bissau** | NR | NR | NR | NR | 3.8 | 4.1 | 4.0 | 0.2 |
| **Guyana** | NR | NR | NR | 4.1 | NR | 5.9 | 6.2 | |
| **Haiti** | NR | NR | 5.4 | 5.7 | 4.7 | 4.6 | 6.2 | 1.5 |
| **Honduras** | NR | 8.1 | 5.5 | 5.5 | 6.2 | 6.9 | 7.0 | 0.8 |
| **Hong Kong** | 9.4 | 9.3 | 9.6 | 9.3 | 9.3 | 9.8 | 9.4 | 0.1 |
| **Hungary** | NR | NR | 4.8 | 4.8 | 4.9 | 6.8 | 7.4 | 2.5 |
| **Iceland** | 6.4 | 4.4 | 5.5 | 5.7 | 7.5 | 8.1 | 8.0 | 0.6 |
| **India** | 4.0 | 3.6 | 4.3 | 4.1 | 4.1 | 5.0 | 5.8 | 1.8 |
| **Indonesia** | 4.8 | 5.0 | 5.2 | 5.9 | 6.8 | 7.3 | 7.2 | 0.4 |
| **Iran** | 6.2 | 6.2 | 3.4 | 3.4 | 4.3 | 3.9 | 5.0 | 0.8 |
| **Ireland** | 6.8 | 6.2 | 6.6 | 6.7 | 7.3 | 8.6 | 8.7 | 1.4 |
| **Israel** | 4.8 | 4.4 | 4.0 | 4.4 | 4.8 | 6.3 | 6.5 | 1.7 |
| **Italy** | 6.8 | 5.5 | 5.5 | 6.0 | 7.4 | 7.5 | 7.9 | 0.5 |
| **Jamaica** | NR | 5.0 | 4.1 | 5.1 | 5.7 | 7.3 | 7.4 | 1.7 |
| **Japan** | 7.3 | 7.0 | 7.4 | 7.7 | 8.3 | 8.2 | 8.3 | 0.0 |
| **Jordan** | NR | 5.6 | 5.6 | 6.1 | 4.9 | 6.1 | 6.1 | 1.2 |
| **Kenya** | 5.0 | 4.8 | 4.8 | 5.1 | 5.1 | 6.2 | 6.8 | 1.7 |

| | 1970 | 1975 | 1980 | 1985 | 1990 | 1995 | 1997 | Change during 1990s |
|---|---|---|---|---|---|---|---|---|
| **Kuwait** | NR | NR | 5.1 | 7.1 | 5.8 | 7.1 | 7.5 | 1.7 |
| **Latvia** | NR | NR | NR | NR | NR | 5.7 | 6.7 | |
| **Lithuania** | NR | NR | NR | NR | NR | 5.7 | 6.6 | |
| **Luxembourg** | 9.1 | 8.8 | 9.0 | 9.4 | 8.3 | 8.4 | 8.5 | 0.2 |
| **Madagascar** | 5.6 | 4.1 | 4.1 | 4.4 | 3.8 | 3.9 | 3.9 | 0.0 |
| **Malawi** | NR | 5.0 | 3.9 | 4.4 | 4.7 | 4.1 | 4.6 | -0.1 |
| **Malaysia** | 6.5 | 6.4 | 7.1 | 7.3 | 7.7 | 7.6 | 7.5 | -0.2 |
| **Mali** | NR | 4.8 | 5.3 | 5.3 | 5.0 | 5.1 | 4.7 | -0.2 |
| **Malta** | 6.2 | 5.6 | 5.2 | 5.1 | 5.2 | 6.5 | 6.3 | 1.1 |
| **Mauritius** | NR | 4.6 | 4.7 | 6.4 | 6.0 | 7.9 | 7.6 | 1.6 |
| **Mexico** | 7.0 | 5.7 | 4.9 | 4.5 | 6.4 | 7.4 | 7.7 | 1.3 |
| **Morocco** | 5.5 | 4.9 | 4.0 | 4.8 | 4.6 | 5.9 | 6.0 | 1.4 |
| **Myanmar** | NR | NR | 2.4 | 2.1 | 1.3 | 1.6 | 2.1 | 0.9 |
| **Namibia** | NR | NR | NR | NR | 5.2 | 5.3 | 6.4 | 1.2 |
| **Nepal** | NR | NR | 5.4 | 5.4 | 4.9 | 5.2 | 5.3 | 0.4 |
| **Netherlands** | 8.6 | 7.4 | 7.8 | 7.8 | 8.1 | 8.4 | 8.5 | 0.5 |
| **New Zealand** | 7.0 | 6.0 | 6.4 | 6.2 | 8.1 | 9.1 | 9.1 | 1.0 |
| **Nicaragua** | NR | 7.6 | 3.7 | 2.0 | 2.9 | 5.7 | 6.9 | 4.1 |
| **Niger** | NR | 5.5 | 5.1 | 5.0 | 4.4 | 4.6 | 4.8 | 0.4 |
| **Nigeria** | 4.0 | 3.8 | 3.1 | 3.6 | 3.6 | 3.4 | 4.7 | 1.0 |
| **Norway** | 7.0 | 6.1 | 6.2 | 6.8 | 7.7 | 8.1 | 8.1 | 0.4 |
| **Oman** | NR | NR | 6.6 | 7.5 | 6.8 | 7.7 | 7.6 | 0.8 |
| **Pakistan** | 3.6 | 2.9 | 3.5 | 4.2 | 4.4 | 5.6 | 5.6 | 1.2 |
| **Panama** | NR | 7.7 | 6.7 | 7.0 | 6.9 | 8.1 | 8.3 | 1.5 |
| **Papua New Guinea** | NR | 4.6 | 4.9 | 6.3 | 6.0 | 5.9 | 5.6 | -0.4 |
| **Paraguay** | NR | NR | 6.2 | 6.0 | 6.3 | 7.8 | 7.6 | 1.3 |
| **Peru** | 4.7 | 3.5 | 3.4 | 2.3 | 3.7 | 7.5 | 7.9 | 4.2 |
| **Philippines** | 5.1 | 4.9 | 5.1 | 4.9 | 5.6 | 7.7 | 7.9 | 2.3 |
| **Poland** | NR | NR | NR | 3.5 | 4.0 | 6.4 | 6.0 | 1.9 |
| **Portugal** | 5.6 | 3.4 | 5.6 | 5.7 | 6.4 | 7.8 | 8.0 | 1.7 |
| **Romania** | NR | NR | NR | 3.5 | 4.2 | 4.5 | 4.6 | 0.5 |
| **Russia** | NR | 1.8 | 1.8 | 1.8 | 1.7 | 5.0 | 5.4 | 3.7 |

| | 1970 | 1975 | 1980 | 1985 | 1990 | 1995 | 1997 | Change during 1990s |
|---|---|---|---|---|---|---|---|---|
| **Rwanda** | NR | 2.1 | 3.7 | NR | 3.9 | 3.9 | 3.7 | -0.1 |
| **Senegal** | NR | NR | 5.0 | 4.9 | 5.0 | 4.2 | 4.7 | -0.3 |
| **Sierra Leone** | NR | 3.9 | 4.1 | 3.0 | 2.9 | 3.7 | 3.2 | 0.3 |
| **Singapore** | 7.7 | 7.6 | 8.0 | 8.4 | 9.1 | 9.4 | 9.4 | 0.3 |
| **Slovakia** | NR | NR | NR | NR | 3.9 | 6.2 | 6.1 | 2.2 |
| **Slovenia** | NR | NR | NR | NR | NR | 5.6 | 6.3 | |
| **Somalia** | NR | NR | NR | 3.3 | NR | NR | NR | |
| **South Africa** | 7.6 | 6.2 | 6.0 | 5.6 | 5.9 | 6.6 | 7.3 | 1.5 |
| **South Korea** | 6.3 | 5.6 | 5.7 | 6.0 | 6.6 | 7.7 | 7.3 | 0.7 |
| **Spain** | 6.5 | 5.9 | 6.2 | 6.3 | 7.0 | 7.9 | 8.2 | 1.3 |
| **Sri Lanka** | NR | NR | 4.2 | 4.8 | 4.5 | 6.3 | 6.5 | 2.0 |
| **Sweden** | 6.2 | 6.2 | 6.3 | 7.0 | 7.5 | 7.9 | 8.0 | 0.4 |
| **Switzerland** | 8.9 | 8.0 | 8.4 | 8.7 | 8.6 | 8.5 | 8.5 | -0.1 |
| **Syria** | 4.3 | 5.4 | 3.5 | 2.9 | 2.8 | 3.9 | 4.4 | 1.6 |
| **Taiwan** | 6.6 | 6.1 | 6.8 | 7.1 | 7.6 | 7.8 | 7.1 | -0.5 |
| **Tanzania** | 4.3 | 3.2 | 4.1 | 3.0 | 3.5 | 5.0 | 5.6 | 2.0 |
| **Thailand** | 6.4 | 5.6 | 5.8 | 6.1 | 6.8 | 7.6 | 8.2 | 1.4 |
| **Togo** | NR | NR | 4.4 | 5.9 | 4.9 | 4.7 | 4.6 | -0.3 |
| **Trinidad & Tobago** | NR | 4.7 | 5.0 | 4.8 | 5.4 | 7.2 | 7.5 | 2.1 |
| **Tunisia** | 4.3 | 4.5 | 4.4 | 4.1 | 5.0 | 6.1 | 6.3 | 1.3 |
| **Turkey** | 3.0 | 3.3 | 3.3 | 4.5 | 5.1 | 6.3 | 6.6 | 1.5 |
| **Uganda** | NR | NR | 2.8 | 2.7 | 2.7 | 4.6 | 6.1 | 3.5 |
| **Ukraine** | NR | NR | NR | NR | NR | 3.1 | 4.5 | |
| **United Arab Emirates** | NR | NR | 6.1 | 6.9 | 7.6 | NR | 7.2 | -0.5 |
| **United Kingdom** | 6.6 | 5.9 | 6.8 | 8.2 | 8.6 | 8.8 | 8.9 | 0.3 |
| **United States** | 8.0 | 8.1 | 8.5 | 8.6 | 8.8 | 8.9 | 9.0 | 0.1 |
| **Uruguay** | NR | 6.5 | 6.3 | 6.8 | 6.9 | 7.2 | 7.4 | 0.6 |
| **Venezuela** | 7.8 | 6.5 | 6.9 | 5.8 | 5.8 | 4.5 | 6.0 | 0.2 |
| **Zambia** | NR | 4.3 | 4.7 | 3.1 | 2.5 | 4.5 | 5.5 | 2.9 |
| **Zimbabwe** | NR | NR | 4.1 | 4.0 | 4.5 | 5.4 | 5.0 | 0.4 |

# Economic Freedom and Economic Performance

Although the economic freedom index has been designed as a measurement of economic freedom in its own right, we recognize the interest in how the index correlates with other measures of human well-being. Exhibit 4 shows the relationship between the 1997 Summary Rating and the level of GDP per capita (measured in purchasing power parity US dollars). The countries were grouped into quintile groups for easy comparison. The relationship between the economic freedom rating and income is quite striking. Greater economic freedom is strongly related with higher levels of income. Exhibit 5 shows the same economic freedom quintiles with the rate of economic growth in the 1990s. The general pattern repeats itself when looking at economic growth.

**Exhibit 4 Economic Freedom and Income, 1995–1997**

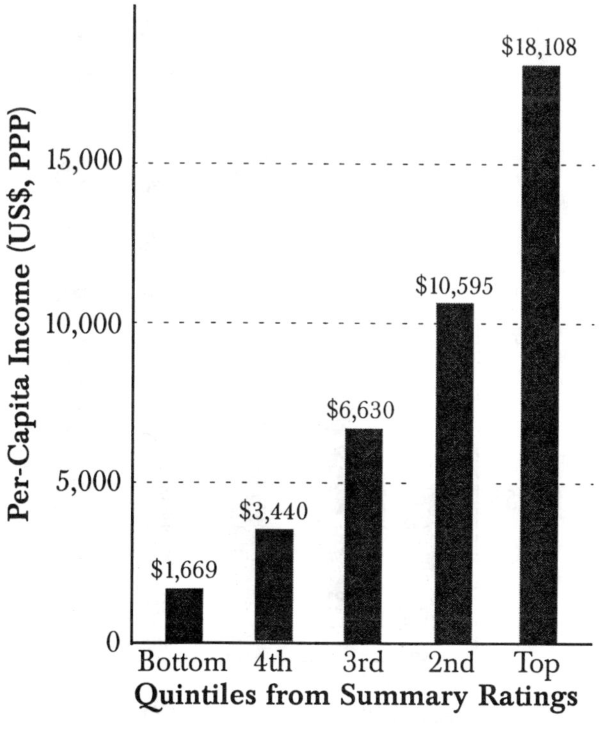


Source: *1999 World Development Indicators* (Washington, DC: The World Bank, 1999).

**Exhibit 5 Economic Freedom and Economic Growth during the 1990s**

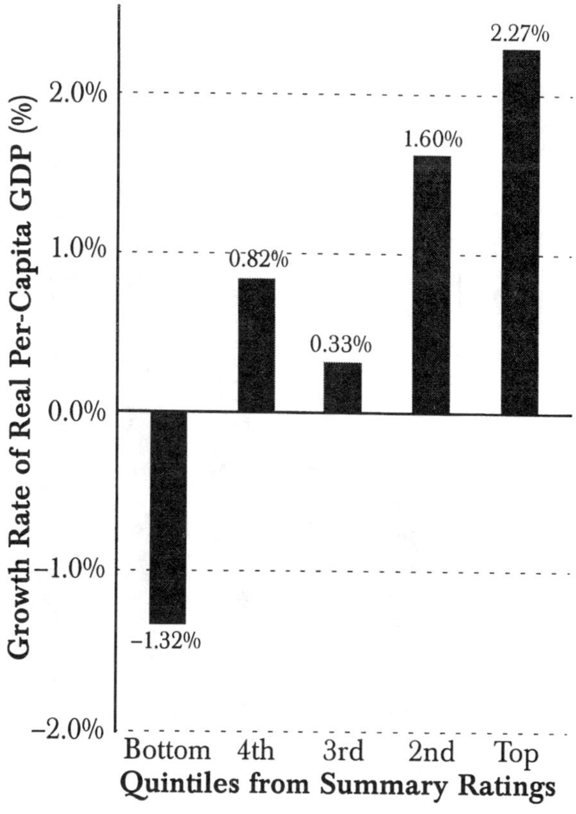


Source: *1999 World Development Indicators* (Washington, DC: The World Bank, 1999).

# Economic Freedom and Social Welfare

Economists have been criticized, perhaps justifiably, for considering only the material side of things. This section presents some simple charts that relate the economic freedom ratings to non-monetary aspects of human well-being. Exhibit 6 shows the relationship between the five economic freedom quintiles and cereal production per hectare. Again we see a clear positive relationship. Exhibit 7 looks at life expectancy, which is, in many ways, a summary statistic of the overall well-being of a group of people. Exhibit 7 shows the strong positive correlation between economic freedom and life expectancy. People living in the top economic-freedom quintile live 20 years longer, on average, than do those living in the bottom quintile. It should also be noted

**Exhibit 6 Economic Freedom and Cereal Yields (1997)**

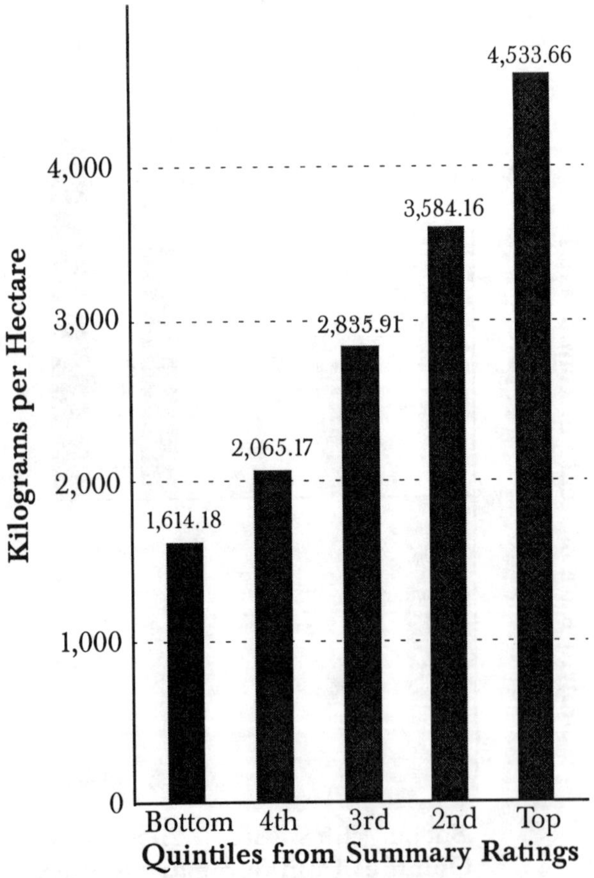


Source: *1999 World Development Indicators* (Washington, DC: The World Bank, 1999).

**Exhibit 7 Economic Freedom and Life Expectancy (1997)**

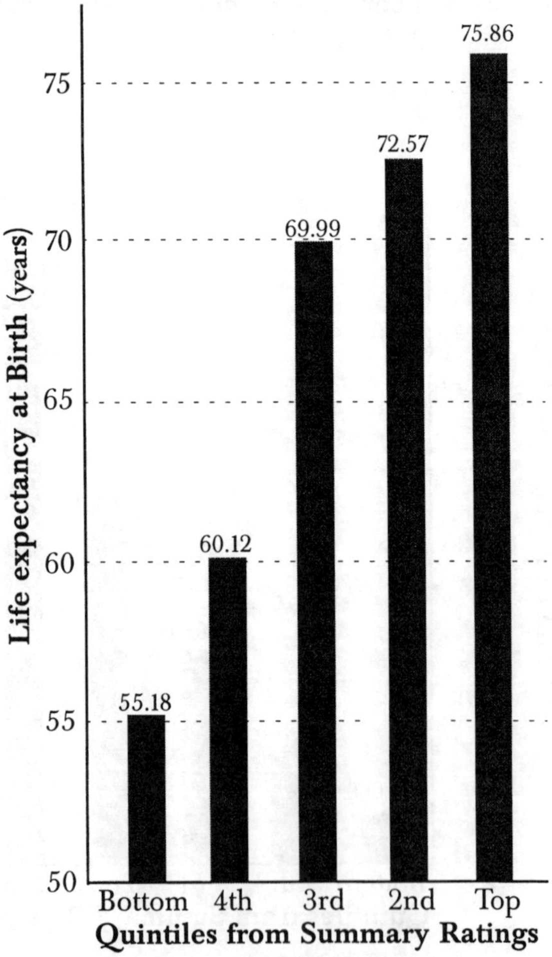


Source: *1999 World Development Indicators* (Washington, DC: The World Bank, 1999).

that these are not the only social statistics that are positively correlated with economic freedom. Other work has looked at infant mortality, literacy, access to safe drinking water, and corruption, all of which show better outcomes with higher levels of economic freedom.[5]

Without question, the most persistent criticism of the market economy is its supposed failure to achieve a "fair" distribution of income. Although the question of what a "fair" distribution of income actually means is not simple to answer, many people find apparent income inequality disturbing. The empirical question, however, is this: Do market-oriented economies actually show a more unequal distribution of income than other types of economies? Exhibit 8 is an attempt to answer that question. This exhibit shows the economic freedom quintiles related to a measure of income inequality. The measure used is the ratio of the income of the top 10 percent (decile) of income earners to the bottom 10 percent. A ratio of 1, for instance, would indicate perfect equality, as the top and bottom deciles would have the same amount of income. The further this ratio moves away from 1, the more unequal the distribution of income. Exhibit 8 clearly shows that the distribution of income is not closely related to economic freedom. It appears that non-market (i.e., less economically free) countries have a distribution of income just as unequal as the market-oriented nations or, in some cases, even more unequal. If anything, it seems that market-oriented economies have slightly more equal distributions of income.

**Exhibit 8: Economic Freedom and Income Inequality**

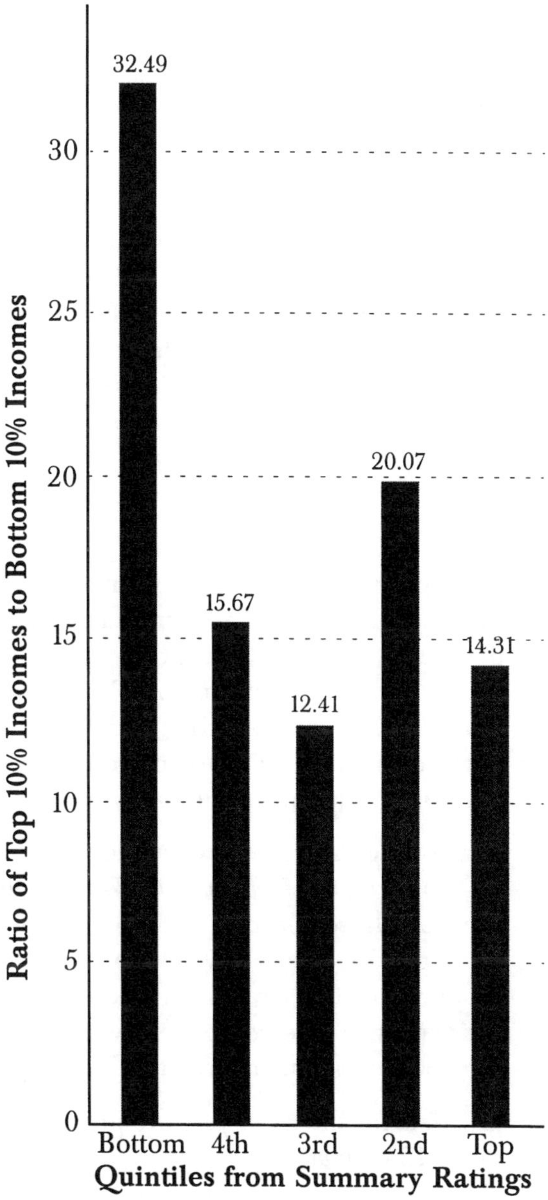


Source: *1999 World Development Indicators* (Washington, DC: The World Bank, 1999).

# NOTES

(1) See Michael Walker (ed.), *Freedom, Democracy, and Economic Welfare* (Vancouver: The Fraser Institute, 1988); Walter Block (ed.), *Economic Freedom: Toward a Theory of Measurement* (Vancouver: The Fraser Institute, 1991); Stephen Easton and Michael Walker (eds.), *Rating Global Economic Freedom* (Vancouver: The Fraser Institute, 1992); James Gwartney, Robert Lawson and Walter Block, *Economic Freedom of the World: 1975–1995* (Vancouver: The Fraser Institute, 1996); James Gwartney and Robert Lawson, *Economic Freedom of the World: 1997 Report* (Vancouver: The Fraser Institute, 1997); and James Gwartney and Robert Lawson, *Economic Freedom of the World: 1998/1999 Interim Report* (Vancouver: The Fraser Institute, 1998). These publications provide the foundation for this work.

(2) One component (freedom to convert domestic currency to foreign currencies in order to engage in current and capital account transactions) was dropped from the index because the representatives from the network expressed concern about its reliability. The black-market exchange rate variable was moved from Area VI to Area IV. Also, two variables (freedom to hold foreign currency bank accounts abroad and domestically) were combined into one component. Area V has been rescaled for all years in order to control for an upward drift in the data that did not reflect real changes in the institutional arrangements.

(3) These weights, with the exception of those used in Area VI, have not changed from what they were in *Economic Freedom of the World: 1998/1999 Interim Report*. Weights used in Area VI had to be recalculated because the black-market exchange rate variable was moved from Area VI to Area IV. Area IV was left with two components after the currency-convertibility component was dropped, the two foreign-currency bank account components were combined, and the black-market exchange rate component was added. Principal component analysis assigns equal weights (e.g., 50%) when there are just two components.

(4) The data for the latest year are primarily 1997. In some cases, 1998 data were used and, in a few cases, 1996 data.

(5) For more information about these correlations, please visit our website: www.freetheworld.com.

# COUNTRY REPORTS

This chapter presents an overview of the level of economic freedom in some of the countries included in this study. Included for each country is a background description of the levels and changes in economic freedom and, in some cases, the future outlook for economic freedom. These reports were produced with the help of the members of the Economic Freedom Network, who contributed specific knowledge of their own country's circumstances. More countries are not included because it is difficult to have a detailed understanding about the level of economic freedom in every single country.

For each country, we present two charts (showing data from 1970, 1975, 1980, 1985, 1990, 1995, and 1997, where data are available.) The first, which appears in the upper left-hand side of the page, shows the summary economic freedom rating along with that country's overall rank. The left axis and the bars correspond to the country's summary ratings. The right axis and the line correspond to the country's overall rank. (The number of countries rated and ranked varies each year.) The chart to the right of this shows total government expenditure as a percentage of GDP over the measurement period. For years, this ratio was considered the most objective measure of the size of the government sector as compared to the market sector. While revealing, it neglects other important aspects of economic freedom that are highlighted in our index, including the structure of the economy, monetary policy, freedom to use alternative currencies, legal structure and property rights, freedom to trade with foreigners, and the freedom of exchange in capital and financial markets. Some would argue that these "other factors" should have less (or more) weight in the measurement of economic freedom. Observation of changes in both economic freedom and government expenditures will help us to interpret the trends in, and meaning of, these two different but interrelated indicators with greater understanding.

More detailed information on the 23 components that compose the economic freedom index can be found in the next section, Country Data Tables, which includes all the countries in this study.

# ALBANIA

### Economic Freedom Rating (bar) and Rank (line)

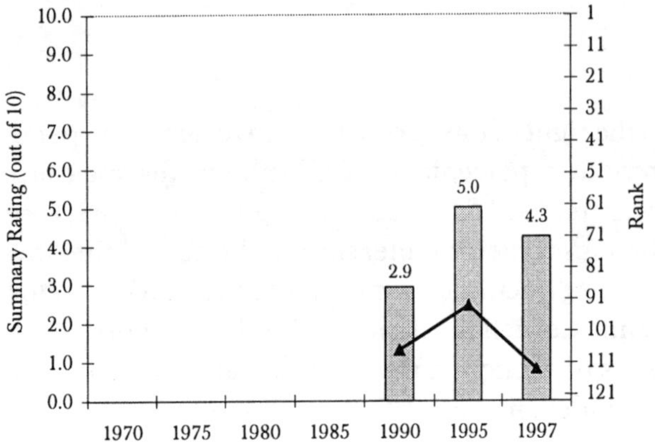


### Total Government Expenditure as a Percentage of GDP

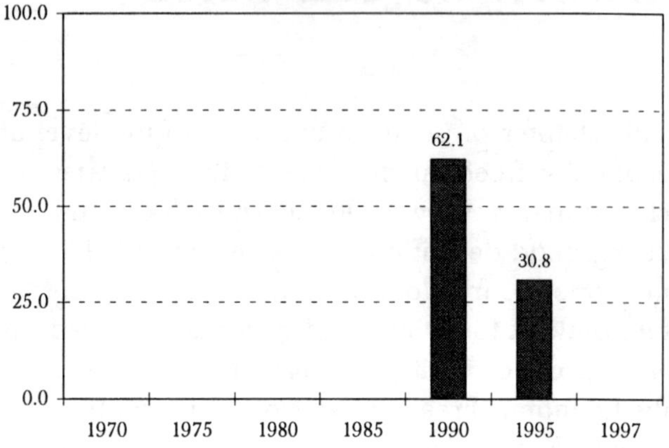


This troubled Balkan country saw its already low rating fall from 5.0 in 1995 to 4.3 in 1997. This places Albania 113th out of the 123 countries rated in this edition of *Economic Freedom of the World.* Widespread use of government enterprises, price controls, and credit and currency-market controls contribute to the low rating. The monetary regime has all but collapsed as Albania's rating in Area III has fallen to 2.5, reflecting an inflationary and volatile monetary policy. But, the financial crisis of 1997 appears to be over and there are signs that the situation is stabilizing as the inflation rate is falling.

Among the most important areas that threaten the economy are corruption, lack of public order, the political tensions in Albania as well as the recent events in Kosovo.

The growth rate of GDP in 1998 was 8 percent, which is comparable with growth prior to the financial crisis of 1997. Unemployment continues at an exceedingly high rate (17.5 percent in 1998).

The privatization of strategic sectors is supposed to start with the telecommunication companies (Albanian Mobile Communication, Albtelecom). Other companies that are supposed to enter the process of strategic-sector privatization include those active in mines, energy, petrol, and banking.

# ALGERIA

### Economic Freedom Rating (bar) and Rank (line)

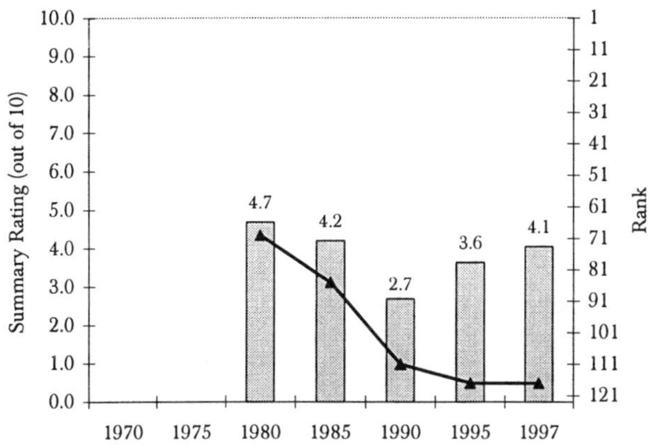


### Total Government Expenditure as a Percentage of GDP

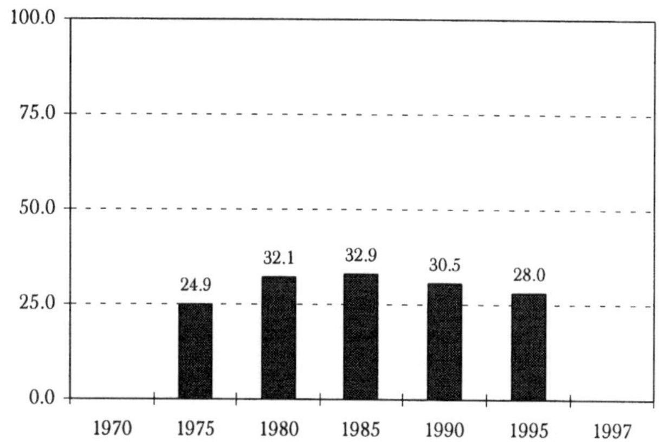


Since the 1990s, Algeria has been near the bottom of the rated countries. In 1997, Algeria was 117th of 123 countries. This poor performance can be attributed to the prevailing unstable political situation, the aftermath of bloody independence and a socialistic approach to policy.

The relatively high share of government consumption (22 percent) and government enterprises (rating 0.0), the remaining price controls (rating 4.0), limited freedom in financial markets, and military conscription drag this country's rating downward.

Monetary policy seems to be improving. The annual money growth has been slightly curbed, the inflation variability has been reduced, and the recent inflation rate declined from 28.5 percent in 1995 to 6.3 percent in 1997, which correspond to ratings of 4.3 (1995) and 8.7 (1997).

Due to restrictions on the ownership of foreign currencies and a soaring black-market exchange-rate differential, Area IV, Freedom to Use Alternative Currencies, got a rating of 0.0. As well, Area VII, Freedom of Exchange in Capital and Financial Markets, received a rating of 0.7.

# ARGENTINA

**Economic Freedom Rating (bar) and Rank (line)**

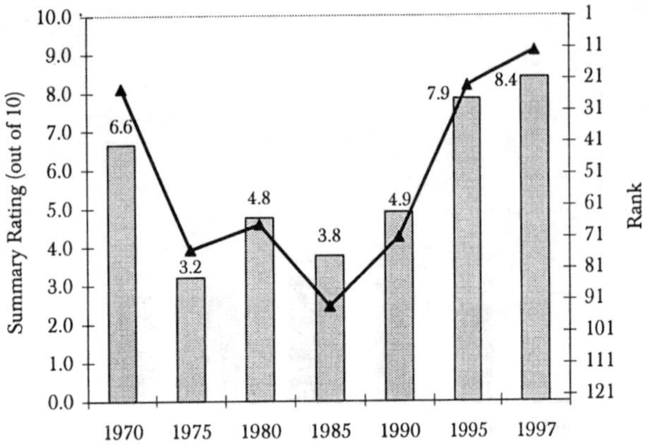


**Total Government Expenditure as a Percentage of GDP**

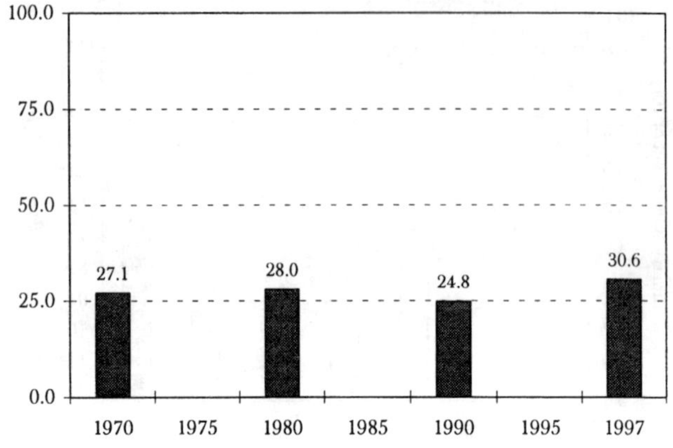


Argentina is one of the real success stories in economic freedom. As recently as 1985, Argentina was ranked 93rd in the world with an abysmal 3.8 rating. Its current rating of 8.4 places Argentina in 12th place.

Rapid and widespread privatization, de-control of prices, a shift to a volunteer military and, most importantly, a radically improved monetary regime are all responsible for the improvement. Argentina's currency-board arrangement has turned one of the world's most notorious inflation records into one of the best. Having the Argentine peso tied to the American dollar has brought inflation from over 2000 percent as recently as 1990 to under 1 percent. There is even serious talk about dollarization; i.e., using American dollars instead of a domestic currency.

Argentina's most significant weak spot is in the area of international trade, where it records some fairly high tariffs and a smaller trade sector than one would expect. Privatization of the remaining government-owned banks also remains on the agenda.

# AUSTRALIA

### Economic Freedom Rating (bar) and Rank (line)

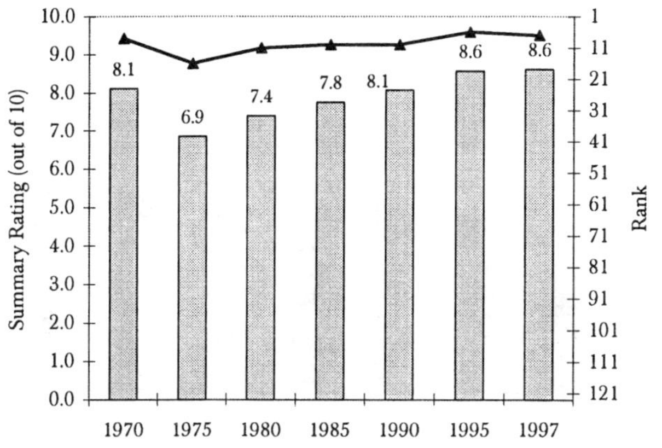


### Total Government Expenditure as a Percentage of GDP

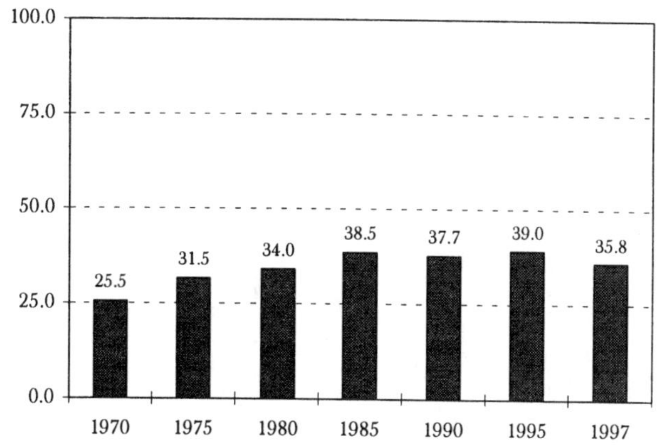


Australia's 8.6 rating placed it 7th among the 123 countries rated.

Two core elements of Australia's high rating are: an established legal structure guaranteeing secure property rights and stable monetary policy, which maintains low inflation rates (1 percent for 1997).

Institutional arrangements provide for substantial capital mobility. Citizens are free to own foreign currency accounts, although some limitations in engaging in capital transactions with foreigners are imposed. In financial markets, the trend of replacing credit extended to the government with private investments is proceeding, with just 5.5 percent of the credit allocated to the non-private sector. Australia possesses a free and liberalized international trade sector; the few existing taxes and tariffs are almost negligible.

Although the share of government consumption is shrinking, transfers and subsidies have been increasing since the mid-1970s.

# AUSTRIA

**Economic Freedom Rating (bar) and Rank (line)**

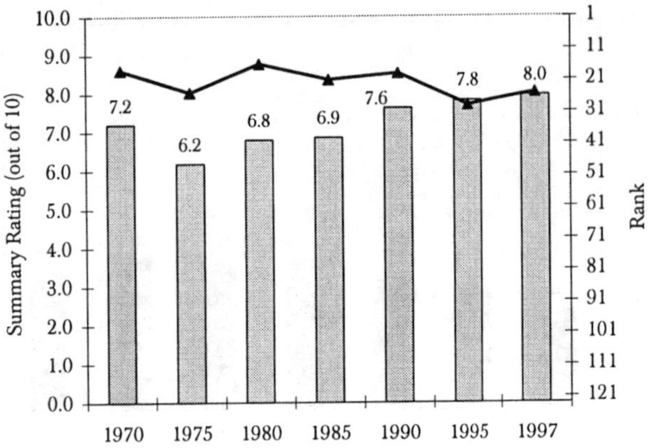


**Total Government Expenditure as a Percentage of GDP**

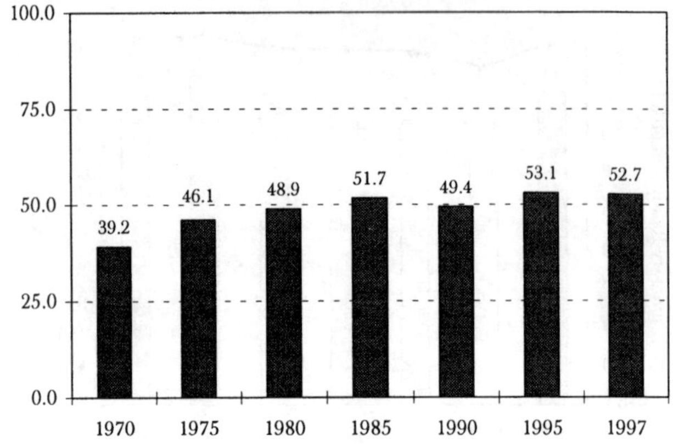


Austria's rating of 8.0 in 1997 placed it 25th among the 123 countries of this study. Its ranking during the past three decades has been relatively constant. Its strengths are a trustworthy established legal structure, a credible monetary policy, and the freedom to maintain foreign currency accounts domestically and abroad.

In preparation for European single-market integration, the trade sector has been liberalized and tariffs almost abolished.

But, as in most European nations, the size of government is relatively high. This is especially the case in the area of transfers and subsidies. A top marginal tax rate of 50 percent is needed to finance this income redistribution.

Privatization is moving along smoothly. Since 1990, over €2.5 billion worth of assets have been privatized. The government telecom monopoly has been eliminated and prices have plummeted while service has increased. A choice among several sources of electricity is now available for large industrial users. About 50 private radio broadcasters now compete with the state-owned enterprise though television remains a state monopoly. Deregulation and privatization of banking and finance is still needed.

# Bahamas

### Economic Freedom Rating (bar) and Rank (line)

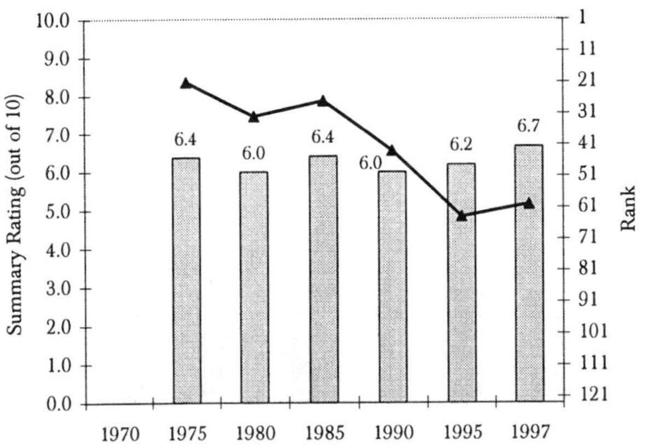


### Total Government Expenditure as a Percentage of GDP

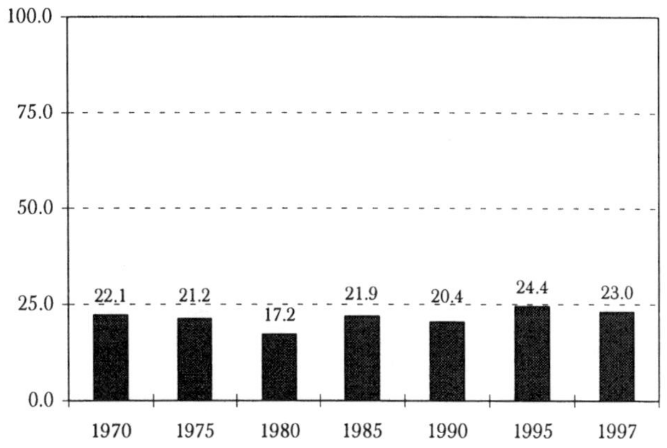


The Bahamas is a very small island country that has a highly regulated, centrally managed economy. All business ventures face a complex set of often-contradictory entry restraints, tax breaks, and subsidies. For instance, a licensing system restrains and controls business entry so that a business venture may get a construction permit, construct its facilities and then not receive the necessary operating license. Foreigners are excluded from the wholesale and retail business sector but qualify for tax breaks in other areas. Expatriate employees must have work permits that are increasingly costly. The Government has invested heavily in the tourist industry and still owns the utilities.

Consequently, the Bahamas has a rating of 6.7, which places it 60th in the world. Most disturbing, though, is the Bahamas' relative decline: it ranked 43rd in the world as late as 1990 and 21st in 1975. Its lowest rated areas are Area II, Use of Markets, Area IV, Use of Alternative Currencies, and, oddly for a island nation, Area VI, International Exchange.

However, a new administration in 1992 promised and subsequently produced a more honest government, sought foreign investment, and sold its largest hotels. This has produced four years of real per-capita growth in the range of 1 ½ to 2 ½ percent per year, reduced unemployment, and increased wage rates.

Despite the new-found prosperity, the government has problems. It created a fast track through the maze of bureaucratic controls for selected investments but it has not changed the maze. Its efforts to privatize the utilities have been slow. The first project, Bahamas Telecommunications, has not been concluded. A 62 percent reduction in staff, an apparent prerequisite to a sale, has produced exceedingly high separation costs and significant labour unrest. This case illustrates how political factors can sometimes undermine movement toward a more efficient and competitive economy.

# BARBADOS

### Economic Freedom Rating (bar) and Rank (line)

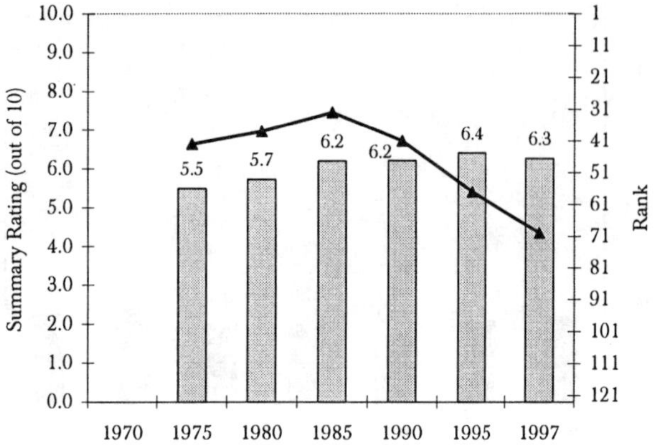


### Total Government Expenditure as a Percentage of GDP

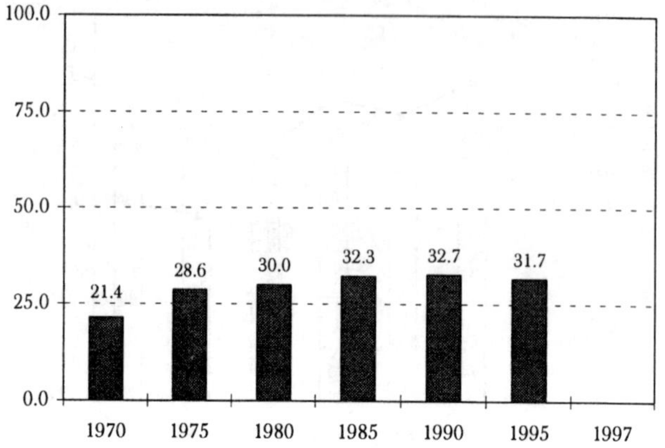


The economic freedom rating of Barbados has remained fairly constant during recent years; its rating was 6.2 in 1990 and 6.3 in 1997. This has resulted in a drop in its relative position from 41st in 1990 to 70th currently.

The main weaknesses of this country are price controls, economic intervention through state-owned companies, lack of trade openness to the rest of the world and capital-mobility controls. All these aspects create market distortions and reduce resource allocation efficiency in the economy. Government consumption as a percentage of the total is over 20 percent. This has not changed in the last ten years.

Among the capital controls that are worth mentioning are the prohibitions on holding foreign bank accounts and the use of foreign currency for economic transactions. These restrictions hold back many commercial activities. In addition, high and selective tariffs contribute to an unusually small amount of trade (especially for an island nation).

However, Barbados has made modest advances in terms of lowering top marginal tax rates. There has also been some improvement concerning property rights and contract enforcement.

# Belgium

**Economic Freedom Rating (bar) and Rank (line)**

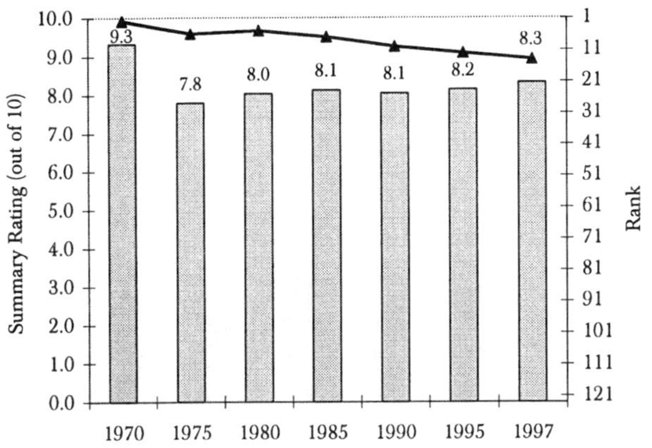


**Total Government Expenditure as a Percentage of GDP**

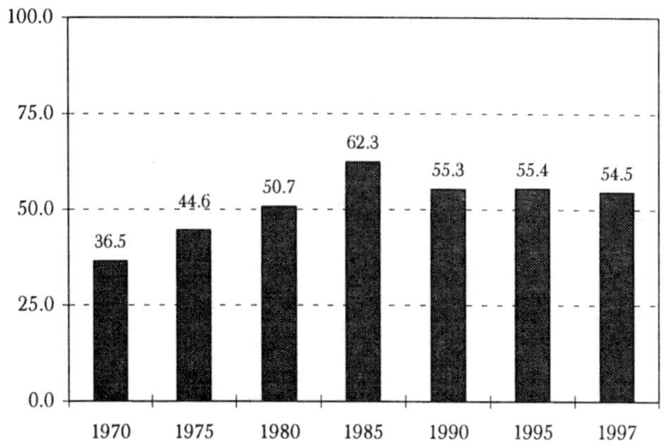


Belgium's summary rating of 8.3 for 1997 does not differ significantly from its historical norm. Its overall ranking for 1997 was 14th of 123, down somewhat from earlier years.

Belgium's strengths are in the areas of legal structure, monetary policy, freedom to use alternative currencies and international trade. By conducting a tight and strict anti-inflationary policy, Belgium has kept its inflation rate at a low level (1.5 percent in 1997). The Belgium Franc is fully convertible and citizens are free to engage in capital transactions with foreigners and to own foreign-currency bank accounts. The international trade sector is well developed and existing barriers will be reduced soon. Also a well-established legal structure is provided but there exists a highly bureaucratic system and space for an erosion of the rule of law (rating 7.0).

Looking to the banking sector, while savings are held by the private financial institutions, only 45.3 percent of total credit is extended to the private sector.

Like the western welfare economies, Belgium's government consumption is relatively high at 18.7 percent. The unemployment rate of almost 10 percent is in part financed by excessive top marginal tax rates (58 percent to 64 percent). Therefore, a slimming of the government, tax cuts, and lifting of existing price controls are recommended.

# BELIZE

**Economic Freedom Rating (bar) and Rank (line)**

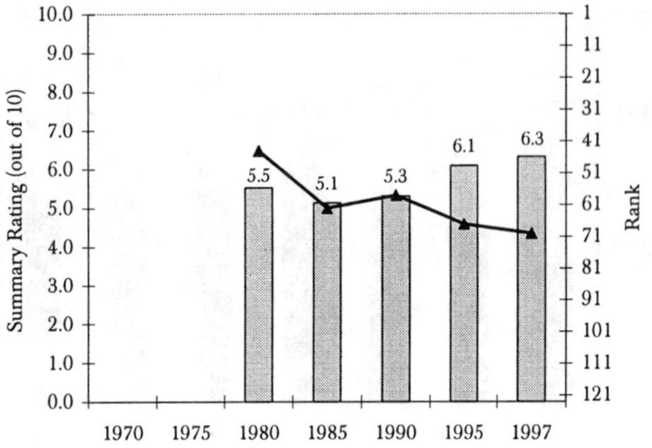


**Total Government Expenditure as a Percentage of GDP**

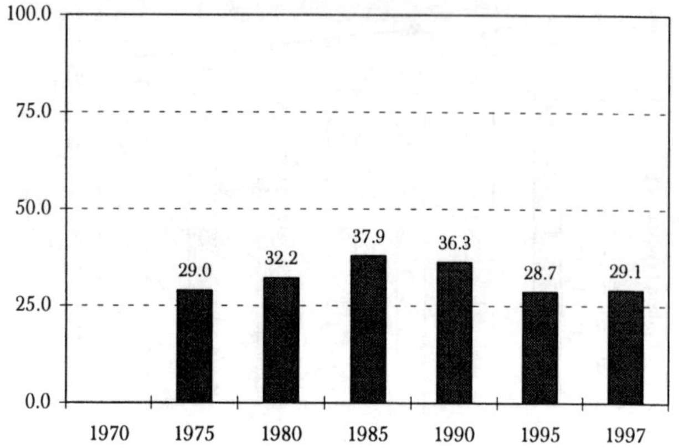


Like other Caribbean countries, Belize's rating has not changed too much recently. Its rating in 1990 was 5.3 and in 1997 it was 6.3. Despite this slight improvement, its ranking relative to other countries was set back several positions. Belize was ranked 58th in 1990 and 70th in 1997.

This country has shown important improvements in several areas. Belize's strength is in monetary policy. The growth of the money supply has slowed and price instability has been reduced. In addition, currency exchange restrictions have been reduced to the point where only minimal black-market activity remains.

However, there are also several factors that have not improved, holding back economic freedom. Belize still has high trade barriers that reduce the size of the trade sector. The size of imports plus exports as a percentage of GDP is very low compared with its expected size. Also, the financial system and capital market are highly regulated, which reduces Belize's access to international funds.

Another liability is the number of state-owned enterprises that participate in the economy, inhibiting the private sector.

# BENIN

### Economic Freedom Rating (bar) and Rank (line)

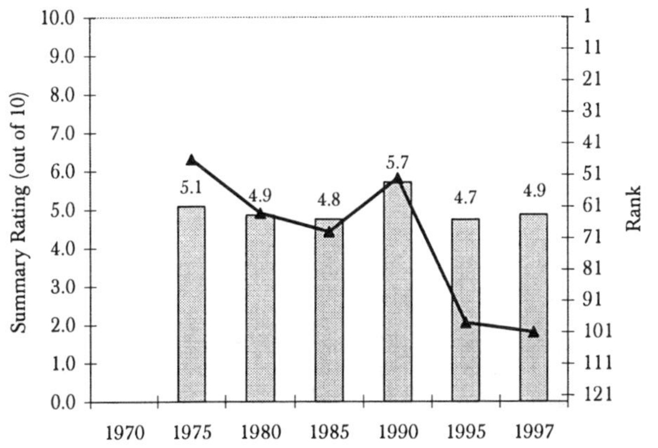


### Total Government Expenditure as a Percentage of GDP

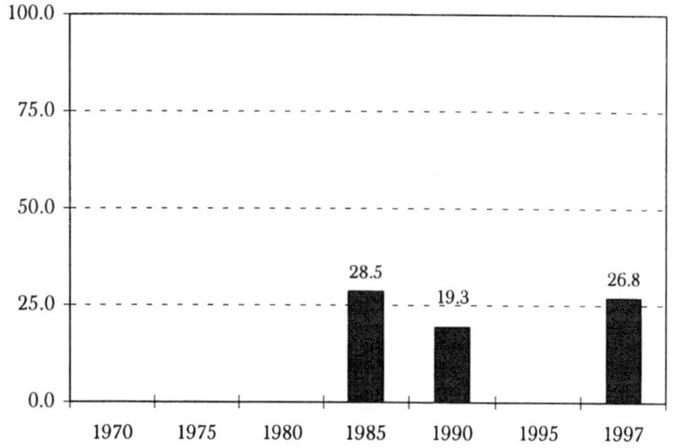


Benin's rating fell from 5.7 to 4.9 and its rank from 52nd in 1990 to 101st in 1997. Its economy remains underdeveloped and dependent upon agriculture, cotton production, and regional trade. The agricultural sector makes up 38.4 percent of GDP while the industrial sector makes up only 13.9 percent.

Although the size of government consumption is relatively low, a large number of government enterprises exist within the economy. Price controls are still prevalent.

Despite some problems in the mid-1990s (the inflation rate in 1995 was 15.4 percent), positive developments can be seen more recently as inflation has fallen to single digits. The banking sector is completely private with all deposits held in private banks.

There are still strong restrictions on capital transactions with foreigners and the ability to own foreign currencies remains unchanged receiving a rating of 0. Problems also remain in generating a trustworthy established legal structure. Benin needs to contend with corruption, encourage competition and adopt market-based policies if its prospects for growth are to improve.

# BOLIVIA

**Economic Freedom Rating (bar) and Rank (line)**

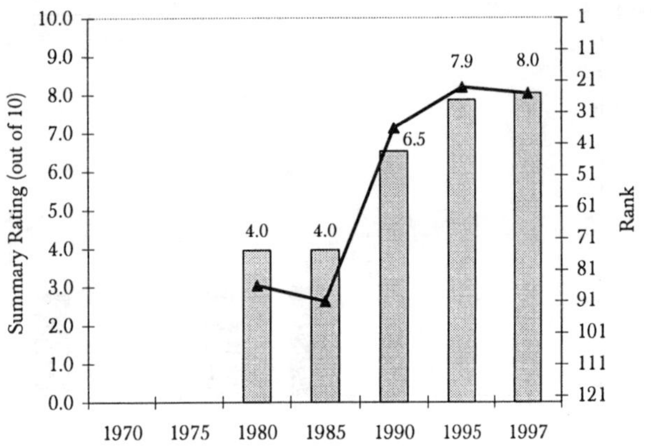


**Total Government Expenditure as a Percentage of GDP**

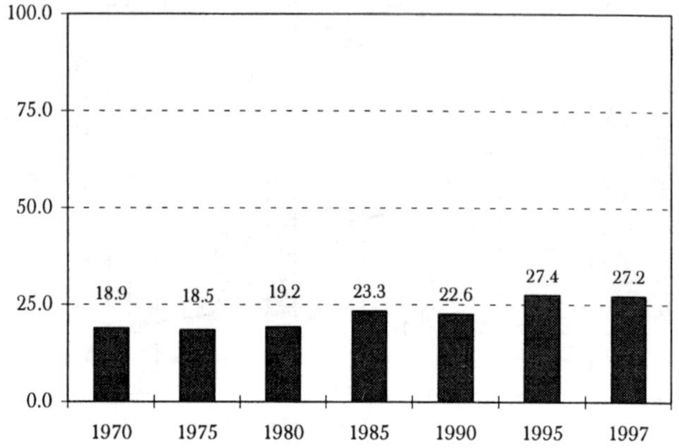


Bolivia's economic freedom rating was flat during the 1980s but it has rebounded during the last decade. Bolivia's rating improved from 4.0 in 1985 to 8.0 most recently. It now ranks 25$^{th}$ in the world. Historically, the potential of this country has been stifled by monetary instability and hyperinflation. In 1985, Bolivia's inflation rate soared to nearly 13,000 percent. Inflation rates of this magnitude undermine economic progress, regardless of the policies in other areas.

Seeking to rebound from this catastrophic situation, Bolivia has taken a number of constructive steps. The freedom to maintain foreign currency bank accounts, which was denied during the inflation of the mid-1980s, has been restored. The top marginal tax rate was reduced from 48 percent in 1980 to 10 percent in 1990 and 13 percent in 1995. Tariff rates were reduced sharply and most of the discriminatory treatment among product categories eliminated. Relaxation of exchange rate controls has virtually eliminated the black market. There has also been some liberalization of the restrictions on the movement of capital.

The privatization program has transferred the management of almost all state-owned companies to the private sector. In order to modernize mandatory social security for the Bolivian employees and workers, the Pensions Law has been passed with the objective that everyone saves with an individual account by means of obligatory savings in private institutions.

# BRAZIL

### Economic Freedom Rating (bar) and Rank (line)

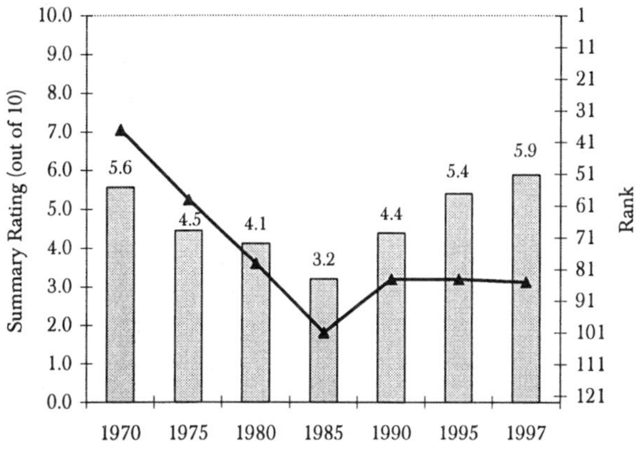


### Total Government Expenditure as a Percentage of GDP

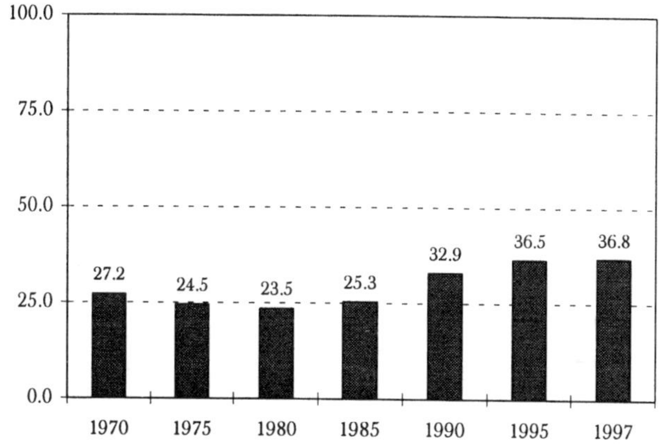


Throughout the last two decades, Brazil's ranking has been low. In 1997, Brazil ranked 85th among 123 countries. Its relative position in the world has been more or less unchanged throughout the period.

The large share of government enterprises is a sign of the government's control over important sectors of the economy. Furthermore, monetary policy remains poor, even following a sharp decrease in annual money growth and the accompanying decrease of the inflation rate from 2,506.5 percent in 1990 to 77.6 percent in 1995 to 7.9 percent in 1997. The high level of inflation variability implies danger.

Remarkable improvement has been made in avoiding negative interest rates: in 1995 the rating was still 0.0 and by 1997, 8.0. The field of government consumption shows a slight improvement, a sign of further reforms under Mr. Cardoso. The share of transfers remains high despite recent efforts to cut the budget. One positive note has been the relaxation of price controls during the 1990s. Brazil's rating in this area rose from 0.0 in 1990 to 8.0 in 1997.

While protectionism remains at a high level, Brazil has moved toward trade liberalization during the 1990s. The mean tariff rate was reduced from 30 percent in 1990 to 11.9 percent in 1997. The standard deviation of tariff rates followed a similar pattern. As the world's 9th largest economy and the main player within the MERCOSUR, reforms of the trade sector would be advantageous for all parties involved.

# BULGARIA

**Economic Freedom Rating (bar) and Rank (line)**

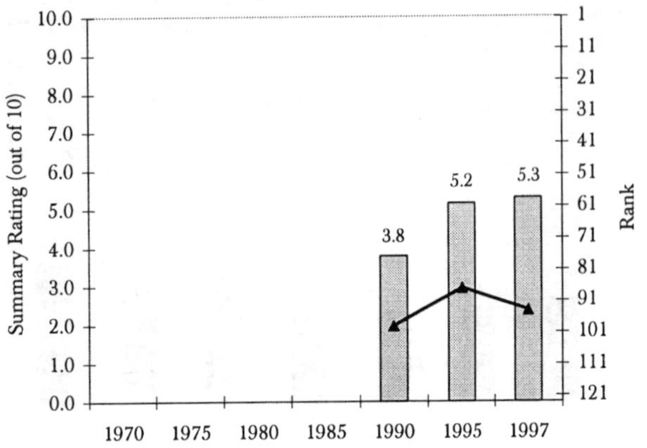


**Total Government Expenditure as a Percentage of GDP**

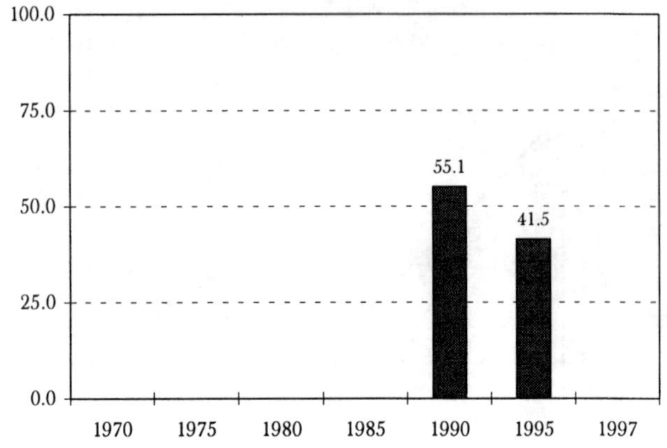


The transition to a market economy in Bulgaria is now ten years old. The reform has been painful, output has declined, and the population has suffered high social costs. However, real GDP growth reached 3.2 percent in 1998. The improvement in economic performance is due to the introduction of a currency-board regime in July of 1997. Even though significant progress has been made in the areas of trade and price liberalization, the prices of energy products, tobacco, and telecom services are still controlled by the government.

Bulgaria's economic freedom rating has grown slowly during the decade, reaching 5.3 in 1997, up from 3.8 in 1990. The former communist country ranks 94$^{th}$ out of 123 in the world. In fact, if Bulgaria's new currency board works as expected, its extremely low monetary area rating (0.0) should be on the rise in the next few years.

1998 also saw the privatization of small and medium enterprises. The privatization of big unprofitable enterprises, however, has gone slowly. If privatization takes hold, Bulgaria's other weak spot (Area II) should improve. If these improvements come to pass, then Bulgaria's overall rating could improve significantly.

# CANADA

## Economic Freedom Rating (bar) and Rank (line)

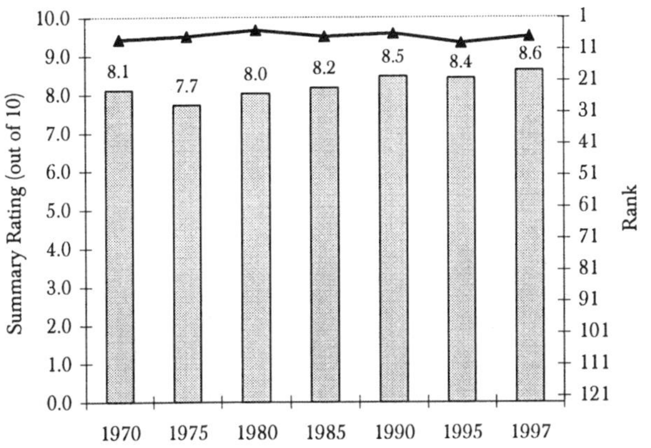


## Total Government Expenditure as a Percentage of GDP

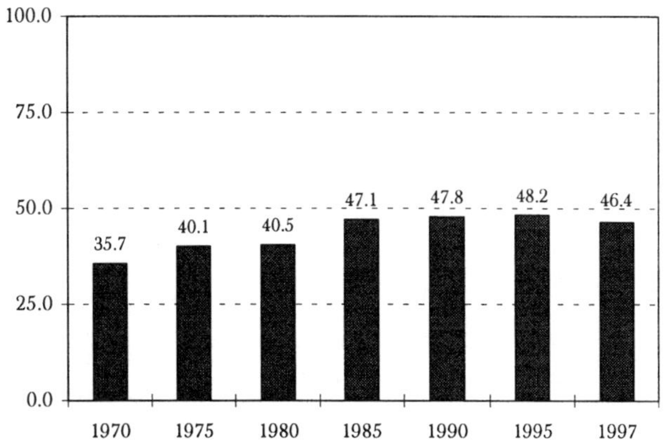


Canada currently ranks 7th overall in economic freedom with a score of 8.6, its highest rating ever. While its ranking of 7th is an improvement over 1995, when it placed 9th, it is still below its ranking of 5th in 1980. The fact that its rating has risen steadily during that time but its ranking has also fallen reflects the faster growth of economic freedom in the rest of the world.

Canada rates well in most of the areas of the index. Its highest scores are earned in Area IV, Freedom to Use Alternative Currencies (a score of 10) and Area V, Legal Structure and Property Rights (a score of 9.4). Canada also does well in monetary policy and freedom of exchange in financial markets. However, the substantial size of government in the Canadian economy along with mediocre scores in Area II, Structure of the Economy and Use of the Markets, drag down Canada's overall rating.

Areas of improvement since the 1970s include Area II, Structure of the Economy and the Use of Markets and Area VII, Freedom of Exchange in Financial Markets. The improvement in Area II stems from declines in the importance of government enterprises, less reliance on price controls, and reductions in the top marginal tax rate. Canada has followed the general worldwide trend in lowering top marginal rates since the 1970s, when the top marginal rate was over 90 percent in some provinces! Despite its improvement, Canada still scores fairly low in this component, receiving a 4. Nevertheless, some of this nation's provinces have made progress in lowering their marginal tax rates and other provinces and the federal government might be expected to follow. The improvements in Area VII derive from an increase in the percent of credit extended to the private sector. This corresponds with a decrease in the importance of government-operated enterprises in the economy.

In other areas of the index, Canada's performance has remained fairly steady, with notable exceptions in Area III, Monetary Policy and Price Stability, and Area V, Legal Structure and Property Rights. After falling during the 1970s, Canada's score in both areas has increased in recent years. In the case of Area III, its initial score has been surpassed while Area V's rating, although increasing, is lower today than it was in 1970.

Much of the current debate in Canada about economic freedom concerns marginal tax rates. Little of this debate has been on the appropriate size of government (where Canada ranks quite poorly) or its functions. The lack of attention to the current substantial size of government, unfortunately, implies a low likelihood of great improvements in Canada's overall score.

# CHILE

### Economic Freedom Rating (bar) and Rank (line)

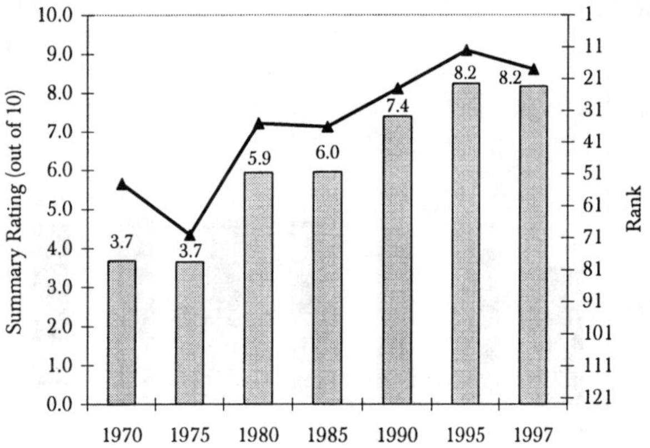


### Total Government Expenditure as a Percentage of GDP

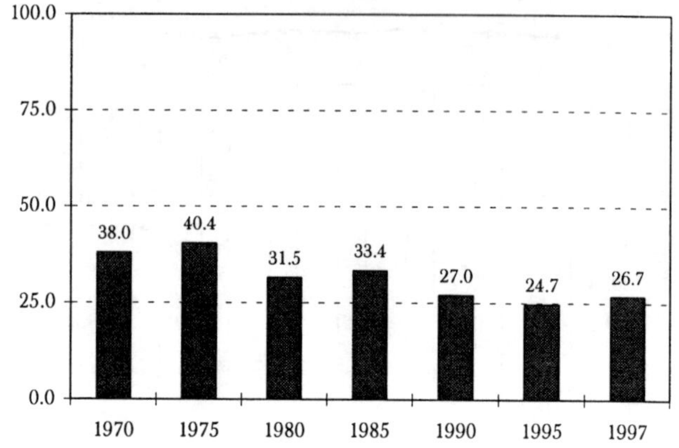


Chile's rating of 3.7 (54th rank) in 1970 was almost the worst rating in the world for that year. Its current rating of 8.2 is good for 18th place. There has been significant privatization of state-owned enterprises, liberalization of trade (note the reduction in the mean tariff rate from 105 percent in 1970 to 9.4 percent in 1997), private ownership of banks, and much improved legal framework. Chile's much celebrated privatized pension plan, though not directly measured in this index, is reflected in the reductions in the transfer sector: 15.3 percent in 1985 and 10.8 percent in 1997.

The recent re-establishment of democracy coupled with this degree of economic freedom surely makes Chile one of the most free Latin nations. It is not a surprise, then, that Chile has grown at a 5.7 percent annual rate in real per-capita income in the 1990s.

# CHINA

## Economic Freedom Rating (bar) and Rank (line)

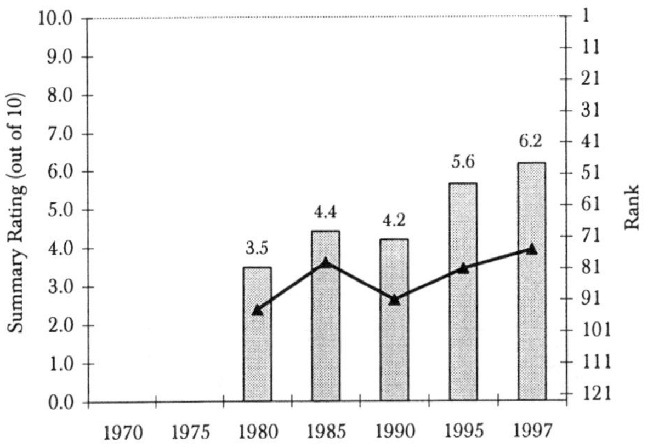


## Total Government Expenditure as a Percentage of GDP

NO RELIABLE DATA AVAILABLE

The most populous country in the world continues a slow march toward economic liberalism. China's rating in the 1990s has improved 2 points to 6.2 while per-capita GDP growth remained very high at 8.65 percent per year. However, despite the positive press about China's economic reforms, it still ranks only 75th in the world.

Most of the positive changes have taken place in the area of economic structure and use of markets, one of China's weakest areas in the economic freedom index. Likewise, the financial market and the country's legal structure have seen a number of positive changes. The rating in Area VII, Freedom of Exchange in Capital and Financial Markets, has risen from 0.0 in 1980 to 3.0 in 1997, still very low but a nice improvement nevertheless. The rating for Area V, Legal Structure and Property Rights, has improved from 6.5 in 1990 to its current 8.5 and rating for Area IV, Freedom to Use Alternative Currencies, improved from 2.5 to 6.8 during the 1990s.

The greatest fear for the Chinese is a possible backward move in the international trade area where additional restrictions on foreign exchange have been imposed as a result of the Asian financial crisis. Also, tariff reductions as a part of the negotiations for entering into the WTO may be slowing under domestic pressures.

# Costa Rica

**Economic Freedom Rating (bar) and Rank (line)**

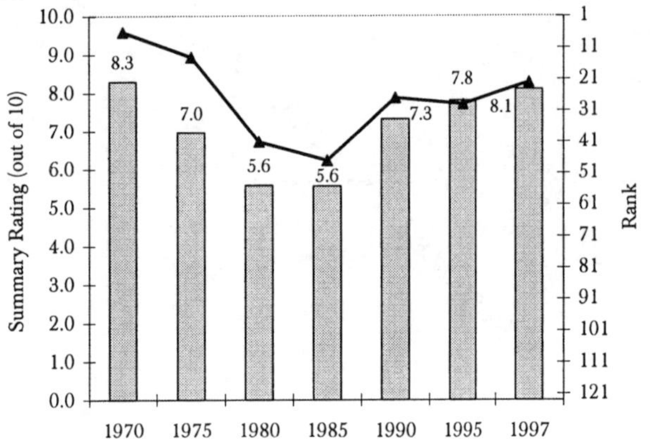


**Total Government Expenditure as a Percentage of GDP**

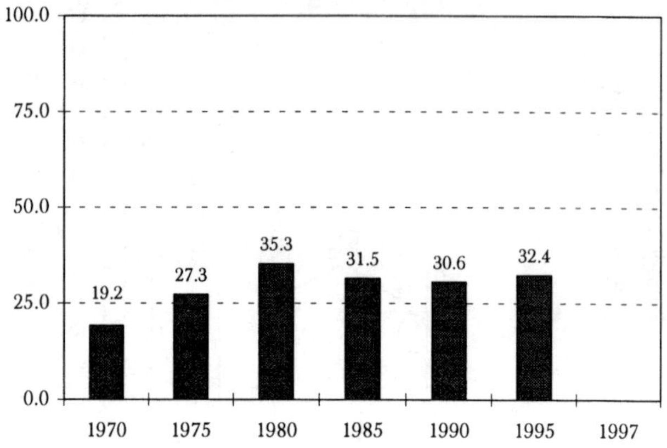


Costa Rica has improved its economic freedom rating in the last few years. Its rating of 8.1 places it 22nd in the world. During the period from 1990 to 1998, the average growth of real GDP was 4.1 percent. With an annual rate of population increase of 2.3 percent (1985–1996), the average real per-capita growth in the last eight years averaged 1.8 percent, similar to that of the United States over the same period.

Government consumption expenditures as a percent of total consumption have fallen from 22.9 percent in 1995 to 17.2 percent in 1997. Although low with respect to public expenditures in many developed countries, this rate is still high when contrasted with developing nations and with the services provided.

The data of the Central Bank of Costa Rica indicate that the average annual inflation rate (CPI) for the 13-year period from 1986 to 1998 was 17.3 percent and the average growth of the money supply (M1), 18.2 percent. The growth of the money supply slowed in the 1990s, as did inflation.

Although residents may freely hold bank accounts in foreign currency, domestically and abroad, foreign banks face many restrictions and regulations that prevent them from operating freely in the country. This severely limits the number of participants in the banking system, a fact that is reflected in a very high spread between the deposit rate and the lending rate and high real interest rates.

# Czech Republic

### Economic Freedom Rating (bar) and Rank (line)

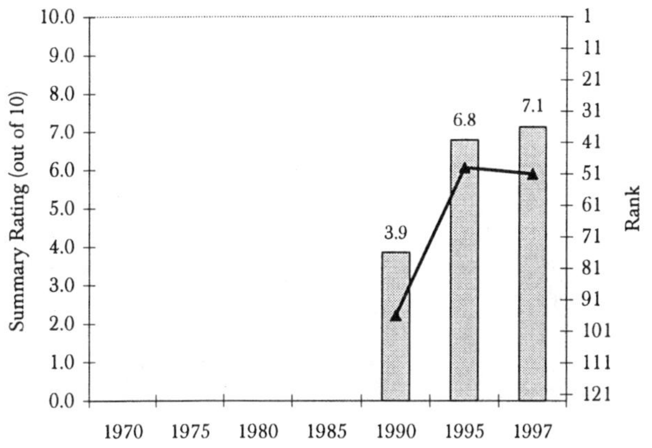


### Total Government Expenditure as a Percentage of GDP

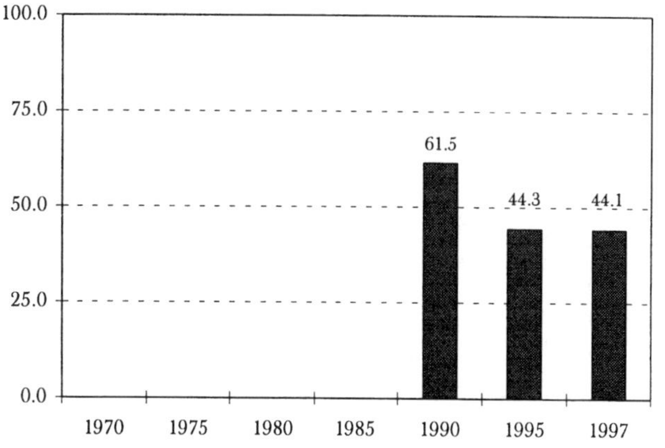


The Czech Republic has made significant moves toward economic freedom since the fall of communism and the Velvet Revolution of 1989. Its summary rating increased from 3.9 in 1990 to 7.1 in 1997 (note that the 1990 figure is for the former Czechoslovakia). This increased the country's ranking from 96th (out of 115) to its current 51st (out of 123). But, after 1995 political deadlock ensued. There has been very little increase in economic freedom since 1995. Virtually no additional moves in the areas of privatization and deregulation have been made.

The Czech Republic made the transition to a market economy more smoothly than most former socialist countries. This country was spared the hyperinflation that beset most other transitional economies. Price controls have been eliminated from most products and the size and scope of state-operated enterprises has been reduced by voucher privatization. Exchange-rate controls have been eliminated and the Czech koruna is now a fully convertible currency. As trade barriers have fallen, the size of the trade sector has grown. Government expenditures for both consumption and income transfers have been curtailed.

However, it is expected that transfers and subsidies as a percent of GDP, already high at 27.2 percent, will increase. Many other problems remain. The economy is still fighting the consequences of a halfway privatization of the banking sector, which is still heavily subsidized. Fiscal policy is highly expansionary; the fiscal deficit is expected to move to an all-time high. The inflation rate is relatively stable and in the single digits. However, high fiscal deficits often invite inflationary monetary policies. This may lead to future problems.

# DENMARK

**Economic Freedom Rating (bar) and Rank (line)**

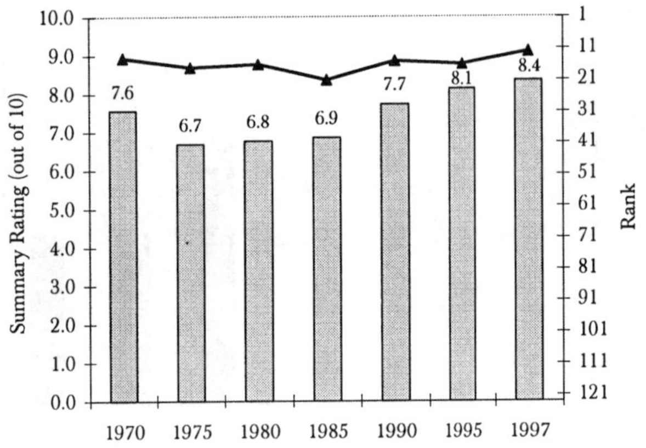


**Total Government Expenditure as a Percentage of GDP**

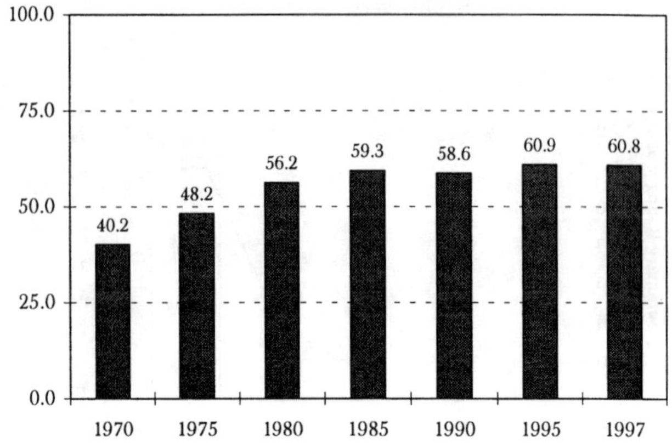


Denmark's ranking has improved from 21st in 1985 to 12th in 1997. The strengths of its economy are the freedom to use alternative currencies as well as its legal structure and guarantee of property rights. Further, the achievements of a consistent monetary policy should be mentioned. The area of capital transactions with foreigners has been improved and got a perfect rating of 10; the previous rating in 1995 was 8.0.

However, the share of government consumption–governmental expenditure and transfers–is particularly high. This consumption is financed to the detriment of the taxpayer and is reflected in an enormous top marginal tax rate (55 percent to 60 percent). For that reason, in this category Denmark receives a rating of 2.0. The Extension of Credit also deserves note. Only 58.7 percent of available credit is given to the private sector, remarkably low in international comparison. As an EU nation, Denmark's revenues on Taxes on International Trade are almost negligible (0.3 percent of trade value) but there is still potential for improving the Mean Tariff Rate (rating 8.6) and Standard Deviation of Tariff rates (rating 7.6) in all the EU nations.

# Dominican Republic

### Economic Freedom Rating (bar) and Rank (line)

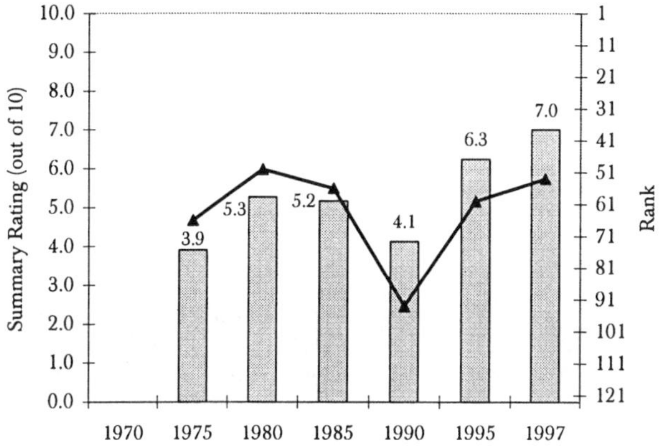


### Total Government Expenditure as a Percentage of GDP

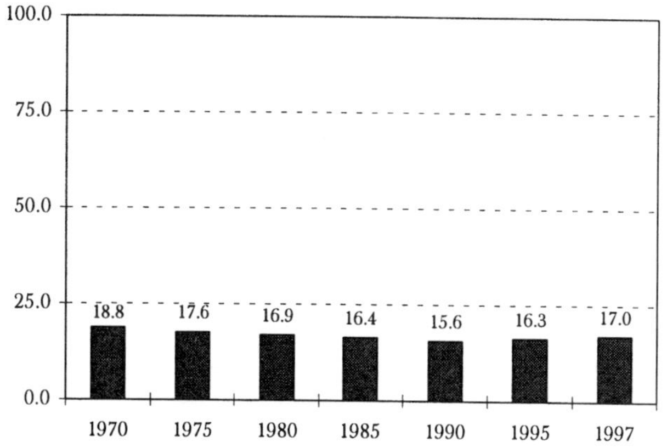


The Dominican Republic rated a 7.0 in 1997, placing it 53rd out of 123 countries. This represents a large increase from the 4.1 rating (93rd ranking) of 1990.

This country has made important improvements in monetary, exchange, and credit policies. The top marginal tax rate has been reduced and mandatory military service has been eliminated.

There was a significant advance over previous years with respect to the enforcement of contracts (Area V-B). In improving its legal structure, the system has more credibility, which would grant confidence to investors.

However, the Dominican Republic could improve other aspects to drive the country towards a higher degree of economic freedom. In particular, lower tariffs and reduction of other trade restrictions are needed. Concerning financial and capital markets, it is still necessary to break barriers that impede the mobility of capital. Dominican Republic needs to eliminate remaining restrictions on currency convertibility.

# ECUADOR

**Economic Freedom Rating (bar) and Rank (line)**

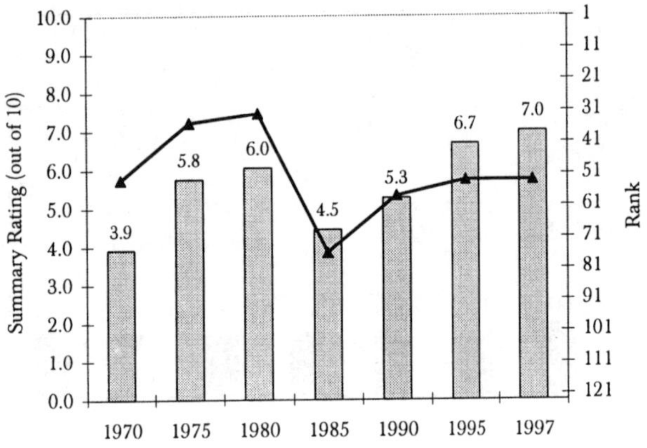


**Total Government Expenditure as a Percentage of GDP**

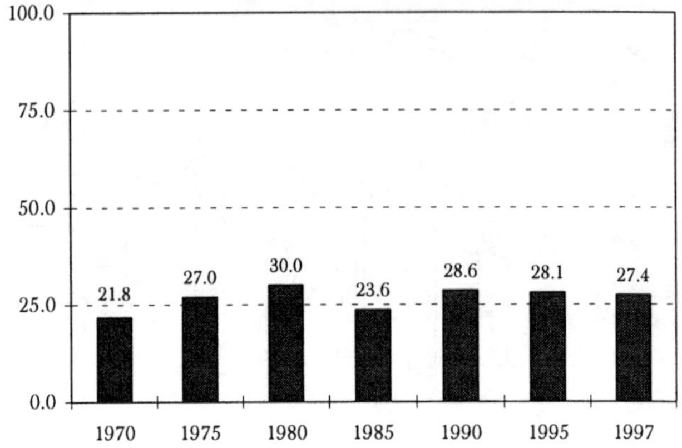


In 1990, Ecuador ranked 58th among the 115 countries in the study. In 1997, Ecuador ranked 53rd among the 123 countries studied. With few exceptions, such as in the area of freedom of exchange in capital and financial markets (Area VII), little improvement in economic freedom can be found. Monetary expansion during the 1990s has led to an annual inflation rate of 26 percent in 1997. The country is in a state of stagnation; per-capita economic growth in the 1990s has been an abysmal 0.90 percent.

Unlike other countries in the region, Ecuador has done almost nothing to privatize government enterprises and little to reduce price controls on gas, electricity, and telephone service. The property-rights structure and legal system is weak and sensitive to political manipulation.

Monetary reform to reduce the discretionary power of the central bank to print money and bail out banks, a cut in tax rates, a reduction in government expenditures, and privatization of government enterprises would help to enhance the health of this economy.

# EL SALVADOR

**Economic Freedom Rating (bar) and Rank (line)**

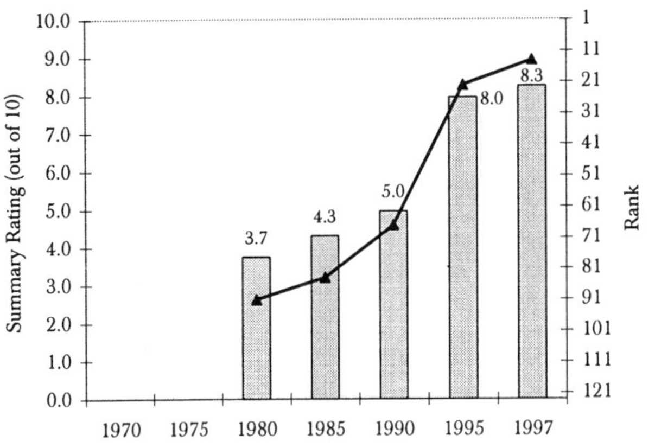


**Total Government Expenditure as a Percentage of GDP**

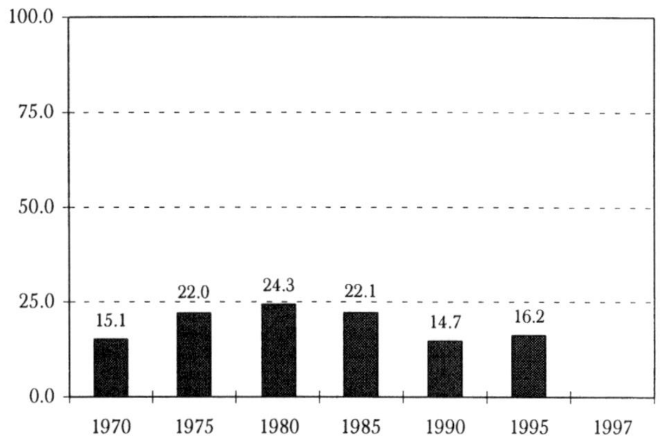


El Salvador is one of the Latin American countries that showed a dramatic improvement in its economic freedom. Its rating of 5.0 in 1990 increased to 8.3 in 1997. El Salvador jumped from the 67th position to the 14th in the world ranking. A more market-oriented program is the main reason for this improvement. Price controls in many markets have been eliminated and government participation in the economy has been reduced through an ambitious privatization process, especially in strategic sectors such as communications and electricity. Moreover, policies promoting trade liberalization and more freedom in financial and capital-market transactions have been adopted.

Monetary policy has been less expansionary. The annual rate of monetary growth has been curtailed from 11.5 percent in 1990 to 5.0 percent in 1997. This allowed the country to reduce its inflation rate from 23 percent in 1990 to 4.6 percent in 1997, one of the lowest rates in the Central America region. In addition, legalization of foreign-currency bank accounts, a reduction in government consumption expenditure, relaxation of exchange-rate controls, a stronger legal system and a lower exchange-rate premium in the black market have contributed to the improvement in El Salvador's economic freedom rating.

# ESTONIA

**Economic Freedom Rating (bar) and Rank (line)**

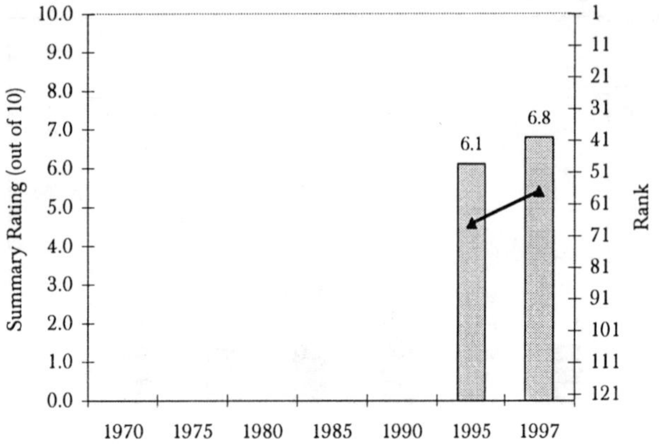


**Total Government Expenditure as a Percentage of GDP**

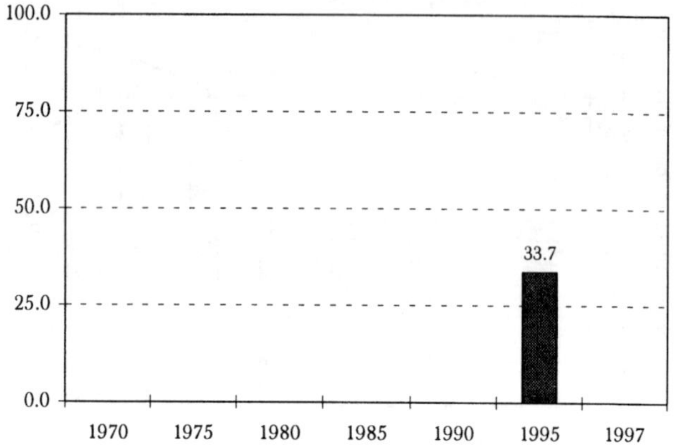


In 1997, Estonia ranks 57th in terms of economic freedom among 123 countries. Estonia's strength is its liberalized trade sector; taxes on international trade are negligible. Its efforts to regain monetary stability have also borne some fruit. The annual money growth for the past five years (relative to economic growth) shrank from 74.6 percent in 1995 to 38.4 percent, and the inflation rate has gone from 29.0 percent to 11.4 percent. Broad goals to reach firm monetary stability and credibility still remain.

The share of government consumption and transfers, though modest by European standards, is relatively high compared to the rest of the world. Reforms leading to privatization are under way to reduce the government enterprises. For example, in 1997, a partial privatization of Estonian Telecom was conducted to reduce the government's stake to 27 percent. Visible restructuring of the banking sector was also undertaken. However, restrictions on ownership of foreign currencies still remain.

One point for consideration is the lack of a fully guaranteed rule of law and viability of contracts, a characteristic of all three Baltic States.

A threat for Estonia's economic prosperity is the economic situation in Russia, although the bilateral trade dependencies are declining since Estonia has gained independence. Estonia ambitiously continues structural reforms to match EU accession requirements for membership as a long-term target. The growth of real GDP moved forward from 4.3 percent in 1995 to 10.6 percent in 1997.

# FINLAND

**Economic Freedom Rating (bar) and Rank (line)**

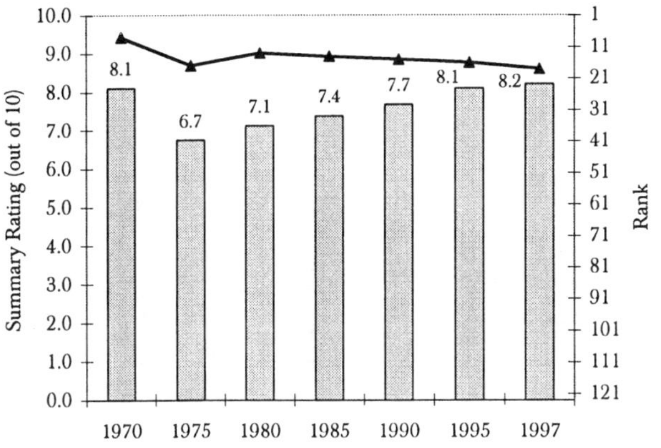


**Total Government Expenditure as a Percentage of GDP**

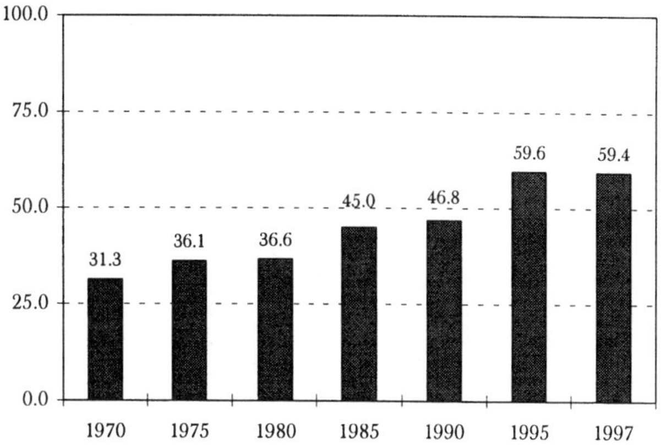


Finland's 8.2 rating places it at 18th position among 123 countries in 1997, about the same as its 8.1 rating and 8th place finish (out of 57) in 1970.

Despite the recent economic revival the government shows no significant structural realignment in terms of the size and share of government consumption. Further, transfers and subsidies remain high–21.9 percent of GDP–and are financed by top marginal tax rates of 53 percent to 60 percent.

A receding governmental share of the economy would increase the potential for economic growth.

Finland's economic strengths are an established and reliable legal structure, the freedom of citizens to maintain foreign currency accounts domestically and abroad, and an almost fully liberalized foreign-trade sector. Also, attempts to control the annual money supply were effective as the inflation rate shrank to 1.5 percent.

# FRANCE

**Economic Freedom Rating (bar) and Rank (line)**

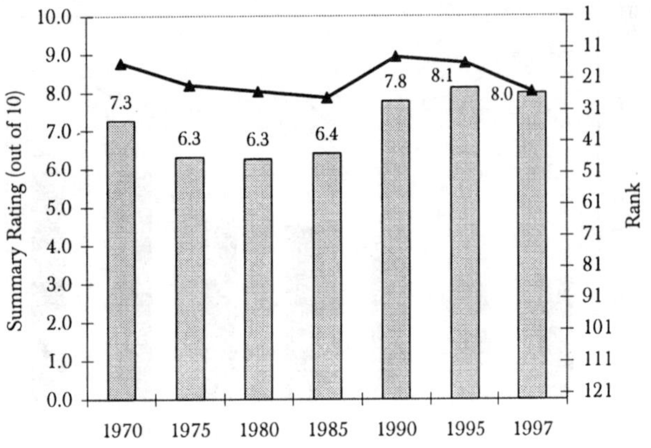


**Total Government Expenditure as a Percentage of GDP**

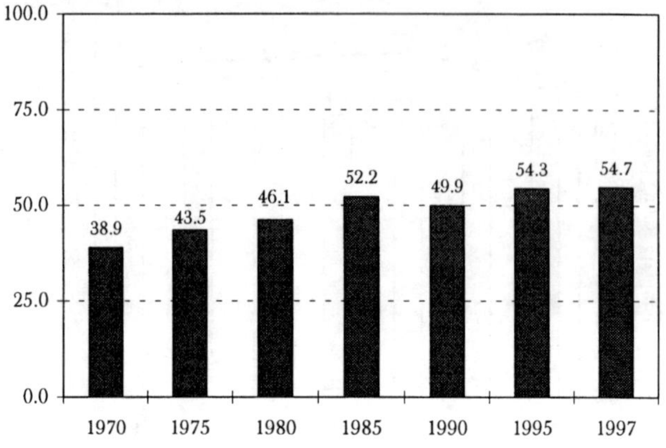


In 1995, France ranked 16th and slipped to 25th in 1997. The most obvious reduction was in the rule of law component–from 10.0 in 1995 to 7.0. Nevertheless, the credibility of its legal structure is far from seriously damaged and remains reliable.

France's monetary administration pursues strict policies of price stability. Its achievements culminated in an inflation rate of 1 percent in 1997 with an inflation variability of 0.5 for the recent five years. Citizens are free to own foreign currencies and the banking sector is fully deregulated. But, in the area of capital transactions with foreigners, constraints still exist. As one of the countries pushing European integration energetically, its foreign-trade sector receives good scores.

France's problem areas are the large share of government consumption, huge transfers and business subsidies, and a stalled deregulation and privatization program. Government consumption, 24.2 percent (1997) of total consumption, resembles the shares of leading western industrial countries. A significant portion of the economy, 28.8 percent of GDP, was redistributed as transfers and subsidies, financing double-digit unemployment (12.3 percent) and distorting market competition.

The real GDP growth rate for 1997 was 2.3 percent but going forward with structural reforms within the government apparatus and more liberalization efforts would enable higher potential growth rates.

# GERMANY

**Economic Freedom Rating (bar) and Rank (line)**

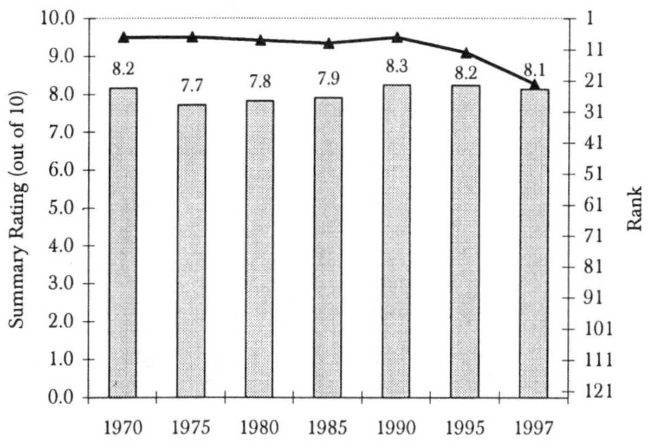


**Total Government Expenditure as a Percentage of GDP**

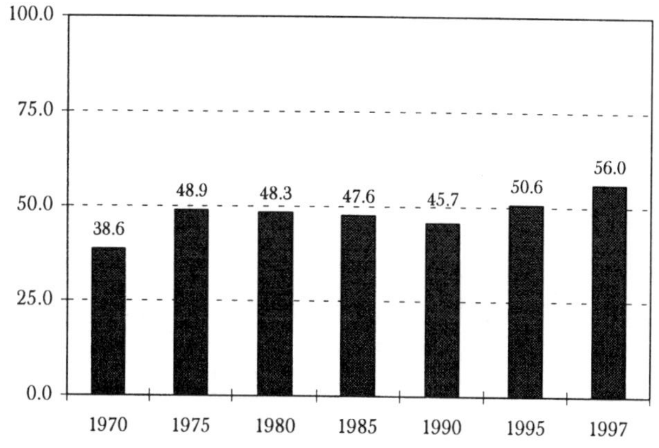


In the immediate post-war years, Germany had been one of the most free economies in the world. This was the basic reason for the "economic miracle" at the time, when the country had one of the fastest growing economies in the world. Since the 1970s, stagnation has been the characteristic feature of Germany's economic policy. The economic-freedom rating has fallen slightly during the last two decades (from 8.2 in 1970 to 8.1 most recently). The relative decline is even more worrisome than the absolute one: because most other countries have liberalized their economies since the 1980s, Germany's relative decline, if compared to the development of the rest of the world, is fairly dramatic. In 1970, Germany's 8.2 rating made it the 7th most free economy in the world; its current 8.1 rating places it at only 22nd place.

There are, of course, positive aspects to be noted. Stability in monetary policy and prices was boldly maintained by the independent Deutsche Bundesbank (German Federal Bank, i.e. the central bank). Trade policies have been oriented toward free trade and the trade sector has consistently registered a strong performance.

There are three major weaknesses, however, which have not been dealt with by government for decades despite growing pressure. One of them is high government consumption, which hovers around 25 percent of total consumption. Another is the highly developed welfare state of Germany, which contributes to a large transfer sector (over 20 percent of GDP). The third problem is taxation. With a 56-percent top marginal tax rate, Germany imposes one of the highest top tax rates in the world. In 1997, the government tried to implement a radical tax reform to reduce this tax rate but it was defeated by the opposition in the Bundesrat (Second Chamber). The new government, elected in 1998, is also planning a tax reform, the outcome of which remains unclear.

Germany also still has a highly regulated economy. There have been major successful reforms in some areas, such as telecommunications and electricity. However, the German labour market remains as highly regulated as ever and, therefore, the main problem of the German economy will also remain unsolved. While, on the whole, the German economy may still perform fairly well in the future under the given circumstances, unemployment will continue to stay at an intolerably high level.

# GREECE

**Economic Freedom Rating (bar) and Rank (line)**

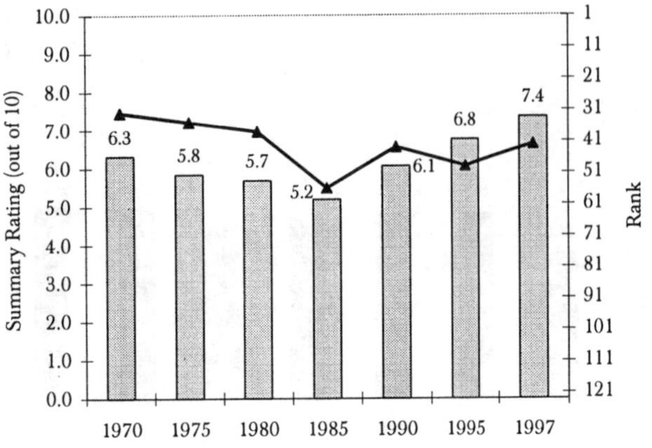


**Total Government Expenditure as a Percentage of GDP**

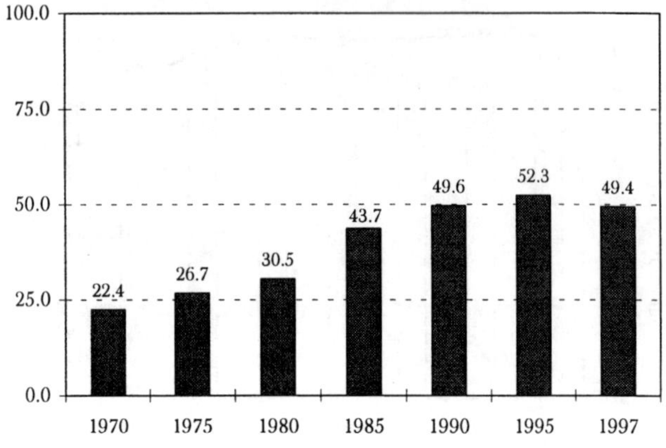


Greece has improved its rating somewhat since 1970 but has been on an erratic path towards greater economic freedom. In 1997, Greece climbed up to 42nd position from a previous rank of 49th in 1995.

One area of improvement is the freedom to hold foreign currencies, still limited as late as 1995. Further positive aspects are the provision of a functional legal structure and the guarantee of property rights, although deficiencies still exist in this area. Greece scores quite low in the Structure of the Economy and Use of Markets, in part due to its reliance on conscription for military recruits and a large government enterprise sector. The 45 percent top marginal tax rate also lowers Greece's score in Area II.

There is a push toward further liberalization of financial markets. Around 50 percent of available credit is channelled to the private sector, up from 39 percent in 1990, and capital transactions with foreigners are less restricted. Since 1995 the government has moved to dam the abundant flow of transfers and subsidies. Compared to 1990, where 20.5 percent of GDP was redistributed as transfers and subsidies, in 1995 19 percent and, in 1997, 17 percent of GDP was used. This is still high but it is a move in the right direction.

# GUATEMALA

### Economic Freedom Rating (bar) and Rank (line)

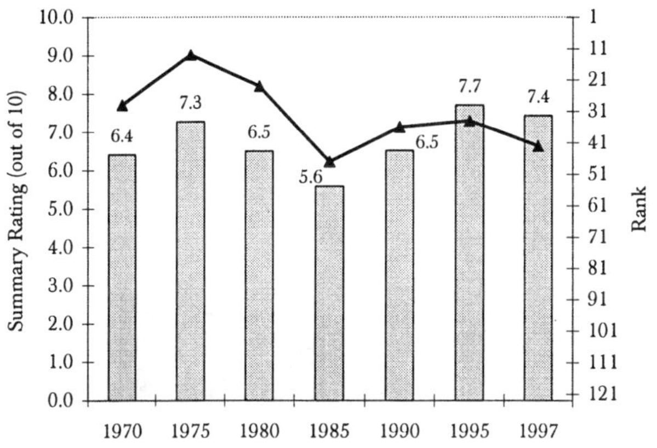


### Total Government Expenditure as a Percentage of GDP

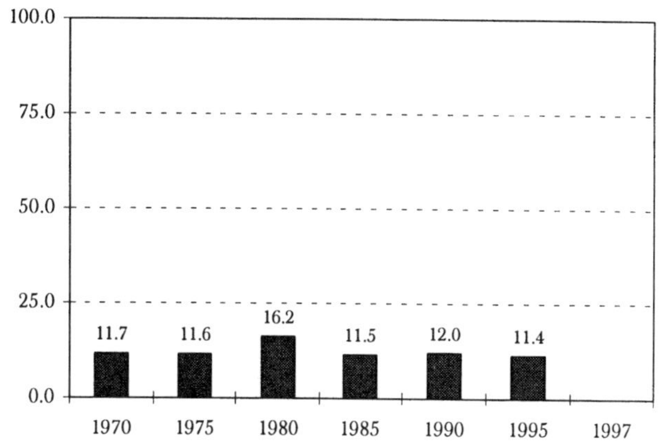


Guatemala ranks 42nd among the countries in this study. This represents little change: in 1990, it ranked in 36th place. Except for a decline during the 1980s that was primarily the result of high government consumption, monetary instability, restrictive exchange rate controls, higher trade tariffs, and many price controls, Guatemala's summary rating has been fairly steady throughout the last two decades.

Inflation has declined to 8.4 percent in 1997. Price controls were relaxed. Several previously regulated markets were opened. A number of state-owned companies have been privatized. Government consumption as a percentage of GDP has declined and transfers and subsidies have been reduced. Moreover, the top marginal tax was reduced from 34 percent in 1995 to 25 percent in 1997.

Modest steps towards more economic freedom have been taken in the commercial area. Within the Northern Triangle (Guatemala, Honduras and El Salvador), duties on international trade have declined slightly during recent years and some other steps have been taken to reduce non-tariff restrictions.

Although positive steps toward more economic freedom have been adopted in recent years, Guatemala still needs to make progress in other key areas where freedom could be improved: it still needs to liberalize currency convertibility and advance on reforms that allow its legal structure to move closer to a true rule-of-law. In addition, Guatemala's use of military conscription hurts its economic freedom rating.

# HONDURAS

**Economic Freedom Rating (bar) and Rank (line)**

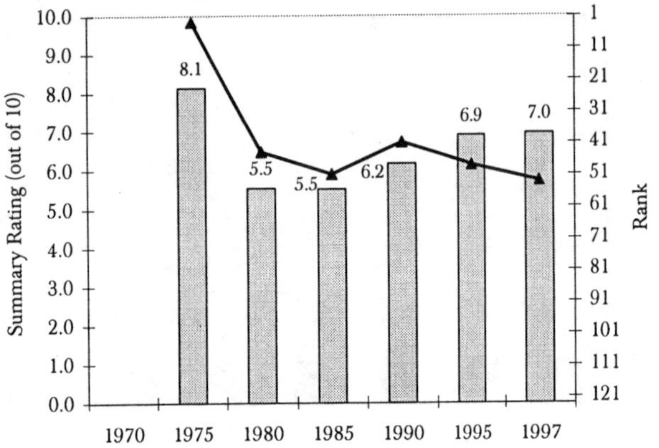


**Total Government Expenditure as a Percentage of GDP**

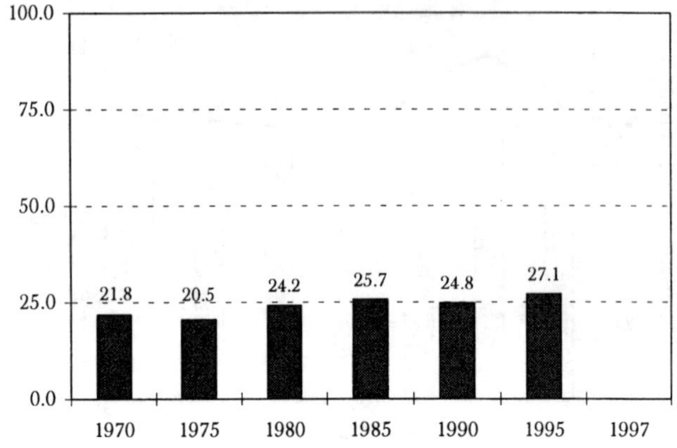


Although Honduras has increased its summary rating from 6.2 in 1990 to 7.0 in 1997, it has dropped from 41st to 53rd place. This relative movement away from more economic freedom is explained by uncertainty in monetary policy, an increase in the top marginal tax rate, and the existence of price and exchange controls.

Although Honduras has made efforts to have a less expansionary monetary policy, to reduce the top marginal tax rate, and to increase the size of its commercial sector (as a percentage of GDP), results are still very poor. The inflation rate still remains high. In 1990, the inflation rate was 23.3 percent and, in 1997, 20.2 percent. Some efforts have been made to reduce the size of government through privatization of state-owned companies but results are very poor and no significant improvement has been achieved in this area.

Actions were taken to remove financial and capital-market controls and to fortify the legal structure. This explained the improvements shown for this country in its effort to approach to a rule-of-law. Nonetheless, the current ranking of Honduras is well below that achieved during the mid-1970s.

# HONG KONG

### Economic Freedom Rating (bar) and Rank (line)

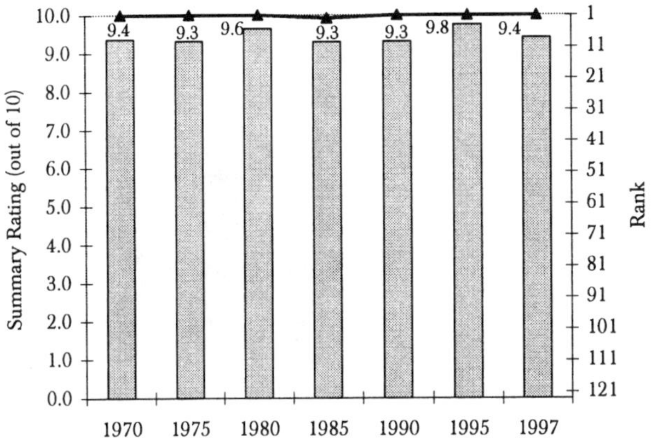


### Total Government Expenditure as a Percentage of GDP

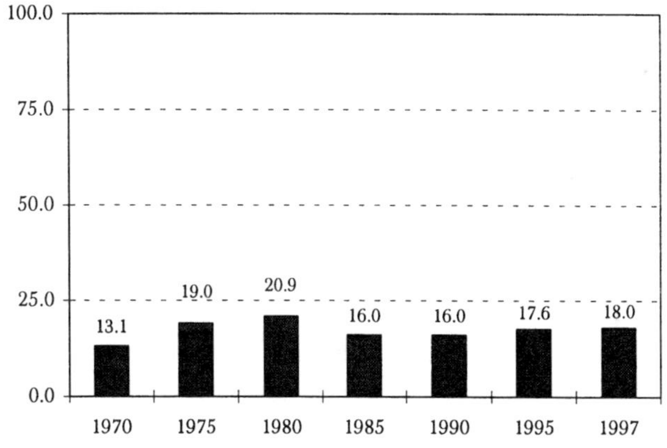


The resumption of sovereignty over Hong Kong by China on July 1, 1997 has not materially hurt the economic freedom long enjoyed by the people of the territory. The latest economic freedom index stands at a level of 9.4, maintaining Hong Kong's primacy as the most economically free place on earth. This year, though, they will share that title with Singapore whose rating was also 9.4. The concept of "One Country, Two Systems" seems to be working. On the whole, the government of the Hong Kong Special Administration Region has been given considerable autonomy by the central government in Beijing in conducting its affairs.

The Asian financial turmoil has taken its toll on Hong Kong. After decades of high growth, real GDP shrank by 3 percent in 1998. The unemployment rate shot up from 3 percent to 6 percent, property values decreased by one-third, and the stock market took a beating. Given the severity of the economic downturn, many suggested that the old policy of "positive non-intervention" could not be maintained.

The government did respond to this crisis. The two most controversial moves were the suspension of public land sales for a year and the purchase of more than HK$100 billion worth of shares of Hong Kong blue chip companies in August 1998. Such overt intervention in the market was prompted by the desire to avoid a collapse in the property market, the concern over bank failures, and the support for the Hong Kong dollar. The government intervention, though condemned in some quarters, had the support of the public.

Concerned by the heavy dependence of the economy on the property and financial sectors, the government has taken steps to diversify the economy. A cyberport on multimedia and internet services will be developed; Disneyland is being courted to build a theme park; there are talks of science parks, a silicon harbour, and a Chinese Medicine Centre.

The government has adopted a policy to sell public rental housing units to their incumbent tenants. This policy, championed by the Hong Kong Centre for Economic Research for close to a decade, will enhance the efficiency of the housing market, and make the distribution of public housing subsidies more equitable. The telecommunication market is being further liberalized. More competition was introduced into the transportation sector. There are more franchised bus companies and more routes. The interest rate agreement as maintained by the banking cartel is scheduled to be completely abolished next year.

*(Continued on page 82)*

# HUNGARY

**Economic Freedom Rating (bar) and Rank (line)**

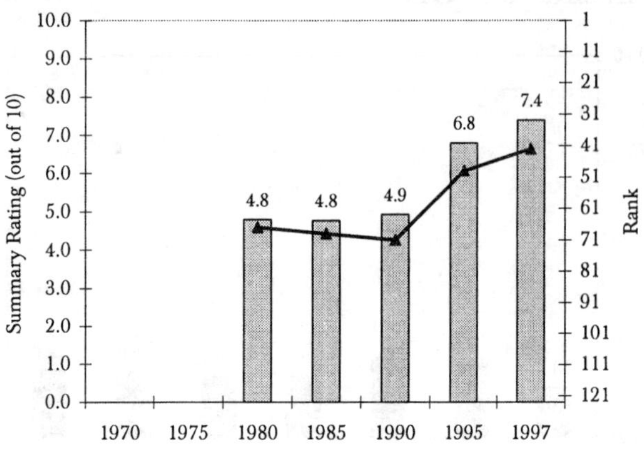


**Total Government Expenditure as a Percentage of GDP**

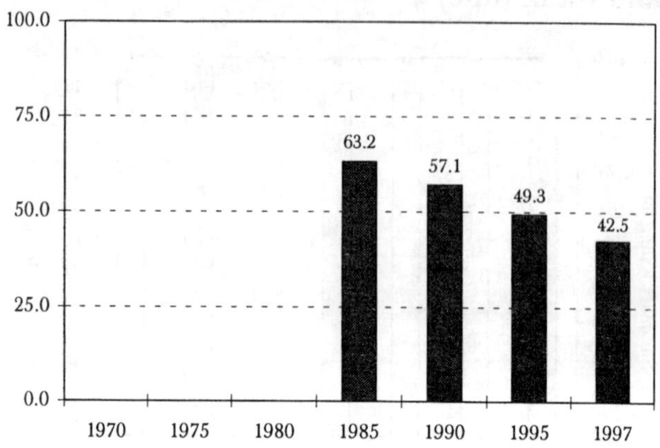


In transforming itself from an economy that was centrally (or, semi-centrally) planned toward one that is market-driven, Hungary made significant progress towards economic freedom, the results of which are captured by its economic freedom rating. In this decade, Hungary showed solid improvement in the rating, which jumped from 4.9 in 1990 to 6.8 in 1995 and further to 7.4 in 1997. This ranked it 42nd in 1997, up from 71st in 1990.

The comprehensive stabilization package introduced in 1995 had some temporary negative effects on the assessment of economic freedom: (1) the Consumer Price Index jumped abruptly, increasing temporarily the uncertainty among the economic actors and the variability of the prices; (2) the levied temporary import surcharge decreased the free international exchange of goods (by 1997 the import surcharge had been gradually abandoned).

Nevertheless, some good resulted: (1) the tight monetary and restrictive fiscal policy reduced the rate of inflation; (2) the new exchange-rate regime became credible; (3) the internal and external equilibrium was restored; (4) the size of the government sector decreased; (5) the competitiveness of the private sector strengthened; (6) Hungary remained attractive to foreign capital.

Institutional measures were also taken to liberalize the economy and to cut back the government sector. Privatization went ahead rapidly. Restrictions on foreigners entering the Hungarian money market were eased. The pay-as-you-go pension system was replaced by a 3-pillar system, including a new fully-funded pillar as well.

Marginal tax rates were decreased slightly after the temporary rise in the 1995 stabilization package. The top rate jumped from 44 percent in 1995 to 48 percent in 1996, then fell to 42 percent in 1997 and remained the same in 1998. After the general elections in 1998, the new government declared a new tax and contribution policy to reduce the private sector's burden. Accordingly, the top rate for 1999 fell to 40 percent. Social insurance contributions paid by companies have also fallen. A special sort of tax is conscription. It remained in force but the duration was shortened significantly. Early in the 1990s, it lasted 18 months; this was cut back to 12 months and then to 9 months in 1994, giving more room for individual freedom.

*(Continued on page 82)*

# ICELAND

### Economic Freedom Rating (bar) and Rank (line)

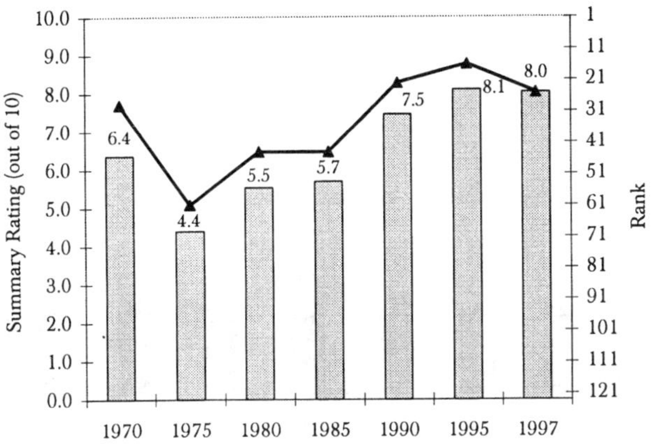


### Total Government Expenditure as a Percentage of GDP

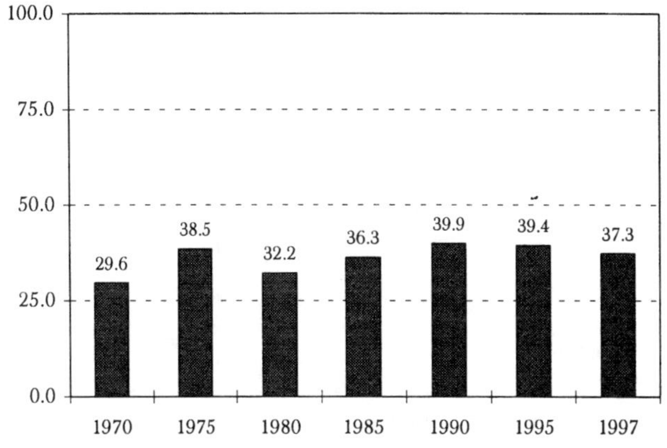


Iceland's rating of 8.0 placed it 25th among the 123 countries in our study. In 1995, it placed 16th with a rating of 8.1. This decline in rank is due to the more vigorous efforts of other countries towards greater economic freedom. But all told, Iceland has rebounded nicely from the doldrums of the 1970s and 1980s when its rating fell to very low levels largely as a result of unstable money and price policies.

The share of government consumption is, as in all western European economies, relatively high and, during the last decades, there has been a tendency for it to increase. Since 1985, the sector of transfers and subsidies has shrunk. The cut in the top marginal tax rate (42 percent) and deregulation of the banking sector in the field of saving deposits in government-owned financial institutions are other positive signs.

The citizens of Iceland are free to own foreign currency accounts and the country has a functional and well-established legal structure that provides a sound base for stable economic activities. Its monetary policies are showing promise in maintaining the inflation rate at a level that will fulfill the Maastricht-criteria–for 1997 the inflation rate was only 1.6 percent.

# INDIA

**Economic Freedom Rating (bar) and Rank (line)**

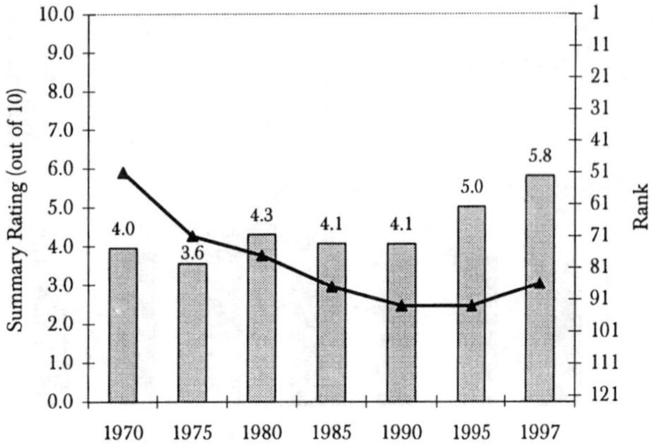


**Total Government Expenditure as a Percentage of GDP**

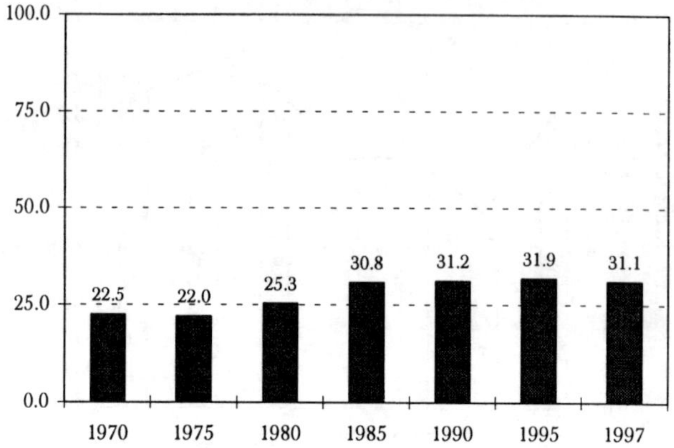


A shift in India's economic policy took place in 1991 when central planning appeared to give way to market forces. The large increase in the economic freedom rating of 1.7 points during the 1990s in the Summary Rating marks that shift. But, in relative terms this improvement has barely kept pace with the liberalization of the rest of the world. India's rank only improved from 93rd (out of 115) to 86th (out of 123) in the 1990s.

The score of 4.1 on Component VI: International Exchange clearly indicates the long path India still has to travel, even though this is the area where India has seen the most improvement. The ratings for Area II: Structure of the Economy and Use of Markets and Area VII: Freedom of Exchange in Capital and Financial Markets suggest that the state control of the domestic economy through price controls, nationalized banking and insurance industry, and public sector enterprises has seen little change.

The improvement in Area V: Legal Structure and Property Rights indicates the increasing independence of the judiciary and of the agencies that supervise the government, like Central Vigilance Commission, Comptroller and Auditor General, and especially the Election Commission, which has curtailed sops given by ruling parties just before elections. The changes in the components of the Index provide reason for guarded optimism.

# IRELAND

### Economic Freedom Rating (bar) and Rank (line)

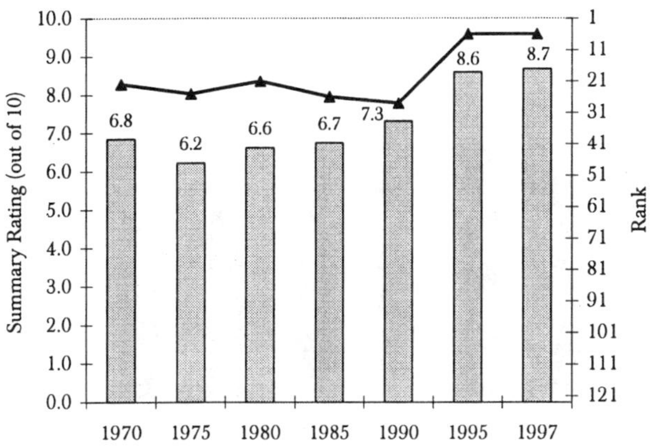


### Total Government Expenditure as a Percentage of GDP

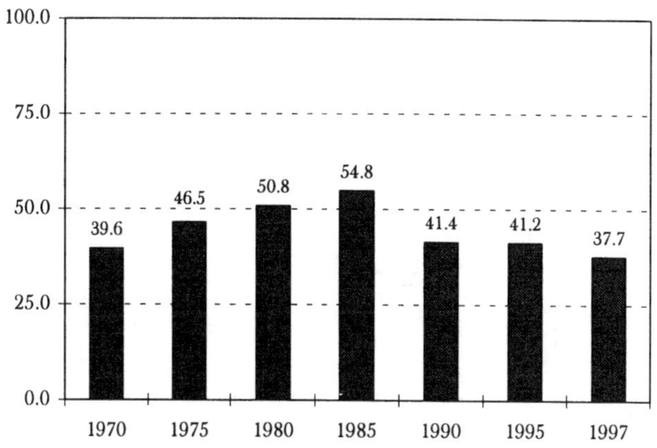


Ireland has been one of the few real success stories of Europe. Beginning in the early 1990s, Ireland embarked on an impressive liberalization program and has now achieved a rating of 8.7 to gain 6th position.

Ireland's economy is one of the most explosive economies in Western Europe. Its growth rate of real GDP for 1997 was a formidable 10.5 percent and, on average, from 1990 to 1997 it grew annually by 6.6 percent.

Ireland's government spending has fallen mostly by reducing the size of the national debt and the accompanying interest payments (a factor that is not fully captured by the government consumption and transfer data). Between 1986 and 1989, government employment fell by 10 percent. Marginal tax rates for high-income individuals have been reduced from the brutal 1975 rate of 80 percent to 58 percent in 1986 and 48 percent in the period from 1992 to 1997. In 1998, the top rate was reduced to 46 percent. Even so, the 3 rating in the marginal tax component is the only really significant blight on Ireland's economic freedom rating.

Supporting these developments was the contribution of monetary policy and legal structure. The latter got a perfect 10 rating. Since the 1990s, the inflation rate has fallen to 1.8 percent in 1997. There are no restrictions upon citizens who wish to maintain foreign currency accounts domestically and abroad.

# ISRAEL

**Economic Freedom Rating (bar) and Rank (line)**

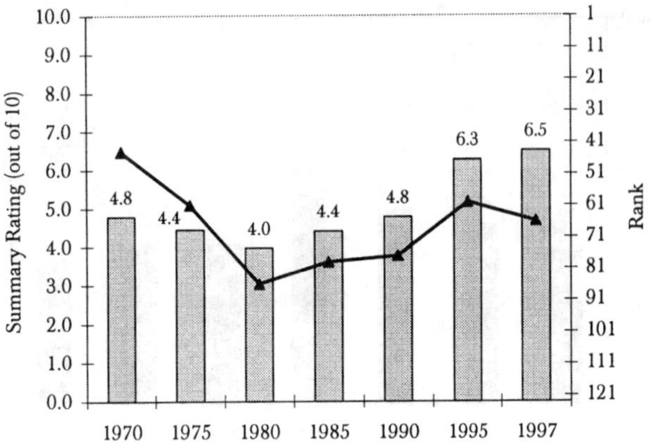


**Total Government Expenditure as a Percentage of GDP**

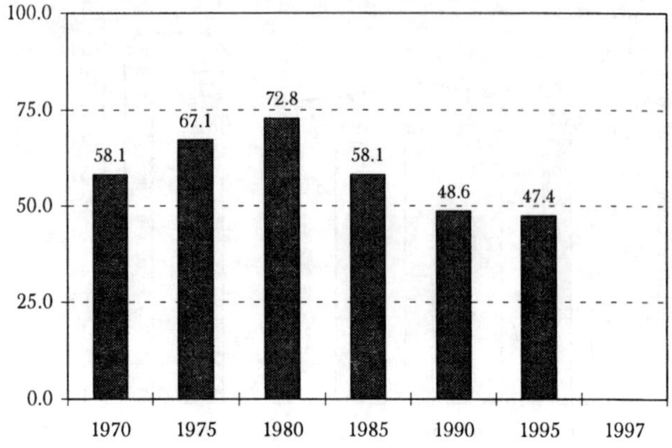


Israel's rating has improved only slightly over the last three decades from 4.8 to 6.5. At times it has been ranked near to the bottom of the list (86th in 1980, for instance) but now holds 66th place.

Israel's government consumes a large portion of the nation's resources; it also has a huge regulatory presence. State-owned enterprises abound, price controls are quite extensive, marginal tax rates are high and apply at low levels of income, and military conscription is used. Banks are all but nationalized, ownership of foreign currency is partially restricted, capital transactions are restricted, and trade is reduced by non-tariff barriers.

The only bright spot for Israel is that it has managed to get its monetary regime under control. The recent single digit inflation rates represent a huge improvement over the three digit rates in the 1980s.

# ITALY

### Economic Freedom Rating (bar) and Rank (line)

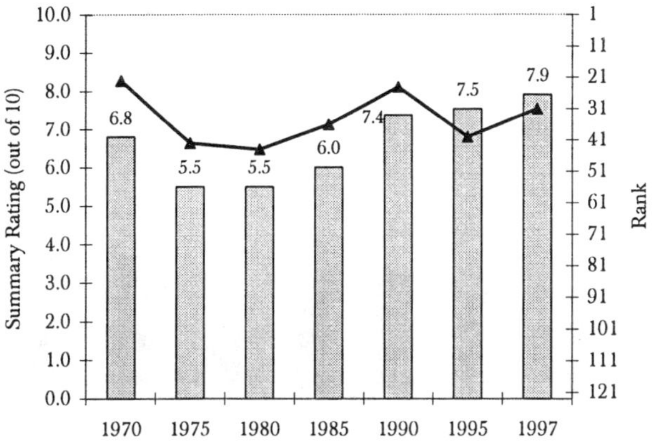


### Total Government Expenditure as a Percentage of GDP

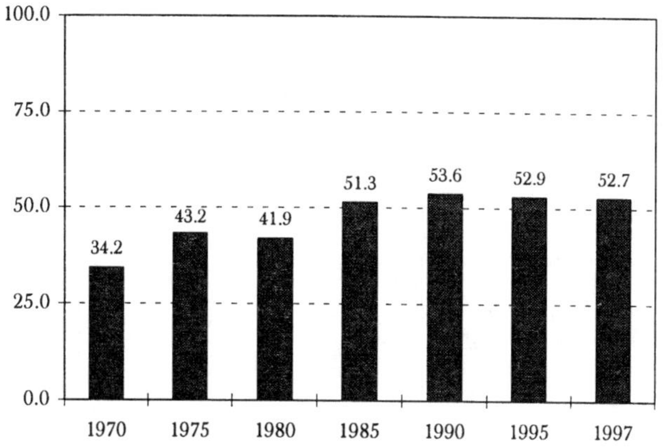


Italy ranked 31st in 1997, down from its rank of 24th in 1990. Among the major industrial countries, Italy lags behind in terms of economic freedom, doing better than only a handful of its European neighbours.

The bright spots are freedom of exchange in capital and financial markets, use of alternative currencies, legal structure, security of property rights and international trade. These results have been achieved through the effort to join the European Monetary Union (EMU). As a co-founder of EMU, Italy has been stimulated to deregulate the financial market and other important areas of the economy. Moreover, in order to fulfill the Maastricht's criteria, Italy reduced its historically high inflation rate and cut the public deficit below the level of 3 percent of GDP.

The size of the government in terms of consumption, transfers, and subsidies has been slightly reduced but remains huge: in 1997, government consumption was over 20 percent of total consumption and transfers and subsidies accounted for more than 20 percent of GDP.

The structure of the economy represents the most critical issue. Although the privatization plan is proceeding, it seems to gain ground too slowly. In 1997, state-owned enterprises still represented more than a quarter of the national economy. The national power-generating utility (ENEL) is state owned and the state directly owns the national railway system. The national Mail Service is state-owned. Some privatization is expected to be realized during the next year but, as in the past, some of it will undoubtedly be deferred.

Most of the prices are determined by the market forces; a few controls are levied on energy and agriculture in accordance with the framework set by the European Union. The Italian top personal marginal tax rate ranks near the top level worldwide though there is some prospect for tax reform in the future.

# JAPAN

### Economic Freedom Rating (bar) and Rank (line)

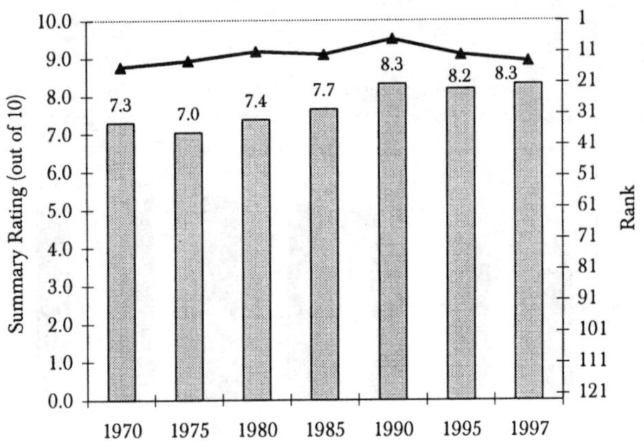


### Total Government Expenditure as a Percentage of GDP

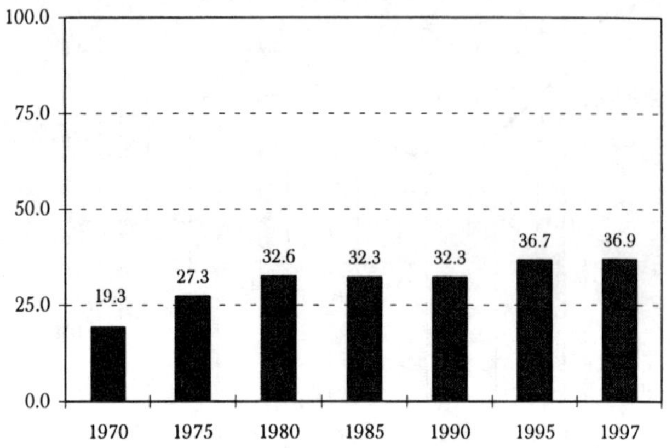


Japan's ranking moved modestly higher between 1970 and 1990. Faced with consequences of the Asian flu at the beginning of the 1990s, the government's trend toward greater economic freedom lost momentum. This allowed other countries to move past Japan in terms of ranking even as its summary rating remained relatively the same. Japan fell from 7th position in 1990 to 14th in 1997.

Japan's strength remains in the field of money and inflation but the incomplete reformation of the banking sector (bad loans), the outflow of private savings from government-owned Post-Banks, and the endangered independence of the Bank of Japan could cast doubt on future positive developments. The figures for ownership of banks remain constant (rating 5.0) because of the size and presumed importance of the government-owned banks for Japan's economy. Successful deregulation policies are, however, being finalized.

Japan also needs to improve in Area II (Economic Structure and Use of Markets) since it had poor ratings in IIA (Government Enterprises) and IIB (Price Controls). The marginal tax rate (65 percent) that applies to its most productive citizens is out of line with the rest of the world and warrants a rating of 2 in that component. Japan's use of non-tariff (and even non-quota) trade barriers is reflected in the unusually small size of its trade sector when compared to expectations.

# Latvia

### Economic Freedom Rating (bar) and Rank (line)

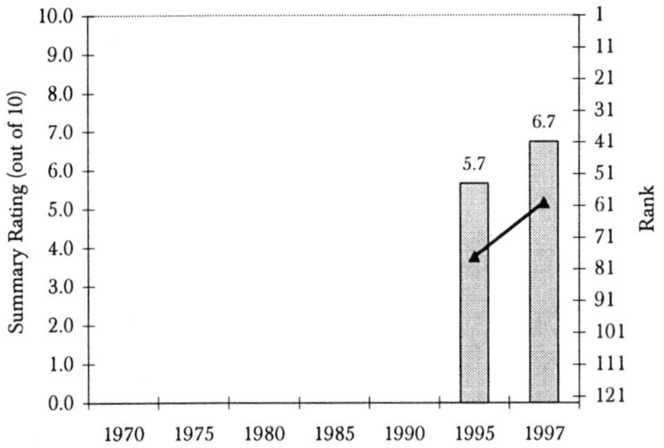


### Total Government Expenditure as a Percentage of GDP

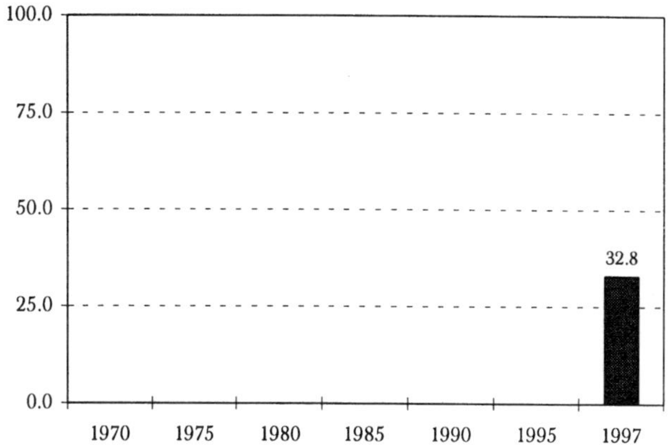


Latvia improved its relative position from 77th in 1995 to 60th in 1997.

Latvia shares some of the characteristics of the other Baltic states. Latvia reduced its annual money growth (relative to economic growth) for the past five years from 49.5 percent in 1995 to 18.5 percent in 1997. At the same time, its inflation rate fell from 16.0 percent to 6.6 percent.

There are also problems with the rule of law and recognition of property rights. Ownership of foreign currencies is not fully allowed–a measure to avert outflow of foreign capital resources–and the relatively high share of government consumption, though modest by European Standards, is significant.

The reduction of government enterprises is worthy of mention. Latvia has improved its rating from 0.0 in 1995 to 4.0 in 1997. Although Latvia's privatization reforms lagged behind other reforms, privatization got a refreshing impetus in 1997 when a new competition law was approved.

# LITHUANIA

**Economic Freedom Rating (bar) and Rank (line)**

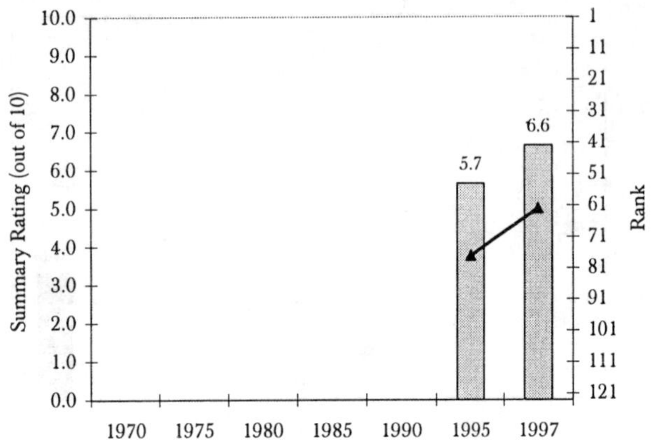


**Total Government Expenditure as a Percentage of GDP**

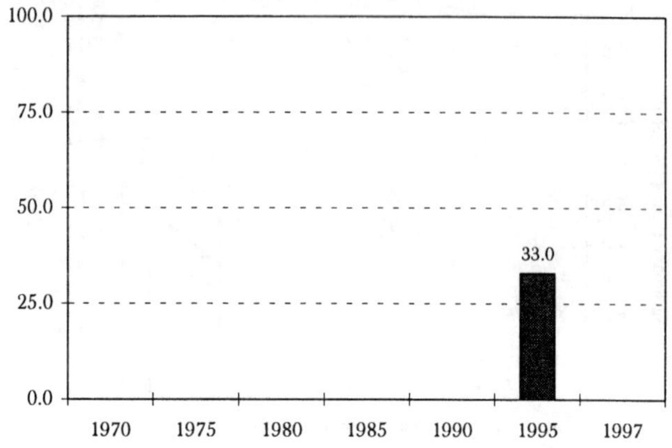


Consistent market reforms have allowed Lithuania to improve its rating to 6.6 from 5.7 in 1995. It now ranks 62nd out of the 123 countries in this study.

Lithuania's tax system is based on an income tax that is almost flat (the regular rate is 33 percent, compared to a top rate of only 35 percent). The VAT (which is the basic source of budget income) is now applied universally at the rate of 18 per cent, with very few items still exempt. It is in the official program of the government to abolish corporate income tax and all companies are already allowed to deduct their investments fully from taxable profits.

The private sector, which employs two-thirds of the country's work force, contributes up to 75 per cent of GDP. Privatization has reached areas of the infrastructure that earlier were "non-touchable." Even the government's 60 percent stake of the Telecommunication Company was privatized in 1998. Of course, given the low rating in this area, there is more to be done.

The currency is protected from political and other interventions by the Currency Board, introduced in 1994. Since that time, the national currency, Litas, is fully backed by foreign reserves and is freely changed into foreign currency at the rate of 4 Litas for US$1. Thanks to the Currency Board, interest rates went down significantly and private investment, both domestic and foreign, boomed. People's savings and other assets are protected from devaluation and income is consistently rising. Since this component is calculated for a period of five years, Lithuania's rating is still affected by the problems of post-Soviet times and will see improvement in the coming years.

Lithuania can also expect further increases in economic freedom if it proceeds further with privatization (including privatization of financial services) and eliminates conscription and price controls.

# LUXEMBOURG

### Economic Freedom Rating (bar) and Rank (line)

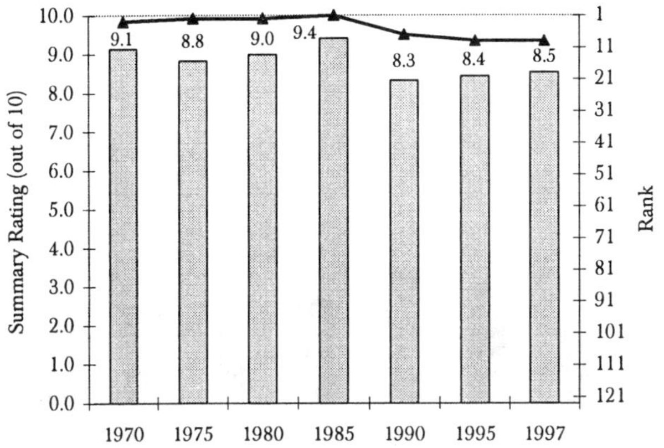


### Total Government Expenditure as a Percentage of GDP

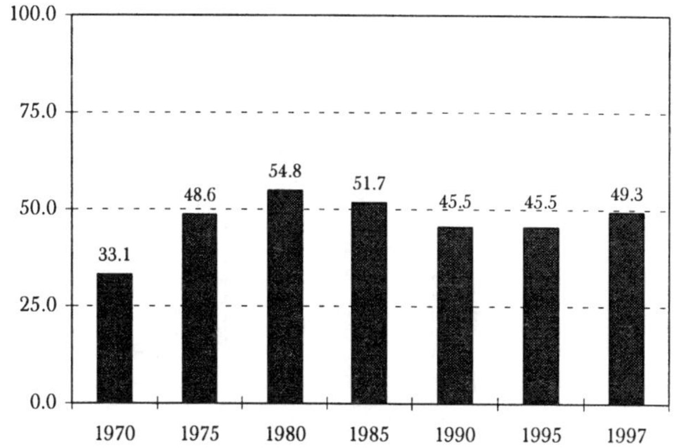


Luxembourg's 8.5 rating places it at 9th position among the 123 countries in our study. Luxembourg lost the high ranking that it held through the 1980s because of rapid development in other countries and, to a certain extent, problems in Luxembourg itself.

There has been a tendency towards government growth during the recent decades. Government's share of total consumption has grown from 13.6 percent in 1970 to 19.8 percent in 1997. Transfers and subsidies absorbed 26 percent of the GDP in 1997 and were financed by very high marginal tax rates.

However, in other fields of examination Luxembourg's performance is one of the best. Citizens are fully free to maintain foreign currency accounts domestically and abroad and suffer no constraints in capital transactions with foreigners. There is a reliable, well-established legal structure providing for the protection of property rights. Its international trade sector has been almost completely liberalized as a precondition for integration into the EU. Since the middle 1980s, the monetary authorities have kept control over inflation. Another important quality of Luxembourg is its functional and liberal banking sector.

# MAURITIUS

**Economic Freedom Rating (bar) and Rank (line)**

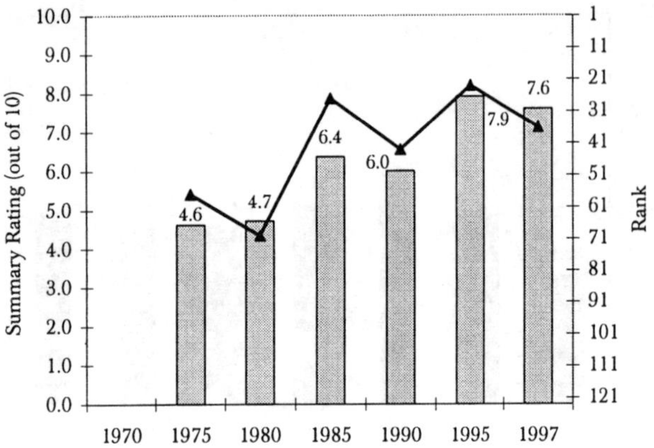


**Total Government Expenditure as a Percentage of GDP**

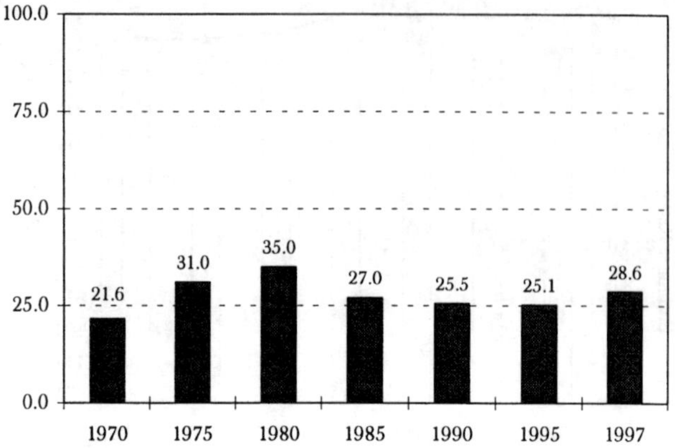


This small African country of approximately 1.2 million people has seen impressive increases in its level of economic freedom, rising from an overall score of 4.6 in 1975 (70th in rank) to a peak of 7.9 in 1995 (23rd in rank). In 1997, Mauritius had an overall score of 7.6 (36th in rank).

Improvements in their overall score can be attributed to improvements in three areas: (I) Structure of the Economy and Use of Markets, (IV) Freedom to Use Alternative Currencies and (VII) Freedom of Exchange in Financial Markets. In particular, Mauritius has made significant improvements in its top marginal tax rate, going from a score of 3 in 1980 to 8 by 1995. Mauritius has also increased the reliance on the private sector by moving toward more private banks and allocating credit more to the private sector rather than the public.

The mean tariff rate remains high but was showing some signs of improvement until it increased between 1995 and 1997. The standard deviation of tariff rates is also unacceptably high, garnering them the lowest score possible of 0.

The overall effect of the increase in economic freedom has been tremendous. The average annual growth rate in GNP per capita between 1977 and 1987 was 1.8 percent per year. From 1988 to 1998, this rate jumped to 4.1 percent per year. In 1997, it was 5 percent and in 1998 it was 4 percent.

# MEXICO

### Economic Freedom Rating (bar) and Rank (line)

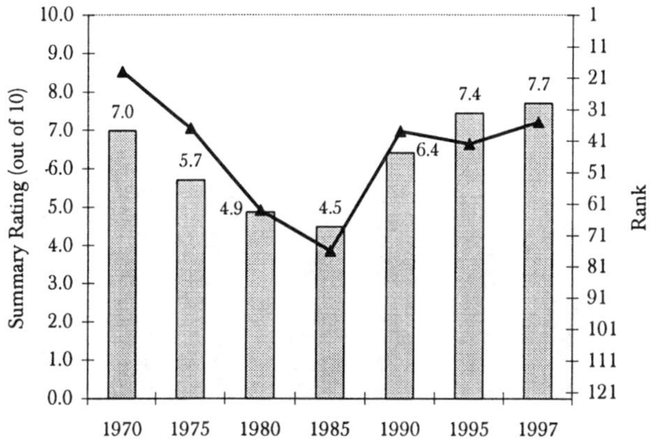


### Total Government Expenditure as a Percentage of GDP

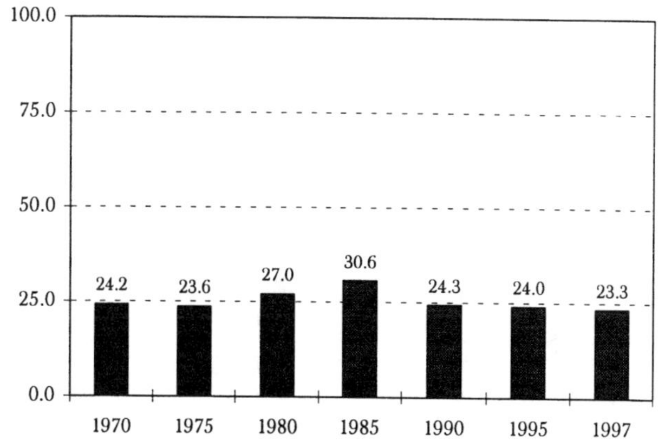


During the past 15 years, Mexico has steadily improved its rating. Its 7.7 rating in 1997 places it 35th among 123 countries in our study; this is up from its 4.5 rating and 76th ranking in 1985.

Mexico has been a fast-growing economy; its real GDP grew by 6.8 percent in 1997. Positive aspects are its small share of government consumption (only 11.3 percent in 1997), low transfers and subsidies (7.5 percent in 1997), and the relatively liberal foreign-trade sector. Although it still suffers from corruption and bureaucratic ineffectiveness, the legal structure has improved significantly since 1985. Compared with 1995, some price controls have been relaxed.

Mexico has problems with its monetary policy. The authorities are struggling to curb annual money growth and an inflation rate of 19 percent cannot be a basis for sustainable growth. While citizens are free to own and maintain foreign currency accounts, there are constraints on capital transactions with foreigners. The recent decline in credit extended to the private sector represents a step backwards. In 1997, just 60.5 percent of total credit was extended to the private sector, down from 83 percent in 1995.

# THE NETHERLANDS

**Economic Freedom Rating (bar) and Rank (line)**

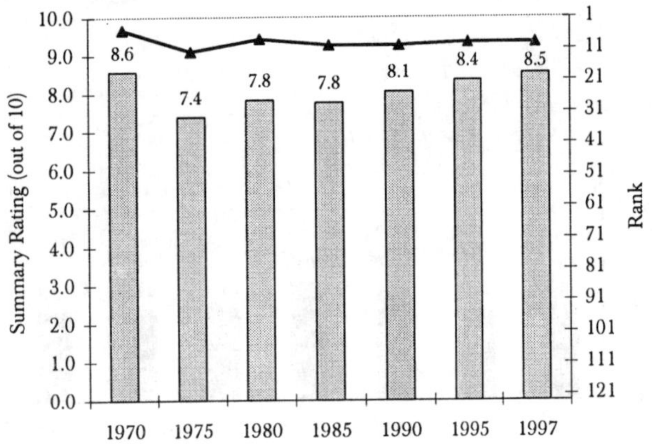


**Total Government Expenditure as a Percentage of GDP**

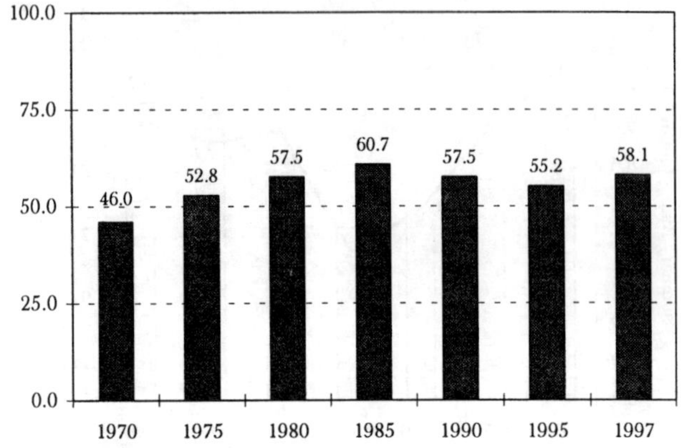


The Netherlands' 8.5 rating in 1997 places it 9th among the 123 countries in our study. The Netherlands has one of the most agile economies among western European countries. It has a moderate unemployment rate and a healthy rate of growth in real GDP. The Netherlands gets high ratings in the areas of monetary policy, international trade, financial markets, and alternative currencies. Its reputation is as a successful anti-inflationary regime. Since the change from full monetary sovereignty to reliance on German Bundesbank policies in the 1980s, the inflation rate has been maintained at a low level by its authorities. Citizens are free to hold foreign currency accounts domestically and abroad and are not bound by restrictions to engage in capital transactions with foreigners. The trade sector is liberalized; remaining tariffs and taxes are negligible.

Even in the area of government operations improvements are visible. Even though government consumption, at 19 percent of total consumption, is relatively high, it has declined slightly during the past 20 years. Also, the transfers and subsidies sector fell modestly from 29.7 percent of GDP in 1995 to 27 percent in 1997, though it remains at a very high level and is financed by a very high top marginal tax rate of 60 percent. The government relaxed some price controls and abandoned conscription. The government provides a well-established legal structure supportive of sound economic development.

# NEW ZEALAND

**Economic Freedom Rating (bar) and Rank (line)**

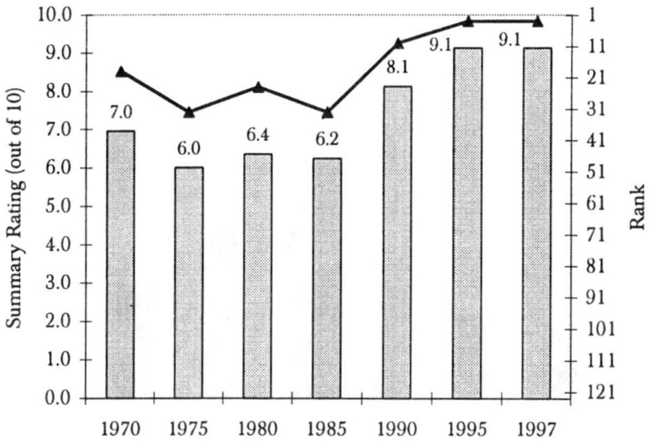


**Total Government Expenditure as a Percentage of GDP**

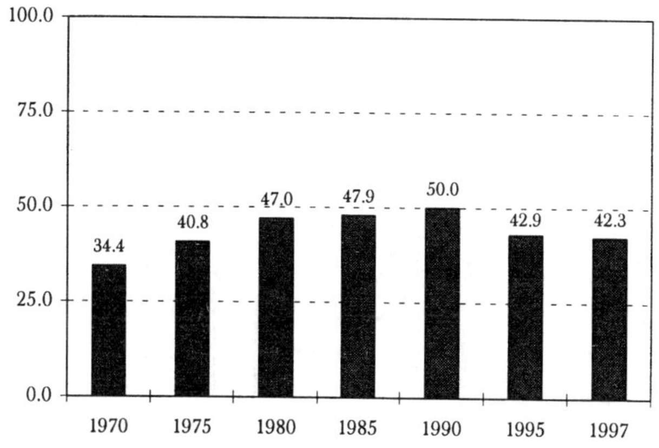


In recent years, New Zealand has moved to the top ranks of this index more rapidly than any other country. In 1997, as in 1995, it ranked in 3rd place. As recently as 1985, though, New Zealand rated just 6.2 and ranked 32nd of 111 nations.

The key components of New Zealand's prosperous economy are a well-established legal structure (note the perfect 10 rating) and a consistent anti-inflationary monetary policy–the inflation rate for 1997 was –0.5 percent.

The reductions in government expenditures in the early 1990s were remarkable. The share of government consumption remains relatively high but has fallen. The reduction in the transfers and subsidies area has been even more impressive–from 27.5 percent in 1990 to 12.4 percent in 1997, financed by a comparatively low top marginal tax rate of 33 percent. Government enterprises are more completely privatized and price controls abolished.

New Zealand's international trade sector is almost completely liberalized and only some minor taxes and tariffs still exist. Even so, the size of the trade sector (in percent of GDP) has declined slightly.

# NICARAGUA

### Economic Freedom Rating (bar) and Rank (line)

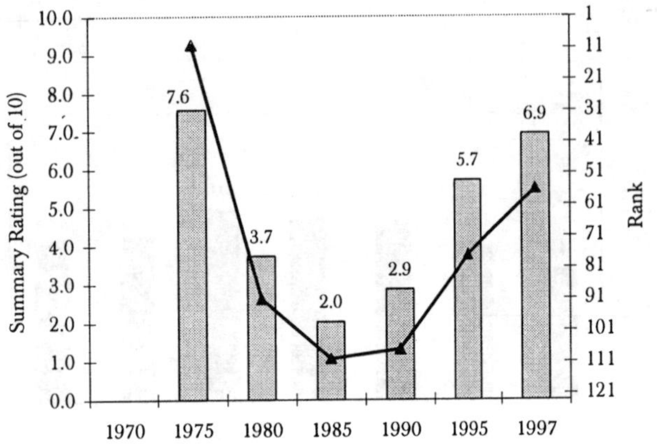


### Total Government Expenditure as a Percentage of GDP

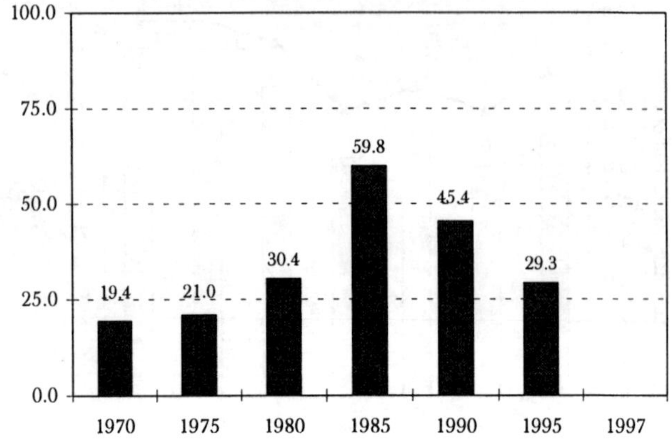


The policies of the 1980s caused Nicaragua's economic freedom rating to plunge from 7.6 in 1975 to 2.0 in 1985. Through reforms in the 1990s, Nicaragua has dramatically changed its policy making and this has improved its rating for economic freedom substantially. It has now recovered to the level it had before the Sandinista Revolution and has moved from 109th position (out of 111 countries) in 1985 to 56th in 1997.

What has produced the increase in Nicaragua's ranking? Price stability and freedom to have foreign currency accounts have played a role. Price controls were also relaxed. Another substantial achievement was met when controls on interest rates and capital markets were eliminated. Nicaragua has also made efforts to reduce its government's consumption and to respect contracts and property rights.

The risk of expropriation and the lack of attention to the principles of a rule-of-law are still weaknesses of Nicaragua's economy. The country still has a lot to do if it wants to regain the confidence of citizens and foreigners.

# NORWAY

## Economic Freedom Rating (bar) and Rank (line)

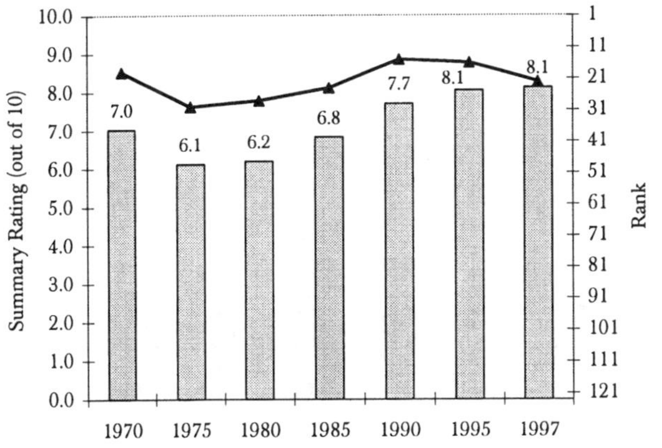


## Total Government Expenditure as a Percentage of GDP

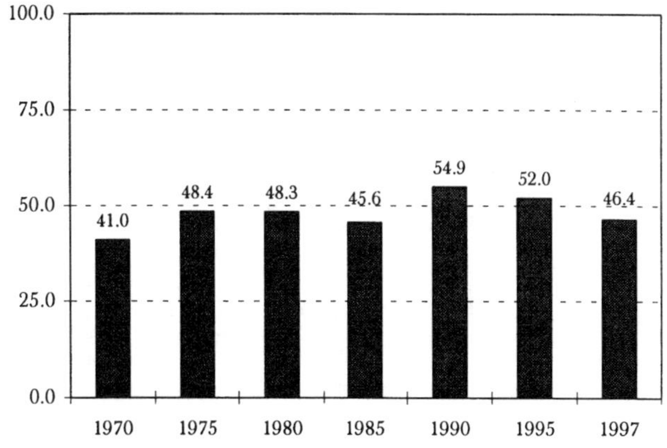


Although Norway received the same rating of 8.1 in 1997 and in 1995, its ranking fell from 16th position to 22nd in 1997.

Norway's share of government consumption is high, as it is in other European welfare states. However, since 1990 there has been a slimming of the transfer and subsidies sector: the share of this sector fell from 27.3 percent of GDP in 1990 to 19.5 percent in 1997. Furthermore, in some areas, price controls were abandoned. There is still an opportunity to reduce the number of government enterprises and its investments.

Norway provides a progressive and functional legal structure supporting economic development. While tariffs are low, their standard deviation increased during the 1990s. Citizens are free to own foreign currencies and to maintain those accounts domestically and abroad. A characteristic feature of Norway's macroeconomic indicators is its successful monetary policy pursuing monetary stability.

# PANAMA

## Economic Freedom Rating (bar) and Rank (line)

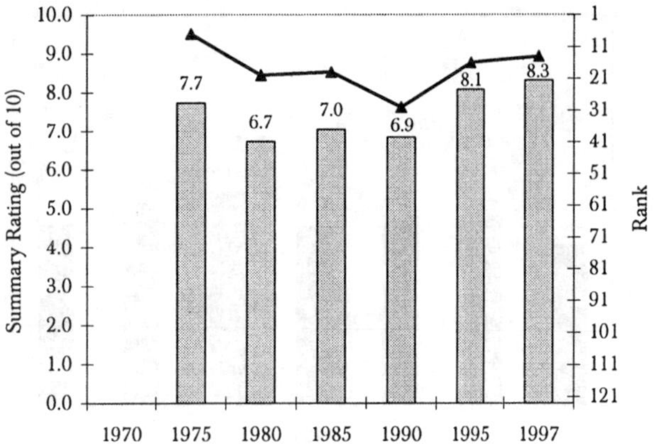


## Total Government Expenditure as a Percentage of GDP

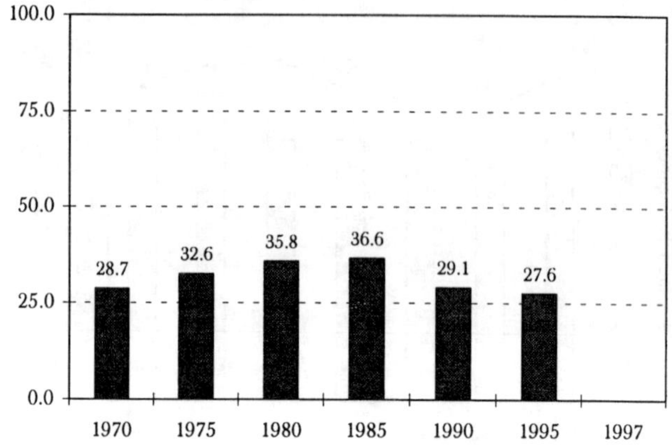


In 1997, Panama's rating was 8.3, up from 6.9 in 1990. Its ranking rose from 30th in 1990 to 14th in 1997. Panama has made substantial moves toward economic freedom during the last decade: tariffs have been reduced and financial and capital markets have been liberalized. The strengths of the Panamanian economy are price stability and its highly convertible currency. Beginning in 1904, Panama adopted the American dollar as its official currency. This provides Panama with a highly credible currency that is readily accepted throughout the world.

There are still weaknesses to be overcome. The legal structure (respect of contracts and the security of private property) would benefit from the removal of barriers that reduce the trust of investors, both foreign and domestic. The state continues to operate a number of government enterprises. Moreover, the size of government is quite large, particularly for a country with a low per-capita income. In spite of these negative factors, Panama has the best economic freedom rating in Central America.

# PHILIPPINES

### Economic Freedom Rating (bar) and Rank (line)

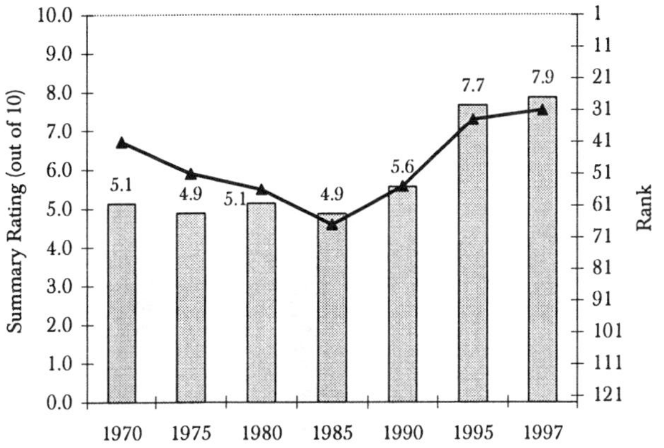


### Total Government Expenditure as a Percentage of GDP

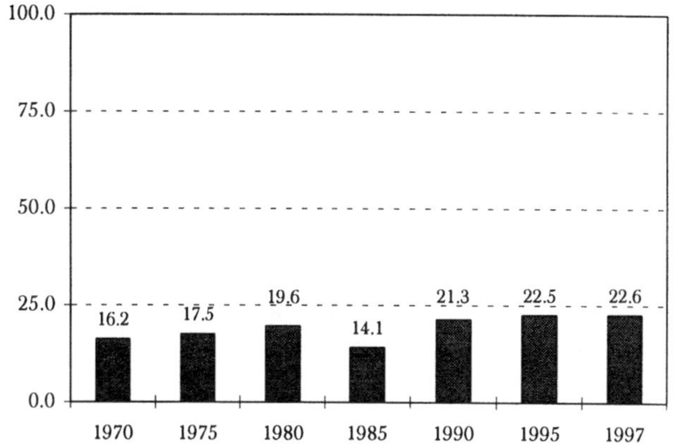


The Philippines' rating has moved up to 7.9 from 4.9 in 1985 and has secured a 31st place ranking. One weak area is Area II, Structure of the Economy and Use of Markets, with a fairly low rating (5 out of 10) for the Price Control Component. The ratings in Area V, Legal Structure and Property rights, were quite low with a very poor 4.1 rating for the Rule of Law component. Relatively high tariffs and restrictions on capital-account transactions are also problem areas.

On the positive side, money and prices are relatively stable and the citizens have access to alternative currencies. Government consumption and direct transfers are fairly small as well.

The Philippines, like so many of the emerging Asian economies, needs a healthy dose of transparency and reduced corruption if it is to continue its trek toward the industrialized world.

# POLAND

**Economic Freedom Rating (bar) and Rank (line)**

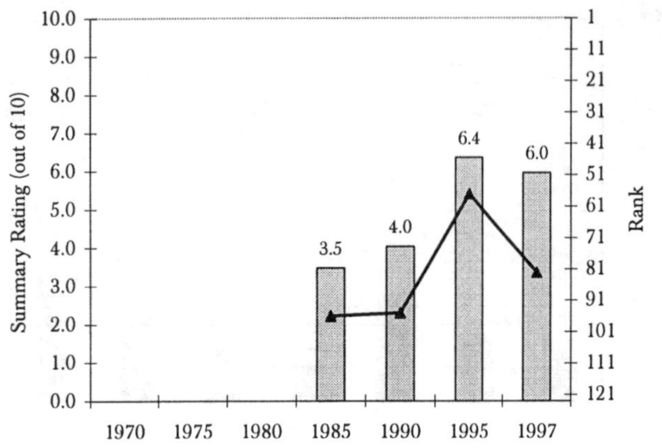


**Total Government Expenditure as a Percentage of GDP**

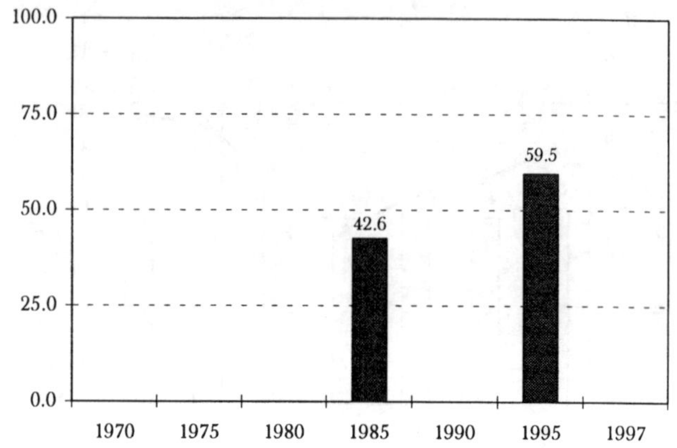


Since 1989, Poland has been on a steady path toward a market economy. Its economic freedom score increased from 3.5 in 1985 to 4.0 in 1990 and 6.4 in 1995, while its rank rose from 96th (out of 111) in 1985 to 95th (out of 115) in 1990, and 57th (out of 122) in 1995. However, in 1996/1997 it recorded a slight decline to 6.0, which gave it a ranking of 82nd place.

Between 1995 and 1997, economic freedom of other eastern European countries went up while Poland experienced a slow-down from its earlier fast pace of transformation toward a freer economy. This, however, was not reflected by any substantial decline in economic growth or in the worsening of other major macroeconomic indicators. A decline in rating for Area VI, International Exchange: Freedom to Trade with Foreigners, from 6.2 in 1995 to 5.0 and another in Area II, Structure of the Economy and Use of Markets, from 4.1 to 3.4 should be noted. There would have been no fall in the overall score if not for the deterioration in these two categories. It may be expected that the scores in Area VI will improve shortly, as Polish trade and competition policies will have to be harmonized with those of the European Union. Scores in Area II will be positively influenced by recent reductions in marginal tax rates and the shortening of compulsory military service.

The Central Bank continued to be a guardian of sound national money. In February 1998, a new body–the Monetary Policy Council–was established to monitor and, to a degree, control decisions of the President of the Central Bank. Nevertheless, the Council itself proved to be largely independent of any direct political influence. In short, the Central Bank maintained a stable money supply and interest rates, retained its traditionally liberal stance in the area of citizens' access to foreign currencies, implemented progressive though not hasty liberalization of the financing of capital transactions and exchange-rate determination (moving toward floating regime). The pace of privatization of commercial banking was rather slow although there are good prospects for a more visible change in this respect in the immediate future.

Problems were exacerbated by the fact that crucial systemic reforms had not been undertaken before the end of 1997 (social security, health care, territorial administration, and education). They were finally prepared and introduced in 1998 and 1999 and may substantially improve the country's economic-freedom score in the years to come. These positive tendencies may, however, be offset by rising demands for redistribution by social groups like the coal miners and peasant farmers influenced by populist ideology and trade-union leaders.

# PORTUGAL

**Economic Freedom Rating (bar) and Rank (line)**

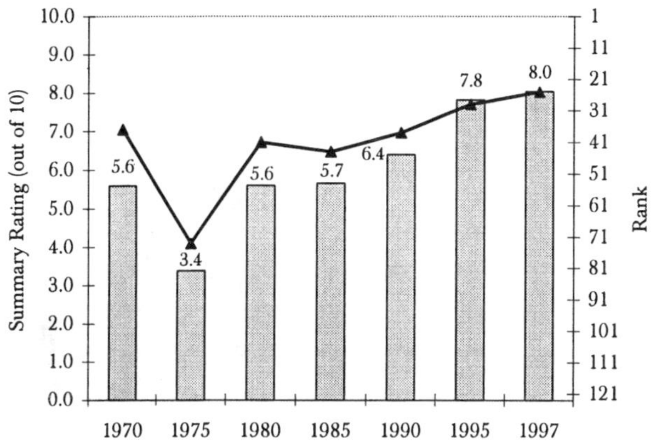


**Total Government Expenditure as a Percentage of GDP**

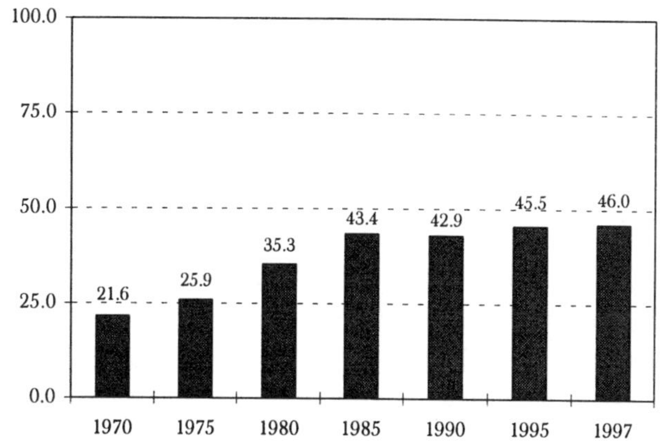


In 1997, Portugal ranked 25th among the 123 countries in our study. This is the best ranking Portugal has ever received. Its rating has improved steadily since 1975's low rating of 3.4 (73rd out of 83 nations) to its current rating of 8.0.

Portugal's monetary policy has shown strong improvement toward monetary stability in order to qualify for membership in the EMU. After more than 20 years of high inflation, the inflation rate declined to a narrow range between 2 percent and 3 percent. The citizens are free to maintain foreign currency accounts domestically and abroad. The recent economic achievements are backed by a well-established legal structure providing a nearly perfect score in Area V. Portugal's international trade sector is very liberalized as it is part of the EU. Progress is also found in the deregulation of the banking sector, where an increasing share of deposits are held in private banks.

The share of government consumption remains relatively high (though moderate by European standards) and transfers and subsidies appear to be coming down. Price controls exist in some sectors and there is ample opportunity for additional privatization of government enterprises.

# SLOVAKIA

### Economic Freedom Rating (bar) and Rank (line)

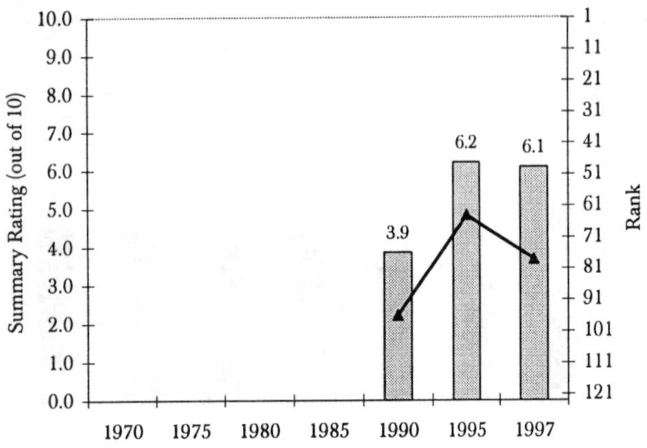


### Total Government Expenditure as a Percentage of GDP

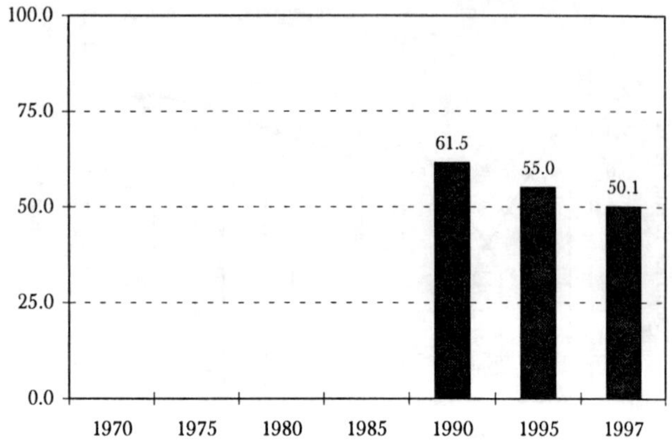


Slovakia's 1997 rating of 6.1 placed it 78th among 123 countries. This rating was a marked improvement over the 3.9 rating (and 96th ranking) of the former Czechoslovakia in 1990 but leaves a lot of room for improvement.

Slovakia has one of the most open economies and some of the lowest tariff barriers in the region. Even though it has made significant progress in the legal protection of private-property rights, it has still a long way to go in the enforcement and viability of contracts. Restrictive monetary policy contributed to one of the lowest inflation rates in the region (around 6 percent in 1996/1997). On the other hand, there have been delays in deregulating prices, especially those for electricity, gas, and rents. Slovakia is gradually liberalizing its capital flows and foreign-currency regime, where further lifting of controls are expected. High marginal tax rates are used to support the still significant share of general government expenditures (50.1 percent of GDP in 1997). The largest banks are still in the hands of the state, as are public utilities.

Slovakia will be able to improve its ranking significantly only if restructuring and privatization are accelerated both in banking and in corporate sectors and if there is a far-reaching reform of public finances aimed at reductions in income redistribution.

# SLOVENIA

**Economic Freedom Rating (bar) and Rank (line)**

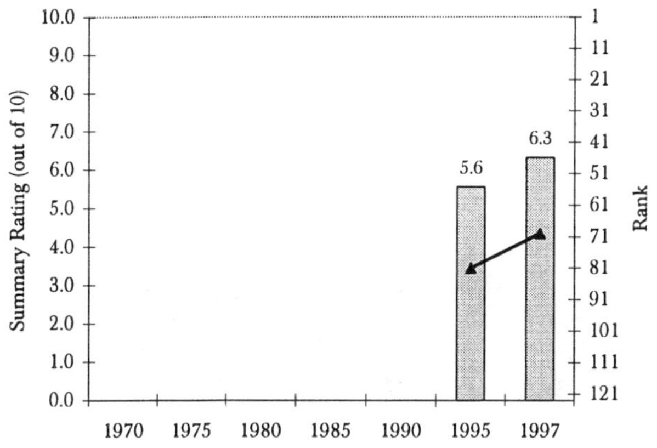


**Total Government Expenditure as a Percentage of GDP**

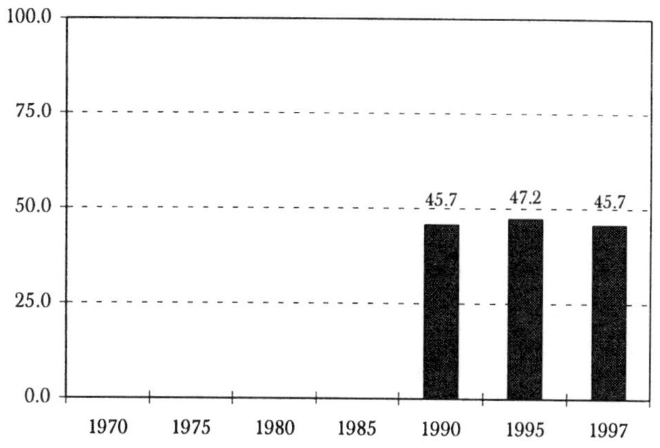


Slovenia's 1997 rating of 6.3 placed it 70th among 123 countries. Slovenia's low rating stems from its weaknesses in Area II: Structure of the Economy and Use of Markets. In particular, it received low ratings because of the large number of government enterprises, the size of its government, and restrictions on the mobility of capital.

There is some good news that will be reflected in up-coming indexes. The privatization of trade and industry has been completed. However, a few enterprises (2 percent of equity) showing losses are still state-owned. Several steps forward in the expected privatization of insurance companies, banks and public utilities have been undertaken recently. A draft version of Proposal of Law of State Property Privatization has been prepared.

The new Foreign Exchange Operations Act, which regulates operations between residents and non-residents, went into force in April 1999. It represents a major step towards full liberalization in the flow of capital. A number of restrictions on foreign investment in Slovenia have been phased out; at the same time, there are almost no restrictions left on residents' investments abroad. Nevertheless, foreign-currency bank accounts abroad for residents are still not permitted.

Further steps must also be taken to lower general government expenditures, especially transfers and subsidies, which constitute an astounding 33 percent of GDP. Since Slovenia is a candidate for full EU membership, it is reasonable to expect that structural reforms towards more economic freedom will be coming.

# South Africa

### Economic Freedom Rating (bar) and Rank (line)

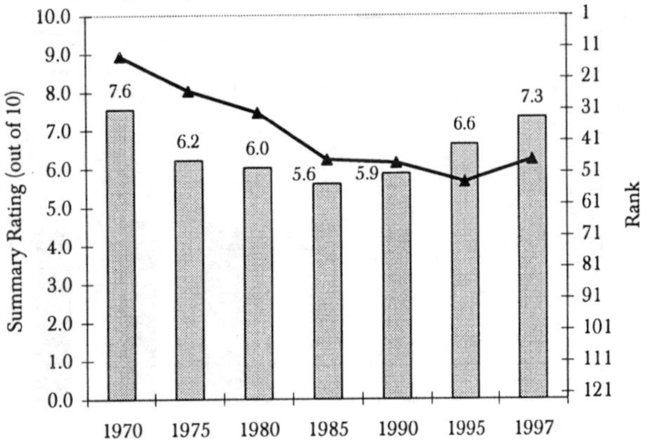


### Total Government Expenditure as a Percentage of GDP

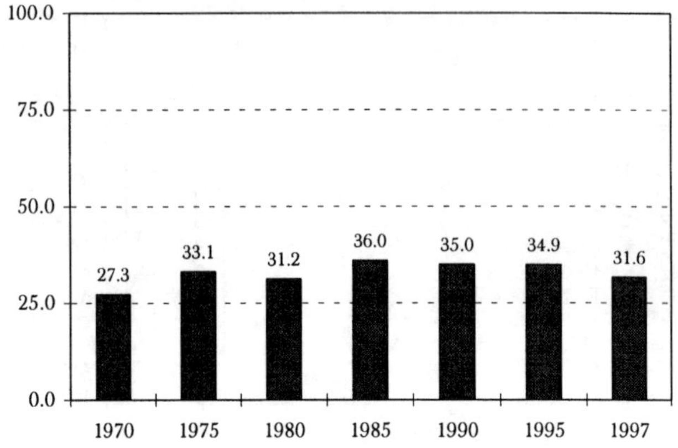


Despite slow improvement during the 1990s, South Africa's economic-freedom rating continues to fall midway among rated countries: its ranking remained steady, 48th (out of 115) in 1990 and 47th (out of 123) in 1997. Government expenditure (31.6 percent of GDP in 1997) remains extremely high for a low-income country ($4,513 per-capita GDP in 1996) but fiscal discipline has been improved and the level of expenditure as well as the size of the budget deficit is declining.

With the disappearance of apartheid, the first government of the new democracy and the 1996 Constitution greatly improved the overall legal structure. Conscription has been abolished and other pro-market changes have been made. However, while controls on the movement of capital have been substantially reduced, exchange controls remain in place and the inflation rate, while declining, has been consistently higher than the rates of South Africa's major trading partners. The currency exchange rate has consequently been falling continuously.

Trade tariffs have been reduced and the powers of the former agricultural marketing boards removed. Farmers and long-protected industries have had to adjust to the changed circumstances and formal unemployment has consequently increased to around one-third of the potential workforce. New labour laws have exacerbated the problem by imposing increased costs on employers. The high unemployment level and restrictive labour laws also make it difficult for the government to implement its planned reduction in the number of civil servants and employees at state-owned industries. The government has re-stated its commitment to privatization but the process is proceeding very slowly.

South Africa can improve its economic freedom rating and prospects of higher growth by continuing to reduce the growth rate of the money supply, replacing the existing limited rights to own foreign currency with total freedom to maintain foreign currency accounts in local banks, abolishing the remaining limitations on the ownership of bank accounts abroad, substantially reducing government expenditure as a percentage of GDP, privatizing rapidly, and reducing marginal tax rates.

# SOUTH KOREA

### Economic Freedom Rating (bar) and Rank (line)

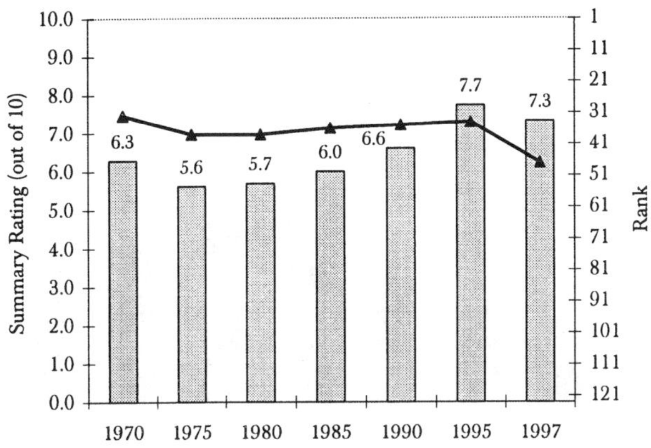


### Total Government Expenditure as a Percentage of GDP

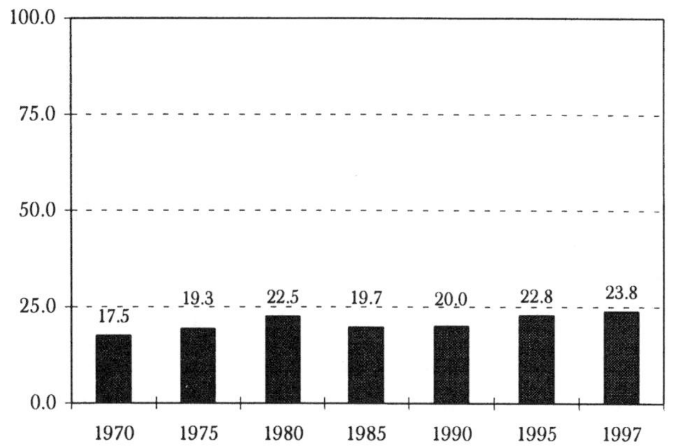


Although South Korea's rating declined only slightly from 7.7 in 1995 to 7.3 in 1997, its ranking fell from 34th in 1995 to 47th in 1997. Reasons for this decline are the successful efforts of other countries pushing forward economic development and freedom.

Korea is well known for its economic growth. However, for a sustainable future development, the Korean government must deregulate the density and supremacy of affiliated trusts (Chaebol) in order to foster flexibility, competition, and efficient allocation of investments.

For the last several decades, governmental consumption and spending on transfers and subsidies have been increasing but remain within a modest range. Particular strengths are the monetary policy, freedom to use alternative currencies and a well-established legal structure. The credibility of its monetary policies has been improved through curbing annual money growth and reducing inflation.

Korea has a large functional foreign-trade sector but there is a relatively high Mean Tariff Rate. The standard deviation of tariff rates indicates a prevailing protectionism toward domestic industries. In the recent decades there have been no significant efforts to liberalize the banking sector. Like Japan, private savings held as deposits in government-owned financial institutions are very large.

# SPAIN

**Economic Freedom Rating (bar) and Rank (line)**

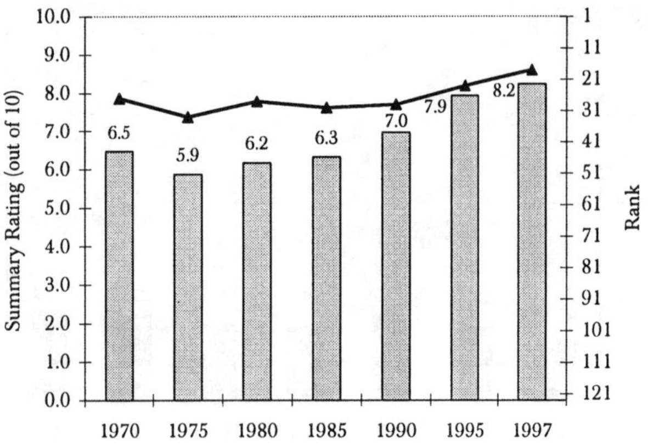


**Total Government Expenditure as a Percentage of GDP**

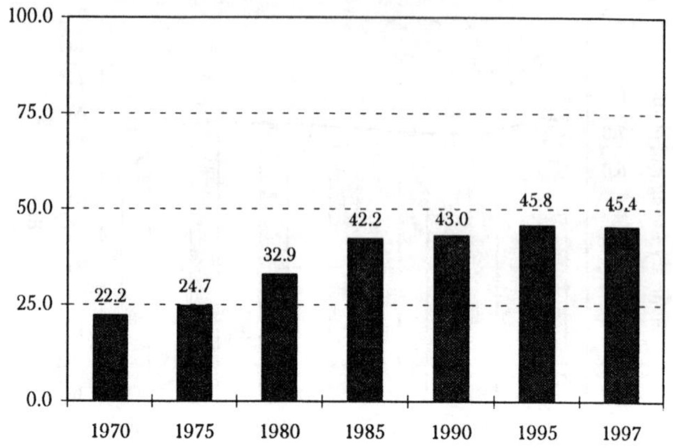


Spain improved its performance steadily during the last decades and the 8.2 rating places it at 18th place, the best that it has yet attained. This is a fairly sound improvement over its 29th ranking in 1990 .

Spain's strengths are international exchange, a fully convertible currency, its legal structure and its monetary policy. Since 1985, the monetary authorities have successfully moved the inflation rate down to 2.1 percent. Obviously, the Maastricht-criteria for accession to the EMU were partly the reason for this. The citizens are not subject to restrictions infringing their right to own foreign currencies domestically and abroad. There is a well-established, trustworthy legal structure providing support for economic development. Spain's foreign-trade sector could be expanded and is almost completely liberalized.

Transfers and subsidies, as well as government consumption, still remain high. Moreover, during the recent decades there has been a tendency towards the expansion of total government consumption. Signs of liberalization of government enterprises and price controls are hard to find and point to an obvious area for improvement.

# SWEDEN

### Economic Freedom Rating (bar) and Rank (line)

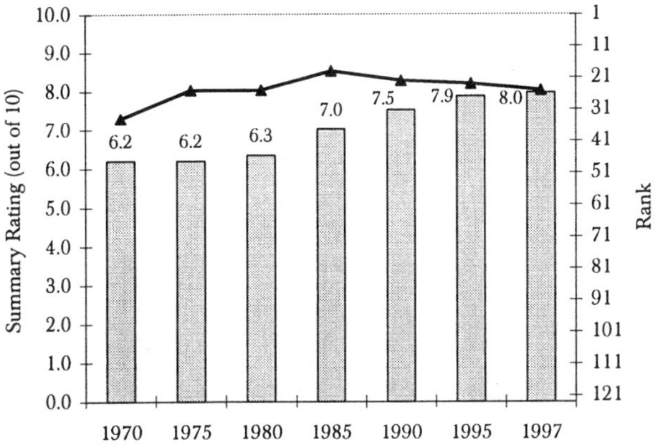


### Total Government Expenditure as a Percentage of GDP

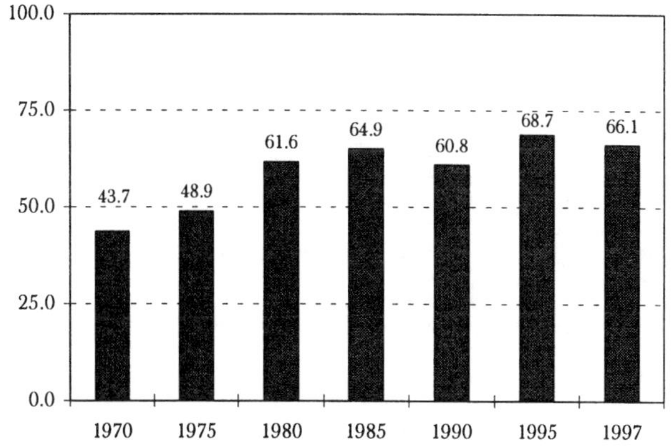


The Swedish figures have been fairly stable over time, varying from a summary rating of 6.2 in 1970 to a rating of 8.0 most recently. Sweden's ranking consequently has not changed much either: 34$^{th}$ in 1970 and 25$^{th}$ in 1997. Two trends are discernable: the variables associated with Area I, Size of Government, and Area II, Structure of the Economy and Use of Markets, have received lower scores, while the variables in Area VI, International Exchange, and Area VII, Freedom of Exchange in Capital and Financial Markets, have improved.

It is in the two first areas that the main problems can be found. The Swedish government has continued to expand and to increase the level of taxation, especially since 1970, which has caused long-term economic growth to slow down and economic freedom to be curtailed. The Swedish welfare state consumes over one third of the total consumption of the nation and redistributes another third.

Two important markets that are not included in the index at present, the labour and housing markets, represent some of Sweden's biggest challenges. The former is plagued by a compressed wage structure and rigid laws regulating hiring and firing decisions, which have resulted in high unemployment. The housing market is likewise highly regulated, with price ceilings, subsidies, poor competition, building requirements, and so on. Were these to be included in the index, Sweden's freedom score would surely drop. Even so, Sweden is near the bottom of the industrialized European nations in terms of economic liberty.

It is hard to say if substantial structural reforms are forthcoming. Many economists advocate them; certain influential interest groups oppose them. Reality, however, may force some liberal reforms to be implemented, which would prove beneficial for both economic freedom and the functioning of the economy.

# SWITZERLAND

**Economic Freedom Rating (bar) and Rank (line)**

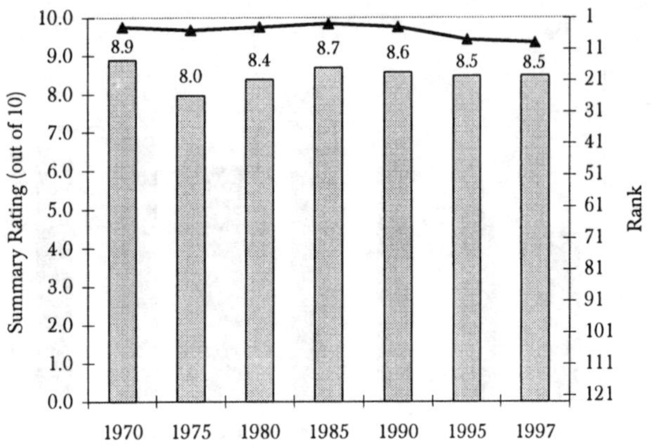


**Total Government Expenditure as a Percentage of GDP**

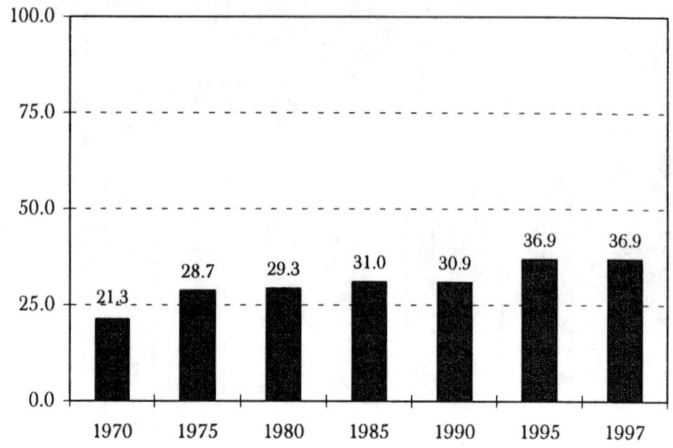


Switzerland's 8.5 rating places it 9th in our 1997 index. Switzerland has sustained its high position during the past decades and has never been ranked below 10th position.

The characteristics of the Swiss economy are its credible and stable monetary regime and well-established legal structure (note the almost perfect rating in that area). Further, a free foreign-trade sector–in the last two years nearly all taxes on international trade were abandoned–as well as the freedom of owning foreign currencies and the small number of government enterprises are positive attributes.

Like its highly developed neighbouring countries, both government consumption and transfers are high. Switzerland's practice of military conscription, famous around the world, hurts its rating. Also, despite being a world center for banking, a large percentage of deposits are held in government-owned banks.

While the growth rate of real GDP has been meagre–an average of 0.4 percent annually between 1990 and 1997–the Swiss economy remains one of the most free in Europe.

# TAIWAN

### Economic Freedom Rating (bar) and Rank (line)

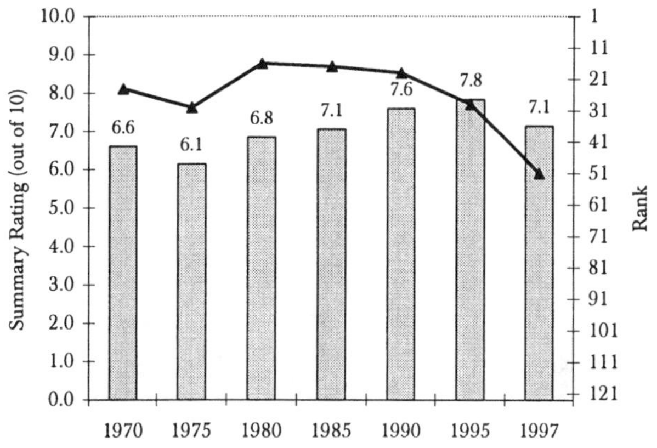


### Total Government Expenditure as a Percentage of GDP

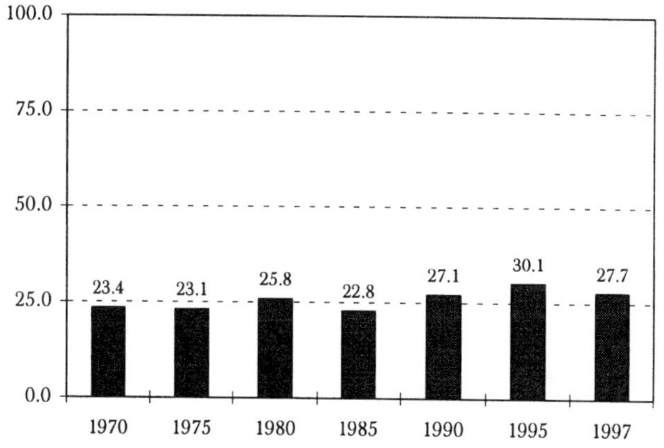


Taiwan's rating has hovered in the low to middle 7s since the 1980s. The 1997 rating of 7.1, however, has not kept pace with other countries and, as a consequence, Taiwan has fallen to 51st place.

Taiwan does a good job in most areas but in two areas significant problems remain. Heavy use of government-owned enterprises, price controls, and conscription generate a very low 3.1 rating in Area II, Structure of the Economy and Use of Markets. Widespread government ownership of banks and capital-account restrictions contribute to a 5.5 rating in Area VII, Freedom of Exchange in Capital and Financial Markets.

Taiwan could easily move its ranking into the top 20 or higher by privatizing public-sector firms and deregulating prices.

# THAILAND

### Economic Freedom Rating (bar) and Rank (line)

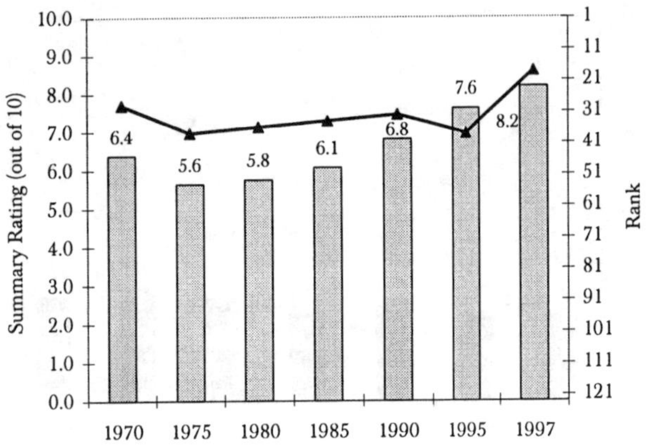


### Total Government Expenditure as a Percentage of GDP

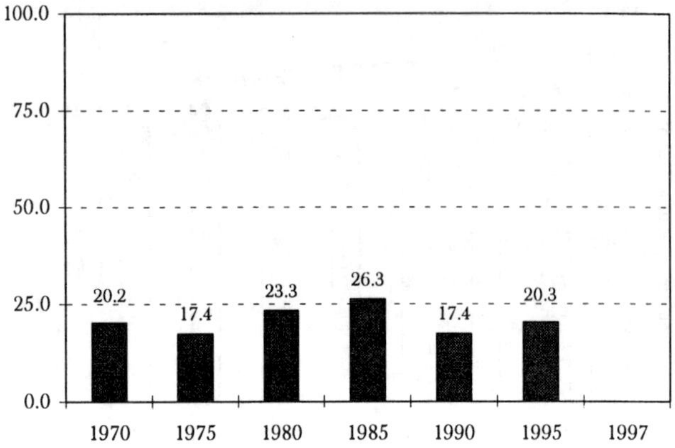


Thailand is on the path to improved economic freedom. In 1975, the economic freedom rating of Thailand was only 5.6 but, in 1997, had improved to 8.2, pushing Thailand to the 18th rank. The continual improvement in economic freedom from 1985 to 1997 can be attributed to the following factors.

(1) Government transfer and subsidies have long been relatively low compared with the gross domestic product.

(2) The role of state enterprises has been reduced. The rating in this category rose to 7 in 1997, up from 4 in 1985. The decreasing role of state enterprises in the 1990s can be attributed to the government's privatizing plan in the 1980s. In addition, the latest financial rescue package from the IMF also requires Thailand to privatize key state enterprises, such as the Transportation Company and the Telephone Organisation of Thailand, to name a few.

(3) The price level in Thailand, as measured by the standard deviation of the inflation rate, is relatively stable and Thai residents may now freely hold foreign-currency bank accounts, which was not allowed in 1975.

(4) Thailand's tariffs are declining although they remain high.

Although Thailand has improved economic freedom in certain areas, the country still faces several challenges to become an economically free country. The government uses a 24-month conscription to obtain military personnel. Prices of certain products remain under the government's control: in 1997, the government still formally controlled the prices of gas and sugar, setting the "maximum" price for gas and the "minimum" price for sugar. For approximately 22 basic consumption products, it oversees the price administration system, which accounts for the rating of 5 in the price-control component. Residents of Thailand are not totally free to engage in capital transactions with foreigners. If Thailand's rating is to improve, it must remove controls on capital transactions, strengthen the rule of law, streamline its tariff structure and reduce price controls.

# TURKEY

### Economic Freedom Rating (bar) and Rank (line)

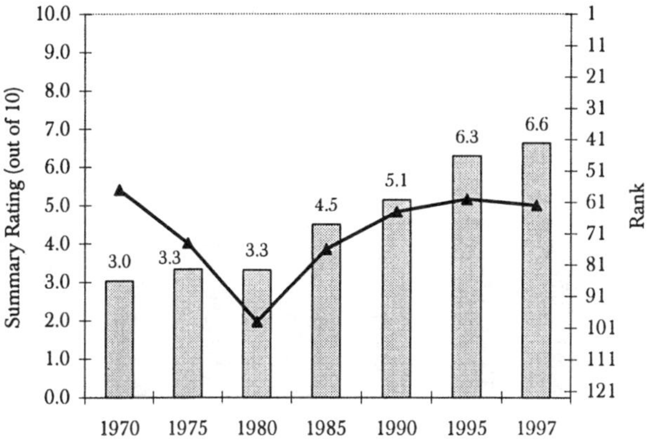


### Total Government Expenditure as a Percentage of GDP

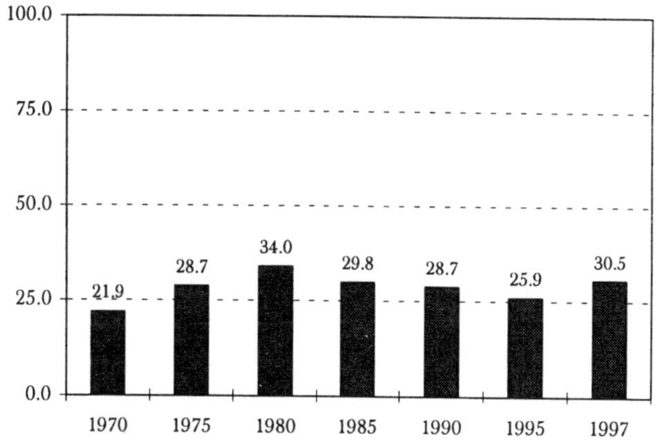


Turkey's most recent rating of 6.6 places it 62nd out of the 123 countries rated. This represents some considerable improvement from the 3.0 rating and dead-last placement in 1970.

Turkey's biggest problem is in the monetary area, for which it received a rating of just 1.6. The situation seems to be getting worse on this front. The inflation rate was 65 percent in August 1999, and the interest rate on government bonds has risen to nearly 100 percent. Other problems include state-owned enterprises, price controls, and military conscription. Privatization efforts have been stymied by trade unions and other interest groups.

Political freedoms are even less protected than economic freedoms. Liberals are either sacked from their jobs if they are journalists or harassed if they are government officials. Still, freedom of thought was improved during the recent election and development of relations with the EU has brought about a better climate.

The tax reform in 1998 tried to increase the tax burden but decrease marginal tax rates. But Turkey ended up with an economic crisis: GDP fell 5.8 percent in the last six months of 1999. The tragic earthquake has only made matters worse.

# UNITED KINGDOM

**Economic Freedom Rating (bar) and Rank (line)**

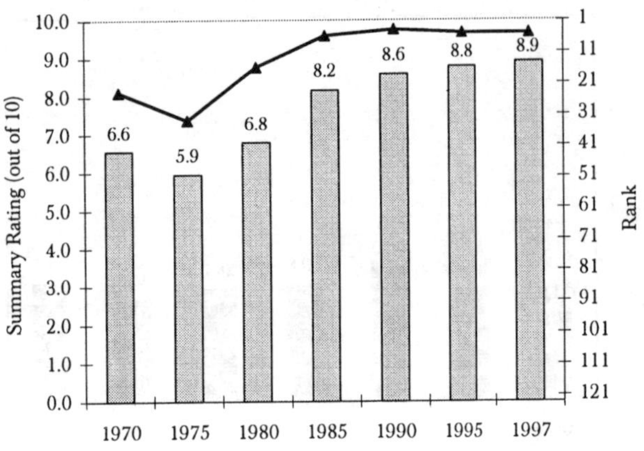


**Total Government Expenditure as a Percentage of GDP**

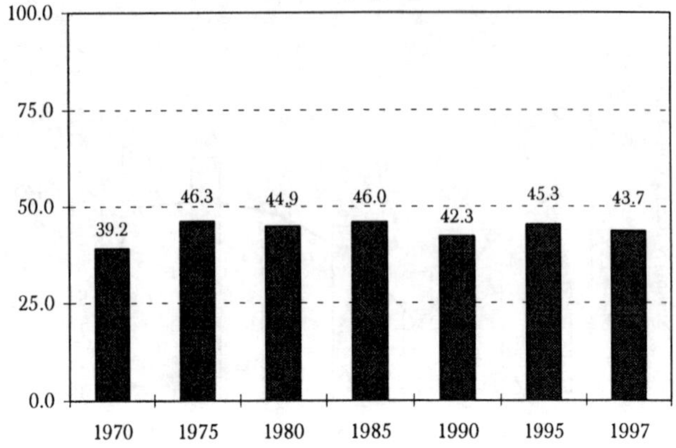


The United Kingdom is now one of the freest economies in the world, following the policy changes brought about by Margaret Thatcher's government. In 1980, the United Kingdom ranked 16th but has now risen to 5th place. The principal reasons for this improvement have been greater monetary and price stability, removal of exchange controls, a substantial privatization program and sharply reduced top marginal personal tax rates (from 83 percent in 1980 to 40 percent at present).

In several respects, trends in the United Kingdom have been different from those in continental Europe. Government expenditures as a proportion of GDP have changed little whereas they have increased in other major European countries. Government transfers and subsidies as a proportion of GDP have also remained fairly stable instead of increasing. The British labour market is less regulated than most Continental markets and in recent years unemployment has been significantly lower than in those countries.

The "New Labour" government, elected in 1997, has emphasized monetary stability and a prudent fiscal policy and has given the Bank of England operational independence to pursue an inflation target of 2½ percent each year. After six years of economic growth, the economy slowed in 1998 but growth now appears to have resumed.

There are still some serious economic problems to be overcome in the United Kingdom. The government sector is large and regulation is extensive. The new government has imposed a minimum wage, agreed to the European Union's working time and other "social" regulations that the previous government would not accept. The mobility of labour is also reduced by the large "public" housing sector and the presence of controls, taxes, and subsidies in the housing market. The big issues to be tackled if economic freedom is to increase are fundamental reform of the "welfare state" and a radical attack on regulation to reduce the power of the government.

# UNITED STATES

**Economic Freedom Rating (bar) and Rank (line)**

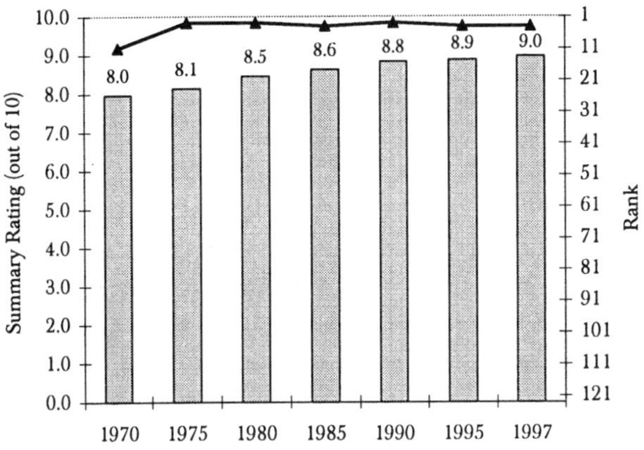


**Total Government Expenditure as a Percentage of GDP**

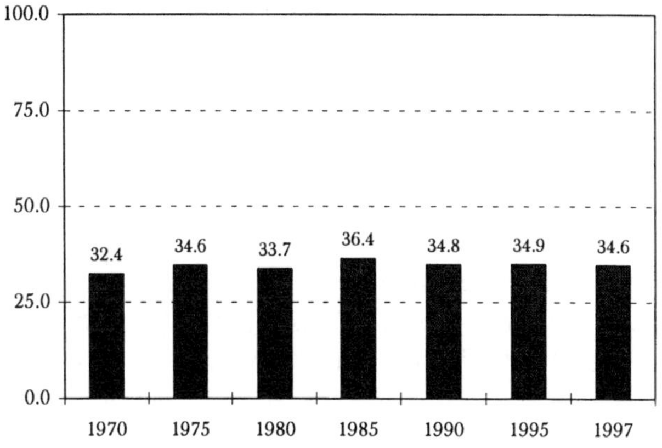


The economic freedom rating of the United States has remained remarkably consistent over the last three decades. The 8.0 rating of 1970 was good for 11th place but the United States has held the 3rd or 4th position ever since. Its 1997 rating of 9.0 earned the United States 4th place. Whatever improvement the index captures reflects a much improved monetary regime. The rating for Area III, Monetary Policy and Price Stability, went from 3.4 in 1970 to 9.8 in 1997. The fiscal size of government has grown only modestly over the years and has actually fallen slightly in the 1990s. Most of all, the United States deserves credit for not increasing the size of government as so many high-income industrial nations have done.

The greatest threats to economic liberty in the United States are in areas that the index does not capture well. For instance, there have been several minimum-wage increases in the last few years. The regulation of the labour market through anti-discrimination laws (for example, the American's with Disabilities Act) has become burdensome as well. Health-care regulations, especially price controls in the Medicare and Medicaid programs, are also a great concern.

Although little gain can been seen in the budget figures, welfare reform has been a success. Literally millions of people have been moved off the social welfare rolls into the job market without the dire consequences so many predicted.

Protectionist and other anti-foreign (especially anti-immigrant) sentiment appear to be on the rise. This has delayed attempts to bring Chile and other Latin American nations into the North American Free Trade Agreement. Indeed the United States' rating in Area VI, International Exchange, has recently fallen to 7.8 from 8.4 in 1980.

Also, despite leading the wave in cutting marginal income taxes that swept the world beginning in the 1980s, the top marginal tax rate has crept up to 39.6 percent at the federal level (and additional state and local income taxes usually apply). Thus the United States' rating for that component is just 7.0.

For the United States to maintain its top-five status, it must refrain from adding burdensome labour and environmental regulations and it must move to privatize social security. Maintaining its leadership in the international arena over freer trade and fundamental tax reform are also critical to future economic freedom and prosperity.

*(Hong Kong continued from page 49)*

The Hong Kong government has indeed taken a more active role in the economy. The widened scope of policy initiatives may only be a cyclical phenomenon. When the economy starts to grow again, the government can then afford to have more faith in the market mechanism and to revert to its "positive non-intervention" principle. This will bode well for long term continuation of Hong Kong's economic freedom.

*(Hungary continued from page 50)*

The transition towards a free economy has not been smooth. Although the freedom of choice keeps increasing, low incomes limit the actual options available to individuals. But GDP in 1998 exceeded the 1989 level, so Hungary is the second country in the region–after Poland–that exceeded the pre-transformation GDP level in real terms. Now the country is on a sustainable growth path with a projected annual rate of growth of 4 percent to 5 percent for the coming years.

# Country Data Tables

This chapter presents detailed data on the economic freedom of the countries included in this study. For each country, we present the overall score of economic freedom and the rank of that country for the years 1970, 1975, 1980, 1985, 1990, 1995, and 1997 (where enough data exists.) Like all the scores in the index, these are values out of 10; 10 is the highest possible score and zero (0) is the lowest. To see how these scores were derived, please refer to the section, Methodology of the Index, earlier in this volume (page 5).

Under the column, Components of Economic Freedom, the titles in bold-face indicate the seven areas of economic freedom that are combined to generate an overall score. Each of the rows in bold-face gives the scores (out of 10) for that particular area for each year. Appendix 1 shows the ratings for each of the seven areas that combine to form the overall summary ratings for the period from 1990 to 1997.

Underneath each area title are the titles of the components that are combined to generate that particular area's score. Beside these titles are the scores (out of 10) for each year for which we have data. In parentheses beside some scores is the actual data used to derive that particular score.

A more complete description of each component can be found in Appendix 2: Explanatory Notes and Data Sources. The full data-set is available online at www.freetheworld.com/download.html.

# ALBANIA

| | 1970 | 1975 | 1980 | 1985 | 1990 | 1995 | 1997 |
|---|---|---|---|---|---|---|---|
| **Summary Ratings** | | | | | 2.9 | 5.0 | 4.3 |
| **Rank** | | | | | 107 | 93 | 113 |

| Components of Economic Freedom | 1970 | | 1975 | | 1980 | | 1985 | | 1990 | | 1995 | | 1997 | |
|---|---|---|---|---|---|---|---|---|---|---|---|---|---|---|
| **I. Size of Government** | | | | | **8.3** | | **8.4** | | **5.0** | | **8.1** | | **9.1** | |
| (a) Government Consumption (% of Total) | | | | | 8.3 | (13.8) | 8.4 | (13.4) | 6.5 | (23.4) | 8.3 | (13.6) | 9.1 | (9.4) |
| (b) Transfers and Subsidies (% of GDP) | | | | | | | | | 3.5 | (24.3) | 7.8 | (8.4) | | |
| **II. Structure of the Economy and Use of Markets** | | | | | | | | | **0.0** | | **2.1** | | **3.0** | |
| (a) Government Enterprises | | | 0.0 | | 0.0 | | 0.0 | | 0.0 | | 0.0 | | 0.0 | |
| (b) Price Controls | | | | | | | | | 0.0 | | 4.0 | | 4.0 | |
| (c) Top Marginal Tax Rate | | | | | | | | | | | | | | |
| (d) Conscription | 0.0 | | 0.0 | | 0.0 | | 0.0 | | 0.0 | | 3.0 | | 10.0 | |
| **III. Monetary Policy and Price Stability** | | | | | | | **9.8** | | **9.8** | | **2.7** | | **2.5** | |
| (a) Annual Money Growth (last 5 yrs.) | | | | | | | | | | | 0.0 | (78.9) | 3.4 | (33.1) |
| (b) Inflation Variability (last 5 yrs.) | | | | | | | 9.6 | (0.9) | 9.6 | (1.0) | 0.0 | (86.9) | 0.0 | (38.1) |
| (c) Recent Inflation Rate | | | | | | | 9.9 | (0.4) | 10.0 | (0.0) | 8.0 | (9.8) | 4.1 | (29.7) |
| **IV. Freedom to Use Alternative Currencies** | **0.0** | | **0.0** | | **0.0** | | **0.0** | | **0.0** | | **7.5** | | **4.6** | |
| (a) Ownership of Foreign Currency | 0.0 | | 0.0 | | 0.0 | | 0.0 | | 0.0 | | 5.0 | | 5.0 | |
| (b) Black Market Exchange Rates (Prem.) | 0.0 | (1100.0) | 0.0 | (745.0) | 0.0 | (866.0) | 0.0 | (818.0) | 0.0 | (800.0) | 10.0 | (0.0) | 4.2 | (29.0) |
| **V. Legal Structure and Property Rights** | | | | | | | **6.3** | | **5.9** | | **8.0** | | **2.5** | |
| (a) Private Ownership Rights | | | | | | | 4.8 | | 4.6 | | 10.0 | | 7.2 | |
| (b) Viability of Contracts | | | | | | | 7.6 | | 6.4 | | 6.8 | | 0.0 | |
| (c) Rule of Law | | | | | | | 6.6 | | 6.7 | | 7.0 | | 0.0 | |
| **VI. International Exchange** | | | | | | | | | | | **4.2** | | **5.8** | |
| (a) Taxes on International Trade | | | | | | | | | | | | | | |
| i. Taxes as a Percentage of Exports and Imports | | | | | | | | | | | 5.8 | (6.3) | | |
| ii. Mean Tariff Rate | | | | | | | | | | | | | 6.8 | (15.9) |
| iii. Standard Deviation of Tariff Rates | | | | | | | | | | | | | 6.7 | (8.3) |
| (b) Non-tariff Regulatory Trade Barriers | | | | | | | | | | | | | | |
| i. Non-tariff Trade Restraints (% of trade covered) | | | | | | | | | | | | | | |
| ii. Size of Trade Sector (% of GDP) | | | | | 1.0 | (45.8) | 0.0 | (34.7) | 0.0 | (38.1) | 0.0 | (47.0) | 0.7 | (52.5) |
| **VII. Freedom of Exchange in Financial Markets** | | | | | | | | | **0.0** | | **2.6** | | **3.1** | |
| (a) Ownership of Banks | | | | | | | | | 0.0 | (0) | 2.0 | (10-40) | 2.0 | (10-40) |
| (b) Extension of Credit | | | | | | | | | | | 0.0 | (7.0) | 0.0 | (6.9) |
| (c) Avoidance of Negative Interest Rates | | | | | | | | | 0.0 | | 6.0 | | 8.0 | |
| (d) Capital Transactions with Foreigners | 0.0 | | 0.0 | | 0.0 | | 0.0 | | 0.0 | | 2.0 | | 2.0 | |

# ALGERIA

| | 1970 | 1975 | 1980 | 1985 | 1990 | 1995 | 1997 |
|---|---|---|---|---|---|---|---|
| **Summary Ratings** | | | 4.7 | 4.2 | 2.7 | 3.6 | 4.1 |
| **Rank** | | | 70 | 85 | 111 | 117 | 117 |

| Components of Economic Freedom | 1970 | | 1975 | | 1980 | | 1985 | | 1990 | | 1995 | | 1997 | |
|---|---|---|---|---|---|---|---|---|---|---|---|---|---|---|
| **I. Size of Government** | **6.9** | | **7.1** | | **6.4** | | **6.3** | | **6.7** | | **7.3** | | **6.8** | |
| (a) Government Consumption (% of Total) | 6.9 | (21.2) | 7.1 | (20.3) | 6.4 | (24.2) | 6.3 | (24.7) | 6.7 | (22.3) | 6.8 | (22.0) | 6.8 | (22.0) |
| (b) Transfers and Subsidies (% of GDP) | | | | | | | | | | | 7.8 | (8.4) | | |
| **II. Structure of the Economy and Use of Markets** | | | | | | | | | **1.0** | | **1.0** | | **1.9** | |
| (a) Government Enterprises | 2.0 | (23.8) | 0.0 | (25.4) | 0.0 | (34.6) | 0.0 | (55.8) | 0.0 | (57.6) | 0.0 | | 0.0 | |
| (b) Price Controls | | | | | | | | | 2.0 | | 2.0 | | 4.0 | |
| (c) Top Marginal Tax Rate | | | | | | | | | | | | | | |
| (d) Conscription | 3.0 | | 10.0 | | 5.0 | | 5.0 | | 1.0 | | 1.0 | | 1.0 | |
| **III. Monetary Policy and Price Stability** | **8.5** | | **6.1** | | **6.5** | | **8.2** | | **6.0** | | **5.2** | | **7.6** | |
| (a) Annual Money Growth (last 5 yrs.) | 7.2 | (14.0) | 6.7 | (16.4) | 6.9 | (15.5) | 7.3 | (13.4) | 9.3 | (3.4) | 7.2 | (13.9) | 7.7 | (11.6) |
| (b) Inflation Variability (last 5 yrs.) | 9.4 | (1.6) | 2.6 | (18.5) | 7.7 | (5.8) | 8.3 | (4.2) | 5.5 | (11.2) | 4.1 | (14.8) | 6.3 | (9.2) |
| (c) Recent Inflation Rate | 8.9 | (5.4) | 8.9 | (5.5) | 4.9 | (25.7) | 9.1 | (4.6) | 3.1 | (34.4) | 4.3 | (28.5) | 8.7 | (6.3) |
| **IV. Freedom to Use Alternative Currencies** | **0.0** | | **0.0** | | **0.0** | | **0.0** | | **0.0** | | **0.0** | | **0.0** | |
| (a) Ownership of Foreign Currency | 0.0 | | 0.0 | | 0.0 | | 0.0 | | 0.0 | | 0.0 | | 0.0 | |
| (b) Black Market Exchange Rates (Prem.) | 0.0 | (59.0) | 0.0 | (56.0) | 0.0 | (263.0) | 0.0 | (335.0) | 0.0 | (140.0) | 0.0 | (201.0) | 0.0 | (122.0) |
| **V. Legal Structure and Property Rights** | **3.2** | | **2.5** | | **3.4** | | **3.7** | | **3.5** | | **7.4** | | **8.5** | |
| (a) Private Ownership Rights | 3.6 | | 3.0 | | 4.0 | | 3.5 | | 3.2 | | 10.0 | | 10.0 | |
| (b) Viability of Contracts | 2.7 | | 1.9 | | 3.0 | | 4.6 | | 4.0 | | 5.2 | | 8.3 | |
| (c) Rule of Law | | | | | 3.3 | | 3.1 | | 3.3 | | 7.0 | | 7.0 | |
| **VI. International Exchange** | | | | | **7.8** | | **4.7** | | **3.6** | | **5.0** | | **4.7** | |
| (a) Taxes on International Trade | | | | | | | | | | | | | | |
| i. Taxes as a Percentage of Exports and Imports | | | | | | | | | | | 3.6 | (9.6) | 4.1 | (8.8) |
| ii. Mean Tariff Rate | | | | | 7.7 | (11.7) | 5.7 | (21.7) | 5.1 | (24.6) | 5.4 | (22.9) | | |
| iii. Standard Deviation of Tariff Rates | | | | | | | | | | | 2.2 | (19.6) | | |
| (b) Non-tariff Regulatory Trade Barriers | | | | | | | | | | | | | | |
| i. Non-tariff Trade Restraints (% of trade covered) | | | | | | | 3.2 | (67.8) | 0.7 | (93.0) | 9.1 | (9.5) | | |
| ii. Size of Trade Sector (% of GDP) | 7.1 | (51.0) | 10.0 | (76.5) | 8.4 | (64.7) | 5.5 | (43.9) | 5.8 | (48.4) | 6.7 | (58.6) | 6.3 | (56.2) |
| **VII. Freedom of Exchange in Financial Markets** | | | | | | | | | **0.3** | | **0.7** | | **0.7** | |
| (a) Ownership of Banks | 0.0 | (0-10) | 0.0 | (0-10) | 0.0 | (0-10) | 0.0 | (0-10) | 0.0 | (0-10) | 0.0 | (0-10) | 0.0 | (0-10) |
| (b) Extension of Credit | | | | | | | | | 1.1 | (19.7) | 0.6 | (15.2) | 0.7 | (16.5) |
| (c) Avoidance of Negative Interest Rates | | | | | | | | | | | 0.0 | | 0.0 | |
| (d) Capital Transactions with Foreigners | 0.0 | | 0.0 | | 0.0 | | 0.0 | | 0.0 | | 2.0 | | 2.0 | |

# ARGENTINA

| | 1970 | 1975 | 1980 | 1985 | 1990 | 1995 | 1997 |
|---|---|---|---|---|---|---|---|
| **Summary Ratings** | 6.6 | 3.2 | 4.8 | 3.8 | 4.9 | 7.9 | 8.4 |
| **Rank** | 24 | 75 | 67 | 93 | 71 | 23 | 12 |

| Components of Economic Freedom | 1970 | | 1975 | | 1980 | | 1985 | | 1990 | | 1995 | | 1997 | |
|---|---|---|---|---|---|---|---|---|---|---|---|---|---|---|
| **I. Size of Government** | **8.4** | | **7.8** | | **7.6** | | **7.7** | | **8.5** | | **7.9** | | **7.8** | |
| (a) Government Consumption (% of Total) | 8.4 | (13.0) | 7.6 | (17.8) | 7.8 | (16.5) | 8.4 | (13.0) | 8.8 | (11.0) | 8.5 | (12.6) | 8.2 | (14.6) |
| (b) Transfers and Subsidies (% of GDP) | | | 8.0 | (7.9) | 7.5 | (9.7) | 6.9 | (11.7) | 8.2 | (7.2) | 7.3 | (10.3) | 7.4 | (9.9) |
| **II. Structure of the Economy and Use of Markets** | | | **3.6** | | **4.4** | | **2.9** | | **3.8** | | **8.4** | | **9.5** | |
| (a) Government Enterprises | 4.0 | (33.6) | 4.0 | (33.6) | 4.0 | (39.5) | 4.0 | (38.3) | 6.0 | (30.0) | 8.0 | (12.8) | 10.0 | |
| (b) Price Controls | | | | | | | | | 0.0 | | 8.0 | | 10.0 | |
| (c) Top Marginal Tax Rate | | | 4.0 | (51) | 6.0 | (45) | 2.0 | (62) | 7.0 | (35) | 9.0 | (30) | 8.0 | (33) |
| (d) Conscription | 0.0 | | 1.0 | | 1.0 | | 1.0 | | 1.0 | | 10.0 | | 10.0 | |
| **III. Monetary Policy and Price Stability** | **6.7** | | **0.0** | | **0.0** | | **0.0** | | **0.0** | | **4.0** | | **8.9** | |
| (a) Annual Money Growth (last 5 yrs.) | 5.0 | (24.8) | 0.0 | (78.3) | 0.0 | (150.0) | 0.0 | (295.2) | 0.0 | (515.6) | 2.5 | (37.5) | 7.9 | (10.5) |
| (b) Inflation Variability (last 5 yrs.) | 6.2 | (9.5) | 0.0 | (61.9) | 0.0 | (119.8) | 0.0 | (208.3) | 0.0 | (1198.8) | 0.0 | (52.4) | 9.0 | (2.6) |
| (c) Recent Inflation Rate | 8.8 | (5.8) | 0.0 | (198.2) | 0.0 | (92.0) | 0.0 | (620.8) | 0.0 | (2064.2) | 9.2 | (3.9) | 10.0 | (0.2) |
| **IV. Freedom to Use Alternative Currencies** | **10.0** | | **5.0** | | **9.9** | | **6.0** | | **10.0** | | **10.0** | | **10.0** | |
| (a) Ownership of Foreign Currency | 10.0 | | 10.0 | | 10.0 | | 10.0 | | 10.0 | | 10.0 | | 10.0 | |
| (b) Black Market Exchange Rates (Prem.) | 10.0 | (0.0) | 0.0 | (124.0) | 9.8 | (1.0) | 2.0 | (40.0) | 10.0 | (0.0) | 10.0 | (0.0) | 10.0 | (0.0) |
| **V. Legal Structure and Property Rights** | **4.2** | | **1.2** | | **4.5** | | **3.2** | | **5.2** | | **8.0** | | **8.5** | |
| (a) Private Ownership Rights | 3.6 | | 0.6 | | 5.2 | | 1.2 | | 5.3 | | 10.0 | | 10.0 | |
| (b) Viability of Contracts | 4.7 | | 1.8 | | 4.9 | | 0.4 | | 2.2 | | 6.8 | | 8.3 | |
| (c) Rule of Law | | | | | 3.3 | | 8.2 | | 8.3 | | 7.0 | | 7.0 | |
| **VI. International Exchange** | | | **0.6** | | **3.4** | | **3.7** | | **3.9** | | **7.3** | | **6.6** | |
| (a) Taxes on International Trade | | | | | | | | | | | | | | |
| i. Taxes as a Percentage of Exports and Imports | | | 1.4 | (12.9) | 3.7 | (9.5) | 1.5 | (12.7) | 3.4 | (9.9) | 7.4 | (3.9) | 7.1 | (4.3) |
| ii. Mean Tariff Rate | | | 0.0 | (55.9) | 4.4 | (27.8) | 4.6 | (27.0) | 5.9 | (20.5) | 7.9 | (10.5) | 7.7 | (11.3) |
| iii. Standard Deviation of Tariff Rates | | | | | | | | | 0.3 | (24.3) | 7.0 | (7.6) | 7.3 | (6.8) |
| (b) Non-tariff Regulatory Trade Barriers | | | | | | | | | | | | | | |
| i. Non-tariff Trade Restraints (% of trade covered) | | | | | | | 6.8 | (31.9) | 8.4 | (16.1) | 10.0 | (0.2) | | |
| ii. Size of Trade Sector (% of GDP) | 0.0 | (10.3) | 0.0 | (11.8) | 0.0 | (11.5) | 0.0 | (18.0) | 0.0 | (15.0) | 0.0 | (17.0) | 0.0 | (18.7) |
| **VII. Freedom of Exchange in Financial Markets** | **5.0** | | **4.7** | | **3.1** | | **2.9** | | **2.6** | | **8.1** | | **8.1** | |
| (a) Ownership of Banks | 5.0 | (40-60) | 5.0 | (40-60) | 5.0 | (40-60) | 5.0 | (40-60) | 5.0 | (40-50) | 5.0 | (60) | 5.0 | (60) |
| (b) Extension of Credit | 8.8 | (89.5) | 7.9 | (81.0) | 8.2 | (83.3) | 7.3 | (76.0) | 5.7 | (60.8) | 7.3 | (76.0) | 7.2 | (74.8) |
| (c) Avoidance of Negative Interest Rates | | | | | 0.0 | | 0.0 | | 0.0 | | 10.0 | | 10.0 | |
| (d) Capital Transactions with Foreigners | 2.0 | | 2.0 | | 0.0 | | 0.0 | | 0.0 | | 10.0 | | 10.0 | |

# AUSTRALIA

| | 1970 | 1975 | 1980 | 1985 | 1990 | 1995 | 1997 |
|---|---|---|---|---|---|---|---|
| **Summary Ratings** | 8.1 | 6.9 | 7.4 | 7.8 | 8.1 | 8.6 | 8.6 |
| **Rank** | 8 | 16 | 11 | 10 | 10 | 6 | 7 |

| Components of Economic Freedom | 1970 | | 1975 | | 1980 | | 1985 | | 1990 | | 1995 | | 1997 | |
|---|---|---|---|---|---|---|---|---|---|---|---|---|---|---|
| **I. Size of Government** | **7.3** | | **7.2** | | **7.0** | | **6.7** | | **7.0** | | **6.6** | | **6.6** | |
| (a) Government Consumption (% of Total) | 7.3 | (19.0) | 6.6 | (22.9) | 6.6 | (23.2) | 6.5 | (23.8) | 6.7 | (22.3) | 6.9 | (21.4) | 6.9 | (21.3) |
| (b) Transfers and Subsidies (% of GDP) | | | 7.8 | (8.5) | 7.4 | (10.1) | 6.9 | (11.9) | 7.2 | (10.7) | 6.3 | (14.2) | 6.3 | (14.2) |
| **II. Structure of the Economy and Use of Markets** | | | **5.0** | | **5.0** | | **5.0** | | **5.6** | | **6.5** | | **6.3** | |
| (a) Government Enterprises | 6.0 | (30.0) | 6.0 | (37.1) | 6.0 | (28.4) | 6.0 | (30.2) | 6.0 | (25.2) | 7.0 | (20.4) | 7.0 | (18.7) |
| (b) Price Controls | | | | | | | | | 6.0 | | 7.0 | | 7.0 | |
| (c) Top Marginal Tax Rate | | | 2.0 | (64) | 2.0 | (62) | 2.0 | (60) | 3.0 | (49) | 4.0 | (47) | 3.0 | (47) |
| (d) Conscription | 0.0 | | 10.0 | | 10.0 | | 10.0 | | 10.0 | | 10.0 | | 10.0 | |
| **III. Monetary Policy and Price Stability** | **9.4** | | **7.9** | | **8.6** | | **9.1** | | **8.7** | | **9.1** | | **9.2** | |
| (a) Annual Money Growth (last 5 yrs.) | 9.7 | (1.6) | 8.4 | (7.8) | 8.3 | (8.6) | 9.4 | (3.2) | 7.6 | (12.0) | 8.1 | (9.3) | 8.1 | (9.6) |
| (b) Inflation Variability (last 5 yrs.) | 9.6 | (1.0) | 8.3 | (4.2) | 9.4 | (1.5) | 9.1 | (2.2) | 9.2 | (2.0) | 9.7 | (0.6) | 9.7 | (0.7) |
| (c) Recent Inflation Rate | 8.9 | (5.5) | 7.0 | (14.9) | 8.0 | (9.8) | 8.8 | (6.1) | 9.3 | (3.3) | 9.4 | (2.9) | 9.8 | (1.0) |
| **IV. Freedom to Use Alternative Currencies** | **10.0** | | **9.9** | | **9.9** | | **10.0** | | **10.0** | | **10.0** | | **10.0** | |
| (a) Ownership of Foreign Currency | 10.0 | | 10.0 | | 10.0 | | 10.0 | | 10.0 | | 10.0 | | 10.0 | |
| (b) Black Market Exchange Rates (Prem.) | 10.0 | (0.0) | 9.8 | (1.0) | 9.8 | (1.0) | 10.0 | (0.0) | 10.0 | (0.0) | 10.0 | (0.0) | 10.0 | (0.0) |
| **V. Legal Structure and Property Rights** | **9.3** | | **7.2** | | **8.0** | | **8.7** | | **8.9** | | **10.0** | | **10.0** | |
| (a) Private Ownership Rights | 9.6 | | 5.5 | | 7.0 | | 8.7 | | 8.6 | | 10.0 | | 10.0 | |
| (b) Viability of Contracts | 9.1 | | 9.0 | | 7.2 | | 7.6 | | 8.2 | | 10.0 | | 10.0 | |
| (c) Rule of Law | | | | | 10.0 | | 10.0 | | 10.0 | | 10.0 | | 10.0 | |
| **VI. International Exchange** | **7.0** | | **6.6** | | **7.1** | | **7.3** | | **6.9** | | **8.0** | | **8.4** | |
| (a) Taxes on International Trade | | | | | | | | | | | | | | |
| i. Taxes as a Percentage of Exports and Imports | 7.5 | (3.7) | 7.1 | (4.4) | 7.6 | (3.6) | 7.9 | (3.2) | 7.9 | (3.1) | 8.7 | (1.9) | 9.0 | (1.5) |
| ii. Mean Tariff Rate | | | 6.6 | (17.0) | 7.1 | (14.5) | 7.3 | (13.3) | 7.2 | (14.2) | 8.4 | (8.2) | 8.9 | (5.7) |
| iii. Standard Deviation of Tariff Rates | | | | | | | | | 4.3 | (14.3) | 6.0 | (10.1) | 6.7 | (8.2) |
| (b) Non-tariff Regulatory Trade Barriers | | | | | | | | | | | | | | |
| i. Non-tariff Trade Restraints (% of trade covered) | | | | | | | | | 9.1 | (8.9) | 10.0 | (0.4) | 10.0 | (0.1) |
| ii. Size of Trade Sector (% of GDP) | 5.6 | (29.0) | 5.3 | (28.9) | 5.9 | (33.9) | 5.8 | (35.2) | 5.4 | (34.6) | 6.1 | (41.7) | 6.0 | (41.5) |
| **VII. Freedom of Exchange in Financial Markets** | **6.3** | | **5.0** | | **6.6** | | **7.6** | | **9.2** | | **9.3** | | **9.3** | |
| (a) Ownership of Banks | 8.0 | (85-95) | 8.0 | (85-95) | 8.0 | (85-95) | 8.0 | (85-95) | 10.0 | (95-100) | 10.0 | (95-100) | 10.0 | (95-100) |
| (b) Extension of Credit | 5.3 | (57.6) | 6.0 | (63.6) | 6.8 | (71.3) | 7.8 | (79.9) | 8.9 | (90.2) | 9.1 | (91.8) | 9.4 | (94.5) |
| (c) Avoidance of Negative Interest Rates | 10.0 | | 4.0 | | 10.0 | | 10.0 | | 10.0 | | 10.0 | | 10.0 | |
| (d) Capital Transactions with Foreigners | 2.0 | | 2.0 | | 2.0 | | 5.0 | | 8.0 | | 8.0 | | 8.0 | |

# AUSTRIA

| | 1970 | 1975 | 1980 | 1985 | 1990 | 1995 | 1997 |
|---|---|---|---|---|---|---|---|
| **Summary Ratings** | 7.2 | 6.2 | 6.8 | 6.9 | 7.6 | 7.8 | 8.0 |
| **Rank** | 18 | 25 | 16 | 21 | 19 | 29 | 25 |

| Components of Economic Freedom | 1970 | | 1975 | | 1980 | | 1985 | | 1990 | | 1995 | | 1997 | |
|---|---|---|---|---|---|---|---|---|---|---|---|---|---|---|
| **I. Size of Government** | **6.5** | | **5.7** | | **5.2** | | **5.0** | | **5.1** | | **4.6** | | **4.7** | |
| (a) Government Consumption (% of Total) | 6.9 | (21.5) | 6.5 | (23.8) | 6.3 | (24.8) | 6.2 | (25.2) | 6.2 | (25.0) | 6.0 | (26.4) | 6.1 | (25.8) |
| (b) Transfers and Subsidies (% of GDP) | 6.1 | (14.9) | 4.9 | (19.4) | 4.1 | (22.1) | 3.8 | (23.1) | 4.0 | (22.4) | 3.3 | (25.2) | 3.2 | (25.3) |
| **II. Structure of the Economy and Use of Markets** | | | **3.1** | | **2.4** | | **2.4** | | **3.8** | | **4.6** | | **4.9** | |
| (a) Government Enterprises | 2.0 | | 2.0 | (45.0) | 2.0 | (44.5) | 2.0 | (42.0) | 2.0 | | 2.0 | | 4.0 | |
| (b) Price Controls | | | | | | | | | 5.0 | | 8.0 | | 7.0 | |
| (c) Top Marginal Tax Rate | | | 4.0 | (54) | 2.0 | (62) | 2.0 | (62) | 4.0 | (50) | 4.0 | (50) | 4.0 | (50) |
| (d) Conscription | 0.0 | | 5.0 | | 5.0 | | 5.0 | | 5.0 | | 3.0 | | 3.0 | |
| **III. Monetary Policy and Price Stability** | **9.5** | | **8.9** | | **9.5** | | **9.5** | | **9.4** | | **9.3** | | **9.5** | |
| (a) Annual Money Growth (last 5 yrs.) | 9.6 | (1.8) | 8.5 | (7.7) | 9.8 | (1.0) | 9.5 | (2.3) | 9.2 | (4.0) | 8.6 | (6.8) | 8.9 | (5.5) |
| (b) Inflation Variability (last 5 yrs.) | 9.7 | (0.7) | 9.5 | (1.2) | 9.6 | (0.9) | 9.5 | (1.2) | 9.7 | (0.6) | 9.7 | (0.8) | 9.6 | (1.0) |
| (c) Recent Inflation Rate | 9.1 | (4.7) | 8.7 | (6.5) | 9.0 | (5.0) | 9.4 | (3.1) | 9.3 | (3.5) | 9.6 | (2.1) | 10.0 | (-0.1) |
| **IV. Freedom to Use Alternative Currencies** | **7.5** | | **7.5** | | **7.5** | | **7.5** | | **10.0** | | **10.0** | | **10.0** | |
| (a) Ownership of Foreign Currency | 5.0 | | 5.0 | | 5.0 | | 5.0 | | 10.0 | | 10.0 | | 10.0 | |
| (b) Black Market Exchange Rates (Prem.) | 10.0 | (0.0) | 10.0 | (0.0) | 10.0 | (0.0) | 10.0 | (0.0) | 10.0 | (0.0) | 10.0 | (0.0) | 10.0 | (0.0) |
| **V. Legal Structure and Property Rights** | | | | | **9.3** | | **9.1** | | **10.0** | | **10.0** | | **10.0** | |
| (a) Private Ownership Rights | | | | | 9.2 | | 8.7 | | 10.0 | | 10.0 | | 10.0 | |
| (b) Viability of Contracts | | | | | 8.7 | | 8.8 | | 10.0 | | 10.0 | | 10.0 | |
| (c) Rule of Law | | | | | 10.0 | | 10.0 | | 10.0 | | 10.0 | | 10.0 | |
| **VI. International Exchange** | **7.8** | | **7.6** | | **8.3** | | **8.5** | | **8.2** | | **8.7** | | **8.5** | |
| (a) Taxes on International Trade | | | | | | | | | | | | | | |
| i. Taxes as a Percentage of Exports and Imports | 8.3 | (2.6) | 8.9 | (1.7) | 9.5 | (0.7) | 9.6 | (0.6) | 9.5 | (0.7) | 9.9 | (0.2) | 9.9 | (0.1) |
| ii. Mean Tariff Rate | | | 6.9 | (15.4) | 7.7 | (11.6) | 8.0 | (10.0) | 8.3 | (8.7) | 8.7 | (6.7) | 8.6 | (6.9) |
| iii. Standard Deviation of Tariff Rates | | | | | | | | | 6.0 | (10.1) | 7.6 | (5.9) | 7.6 | (6.0) |
| (b) Non-tariff Regulatory Trade Barriers | | | | | | | | | | | | | | |
| i. Non-tariff Trade Restraints (% of trade covered) | | | | | | | | | 9.7 | (2.6) | 9.7 | (2.6) | | |
| ii. Size of Trade Sector (% of GDP) | 6.5 | (59.7) | 6.3 | (61.6) | 7.0 | (74.0) | 7.0 | (79.1) | 6.6 | (79.0) | 6.1 | (78.2) | 6.5 | (85.0) |
| **VII. Freedom of Exchange in Financial Markets** | **5.6** | | **5.0** | | **5.5** | | **6.0** | | **6.7** | | **7.0** | | **7.6** | |
| (a) Ownership of Banks | 5.0 | (40-60) | 5.0 | (40-75) | 5.0 | (40-75) | 5.0 | (63) | 5.0 | (40-75) | 5.0 | (54) | 5.0 | (74) |
| (b) Extension of Credit | 8.3 | (84.6) | 7.9 | (80.6) | 7.6 | (78.7) | 7.5 | (77.7) | 7.1 | (73.8) | 7.0 | (72.8) | 7.4 | (76.8) |
| (c) Avoidance of Negative Interest Rates | 8.0 | | 6.0 | | 8.0 | | 10.0 | | 10.0 | | 8.0 | | 10.0 | |
| (d) Capital Transactions with Foreigners | 2.0 | | 2.0 | | 2.0 | | 2.0 | | 5.0 | | 8.0 | | 8.0 | |

# BAHAMAS

| | 1970 | 1975 | 1980 | 1985 | 1990 | 1995 | 1997 |
|---|---|---|---|---|---|---|---|
| **Summary Ratings** | | 6.4 | 6.0 | 6.4 | 6.0 | 6.2 | 6.7 |
| **Rank** | | 21 | 32 | 27 | 43 | 64 | 60 |

| Components of Economic Freedom | 1970 | | 1975 | | 1980 | | 1985 | | 1990 | | 1995 | | 1997 | |
|---|---|---|---|---|---|---|---|---|---|---|---|---|---|---|
| **I. Size of Government** | **9.8** | | **8.8** | | **8.9** | | **8.9** | | **8.9** | | **8.5** | | | |
| (a) Government Consumption (% of Total) | | | 7.6 | (17.6) | 7.7 | (16.9) | 7.8 | (16.5) | 8.0 | (15.6) | 7.4 | (18.9) | | |
| (b) Transfers and Subsidies (% of GDP) | 9.8 | (1.4) | 10.0 | (0.5) | 10.0 | (0.5) | 10.0 | (0.1) | 9.9 | (1.0) | 9.7 | (1.6) | | |
| **II. Structure of the Economy and Use of Markets** | | | **8.0** | | **7.1** | | **6.1** | | **5.4** | | **6.7** | | **6.7** | |
| (a) Government Enterprises | 6.0 | | 6.0 | (24.2) | 4.0 | | 2.0 | | 2.0 | | 6.0 | | 6.0 | |
| (b) Price Controls | | | | | | | | | 4.0 | | 4.0 | | 4.0 | |
| (c) Top Marginal Tax Rate | | | 10.0 | (0) | 10.0 | (0) | 10.0 | (0) | 10.0 | (0) | 10.0 | (0) | 10.0 | (0) |
| (d) Conscription | | | 10.0 | | 10.0 | | 10.0 | | 10.0 | | 10.0 | | 10.0 | |
| **III. Monetary Policy and Price Stability** | **9.0** | | **8.7** | | **8.2** | | **8.6** | | **9.1** | | **9.3** | | **9.6** | |
| (a) Annual Money Growth (last 5 yrs.) | | | 9.6 | (-1.9) | 7.9 | (10.3) | 9.6 | (2.2) | 8.7 | (6.6) | 9.1 | (4.6) | 9.0 | (4.8) |
| (b) Inflation Variability (last 5 yrs.) | 9.3 | (1.8) | 8.7 | (3.3) | 8.6 | (3.5) | 7.9 | (5.3) | 9.3 | (1.7) | 9.3 | (1.6) | 9.8 | (0.4) |
| (c) Recent Inflation Rate | 8.8 | (6.2) | 7.9 | (10.7) | 8.0 | (10.0) | 8.3 | (8.5) | 9.4 | (3.2) | 9.4 | (2.8) | 9.9 | (0.5) |
| **IV. Freedom to Use Alternative Currencies** | **7.2** | | **3.6** | | **3.0** | | **3.9** | | **3.7** | | **4.8** | | **4.6** | |
| (a) Ownership of Foreign Currency | | | 0.0 | | 0.0 | | 0.0 | | 0.0 | | 0.0 | | 0.0 | |
| (b) Black Market Exchange Rates (Prem.) | 7.2 | (14.0) | 7.2 | (14.0) | 6.0 | (20.0) | 7.8 | (11.0) | 7.4 | (13.0) | 9.6 | (2.0) | 9.2 | (4.0) |
| **V. Legal Structure and Property Rights** | | | | | | | **6.8** | | **6.7** | | **6.3** | | **6.6** | |
| (a) Private Ownership Rights | | | | | | | 6.1 | | 5.9 | | 7.7 | | 7.2 | |
| (b) Viability of Contracts | | | | | | | 7.6 | | 7.6 | | 6.8 | | 8.3 | |
| (c) Rule of Law | | | | | | | 6.6 | | 6.7 | | 4.1 | | 4.1 | |
| **VI. International Exchange** | | | **4.6** | | **4.4** | | **5.3** | | **3.4** | | **3.0** | | | |
| (a) Taxes on International Trade | | | | | | | | | | | | | | |
| i. Taxes as a Percentage of Exports and Imports | 4.7 | (7.9) | 4.1 | (8.8) | 4.6 | (8.1) | 3.8 | (9.3) | 3.6 | (9.6) | 3.1 | (10.3) | | |
| ii. Mean Tariff Rate | | | | | 4.0 | (29.8) | 3.5 | (32.3) | | | | | 3.0 | (35.0) |
| iii. Standard Deviation of Tariff Rates | | | | | | | | | | | | | | |
| (b) Non-tariff Regulatory Trade Barriers | | | | | | | | | | | | | | |
| i. Non-tariff Trade Restraints (% of trade covered) | | | | | | | 10.0 | (0.1) | | | | | | |
| ii. Size of Trade Sector (% of GDP) | | | 5.6 | (151.9) | 4.7 | (133.3) | 4.0 | (124.1) | 2.8 | (108.7) | 2.8 | (114.0) | | |
| **VII. Freedom of Exchange in Financial Markets** | **6.2** | | **6.3** | | **6.3** | | **6.9** | | **6.8** | | **6.9** | | **6.9** | |
| (a) Ownership of Banks | 10.0 | (95-100) | 10.0 | (95-100) | 10.0 | (95-100) | 10.0 | (95-100) | 10.0 | (95-100) | 10.0 | (95-100) | 10.0 | (95-100) |
| (b) Extension of Credit | 9.4 | (94.7) | 7.8 | (80.2) | 7.6 | (78.5) | 7.9 | (81.2) | 7.7 | (78.9) | 8.0 | (81.7) | 8.3 | (84.3) |
| (c) Avoidance of Negative Interest Rates | | | 8.0 | | 8.0 | | 10.0 | | 10.0 | | 10.0 | | 10.0 | |
| (d) Capital Transactions with Foreigners | 0.0 | | 0.0 | | 0.0 | | 0.0 | | 0.0 | | 0.0 | | 0.0 | |

# BAHRAIN

| | 1970 | 1975 | 1980 | 1985 | 1990 | 1995 | 1997 |
|---|---|---|---|---|---|---|---|
| **Summary Ratings** | | | 7.6 | 7.4 | 7.4 | 7.9 | 7.9 |
| **Rank** | | | 10 | 14 | 24 | 23 | 31 |

| Components of Economic Freedom | 1970 | | 1975 | | 1980 | | 1985 | | 1990 | | 1995 | | 1997 | |
|---|---|---|---|---|---|---|---|---|---|---|---|---|---|---|
| **I. Size of Government** | | | | | **7.7** | | **6.4** | | **6.4** | | **7.2** | | **7.1** | |
| (a) Government Consumption (% of Total) | | | | | 5.5 | (29.0) | 2.8 | (43.5) | 2.8 | (43.8) | 4.4 | (35.2) | 4.8 | (32.7) |
| (b) Transfers and Subsidies (% of GDP) | | | | | 9.8 | (1.2) | 10.0 | (0.0) | 10.0 | (0.5) | 10.0 | (0.0) | 9.4 | (2.6) |
| **II. Structure of the Economy and Use of Markets** | | | **6.1** | | **7.1** | | **7.1** | | **6.0** | | **6.0** | | **6.0** | |
| (a) Government Enterprises | 0.0 | | 2.0 | (76.4) | 4.0 | (29.8) | 4.0 | (31.7) | 4.0 | | 4.0 | | 4.0 | |
| (b) Price Controls | | | | | | | | | 4.0 | | 4.0 | | 4.0 | |
| (c) Top Marginal Tax Rate | | | 10.0 | (0) | 10.0 | (0) | 10.0 | (0) | 10.0 | (0) | 10.0 | (0) | 10.0 | (0) |
| (d) Conscription | | | 10.0 | | 10.0 | | 10.0 | | 10.0 | | 10.0 | | 10.0 | |
| **III. Monetary Policy and Price Stability** | **9.0** | | **7.0** | | **7.5** | | **8.2** | | **8.3** | | **9.4** | | **9.0** | |
| (a) Annual Money Growth (last 5 yrs.) | 7.9 | (10.5) | 7.1 | (14.4) | 6.4 | (18.1) | 8.5 | (7.7) | 9.5 | (2.7) | 9.6 | (-2.1) | 8.8 | (-6.2) |
| (b) Inflation Variability (last 5 yrs.) | 9.4 | (1.4) | 7.1 | (7.2) | 6.8 | (8.0) | 6.3 | (9.2) | 6.9 | (7.7) | 8.7 | (3.3) | 8.8 | (2.9) |
| (c) Recent Inflation Rate | 9.7 | (1.6) | 6.8 | (16.1) | 9.2 | (3.9) | 9.6 | (-1.8) | 8.6 | (6.8) | 9.8 | (1.0) | 9.5 | (2.7) |
| **IV. Freedom to Use Alternative Currencies** | | | **10.0** | | **10.0** | | **10.0** | | **10.0** | | **10.0** | | **10.0** | |
| (a) Ownership of Foreign Currency | | | 10.0 | | 10.0 | | 10.0 | | 10.0 | | 10.0 | | 10.0 | |
| (b) Black Market Exchange Rates (Prem.) | | | 10.0 | (0.0) | 10.0 | (0.0) | 10.0 | (0.0) | 10.0 | (0.0) | 10.0 | (0.0) | 10.0 | (0.0) |
| **V. Legal Structure and Property Rights** | | | | | | | **5.9** | | **5.9** | | **8.5** | | **8.5** | |
| (a) Private Ownership Rights | | | | | | | 6.1 | | 5.9 | | 10.0 | | 10.0 | |
| (b) Viability of Contracts | | | | | | | 5.2 | | 5.2 | | 8.4 | | 8.3 | |
| (c) Rule of Law | | | | | | | 6.6 | | 6.7 | | 7.0 | | 7.0 | |
| **VI. International Exchange** | | | | | | | **8.6** | | **8.4** | | **8.0** | | **8.0** | |
| (a) Taxes on International Trade | | | | | | | | | | | | | | |
| i. Taxes as a Percentage of Exports and Imports | | | | | | | 9.5 | (0.7) | 9.3 | (1.1) | 9.1 | (1.4) | 9.1 | (1.4) |
| ii. Mean Tariff Rate | | | | | | | 8.8 | (6.0) | | | | | | |
| iii. Standard Deviation of Tariff Rates | | | | | | | | | | | | | | |
| (b) Non-tariff Regulatory Trade Barriers | | | | | | | | | | | | | | |
| i. Non-tariff Trade Restraints (% of trade covered) | | | | | | | | | | | | | | |
| ii. Size of Trade Sector (% of GDP) | | | 7.1 | (241.2) | 6.9 | (239.3) | 5.4 | (191.6) | 6.0 | (221.7) | 5.1 | (195.4) | 5.4 | (206.9) |
| **VII. Freedom of Exchange in Financial Markets** | | | **6.4** | | **6.2** | | **6.0** | | **6.7** | | **6.5** | | **7.0** | |
| (a) Ownership of Banks | | | 8.0 | (80-90) | 8.0 | (80-90) | 8.0 | (80-90) | 8.0 | (90-95) | 8.0 | (90-95) | 8.0 | (90-95) |
| (b) Extension of Credit | 10.0 | (99.9) | 9.9 | (99.2) | 9.4 | (94.1) | 8.6 | (87.0) | 7.2 | (74.6) | 8.6 | (87.3) | 8.7 | (88.4) |
| (c) Avoidance of Negative Interest Rates | | | | | | | | | 10.0 | | 8.0 | | 10.0 | |
| (d) Capital Transactions with Foreigners | 2.0 | | 2.0 | | 2.0 | | 2.0 | | 2.0 | | 2.0 | | 2.0 | |

# BANGLADESH

| | 1970 | 1975 | 1980 | 1985 | 1990 | 1995 | 1997 |
|---|---|---|---|---|---|---|---|
| **Summary Ratings** | | 2.9 | 2.9 | 3.3 | 3.7 | 4.1 | 5.3 |
| **Rank** | | 79 | 102 | 99 | 102 | 109 | 94 |

| Components of Economic Freedom | 1970 | | 1975 | | 1980 | | 1985 | | 1990 | | 1995 | | 1997 | |
|---|---|---|---|---|---|---|---|---|---|---|---|---|---|---|
| **I. Size of Government** | | | **10.0** | | **10.0** | | **10.0** | | **10.0** | | **9.9** | | **9.9** | |
| (a) Government Consumption (% of Total) | | | 10.0 | (1.0) | 10.0 | (2.0) | 10.0 | (2.4) | 10.0 | (4.6) | 9.9 | (5.2) | 9.9 | (5.0) |
| (b) Transfers and Subsidies (% of GDP) | | | | | | | | | | | | | | |
| **II. Structure of the Economy and Use of Markets** | | | | | **2.7** | | **2.7** | | | | **2.0** | | **2.0** | |
| (a) Government Enterprises | 2.0 | | 2.0 | (50.4) | 2.0 | (44.4) | 2.0 | (46.6) | 2.0 | (47.1) | 2.0 | (46.4) | 2.0 | |
| (b) Price Controls | | | | | | | | | 0.0 | | 0.0 | | 0.0 | |
| (c) Top Marginal Tax Rate | | | | | 1.0 | (60) | 1.0 | (60) | | | | | | |
| (d) Conscription | | | 10.0 | | 10.0 | | 10.0 | | 10.0 | | 10.0 | | 10.0 | |
| **III. Monetary Policy and Price Stability** | **8.5** | | **2.6** | | **6.0** | | **8.0** | | **9.2** | | **8.5** | | **9.0** | |
| (a) Annual Money Growth (last 5 yrs.) | | | 7.8 | (10.9) | 6.4 | (18.0) | 7.4 | (13.1) | 9.5 | (2.7) | 7.7 | (11.3) | 8.2 | (9.2) |
| (b) Inflation Variability (last 5 yrs.) | 7.0 | (7.5) | 0.0 | (29.1) | 4.2 | (14.4) | 8.8 | (3.1) | 9.2 | (2.1) | 9.0 | (2.4) | 9.1 | (2.2) |
| (c) Recent Inflation Rate | 9.9 | (0.5) | 0.0 | (74.5) | 7.3 | (13.4) | 7.8 | (11.1) | 9.0 | (4.9) | 8.7 | (6.7) | 9.7 | (1.3) |
| **IV. Freedom to Use Alternative Currencies** | | | **0.0** | | **0.0** | | **0.0** | | **0.0** | | **2.2** | | **3.2** | |
| (a) Ownership of Foreign Currency | | | 0.0 | | 0.0 | | 0.0 | | 0.0 | | 0.0 | | 0.0 | |
| (b) Black Market Exchange Rates (Prem.) | | | 0.0 | (51.0) | 0.0 | (111.0) | 0.0 | (168.0) | 0.0 | (165.0) | 4.4 | (28.0) | 6.4 | (18.0) |
| **V. Legal Structure and Property Rights** | | | | | **1.9** | | **2.2** | | **1.7** | | **5.3** | | **6.9** | |
| (a) Private Ownership Rights | | | | | 2.2 | | 2.2 | | 1.9 | | 5.5 | | 7.2 | |
| (b) Viability of Contracts | | | | | 1.8 | | 2.8 | | 1.6 | | 3.7 | | 6.6 | |
| (c) Rule of Law | | | | | 1.7 | | 1.4 | | 1.7 | | 7.0 | | 7.0 | |
| **VI. International Exchange** | | | **3.4** | | **0.8** | | **1.6** | | **1.5** | | **0.7** | | | |
| (a) Taxes on International Trade | | | | | | | | | | | | | | |
| i. Taxes as a Percentage of Exports and Imports | | | 4.7 | (7.9) | 1.1 | (13.4) | 0.0 | (17.9) | 1.9 | (12.1) | | | | |
| ii. Mean Tariff Rate | | | | | 0.0 | (99.9) | 0.0 | (86.0) | 0.0 | (102.2) | 0.0 | (81.2) | | |
| iii. Standard Deviation of Tariff Rates | | | | | | | | | 0.0 | (50.4) | 0.0 | (26.1) | | |
| (b) Non-tariff Regulatory Trade Barriers | | | | | | | | | | | | | | |
| i. Non-tariff Trade Restraints (% of trade covered) | | | | | | | 5.1 | (49.4) | 4.3 | (57.5) | | | | |
| ii. Size of Trade Sector (% of GDP) | 1.9 | (20.8) | 0.0 | (11.0) | 2.3 | (24.1) | 2.5 | (25.8) | 2.5 | (27.1) | 4.2 | (36.7) | 4.4 | (38.7) |
| **VII. Freedom of Exchange in Financial Markets** | | | **0.6** | | **2.3** | | **2.8** | | **3.9** | | **3.5** | | **3.5** | |
| (a) Ownership of Banks | 0.0 | (0-10) | 0.0 | (0-10) | 0.0 | (0-10) | 0.0 | (0-10) | 0.0 | (0-10) | 0.0 | (0-10) | 0.0 | (0-10) |
| (b) Extension of Credit | | | 2.0 | (27.8) | 3.7 | (43.1) | 6.2 | (65.5) | 7.0 | (72.7) | 7.1 | (73.6) | 7.1 | (74.2) |
| (c) Avoidance of Negative Interest Rates | | | | | 6.0 | | 6.0 | | 10.0 | | 8.0 | | 8.0 | |
| (d) Capital Transactions with Foreigners | 0.0 | | 0.0 | | 0.0 | | 0.0 | | 0.0 | | 0.0 | | 0.0 | |

# BARBADOS

| | 1970 | 1975 | 1980 | 1985 | 1990 | 1995 | 1997 |
|---|---|---|---|---|---|---|---|
| **Summary Ratings** | | 5.5 | 5.7 | 6.2 | 6.2 | 6.4 | 6.3 |
| **Rank** | | 42 | 38 | 32 | 41 | 57 | 70 |

| Components of Economic Freedom | 1970 | | 1975 | | 1980 | | 1985 | | 1990 | | 1995 | | 1997 | |
|---|---|---|---|---|---|---|---|---|---|---|---|---|---|---|
| **I. Size of Government** | **8.6** | | **8.7** | | **8.6** | | **8.2** | | **8.2** | | **8.3** | | **6.3** | |
| (a) Government Consumption (% of Total) | 7.9 | (16.2) | 7.5 | (18.3) | 7.3 | (19.3) | 6.3 | (24.6) | 6.4 | (24.1) | 6.7 | (22.7) | 6.3 | (24.8) |
| (b) Transfers and Subsidies (% of GDP) | 9.3 | (2.9) | 10.0 | (0.2) | 10.0 | (0.2) | 10.0 | (0.0) | 10.0 | (0.5) | 10.0 | (0.0) | | |
| **II. Structure of the Economy and Use of Markets** | | | **4.7** | | **4.7** | | **4.7** | | **5.9** | | **6.1** | | **6.1** | |
| (a) Government Enterprises | 8.0 | (19.2) | 6.0 | (26.8) | 6.0 | (22.8) | 6.0 | (22.5) | 6.0 | | 6.0 | | 6.0 | |
| (b) Price Controls | | | | | | | | | 6.0 | | 6.0 | | 6.0 | |
| (c) Top Marginal Tax Rate | | | 1.0 | (65) | 1.0 | (60) | 1.0 | (60) | 4.0 | (50) | 5.0 | (40) | 5.0 | (40) |
| (d) Conscription | | | 10.0 | | 10.0 | | 10.0 | | 10.0 | | 10.0 | | 10.0 | |
| **III. Monetary Policy and Price Stability** | **8.8** | | **7.4** | | **6.7** | | **8.9** | | **8.7** | | **9.5** | | **8.8** | |
| (a) Annual Money Growth (last 5 yrs.) | | | 8.1 | (9.5) | 6.9 | (15.3) | 8.8 | (5.8) | 8.6 | (7.1) | 8.9 | (-5.4) | 8.3 | (8.7) |
| (b) Inflation Variability (last 5 yrs.) | 9.1 | (2.3) | 6.3 | (9.2) | 7.6 | (6.0) | 8.6 | (3.5) | 8.6 | (3.4) | 9.5 | (1.3) | 9.7 | (0.8) |
| (c) Recent Inflation Rate | 8.5 | (7.3) | 7.7 | (11.7) | 5.5 | (22.6) | 9.2 | (4.1) | 8.9 | (5.5) | 10.0 | (0.3) | 8.5 | (7.7) |
| **IV. Freedom to Use Alternative Currencies** | | | **3.0** | | **3.9** | | **3.9** | | **4.0** | | **4.7** | | **4.9** | |
| (a) Ownership of Foreign Currency | | | 0.0 | | 0.0 | | 0.0 | | 0.0 | | 0.0 | | 0.0 | |
| (b) Black Market Exchange Rates (Prem.) | | | 6.0 | (20.0) | 7.8 | (11.0) | 7.8 | (11.0) | 8.0 | (10.0) | 9.4 | (3.0) | 9.8 | (1.0) |
| **V. Legal Structure and Property Rights** | | | | | | | **6.8** | | **6.7** | | **6.3** | | **6.6** | |
| (a) Private Ownership Rights | | | | | | | 6.1 | | 5.9 | | 7.7 | | 7.2 | |
| (b) Viability of Contracts | | | | | | | 7.6 | | 7.6 | | 6.8 | | 8.3 | |
| (c) Rule of Law | | | | | | | 6.6 | | 6.7 | | 4.1 | | 4.1 | |
| **VI. International Exchange** | **5.8** | | **5.6** | | **6.3** | | **6.3** | | **5.5** | | **5.8** | | | |
| (a) Taxes on International Trade | | | | | | | | | | | | | | |
| i. Taxes as a Percentage of Exports and Imports | 6.6 | (5.1) | 7.1 | (4.4) | 7.5 | (3.7) | 7.7 | (3.4) | 7.6 | (3.6) | 7.8 | (3.3) | | |
| ii. Mean Tariff Rate | | | | | | | 6.6 | (17.0) | | | 7.2 | (14.1) | | |
| iii. Standard Deviation of Tariff Rates | | | | | | | | | 4.5 | (13.7) | 4.8 | (13.1) | | |
| (b) Non-tariff Regulatory Trade Barriers | | | | | | | | | | | | | | |
| i. Non-tariff Trade Restraints (% of trade covered) | | | | | | | | | 6.6 | (33.9) | | | | |
| ii. Size of Trade Sector (% of GDP) | 3.9 | (138.1) | 1.9 | (110.8) | 3.3 | (142.2) | 2.0 | (127.8) | 0.0 | (100.8) | 0.0 | (115.8) | 0.0 | (113.2) |
| **VII. Freedom of Exchange in Financial Markets** | | | **5.1** | | **5.2** | | **6.1** | | **6.0** | | **6.0** | | **5.9** | |
| (a) Ownership of Banks | | | 8.0 | (75-90) | 8.0 | (75-90) | 8.0 | (75-90) | 8.0 | (75-90) | 8.0 | (75-90) | 8.0 | (75-90) |
| (b) Extension of Credit | 9.5 | (95.4) | 7.9 | (80.9) | 7.3 | (75.7) | 6.8 | (70.7) | 6.4 | (67.3) | 6.2 | (66.1) | 5.9 | (63.1) |
| (c) Avoidance of Negative Interest Rates | | | | | 6.0 | | 10.0 | | 10.0 | | 10.0 | | 10.0 | |
| (d) Capital Transactions with Foreigners | 0.0 | | 0.0 | | 0.0 | | 0.0 | | 0.0 | | 0.0 | | 0.0 | |

# BELGIUM

| | 1970 | 1975 | 1980 | 1985 | 1990 | 1995 | 1997 |
|---|---|---|---|---|---|---|---|
| **Summary Ratings** | 9.3 | 7.8 | 8.0 | 8.1 | 8.1 | 8.2 | 8.3 |
| **Rank** | 2 | 6 | 5 | 7 | 10 | 12 | 14 |

| Components of Economic Freedom | 1970 | | 1975 | | 1980 | | 1985 | | 1990 | | 1995 | | 1997 | |
|---|---|---|---|---|---|---|---|---|---|---|---|---|---|---|
| **I. Size of Government** | **6.0** | | **4.7** | | **5.0** | | **4.9** | | **5.4** | | **5.2** | | **7.4** | |
| (a) Government Consumption (% of Total) | 7.5 | (18.3) | 7.0 | (20.9) | 6.9 | (21.6) | 7.1 | (20.3) | 7.5 | (18.1) | 7.4 | (18.9) | 7.4 | (18.7) |
| (b) Transfers and Subsidies (% of GDP) | 4.5 | (20.8) | 2.4 | (28.5) | 3.1 | (26.0) | 2.6 | (27.6) | 3.3 | (25.0) | 3.0 | (26.3) | | |
| **II. Structure of the Economy and Use of Markets** | | | **4.1** | | **3.3** | | **3.3** | | **3.4** | | **4.8** | | **4.8** | |
| (a) Government Enterprises | 6.0 | | 6.0 | (25.0) | 6.0 | (26.8) | 6.0 | (25.3) | 6.0 | (27.0) | 6.0 | | 6.0 | |
| (b) Price Controls | | | | | | | | | 2.0 | | 5.0 | | 5.0 | |
| (c) Top Marginal Tax Rate | | | 2.0 | (64) | 0.0 | (76) | 0.0 | (76) | 2.0 | (55-61) | 1.0 | (58-68) | 1.0 | (58-64) |
| (d) Conscription | 1.0 | | 3.0 | | 3.0 | | 3.0 | | 3.0 | | 10.0 | | 10.0 | |
| **III. Monetary Policy and Price Stability** | **9.5** | | **8.3** | | **9.4** | | **9.4** | | **9.5** | | **9.6** | | **9.7** | |
| (a) Annual Money Growth (last 5 yrs.) | 9.7 | (-1.3) | 8.6 | (6.9) | 9.6 | (1.9) | 9.7 | (1.6) | 9.4 | (2.9) | 9.4 | (3.0) | 9.9 | (-0.4) |
| (b) Inflation Variability (last 5 yrs.) | 9.7 | (0.7) | 8.8 | (3.0) | 9.4 | (1.6) | 9.8 | (0.6) | 9.6 | (1.0) | 9.6 | (0.9) | 9.6 | (1.0) |
| (c) Recent Inflation Rate | 9.1 | (4.6) | 7.5 | (12.3) | 9.2 | (4.2) | 8.8 | (6.1) | 9.4 | (3.1) | 9.7 | (1.7) | 9.7 | (1.5) |
| **IV. Freedom to Use Alternative Currencies** | **10.0** | | **10.0** | | **10.0** | | **10.0** | | **10.0** | | **10.0** | | **10.0** | |
| (a) Ownership of Foreign Currency | 10.0 | | 10.0 | | 10.0 | | 10.0 | | 10.0 | | 10.0 | | 10.0 | |
| (b) Black Market Exchange Rates (Prem.) | 10.0 | (0.0) | 10.0 | (0.0) | 10.0 | (0.0) | 10.0 | (0.0) | 10.0 | (0.0) | 10.0 | (0.0) | 10.0 | (0.0) |
| **V. Legal Structure and Property Rights** | **9.9** | | **8.6** | | **8.6** | | **9.1** | | **10.0** | | **9.5** | | **9.0** | |
| (a) Private Ownership Rights | 10.0 | | 8.6 | | 8.6 | | 8.7 | | 10.0 | | 10.0 | | 10.0 | |
| (b) Viability of Contracts | 9.9 | | 8.5 | | 7.2 | | 8.8 | | 10.0 | | 8.4 | | 10.0 | |
| (c) Rule of Law | | | | | 10.0 | | 10.0 | | 10.0 | | 10.0 | | 7.0 | |
| **VI. International Exchange** | **9.5** | | **9.0** | | **9.0** | | **9.1** | | **8.7** | | **8.8** | | **8.6** | |
| (a) Taxes on International Trade | | | | | | | | | | | | | | |
| i. Taxes as a Percentage of Exports and Imports | 9.7 | (0.4) | 10.0 | (0.0) | 9.8 | (0.3) | 9.8 | (0.3) | 9.7 | (0.4) | 9.7 | (0.4) | 9.7 | (0.4) |
| ii. Mean Tariff Rate | | | 8.1 | (9.4) | 8.2 | (8.8) | 8.5 | (7.5) | 8.5 | (7.4) | 8.7 | (6.7) | 8.6 | (6.9) |
| iii. Standard Deviation of Tariff Rates | | | | | | | | | 7.1 | (7.2) | 7.6 | (5.9) | 7.6 | (6.0) |
| (b) Non-tariff Regulatory Trade Barriers | | | | | | | | | | | | | | |
| i. Non-tariff Trade Restraints (% of trade covered) | | | | | 8.7 | (12.6) | 8.6 | (14.3) | 8.9 | (10.9) | 9.1 | (9.0) | | |
| ii. Size of Trade Sector (% of GDP) | 9.0 | (101.1) | 8.9 | (106.6) | 9.9 | (127.3) | 10.0 | (149.9) | 9.8 | (143.5) | 9.0 | (140.4) | 8.7 | (139.4) |
| **VII. Freedom of Exchange in Financial Markets** | **10.0** | | **8.7** | | **10.0** | | **10.0** | | **8.7** | | **8.6** | | **8.7** | |
| (a) Ownership of Banks | 10.0 | (95-100) | 10.0 | (95-100) | 10.0 | (95-100) | 10.0 | (95-100) | 10.0 | (95-100) | 10.0 | (95-100) | 10.0 | (95-100) |
| (b) Extension of Credit | | | | | | | | | 3.9 | (44.8) | 3.6 | (42.5) | 3.9 | (45.3) |
| (c) Avoidance of Negative Interest Rates | 10.0 | | 6.0 | | 10.0 | | 10.0 | | 10.0 | | 10.0 | | 10.0 | |
| (d) Capital Transactions with Foreigners | 10.0 | | 10.0 | | 10.0 | | 10.0 | | 10.0 | | 10.0 | | 10.0 | |

# BELIZE

| | 1970 | 1975 | 1980 | 1985 | 1990 | 1995 | 1997 |
|---|---|---|---|---|---|---|---|
| **Summary Ratings** | | | 5.5 | 5.1 | 5.3 | 6.1 | 6.3 |
| **Rank** | | | 44 | 62 | 58 | 67 | 70 |

| Components of Economic Freedom | 1970 | | 1975 | | 1980 | | 1985 | | 1990 | | 1995 | | 1997 | |
|---|---|---|---|---|---|---|---|---|---|---|---|---|---|---|
| **I. Size of Government** | | | **7.8** | | **8.4** | | **7.9** | | **8.4** | | **8.7** | | **8.0** | |
| (a) Government Consumption (% of Total) | | | 7.8 | (16.4) | 7.3 | (19.3) | 6.6 | (23.1) | 7.0 | (20.9) | 7.6 | (17.7) | 6.3 | (24.6) |
| (b) Transfers and Subsidies (% of GDP) | | | | | 9.4 | (2.6) | 9.2 | (3.6) | 9.8 | (1.2) | 9.8 | (1.2) | 9.7 | (1.6) |
| **II. Structure of the Economy and Use of Markets** | | | | | | | **4.8** | | **2.5** | | **4.8** | | **4.7** | |
| (a) Government Enterprises | | | 6.0 | (34.9) | 2.0 | (54.6) | 4.0 | (36.5) | 2.0 | (55.5) | 2.0 | (47.6) | 2.0 | |
| (b) Price Controls | | | | | | | | | 0.0 | | 6.0 | | 6.0 | |
| (c) Top Marginal Tax Rate | | | | | | | 4.0 | (50) | 4.0 | (45) | 5.0 | (45) | | |
| (d) Conscription | | | | | 10.0 | | 10.0 | | 10.0 | | 10.0 | | 10.0 | |
| **III. Monetary Policy and Price Stability** | **8.7** | | **6.6** | | **8.3** | | **8.8** | | **9.1** | | **9.5** | | **9.6** | |
| (a) Annual Money Growth (last 5 yrs.) | | | | | 8.8 | (6.2) | 9.3 | (3.3) | 8.5 | (7.6) | 9.8 | (1.0) | 10.0 | (-0.1) |
| (b) Inflation Variability (last 5 yrs.) | 9.0 | (2.6) | 6.7 | (8.3) | 8.5 | (3.8) | 7.5 | (6.3) | 8.8 | (3.0) | 9.6 | (1.0) | 8.9 | (2.6) |
| (c) Recent Inflation Rate | 8.5 | (7.4) | 6.6 | (16.9) | 7.7 | (11.4) | 9.6 | (-1.9) | 9.9 | (0.3) | 9.2 | (3.9) | 9.8 | (-1.1) |
| **IV. Freedom to Use Alternative Currencies** | | | **3.6** | | **1.6** | | **0.0** | | **2.5** | | **4.7** | | **4.6** | |
| (a) Ownership of Foreign Currency | | | | | 0.0 | | 0.0 | | 0.0 | | 0.0 | | 0.0 | |
| (b) Black Market Exchange Rates (Prem.) | | | 3.6 | (32.0) | 3.2 | (34.0) | 0.0 | (63.0) | 5.0 | (25.0) | 9.4 | (3.0) | 9.2 | (4.0) |
| **V. Legal Structure and Property Rights** | | | | | | | | | | | | | | |
| (a) Private Ownership Rights | | | | | | | | | | | | | | |
| (b) Viability of Contracts | | | | | | | | | | | | | | |
| (c) Rule of Law | | | | | | | | | | | | | | |
| **VI. International Exchange** | | | | | **4.2** | | **4.5** | | **3.1** | | **2.6** | | **4.7** | |
| (a) Taxes on International Trade | | | | | | | | | | | | | | |
| i. Taxes as a Percentage of Exports and Imports | | | | | 4.2 | (8.7) | 2.7 | (10.9) | 2.8 | (10.8) | 2.7 | (10.9) | 5.6 | (6.6) |
| ii. Mean Tariff Rate | | | | | | | 6.6 | (17.0) | | | | | | |
| iii. Standard Deviation of Tariff Rates | | | | | | | | | | | | | | |
| (b) Non-tariff Regulatory Trade Barriers | | | | | | | | | | | | | | |
| i. Non-tariff Trade Restraints (% of trade covered) | | | | | | | | | | | | | | |
| ii. Size of Trade Sector (% of GDP) | | | 6.0 | (165.1) | 4.2 | (124.0) | 3.2 | (109.8) | 3.8 | (125.4) | 2.1 | (103.2) | 2.4 | (109.3) |
| **VII. Freedom of Exchange in Financial Markets** | | | | | **6.9** | | **6.7** | | **8.2** | | **8.3** | | **7.9** | |
| (a) Ownership of Banks | | | | | | | | | 10.0 | (95-100) | 10.0 | (95-100) | 10.0 | (95-100) |
| (b) Extension of Credit | | | 9.0 | (91.1) | 8.0 | (82.1) | 7.4 | (76.6) | 8.0 | (82.1) | 8.5 | (86.8) | 8.8 | (88.9) |
| (c) Avoidance of Negative Interest Rates | | | | | 8.0 | | 8.0 | | 10.0 | | 10.0 | | 8.0 | |
| (d) Capital Transactions with Foreigners | | | | | 5.0 | | 5.0 | | 5.0 | | 5.0 | | 5.0 | |

# BENIN

| | 1970 | 1975 | 1980 | 1985 | 1990 | 1995 | 1997 |
|---|---|---|---|---|---|---|---|
| **Summary Ratings** | | 5.1 | 4.9 | 4.8 | 5.7 | 4.7 | 4.9 |
| **Rank** | | 46 | 63 | 69 | 52 | 98 | 101 |

| Components of Economic Freedom | 1970 | | 1975 | | 1980 | | 1985 | | 1990 | | 1995 | | 1997 | |
|---|---|---|---|---|---|---|---|---|---|---|---|---|---|---|
| **I. Size of Government** | **9.0** | | **9.1** | | **9.3** | | **8.0** | | **8.7** | | **8.5** | | **8.7** | |
| (a) Government Consumption (% of Total) | 9.0 | (10.3) | 9.1 | (9.4) | 9.3 | (8.2) | 8.0 | (15.5) | 8.7 | (11.7) | 8.5 | (12.5) | 8.7 | (11.7) |
| (b) Transfers and Subsidies (% of GDP) | | | | | | | | | | | | | | |
| **II. Structure of the Economy and Use of Markets** | | | | | | | | | | | **1.9** | | **1.9** | |
| (a) Government Enterprises | 2.0 | (50.0) | 2.0 | (45.9) | 2.0 | (53.7) | 2.0 | (53.5) | 2.0 | (42.9) | 2.0 | (50.0) | 2.0 | |
| (b) Price Controls | | | | | | | | | | | 2.0 | | 2.0 | |
| (c) Top Marginal Tax Rate | | | | | | | | | | | | | | |
| (d) Conscription | | | | | | | 1.0 | | 1.0 | | 1.0 | | 1.0 | |
| **III. Monetary Policy and Price Stability** | **9.0** | | **6.9** | | **8.4** | | **8.1** | | **9.0** | | **6.9** | | **7.9** | |
| (a) Annual Money Growth (last 5 yrs.) | 8.6 | (6.8) | 5.8 | (20.8) | 8.4 | (8.0) | 8.0 | (10.0) | 9.9 | (0.7) | 8.7 | (6.3) | 9.1 | (4.7) |
| (b) Inflation Variability (last 5 yrs.) | 9.3 | (1.8) | 7.8 | (5.4) | 8.7 | (3.2) | 7.2 | (6.9) | 8.3 | (4.2) | 5.0 | (12.5) | 5.4 | (11.6) |
| (c) Recent Inflation Rate | 9.0 | (5.1) | 7.2 | (14.3) | 8.0 | (10.2) | 9.0 | (-4.9) | 8.8 | (6.1) | 6.9 | (15.4) | 9.1 | (4.7) |
| **IV. Freedom to Use Alternative Currencies** | **4.8** | | **4.8** | | **4.8** | | **4.9** | | **4.6** | | **4.9** | | **4.8** | |
| (a) Ownership of Foreign Currency | 0.0 | | 0.0 | | 0.0 | | 0.0 | | 0.0 | | 0.0 | | 0.0 | |
| (b) Black Market Exchange Rates (Prem.) | 9.6 | (2.0) | 9.6 | (2.0) | 9.6 | (2.0) | 9.8 | (1.0) | 9.2 | (4.0) | 9.8 | (1.0) | 9.6 | (2.0) |
| **V. Legal Structure and Property Rights** | | | | | **4.2** | | **4.1** | | **4.3** | | **3.6** | | **3.6** | |
| (a) Private Ownership Rights | | | | | 4.0 | | 3.8 | | 3.8 | | 2.7 | | 2.8 | |
| (b) Viability of Contracts | | | | | 2.8 | | 3.9 | | 4.0 | | 3.0 | | 3.1 | |
| (c) Rule of Law | | | | | 5.8 | | 4.8 | | 5.3 | | 5.2 | | 5.2 | |
| **VI. International Exchange** | | | **4.0** | | **2.2** | | **2.1** | | | | | | | |
| (a) Taxes on International Trade | | | | | | | | | | | | | | |
| i. Taxes as a Percentage of Exports and Imports | | | 3.9 | (9.2) | 2.9 | (10.6) | | | | | | | | |
| ii. Mean Tariff Rate | | | | | | | 2.5 | (37.4) | | | | | | |
| iii. Standard Deviation of Tariff Rates | | | | | | | | | | | | | | |
| (b) Non-tariff Regulatory Trade Barriers | | | | | | | | | | | | | | |
| i. Non-tariff Trade Restraints (% of trade covered) | | | | | 0.0 | (100.0) | 0.0 | (100.0) | 0.0 | (100.0) | 8.3 | (17.0) | | |
| ii. Size of Trade Sector (% of GDP) | 3.8 | (50.4) | 4.5 | (59.9) | 4.8 | (66.3) | 5.4 | (76.9) | 2.9 | (52.3) | 3.9 | (62.9) | 3.6 | (61.4) |
| **VII. Freedom of Exchange in Financial Markets** | **2.7** | | **2.8** | | **3.6** | | **4.0** | | **4.3** | | **4.5** | | **4.6** | |
| (a) Ownership of Banks | 0.0 | (0) | 0.0 | (0) | 0.0 | (0) | 0.0 | (0) | 2.0 | (10-40) | 10.0 | (100) | 10.0 | (100) |
| (b) Extension of Credit | 9.7 | (97.5) | 10.0 | (99.9) | 9.9 | (99.3) | 9.7 | (97.5) | 8.6 | (87.5) | 6.2 | (65.9) | 6.5 | (68.5) |
| (c) Avoidance of Negative Interest Rates | | | | | 6.0 | | 8.0 | | 8.0 | | 2.0 | | 2.0 | |
| (d) Capital Transactions with Foreigners | 0.0 | | 0.0 | | 0.0 | | 0.0 | | 0.0 | | 0.0 | | 0.0 | |

# BOLIVIA

| | 1970 | 1975 | 1980 | 1985 | 1990 | 1995 | 1997 |
|---|---|---|---|---|---|---|---|
| **Summary Ratings** | | | 4.0 | 4.0 | 6.5 | 7.9 | 8.0 |
| **Rank** | | | 86 | 91 | 36 | 23 | 25 |

| Components of Economic Freedom | 1970 | | 1975 | | 1980 | | 1985 | | 1990 | | 1995 | | 1997 | |
|---|---|---|---|---|---|---|---|---|---|---|---|---|---|---|
| **I. Size of Government** | **9.9** | | **8.9** | | **8.7** | | **9.1** | | **8.9** | | **8.7** | | **8.0** | |
| (a) Government Consumption (% of Total) | | | 8.1 | (15.1) | 7.7 | (17.1) | 8.5 | (12.5) | 8.4 | (13.3) | 8.0 | (15.2) | 7.7 | (16.9) |
| (b) Transfers and Subsidies (% of GDP) | 9.9 | (1.0) | 9.8 | (1.3) | 9.7 | (1.6) | 9.6 | (1.8) | 9.4 | (2.8) | 9.5 | (2.5) | 8.3 | (6.8) |
| **II. Structure of the Economy and Use of Markets** | | | | | **2.5** | | **4.4** | | **4.8** | | **6.1** | | **7.1** | |
| (a) Government Enterprises | 2.0 | (44.0) | 4.0 | (28.9) | 2.0 | (50.1) | 2.0 | (42.5) | 0.0 | (64.3) | 2.0 | (51.2) | 4.0 | (40.3) |
| (b) Price Controls | | | | | | | | | 6.0 | | 8.0 | | 9.0 | |
| (c) Top Marginal Tax Rate | | | | | 3.0 | (48) | 8.0 | (30) | 10.0 | (10) | 10.0 | (13) | 10.0 | (13) |
| (d) Conscription | 3.0 | | 3.0 | | 3.0 | | 3.0 | | 3.0 | | 3.0 | | 3.0 | |
| **III. Monetary Policy and Price Stability** | **9.2** | | **5.1** | | **3.5** | | **0.0** | | **3.1** | | **6.8** | | **7.9** | |
| (a) Annual Money Growth (last 5 yrs.) | 8.9 | (5.6) | 5.8 | (20.9) | 6.2 | (19.1) | 0.0 | (566.0) | 2.4 | (38.0) | 4.3 | (28.3) | 6.0 | (20.2) |
| (b) Inflation Variability (last 5 yrs.) | 9.4 | (1.5) | 1.0 | (22.5) | 3.8 | (15.5) | 0.0 | (4769.2) | 0.0 | (85.9) | 8.4 | (4.0) | 8.8 | (3.1) |
| (c) Recent Inflation Rate | 9.2 | (3.8) | 8.4 | (7.8) | 0.5 | (47.3) | 0.0 | (12336.7) | 6.7 | (16.3) | 7.7 | (11.4) | 8.9 | (5.4) |
| **IV. Freedom to Use Alternative Currencies** | 6.1 | | 9.5 | | 7.8 | | 4.1 | | 9.7 | | 9.9 | | 9.9 | |
| (a) Ownership of Foreign Currency | 10.0 | | 10.0 | | 10.0 | | 0.0 | | 10.0 | | 10.0 | | 10.0 | |
| (b) Black Market Exchange Rates (Prem.) | 2.2 | (39.0) | 9.0 | (5.0) | 5.6 | (22.0) | 8.2 | (9.0) | 9.4 | (3.0) | 9.8 | (1.0) | 9.8 | (1.0) |
| **V. Legal Structure and Property Rights** | | | | | **1.7** | | **0.5** | | **3.4** | | **7.2** | | **6.9** | |
| (a) Private Ownership Rights | | | | | 1.6 | | 0.0 | | 3.9 | | 7.7 | | 7.2 | |
| (b) Viability of Contracts | | | | | 1.8 | | 0.0 | | 4.6 | | 6.8 | | 6.6 | |
| (c) Rule of Law | | | | | 1.7 | | 1.4 | | 1.7 | | 7.0 | | 7.0 | |
| **VI. International Exchange** | **3.6** | | **4.9** | | **3.3** | | **5.8** | | **7.8** | | **8.6** | | **8.3** | |
| (a) Taxes on International Trade | | | | | | | | | | | | | | |
| i. Taxes as a Percentage of Exports and Imports | 2.6 | (11.1) | 4.1 | (8.9) | 4.8 | (7.8) | 5.3 | (7.0) | 8.5 | (2.3) | 8.6 | (2.1) | 8.5 | (2.2) |
| ii. Mean Tariff Rate | | | | | | | 6.0 | (19.8) | 6.7 | (16.7) | 8.1 | (9.7) | 8.1 | (9.7) |
| iii. Standard Deviation of Tariff Rates | | | | | | | | | | | 9.6 | (1.1) | 9.5 | (1.3) |
| (b) Non-tariff Regulatory Trade Barriers | | | | | | | | | | | | | | |
| i. Non-tariff Trade Restraints (% of trade covered) | | | | | 1.0 | (90.0) | 7.5 | (25.0) | 9.8 | (2.0) | 9.8 | (2.0) | | |
| ii. Size of Trade Sector (% of GDP) | 6.1 | (48.9) | 7.0 | (58.2) | 4.2 | (37.7) | 2.4 | (30.3) | 4.9 | (47.0) | 4.9 | (49.7) | 4.8 | (49.5) |
| **VII. Freedom of Exchange in Financial Markets** | | | | | **2.0** | | | | **7.3** | | **7.5** | | **8.3** | |
| (a) Ownership of Banks | | | | | | | | | 10.0 | (100) | 8.0 | (93) | 8.0 | (93) |
| (b) Extension of Credit | 2.6 | (33.4) | 6.1 | (65.1) | 4.4 | (49.7) | | | 10.0 | (99.9) | 9.6 | (96.4) | 9.2 | (92.9) |
| (c) Avoidance of Negative Interest Rates | | | | | 0.0 | | 0.0 | | 8.0 | | 8.0 | | 8.0 | |
| (d) Capital Transactions with Foreigners | 2.0 | | 2.0 | | 2.0 | | 2.0 | | 2.0 | | 5.0 | | 8.0 | |

# BOTSWANA

| | 1970 | 1975 | 1980 | 1985 | 1990 | 1995 | 1997 |
|---|---|---|---|---|---|---|---|
| **Summary Ratings** | | 3.9 | 4.7 | 5.6 | 6.0 | 6.8 | 6.6 |
| **Rank** | | 66 | 70 | 47 | 43 | 49 | 62 |

| Components of Economic Freedom | 1970 | | 1975 | | 1980 | | 1985 | | 1990 | | 1995 | | 1997 | |
|---|---|---|---|---|---|---|---|---|---|---|---|---|---|---|
| **I. Size of Government** | **8.4** | | **7.5** | | **7.3** | | **6.1** | | **6.4** | | **5.3** | | **5.0** | |
| (a) Government Consumption (% of Total) | 7.0 | (21.0) | 6.3 | (24.8) | 5.8 | (27.5) | 4.1 | (36.7) | 4.5 | (34.4) | 2.4 | (45.9) | 1.9 | (48.5) |
| (b) Transfers and Subsidies (% of GDP) | 9.7 | (1.5) | 8.6 | (5.5) | 8.8 | (4.9) | 8.1 | (7.3) | 8.3 | (6.6) | 8.2 | (7.2) | 8.0 | (7.7) |
| **II. Structure of the Economy and Use of Markets** | | | **2.3** | | **2.3** | | **3.1** | | **4.3** | | **5.9** | | **6.2** | |
| (a) Government Enterprises | 2.0 | (34.6) | 2.0 | (46.3) | 2.0 | (44.9) | 2.0 | (53.2) | 2.0 | | 4.0 | | 4.0 | |
| (b) Price Controls | | | | | | | | | 6.0 | | 6.0 | | 6.0 | |
| (c) Top Marginal Tax Rate | | | 0.0 | (75) | 0.0 | (75) | 2.0 | (60) | 3.0 | (50) | 7.0 | (35) | 8.0 | (30) |
| (d) Conscription | | | 10.0 | | 10.0 | | 10.0 | | 10.0 | | 10.0 | | 10.0 | |
| **III. Monetary Policy and Price Stability** | **9.6** | | **6.6** | | **7.1** | | **7.0** | | **7.4** | | **8.8** | | **8.2** | |
| (a) Annual Money Growth (last 5 yrs.) | | | | | 8.6 | (6.8) | 9.2 | (4.1) | 6.9 | (15.3) | 10.0 | (0.0) | 9.1 | (4.4) |
| (b) Inflation Variability (last 5 yrs.) | 9.5 | (1.3) | 6.9 | (7.7) | 6.4 | (8.9) | 6.5 | (8.9) | 6.6 | (8.6) | 8.3 | (4.3) | 8.6 | (3.4) |
| (c) Recent Inflation Rate | 9.8 | (1.1) | 6.3 | (18.8) | 6.2 | (19.1) | 5.5 | (22.7) | 8.8 | (6.0) | 8.1 | (9.3) | 7.0 | (15.2) |
| **IV. Freedom to Use Alternative Currencies** | | | **0.6** | | **4.0** | | **2.8** | | **4.3** | | **7.3** | | **7.3** | |
| (a) Ownership of Foreign Currency | | | 0.0 | | 0.0 | | 0.0 | | 0.0 | | 5.0 | | 5.0 | |
| (b) Black Market Exchange Rates (Prem.) | | | 1.2 | (44.0) | 8.0 | (10.0) | 5.6 | (22.0) | 8.6 | (7.0) | 9.6 | (2.0) | 9.6 | (2.0) |
| **V. Legal Structure and Property Rights** | | | | | | | 6.5 | | 6.4 | | 8.0 | | 7.6 | |
| **(a) Private Ownership Rights** | | | | | | | 6.1 | | 5.9 | | 10.0 | | 10.0 | |
| (b) Viability of Contracts | | | | | | | 5.2 | | 5.2 | | 6.8 | | 8.3 | |
| (c) Rule of Law | | | | | | | 8.2 | | 8.3 | | 7.0 | | 4.1 | |
| **VI. International Exchange** | | | **4.3** | | **3.2** | | **6.8** | | **7.6** | | **6.9** | | **5.6** | |
| (a) Taxes on International Trade | | | | | | | | | | | | | | |
| i. Taxes as a Percentage of Exports and Imports | | | 3.1 | (10.4) | 1.5 | (12.8) | 5.3 | (7.1) | 5.6 | (6.6) | 4.8 | (7.8) | 5.3 | (7.1) |
| ii. Mean Tariff Rate | | | | | | | | | | | | | | |
| iii. Standard Deviation of Tariff Rates | | | | | | | | | | | | | | |
| (b) Non-tariff Regulatory Trade Barriers | | | | | | | | | | | | | | |
| i. Non-tariff Trade Restraints (% of trade covered) | | | | | | | 8.3 | (17.1) | 10.0 | (0.3) | 10.0 | (0.3) | | |
| ii. Size of Trade Sector (% of GDP) | 5.9 | (70.9) | 7.4 | (92.0) | 7.7 | (99.3) | 7.4 | (99.1) | 7.8 | (107.5) | 5.6 | (81.7) | 6.4 | (93.9) |
| **VII. Freedom of Exchange in Financial Markets** | | | | | **5.8** | | **6.9** | | **5.5** | | **6.0** | | **6.6** | |
| (a) Ownership of Banks | | | | | | | | | 5.0 | (40-75) | 5.0 | (40-75) | 5.0 | (40-75) |
| (b) Extension of Credit | | | 9.0 | (91.1) | 8.8 | (89.4) | 7.9 | (81.3) | 8.6 | (87.5) | 8.6 | (87.6) | 9.3 | (93.5) |
| (c) Avoidance of Negative Interest Rates | | | | | 4.0 | | 8.0 | | 4.0 | | 6.0 | | 8.0 | |
| (d) Capital Transactions with Foreigners | | | | | 5.0 | | 5.0 | | 5.0 | | 5.0 | | 5.0 | |

# BRAZIL

| | 1970 | 1975 | 1980 | 1985 | 1990 | 1995 | 1997 |
|---|---|---|---|---|---|---|---|
| **Summary Ratings** | 5.6 | 4.5 | 4.1 | 3.2 | 4.4 | 5.4 | 5.9 |
| **Rank** | 37 | 59 | 79 | 101 | 84 | 84 | 85 |

| Components of Economic Freedom | 1970 | | 1975 | | 1980 | | 1985 | | 1990 | | 1995 | | 1997 | |
|---|---|---|---|---|---|---|---|---|---|---|---|---|---|---|
| **I. Size of Government** | **7.1** | | **6.5** | | **7.7** | | **7.9** | | **6.8** | | **6.4** | | **6.7** | |
| (a) Government Consumption (% of Total) | 8.2 | (14.2) | 8.3 | (13.8) | 8.7 | (11.6) | 8.4 | (13.0) | 6.3 | (24.5) | 6.3 | (24.7) | 6.7 | (22.3) |
| (b) Transfers and Subsidies (% of GDP) | 5.9 | (15.5) | 4.7 | (19.9) | 6.8 | (12.4) | 7.4 | (10.0) | 7.2 | (10.7) | 6.5 | (13.3) | | |
| **II. Structure of the Economy and Use of Markets** | **5.0** | | **4.2** | | **2.9** | | **2.7** | | **4.5** | | **6.2** | | **7.2** | |
| (a) Government Enterprises | 4.0 | (38.3) | 4.0 | (35.8) | 2.0 | (49.2) | 4.0 | (36.0) | 6.0 | (24.9) | 6.0 | (19.3) | 6.0 | |
| (b) Price Controls | | | | | | | | | 0.0 | | 6.0 | | 8.0 | |
| (c) Top Marginal Tax Rate | 7.0 | (45) | 5.0 | (50) | 4.0 | (55) | 1.0 | (60) | 9.0 | (25) | 8.0 | (35) | 9.0 | (25) |
| (d) Conscription | 3.0 | | 3.0 | | 3.0 | | 3.0 | | 3.0 | | 3.0 | | 3.0 | |
| **III. Monetary Policy and Price Stability** | **6.2** | | **4.8** | | **1.7** | | **0.0** | | **0.0** | | **0.0** | | **2.8** | |
| (a) Annual Money Growth (last 5 yrs.) | 5.1 | (24.3) | 3.9 | (30.6) | 1.6 | (41.8) | 0.0 | (137.8) | 0.0 | (648.7) | 0.0 | (708.0) | 0.0 | (293.7) |
| (b) Inflation Variability (last 5 yrs.) | 6.9 | (7.7) | 7.3 | (6.7) | 3.4 | (16.6) | 0.0 | (53.1) | 0.0 | (878.9) | 0.0 | (851.5) | 0.0 | (1023.9) |
| (c) Recent Inflation Rate | 6.6 | (17.1) | 3.2 | (34.0) | 0.0 | (87.5) | 0.0 | (231.7) | 0.0 | (2509.5) | 0.0 | (77.6) | 8.4 | (7.9) |
| **IV. Freedom to Use Alternative Currencies** | **6.1** | | **0.1** | | **3.2** | | **0.1** | | **4.0** | | **4.7** | | **4.9** | |
| (a) Ownership of Foreign Currency | 5.0 | | 0.0 | | 0.0 | | 0.0 | | 0.0 | | 0.0 | | 0.0 | |
| (b) Black Market Exchange Rates (Prem.) | 7.2 | (14.0) | 0.2 | (49.0) | 6.4 | (18.0) | 0.2 | (49.0) | 8.0 | (10.0) | 9.4 | (3.0) | 9.8 | (1.0) |
| **V. Legal Structure and Property Rights** | 6.2 | | 5.6 | | 6.0 | | 5.6 | | 6.4 | | 8.0 | | 7.9 | |
| (a) Private Ownership Rights | 7.0 | | 5.9 | | 6.4 | | 6.1 | | 7.3 | | 10.0 | | 10.0 | |
| (b) Viability of Contracts | 5.4 | | 5.4 | | 4.9 | | 4.3 | | 5.2 | | 6.8 | | 6.6 | |
| (c) Rule of Law | | | | | 6.7 | | 6.6 | | 6.7 | | 7.0 | | 7.0 | |
| **VI. International Exchange** | **4.7** | | **5.6** | | **3.5** | | **3.4** | | **5.2** | | **7.4** | | **6.2** | |
| (a) Taxes on International Trade | | | | | | | | | | | | | | |
| i. Taxes as a Percentage of Exports and Imports | 5.6 | (6.6) | 6.2 | (5.7) | 3.3 | (10.0) | 7.9 | (3.2) | 7.5 | (3.7) | 8.1 | (2.8) | | |
| ii. Mean Tariff Rate | | | | | | | 0.0 | (55.6) | 4.0 | (30.0) | 7.6 | (12.0) | 7.6 | (11.9) |
| iii. Standard Deviation of Tariff Rates | | | | | | | 0.0 | (26.2) | 3.0 | (17.5) | 7.2 | (6.9) | 7.0 | (7.5) |
| (b) Non-tariff Regulatory Trade Barriers | | | | | | | | | | | | | | |
| i. Non-tariff Trade Restraints (% of trade covered) | | | | | | | 6.5 | (35.3) | 9.0 | (10.0) | 9.9 | (1.5) | | |
| ii. Size of Trade Sector (% of GDP) | 2.4 | (14.5) | 3.9 | (19.0) | 4.1 | (20.4) | 3.4 | (19.3) | 0.0 | (12.7) | 0.5 | (14.7) | 0.2 | (14.5) |
| **VII. Freedom of Exchange in Financial Markets** | **4.6** | | **4.6** | | **3.7** | | **2.4** | | **2.7** | | **3.1** | | **4.5** | |
| (a) Ownership of Banks | 5.0 | (40-75) | 5.0 | (40-75) | 5.0 | (40-75) | 5.0 | (40-75) | 5.0 | (54) | 5.0 | (61) | 5.0 | (57) |
| (b) Extension of Credit | 8.1 | (83.2) | 8.2 | (84.0) | 6.4 | (67.8) | 4.8 | (52.9) | 6.5 | (68.4) | 8.0 | (82.2) | 5.7 | (61.4) |
| (c) Avoidance of Negative Interest Rates | 6.0 | | 6.0 | | 4.0 | | 0.0 | | 0.0 | | 0.0 | | 8.0 | |
| (d) Capital Transactions with Foreigners | 0.0 | | 0.0 | | 0.0 | | 0.0 | | 0.0 | | 0.0 | | 0.0 | |

# BULGARIA

| | 1970 | 1975 | 1980 | 1985 | 1990 | 1995 | 1997 |
|---|---|---|---|---|---|---|---|
| **Summary Ratings** | | | | | 3.8 | 5.2 | 5.3 |
| **Rank** | | | | | 99 | 87 | 94 |

| Components of Economic Freedom | 1970 | | 1975 | | 1980 | | 1985 | | 1990 | | 1995 | | 1997 | |
|---|---|---|---|---|---|---|---|---|---|---|---|---|---|---|
| **I. Size of Government** | | | | | **9.1** | | **7.0** | | **4.6** | | **7.1** | | **7.6** | |
| (a) Government Consumption (% of Total) | | | | | 9.1 | (9.3) | 8.6 | (12.4) | 6.5 | (23.3) | 7.6 | (17.8) | 8.0 | (14.7) |
| (b) Transfers and Subsidies (% of GDP) | | | | | | | 5.4 | (17.5) | 2.7 | (27.2) | 6.6 | (13.0) | 7.2 | (10.7) |
| **II. Structure of the Economy and Use of Markets** | | | | | | | | | **0.0** | | **2.2** | | **3.3** | |
| (a) Government Enterprises | 0.0 | | 0.0 | | 0.0 | (76.0) | 0.0 | (66.0) | 0.0 | (64.0) | 0.0 | (55.6) | 0.0 | (55.6) |
| (b) Price Controls | | | | | | | | | 0.0 | | 4.0 | | 6.0 | |
| (c) Top Marginal Tax Rate | | | | | | | | | | | 3.0 | (50) | 5.0 | (40) |
| (d) Conscription | 0.0 | | 0.0 | | 0.0 | | 0.0 | | 0.0 | | 1.0 | | 1.0 | |
| **III. Monetary Policy and Price Stability** | | | | | | | **9.7** | | **5.9** | | **0.0** | | **0.0** | |
| (a) Annual Money Growth (last 5 yrs.) | | | | | | | | | 7.4 | (13.1) | 0.0 | (67.0) | 0.0 | (130.3) |
| (b) Inflation Variability (last 5 yrs.) | | | | | | | 9.4 | (1.4) | 5.6 | (10.9) | 0.0 | (66.4) | 0.0 | (350.5) |
| (c) Recent Inflation Rate | | | | | | | 10.0 | (0.2) | 4.8 | (26.2) | 0.0 | (62.9) | 0.0 | (951.0) |
| **IV. Freedom to Use Alternative Currencies** | **0.0** | | **0.0** | | **0.0** | | **0.0** | | **0.0** | | **7.0** | | **7.1** | |
| (a) Ownership of Foreign Currency | 0.0 | | 0.0 | | 0.0 | | 0.0 | | 0.0 | | 5.0 | | 5.0 | |
| (b) Black Market Exchange Rates (Prem.) | 0.0 | (161.0) | 0.0 | (175.0) | 0.0 | (175.0) | 0.0 | (435.0) | 0.0 | (100.0) | 9.0 | (5.0) | 9.2 | (4.0) |
| **V. Legal Structure and Property Rights** | | | | | | | **7.6** | | **7.4** | | **7.2** | | **4.8** | |
| (a) Private Ownership Rights | | | | | | | 8.7 | | 8.6 | | 7.7 | | 7.2 | |
| (b) Viability of Contracts | | | | | | | 5.8 | | 5.2 | | 6.8 | | 3.1 | |
| (c) Rule of Law | | | | | | | 8.2 | | 8.3 | | 7.0 | | 4.1 | |
| **VI. International Exchange** | | | | | | | **6.6** | | **7.9** | | **6.5** | | **7.7** | |
| (a) Taxes on International Trade | | | | | | | | | | | | | | |
| i. Taxes as a Percentage of Exports and Imports | | | | | | | 6.4 | (5.4) | 9.1 | (1.3) | 7.9 | (3.2) | 8.8 | (1.8) |
| ii. Mean Tariff Rate | | | | | | | | | 7.7 | (11.4) | 6.6 | (17.2) | 6.6 | (17.0) |
| iii. Standard Deviation of Tariff Rates | | | | | | | | | | | 4.7 | (13.3) | | |
| (b) Non-tariff Regulatory Trade Barriers | | | | | | | | | | | | | | |
| i. Non-tariff Trade Restraints (% of trade covered) | | | | | | | | | | | | | | |
| ii. Size of Trade Sector (% of GDP) | | | | | 5.7 | (66.4) | 7.0 | (86.0) | 5.3 | (69.8) | 7.2 | (102.7) | 8.0 | (117.0) |
| **VII. Freedom of Exchange in Financial Markets** | | | | | | | | | **1.0** | | **4.3** | | **4.8** | |
| (a) Ownership of Banks | 0.0 | (0) | 0.0 | (0) | 0.0 | (0) | 0.0 | (0) | 0.0 | (0-10) | 2.0 | (30) | 5.0 | (43) |
| (b) Extension of Credit | | | | | | | | | 0.0 | (10.0) | 2.2 | (29.8) | 5.3 | (57.5) |
| (c) Avoidance of Negative Interest Rates | | | | | | | | | 4.0 | | 8.0 | | 4.0 | |
| (d) Capital Transactions with Foreigners | 0.0 | | 0.0 | | 0.0 | | 0.0 | | 0.0 | | 5.0 | | 5.0 | |

# BURUNDI

| | 1970 | 1975 | 1980 | 1985 | 1990 | 1995 | 1997 |
|---|---|---|---|---|---|---|---|
| **Summary Ratings** | | 3.2 | 3.2 | 4.1 | 3.9 | 3.5 | 4.2 |
| **Rank** | | 75 | 100 | 87 | 96 | 118 | 115 |

| Components of Economic Freedom | 1970 | | 1975 | | 1980 | | 1985 | | 1990 | | 1995 | | 1997 | |
|---|---|---|---|---|---|---|---|---|---|---|---|---|---|---|
| **I. Size of Government** | **9.0** | | **8.8** | | **9.2** | | **9.3** | | **9.0** | | **8.9** | | **8.8** | |
| (a) Government Consumption (% of Total) | 9.0 | (10.1) | 8.8 | (11.2) | 9.2 | (9.2) | 9.3 | (8.2) | 9.0 | (10.3) | 8.5 | (12.5) | 8.1 | (14.9) |
| (b) Transfers and Subsidies (% of GDP) | | | | | | | | | | | 9.3 | (3.2) | 9.4 | (2.6) |
| **II. Structure of the Economy and Use of Markets** | | | | | | | | | **1.2** | | **2.1** | | **3.0** | |
| (a) Government Enterprises | 0.0 | (72.5) | 0.0 | (55.3) | 0.0 | (67.7) | 0.0 | (82.4) | 0.0 | (82.5) | 0.0 | | 0.0 | |
| (b) Price Controls | | | | | | | | | 0.0 | | 2.0 | | 4.0 | |
| (c) Top Marginal Tax Rate | | | | | | | | | | | | | | |
| (d) Conscription | | | 10.0 | | 10.0 | | 10.0 | | 10.0 | | 10.0 | | 10.0 | |
| **III. Monetary Policy and Price Stability** | **8.9** | | **7.2** | | **6.5** | | **8.2** | | **8.6** | | **7.5** | | **6.6** | |
| (a) Annual Money Growth (last 5 yrs.) | 9.2 | (4.1) | 8.8 | (6.1) | 5.3 | (23.3) | 8.5 | (7.3) | 9.9 | (0.8) | 7.6 | (12.0) | 7.5 | (12.5) |
| (b) Inflation Variability (last 5 yrs.) | 8.4 | (3.9) | 7.2 | (7.1) | 7.6 | (6.0) | 7.1 | (7.4) | 7.2 | (6.9) | 8.1 | (4.9) | 7.0 | (7.4) |
| (c) Recent Inflation Rate | 9.0 | (5.2) | 5.8 | (21.1) | 6.7 | (16.4) | 9.0 | (5.1) | 8.8 | (6.0) | 7.0 | (15.2) | 5.3 | (23.3) |
| **IV. Freedom to Use Alternative Currencies** | **5.4** | | **0.4** | | **0.5** | | **2.5** | | **4.4** | | **0.6** | | **4.3** | |
| (a) Ownership of Foreign Currency | | | 0.0 | | 0.0 | | 0.0 | | 0.0 | | 0.0 | | 5.0 | |
| (b) Black Market Exchange Rates (Prem.) | 5.4 | (23.0) | 0.8 | (46.0) | 1.0 | (45.0) | 5.0 | (25.0) | 8.8 | (6.0) | 1.2 | (44.0) | 3.6 | (32.0) |
| **V. Legal Structure and Property Rights** | | | | | **4.2** | | **4.1** | | **4.3** | | **3.6** | | **3.6** | |
| (a) Private Ownership Rights | | | | | 4.0 | | 3.8 | | 3.8 | | 2.7 | | 2.8 | |
| (b) Viability of Contracts | | | | | 2.8 | | 3.9 | | 4.0 | | 3.0 | | 3.1 | |
| (c) Rule of Law | | | | | 5.8 | | 4.8 | | 5.3 | | 5.2 | | 5.2 | |
| **VI. International Exchange** | | | **1.3** | | **0.4** | | **1.0** | | **1.1** | | **3.9** | | **2.9** | |
| (a) Taxes on International Trade | | | | | | | | | | | | | | |
| i. Taxes as a Percentage of Exports and Imports | | | 1.9 | (12.2) | 0.0 | (18.1) | 0.0 | (17.0) | 0.0 | (22.9) | 1.6 | (12.6) | 4.0 | (9.0) |
| ii. Mean Tariff Rate | | | | | | | 2.4 | (37.9) | 2.6 | (37.0) | 2.6 | (36.9) | | |
| iii. Standard Deviation of Tariff Rates | | | | | | | | | | | | | | |
| (b) Non-tariff Regulatory Trade Barriers | | | | | | | | | | | | | | |
| i. Non-tariff Trade Restraints (% of trade covered) | | | | | 1.0 | (90.0) | 1.0 | (90.0) | 1.0 | (90.0) | 10.0 | (0.0) | | |
| ii. Size of Trade Sector (% of GDP) | 0.0 | (28.9) | 0.0 | (27.3) | 0.0 | (32.1) | 0.0 | (31.7) | 0.0 | (35.6) | 0.0 | (32.7) | 0.0 | (23.4) |
| **VII. Freedom of Exchange in Financial Markets** | **1.8** | | **1.7** | | **1.9** | | **2.7** | | **2.1** | | **1.3** | | **2.9** | |
| (a) Ownership of Banks | 2.0 | (10-40) | 2.0 | (10-40) | 2.0 | (10-40) | 2.0 | (10-40) | 0.0 | (0-10) | 0.0 | (0-10) | 0.0 | (0-10) |
| (b) Extension of Credit | 3.7 | (43.0) | 3.6 | (42.5) | 4.2 | (48.1) | 3.2 | (38.7) | 5.3 | (57.7) | | | 6.9 | (72.2) |
| (c) Avoidance of Negative Interest Rates | | | | | 2.0 | | 6.0 | | 4.0 | | 4.0 | | 6.0 | |
| (d) Capital Transactions with Foreigners | 0.0 | | 0.0 | | 0.0 | | 0.0 | | 0.0 | | 0.0 | | 0.0 | |

# CAMEROON

| | 1970 | 1975 | 1980 | 1985 | 1990 | 1995 | 1997 |
|---|---|---|---|---|---|---|---|
| **Summary Ratings** | | | 5.1 | 5.2 | 5.5 | 5.2 | 5.1 |
| **Rank** | | | 56 | 56 | 56 | 87 | 97 |

| Components of Economic Freedom | 1970 | | 1975 | | 1980 | | 1985 | | 1990 | | 1995 | | 1997 | |
|---|---|---|---|---|---|---|---|---|---|---|---|---|---|---|
| **I. Size of Government** | **8.2** | | **9.1** | | **9.3** | | **9.3** | | **8.6** | | **9.3** | | **8.9** | |
| (a) Government Consumption (% of Total) | 8.2 | (14.5) | 8.4 | (13.1) | 8.6 | (12.2) | 8.6 | (12.3) | 7.9 | (16.1) | 8.9 | (10.7) | 8.9 | (10.4) |
| (b) Transfers and Subsidies (% of GDP) | | | 9.8 | (1.4) | 9.9 | (0.8) | 10.0 | (0.6) | 9.4 | (2.7) | 9.7 | (1.6) | | |
| **II. Structure of the Economy and Use of Markets** | | | | | | | **3.1** | | **2.4** | | **2.2** | | **2.2** | |
| (a) Government Enterprises | 2.0 | (47.6) | 2.0 | (54.7) | 4.0 | (27.7) | 2.0 | (41.7) | 4.0 | (32.0) | 4.0 | | 4.0 | |
| (b) Price Controls | | | | | | | | | 0.0 | | 0.0 | | 0.0 | |
| (c) Top Marginal Tax Rate | | | | | | | 2.0 | (60) | 1.0 | (60) | 0.0 | (66) | 0.0 | (65) |
| (d) Conscription | | | 10.0 | | 10.0 | | 10.0 | | 10.0 | | 10.0 | | 10.0 | |
| **III. Monetary Policy and Price Stability** | **7.7** | | **8.6** | | **7.2** | | **8.5** | | **9.4** | | **7.8** | | **8.5** | |
| (a) Annual Money Growth (last 5 yrs.) | 7.7 | (11.6) | 7.9 | (10.4) | 6.8 | (15.8) | 8.5 | (7.7) | 9.2 | (-4.1) | 9.4 | (-3.2) | 8.4 | (8.0) |
| (b) Inflation Variability (last 5 yrs.) | 6.8 | (8.0) | 9.0 | (2.4) | 7.6 | (5.9) | 9.3 | (1.7) | 9.4 | (1.6) | 7.3 | (6.6) | 7.7 | (5.7) |
| (c) Recent Inflation Rate | 8.4 | (7.9) | 8.8 | (6.0) | 7.2 | (14.3) | 7.8 | (11.2) | 9.7 | (1.6) | 6.6 | (17.0) | 9.5 | (2.7) |
| **IV. Freedom to Use Alternative Currencies** | **4.8** | | **4.8** | | **4.8** | | **4.9** | | **4.6** | | **4.9** | | **4.8** | |
| (a) Ownership of Foreign Currency | 0.0 | | 0.0 | | 0.0 | | 0.0 | | 0.0 | | 0.0 | | 0.0 | |
| (b) Black Market Exchange Rates (Prem.) | 9.6 | (2.0) | 9.6 | (2.0) | 9.6 | (2.0) | 9.8 | (1.0) | 9.2 | (4.0) | 9.8 | (1.0) | 9.6 | (2.0) |
| **V. Legal Structure and Property Rights** | | | | | 5.7 | | 6.0 | | 6.0 | | 5.9 | | 5.4 | |
| (a) Private Ownership Rights | | | | | 4.6 | | 4.8 | | 4.6 | | 5.5 | | 4.4 | |
| (b) Viability of Contracts | | | | | 4.3 | | 5.2 | | 5.2 | | 5.2 | | 4.8 | |
| (c) Rule of Law | | | | | 8.3 | | 8.2 | | 8.3 | | 7.0 | | 7.0 | |
| **VI. International Exchange** | | | **2.2** | | **4.0** | | **5.6** | | **6.4** | | **6.1** | | | |
| (a) Taxes on International Trade | | | | | | | | | | | | | | |
| i. Taxes as a Percentage of Exports and Imports | | | 1.1 | (13.4) | 2.7 | (11.0) | 5.9 | (6.1) | 6.4 | (5.4) | 4.9 | (7.7) | | |
| ii. Mean Tariff Rate | | | | | | | | | | | 6.3 | (18.7) | | |
| iii. Standard Deviation of Tariff Rates | | | | | | | | | | | 5.2 | (12.0) | | |
| (b) Non-tariff Regulatory Trade Barriers | | | | | | | | | | | | | | |
| i. Non-tariff Trade Restraints (% of trade covered) | | | | | 5.0 | (50.0) | 5.0 | (50.0) | 8.0 | (20.0) | 9.5 | (5.1) | | |
| ii. Size of Trade Sector (% of GDP) | 5.5 | (50.9) | 5.0 | (48.2) | 5.4 | (54.2) | 6.2 | (65.0) | 2.8 | (37.7) | 3.8 | (45.6) | 0.9 | (31.6) |
| **VII. Freedom of Exchange in Financial Markets** | | | | | **1.9** | | **1.9** | | **3.5** | | **2.7** | | **3.2** | |
| (a) Ownership of Banks | 0.0 | (0-10) | 0.0 | (0-10) | 0.0 | (0-10) | 0.0 | (0-10) | 0.0 | (0-10) | 2.0 | (10-40) | 2.0 | (10-40) |
| (b) Extension of Credit | | | | | | | | | 7.4 | (76.8) | 5.7 | (60.9) | 5.7 | (60.9) |
| (c) Avoidance of Negative Interest Rates | | | | | 6.0 | | 6.0 | | 8.0 | | 4.0 | | 6.0 | |
| (d) Capital Transactions with Foreigners | 0.0 | | 0.0 | | 0.0 | | 0.0 | | 0.0 | | 0.0 | | 0.0 | |

# CANADA

| | 1970 | 1975 | 1980 | 1985 | 1990 | 1995 | 1997 |
|---|---|---|---|---|---|---|---|
| **Summary Ratings** | 8.1 | 7.7 | 8.0 | 8.2 | 8.5 | 8.4 | 8.6 |
| **Rank** | 8 | 7 | 5 | 7 | 6 | 9 | 7 |

| Components of Economic Freedom | 1970 | | 1975 | | 1980 | | 1985 | | 1990 | | 1995 | | 1997 | |
|---|---|---|---|---|---|---|---|---|---|---|---|---|---|---|
| **I. Size of Government** | **5.8** | | **6.6** | | **5.9** | | **5.6** | | **5.7** | | **5.5** | | **6.0** | |
| (a) Government Consumption (% of Total) | 5.8 | (27.2) | 5.5 | (28.9) | 5.5 | (28.8) | 5.5 | (28.8) | 5.6 | (28.6) | 5.8 | (27.5) | 6.0 | (26.5) |
| (b) Transfers and Subsidies (% of GDP) | | | 7.7 | (9.1) | 6.2 | (14.5) | 5.7 | (16.3) | 5.9 | (15.6) | 5.3 | (17.7) | | |
| **II. Structure of the Economy and Use of Markets** | **4.3** | | **5.0** | | **5.0** | | **5.0** | | **6.5** | | **6.2** | | **7.5** | |
| (a) Government Enterprises | 6.0 | (28.2) | 6.0 | (29.1) | 6.0 | (25.2) | 6.0 | (25.6) | 6.0 | (19.8) | 6.0 | (19.9) | 8.0 | (17.7) |
| (b) Price Controls | | | | | | | | | 8.0 | | 7.0 | | 9.0 | |
| (c) Top Marginal Tax Rate | 0.0 | (82-91) | 2.0 | (59-67) | 2.0 | (60-68) | 2.0 | (50-63) | 4.0 | (44-51) | 4.0 | (44-54) | 4.0 | (44-51) |
| (d) Conscription | 10.0 | | 10.0 | | 10.0 | | 10.0 | | 10.0 | | 10.0 | | 10.0 | |
| **III. Monetary Policy and Price Stability** | **9.1** | | **8.4** | | **8.9** | | **8.6** | | **9.4** | | **9.4** | | **9.3** | |
| (a) Annual Money Growth (last 5 yrs.) | 8.4 | (7.8) | 8.7 | (6.5) | 9.7 | (1.7) | 7.6 | (11.9) | 9.2 | (3.9) | 9.0 | (5.1) | 8.5 | (7.5) |
| (b) Inflation Variability (last 5 yrs.) | 9.8 | (0.5) | 8.5 | (3.9) | 9.3 | (1.7) | 8.7 | (3.2) | 9.6 | (0.9) | 9.7 | (0.7) | 9.5 | (1.3) |
| (c) Recent Inflation Rate | 9.0 | (4.8) | 8.0 | (10.2) | 7.8 | (11.0) | 9.5 | (2.4) | 9.4 | (3.1) | 9.5 | (2.7) | 9.8 | (-1.2) |
| **IV. Freedom to Use Alternative Currencies** | **10.0** | | **10.0** | | **10.0** | | **10.0** | | **10.0** | | **10.0** | | **10.0** | |
| (a) Ownership of Foreign Currency | 10.0 | | 10.0 | | 10.0 | | 10.0 | | 10.0 | | 10.0 | | 10.0 | |
| (b) Black Market Exchange Rates (Prem.) | 10.0 | (0.0) | 10.0 | (0.0) | 10.0 | (0.0) | 10.0 | (0.0) | 10.0 | (0.0) | 10.0 | (0.0) | 10.0 | (0.0) |
| **V. Legal Structure and Property Rights** | 9.9 | | 8.2 | | 8.4 | | 9.1 | | 9.6 | | 9.5 | | 9.4 | |
| (a) Private Ownership Rights | 10.0 | | 6.5 | | 6.7 | | 8.7 | | 10.0 | | 10.0 | | 10.0 | |
| (b) Viability of Contracts | 9.9 | | 10.0 | | 8.5 | | 8.8 | | 8.8 | | 8.4 | | 8.3 | |
| (c) Rule of Law | | | | | 10.0 | | 10.0 | | 10.0 | | 10.0 | | 10.0 | |
| **VI. International Exchange** | **8.2** | | **7.6** | | **8.2** | | **8.6** | | **8.2** | | **8.7** | | **8.5** | |
| (a) Taxes on International Trade | | | | | | | | | | | | | | |
| i. Taxes as a Percentage of Exports and Imports | 8.4 | (2.4) | 7.5 | (3.7) | 8.4 | (2.4) | 8.9 | (1.7) | 9.2 | (1.2) | 9.5 | (0.7) | | |
| ii. Mean Tariff Rate | | | 7.4 | (13.0) | 7.8 | (11.2) | 7.9 | (10.5) | 8.1 | (9.4) | 8.0 | (10.1) | 8.8 | (6.0) |
| iii. Standard Deviation of Tariff Rates | | | | | | | | | 6.5 | (8.8) | 7.2 | (6.9) | 6.8 | (8.1) |
| (b) Non-tariff Regulatory Trade Barriers | | | | | | | | | | | | | | |
| i. Non-tariff Trade Restraints (% of trade covered) | | | | | | | 9.4 | (5.7) | 9.5 | (5.0) | 9.6 | (4.3) | 9.6 | (4.0) |
| ii. Size of Trade Sector (% of GDP) | 7.7 | (42.9) | 8.1 | (47.2) | 8.9 | (55.1) | 8.3 | (54.5) | 7.4 | (51.3) | 10.0 | (73.1) | 10.0 | (78.7) |
| **VII. Freedom of Exchange in Financial Markets** | **8.8** | | **8.1** | | **9.3** | | **9.3** | | **9.3** | | **9.1** | | **9.2** | |
| (a) Ownership of Banks | 10.0 | (100) | 10.0 | (100) | 10.0 | (100) | 10.0 | (100) | 10.0 | (100) | 10.0 | (100) | 10.0 | (100) |
| (b) Extension of Credit | 6.9 | (71.9) | 8.2 | (83.9) | 9.1 | (91.5) | 9.2 | (92.4) | 9.1 | (92.0) | 8.1 | (83.0) | 8.6 | (87.4) |
| (c) Avoidance of Negative Interest Rates | 10.0 | | 6.0 | | 10.0 | | 10.0 | | 10.0 | | 10.0 | | 10.0 | |
| (d) Capital Transactions with Foreigners | 8.0 | | 8.0 | | 8.0 | | 8.0 | | 8.0 | | 8.0 | | 8.0 | |

# Central African Republic

| | 1970 | 1975 | 1980 | 1985 | 1990 | 1995 | 1997 |
|---|---|---|---|---|---|---|---|
| **Summary Ratings** | | | 5.2 | 4.6 | 4.4 | 4.4 | 4.3 |
| **Rank** | | | 53 | 74 | 84 | 106 | 113 |

| Components of Economic Freedom | 1970 | | 1975 | | 1980 | | 1985 | | 1990 | | 1995 | | 1997 | |
|---|---|---|---|---|---|---|---|---|---|---|---|---|---|---|
| **I. Size of Government** | **6.8** | | **7.8** | | **8.3** | | **8.0** | | **8.1** | | **8.3** | | **9.0** | |
| (a) Government Consumption (% of Total) | 6.8 | (21.9) | 7.8 | (16.3) | 8.3 | (13.9) | 8.0 | (15.7) | 8.1 | (14.8) | 8.3 | (14.0) | 9.0 | (10.0) |
| (b) Transfers and Subsidies (% of GDP) | | | | | | | | | | | | | | |
| **II. Structure of the Economy and Use of Markets** | | | | | | | | | **0.0** | | **0.0** | | **0.0** | |
| (a) Government Enterprises | 0.0 | (68.3) | 2.0 | (39.0) | 0.0 | (65.7) | 0.0 | (67.0) | 0.0 | (51.8) | 0.0 | (54.8) | 0.0 | |
| (b) Price Controls | | | | | | | | | 0.0 | | 0.0 | | 0.0 | |
| (c) Top Marginal Tax Rate | | | | | | | | | | | | | | |
| (d) Conscription | | | | | 0.0 | | 0.0 | | 0.0 | | 0.0 | | 0.0 | |
| **III. Monetary Policy and Price Stability** | **8.4** | | **7.4** | | **6.5** | | **5.8** | | **9.5** | | **6.8** | | **7.6** | |
| (a) Annual Money Growth (last 5 yrs.) | 8.9 | (5.6) | 8.6 | (7.0) | 5.6 | (22.1) | 8.5 | (7.3) | 10.0 | (-0.2) | 7.0 | (15.0) | 7.0 | (15.1) |
| (b) Inflation Variability (last 5 yrs.) | 7.3 | (6.8) | 7.6 | (6.1) | 7.5 | (6.2) | 5.6 | (10.9) | 8.9 | (2.9) | 6.0 | (9.9) | 6.0 | (9.9) |
| (c) Recent Inflation Rate | 9.1 | (4.5) | 6.1 | (19.3) | 6.3 | (18.3) | 3.2 | (34.2) | 9.5 | (2.3) | 7.3 | (13.4) | 9.7 | (1.6) |
| **IV. Freedom to Use Alternative Currencies** | **4.8** | | **4.8** | | **4.8** | | **4.9** | | **4.6** | | **4.9** | | **4.8** | |
| (a) Ownership of Foreign Currency | 0.0 | | 0.0 | | 0.0 | | 0.0 | | 0.0 | | 0.0 | | 0.0 | |
| (b) Black Market Exchange Rates (Prem.) | 9.6 | (2.0) | 9.6 | (2.0) | 9.6 | (2.0) | 9.8 | (1.0) | 9.2 | (4.0) | 9.8 | (1.0) | 9.6 | (2.0) |
| **V. Legal Structure and Property Rights** | | | | | **4.2** | | **4.1** | | **4.3** | | **3.6** | | **3.6** | |
| (a) Private Ownership Rights | | | | | 4.0 | | 3.8 | | 3.8 | | 2.7 | | 2.8 | |
| (b) Viability of Contracts | | | | | 2.8 | | 3.9 | | 4.0 | | 3.0 | | 3.1 | |
| (c) Rule of Law | | | | | 5.8 | | 4.8 | | 5.3 | | 5.2 | | 5.2 | |
| **VI. International Exchange** | | | | | **3.8** | | **3.9** | | **3.0** | | **5.8** | | | |
| (a) Taxes on International Trade | | | | | | | | | | | | | | |
| i. Taxes as a Percentage of Exports and Imports | | | | | 2.9 | (10.6) | | | 2.3 | (11.5) | | | | |
| ii. Mean Tariff Rate | | | | | | | 3.6 | (32.0) | 3.6 | (32.0) | 6.3 | (18.6) | | |
| iii. Standard Deviation of Tariff Rates | | | | | | | | | | | 6.2 | (9.6) | | |
| (b) Non-tariff Regulatory Trade Barriers | | | | | | | | | | | | | | |
| i. Non-tariff Trade Restraints (% of trade covered) | | | | | | | | | | | | | | |
| ii. Size of Trade Sector (% of GDP) | 7.5 | (73.5) | 5.9 | (61.1) | 6.1 | (66.3) | 4.8 | (54.3) | 3.2 | (43.1) | 3.6 | (48.5) | 2.3 | (40.6) |
| **VII. Freedom of Exchange in Financial Markets** | | | | | | | **2.5** | | **4.4** | | **3.3** | | **3.4** | |
| (a) Ownership of Banks | 0.0 | (0-10) | 0.0 | (0-10) | 0.0 | (0-10) | 0.0 | (0-10) | 2.0 | (10-40) | 2.0 | (10-40) | 2.0 | (10-40) |
| (b) Extension of Credit | | | | | | | | | 6.5 | (68.7) | 6.2 | (65.9) | 6.6 | (69.0) |
| (c) Avoidance of Negative Interest Rates | | | | | | | 8.0 | | 10.0 | | 6.0 | | 6.0 | |
| (d) Capital Transactions with Foreigners | 0.0 | | 0.0 | | 0.0 | | 0.0 | | 0.0 | | 0.0 | | 0.0 | |

# CHAD

| | 1970 | 1975 | 1980 | 1985 | 1990 | 1995 | 1997 |
|---|---|---|---|---|---|---|---|
| **Summary Ratings** | | | | 5.2 | 5.2 | 5.1 | 4.5 |
| **Rank** | | | | 56 | 60 | 91 | 110 |

| Components of Economic Freedom | 1970 | | 1975 | | 1980 | | 1985 | | 1990 | | 1995 | | 1997 | |
|---|---|---|---|---|---|---|---|---|---|---|---|---|---|---|
| **I. Size of Government** | **6.5** | | **6.9** | | **6.1** | | **8.9** | | **9.4** | | **9.5** | | **9.5** | |
| (a) Government Consumption (% of Total) | 6.5 | (23.7) | 6.9 | (21.6) | 6.1 | (26.0) | 8.9 | (10.8) | 8.9 | (10.5) | 9.2 | (9.1) | 9.5 | (7.2) |
| (b) Transfers and Subsidies (% of GDP) | | | | | | | | | 9.9 | (0.9) | 9.9 | (0.8) | | |
| **II. Structure of the Economy and Use of Markets** | | | | | | | | | **1.8** | | **1.8** | | **1.8** | |
| (a) Government Enterprises | 0.0 | | 0.0 | | 0.0 | | 0.0 | (95.7) | 0.0 | (94.0) | 0.0 | | 0.0 | |
| (b) Price Controls | | | | | | | | | 4.0 | | 4.0 | | 4.0 | |
| (c) Top Marginal Tax Rate | | | | | | | | | | | | | | |
| (d) Conscription | | | 10.0 | | 10.0 | | 0.0 | | 0.0 | | 0.0 | | 0.0 | |
| **III. Monetary Policy and Price Stability** | **9.2** | | **8.4** | | **8.4** | | **7.0** | | **7.7** | | **6.9** | | **7.5** | |
| (a) Annual Money Growth (last 5 yrs.) | 9.1 | (4.5) | 7.7 | (11.5) | 7.3 | (13.5) | 5.8 | (20.9) | 9.3 | (-3.7) | 9.7 | (1.6) | 8.8 | (6.1) |
| (b) Inflation Variability (last 5 yrs.) | 9.4 | (1.5) | 9.2 | (1.9) | 9.8 | (0.6) | 6.0 | (10.0) | 6.2 | (9.5) | 2.8 | (17.9) | 4.6 | (13.5) |
| (c) Recent Inflation Rate | 9.2 | (3.9) | 8.4 | (8.2) | 8.3 | (8.7) | 9.3 | (3.8) | 7.7 | (11.4) | 8.2 | (8.9) | 9.0 | (4.9) |
| **IV. Freedom to Use Alternative Currencies** | **4.8** | | **4.8** | | **4.8** | | **4.9** | | **4.6** | | **4.9** | | **4.8** | |
| (a) Ownership of Foreign Currency | 0.0 | | 0.0 | | 0.0 | | 0.0 | | 0.0 | | 0.0 | | 0.0 | |
| (b) Black Market Exchange Rates (Prem.) | 9.6 | (2.0) | 9.6 | (2.0) | 9.6 | (2.0) | 9.8 | (1.0) | 9.2 | (4.0) | 9.8 | (1.0) | 9.6 | (2.0) |
| **V. Legal Structure and Property Rights** | | | | | **4.2** | | **4.1** | | **4.3** | | **3.6** | | **3.6** | |
| (a) Private Ownership Rights | | | | | 4.0 | | 3.8 | | 3.8 | | 2.7 | | 2.8 | |
| (b) Viability of Contracts | | | | | 2.8 | | 3.9 | | 4.0 | | 3.0 | | 3.1 | |
| (c) Rule of Law | | | | | 5.8 | | 4.8 | | 5.3 | | 5.2 | | 5.2 | |
| **VI. International Exchange** | | | **4.7** | | | | | | **7.1** | | **8.2** | | | |
| (a) Taxes on International Trade | | | | | | | | | | | | | | |
| i. Taxes as a Percentage of Exports and Imports | | | 3.9 | (9.2) | | | | | 7.4 | (3.9) | 8.5 | (2.2) | | |
| ii. Mean Tariff Rate | | | | | | | | | | | | | | |
| iii. Standard Deviation of Tariff Rates | | | | | | | | | | | | | | |
| (b) Non-tariff Regulatory Trade Barriers | | | | | | | | | | | | | | |
| i. Non-tariff Trade Restraints (% of trade covered) | | | | | | | | | | | | | | |
| ii. Size of Trade Sector (% of GDP) | 6.7 | (54.4) | 6.7 | (57.2) | 7.3 | (65.1) | 6.6 | (61.4) | 6.2 | (60.3) | 7.5 | (75.9) | 7.0 | (72.3) |
| **VII. Freedom of Exchange in Financial Markets** | | | | | | | **3.2** | | **3.2** | | **2.2** | | **2.5** | |
| (a) Ownership of Banks | | | 2.0 | (10-40) | 2.0 | (10-40) | 2.0 | (10-40) | 0.0 | (0-10) | 0.0 | (0-10) | 0.0 | (0-10) |
| (b) Extension of Credit | | | | | | | | | 5.9 | (62.8) | 6.0 | (63.7) | 5.0 | (55.3) |
| (c) Avoidance of Negative Interest Rates | | | | | | | 8.0 | | 8.0 | | 4.0 | | 6.0 | |
| (d) Capital Transactions with Foreigners | 0.0 | | 0.0 | | 0.0 | | 0.0 | | 0.0 | | 0.0 | | 0.0 | |

# CHILE

| | 1970 | 1975 | 1980 | 1985 | 1990 | 1995 | 1997 |
|---|---|---|---|---|---|---|---|
| **Summary Ratings** | 3.7 | 3.7 | 5.9 | 6.0 | 7.4 | 8.2 | 8.2 |
| **Rank** | 54 | 70 | 35 | 36 | 24 | 12 | 18 |

| Components of Economic Freedom | 1970 | | 1975 | | 1980 | | 1985 | | 1990 | | 1995 | | 1997 | |
|---|---|---|---|---|---|---|---|---|---|---|---|---|---|---|
| **I. Size of Government** | **7.0** | | **7.4** | | **7.4** | | **6.9** | | **7.8** | | **7.9** | | **7.8** | |
| (a) Government Consumption (% of Total) | 8.0 | (15.5) | 7.6 | (17.7) | 8.1 | (15.0) | 7.8 | (16.7) | 8.3 | (13.6) | 8.3 | (13.6) | 8.4 | (13.2) |
| (b) Transfers and Subsidies (% of GDP) | 5.9 | (15.4) | 7.3 | (10.5) | 6.6 | (12.9) | 6.0 | (15.3) | 7.3 | (10.5) | 7.4 | (10.0) | 7.2 | (10.8) |
| **II. Structure of the Economy and Use of Markets** | | | **2.1** | | **3.1** | | **2.7** | | **5.6** | | **7.1** | | **6.8** | |
| (a) Government Enterprises | 4.0 | (38.8) | 2.0 | (54.1) | 4.0 | | 4.0 | (45.8) | 6.0 | (21.2) | 7.0 | (27.6) | 7.0 | (21.1) |
| (b) Price Controls | | | | | | | | | 8.0 | | 10.0 | | 9.0 | |
| (c) Top Marginal Tax Rate | | | 2.0 | (60) | 2.0 | (58) | 2.0 | (56) | 4.0 | (50) | 6.0 | (45) | 6.0 | (45) |
| (d) Conscription | 3.0 | | 3.0 | | 3.0 | | 0.0 | | 0.0 | | 0.0 | | 0.0 | |
| **III. Monetary Policy and Price Stability** | **3.4** | | **0.0** | | **1.4** | | **6.0** | | **6.3** | | **7.6** | | **8.4** | |
| (a) Annual Money Growth (last 5 yrs.) | 1.0 | (44.9) | 0.0 | (210.7) | 0.0 | (99.5) | 7.9 | (10.7) | 4.8 | (25.9) | 6.4 | (18.1) | 7.8 | (11.2) |
| (b) Inflation Variability (last 5 yrs.) | 7.5 | (6.2) | 0.0 | (233.7) | 0.0 | (80.6) | 6.2 | (9.6) | 8.3 | (4.2) | 8.3 | (4.2) | 8.6 | (3.5) |
| (c) Recent Inflation Rate | 1.9 | (40.7) | 0.0 | (334.7) | 4.2 | (28.8) | 3.9 | (30.7) | 5.8 | (21.2) | 8.1 | (9.3) | 8.8 | (5.8) |
| **IV. Freedom to Use Alternative Currencies** | **5.1** | | **4.5** | | **6.9** | | **7.8** | | **10.0** | | **9.8** | | **9.6** | |
| (a) Ownership of Foreign Currency | 10.0 | | 0.0 | | 5.0 | | 10.0 | | 10.0 | | 10.0 | | 10.0 | |
| (b) Black Market Exchange Rates (Prem.) | 0.2 | (49.0) | 9.0 | (5.0) | 8.8 | (6.0) | 5.6 | (22.0) | 10.0 | (0.0) | 9.6 | (2.0) | 9.2 | (4.0) |
| **V. Legal Structure and Property Rights** | **0.0** | | **2.9** | | **6.5** | | **4.9** | | **7.0** | | **8.5** | | **8.5** | |
| (a) Private Ownership Rights | 0.0 | | 3.8 | | 6.4 | | 4.2 | | 7.3 | | 10.0 | | 10.0 | |
| (b) Viability of Contracts | 0.0 | | 1.9 | | 4.9 | | 4.0 | | 7.0 | | 8.4 | | 8.3 | |
| (c) Rule of Law | | | | | 8.3 | | 6.6 | | 6.7 | | 7.0 | | 7.0 | |
| **VI. International Exchange** | **4.1** | | **4.7** | | **8.5** | | **7.0** | | **8.2** | | **8.3** | | **8.0** | |
| (a) Taxes on International Trade | | | | | | | | | | | | | | |
| i. Taxes as a Percentage of Exports and Imports | 9.2 | (1.2) | 6.3 | (5.6) | 8.1 | (2.8) | 6.2 | (5.7) | 7.5 | (3.7) | 7.1 | (4.3) | 7.1 | (4.4) |
| ii. Mean Tariff Rate | 0.0 | (105.0) | 0.0 | (55.0) | 8.0 | (10.0) | 4.0 | (30.0) | 7.0 | (15.0) | 7.8 | (11.0) | 8.1 | (9.4) |
| iii. Standard Deviation of Tariff Rates | | | | | 10.0 | (0.0) | 10.0 | (0.0) | 10.0 | (0.0) | 10.0 | (0.0) | 10.0 | (0.0) |
| (b) Non-tariff Regulatory Trade Barriers | | | | | | | | | | | | | | |
| i. Non-tariff Trade Restraints (% of trade covered) | 3.6 | (63.0) | 8.0 | (20.0) | 9.0 | (10.0) | 9.0 | (10.1) | 8.9 | (10.6) | 10.0 | (0.1) | | |
| ii. Size of Trade Sector (% of GDP) | 2.8 | (28.6) | 6.1 | (52.8) | 5.4 | (49.8) | 5.6 | (53.9) | 6.4 | (65.5) | 5.2 | (55.4) | 5.1 | (56.1) |
| **VII. Freedom of Exchange in Financial Markets** | | | **3.5** | | **5.9** | | **6.5** | | **6.6** | | **8.1** | | **8.0** | |
| (a) Ownership of Banks | | | 2.0 | (10-40) | 5.0 | (40-75) | 8.0 | (75-85) | 8.0 | (75-85) | 8.0 | (80-90) | 8.0 | (85-95) |
| (b) Extension of Credit | | | 7.2 | (75.0) | 9.6 | (96.2) | 8.4 | (85.5) | 9.2 | (92.7) | 9.8 | (98.5) | 9.7 | (97.5) |
| (c) Avoidance of Negative Interest Rates | | | | | 8.0 | | 8.0 | | 8.0 | | 10.0 | | 10.0 | |
| (d) Capital Transactions with Foreigners | 2.0 | | 2.0 | | 2.0 | | 2.0 | | 2.0 | | 5.0 | | 5.0 | |

# CHINA

| | 1970 | 1975 | 1980 | 1985 | 1990 | 1995 | 1997 |
|---|---|---|---|---|---|---|---|
| **Summary Ratings** | | | 3.5 | 4.4 | 4.2 | 5.6 | 6.2 |
| **Rank** | | | 94 | 79 | 91 | 81 | 75 |

| Components of Economic Freedom | 1970 | | 1975 | | 1980 | | 1985 | | 1990 | | 1995 | | 1997 | |
|---|---|---|---|---|---|---|---|---|---|---|---|---|---|---|
| **I. Size of Government** | **8.9** | | **8.8** | | **6.8** | | **7.1** | | **7.2** | | **7.3** | | **7.3** | |
| (a) Government Consumption (% of Total) | 8.9 | (10.7) | 8.8 | (10.9) | 6.8 | (22.1) | 7.1 | (20.5) | 7.2 | (19.8) | 7.3 | (19.4) | 7.3 | (19.3) |
| (b) Transfers and Subsidies (% of GDP) | | | | | | | | | | | | | | |
| **II. Structure of the Economy and Use of Markets** | | | | | | | **2.3** | | **1.9** | | **2.5** | | **3.2** | |
| (a) Government Enterprises | 0.0 | | 0.0 | | 0.0 | (55.3) | 0.0 | | 0.0 | (61.8) | 0.0 | | 0.0 | |
| (b) Price Controls | | | | | | | | | 2.0 | | 3.0 | | 5.0 | |
| (c) Top Marginal Tax Rate | | | | | | | 6.0 | (45) | 5.0 | (45) | 6.0 | (45) | 6.0 | (45) |
| (d) Conscription | 0.0 | | 0.0 | | 0.0 | | 0.0 | | 0.0 | | 0.0 | | 0.0 | |
| **III. Monetary Policy and Price Stability** | **8.7** | | **9.8** | | **8.2** | | **8.0** | | **8.6** | | **7.0** | | **8.6** | |
| (a) Annual Money Growth (last 5 yrs.) | | | | | 6.0 | (20.0) | 7.3 | (13.3) | 8.1 | (9.3) | 5.4 | (22.9) | 8.1 | (9.5) |
| (b) Inflation Variability (last 5 yrs.) | 8.4 | (4.0) | 9.7 | (0.8) | 9.5 | (1.3) | 8.6 | (3.4) | 8.9 | (2.8) | 8.4 | (4.0) | 8.6 | (3.6) |
| (c) Recent Inflation Rate | 9.1 | (-4.7) | 10.0 | (-0.1) | 9.2 | (3.8) | 8.0 | (10.1) | 8.9 | (5.7) | 7.4 | (13.2) | 9.1 | (4.5) |
| **IV. Freedom to Use Alternative Currencies** | **1.0** | | **2.6** | | **2.5** | | **3.9** | | **2.5** | | **6.8** | | **6.8** | |
| (a) Ownership of Foreign Currency | 0.0 | | 0.0 | | 0.0 | | 0.0 | | 5.0 | | 5.0 | | 5.0 | |
| (b) Black Market Exchange Rates (Prem.) | 2.0 | (40.0) | 5.2 | (24.0) | 5.0 | (25.0) | 7.8 | (11.0) | 0.0 | (159.0) | 8.6 | (7.0) | 8.6 | (7.0) |
| **V. Legal Structure and Property Rights** | | | | | | | **6.5** | | **5.6** | | **8.5** | | **8.5** | |
| (a) Private Ownership Rights | | | | | | | 7.4 | | 4.6 | | 10.0 | | 10.0 | |
| (b) Viability of Contracts | | | | | | | 4.0 | | 4.0 | | 8.4 | | 8.3 | |
| (c) Rule of Law | | | | | | | 8.2 | | 8.3 | | 7.0 | | 7.0 | |
| **VI. International Exchange** | | | | | **3.2** | | **4.8** | | **4.4** | | **5.4** | | **7.2** | |
| (a) Taxes on International Trade | | | | | | | | | | | | | | |
| i. Taxes as a Percentage of Exports and Imports | | | | | 6.2 | (5.7) | 3.3 | (10.0) | 7.5 | (3.7) | 9.2 | (1.2) | 9.3 | (1.0) |
| ii. Mean Tariff Rate | | | | | 0.1 | (49.5) | 2.1 | (39.5) | 1.9 | (40.3) | 2.5 | (37.5) | 6.4 | (17.8) |
| iii. Standard Deviation of Tariff Rates | | | | | | | | | 0.0 | (32.1) | 0.0 | (28.0) | 4.7 | (13.2) |
| (b) Non-tariff Regulatory Trade Barriers | | | | | | | | | | | | | | |
| i. Non-tariff Trade Restraints (% of trade covered) | | | | | | | 8.9 | (10.6) | 7.7 | (23.2) | 8.9 | (11.3) | | |
| ii. Size of Trade Sector (% of GDP) | 0.0 | (5.2) | 2.5 | (10.2) | 3.7 | (12.9) | 7.0 | (24.0) | 7.4 | (26.8) | 10.0 | (40.4) | 10.0 | |
| **VII. Freedom of Exchange in Financial Markets** | | | | | **0.0** | | **0.7** | | **1.7** | | **3.0** | | **3.0** | |
| (a) Ownership of Banks | 0.0 | (0-10) | 0.0 | (0) | 0.0 | (0) | 0.0 | (0) | 0.0 | (0) | 0.0 | (0) | 0.0 | (0) |
| (b) Extension of Credit | | | | | | | | | | | | | | |
| (c) Avoidance of Negative Interest Rates | | | | | 0.0 | | 0.0 | | 0.0 | | 4.0 | | 4.0 | |
| (d) Capital Transactions with Foreigners | 0.0 | | 0.0 | | 0.0 | | 2.0 | | 5.0 | | 5.0 | | 5.0 | |

# COLOMBIA

| | 1970 | 1975 | 1980 | 1985 | 1990 | 1995 | 1997 |
|---|---|---|---|---|---|---|---|
| **Summary Ratings** | 5.1 | 4.7 | 4.6 | 5.2 | 5.1 | 6.4 | 5.6 |
| **Rank** | 41 | 55 | 74 | 56 | 64 | 57 | 88 |

| Components of Economic Freedom | 1970 | | 1975 | | 1980 | | 1985 | | 1990 | | 1995 | | 1997 | |
|---|---|---|---|---|---|---|---|---|---|---|---|---|---|---|
| **I. Size of Government** | **8.8** | | **9.1** | | **8.9** | | **8.7** | | **8.7** | | **8.2** | | **7.3** | |
| (a) Government Consumption (% of Total) | 8.8 | (11.3) | 8.8 | (11.0) | 8.5 | (12.6) | 8.4 | (13.4) | 8.3 | (13.6) | 7.5 | (18.3) | 7.3 | (19.4) |
| (b) Transfers and Subsidies (% of GDP) | | | 9.3 | (3.0) | 9.3 | (2.9) | 8.9 | (4.4) | 9.1 | (3.7) | 9.0 | (4.1) | | |
| **II. Structure of the Economy and Use of Markets** | | | **4.2** | | **1.7** | | **2.9** | | **4.7** | | **5.1** | | **4.5** | |
| (a) Government Enterprises | 4.0 | (31.7) | 4.0 | (32.8) | 2.0 | (41.5) | 2.0 | (53.9) | 2.0 | (43.9) | 4.0 | (34.1) | 4.0 | |
| (b) Price Controls | | | | | | | | | 6.0 | | 5.0 | | 4.0 | |
| (c) Top Marginal Tax Rate | | | 6.0 | (41) | 2.0 | (56) | 5.0 | (49) | 8.0 | (30) | 8.0 | (30) | 7.0 | (35) |
| (d) Conscription | 3.0 | | 0.0 | | 0.0 | | 0.0 | | 0.0 | | 1.0 | | 1.0 | |
| **III. Monetary Policy and Price Stability** | **8.1** | | **6.7** | | **6.0** | | **7.0** | | **5.9** | | **6.6** | | **7.0** | |
| (a) Annual Money Growth (last 5 yrs.) | 7.4 | (13.1) | 6.9 | (15.6) | 5.3 | (23.7) | 6.6 | (17.0) | 4.4 | (27.8) | 4.8 | (26.1) | 6.0 | (19.8) |
| (b) Inflation Variability (last 5 yrs.) | 9.0 | (2.6) | 7.7 | (5.6) | 8.3 | (4.2) | 9.3 | (1.7) | 9.1 | (2.3) | 9.2 | (2.1) | 8.9 | (2.6) |
| (c) Recent Inflation Rate | 8.0 | (9.9) | 5.4 | (22.9) | 4.5 | (27.6) | 5.0 | (24.9) | 4.3 | (28.6) | 6.0 | (19.8) | 6.1 | (19.3) |
| **IV. Freedom to Use Alternative Currencies** | **3.9** | | **2.1** | | **3.4** | | **6.6** | | **3.3** | | **4.3** | | **3.6** | |
| (a) Ownership of Foreign Currency | 0.0 | | 0.0 | | 0.0 | | 5.0 | | 0.0 | | 0.0 | | 0.0 | |
| (b) Black Market Exchange Rates (Prem.) | 7.8 | (11.0) | 4.2 | (29.0) | 6.8 | (16.0) | 8.2 | (9.0) | 6.6 | (17.0) | 8.6 | (7.0) | 7.2 | (14.0) |
| **V. Legal Structure and Property Rights** | **2.5** | | **3.2** | | **4.5** | | **4.3** | | **3.9** | | **5.8** | | **3.5** | |
| (a) Private Ownership Rights | 2.3 | | 3.0 | | 4.6 | | 4.8 | | 4.6 | | 10.0 | | 7.2 | |
| (b) Viability of Contracts | 2.7 | | 3.3 | | 5.6 | | 6.4 | | 5.2 | | 6.8 | | 3.1 | |
| (c) Rule of Law | | | | | 3.3 | | 1.4 | | 1.7 | | 0.0 | | 0.0 | |
| **VI. International Exchange** | **4.5** | | **4.7** | | **4.0** | | **3.5** | | **4.6** | | **7.6** | | **7.0** | |
| (a) Taxes on International Trade | | | | | | | | | | | | | | |
| i. Taxes as a Percentage of Exports and Imports | 4.6 | (8.1) | 5.1 | (7.4) | 4.8 | (7.8) | 5.0 | (7.5) | 5.3 | (7.1) | 7.3 | (4.0) | | |
| ii. Mean Tariff Rate | | | | | 3.3 | (33.5) | 3.3 | (33.6) | 3.9 | (30.4) | 7.3 | (13.3) | 7.7 | (11.7) |
| iii. Standard Deviation of Tariff Rates | | | | | | | | | 6.7 | (8.3) | 8.0 | (4.9) | 7.5 | (6.3) |
| (b) Non-tariff Regulatory Trade Barriers | | | | | | | | | | | | | | |
| i. Non-tariff Trade Restraints (% of trade covered) | | | | | | | 2.7 | (73.2) | 2.6 | (73.8) | 9.8 | (1.7) | | |
| ii. Size of Trade Sector (% of GDP) | 4.1 | (30.1) | 3.8 | (29.9) | 3.9 | (31.8) | 2.3 | (26.3) | 4.0 | (35.4) | 3.8 | (36.3) | 3.8 | (36.5) |
| **VII. Freedom of Exchange in Financial Markets** | | | | | **5.3** | | **5.3** | | **5.9** | | **7.2** | | **7.1** | |
| (a) Ownership of Banks | | | 8.0 | (75-90) | 8.0 | (75-90) | 8.0 | (75-90) | 8.0 | (75-95) | 8.0 | (75-95) | 8.0 | (75-95) |
| (b) Extension of Credit | | | | | | | | | 8.5 | (86.0) | 7.9 | (81.0) | 7.5 | (77.1) |
| (c) Avoidance of Negative Interest Rates | | | | | 8.0 | | 8.0 | | 8.0 | | 8.0 | | 8.0 | |
| (d) Capital Transactions with Foreigners | 0.0 | | 0.0 | | 0.0 | | 0.0 | | 0.0 | | 5.0 | | 5.0 | |

# Democratic Republic of Congo

| | 1970 | 1975 | 1980 | 1985 | 1990 | 1995 | 1997 |
|---|---|---|---|---|---|---|---|
| **Summary Ratings** | 4.6 | 3.2 | 2.7 | 3.7 | 3.2 | 3.2 | 3.1 |
| **Rank** | 47 | 75 | 104 | 94 | 106 | 120 | 122 |

| Components of Economic Freedom | 1970 | | 1975 | | 1980 | | 1985 | | 1990 | | 1995 | | 1997 | |
|---|---|---|---|---|---|---|---|---|---|---|---|---|---|---|
| **I. Size of Government** | **8.0** | | **9.1** | | **9.6** | | **9.2** | | **9.2** | | **9.9** | | **9.1** | |
| (a) Government Consumption (% of Total) | 8.0 | (15.5) | 8.4 | (13.4) | 9.1 | (9.3) | 9.2 | (9.0) | 8.5 | (12.7) | 9.8 | (5.7) | 9.1 | (9.3) |
| (b) Transfers and Subsidies (% of GDP) | | | 9.9 | (1.0) | 10.0 | (0.6) | | | 9.9 | (0.8) | 10.0 | (0.5) | | |
| **II. Structure of the Economy and Use of Markets** | | | **2.1** | | **1.7** | | **1.7** | | **2.5** | | **2.5** | | **3.0** | |
| (a) Government Enterprises | 0.0 | (56.8) | 0.0 | (58.8) | 0.0 | (60.2) | 0.0 | (45.5) | 2.0 | (31.1) | 2.0 | | 2.0 | |
| (b) Price Controls | | | | | | | | | 2.0 | | 2.0 | | 2.0 | |
| (c) Top Marginal Tax Rate | | | 2.0 | (60) | 1.0 | (60) | 1.0 | (60) | 1.0 | (60) | 1.0 | (60) | 3.0 | (50) |
| (d) Conscription | 10.0 | | 10.0 | | 10.0 | | 10.0 | | 10.0 | | 10.0 | | 10.0 | |
| **III. Monetary Policy and Price Stability** | **5.1** | | **7.5** | | **0.5** | | **1.6** | | **0.0** | | **0.0** | | **0.0** | |
| (a) Annual Money Growth (last 5 yrs.) | 5.7 | (21.7) | 6.7 | (16.6) | 1.6 | (42.2) | 0.0 | (52.5) | 0.0 | (99.5) | 0.0 | (2294.3) | 0.0 | (2290.0) |
| (b) Inflation Variability (last 5 yrs.) | 0.0 | (26.2) | 8.4 | (3.9) | 0.0 | (25.5) | 0.0 | (25.3) | 0.0 | (30.2) | 0.0 | (9932.5) | 0.0 | (10424.0) |
| (c) Recent Inflation Rate | 9.3 | (-3.3) | 7.5 | (12.5) | 0.0 | (51.4) | 4.8 | (25.8) | 0.0 | (109.0) | 0.0 | (466.4) | 0.0 | (187.3) |
| **IV. Freedom to Use Alternative Currencies** | **8.1** | | **0.0** | | **0.0** | | **4.4** | | **3.0** | | **4.6** | | **7.0** | |
| (a) Ownership of Foreign Currency | 10.0 | | 0.0 | | 0.0 | | 0.0 | | 0.0 | | 0.0 | | 5.0 | |
| (b) Black Market Exchange Rates (Prem.) | 6.2 | (19.0) | 0.0 | (120.0) | 0.0 | (131.0) | 8.8 | (6.0) | 6.0 | (20.0) | 9.2 | (4.0) | 9.0 | (5.0) |
| **V. Legal Structure and Property Rights** | | | | | **1.9** | | **2.2** | | **2.1** | | **0.0** | | **0.0** | |
| (a) Private Ownership Rights | | | | | 1.7 | | 2.2 | | 1.9 | | 0.0 | | 0.0 | |
| (b) Viability of Contracts | | | | | 2.4 | | 2.8 | | 2.8 | | 0.0 | | 0.0 | |
| (c) Rule of Law | | | | | 1.7 | | 1.4 | | 1.7 | | 0.0 | | 0.0 | |
| **VI. International Exchange** | **1.4** | | **0.9** | | **3.2** | | **4.0** | | **4.0** | | **4.0** | | | |
| (a) Taxes on International Trade | | | | | | | | | | | | | | |
| i. Taxes as a Percentage of Exports and Imports | 0.0 | (19.7) | 0.0 | (19.0) | 3.1 | (10.3) | 4.4 | (8.4) | 3.9 | (9.1) | 5.9 | (6.1) | | |
| ii. Mean Tariff Rate | | | | | 5.3 | (23.6) | 5.5 | (22.4) | 5.9 | (20.7) | | | | |
| iii. Standard Deviation of Tariff Rates | | | | | | | | | | | | | | |
| (b) Non-tariff Regulatory Trade Barriers | | | | | | | | | | | | | | |
| i. Non-tariff Trade Restraints (% of trade covered) | | | | | 0.0 | (100.0) | 0.0 | (100.0) | 0.0 | (100.0) | 0.0 | (100.0) | | |
| ii. Size of Trade Sector (% of GDP) | 5.2 | (34.6) | 3.1 | (25.1) | 4.5 | (32.8) | 7.1 | (53.1) | 7.5 | (58.7) | 7.3 | (59.0) | 8.4 | (68.4) |
| **VII. Freedom of Exchange in Financial Markets** | **2.6** | | **2.8** | | **3.1** | | **3.4** | | **2.3** | | **2.5** | | **0.7** | |
| (a) Ownership of Banks | 0.0 | (0) | 0.0 | (0) | 0.0 | (0) | 0.0 | (0) | 0.0 | (0) | 0.0 | (0) | 0.0 | (0) |
| (b) Extension of Credit | 6.5 | (68.7) | 7.5 | (77.7) | 8.5 | (86.8) | 9.4 | (94.9) | 8.5 | (86.4) | 9.3 | (93.4) | | |
| (c) Avoidance of Negative Interest Rates | | | | | | | | | 0.0 | | 0.0 | | 0.0 | |
| (d) Capital Transactions with Foreigners | 2.0 | | 2.0 | | 2.0 | | 2.0 | | 2.0 | | 2.0 | | 2.0 | |

# REPUBLIC OF CONGO

| | 1970 | 1975 | 1980 | 1985 | 1990 | 1995 | 1997 |
|---|---|---|---|---|---|---|---|
| **Summary Ratings** | | | 5.1 | 4.4 | 4.4 | 4.8 | 4.2 |
| **Rank** | | | 56 | 79 | 84 | 97 | 115 |

| Components of Economic Freedom | 1970 | | 1975 | | 1980 | | 1985 | | 1990 | | 1995 | | 1997 | |
|---|---|---|---|---|---|---|---|---|---|---|---|---|---|---|
| **I. Size of Government** | **8.7** | | **7.1** | | **5.8** | | **6.4** | | **7.5** | | **7.5** | | **5.4** | |
| (a) Government Consumption (% of Total) | 7.7 | (17.2) | 7.1 | (20.3) | 5.8 | (27.3) | 6.4 | (23.9) | 7.5 | (18.2) | 7.5 | (17.9) | 5.4 | (29.5) |
| (b) Transfers and Subsidies (% of GDP) | 9.7 | (1.4) | | | | | | | | | | | | |
| **II. Structure of the Economy and Use of Markets** | | | | | | | | | **1.9** | | **1.6** | | **1.6** | |
| (a) Government Enterprises | 4.0 | (24.8) | 0.0 | (44.6) | 0.0 | (44.2) | 0.0 | (59.4) | 0.0 | | 0.0 | | 0.0 | |
| (b) Price Controls | | | | | | | | | 0.0 | | 0.0 | | 0.0 | |
| (c) Top Marginal Tax Rate | | | | | | | | | 4.0 | (50) | 3.0 | (50) | 3.0 | (50) |
| (d) Conscription | | | 10.0 | | 10.0 | | 10.0 | | 10.0 | | 10.0 | | 10.0 | |
| **III. Monetary Policy and Price Stability** | **8.7** | | **8.8** | | **7.1** | | **8.1** | | **7.8** | | **7.7** | | **7.5** | |
| (a) Annual Money Growth (last 5 yrs.) | 8.3 | (8.7) | 8.1 | (9.3) | 8.3 | (8.6) | 8.3 | (8.4) | 9.3 | (-3.6) | 9.6 | (2.1) | 8.9 | (5.7) |
| (b) Inflation Variability (last 5 yrs.) | 8.6 | (3.6) | 9.9 | (0.3) | 7.0 | (7.4) | 6.4 | (9.0) | 4.2 | (14.5) | 4.0 | (14.9) | 4.6 | (13.5) |
| (c) Recent Inflation Rate | 9.3 | (3.7) | 8.3 | (8.3) | 6.0 | (20.1) | 9.5 | (2.5) | 9.8 | (-0.8) | 9.3 | (3.4) | 8.9 | (5.7) |
| **IV. Freedom to Use Alternative Currencies** | **4.8** | | **4.8** | | **4.8** | | **4.9** | | **4.6** | | **4.9** | | **4.8** | |
| (a) Ownership of Foreign Currency | 0.0 | | 0.0 | | 0.0 | | 0.0 | | 0.0 | | 0.0 | | 0.0 | |
| (b) Black Market Exchange Rates (Prem.) | 9.6 | (2.0) | 9.6 | (2.0) | 9.6 | (2.0) | 9.8 | (1.0) | 9.2 | (4.0) | 9.8 | (1.0) | 9.6 | (2.0) |
| **V. Legal Structure and Property Rights** | | | | | **4.2** | | **2.9** | | **2.6** | | **4.8** | | **4.8** | |
| (a) Private Ownership Rights | | | | | 4.0 | | 2.2 | | 1.9 | | 5.5 | | 4.4 | |
| (b) Viability of Contracts | | | | | 2.8 | | 3.4 | | 2.8 | | 2.1 | | 3.1 | |
| (c) Rule of Law | | | | | 5.8 | | 3.1 | | 3.3 | | 7.0 | | 7.0 | |
| **VI. International Exchange** | | | **6.7** | | **7.8** | | **4.3** | | **5.1** | | **7.0** | | | |
| (a) Taxes on International Trade | | | | | | | | | | | | | | |
| i. Taxes as a Percentage of Exports and Imports | | | 6.4 | (5.4) | 7.5 | (3.8) | | | 4.5 | (8.2) | 7.8 | (3.3) | | |
| ii. Mean Tariff Rate | | | | | | | 3.6 | (32.0) | | | 6.3 | (18.6) | | |
| iii. Standard Deviation of Tariff Rates | | | | | | | | | | | 6.2 | (9.5) | | |
| (b) Non-tariff Regulatory Trade Barriers | | | | | | | | | | | | | | |
| i. Non-tariff Trade Restraints (% of trade covered) | | | | | | | 3.5 | (65.0) | | | 7.2 | (28.0) | | |
| ii. Size of Trade Sector (% of GDP) | 7.1 | (92.5) | 7.4 | (99.6) | 8.5 | (120.1) | 7.7 | (112.8) | 6.4 | (97.9) | 8.1 | (127.6) | 10.0 | (164.3) |
| **VII. Freedom of Exchange in Financial Markets** | | | | | **1.9** | | **2.5** | | **3.7** | | **1.8** | | **2.9** | |
| (a) Ownership of Banks | 0.0 | (0) | 0.0 | (0) | 0.0 | (0) | 0.0 | (0) | 0.0 | (0) | 0.0 | (0) | 0.0 | (0) |
| (b) Extension of Credit | | | | | | | | | 6.0 | (63.5) | 6.3 | (66.3) | 6.9 | (72.4) |
| (c) Avoidance of Negative Interest Rates | | | | | 6.0 | | 8.0 | | 10.0 | | 2.0 | | 6.0 | |
| (d) Capital Transactions with Foreigners | 0.0 | | 0.0 | | 0.0 | | 0.0 | | 0.0 | | 0.0 | | 0.0 | |

# COSTA RICA

| | 1970 | 1975 | 1980 | 1985 | 1990 | 1995 | 1997 |
|---|---|---|---|---|---|---|---|
| **Summary Ratings** | 8.3 | 7.0 | 5.6 | 5.6 | 7.3 | 7.8 | 8.1 |
| **Rank** | 6 | 14 | 41 | 47 | 27 | 29 | 22 |

| Components of Economic Freedom | 1970 | | 1975 | | 1980 | | 1985 | | 1990 | | 1995 | | 1997 | |
|---|---|---|---|---|---|---|---|---|---|---|---|---|---|---|
| **I. Size of Government** | **9.0** | | **8.3** | | **7.7** | | **7.6** | | **7.7** | | **7.4** | | **7.9** | |
| (a) Government Consumption (% of Total) | 8.2 | (14.6) | 7.6 | (17.5) | 6.8 | (21.8) | 7.0 | (20.8) | 6.6 | (22.9) | 6.6 | (22.9) | 7.7 | (17.2) |
| (b) Transfers and Subsidies (% of GDP) | 9.8 | (1.2) | 9.0 | (4.1) | 8.5 | (6.0) | 8.2 | (7.2) | 8.8 | (5.0) | 8.2 | (7.0) | 8.2 | (7.0) |
| **II. Structure of the Economy and Use of Markets** | | | **6.2** | | **5.2** | | **4.4** | | **7.4** | | **7.4** | | **8.1** | |
| (a) Government Enterprises | 6.0 | (28.2) | 6.0 | (29.7) | 4.0 | (36.2) | 4.0 | (34.1) | 7.0 | (21.0) | 7.0 | (21.0) | 7.0 | |
| (b) Price Controls | | | | | | | | | 6.0 | | 6.0 | | 8.0 | |
| (c) Top Marginal Tax Rate | | | 5.0 | (50) | 5.0 | (50) | 3.0 | (50) | 9.0 | (25) | 9.0 | (25) | 9.0 | (25) |
| (d) Conscription | | | 10.0 | | 10.0 | | 10.0 | | 10.0 | | 10.0 | | 10.0 | |
| **III. Monetary Policy and Price Stability** | **8.9** | | **6.1** | | **7.1** | | **3.3** | | **7.4** | | **6.9** | | **7.5** | |
| (a) Annual Money Growth (last 5 yrs.) | 9.0 | (4.9) | 6.8 | (16.0) | 6.9 | (15.6) | 3.6 | (32.1) | 7.4 | (13.0) | 7.3 | (13.4) | 6.7 | (16.3) |
| (b) Inflation Variability (last 5 yrs.) | 9.1 | (2.2) | 6.5 | (8.8) | 8.2 | (4.5) | 0.2 | (24.4) | 8.7 | (3.3) | 7.6 | (6.0) | 8.6 | (3.4) |
| (c) Recent Inflation Rate | 8.5 | (7.3) | 5.1 | (24.5) | 6.2 | (18.8) | 5.9 | (20.5) | 6.3 | (18.6) | 5.7 | (21.3) | 7.1 | (14.5) |
| **IV. Freedom to Use Alternative Currencies** | **10.0** | | **9.2** | | **5.0** | | **7.6** | | **10.0** | | **10.0** | | **10.0** | |
| (a) Ownership of Foreign Currency | 10.0 | | 10.0 | | 10.0 | | 10.0 | | 10.0 | | 10.0 | | 10.0 | |
| (b) Black Market Exchange Rates (Prem.) | 10.0 | (0.0) | 8.4 | (8.0) | 0.0 | (69.0) | 5.2 | (24.0) | 10.0 | (0.0) | 10.0 | (0.0) | 10.0 | (0.0) |
| **V. Legal Structure and Property Rights** | | | | | **4.5** | | **5.1** | | **5.3** | | **6.3** | | **6.0** | |
| (a) Private Ownership Rights | | | | | 4.6 | | 4.8 | | 5.3 | | 7.7 | | 7.2 | |
| (b) Viability of Contracts | | | | | 2.4 | | 4.0 | | 4.0 | | 6.8 | | 6.6 | |
| (c) Rule of Law | | | | | 6.7 | | 6.6 | | 6.7 | | 4.1 | | 4.1 | |
| **VI. International Exchange** | **6.4** | | **5.6** | | **4.9** | | **3.5** | | **6.4** | | **7.6** | | **7.9** | |
| (a) Taxes on International Trade | | | | | | | | | | | | | | |
| i. Taxes as a Percentage of Exports and Imports | 7.3 | (4.1) | 6.1 | (5.9) | 6.5 | (5.3) | 5.4 | (6.9) | 5.3 | (7.0) | 6.9 | (4.6) | 9.0 | (1.5) |
| ii. Mean Tariff Rate | | | | | 0.0 | (55.0) | 0.0 | (53.0) | 6.7 | (16.4) | 8.0 | (10.2) | | |
| iii. Standard Deviation of Tariff Rates | | | | | | | 0.0 | (61.8) | 4.8 | (12.9) | 6.9 | (7.7) | | |
| (b) Non-tariff Regulatory Trade Barriers | | | | | | | | | | | | | | |
| i. Non-tariff Trade Restraints (% of trade covered) | | | | | 9.9 | (1.0) | 9.9 | (0.8) | 10.0 | (0.0) | 10.0 | (0.0) | | |
| ii. Size of Trade Sector (% of GDP) | 4.2 | (63.2) | 4.4 | (68.6) | 3.7 | (63.3) | 3.4 | (63.2) | 4.3 | (76.0) | 4.7 | (85.6) | 5.3 | (97.6) |
| **VII. Freedom of Exchange in Financial Markets** | **8.0** | | **6.7** | | **6.0** | | **7.3** | | **7.6** | | **8.7** | | **9.1** | |
| (a) Ownership of Banks | 10.0 | (95-100) | 10.0 | (95-100) | 10.0 | (95-100) | 10.0 | (95-100) | 10.0 | (100) | 10.0 | (100) | 10.0 | (100) |
| (b) Extension of Credit | 9.3 | (93.5) | 8.5 | (86.3) | 6.0 | (63.6) | 8.1 | (82.7) | 7.2 | (75.0) | 8.7 | (87.8) | 8.0 | (82.1) |
| (c) Avoidance of Negative Interest Rates | | | | | | | 6.0 | | 8.0 | | 8.0 | | 8.0 | |
| (d) Capital Transactions with Foreigners | 5.0 | | 2.0 | | 2.0 | | 5.0 | | 5.0 | | 8.0 | | 10.0 | |

# COTE D'IVOIRE

| | 1970 | 1975 | 1980 | 1985 | 1990 | 1995 | 1997 |
|---|---|---|---|---|---|---|---|
| **Summary Ratings** | | | 4.9 | 5.4 | 4.9 | 5.2 | 5.7 |
| **Rank** | | | 63 | 52 | 71 | 87 | 87 |

| Components of Economic Freedom | 1970 | | 1975 | | 1980 | | 1985 | | 1990 | | 1995 | | 1997 | |
|---|---|---|---|---|---|---|---|---|---|---|---|---|---|---|
| **I. Size of Government** | **7.3** | | **6.8** | | **8.0** | | **7.3** | | **7.4** | | **8.1** | | **8.1** | |
| (a) Government Consumption (% of Total) | 7.3 | (19.2) | 6.8 | (22.0) | 6.9 | (21.2) | 7.3 | (19.4) | 7.4 | (18.9) | 8.1 | (15.0) | 8.1 | (15.1) |
| (b) Transfers and Subsidies (% of GDP) | | | | | 9.0 | (4.2) | | | | | | | | |
| **II. Structure of the Economy and Use of Markets** | | | | | **3.2** | | **2.5** | | **1.4** | | **2.5** | | **3.0** | |
| (a) Government Enterprises | 2.0 | (39.6) | 2.0 | (39.7) | 0.0 | (52.4) | 0.0 | (66.7) | 0.0 | (52.5) | 2.0 | (43.7) | 2.0 | |
| (b) Price Controls | | | | | | | | | 0.0 | | 2.0 | | 2.0 | |
| (c) Top Marginal Tax Rate | | | | | 5.0 | (45) | 5.0 | (45) | 4.0 | (45) | 3.0 | (49) | 5.0 | (39) |
| (d) Conscription | 0.0 | | 10.0 | | 10.0 | | 5.0 | | 5.0 | | 5.0 | | 5.0 | |
| **III. Monetary Policy and Price Stability** | **9.1** | | **7.8** | | **6.2** | | **8.9** | | **9.2** | | **6.6** | | **6.8** | |
| (a) Annual Money Growth (last 5 yrs.) | 8.8 | (5.9) | 8.3 | (8.5) | 7.2 | (14.3) | 9.0 | (5.0) | 9.2 | (-3.9) | 7.8 | (10.9) | 7.1 | (14.8) |
| (b) Inflation Variability (last 5 yrs.) | 9.2 | (2.0) | 6.0 | (9.9) | 6.2 | (9.6) | 7.6 | (6.1) | 9.3 | (1.6) | 3.6 | (16.1) | 3.9 | (15.4) |
| (c) Recent Inflation Rate | 9.4 | (3.0) | 9.1 | (4.3) | 5.2 | (24.1) | 9.9 | (0.3) | 9.1 | (-4.5) | 8.3 | (8.5) | 9.4 | (3.2) |
| **IV. Freedom to Use Alternative Currencies** | **4.8** | | **4.8** | | **4.8** | | **4.9** | | **4.6** | | **4.9** | | **4.8** | |
| (a) Ownership of Foreign Currency | 0.0 | | 0.0 | | 0.0 | | 0.0 | | 0.0 | | 0.0 | | 0.0 | |
| (b) Black Market Exchange Rates (Prem.) | 9.6 | (2.0) | 9.6 | (2.0) | 9.6 | (2.0) | 9.8 | (1.0) | 9.2 | (4.0) | 9.8 | (1.0) | 9.6 | (2.0) |
| **V. Legal Structure and Property Rights** | | | | | | | **6.4** | | **5.1** | | **4.5** | | **3.8** | |
| (a) Private Ownership Rights | | | | | | | 6.1 | | 5.9 | | 3.2 | | 1.7 | |
| (b) Viability of Contracts | | | | | | | 6.4 | | 5.2 | | 3.7 | | 3.1 | |
| (c) Rule of Law | | | | | | | 6.6 | | 4.2 | | 7.0 | | 7.0 | |
| **VI. International Exchange** | | | | | **4.3** | | **4.8** | | **4.1** | | **6.3** | | **8.8** | |
| (a) Taxes on International Trade | | | | | | | | | | | | | | |
| i. Taxes as a Percentage of Exports and Imports | | | | | 1.5 | (12.8) | 2.1 | (11.8) | 2.7 | (10.9) | 6.1 | (5.8) | | |
| ii. Mean Tariff Rate | | | | | 4.5 | (27.5) | 5.3 | (23.3) | 3.4 | (33.0) | 3.4 | (33.0) | 9.0 | (4.8) |
| iii. Standard Deviation of Tariff Rates | | | | | | | | | | | 9.4 | (1.5) | 9.6 | (1.1) |
| (b) Non-tariff Regulatory Trade Barriers | | | | | | | | | | | | | | |
| i. Non-tariff Trade Restraints (% of trade covered) | | | | | 6.0 | (40.0) | 6.3 | (37.5) | 6.3 | (37.5) | 6.3 | (37.5) | | |
| ii. Size of Trade Sector (% of GDP) | 6.5 | (64.9) | 7.2 | (73.3) | 7.2 | (76.2) | 7.3 | (79.2) | 5.2 | (58.8) | 6.6 | (76.9) | 6.4 | (76.6) |
| **VII. Freedom of Exchange in Financial Markets** | | | | | **4.6** | | **5.0** | | **4.4** | | **4.6** | | **5.1** | |
| (a) Ownership of Banks | | | 2.0 | (10-40) | 2.0 | (10-40) | 2.0 | (10-40) | 2.0 | (10-40) | 8.0 | (75-95) | 8.0 | (90-95) |
| (b) Extension of Credit | | | | | 9.6 | (96.6) | 9.3 | (93.4) | 9.1 | (91.6) | 7.0 | (72.8) | 7.1 | (73.4) |
| (c) Avoidance of Negative Interest Rates | | | | | 8.0 | | 10.0 | | 8.0 | | 4.0 | | 6.0 | |
| (d) Capital Transactions with Foreigners | 0.0 | | 0.0 | | 0.0 | | 0.0 | | 0.0 | | 0.0 | | 0.0 | |

# CROATIA

| | 1970 | 1975 | 1980 | 1985 | 1990 | 1995 | 1997 |
|---|---|---|---|---|---|---|---|
| **Summary Ratings** | | | | | | 4.3 | 4.7 |
| **Rank** | | | | | | 107 | 103 |

| Components of Economic Freedom | 1970 | | 1975 | | 1980 | | 1985 | | 1990 | | 1995 | | 1997 | |
|---|---|---|---|---|---|---|---|---|---|---|---|---|---|---|
| **I. Size of Government** | | | | | | | | | | | **5.3** | | **5.2** | |
| (a) Government Consumption (% of Total) | | | | | | | | | | | 4.7 | (33.4) | 5.1 | (31.4) |
| (b) Transfers and Subsidies (% of GDP) | | | | | | | | | | | 5.9 | (15.5) | 5.3 | (17.9) |
| **II. Structure of the Economy and Use of Markets** | | | | | | | | | | | **1.2** | | **2.6** | |
| (a) Government Enterprises | | | | | | | | | | | 0.0 | | 0.0 | |
| (b) Price Controls | | | | | | | | | 0.0 | | 2.0 | | 4.0 | |
| (c) Top Marginal Tax Rate | | | | | | | | | | | | | 4.0 | (35-53) |
| (d) Conscription | | | | | | | | | | | 3.0 | | 3.0 | |
| **III. Monetary Policy and Price Stability** | | | | | | | | | | | **2.8** | | **3.6** | |
| (a) Annual Money Growth (last 5 yrs.) | | | | | | | | | | | 0.0 | (62.4) | 1.4 | (42.8) |
| (b) Inflation Variability (last 5 yrs.) | | | | | | | | | | | 0.0 | (573.3) | 0.0 | (649.3) |
| (c) Recent Inflation Rate | | | | | | | | | 0.0 | (500.0) | 8.4 | (8.0) | 9.2 | (4.1) |
| **IV. Freedom to Use Alternative Currencies** | | | | | | | | | **2.5** | | **6.7** | | **5.2** | |
| (a) Ownership of Foreign Currency | | | | | | | | | 5.0 | | 5.0 | | 10.0 | |
| (b) Black Market Exchange Rates (Prem.) | | | | | | | | | 0.0 | (106.0) | 8.4 | (8.0) | 0.4 | (48.0) |
| **V. Legal Structure and Property Rights** | | | | | | | | | | | | | | |
| (a) Private Ownership Rights | | | | | | | | | | | | | | |
| (b) Viability of Contracts | | | | | | | | | | | | | | |
| (c) Rule of Law | | | | | | | | | | | | | | |
| **VI. International Exchange** | | | | | | | | | | | **6.7** | | **7.0** | |
| (a) Taxes on International Trade | | | | | | | | | | | | | | |
| i. Taxes as a Percentage of Exports and Imports | | | | | | | | | | | 7.1 | (4.3) | 7.5 | (3.7) |
| ii. Mean Tariff Rate | | | | | | | | | | | | | | |
| iii. Standard Deviation of Tariff Rates | | | | | | | | | | | | | | |
| (b) Non-tariff Regulatory Trade Barriers | | | | | | | | | | | | | | |
| i. Non-tariff Trade Restraints (% of trade covered) | | | | | | | | | | | | | | |
| ii. Size of Trade Sector (% of GDP) | | | | | | | | | | | 5.5 | (93.0) | 5.6 | (95.5) |
| **VII. Freedom of Exchange in Financial Markets** | | | | | | | | | | | **2.7** | | **4.0** | |
| (a) Ownership of Banks | | | | | | | | | 0.0 | (0-10) | 0.0 | (0-10) | 0.0 | (0-10) |
| (b) Extension of Credit | | | | | | | | | | | 5.7 | (61.0) | 6.9 | (71.6) |
| (c) Avoidance of Negative Interest Rates | | | | | | | | | | | 4.0 | | 8.0 | |
| (d) Capital Transactions with Foreigners | | | | | | | | | 0.0 | | 2.0 | | 2.0 | |

# CYPRUS

| | 1970 | 1975 | 1980 | 1985 | 1990 | 1995 | 1997 |
|---|---|---|---|---|---|---|---|
| **Summary Ratings** | | 6.3 | 5.8 | 5.8 | 5.9 | 6.6 | 6.8 |
| **Rank** | | 23 | 36 | 42 | 48 | 54 | 57 |

| Components of Economic Freedom | 1970 | | 1975 | | 1980 | | 1985 | | 1990 | | 1995 | | 1997 | |
|---|---|---|---|---|---|---|---|---|---|---|---|---|---|---|
| **I. Size of Government** | **9.1** | | **7.5** | | **8.0** | | **7.7** | | **7.3** | | **7.1** | | **7.0** | |
| (a) Government Consumption (% of Total) | | | 7.6 | (17.7) | 7.7 | (17.0) | 7.5 | (18.1) | 6.7 | (22.4) | 6.9 | (21.2) | 6.6 | (22.8) |
| (b) Transfers and Subsidies (% of GDP) | 9.1 | (3.9) | 7.3 | (10.3) | 8.3 | (6.6) | 7.9 | (8.1) | 7.9 | (8.3) | 7.3 | (10.3) | 7.4 | (9.9) |
| **II. Structure of the Economy and Use of Markets** | | | | | **4.3** | | **4.3** | | **2.6** | | **4.3** | | **4.3** | |
| (a) Government Enterprises | 8.0 | (11.1) | 8.0 | (12.3) | 8.0 | (18.1) | 8.0 | (17.4) | 8.0 | | 8.0 | | 8.0 | |
| (b) Price Controls | | | | | | | | | 0.0 | | 2.0 | | 2.0 | |
| (c) Top Marginal Tax Rate | | | 3.0 | (54) | 1.0 | (60) | 1.0 | (60) | 0.0 | (62) | 4.0 | (42) | 4.0 | (42) |
| (d) Conscription | | | | | 0.0 | | 0.0 | | 0.0 | | 0.0 | | 0.0 | |
| **III. Monetary Policy and Price Stability** | | | **7.9** | | **7.6** | | **8.9** | | **9.4** | | **9.6** | | **9.6** | |
| (a) Annual Money Growth (last 5 yrs.) | | | | | 6.4 | (18.0) | 9.1 | (4.6) | 9.5 | (2.3) | 9.8 | (1.1) | 9.9 | (0.6) |
| (b) Inflation Variability (last 5 yrs.) | | | 8.6 | (3.6) | 9.1 | (2.4) | 8.9 | (2.8) | 9.7 | (0.7) | 9.6 | (0.9) | 9.6 | (0.9) |
| (c) Recent Inflation Rate | 9.5 | (2.4) | 7.2 | (14.2) | 7.3 | (13.5) | 8.9 | (5.7) | 8.9 | (5.3) | 9.5 | (2.6) | 9.3 | (3.6) |
| **IV. Freedom to Use Alternative Currencies** | **4.9** | | **4.4** | | **4.6** | | **4.9** | | **4.5** | | **4.5** | | **5.0** | |
| (a) Ownership of Foreign Currency | 0.0 | | 0.0 | | 0.0 | | 0.0 | | 0.0 | | 0.0 | | 0.0 | |
| (b) Black Market Exchange Rates (Prem.) | 9.8 | (1.0) | 8.8 | (6.0) | 9.2 | (4.0) | 9.8 | (1.0) | 9.0 | (5.0) | 9.0 | (5.0) | 10.0 | (0.0) |
| **V. Legal Structure and Property Rights** | | | | | | | **4.4** | | **7.3** | | **8.5** | | **9.0** | |
| (a) Private Ownership Rights | | | | | | | 4.8 | | 8.6 | | 10.0 | | 10.0 | |
| (b) Viability of Contracts | | | | | | | 5.2 | | 6.4 | | 8.4 | | 10.0 | |
| (c) Rule of Law | | | | | | | 3.1 | | 6.7 | | 7.0 | | 7.0 | |
| **VI. International Exchange** | **5.5** | | **6.6** | | **6.5** | | **6.3** | | **5.3** | | **6.9** | | | |
| (a) Taxes on International Trade | | | | | | | | | | | | | | |
| i. Taxes as a Percentage of Exports and Imports | 6.2 | (5.7) | 7.7 | (3.5) | 7.3 | (4.0) | 7.1 | (4.4) | 7.2 | (4.2) | 8.3 | (2.6) | | |
| ii. Mean Tariff Rate | | | | | 6.6 | (17.1) | 6.5 | (17.6) | 6.7 | (16.5) | 7.2 | (14.0) | | |
| iii. Standard Deviation of Tariff Rates | | | | | | | | | 2.5 | (18.7) | | | | |
| (b) Non-tariff Regulatory Trade Barriers | | | | | | | | | | | | | | |
| i. Non-tariff Trade Restraints (% of trade covered) | | | | | | | | | 5.1 | (49.0) | | | | |
| ii. Size of Trade Sector (% of GDP) | 3.8 | (85.4) | 3.9 | (92.2) | 4.4 | (108.3) | 4.1 | (107.6) | 3.8 | (109.0) | 2.6 | (96.8) | 2.7 | (99.5) |
| **VII. Freedom of Exchange in Financial Markets** | **5.3** | | **6.1** | | **5.1** | | **6.0** | | **6.4** | | **6.5** | | **6.4** | |
| (a) Ownership of Banks | | | 8.0 | (75-95) | 8.0 | (75-95) | 8.0 | (75-95) | 8.0 | (75-95) | 8.0 | (75-95) | 8.0 | (75-95) |
| (b) Extension of Credit | 9.0 | (90.7) | 9.1 | (92.1) | 9.2 | (92.7) | 8.8 | (88.9) | 8.3 | (84.9) | 8.6 | (87.4) | 8.1 | (83.1) |
| (c) Avoidance of Negative Interest Rates | 8.0 | | 8.0 | | 4.0 | | 8.0 | | 10.0 | | 10.0 | | 10.0 | |
| (d) Capital Transactions with Foreigners | 0.0 | | 0.0 | | 0.0 | | 0.0 | | 0.0 | | 0.0 | | 0.0 | |

# CZECH REPUBLIC

| | 1970 | 1975 | 1980 | 1985 | 1990 | 1995 | 1997 |
|---|---|---|---|---|---|---|---|
| **Summary Ratings** | | | | | 3.9 | 6.8 | 7.1 |
| **Rank** | | | | | 96 | 49 | 51 |

| Components of Economic Freedom | 1970 | | 1975 | | 1980 | | 1985 | | 1990 | | 1995 | | 1997 | |
|---|---|---|---|---|---|---|---|---|---|---|---|---|---|---|
| **I. Size of Government** | | | **5.9** | | **5.8** | | **5.3** | | **2.7** | | **3.9** | | **4.2** | |
| (a) Government Consumption (% of Total) | | | 5.9 | (26.6) | 5.8 | (27.3) | 5.3 | (30.1) | 5.3 | (29.9) | 5.4 | (29.7) | 5.6 | (28.3) |
| (b) Transfers and Subsidies (% of GDP) | | | | | | | | | 0.0 | (37.2) | 2.4 | (28.4) | 2.7 | (27.2) |
| **II. Structure of the Economy and Use of Markets** | | | | | | | | | **1.0** | | **4.8** | | **5.2** | |
| (a) Government Enterprises | 0.0 | | 0.0 | | 0.0 | | 0.0 | | 0.0 | | 4.0 | | 6.0 | |
| (b) Price Controls | | | | | | | | | 0.0 | | 6.0 | | 5.0 | |
| (c) Top Marginal Tax Rate | | | | | | | | | 4.0 | (55) | 5.0 | (43) | 5.0 | (40) |
| (d) Conscription | 0.0 | | 0.0 | | 0.0 | | 0.0 | | 0.0 | | 3.0 | | 3.0 | |
| **III. Monetary Policy and Price Stability** | | | | | | | **9.4** | | **8.8** | | **6.3** | | **8.1** | |
| (a) Annual Money Growth (last 5 yrs.) | | | | | | | 9.4 | (3.0) | 9.9 | (0.4) | 6.0 | (20.0) | 8.1 | (9.7) |
| (b) Inflation Variability (last 5 yrs.) | | | | | | | 9.1 | (2.2) | 8.4 | (4.0) | 4.9 | (12.8) | 7.7 | (5.8) |
| (c) Recent Inflation Rate | | | 9.9 | (0.7) | 9.4 | (2.9) | 9.7 | (1.7) | 8.1 | (9.5) | 7.9 | (10.4) | 8.7 | (6.6) |
| **IV. Freedom to Use Alternative Currencies** | **0.0** | | **0.0** | | **0.0** | | **0.0** | | **0.0** | | **7.5** | | **7.5** | |
| (a) Ownership of Foreign Currency | 0.0 | | 0.0 | | 0.0 | | 0.0 | | 0.0 | | 5.0 | | 5.0 | |
| (b) Black Market Exchange Rates (Prem.) | 0.0 | (525.0) | 0.0 | (359.0) | 0.0 | (387.0) | 0.0 | (423.0) | 0.0 | (61.0) | 10.0 | (0.0) | 10.0 | (0.0) |
| **V. Legal Structure and Property Rights** | | | | | | | **7.3** | | **7.8** | | **9.5** | | **10.0** | |
| (a) Private Ownership Rights | | | | | | | 7.4 | | 8.6 | | 10.0 | | 10.0 | |
| (b) Viability of Contracts | | | | | | | 6.4 | | 6.4 | | 8.4 | | 10.0 | |
| (c) Rule of Law | | | | | | | 8.2 | | 8.3 | | 10.0 | | 10.0 | |
| **VI. International Exchange** | | | | | | | | | | | **8.6** | | **8.7** | |
| (a) Taxes on International Trade | | | | | | | | | | | | | | |
| i. Taxes as a Percentage of Exports and Imports | | | | | | | | | 7.3 | (4.0) | 9.2 | (1.1) | 9.5 | (0.8) |
| ii. Mean Tariff Rate | | | | | | | | | | | 8.7 | (6.7) | 9.0 | (4.8) |
| iii. Standard Deviation of Tariff Rates | | | | | | | | | | | 7.4 | (6.4) | 7.1 | (7.2) |
| (b) Non-tariff Regulatory Trade Barriers | | | | | | | | | | | | | | |
| i. Non-tariff Trade Restraints (% of trade covered) | | | | | | | | | | | | | | |
| ii. Size of Trade Sector (% of GDP) | | | | | | | | | | | 10.0 | (123.1) | 9.6 | (120.6) |
| **VII. Freedom of Exchange in Financial Markets** | | | | | | | | | | | **5.5** | | **5.4** | |
| (a) Ownership of Banks | 0.0 | (0) | 0.0 | (0) | 0.0 | (0) | 0.0 | (0) | 0.0 | (0) | 5.0 | (40-75) | 2.0 | (10-20) |
| (b) Extension of Credit | | | | | | | | | | | 6.1 | (65.2) | 7.5 | (77.2) |
| (c) Avoidance of Negative Interest Rates | | | | | | | | | | | 6.0 | | 8.0 | |
| (d) Capital Transactions with Foreigners | 0.0 | | 0.0 | | 0.0 | | 0.0 | | 0.0 | | 5.0 | | 5.0 | |

# DENMARK

| | 1970 | 1975 | 1980 | 1985 | 1990 | 1995 | 1997 |
|---|---|---|---|---|---|---|---|
| **Summary Ratings** | 7.6 | 6.7 | 6.8 | 6.9 | 7.7 | 8.1 | 8.4 |
| **Rank** | 14 | 17 | 16 | 21 | 15 | 16 | 12 |

| Components of Economic Freedom | 1970 | | 1975 | | 1980 | | 1985 | | 1990 | | 1995 | | 1997 | |
|---|---|---|---|---|---|---|---|---|---|---|---|---|---|---|
| **I. Size of Government** | **5.8** | | **5.1** | | **4.5** | | **4.6** | | **4.3** | | **3.8** | | **4.6** | |
| (a) Government Consumption (% of Total) | 5.8 | (27.3) | 4.9 | (32.4) | 4.6 | (34.0) | 4.7 | (33.2) | 4.5 | (34.3) | 4.6 | (33.6) | 4.6 | (33.6) |
| (b) Transfers and Subsidies (% of GDP) | | | 5.3 | (17.8) | 4.5 | (20.8) | 4.6 | (20.4) | 4.0 | (22.6) | 2.9 | (26.5) | | |
| **II. Structure of the Economy and Use of Markets** | | | **3.7** | | **3.3** | | **3.3** | | **4.2** | | **5.8** | | **6.1** | |
| (a) Government Enterprises | 6.0 | | 6.0 | (27.3) | 6.0 | (25.0) | 6.0 | (26.0) | 6.0 | (20.3) | 7.0 | (24.9) | 7.0 | |
| (b) Price Controls | | | | | | | | | 6.0 | | 9.0 | | 9.0 | |
| (c) Top Marginal Tax Rate | | | 1.0 | (63) | 0.0 | (66) | 0.0 | (73) | 0.0 | (68) | 1.0 | (64) | 2.0 | (55-60) |
| (d) Conscription | 3.0 | | 3.0 | | 3.0 | | 3.0 | | 3.0 | | 3.0 | | 3.0 | |
| **III. Monetary Policy and Price Stability** | **9.0** | | **8.2** | | **8.9** | | **8.6** | | **9.2** | | **9.6** | | **9.5** | |
| (a) Annual Money Growth (last 5 yrs.) | 8.9 | (5.6) | 8.0 | (9.8) | 8.6 | (7.0) | 7.5 | (12.5) | 8.5 | (7.4) | 9.6 | (1.9) | 9.2 | (4.1) |
| (b) Inflation Variability (last 5 yrs.) | 9.7 | (0.7) | 9.2 | (2.0) | 9.7 | (0.8) | 9.0 | (2.4) | 9.7 | (0.7) | 9.8 | (0.6) | 9.8 | (0.5) |
| (c) Recent Inflation Rate | 8.3 | (8.3) | 7.5 | (12.4) | 8.4 | (8.2) | 9.1 | (4.3) | 9.3 | (3.4) | 9.6 | (2.1) | 9.6 | (2.0) |
| **IV. Freedom to Use Alternative Currencies** | **5.0** | | **4.9** | | **4.8** | | **5.0** | | **10.0** | | **10.0** | | **10.0** | |
| (a) Ownership of Foreign Currency | 0.0 | | 0.0 | | 0.0 | | 0.0 | | 10.0 | | 10.0 | | 10.0 | |
| (b) Black Market Exchange Rates (Prem.) | 10.0 | (0.0) | 9.8 | (1.0) | 9.6 | (2.0) | 10.0 | (0.0) | 10.0 | (0.0) | 10.0 | (0.0) | 10.0 | (0.0) |
| **V. Legal Structure and Property Rights** | **9.7** | | **8.2** | | **8.4** | | **9.1** | | **9.6** | | **10.0** | | **10.0** | |
| (a) Private Ownership Rights | 9.9 | | 7.0 | | 6.7 | | 8.7 | | 10.0 | | 10.0 | | 10.0 | |
| (b) Viability of Contracts | 9.5 | | 9.4 | | 8.7 | | 8.8 | | 8.8 | | 10.0 | | 10.0 | |
| (c) Rule of Law | | | | | 10.0 | | 10.0 | | 10.0 | | 10.0 | | 10.0 | |
| **VI. International Exchange** | **7.6** | | **8.1** | | **8.5** | | **8.6** | | **8.1** | | **8.3** | | **8.3** | |
| (a) Taxes on International Trade | | | | | | | | | | | | | | |
| i. Taxes as a Percentage of Exports and Imports | 8.7 | (1.9) | 9.4 | (0.9) | 9.7 | (0.5) | 9.7 | (0.4) | 9.8 | (0.3) | 9.8 | (0.3) | 9.8 | (0.3) |
| ii. Mean Tariff Rate | | | 8.2 | (9.0) | 8.2 | (8.8) | 8.5 | (7.5) | 8.5 | (7.4) | 8.7 | (6.7) | 8.6 | (6.9) |
| iii. Standard Deviation of Tariff Rates | | | | | | | | | 7.1 | (7.2) | 7.6 | (5.9) | 7.6 | (6.0) |
| (b) Non-tariff Regulatory Trade Barriers | | | | | | | | | | | | | | |
| i. Non-tariff Trade Restraints (% of trade covered) | | | | | 9.3 | (6.7) | 9.2 | (7.9) | 8.9 | (10.9) | 9.1 | (9.0) | 9.3 | (6.7) |
| ii. Size of Trade Sector (% of GDP) | 4.8 | (58.8) | 4.6 | (61.1) | 4.7 | (66.5) | 4.9 | (73.0) | 3.9 | (65.6) | 3.4 | (64.2) | 3.6 | (68.7) |
| **VII. Freedom of Exchange in Financial Markets** | **8.0** | | **8.0** | | **8.2** | | **7.9** | | **8.0** | | **8.5** | | **9.0** | |
| (a) Ownership of Banks | 10.0 | (100) | 10.0 | (100) | 10.0 | (100) | 10.0 | (100) | 10.0 | (100) | 10.0 | (100) | 10.0 | (100) |
| (b) Extension of Credit | 9.5 | (95.5) | 9.2 | (93.1) | 8.0 | (82.3) | 6.5 | (68.3) | 6.8 | (70.8) | 5.4 | (58.2) | 5.4 | (58.7) |
| (c) Avoidance of Negative Interest Rates | 8.0 | | 8.0 | | 10.0 | | 10.0 | | 10.0 | | 10.0 | | 10.0 | |
| (d) Capital Transactions with Foreigners | 5.0 | | 5.0 | | 5.0 | | 5.0 | | 5.0 | | 8.0 | | 10.0 | |

# Dominican Republic

| | 1970 | 1975 | 1980 | 1985 | 1990 | 1995 | 1997 |
|---|---|---|---|---|---|---|---|
| **Summary Ratings** | | 3.9 | 5.3 | 5.2 | 4.1 | 6.3 | 7.0 |
| **Rank** | | 66 | 50 | 56 | 93 | 60 | 53 |

| Components of Economic Freedom | 1970 | | 1975 | | 1980 | | 1985 | | 1990 | | 1995 | | 1997 | |
|---|---|---|---|---|---|---|---|---|---|---|---|---|---|---|
| **I. Size of Government** | **9.0** | | **9.4** | | **9.4** | | **9.4** | | **9.7** | | **9.7** | | **9.2** | |
| (a) Government Consumption (% of Total) | 8.4 | (13.1) | 9.4 | (7.9) | 9.2 | (9.0) | 9.3 | (8.2) | 9.7 | (6.0) | 9.7 | (6.4) | 9.0 | (9.9) |
| (b) Transfers and Subsidies (% of GDP) | 9.6 | (2.0) | 9.5 | (2.5) | 9.7 | (1.6) | 9.5 | (2.5) | 9.7 | (1.5) | 9.7 | (1.7) | 9.4 | (2.7) |
| **II. Structure of the Economy and Use of Markets** | | | **2.4** | | **3.3** | | **3.3** | | **3.5** | | **6.4** | | **6.4** | |
| (a) Government Enterprises | 4.0 | (39.2) | 4.0 | (37.7) | 4.0 | (21.0) | 4.0 | (26.2) | 4.0 | (28.5) | 4.0 | (38.3) | 4.0 | |
| (b) Price Controls | | | | | | | | | 4.0 | | 6.0 | | 6.0 | |
| (c) Top Marginal Tax Rate | | | 0.0 | (73) | 0.0 | (73) | 0.0 | (73) | 0.0 | (73) | 9.0 | (25) | 9.0 | (25) |
| (d) Conscription | 3.0 | | 3.0 | | 10.0 | | 10.0 | | 10.0 | | 10.0 | | 10.0 | |
| **III. Monetary Policy and Price Stability** | **9.6** | | **7.4** | | **8.2** | | **3.4** | | **2.0** | | **5.7** | | **8.1** | |
| (a) Annual Money Growth (last 5 yrs.) | 10.0 | (-0.1) | 8.3 | (8.6) | 9.3 | (3.7) | 7.3 | (13.5) | 2.7 | (36.6) | 7.5 | (12.7) | 7.2 | (14.0) |
| (b) Inflation Variability (last 5 yrs.) | 9.1 | (2.2) | 7.4 | (6.6) | 8.1 | (4.6) | 3.0 | (17.5) | 3.5 | (16.3) | 2.0 | (20.0) | 8.9 | (2.7) |
| (c) Recent Inflation Rate | 9.6 | (2.1) | 6.6 | (17.0) | 7.3 | (13.7) | 0.0 | (50.5) | 0.0 | (51.1) | 7.5 | (12.6) | 8.3 | (8.4) |
| **IV. Freedom to Use Alternative Currencies** | **2.8** | | **2.2** | | **3.8** | | **6.1** | | **0.0** | | **4.8** | | **7.1** | |
| (a) Ownership of Foreign Currency | 0.0 | | 0.0 | | 5.0 | | 5.0 | | 0.0 | | 0.0 | | 5.0 | |
| (b) Black Market Exchange Rates (Prem.) | 5.6 | (22.0) | 4.4 | (28.0) | 2.6 | (37.0) | 7.2 | (14.0) | 0.0 | (66.0) | 9.6 | (2.0) | 9.2 | (4.0) |
| **V. Legal Structure and Property Rights** | | | | | **5.4** | | **3.9** | | **4.5** | | **5.2** | | **4.8** | |
| (a) Private Ownership Rights | | | | | 4.6 | | 3.5 | | 3.2 | | 7.7 | | 7.2 | |
| (b) Viability of Contracts | | | | | 3.7 | | 0.4 | | 2.2 | | 3.7 | | 3.1 | |
| (c) Rule of Law | | | | | 8.3 | | 8.2 | | 8.3 | | 4.1 | | 4.1 | |
| **VI. International Exchange** | **0.7** | | **1.2** | | **3.3** | | **5.1** | | **4.6** | | **5.6** | | **6.6** | |
| (a) Taxes on International Trade | | | | | | | | | | | | | | |
| i. Taxes as a Percentage of Exports and Imports | 0.0 | (16.5) | 0.0 | (16.1) | 3.5 | (9.8) | 5.7 | (6.5) | 4.5 | (8.2) | 5.9 | (6.1) | 6.8 | (4.8) |
| ii. Mean Tariff Rate | | | | | | | | | 4.4 | (28.0) | 6.0 | (20.0) | | |
| iii. Standard Deviation of Tariff Rates | | | | | | | | | | | | | | |
| (b) Non-tariff Regulatory Trade Barriers | | | | | | | | | | | | | | |
| i. Non-tariff Trade Restraints (% of trade covered) | | | | | | | | | | | | | | |
| ii. Size of Trade Sector (% of GDP) | 2.6 | (41.8) | 4.4 | (57.7) | 3.0 | (48.1) | 3.8 | (57.2) | 5.2 | (77.8) | 3.8 | (62.6) | 6.1 | (98.2) |
| **VII. Freedom of Exchange in Financial Markets** | | | | | **5.6** | | **5.4** | | **4.9** | | **7.1** | | **7.8** | |
| (a) Ownership of Banks | | | | | 8.0 | (90-95) | 8.0 | (90-95) | 10.0 | (95-100) | 10.0 | (95-100) | 10.0 | (95-100) |
| (b) Extension of Credit | 6.4 | (67.2) | 7.3 | (75.9) | 7.3 | (75.7) | 6.3 | (66.7) | 7.7 | (79.6) | 8.8 | (88.9) | 8.5 | (86.2) |
| (c) Avoidance of Negative Interest Rates | | | | | | | | | 0.0 | | 8.0 | | 8.0 | |
| (d) Capital Transactions with Foreigners | 2.0 | | 2.0 | | 2.0 | | 2.0 | | 2.0 | | 2.0 | | 5.0 | |

# ECUADOR

| | 1970 | 1975 | 1980 | 1985 | 1990 | 1995 | 1997 |
|---|---|---|---|---|---|---|---|
| **Summary Ratings** | 3.9 | 5.8 | 6.0 | 4.5 | 5.3 | 6.7 | 7.0 |
| **Rank** | 53 | 35 | 32 | 76 | 58 | 53 | 53 |

| Components of Economic Freedom | 1970 | | 1975 | | 1980 | | 1985 | | 1990 | | 1995 | | 1997 | |
|---|---|---|---|---|---|---|---|---|---|---|---|---|---|---|
| **I. Size of Government** | **8.5** | | **7.5** | | **8.0** | | **8.6** | | **9.1** | | **8.8** | | **8.1** | |
| (a) Government Consumption (% of Total) | 8.5 | (12.8) | 7.5 | (18.2) | 7.2 | (19.6) | 8.1 | (15.1) | 8.8 | (11.2) | 8.0 | (15.7) | 8.1 | (14.7) |
| (b) Transfers and Subsidies (% of GDP) | | | | | 8.8 | (4.9) | 9.0 | (4.0) | 9.5 | (2.3) | 9.7 | (1.5) | | |
| **II. Structure of the Economy and Use of Markets** | | | **3.8** | | **3.8** | | **2.7** | | **2.8** | | **5.2** | | **5.2** | |
| (a) Government Enterprises | 4.0 | (39.5) | 4.0 | (40.8) | 4.0 | (39.5) | 4.0 | (41.3) | 4.0 | (38.9) | 4.0 | (35.2) | 4.0 | |
| (b) Price Controls | | | | | | | | | 0.0 | | 4.0 | | 4.0 | |
| (c) Top Marginal Tax Rate | | | 5.0 | (50) | 5.0 | (50) | 2.0 | (58) | 5.0 | (40) | 9.0 | (25) | 9.0 | (25) |
| (d) Conscription | 0.0 | | 0.0 | | 0.0 | | 0.0 | | 3.0 | | 3.0 | | 3.0 | |
| **III. Monetary Policy and Price Stability** | **8.3** | | **6.4** | | **7.2** | | **5.2** | | **1.7** | | **4.7** | | **5.8** | |
| (a) Annual Money Growth (last 5 yrs.) | 7.4 | (13.3) | 6.7 | (16.5) | 7.3 | (13.7) | 6.0 | (19.9) | 1.9 | (40.5) | 3.1 | (34.4) | 4.7 | (26.5) |
| (b) Inflation Variability (last 5 yrs.) | 9.3 | (1.8) | 4.5 | (13.7) | 8.4 | (4.1) | 5.9 | (10.4) | 3.3 | (16.8) | 5.8 | (10.5) | 7.9 | (5.3) |
| (c) Recent Inflation Rate | 8.2 | (9.1) | 8.0 | (10.0) | 6.1 | (19.5) | 3.8 | (30.9) | 0.0 | (54.0) | 5.4 | (23.2) | 4.8 | (25.9) |
| **IV. Freedom to Use Alternative Currencies** | **2.8** | | **9.5** | | **8.7** | | **5.2** | | **10.0** | | **8.8** | | **9.5** | |
| (a) Ownership of Foreign Currency | 0.0 | | 10.0 | | 10.0 | | 10.0 | | 10.0 | | 10.0 | | 10.0 | |
| (b) Black Market Exchange Rates (Prem.) | 5.6 | (22.0) | 9.0 | (5.0) | 7.4 | (13.0) | 0.4 | (48.0) | 10.0 | (0.0) | 7.6 | (12.0) | 9.0 | (5.0) |
| **V. Legal Structure and Property Rights** | **2.5** | | **3.8** | | **6.4** | | **3.9** | | **5.1** | | **5.5** | | **5.1** | |
| (a) Private Ownership Rights | 2.3 | | 3.8 | | 6.4 | | 4.8 | | 4.6 | | 5.5 | | 4.4 | |
| (b) Viability of Contracts | 2.7 | | 3.9 | | 6.2 | | 0.4 | | 4.0 | | 6.8 | | 6.6 | |
| (c) Rule of Law | | | | | 6.7 | | 6.6 | | 6.7 | | 4.1 | | 4.1 | |
| **VI. International Exchange** | **1.0** | | **4.5** | | **5.1** | | **4.1** | | **3.5** | | **6.6** | | **7.1** | |
| (a) Taxes on International Trade | | | | | | | | | | | | | | |
| i. Taxes as a Percentage of Exports and Imports | 0.4 | (14.4) | 4.1 | (8.9) | 5.2 | (7.2) | 5.9 | (6.2) | 7.3 | (4.0) | 7.7 | (3.5) | | |
| ii. Mean Tariff Rate | | | | | | | 2.5 | (37.7) | 2.6 | (37.1) | 7.5 | (12.3) | 7.7 | (11.4) |
| iii. Standard Deviation of Tariff Rates | | | | | | | | | 0.0 | (27.0) | 7.8 | (5.6) | 7.4 | (6.4) |
| (b) Non-tariff Regulatory Trade Barriers | | | | | | | | | | | | | | |
| i. Non-tariff Trade Restraints (% of trade covered) | | | | | | | 4.1 | (59.3) | 3.6 | (63.6) | 3.6 | (63.6) | | |
| ii. Size of Trade Sector (% of GDP) | 2.4 | (32.6) | 5.7 | (58.9) | 4.7 | (50.6) | 4.1 | (47.6) | 5.1 | (60.1) | 4.7 | (58.3) | 4.7 | (59.0) |
| **VII. Freedom of Exchange in Financial Markets** | | | | | **4.4** | | **3.1** | | **4.7** | | **7.0** | | **8.1** | |
| (a) Ownership of Banks | | | | | 5.0 | (47) | 5.0 | (74) | 8.0 | (87) | 8.0 | (91) | 8.0 | (92) |
| (b) Extension of Credit | 4.8 | (53.1) | 5.3 | (57.4) | 7.0 | (72.6) | 5.8 | (62.0) | 9.3 | (93.6) | 9.3 | (93.2) | 8.6 | (87.3) |
| (c) Avoidance of Negative Interest Rates | | | | | 4.0 | | 0.0 | | 0.0 | | 6.0 | | 8.0 | |
| (d) Capital Transactions with Foreigners | 2.0 | | 2.0 | | 2.0 | | 2.0 | | 2.0 | | 5.0 | | 8.0 | |

# EGYPT

| | 1970 | 1975 | 1980 | 1985 | 1990 | 1995 | 1997 |
|---|---|---|---|---|---|---|---|
| **Summary Ratings** | | 4.2 | 4.1 | 4.6 | 4.3 | 6.0 | 6.6 |
| **Rank** | | 64 | 79 | 74 | 89 | 73 | 62 |

| Components of Economic Freedom | 1970 | | 1975 | | 1980 | | 1985 | | 1990 | | 1995 | | 1997 | |
|---|---|---|---|---|---|---|---|---|---|---|---|---|---|---|
| **I. Size of Government** | **5.8** | | **4.5** | | **6.4** | | **6.7** | | **8.0** | | **8.2** | | **8.6** | |
| (a) Government Consumption (% of Total) | 5.8 | (27.4) | 5.6 | (28.4) | 7.4 | (18.5) | 7.1 | (20.2) | 8.3 | (13.6) | 8.6 | (12.4) | 8.6 | (11.9) |
| (b) Transfers and Subsidies (% of GDP) | | | 3.3 | (25.0) | 5.4 | (17.2) | 6.3 | (13.9) | 7.7 | (8.9) | 7.8 | (8.5) | | |
| **II. Structure of the Economy and Use of Markets** | | | | | **1.0** | | **1.7** | | **1.2** | | **2.1** | | **2.5** | |
| (a) Government Enterprises | 2.0 | (47.0) | 2.0 | (43.8) | 2.0 | (39.7) | 2.0 | (30.7) | 0.0 | (55.5) | 2.0 | (35.1) | 2.0 | |
| (b) Price Controls | | | | | | | | | 2.0 | | 2.0 | | 4.0 | |
| (c) Top Marginal Tax Rate | | | | | 0.0 | (80) | 2.0 | (65) | 2.0 | (65) | 3.0 | (50) | 2.0 | (52) |
| (d) Conscription | 0.0 | | 0.0 | | 0.0 | | 0.0 | | 0.0 | | 0.0 | | 0.0 | |
| **III. Monetary Policy and Price Stability** | **9.6** | | **7.7** | | **6.6** | | **8.4** | | **7.4** | | **8.4** | | **9.1** | |
| (a) Annual Money Growth (last 5 yrs.) | 9.6 | (-1.8) | 6.9 | (15.5) | 5.4 | (22.9) | 8.3 | (8.5) | 8.6 | (6.8) | 8.8 | (5.9) | 9.0 | (5.2) |
| (b) Inflation Variability (last 5 yrs.) | 9.5 | (1.3) | 8.3 | (4.2) | 8.1 | (4.7) | 8.6 | (3.4) | 7.4 | (6.6) | 8.2 | (4.5) | 9.4 | (1.5) |
| (c) Recent Inflation Rate | 9.6 | (2.2) | 7.9 | (10.4) | 6.4 | (18.0) | 8.2 | (9.0) | 6.3 | (18.4) | 8.1 | (9.4) | 8.8 | (5.9) |
| **IV. Freedom to Use Alternative Currencies** | **0.0** | | **4.9** | | **9.1** | | **5.0** | | **5.0** | | **7.2** | | **7.5** | |
| (a) Ownership of Foreign Currency | 0.0 | | 0.0 | | 10.0 | | 10.0 | | 10.0 | | 5.0 | | 5.0 | |
| (b) Black Market Exchange Rates (Prem.) | 0.0 | (83.0) | 9.8 | (1.0) | 8.2 | (9.0) | 0.0 | (146.0) | 0.0 | (56.0) | 9.4 | (3.0) | 10.0 | (0.0) |
| **V. Legal Structure and Property Rights** | **0.3** | | **3.4** | | **2.5** | | **5.2** | | **3.5** | | **7.6** | | **7.6** | |
| (a) Private Ownership Rights | 0.0 | | 3.0 | | 2.8 | | 3.5 | | 3.2 | | 10.0 | | 10.0 | |
| (b) Viability of Contracts | 0.7 | | 3.7 | | 3.0 | | 4.0 | | 4.0 | | 8.4 | | 8.3 | |
| (c) Rule of Law | | | | | 1.7 | | 8.2 | | 3.3 | | 4.1 | | 4.1 | |
| **VI. International Exchange** | | | **2.5** | | **2.3** | | **3.6** | | **3.9** | | **3.8** | | | |
| (a) Taxes on International Trade | | | | | | | | | | | | | | |
| i. Taxes as a Percentage of Exports and Imports | | | 0.0 | (16.7) | 1.3 | (13.1) | 1.9 | (12.1) | 6.1 | (5.9) | 4.8 | (7.8) | | |
| ii. Mean Tariff Rate | | | | | 0.5 | (47.4) | 1.4 | (42.8) | 3.3 | (33.5) | 4.3 | (28.3) | | |
| iii. Standard Deviation of Tariff Rates | | | | | | | | | 0.0 | (425.8) | 0.0 | (28.9) | | |
| (b) Non-tariff Regulatory Trade Barriers | | | | | | | | | | | | | | |
| i. Non-tariff Trade Restraints (% of trade covered) | | | | | | | 6.7 | (32.9) | 5.5 | (45.2) | 5.5 | (45.2) | | |
| ii. Size of Trade Sector (% of GDP) | 5.0 | (32.9) | 8.8 | (61.5) | 10.0 | (73.4) | 6.8 | (52.0) | 6.6 | (52.8) | 6.4 | (53.0) | 5.4 | (45.5) |
| **VII. Freedom of Exchange in Financial Markets** | | | | | **2.8** | | **3.7** | | **3.6** | | **6.0** | | **5.7** | |
| (a) Ownership of Banks | | | 5.0 | (40-60) | 5.0 | (40-60) | 5.0 | (40-60) | 5.0 | (40-60) | 5.0 | (40-45) | 5.0 | (40-50) |
| (b) Extension of Credit | | | | | 2.0 | (28.0) | 4.0 | (46.0) | 3.7 | (43.4) | 4.1 | (46.5) | 4.7 | (52.3) |
| (c) Avoidance of Negative Interest Rates | | | | | 4.0 | | 6.0 | | 6.0 | | 10.0 | | 8.0 | |
| (d) Capital Transactions with Foreigners | 0.0 | | 0.0 | | 0.0 | | 0.0 | | 0.0 | | 5.0 | | 5.0 | |

# El Salvador

| | 1970 | 1975 | 1980 | 1985 | 1990 | 1995 | 1997 |
|---|---|---|---|---|---|---|---|
| **Summary Ratings** | | | 3.7 | 4.3 | 5.0 | 8.0 | 8.3 |
| **Rank** | | | 91 | 84 | 67 | 22 | 14 |

| Components of Economic Freedom | 1970 | | 1975 | | 1980 | | 1985 | | 1990 | | 1995 | | 1997 | |
|---|---|---|---|---|---|---|---|---|---|---|---|---|---|---|
| **I. Size of Government** | **8.6** | | **8.9** | | **8.6** | | **8.7** | | **9.4** | | **9.2** | | **9.3** | |
| (a) Government Consumption (% of Total) | 8.6 | (12.4) | 8.4 | (13.5) | 7.8 | (16.3) | 7.9 | (16.0) | 9.0 | (10.0) | 9.2 | (9.0) | 9.1 | (9.5) |
| (b) Transfers and Subsidies (% of GDP) | | | 9.5 | (2.5) | 9.4 | (2.7) | 9.6 | (2.0) | 9.8 | (1.4) | 9.2 | (3.3) | 9.5 | (2.4) |
| **II. Structure of the Economy and Use of Markets** | | | | | **4.5** | | **4.1** | | **4.5** | | **6.6** | | **7.6** | |
| (a) Government Enterprises | 8.0 | (11.2) | 8.0 | (10.8) | 6.0 | (20.2) | 6.0 | (28.4) | 8.0 | (20.0) | 8.0 | (19.0) | 8.0 | |
| (b) Price Controls | | | | | | | | | 4.0 | | 6.0 | | 8.0 | |
| (c) Top Marginal Tax Rate | | | 4.0 | (55) | 3.0 | (60) | 3.0 | (48) | 2.0 | (60) | 8.0 | (30) | 8.0 | (30) |
| (d) Conscription | 3.0 | | | | 3.0 | | 0.0 | | 0.0 | | 0.0 | | 3.0 | |
| **III. Monetary Policy and Price Stability** | **9.3** | | **7.9** | | **7.0** | | **7.3** | | **6.7** | | **8.2** | | **9.0** | |
| (a) Annual Money Growth (last 5 yrs.) | 9.8 | (-0.9) | 7.5 | (12.5) | 7.0 | (14.9) | 7.8 | (10.9) | 7.5 | (12.7) | 7.4 | (12.8) | 9.0 | (5.1) |
| (b) Inflation Variability (last 5 yrs.) | 9.2 | (2.1) | 8.3 | (4.4) | 7.4 | (6.5) | 8.2 | (4.4) | 7.0 | (7.5) | 9.4 | (1.5) | 8.8 | (2.9) |
| (c) Recent Inflation Rate | 9.0 | (4.8) | 8.0 | (9.9) | 6.6 | (17.0) | 6.0 | (20.2) | 5.5 | (22.5) | 7.9 | (10.4) | 9.1 | (4.6) |
| **IV. Freedom to Use Alternative Currencies** | **3.2** | | **3.0** | | **0.0** | | **0.0** | | **2.6** | | **9.9** | | **9.7** | |
| (a) Ownership of Foreign Currency | 0.0 | | 0.0 | | 0.0 | | 0.0 | | 0.0 | | 10.0 | | 10.0 | |
| (b) Black Market Exchange Rates (Prem.) | 6.4 | (18.0) | 6.0 | (20.0) | 0.0 | (100.0) | 0.0 | (195.0) | 5.2 | (24.0) | 9.8 | (1.0) | 9.4 | (3.0) |
| **V. Legal Structure and Property Rights** | | | | | **1.9** | | **1.7** | | **1.7** | | **7.2** | | **6.9** | |
| (a) Private Ownership Rights | | | | | 2.2 | | 0.9 | | 0.5 | | 7.7 | | 7.2 | |
| (b) Viability of Contracts | | | | | 1.8 | | 2.8 | | 2.8 | | 6.8 | | 6.6 | |
| (c) Rule of Law | | | | | 1.7 | | 1.4 | | 1.7 | | 7.0 | | 7.0 | |
| **VI. International Exchange** | **3.5** | | **5.5** | | **3.3** | | **4.4** | | **5.7** | | **7.2** | | **7.0** | |
| (a) Taxes on International Trade | | | | | | | | | | | | | | |
| i. Taxes as a Percentage of Exports and Imports | 3.7 | (9.4) | 5.7 | (6.4) | 5.9 | (6.2) | 5.3 | (7.1) | 7.3 | (4.1) | 7.6 | (3.6) | 8.5 | (2.2) |
| ii. Mean Tariff Rate | | | | | 0.4 | (48.0) | | | 5.8 | (21.1) | 8.0 | (10.2) | 7.2 | (13.9) |
| iii. Standard Deviation of Tariff Rates | | | | | | | | | | | 7.0 | (7.6) | | |
| (b) Non-tariff Regulatory Trade Barriers | | | | | | | | | | | | | | |
| i. Non-tariff Trade Restraints (% of trade covered) | | | | | | | | | | | 8.1 | (19.2) | | |
| ii. Size of Trade Sector (% of GDP) | 2.9 | (49.4) | 4.9 | (71.3) | 4.3 | (67.4) | 2.2 | (52.2) | 1.3 | (49.8) | 2.4 | (59.3) | 2.3 | (59.2) |
| **VII. Freedom of Exchange in Financial Markets** | | | | | | | **6.1** | | **6.1** | | **8.0** | | **9.2** | |
| (a) Ownership of Banks | | | | | | | | | | | | | | |
| (b) Extension of Credit | 9.9 | (98.8) | 9.8 | (98.4) | 9.8 | (98.4) | 9.2 | (93.1) | 9.2 | (92.9) | 9.4 | (94.7) | 9.6 | (96.7) |
| (c) Avoidance of Negative Interest Rates | | | | | | | 8.0 | | 8.0 | | 10.0 | | 10.0 | |
| (d) Capital Transactions with Foreigners | 2.0 | | 2.0 | | 2.0 | | 2.0 | | 2.0 | | 5.0 | | 8.0 | |

# ESTONIA

| | 1970 | 1975 | 1980 | 1985 | 1990 | 1995 | 1997 |
|---|---|---|---|---|---|---|---|
| Summary Ratings | | | | | | 6.1 | 6.8 |
| Rank | | | | | | 67 | 57 |

| Components of Economic Freedom | 1970 | | 1975 | | 1980 | | 1985 | | 1990 | | 1995 | | 1997 | |
|---|---|---|---|---|---|---|---|---|---|---|---|---|---|---|
| **I. Size of Government** | | | | | | | | | **7.1** | | **6.0** | | **5.9** | |
| (a) Government Consumption (% of Total) | | | | | | | | | 7.1 | (20.5) | 5.5 | (29.1) | 5.7 | (28.1) |
| (b) Transfers and Subsidies (% of GDP) | | | | | | | | | | | 6.4 | (13.6) | 6.1 | (14.7) |
| **II. Structure of the Economy and Use of Markets** | | | | | | | | | | | **4.9** | | **5.6** | |
| (a) Government Enterprises | | | | | | | | | | | 2.0 | | 4.0 | |
| (b) Price Controls | | | | | | | | | 0.0 | | 6.0 | | 6.0 | |
| (c) Top Marginal Tax Rate | | | | | | | | | | | 8.0 | (26) | 8.0 | (26) |
| (d) Conscription | | | | | | | | | 0.0 | | 3.0 | | 3.0 | |
| **III. Monetary Policy and Price Stability** | | | | | | | **8.8** | | **4.2** | | **1.4** | | **3.4** | |
| (a) Annual Money Growth (last 5 yrs.) | | | | | | | | | | | 0.0 | (74.6) | 2.3 | (38.4) |
| (b) Inflation Variability (last 5 yrs.) | | | | | | | 8.7 | (3.4) | 5.2 | (12.1) | 0.0 | (323.0) | 0.0 | (24.9) |
| (c) Recent Inflation Rate | | | | | | | 8.9 | (-5.6) | 3.3 | (33.7) | 4.2 | (29.0) | 7.7 | (11.4) |
| **IV. Freedom to Use Alternative Currencies** | | | | | | | | | **2.5** | | **7.5** | | **7.5** | |
| (a) Ownership of Foreign Currency | | | | | | | | | 5.0 | | 5.0 | | 5.0 | |
| (b) Black Market Exchange Rates (Prem.) | | | | | | | | | 0.0 | (1969.0) | 10.0 | (0.0) | 10.0 | (0.0) |
| **V. Legal Structure and Property Rights** | | | | | | | | | | | | | **7.2** | |
| (a) Private Ownership Rights | | | | | | | | | | | | | 8.6 | |
| (b) Viability of Contracts | | | | | | | | | | | | | 7.4 | |
| (c) Rule of Law | | | | | | | | | | | | | 5.5 | |
| **VI. International Exchange** | | | | | | | | | | | **9.5** | | **9.2** | |
| (a) Taxes on International Trade | | | | | | | | | | | | | | |
| i. Taxes as a Percentage of Exports and Imports | | | | | | | | | 9.8 | (0.3) | 9.9 | (0.1) | 10.0 | (0.0) |
| ii. Mean Tariff Rate | | | | | | | | | | | 10.0 | (0.1) | | |
| iii. Standard Deviation of Tariff Rates | | | | | | | | | | | 9.5 | (1.2) | | |
| (b) Non-tariff Regulatory Trade Barriers | | | | | | | | | | | | | | |
| i. Non-tariff Trade Restraints (% of trade covered) | | | | | | | | | | | | | | |
| ii. Size of Trade Sector (% of GDP) | | | | | | | | | | | 7.5 | (159.7) | 7.3 | (158.5) |
| **VII. Freedom of Exchange in Financial Markets** | | | | | | | | | | | **5.1** | | **6.8** | |
| (a) Ownership of Banks | | | | | | | | | 0.0 | (0) | 5.0 | (50-75) | 8.0 | (80-90) |
| (b) Extension of Credit | | | | | | | | | | | 7.7 | (78.9) | 6.9 | (72.2) |
| (c) Avoidance of Negative Interest Rates | | | | | | | | | | | 0.0 | | 4.0 | |
| (d) Capital Transactions with Foreigners | | | | | | | | | 0.0 | | 8.0 | | 8.0 | |

# FIJI

| | 1970 | 1975 | 1980 | 1985 | 1990 | 1995 | 1997 |
|---|---|---|---|---|---|---|---|
| **Summary Ratings** | | 5.0 | 5.3 | 5.4 | 5.7 | 6.1 | 6.1 |
| **Rank** | | 47 | 50 | 52 | 52 | 67 | 78 |

| Components of Economic Freedom | 1970 | | 1975 | | 1980 | | 1985 | | 1990 | | 1995 | | 1997 | |
|---|---|---|---|---|---|---|---|---|---|---|---|---|---|---|
| **I. Size of Government** | **7.6** | | **8.8** | | **8.2** | | **7.7** | | **8.5** | | **8.0** | | **8.4** | |
| (a) Government Consumption (% of Total) | 7.6 | (17.7) | 8.1 | (15.0) | 7.0 | (21.1) | 6.6 | (23.1) | 7.2 | (19.9) | 6.9 | (21.4) | 7.5 | (18.4) |
| (b) Transfers and Subsidies (% of GDP) | | | 9.6 | (1.9) | 9.5 | (2.5) | 8.9 | (4.5) | 9.9 | (1.0) | 9.2 | (3.5) | 9.3 | (2.9) |
| **II. Structure of the Economy and Use of Markets** | | | **4.4** | | **3.1** | | **3.4** | | **4.3** | | **5.3** | | **5.3** | |
| (a) Government Enterprises | 4.0 | (29.8) | 4.0 | (30.0) | 2.0 | (45.0) | 2.0 | (37.0) | 2.0 | (62.0) | 2.0 | | 2.0 | |
| (b) Price Controls | | | | | | | | | 6.0 | | 6.0 | | 6.0 | |
| (c) Top Marginal Tax Rate | | | 3.0 | (53) | 2.0 | (53) | 3.0 | (50) | 3.0 | (50) | 7.0 | (35) | 7.0 | (35) |
| (d) Conscription | | | 10.0 | | 10.0 | | 10.0 | | 10.0 | | 10.0 | | 10.0 | |
| **III. Monetary Policy and Price Stability** | **8.6** | | **6.3** | | **8.0** | | **8.7** | | **8.4** | | **9.3** | | **9.2** | |
| (a) Annual Money Growth (last 5 yrs.) | 8.7 | (6.4) | 7.5 | (11.2) | 9.8 | (-1.3) | 9.1 | (4.5) | 7.5 | (12.3) | 9.0 | (4.9) | 9.2 | (4.2) |
| (b) Inflation Variability (last 5 yrs.) | 8.5 | (3.8) | 6.4 | (9.0) | 7.7 | (5.7) | 8.4 | (3.9) | 9.2 | (2.1) | 9.1 | (2.4) | 9.2 | (1.9) |
| (c) Recent Inflation Rate | 8.6 | (6.8) | 5.1 | (24.3) | 6.5 | (17.3) | 8.5 | (7.5) | 8.6 | (7.1) | 9.7 | (1.6) | 9.2 | (3.8) |
| **IV. Freedom to Use Alternative Currencies** | **4.8** | | **3.3** | | **3.2** | | **4.2** | | **4.6** | | **4.9** | | **4.7** | |
| (a) Ownership of Foreign Currency | | | 0.0 | | 0.0 | | 0.0 | | 0.0 | | 0.0 | | 0.0 | |
| (b) Black Market Exchange Rates (Prem.) | 4.8 | (26.0) | 6.6 | (17.0) | 6.4 | (18.0) | 8.4 | (8.0) | 9.2 | (4.0) | 9.8 | (1.0) | 9.4 | (3.0) |
| **V. Legal Structure and Property Rights** | | | | | | | | | | | | | | |
| (a) Private Ownership Rights | | | | | | | | | | | | | | |
| (b) Viability of Contracts | | | | | | | | | | | | | | |
| (c) Rule of Law | | | | | | | | | | | | | | |
| **VI. International Exchange** | | | **5.4** | | **5.9** | | **4.7** | | **5.9** | | **6.2** | | **6.4** | |
| (a) Taxes on International Trade | | | | | | | | | | | | | | |
| i. Taxes as a Percentage of Exports and Imports | | | 5.6 | (6.6) | 6.1 | (5.8) | 4.7 | (7.9) | 5.7 | (6.4) | 6.6 | (5.1) | 6.9 | (4.7) |
| ii. Mean Tariff Rate | | | | | | | | | | | | | | |
| iii. Standard Deviation of Tariff Rates | | | | | | | | | | | | | | |
| (b) Non-tariff Regulatory Trade Barriers | | | | | | | | | | | | | | |
| i. Non-tariff Trade Restraints (% of trade covered) | | | | | | | | | | | | | | |
| ii. Size of Trade Sector (% of GDP) | 5.9 | (100.0) | 4.9 | (86.6) | 5.4 | (100.5) | 4.5 | (89.1) | 6.3 | (129.6) | 5.3 | (115.1) | 5.1 | (113.6) |
| **VII. Freedom of Exchange in Financial Markets** | | | **3.3** | | **4.8** | | **5.4** | | **4.3** | | **4.8** | | **4.7** | |
| (a) Ownership of Banks | | | 2.0 | (10-40) | 2.0 | (10-40) | 2.0 | (10-40) | 2.0 | (10-40) | 2.0 | (10-40) | 2.0 | (10-40) |
| (b) Extension of Credit | 7.0 | (72.6) | 6.8 | (70.8) | 7.0 | (72.6) | 7.5 | (77.2) | 8.2 | (83.3) | 8.3 | (84.6) | 7.8 | (80.1) |
| (c) Avoidance of Negative Interest Rates | | | 0.0 | | 6.0 | | 8.0 | | 6.0 | | 8.0 | | 8.0 | |
| (d) Capital Transactions with Foreigners | 5.0 | | 5.0 | | 5.0 | | 5.0 | | 2.0 | | 2.0 | | 2.0 | |

# FINLAND

| | 1970 | 1975 | 1980 | 1985 | 1990 | 1995 | 1997 |
|---|---|---|---|---|---|---|---|
| **Summary Ratings** | 8.1 | 6.7 | 7.1 | 7.4 | 7.7 | 8.1 | 8.2 |
| **Rank** | 8 | 17 | 13 | 14 | 15 | 16 | 18 |

| Components of Economic Freedom | 1970 | | 1975 | | 1980 | | 1985 | | 1990 | | 1995 | | 1997 | |
|---|---|---|---|---|---|---|---|---|---|---|---|---|---|---|
| **I. Size of Government** | **7.1** | | **6.4** | | **6.2** | | **5.8** | | **5.7** | | **4.7** | | **4.9** | |
| (a) Government Consumption (% of Total) | 7.1 | (20.3) | 6.5 | (23.4) | 6.3 | (24.9) | 5.9 | (27.0) | 5.6 | (28.7) | 5.6 | (28.7) | 5.6 | (28.7) |
| (b) Transfers and Subsidies (% of GDP) | | | 6.3 | (14.1) | 6.2 | (14.3) | 5.8 | (15.8) | 5.8 | (16.0) | 3.9 | (22.8) | 4.2 | (21.9) |
| **II. Structure of the Economy and Use of Markets** | | | **4.6** | | **4.2** | | **4.2** | | **4.2** | | **5.7** | | **5.4** | |
| (a) Government Enterprises | 7.0 | (22.4) | 7.0 | (18.9) | 7.0 | (23.3) | 7.0 | (24.2) | 6.0 | (29.3) | 6.0 | (42.2) | 6.0 | |
| (b) Price Controls | | | | | | | | | 6.0 | | 9.0 | | 8.0 | |
| (c) Top Marginal Tax Rate | | | 2.0 | (61-68) | 1.0 | (65-71) | 1.0 | (64-70) | 0.0 | (63-69) | 2.0 | (55-61) | 2.0 | (53-60) |
| (d) Conscription | 3.0 | | 3.0 | | 3.0 | | 3.0 | | 3.0 | | 3.0 | | 3.0 | |
| **III. Monetary Policy and Price Stability** | **9.0** | | **7.1** | | **8.7** | | **8.7** | | **9.0** | | **7.7** | | **9.3** | |
| (a) Annual Money Growth (last 5 yrs.) | 8.8 | (5.8) | 6.2 | (18.8) | 8.9 | (5.5) | 7.9 | (10.3) | 8.6 | (6.8) | 3.9 | (30.3) | 8.4 | (8.2) |
| (b) Inflation Variability (last 5 yrs.) | 8.8 | (3.1) | 7.9 | (5.3) | 9.3 | (1.8) | 9.3 | (1.9) | 9.6 | (0.9) | 9.7 | (0.7) | 9.8 | (0.5) |
| (c) Recent Inflation Rate | 9.2 | (3.9) | 7.3 | (13.3) | 8.1 | (9.8) | 8.9 | (5.3) | 8.8 | (5.8) | 9.5 | (2.4) | 9.7 | (1.5) |
| **IV. Freedom to Use Alternative Currencies** | **7.5** | | **7.4** | | **7.4** | | **7.5** | | **10.0** | | **10.0** | | **10.0** | |
| (a) Ownership of Foreign Currency | 5.0 | | 5.0 | | 5.0 | | 5.0 | | 10.0 | | 10.0 | | 10.0 | |
| (b) Black Market Exchange Rates (Prem.) | 10.0 | (0.0) | 9.8 | (1.0) | 9.8 | (1.0) | 10.0 | (0.0) | 10.0 | (0.0) | 10.0 | (0.0) | 10.0 | (0.0) |
| **V. Legal Structure and Property Rights** | **9.1** | | **7.5** | | **8.1** | | **9.1** | | **9.6** | | **10.0** | | **10.0** | |
| (a) Private Ownership Rights | 8.3 | | 5.3 | | 5.8 | | 8.7 | | 10.0 | | 10.0 | | 10.0 | |
| (b) Viability of Contracts | 9.9 | | 9.7 | | 8.6 | | 8.8 | | 8.8 | | 10.0 | | 10.0 | |
| (c) Rule of Law | | | | | 10.0 | | 10.0 | | 10.0 | | 10.0 | | 10.0 | |
| **VI. International Exchange** | **7.9** | | **7.6** | | **8.5** | | **8.6** | | **7.7** | | **8.4** | | **8.4** | |
| (a) Taxes on International Trade | | | | | | | | | | | | | | |
| i. Taxes as a Percentage of Exports and Imports | 9.0 | (1.5) | 8.9 | (1.6) | 9.5 | (0.8) | 9.7 | (0.4) | 9.6 | (0.6) | 9.9 | (0.2) | 9.7 | (0.5) |
| ii. Mean Tariff Rate | | | 7.4 | (13.2) | 7.9 | (10.4) | 8.6 | (7.0) | 8.5 | (7.7) | 8.7 | (6.7) | 8.6 | (6.9) |
| iii. Standard Deviation of Tariff Rates | | | | | | | | | 6.0 | (10.1) | 7.6 | (5.9) | 7.6 | (6.0) |
| (b) Non-tariff Regulatory Trade Barriers | | | | | | | | | | | | | | |
| i. Non-tariff Trade Restraints (% of trade covered) | | | | | 9.2 | (7.9) | 9.2 | (8.0) | 8.8 | (11.7) | 9.0 | (10.1) | 9.3 | (6.7) |
| ii. Size of Trade Sector (% of GDP) | 5.1 | (52.6) | 5.0 | (54.0) | 5.8 | (67.1) | 4.7 | (58.1) | 3.1 | (47.6) | 4.9 | (68.2) | 4.9 | (70.7) |
| **VII. Freedom of Exchange in Financial Markets** | | | **6.4** | | **6.8** | | **7.3** | | **7.3** | | **8.7** | | **8.7** | |
| (a) Ownership of Banks | | | 8.0 | (75-90) | 8.0 | (75-90) | 8.0 | (75-90) | 8.0 | (75-95) | 8.0 | (75-95) | 8.0 | (75-95) |
| (b) Extension of Credit | 9.6 | (96.1) | 9.9 | (99.0) | 9.9 | (98.8) | 9.9 | (99.0) | 10.0 | (99.6) | 8.9 | (90.3) | 8.9 | (89.9) |
| (c) Avoidance of Negative Interest Rates | | | | | 8.0 | | 10.0 | | 10.0 | | 10.0 | | 10.0 | |
| (d) Capital Transactions with Foreigners | 2.0 | | 2.0 | | 2.0 | | 2.0 | | 2.0 | | 8.0 | | 8.0 | |

# FRANCE

| | 1970 | 1975 | 1980 | 1985 | 1990 | 1995 | 1997 |
|---|---|---|---|---|---|---|---|
| **Summary Ratings** | 7.3 | 6.3 | 6.3 | 6.4 | 7.8 | 8.1 | 8.0 |
| **Rank** | 16 | 23 | 25 | 27 | 14 | 16 | 25 |

| Components of Economic Freedom | 1970 | | 1975 | | 1980 | | 1985 | | 1990 | | 1995 | | 1997 | |
|---|---|---|---|---|---|---|---|---|---|---|---|---|---|---|
| **I. Size of Government** | **6.1** | | **5.2** | | **4.8** | | **4.6** | | **4.9** | | **4.5** | | **4.3** | |
| (a) Government Consumption (% of Total) | 7.1 | (20.2) | 6.8 | (22.0) | 6.5 | (23.5) | 6.4 | (24.1) | 6.6 | (23.2) | 6.4 | (24.3) | 6.4 | (24.2) |
| (b) Transfers and Subsidies (% of GDP) | 5.1 | (18.5) | 3.6 | (24.0) | 3.0 | (26.1) | 2.8 | (26.8) | 3.3 | (25.2) | 2.5 | (27.9) | 2.3 | (28.8) |
| **II. Structure of the Economy and Use of Markets** | | | **4.2** | | **3.5** | | **2.7** | | **4.3** | | **5.3** | | **5.5** | |
| (a) Government Enterprises | 4.0 | | 4.0 | | 4.0 | (27.4) | 4.0 | (33.2) | 4.0 | (35.0) | 4.0 | (30.0) | 4.0 | |
| (b) Price Controls | | | | | | | | | 6.0 | | 8.0 | | 8.0 | |
| (c) Top Marginal Tax Rate | | | 5.0 | (48) | 3.0 | (60) | 1.0 | (65) | 3.0 | (53) | 4.0 | (51) | 5.0 | (48) |
| (d) Conscription | 1.0 | | 3.0 | | 3.0 | | 3.0 | | 3.0 | | 3.0 | | 3.0 | |
| **III. Monetary Policy and Price Stability** | **9.4** | | **8.2** | | **8.4** | | **8.8** | | **9.5** | | **9.8** | | **9.7** | |
| (a) Annual Money Growth (last 5 yrs.) | 10.0 | (0.2) | 8.3 | (8.4) | 8.0 | (10.2) | 8.4 | (8.1) | 9.4 | (2.8) | 9.9 | (-0.7) | 9.7 | (1.7) |
| (b) Inflation Variability (last 5 yrs.) | 9.4 | (1.4) | 8.9 | (2.6) | 9.7 | (0.8) | 9.1 | (2.3) | 9.6 | (0.9) | 9.7 | (0.7) | 9.8 | (0.5) |
| (c) Recent Inflation Rate | 8.9 | (5.6) | 7.4 | (13.0) | 7.7 | (11.4) | 8.8 | (5.8) | 9.4 | (3.1) | 9.7 | (1.6) | 9.8 | (1.0) |
| **IV. Freedom to Use Alternative Currencies** | **4.8** | | **5.0** | | **4.7** | | **4.6** | | **10.0** | | **10.0** | | **10.0** | |
| (a) Ownership of Foreign Currency | 0.0 | | 0.0 | | 0.0 | | 0.0 | | 10.0 | | 10.0 | | 10.0 | |
| (b) Black Market Exchange Rates (Prem.) | 9.6 | (2.0) | 10.0 | (0.0) | 9.4 | (3.0) | 9.2 | (4.0) | 10.0 | (0.0) | 10.0 | (0.0) | 10.0 | (0.0) |
| **V. Legal Structure and Property Rights** | **8.5** | | **5.9** | | **6.7** | | **8.3** | | **9.1** | | **10.0** | | **9.0** | |
| (a) Private Ownership Rights | 8.7 | | 5.2 | | 5.8 | | 8.7 | | 10.0 | | 10.0 | | 10.0 | |
| (b) Viability of Contracts | 8.2 | | 6.7 | | 4.7 | | 7.9 | | 8.8 | | 10.0 | | 10.0 | |
| (c) Rule of Law | | | | | 10.0 | | 8.2 | | 8.3 | | 10.0 | | 7.0 | |
| **VI. International Exchange** | **8.3** | | **8.3** | | **8.5** | | **8.5** | | **8.3** | | **8.4** | | **8.5** | |
| (a) Taxes on International Trade | | | | | | | | | | | | | | |
| i. Taxes as a Percentage of Exports and Imports | 9.7 | (0.4) | 9.9 | (0.1) | 9.7 | (0.5) | 9.7 | (0.4) | 9.7 | (0.4) | 9.8 | (0.3) | 9.8 | (0.3) |
| ii. Mean Tariff Rate | | | 7.8 | (11.0) | 8.2 | (8.8) | 8.5 | (7.5) | 8.5 | (7.4) | 8.7 | (6.7) | 8.6 | (6.9) |
| iii. Standard Deviation of Tariff Rates | | | | | | | | | 7.1 | (7.2) | 7.6 | (5.9) | 7.6 | (6.0) |
| (b) Non-tariff Regulatory Trade Barriers | | | | | | | | | | | | | | |
| i. Non-tariff Trade Restraints (% of trade covered) | | | | | 8.4 | (15.7) | 8.1 | (18.6) | 8.9 | (10.9) | 9.1 | (9.0) | 9.3 | (6.7) |
| ii. Size of Trade Sector (% of GDP) | 4.8 | (31.1) | 5.4 | (36.9) | 6.0 | (44.3) | 6.0 | (47.2) | 5.4 | (45.1) | 5.0 | (44.6) | 5.5 | (49.4) |
| **VII. Freedom of Exchange in Financial Markets** | **6.7** | | **7.2** | | **7.0** | | **7.0** | | **7.9** | | **8.3** | | **8.2** | |
| (a) Ownership of Banks | 10.0 | (95-100) | 10.0 | (95-100) | 10.0 | (95-100) | 10.0 | (95-100) | 10.0 | (95-100) | 10.0 | (95-100) | 10.0 | (95-100) |
| (b) Extension of Credit | 9.3 | (93.8) | 9.5 | (95.0) | 8.6 | (87.2) | 8.3 | (84.5) | 8.9 | (90.2) | 8.2 | (83.6) | 7.8 | (80.4) |
| (c) Avoidance of Negative Interest Rates | 6.0 | | 8.0 | | 8.0 | | 8.0 | | 8.0 | | 10.0 | | 10.0 | |
| (d) Capital Transactions with Foreigners | 2.0 | | 2.0 | | 2.0 | | 2.0 | | 5.0 | | 5.0 | | 5.0 | |

# GABON

| | 1970 | 1975 | 1980 | 1985 | 1990 | 1995 | 1997 |
|---|---|---|---|---|---|---|---|
| **Summary Ratings** | | | 3.8 | 5.2 | 5.2 | 5.7 | 5.1 |
| **Rank** | | | 90 | 56 | 60 | 77 | 97 |

| Components of Economic Freedom | 1970 | | 1975 | | 1980 | | 1985 | | 1990 | | 1995 | | 1997 | |
|---|---|---|---|---|---|---|---|---|---|---|---|---|---|---|
| **I. Size of Government** | **4.4** | | **6.9** | | **4.7** | | **6.6** | | **8.4** | | **8.0** | | **5.9** | |
| (a) Government Consumption (% of Total) | 4.4 | (34.9) | 4.5 | (34.2) | 4.7 | (33.6) | 3.7 | (38.7) | 6.9 | (21.2) | 6.2 | (25.3) | 5.9 | (27.0) |
| (b) Transfers and Subsidies (% of GDP) | | | 9.3 | (3.1) | | | 9.4 | (2.7) | 9.8 | (1.2) | 9.8 | (1.2) | | |
| **II. Structure of the Economy and Use of Markets** | | | | | | | | | **2.4** | | **3.1** | | **2.9** | |
| (a) Government Enterprises | 2.0 | (48.4) | 2.0 | (42.6) | 2.0 | (42.6) | 4.0 | (35.3) | 4.0 | | 4.0 | | 4.0 | |
| (b) Price Controls | | | | | | | | | 0.0 | | 2.0 | | 2.0 | |
| (c) Top Marginal Tax Rate | | | | | | | | | 1.0 | (60) | 1.0 | (60) | 0.0 | (60.5) |
| (d) Conscription | | | 10.0 | | 10.0 | | 10.0 | | 10.0 | | 10.0 | | 10.0 | |
| **III. Monetary Policy and Price Stability** | **9.6** | | **4.8** | | **5.9** | | **8.2** | | **7.3** | | **7.2** | | **6.9** | |
| (a) Annual Money Growth (last 5 yrs.) | 9.7 | (1.4) | 5.1 | (24.5) | 9.6 | (2.2) | 7.4 | (13.0) | 9.7 | (-1.5) | 9.6 | (1.8) | 7.8 | (11.0) |
| (b) Inflation Variability (last 5 yrs.) | 9.0 | (2.5) | 0.0 | (26.3) | 5.4 | (11.4) | 7.4 | (6.5) | 5.2 | (12.1) | 1.9 | (20.3) | 2.8 | (18.1) |
| (c) Recent Inflation Rate | 9.9 | (-0.4) | 9.1 | (4.4) | 2.6 | (36.8) | 9.7 | (-1.3) | 6.9 | (15.4) | 9.9 | (-0.5) | 10.0 | (-0.1) |
| **IV. Freedom to Use Alternative Currencies** | **4.8** | | **4.8** | | **4.8** | | **4.9** | | **4.6** | | **4.9** | | **4.8** | |
| (a) Ownership of Foreign Currency | 0.0 | | 0.0 | | 0.0 | | 0.0 | | 0.0 | | 0.0 | | 0.0 | |
| (b) Black Market Exchange Rates (Prem.) | 9.6 | (2.0) | 9.6 | (2.0) | 9.6 | (2.0) | 9.8 | (1.0) | 9.2 | (4.0) | 9.8 | (1.0) | 9.6 | (2.0) |
| **V. Legal Structure and Property Rights** | | | | | **3.6** | | **4.8** | | **5.7** | | **7.2** | | **6.9** | |
| (a) Private Ownership Rights | | | | | 4.5 | | 6.1 | | 7.3 | | 7.7 | | 7.2 | |
| (b) Viability of Contracts | | | | | 3.0 | | 5.2 | | 6.4 | | 6.8 | | 6.6 | |
| (c) Rule of Law | | | | | 3.3 | | 3.1 | | 3.3 | | 7.0 | | 7.0 | |
| **VI. International Exchange** | **4.3** | | **4.9** | | **3.6** | | **6.1** | | **6.0** | | **7.1** | | | |
| (a) Taxes on International Trade | | | | | | | | | | | | | | |
| i. Taxes as a Percentage of Exports and Imports | 3.8 | (9.3) | 4.5 | (8.2) | 5.1 | (7.3) | 5.7 | (6.4) | 6.8 | (4.8) | 5.8 | (6.3) | | |
| ii. Mean Tariff Rate | | | | | 1.3 | (43.3) | 4.1 | (29.6) | | | | | | |
| iii. Standard Deviation of Tariff Rates | | | | | | | | | | | | | | |
| (b) Non-tariff Regulatory Trade Barriers | | | | | | | | | | | | | | |
| i. Non-tariff Trade Restraints (% of trade covered) | | | | | | | 9.3 | (6.6) | | | 9.6 | (4.0) | | |
| ii. Size of Trade Sector (% of GDP) | 5.6 | (87.7) | 6.0 | (97.4) | 5.7 | (96.4) | 5.6 | (98.5) | 4.1 | (76.9) | 4.9 | (93.1) | 5.0 | (96.2) |
| **VII. Freedom of Exchange in Financial Markets** | | | | | **1.9** | | **2.5** | | **3.8** | | **3.3** | | **4.0** | |
| (a) Ownership of Banks | 0.0 | (0-10) | 0.0 | (0-10) | 0.0 | (0-10) | 0.0 | (0-10) | 2.0 | (10-40) | 5.0 | (40-75) | 5.0 | (40-75) |
| (b) Extension of Credit | | | | | | | | | 5.9 | (62.9) | 4.7 | (51.9) | 5.6 | (60.1) |
| (c) Avoidance of Negative Interest Rates | | | | | 6.0 | | 8.0 | | 8.0 | | 4.0 | | 6.0 | |
| (d) Capital Transactions with Foreigners | 0.0 | | 0.0 | | 0.0 | | 0.0 | | 0.0 | | 0.0 | | 0.0 | |

# GERMANY

| | 1970 | 1975 | 1980 | 1985 | 1990 | 1995 | 1997 |
|---|---|---|---|---|---|---|---|
| **Summary Ratings** | 8.2 | 7.7 | 7.8 | 7.9 | 8.3 | 8.2 | 8.1 |
| **Rank** | 7 | 7 | 8 | 9 | 7 | 12 | 22 |

| Components of Economic Freedom | 1970 | | 1975 | | 1980 | | 1985 | | 1990 | | 1995 | | 1997 | |
|---|---|---|---|---|---|---|---|---|---|---|---|---|---|---|
| **I. Size of Government** | **6.4** | | **5.7** | | **5.7** | | **5.5** | | **5.7** | | **5.2** | | **5.2** | |
| (a) Government Consumption (% of Total) | 6.7 | (22.4) | 6.0 | (26.5) | 6.0 | (26.3) | 6.0 | (26.1) | 6.2 | (25.2) | 6.1 | (25.8) | 6.1 | (25.6) |
| (b) Transfers and Subsidies (% of GDP) | 6.1 | (14.8) | 5.4 | (17.4) | 5.3 | (17.6) | 5.0 | (19.0) | 5.3 | (17.9) | 4.3 | (21.6) | 4.4 | (21.2) |
| **II. Structure of the Economy and Use of Markets** | **5.1** | | **5.1** | | **4.7** | | **4.3** | | **5.8** | | **6.0** | | **5.2** | |
| (a) Government Enterprises | 7.0 | | 7.0 | | 7.0 | (25.7) | 7.0 | (24.4) | 6.0 | (24.0) | 6.0 | (25.5) | 6.0 | |
| (b) Price Controls | | | | | | | | | 9.0 | | 9.0 | | 8.0 | |
| (c) Top Marginal Tax Rate | 4.0 | (53) | 4.0 | (56) | 3.0 | (56) | 2.0 | (56) | 3.0 | (56) | 3.0 | (57) | 1.0 | (61.7) |
| (d) Conscription | 1.0 | | 1.0 | | 1.0 | | 1.0 | | 1.0 | | 3.0 | | 3.0 | |
| **III. Monetary Policy and Price Stability** | **9.3** | | **9.1** | | **9.2** | | **9.5** | | **9.0** | | **9.4** | | **9.5** | |
| (a) Annual Money Growth (last 5 yrs.) | 9.4 | (2.9) | 8.8 | (6.2) | 9.2 | (4.1) | 9.5 | (2.6) | 8.1 | (9.7) | 9.0 | (5.0) | 9.0 | (4.8) |
| (b) Inflation Variability (last 5 yrs.) | 9.2 | (2.1) | 9.7 | (0.7) | 9.6 | (0.9) | 9.5 | (1.2) | 9.5 | (1.2) | 9.5 | (1.2) | 9.5 | (1.2) |
| (c) Recent Inflation Rate | 9.3 | (3.4) | 8.8 | (6.0) | 8.9 | (5.5) | 9.6 | (2.2) | 9.5 | (2.7) | 9.6 | (2.1) | 9.8 | (0.8) |
| **IV. Freedom to Use Alternative Currencies** | **10.0** | | **10.0** | | **10.0** | | **10.0** | | **10.0** | | **10.0** | | **10.0** | |
| (a) Ownership of Foreign Currency | 10.0 | | 10.0 | | 10.0 | | 10.0 | | 10.0 | | 10.0 | | 10.0 | |
| (b) Black Market Exchange Rates (Prem.) | 10.0 | (0.0) | 10.0 | (0.0) | 10.0 | (0.0) | 10.0 | (0.0) | 10.0 | (0.0) | 10.0 | (0.0) | 10.0 | (0.0) |
| **V. Legal Structure and Property Rights** | **9.9** | | **8.5** | | **8.6** | | **8.8** | | **10.0** | | **10.0** | | **10.0** | |
| (a) Private Ownership Rights | 10.0 | | 7.6 | | 8.2 | | 9.4 | | 10.0 | | 10.0 | | 10.0 | |
| (b) Viability of Contracts | 9.9 | | 9.4 | | 7.8 | | 8.8 | | 10.0 | | 10.0 | | 10.0 | |
| (c) Rule of Law | | | | | 10.0 | | 8.2 | | 10.0 | | 10.0 | | 10.0 | |
| **VI. International Exchange** | **8.5** | | **8.4** | | **8.7** | | **8.8** | | **8.4** | | **8.4** | | **8.5** | |
| (a) Taxes on International Trade | | | | | | | | | | | | | | |
| i. Taxes as a Percentage of Exports and Imports | 9.7 | (0.5) | 9.7 | (0.5) | 9.7 | (0.5) | 9.7 | (0.5) | 9.7 | (0.5) | 9.7 | (0.5) | 9.7 | (0.5) |
| ii. Mean Tariff Rate | | | 8.1 | (9.4) | 8.2 | (8.8) | 8.5 | (7.5) | 8.5 | (7.4) | 8.7 | (6.7) | 8.6 | (6.9) |
| iii. Standard Deviation of Tariff Rates | | | | | | | | | 7.1 | (7.2) | 7.6 | (5.9) | 7.6 | (6.0) |
| (b) Non-tariff Regulatory Trade Barriers | | | | | | | | | | | | | | |
| i. Non-tariff Trade Restraints (% of trade covered) | | | | | 8.8 | (11.8) | 8.5 | (15.4) | 8.9 | (10.9) | 9.1 | (9.0) | 9.3 | (6.7) |
| ii. Size of Trade Sector (% of GDP) | 5.4 | (36.5) | 6.2 | (44.5) | 7.1 | (55.1) | 7.7 | (63.8) | 7.0 | (61.6) | 5.2 | (46.4) | 5.4 | (49.8) |
| **VII. Freedom of Exchange in Financial Markets** | **7.7** | | **7.1** | | **7.6** | | **8.1** | | **8.2** | | **8.1** | | **8.1** | |
| (a) Ownership of Banks | 5.0 | (40-50) | 5.0 | (48-50) | 5.0 | (48-50) | 5.0 | (48-50) | 5.0 | (49) | 5.0 | (49) | 5.0 | (49) |
| (b) Extension of Credit | 8.2 | (84.0) | 7.8 | (79.8) | 7.6 | (78.2) | 7.5 | (77.3) | 7.7 | (79.3) | 7.4 | (76.4) | 7.4 | (76.5) |
| (c) Avoidance of Negative Interest Rates | 10.0 | | 8.0 | | 10.0 | | 10.0 | | 10.0 | | 10.0 | | 10.0 | |
| (d) Capital Transactions with Foreigners | 8.0 | | 8.0 | | 8.0 | | 10.0 | | 10.0 | | 10.0 | | 10.0 | |

# GHANA

| | 1970 | 1975 | 1980 | 1985 | 1990 | 1995 | 1997 |
|---|---|---|---|---|---|---|---|
| **Summary Ratings** | 3.3 | 2.5 | 2.1 | 2.6 | 4.8 | 6.1 | 6.4 |
| **Rank** | 56 | 81 | 106 | 107 | 77 | 67 | 68 |

| Components of Economic Freedom | 1970 | | 1975 | | 1980 | | 1985 | | 1990 | | 1995 | | 1997 | |
|---|---|---|---|---|---|---|---|---|---|---|---|---|---|---|
| **I. Size of Government** | **8.8** | | **8.7** | | **9.1** | | **9.4** | | **9.2** | | **8.8** | | **8.7** | |
| (a) Government Consumption (% of Total) | 8.1 | (14.7) | 8.1 | (15.1) | 8.7 | (11.7) | 9.0 | (10.1) | 9.0 | (9.9) | 8.3 | (13.8) | 8.7 | (11.4) |
| (b) Transfers and Subsidies (% of GDP) | 9.5 | (2.4) | 9.3 | (3.1) | 9.5 | (2.4) | 9.8 | (1.3) | 9.4 | (2.6) | 9.2 | (3.3) | | |
| **II. Structure of the Economy and Use of Markets** | **1.3** | | **1.3** | | **1.7** | | **1.7** | | **2.0** | | **5.3** | | **5.9** | |
| (a) Government Enterprises | 0.0 | (45.8) | 0.0 | (34.1) | 0.0 | (35.4) | 0.0 | | 2.0 | (25.0) | 4.0 | | 4.0 | |
| (b) Price Controls | | | | | | | | | 0.0 | | 4.0 | | 6.0 | |
| (c) Top Marginal Tax Rate | 0.0 | (70) | 0.0 | (70) | 1.0 | (60) | 1.0 | (60) | 2.0 | (55) | 7.0 | (35) | 7.0 | (35) |
| (d) Conscription | 10.0 | | 10.0 | | 10.0 | | 10.0 | | 10.0 | | 10.0 | | 10.0 | |
| **III. Monetary Policy and Price Stability** | **8.9** | | **5.2** | | **1.5** | | **2.4** | | **5.4** | | **3.6** | | **5.4** | |
| (a) Annual Money Growth (last 5 yrs.) | 9.6 | (2.0) | 4.9 | (25.7) | 1.4 | (42.9) | 1.2 | (44.2) | 2.4 | (37.9) | 3.9 | (30.4) | 3.4 | (33.0) |
| (b) Inflation Variability (last 5 yrs.) | 7.6 | (6.0) | 6.7 | (8.3) | 3.2 | (17.1) | 0.0 | (38.3) | 8.0 | (5.0) | 5.6 | (10.9) | 6.7 | (8.3) |
| (c) Recent Inflation Rate | 9.4 | (2.9) | 4.1 | (29.5) | 0.0 | (51.1) | 5.9 | (20.7) | 5.9 | (20.7) | 1.4 | (43.2) | 6.1 | (19.5) |
| **IV. Freedom to Use Alternative Currencies** | **0.0** | | **0.0** | | **0.0** | | **0.0** | | **4.3** | | **7.3** | | **7.4** | |
| (a) Ownership of Foreign Currency | 0.0 | | 0.0 | | 0.0 | | 0.0 | | 0.0 | | 5.0 | | 5.0 | |
| (b) Black Market Exchange Rates (Prem.) | 0.0 | (66.0) | 0.0 | (67.0) | 0.0 | (304.0) | 0.0 | (142.0) | 8.6 | (7.0) | 9.6 | (2.0) | 9.8 | (1.0) |
| **V. Legal Structure and Property Rights** | | | | | **3.0** | | **2.4** | | **6.0** | | **6.6** | | **6.9** | |
| (a) Private Ownership Rights | | | | | 2.8 | | 2.9 | | 4.6 | | 7.7 | | 7.2 | |
| (b) Viability of Contracts | | | | | 4.3 | | 2.8 | | 5.2 | | 5.2 | | 6.6 | |
| (c) Rule of Law | | | | | 1.7 | | 1.4 | | 8.3 | | 7.0 | | 7.0 | |
| **VI. International Exchange** | **1.3** | | **1.0** | | **0.0** | | **2.6** | | **5.7** | | **6.7** | | | |
| (a) Taxes on International Trade | | | | | | | | | | | | | | |
| i. Taxes as a Percentage of Exports and Imports | 0.0 | (15.1) | 0.0 | (20.6) | 0.0 | (17.3) | 0.0 | (21.7) | 2.3 | (11.6) | 4.6 | (8.1) | | |
| ii. Mean Tariff Rate | | | | | | | 4.0 | (30.0) | 6.5 | (17.5) | 7.0 | (15.0) | | |
| iii. Standard Deviation of Tariff Rates | | | | | | | | | | | 6.7 | (8.3) | | |
| (b) Non-tariff Regulatory Trade Barriers | | | | | | | | | | | | | | |
| i. Non-tariff Trade Restraints (% of trade covered) | | | | | | | 5.2 | (48.4) | 9.8 | (2.0) | 9.8 | (2.0) | | |
| ii. Size of Trade Sector (% of GDP) | 4.6 | (44.0) | 3.5 | (37.8) | 0.0 | (17.6) | 0.0 | (23.3) | 3.5 | (42.7) | 5.2 | (59.8) | 5.5 | (65.0) |
| **VII. Freedom of Exchange in Financial Markets** | | | **1.8** | | **1.1** | | **1.6** | | **2.6** | | **4.2** | | **4.4** | |
| (a) Ownership of Banks | | | 2.0 | (10-40) | 2.0 | (10-40) | 2.0 | (10-40) | 2.0 | (10-40) | 5.0 | (40-75) | 5.0 | (40-75) |
| (b) Extension of Credit | 5.6 | (60.7) | 4.0 | (45.7) | 2.5 | (32.9) | 4.9 | (54.4) | 7.5 | (77.8) | 8.9 | (89.8) | 5.2 | (56.5) |
| (c) Avoidance of Negative Interest Rates | | | | | 0.0 | | 0.0 | | 2.0 | | 4.0 | | 8.0 | |
| (d) Capital Transactions with Foreigners | 0.0 | | 0.0 | | 0.0 | | 0.0 | | 0.0 | | 0.0 | | 0.0 | |

# GREECE

| | 1970 | 1975 | 1980 | 1985 | 1990 | 1995 | 1997 |
|---|---|---|---|---|---|---|---|
| **Summary Ratings** | 6.3 | 5.8 | 5.7 | 5.2 | 6.1 | 6.8 | 7.4 |
| **Rank** | 32 | 35 | 38 | 56 | 43 | 49 | 42 |

| Components of Economic Freedom | 1970 | | 1975 | | 1980 | | 1985 | | 1990 | | 1995 | | 1997 | |
|---|---|---|---|---|---|---|---|---|---|---|---|---|---|---|
| **I. Size of Government** | **9.2** | | **8.8** | | **8.4** | | **6.5** | | **6.1** | | **6.4** | | **6.7** | |
| (a) Government Consumption (% of Total) | 8.8 | (11.0) | 8.4 | (13.2) | 8.1 | (14.7) | 7.6 | (17.5) | 7.7 | (17.3) | 7.8 | (16.4) | 7.9 | (16.1) |
| (b) Transfers and Subsidies (% of GDP) | 9.6 | (1.9) | 9.3 | (3.1) | 8.6 | (5.7) | 5.3 | (17.7) | 4.6 | (20.5) | 5.0 | (19.0) | 5.5 | (17.0) |
| **II. Structure of the Economy and Use of Markets** | | | **3.5** | | **2.1** | | **1.4** | | **1.7** | | **4.2** | | **4.6** | |
| (a) Government Enterprises | 6.0 | (28.4) | 4.0 | (29.0) | 2.0 | (32.0) | 2.0 | (41.0) | 2.0 | (37.5) | 4.0 | (35.8) | 4.0 | |
| (b) Price Controls | | | | | | | | | 0.0 | | 5.0 | | 6.0 | |
| (c) Top Marginal Tax Rate | | | 4.0 | (52) | 3.0 | (60) | 1.0 | (63) | 4.0 | (50) | 5.0 | (45) | 5.0 | (45) |
| (d) Conscription | 0.0 | | 0.0 | | 0.0 | | 0.0 | | 0.0 | | 0.0 | | 0.0 | |
| **III. Monetary Policy and Price Stability** | **9.4** | | **7.4** | | **7.6** | | **7.4** | | **7.3** | | **8.0** | | **8.5** | |
| (a) Annual Money Growth (last 5 yrs.) | 9.3 | (3.4) | 7.4 | (12.9) | 7.2 | (14.1) | 6.7 | (16.4) | 6.3 | (18.4) | 7.2 | (14.0) | 7.3 | (13.7) |
| (b) Inflation Variability (last 5 yrs.) | 9.6 | (1.1) | 7.1 | (7.2) | 9.1 | (2.4) | 9.0 | (2.5) | 9.1 | (2.4) | 8.5 | (3.8) | 9.4 | (1.6) |
| (c) Recent Inflation Rate | 9.2 | (3.9) | 7.5 | (12.3) | 6.5 | (17.7) | 6.5 | (17.7) | 6.5 | (17.7) | 8.2 | (8.9) | 8.9 | (5.5) |
| **IV. Freedom to Use Alternative Currencies** | **7.3** | | **7.2** | | **6.8** | | **5.0** | | **7.2** | | **7.5** | | **10.0** | |
| (a) Ownership of Foreign Currency | 5.0 | | 5.0 | | 5.0 | | 5.0 | | 5.0 | | 5.0 | | 10.0 | |
| (b) Black Market Exchange Rates (Prem.) | 9.6 | (2.0) | 9.4 | (3.0) | 8.6 | (7.0) | 5.0 | (25.0) | 9.4 | (3.0) | 10.0 | (0.0) | 10.0 | (0.0) |
| **V. Legal Structure and Property Rights** | **5.7** | | **5.6** | | **5.5** | | **5.6** | | **7.7** | | **7.6** | | **7.5** | |
| (a) Private Ownership Rights | 6.1 | | 5.9 | | 4.0 | | 4.2 | | 7.3 | | 7.7 | | 7.2 | |
| (b) Viability of Contracts | 5.4 | | 5.4 | | 4.3 | | 4.6 | | 7.6 | | 5.2 | | 8.3 | |
| (c) Rule of Law | | | | | 8.3 | | 8.2 | | 8.3 | | 10.0 | | 7.0 | |
| **VI. International Exchange** | **4.9** | | **7.1** | | **7.5** | | **8.0** | | **8.0** | | **8.2** | | **8.1** | |
| (a) Taxes on International Trade | | | | | | | | | | | | | | |
| i. Taxes as a Percentage of Exports and Imports | 6.9 | (4.7) | 7.7 | (3.5) | 7.9 | (3.2) | 9.5 | (0.7) | 9.6 | (0.6) | 9.7 | (0.4) | 9.7 | (0.4) |
| ii. Mean Tariff Rate | | | 8.1 | (9.4) | 8.2 | (8.8) | 8.5 | (7.5) | 8.5 | (7.4) | 8.7 | (6.7) | 8.6 | (6.9) |
| iii. Standard Deviation of Tariff Rates | | | | | | | | | 7.1 | (7.2) | 7.6 | (5.9) | 7.6 | (6.0) |
| (b) Non-tariff Regulatory Trade Barriers | | | | | | | | | | | | | | |
| i. Non-tariff Trade Restraints (% of trade covered) | | | | | 8.4 | (16.2) | 7.9 | (21.0) | 8.9 | (10.9) | 9.1 | (9.0) | 9.3 | (6.7) |
| ii. Size of Trade Sector (% of GDP) | 0.0 | (23.5) | 2.6 | (36.0) | 2.8 | (38.6) | 3.3 | (44.4) | 2.9 | (44.9) | 2.2 | (43.4) | 1.0 | (38.3) |
| **VII. Freedom of Exchange in Financial Markets** | **3.9** | | **2.9** | | **3.4** | | **3.4** | | **4.6** | | **5.6** | | **6.4** | |
| (a) Ownership of Banks | 2.0 | (10-40) | 2.0 | (10-40) | 2.0 | (10-40) | 2.0 | (10-40) | 5.0 | (40-60) | 5.0 | (40-60) | 5.0 | (40-60) |
| (b) Extension of Credit | 4.1 | (47.0) | 4.0 | (46.4) | 4.1 | (47.3) | 3.8 | (43.8) | 3.2 | (39.0) | 4.3 | (49.1) | 4.3 | (48.9) |
| (c) Avoidance of Negative Interest Rates | 8.0 | | 4.0 | | 6.0 | | 6.0 | | 8.0 | | 8.0 | | 8.0 | |
| (d) Capital Transactions with Foreigners | 2.0 | | 2.0 | | 2.0 | | 2.0 | | 2.0 | | 5.0 | | 8.0 | |

# GUATEMALA

| | 1970 | 1975 | 1980 | 1985 | 1990 | 1995 | 1997 |
|---|---|---|---|---|---|---|---|
| **Summary Ratings** | 6.4 | 7.3 | 6.5 | 5.6 | 6.5 | 7.7 | 7.4 |
| **Rank** | 29 | 13 | 23 | 47 | 36 | 34 | 42 |

| Components of Economic Freedom | 1970 | | 1975 | | 1980 | | 1985 | | 1990 | | 1995 | | 1997 | |
|---|---|---|---|---|---|---|---|---|---|---|---|---|---|---|
| **I. Size of Government** | **9.5** | | **9.6** | | **9.5** | | **9.6** | | **9.6** | | **9.9** | | **9.9** | |
| (a) Government Consumption (% of Total) | 9.1 | (9.2) | 9.4 | (8.0) | 9.2 | (9.2) | 9.4 | (7.8) | 9.5 | (7.3) | 9.7 | (6.0) | 9.9 | (5.4) |
| (b) Transfers and Subsidies (% of GDP) | 9.9 | (0.7) | 9.9 | (0.8) | 9.8 | (1.2) | 9.8 | (1.3) | 9.6 | (1.8) | 10.0 | (0.5) | 9.9 | (0.8) |
| **II. Structure of the Economy and Use of Markets** | | | **8.6** | | **8.3** | | **5.8** | | **6.4** | | **6.6** | | **7.3** | |
| (a) Government Enterprises | 8.0 | (19.2) | 8.0 | (20.9) | 8.0 | (37.4) | 8.0 | (32.1) | 8.0 | (21.0) | 8.0 | (17.3) | 8.0 | |
| (b) Price Controls | | | | | | | | | 6.0 | | 6.0 | | 8.0 | |
| (c) Top Marginal Tax Rate | | | 9.0 | (34) | 8.0 | (40) | 5.0 | (48) | 7.0 | (34) | 8.0 | (30) | 8.0 | (30) |
| (d) Conscription | 0.0 | | 10.0 | | 10.0 | | 0.0 | | 0.0 | | 0.0 | | 0.0 | |
| **III. Monetary Policy and Price Stability** | **9.4** | | **7.4** | | **8.1** | | **7.4** | | **5.5** | | **7.2** | | **7.8** | |
| (a) Annual Money Growth (last 5 yrs.) | 9.9 | (-0.5) | 8.1 | (9.7) | 7.9 | (10.7) | 8.0 | (10.1) | 6.3 | (18.3) | 6.9 | (15.5) | 6.1 | (19.4) |
| (b) Inflation Variability (last 5 yrs.) | 9.2 | (2.0) | 6.9 | (7.8) | 8.6 | (3.6) | 7.9 | (5.3) | 3.9 | (15.2) | 6.4 | (9.1) | 9.1 | (2.4) |
| (c) Recent Inflation Rate | 9.0 | (5.0) | 7.4 | (13.1) | 8.0 | (10.0) | 6.2 | (18.8) | 6.2 | (18.8) | 8.3 | (8.7) | 8.3 | (8.4) |
| **IV. Freedom to Use Alternative Currencies** | **4.1** | | **6.5** | | **9.0** | | **5.0** | | **10.0** | | **10.0** | | **9.9** | |
| (a) Ownership of Foreign Currency | 0.0 | | 5.0 | | 10.0 | | 10.0 | | 10.0 | | 10.0 | | 10.0 | |
| (b) Black Market Exchange Rates (Prem.) | 8.2 | (9.0) | 8.0 | (10.0) | 8.0 | (10.0) | 0.0 | (89.0) | 10.0 | (0.0) | 10.0 | (0.0) | 9.8 | (1.0) |
| **V. Legal Structure and Property Rights** | | | | | **2.1** | | **2.1** | | **2.5** | | **5.3** | | **4.8** | |
| (a) Private Ownership Rights | | | | | 2.2 | | 0.9 | | 1.9 | | 5.5 | | 4.4 | |
| (b) Viability of Contracts | | | | | 2.4 | | 4.0 | | 4.0 | | 3.7 | | 3.1 | |
| (c) Rule of Law | | | | | 1.7 | | 1.4 | | 1.7 | | 7.0 | | 7.0 | |
| **VI. International Exchange** | **4.9** | | **5.5** | | **3.3** | | **3.9** | | **5.1** | | **7.3** | | **6.0** | |
| (a) Taxes on International Trade | | | | | | | | | | | | | | |
| i. Taxes as a Percentage of Exports and Imports | 5.9 | (6.1) | 6.3 | (5.6) | 6.8 | (4.8) | 5.0 | (7.5) | 7.6 | (3.6) | 7.1 | (4.4) | 7.7 | (3.4) |
| ii. Mean Tariff Rate | | | | | 0.0 | (50.0) | 0.0 | (50.0) | 5.4 | (23.0) | 8.0 | (10.2) | | |
| iii. Standard Deviation of Tariff Rates | | | | | | | | | 0.0 | (26.7) | 7.0 | (7.4) | | |
| (b) Non-tariff Regulatory Trade Barriers | | | | | | | | | | | | | | |
| i. Non-tariff Trade Restraints (% of trade covered) | | | | | | | 9.3 | (7.4) | 9.3 | (7.0) | 9.4 | (6.0) | | |
| ii. Size of Trade Sector (% of GDP) | 2.3 | (36.3) | 3.6 | (45.3) | 3.6 | (47.1) | 0.0 | (24.9) | 2.4 | (43.5) | 2.4 | (44.8) | 1.7 | (42.0) |
| **VII. Freedom of Exchange in Financial Markets** | **6.3** | | **6.9** | | **7.5** | | **7.5** | | **7.5** | | **8.2** | | **7.6** | |
| (a) Ownership of Banks | 8.0 | (80-90) | 8.0 | (85) | 8.0 | (89) | 8.0 | (90) | 8.0 | (91) | 8.0 | (91) | 8.0 | (91) |
| (b) Extension of Credit | 9.5 | (95.1) | 8.0 | (82.1) | 9.5 | (95.7) | 9.3 | (93.7) | 9.4 | (94.7) | 9.1 | (91.5) | 8.5 | (86.2) |
| (c) Avoidance of Negative Interest Rates | | | | | 8.0 | | 8.0 | | 8.0 | | 8.0 | | 6.0 | |
| (d) Capital Transactions with Foreigners | 2.0 | | 5.0 | | 5.0 | | 5.0 | | 5.0 | | 8.0 | | 8.0 | |

# GUINEA-BISSAU

| | 1970 | 1975 | 1980 | 1985 | 1990 | 1995 | 1997 |
|---|---|---|---|---|---|---|---|
| **Summary Ratings** | | | | | 3.8 | 4.1 | 4.0 |
| **Rank** | | | | | 99 | 109 | 118 |

| Components of Economic Freedom | 1970 | | 1975 | | 1980 | | 1985 | | 1990 | | 1995 | | 1997 | |
|---|---|---|---|---|---|---|---|---|---|---|---|---|---|---|
| **I. Size of Government** | **7.0** | | **6.8** | | | | **8.1** | | **8.9** | | **9.7** | | **9.5** | |
| (a) Government Consumption (% of Total) | 7.0 | (20.6) | 6.8 | (21.7) | | | 8.1 | (14.6) | 8.9 | (10.6) | 9.7 | (6.3) | 9.5 | (7.4) |
| (b) Transfers and Subsidies (% of GDP) | | | | | | | | | | | | | | |
| **II. Structure of the Economy and Use of Markets** | | | | | | | | | **2.1** | | **4.8** | | **4.8** | |
| (a) Government Enterprises | 2.0 | | 2.0 | | 2.0 | | 2.0 | | 4.0 | | 4.0 | | 4.0 | |
| (b) Price Controls | | | | | | | | | 0.0 | | 6.0 | | 6.0 | |
| (c) Top Marginal Tax Rate | | | | | | | | | | | | | | |
| (d) Conscription | | | | | | | 3.0 | | 3.0 | | 3.0 | | 3.0 | |
| **III. Monetary Policy and Price Stability** | | | **8.7** | | **8.1** | | **2.9** | | **1.2** | | **1.8** | | **3.0** | |
| (a) Annual Money Growth (last 5 yrs.) | | | | | | | | | 0.0 | (65.1) | 1.0 | (45.2) | 0.0 | (50.3) |
| (b) Inflation Variability (last 5 yrs.) | | | 8.8 | (3.0) | 8.6 | (3.5) | 2.3 | (19.2) | 0.0 | (28.6) | 3.6 | (16.1) | 6.1 | (9.8) |
| (c) Recent Inflation Rate | | | 8.6 | (7.1) | 7.7 | (11.6) | 3.5 | (32.3) | 3.5 | (32.3) | 1.1 | (44.7) | 2.8 | (35.8) |
| **IV. Freedom to Use Alternative Currencies** | | | **0.0** | | **0.0** | | **2.1** | | **4.1** | | **4.8** | | **1.8** | |
| (a) Ownership of Foreign Currency | | | 0.0 | | 0.0 | | 0.0 | | 0.0 | | 0.0 | | 0.0 | |
| (b) Black Market Exchange Rates (Prem.) | | | | | | | 4.2 | (29.0) | 8.2 | (9.0) | 9.6 | (2.0) | 3.6 | (32.0) |
| **V. Legal Structure and Property Rights** | | | | | | | **1.7** | | **2.6** | | **0.2** | | **0.0** | |
| (a) Private Ownership Rights | | | | | | | 0.9 | | 3.2 | | 0.0 | | 0.0 | |
| (b) Viability of Contracts | | | | | | | 2.8 | | 2.8 | | 0.5 | | 0.0 | |
| (c) Rule of Law | | | | | | | 1.4 | | 1.7 | | 0.0 | | 0.0 | |
| **VI. International Exchange** | | | | | | | | | | | | | | |
| (a) Taxes on International Trade | | | | | | | | | | | | | | |
| i. Taxes as a Percentage of Exports and Imports | | | | | | | | | | | | | | |
| ii. Mean Tariff Rate | | | | | | | | | | | | | | |
| iii. Standard Deviation of Tariff Rates | | | | | | | | | | | | | | |
| (b) Non-tariff Regulatory Trade Barriers | | | | | | | | | | | | | | |
| i. Non-tariff Trade Restraints (% of trade covered) | | | | | | | | | | | | | | |
| ii. Size of Trade Sector (% of GDP) | 0.0 | (34.2) | 0.0 | (31.1) | 0.4 | (52.3) | 1.4 | (61.5) | 0.0 | (53.2) | 0.0 | (46.8) | 0.4 | (62.0) |
| **VII. Freedom of Exchange in Financial Markets** | | | | | | | | | **4.0** | | **4.4** | | **6.1** | |
| (a) Ownership of Banks | | | | | | | | | | | | | | |
| (b) Extension of Credit | | | | | | | | | 7.5 | (77.4) | 8.8 | (89.1) | 9.9 | (98.6) |
| (c) Avoidance of Negative Interest Rates | | | | | | | | | 0.0 | | 0.0 | | 4.0 | |
| (d) Capital Transactions with Foreigners | 0.0 | | 0.0 | | 0.0 | | 0.0 | | 5.0 | | 5.0 | | 5.0 | |

# GUYANA

| | 1970 | 1975 | 1980 | 1985 | 1990 | 1995 | 1997 |
|---|---|---|---|---|---|---|---|
| **Summary Ratings** | | | | 4.1 | | 5.9 | 6.2 |
| **Rank** | | | | 87 | | 74 | 75 |

| Components of Economic Freedom | 1970 | | 1975 | | 1980 | | 1985 | | 1990 | | 1995 | | 1997 | |
|---|---|---|---|---|---|---|---|---|---|---|---|---|---|---|
| **I. Size of Government** | **6.8** | | **5.4** | | **5.2** | | **6.6** | | **7.9** | | **7.0** | | **6.5** | |
| (a) Government Consumption (% of Total) | 6.8 | (21.8) | 5.4 | (29.3) | 5.2 | (30.4) | 6.6 | (23.1) | 7.9 | (15.8) | 7.0 | (20.8) | 6.5 | (23.8) |
| (b) Transfers and Subsidies (% of GDP) | | | | | | | | | | | | | | |
| **II. Structure of the Economy and Use of Markets** | | | | | | | | | | | | | **4.0** | |
| (a) Government Enterprises | 0.0 | | 0.0 | | 0.0 | | 0.0 | | 0.0 | | 0.0 | | 0.0 | |
| (b) Price Controls | | | | | | | | | | | | | | |
| (c) Top Marginal Tax Rate | | | | | | | | | | | | | 7.0 | (33.3) |
| (d) Conscription | | | | | | | | | 10.0 | | 10.0 | | 10.0 | |
| **III. Monetary Policy and Price Stability** | **9.3** | | **5.9** | | **7.7** | | **6.9** | | **2.6** | | **4.1** | | **8.2** | |
| (a) Annual Money Growth (last 5 yrs.) | 9.4 | (2.8) | 5.5 | (22.7) | 8.4 | (7.9) | 5.8 | (20.8) | 0.9 | (45.5) | 4.5 | (27.6) | 6.2 | (19.2) |
| (b) Inflation Variability (last 5 yrs.) | 9.2 | (2.0) | 5.0 | (12.4) | 7.1 | (7.3) | 7.7 | (5.9) | 0.0 | (53.1) | 0.0 | (48.3) | 9.1 | (2.3) |
| (c) Recent Inflation Rate | 9.4 | (3.0) | 7.1 | (14.7) | 7.6 | (11.8) | 7.1 | (14.5) | 6.9 | (15.5) | 7.8 | (11.2) | 9.3 | (3.5) |
| **IV. Freedom to Use Alternative Currencies** | **8.2** | | **0.0** | | **0.0** | | **0.0** | | **4.1** | | **7.1** | | **7.0** | |
| (a) Ownership of Foreign Currency | | | 0.0 | | 0.0 | | 0.0 | | 0.0 | | 5.0 | | 5.0 | |
| (b) Black Market Exchange Rates (Prem.) | 8.2 | (9.0) | | | 0.0 | (267.0) | 0.0 | (743.0) | 8.2 | (9.0) | 9.2 | (4.0) | 9.0 | (5.0) |
| **V. Legal Structure and Property Rights** | | | | | **1.9** | | **2.2** | | **3.5** | | **6.3** | | **7.0** | |
| (a) Private Ownership Rights | | | | | 3.0 | | 1.2 | | 4.6 | | 7.7 | | 10.0 | |
| (b) Viability of Contracts | | | | | 2.7 | | 4.0 | | 4.0 | | 6.8 | | 6.6 | |
| (c) Rule of Law | | | | | 0.0 | | 1.4 | | 1.7 | | 4.1 | | 4.1 | |
| **VI. International Exchange** | | | | | | | **6.5** | | | | | | | |
| (a) Taxes on International Trade | | | | | | | | | | | | | | |
| i. Taxes as a Percentage of Exports and Imports | | | | | | | | | | | | | | |
| ii. Mean Tariff Rate | | | | | | | 6.6 | (17.0) | | | | | | |
| iii. Standard Deviation of Tariff Rates | | | | | | | | | | | | | | |
| (b) Non-tariff Regulatory Trade Barriers | | | | | | | | | | | | | | |
| i. Non-tariff Trade Restraints (% of trade covered) | | | | | | | | | | | | | | |
| ii. Size of Trade Sector (% of GDP) | 7.4 | (113.5) | 9.3 | (149.8) | 10.0 | (174.9) | 6.1 | (110.0) | 7.4 | (142.6) | 8.0 | (164.5) | 7.9 | (166.4) |
| **VII. Freedom of Exchange in Financial Markets** | | | | | | | | | | | **4.8** | | **5.2** | |
| (a) Ownership of Banks | | | | | | | | | | | | | | |
| (b) Extension of Credit | 6.5 | (68.1) | 2.9 | (36.4) | 2.2 | (30.2) | 1.5 | (23.8) | 4.0 | (46.1) | 5.3 | (57.9) | 6.8 | (71.0) |
| (c) Avoidance of Negative Interest Rates | | | | | | | | | | | 4.0 | | 4.0 | |
| (d) Capital Transactions with Foreigners | 0.0 | | 0.0 | | 0.0 | | 0.0 | | 5.0 | | 5.0 | | 5.0 | |

# HAITI

| | 1970 | 1975 | 1980 | 1985 | 1990 | 1995 | 1997 |
|---|---|---|---|---|---|---|---|
| **Summary Ratings** | | | 5.4 | 5.7 | 4.7 | 4.6 | 6.2 |
| **Rank** | | | 48 | 44 | 79 | 100 | 75 |

| Components of Economic Freedom | 1970 | | 1975 | | 1980 | | 1985 | | 1990 | | 1995 | | 1997 | |
|---|---|---|---|---|---|---|---|---|---|---|---|---|---|---|
| **I. Size of Government** | **8.9** | | **9.1** | | **8.8** | | **8.4** | | **9.4** | | **9.6** | | **9.6** | |
| (a) Government Consumption (% of Total) | 8.9 | (10.3) | 9.1 | (9.7) | 8.8 | (11.0) | 8.6 | (11.9) | 9.4 | (7.6) | 9.6 | (6.8) | 9.6 | (6.7) |
| (b) Transfers and Subsidies (% of GDP) | | | | | | | 8.1 | (7.3) | | | | | | |
| **II. Structure of the Economy and Use of Markets** | | | | | | | | | **5.8** | | **2.9** | | | |
| (a) Government Enterprises | 8.0 | (17.9) | 6.0 | (13.1) | 6.0 | (19.0) | 6.0 | (32.7) | 6.0 | (42.0) | 4.0 | | | |
| (b) Price Controls | | | | | | | | | 2.0 | | 0.0 | | 2.0 | |
| (c) Top Marginal Tax Rate | | | | | | | | | 9.0 | (30) | | | | |
| (d) Conscription | 10.0 | | 10.0 | | 10.0 | | 10.0 | | 10.0 | | 10.0 | | 10.0 | |
| **III. Monetary Policy and Price Stability** | **9.0** | | **7.9** | | **6.5** | | **8.3** | | **7.8** | | **5.0** | | **7.0** | |
| (a) Annual Money Growth (last 5 yrs.) | 8.6 | (7.2) | 7.1 | (14.6) | 7.1 | (14.3) | 8.3 | (8.6) | 8.4 | (8.1) | 4.9 | (25.4) | 6.9 | (15.3) |
| (b) Inflation Variability (last 5 yrs.) | 9.3 | (1.7) | 7.7 | (5.9) | 6.7 | (8.3) | 8.7 | (3.1) | 7.0 | (7.5) | 6.3 | (9.2) | 7.2 | (7.1) |
| (c) Recent Inflation Rate | 9.1 | (4.7) | 8.8 | (5.8) | 5.7 | (21.4) | 7.9 | (10.4) | 7.9 | (10.4) | 3.8 | (31.0) | 6.8 | (16.2) |
| **IV. Freedom to Use Alternative Currencies** | **10.0** | | **7.5** | | **8.0** | | **5.0** | | **5.0** | | **5.3** | | **6.9** | |
| (a) Ownership of Foreign Currency | 10.0 | | 5.0 | | 10.0 | | 10.0 | | 10.0 | | 10.0 | | 10.0 | |
| (b) Black Market Exchange Rates (Prem.) | 10.0 | (0.0) | 10.0 | (0.0) | 6.0 | (20.0) | 0.0 | (60.0) | 0.0 | (151.0) | 0.6 | (47.0) | 3.8 | (31.0) |
| **V. Legal Structure and Property Rights** | | | | | **1.9** | | **2.8** | | **0.8** | | **2.7** | | **4.2** | |
| (a) Private Ownership Rights | | | | | 3.0 | | 3.5 | | 0.5 | | 0.9 | | 4.4 | |
| (b) Viability of Contracts | | | | | 2.7 | | 3.4 | | 0.4 | | 0.5 | | 1.4 | |
| (c) Rule of Law | | | | | 0.0 | | 1.4 | | 1.7 | | 7.0 | | 7.0 | |
| **VI. International Exchange** | | | **3.0** | | **3.8** | | **5.8** | | **4.3** | | | | | |
| (a) Taxes on International Trade | | | | | | | | | | | | | | |
| i. Taxes as a Percentage of Exports and Imports | | | 3.8 | (9.3) | 3.4 | (9.9) | 4.7 | (8.0) | 5.5 | (6.7) | | | | |
| ii. Mean Tariff Rate | | | | | 4.5 | (27.7) | 7.7 | (11.6) | | | | | | |
| iii. Standard Deviation of Tariff Rates | | | | | | | | | | | | | | |
| (b) Non-tariff Regulatory Trade Barriers | | | | | | | | | | | | | | |
| i. Non-tariff Trade Restraints (% of trade covered) | | | | | | | 6.9 | (30.8) | | | 6.9 | (30.8) | | |
| ii. Size of Trade Sector (% of GDP) | 0.0 | (31.5) | 0.8 | (37.5) | 3.1 | (52.1) | 1.6 | (45.2) | 1.2 | (45.2) | 0.0 | (36.3) | 0.0 | (34.3) |
| **VII. Freedom of Exchange in Financial Markets** | | | | | | | | | **2.9** | | **3.6** | | **5.0** | |
| (a) Ownership of Banks | | | | | | | | | | | | | | |
| (b) Extension of Credit | 9.1 | (92.2) | 9.2 | (92.4) | 10.0 | (99.9) | 9.7 | (97.0) | 9.9 | (99.3) | 10.0 | (99.8) | 10.0 | (99.9) |
| (c) Avoidance of Negative Interest Rates | | | | | | | | | 0.0 | | 0.0 | | 4.0 | |
| (d) Capital Transactions with Foreigners | 0.0 | | 0.0 | | 0.0 | | 0.0 | | 0.0 | | 2.0 | | 2.0 | |

# HONDURAS

| | 1970 | 1975 | 1980 | 1985 | 1990 | 1995 | 1997 |
|---|---|---|---|---|---|---|---|
| **Summary Ratings** | | 8.1 | 5.5 | 5.5 | 6.2 | 6.9 | 7.0 |
| **Rank** | | 3 | 44 | 51 | 41 | 48 | 53 |

| Components of Economic Freedom | 1970 | | 1975 | | 1980 | | 1985 | | 1990 | | 1995 | | 1997 | |
|---|---|---|---|---|---|---|---|---|---|---|---|---|---|---|
| **I. Size of Government** | **9.2** | | **9.2** | | **8.0** | | **8.8** | | **8.6** | | **8.4** | | **7.2** | |
| (a) Government Consumption (% of Total) | 8.4 | (13.5) | 8.3 | (13.7) | 8.0 | (15.3) | 8.1 | (14.8) | 7.6 | (17.4) | 7.7 | (17.0) | 7.2 | (19.6) |
| (b) Transfers and Subsidies (% of GDP) | 10.0 | (0.6) | 10.0 | (0.5) | | | 9.5 | (2.3) | 9.5 | (2.2) | 9.0 | (4.0) | | |
| **II. Structure of the Economy and Use of Markets** | | | **7.7** | | **7.3** | | **4.8** | | **4.6** | | **5.9** | | **6.2** | |
| (a) Government Enterprises | 6.0 | (35.1) | 6.0 | (31.1) | 6.0 | (37.4) | 6.0 | (62.6) | 6.0 | (32.0) | 6.0 | (37.2) | 6.0 | |
| (b) Price Controls | | | | | | | | | 4.0 | | 4.0 | | 4.0 | |
| (c) Top Marginal Tax Rate | | | 9.0 | (27) | 8.0 | (40) | 5.0 | (46) | 5.0 | (46) | 7.0 | (40) | 8.0 | (30) |
| (d) Conscription | 10.0 | | 10.0 | | 10.0 | | 0.0 | | 0.0 | | 10.0 | | 10.0 | |
| **III. Monetary Policy and Price Stability** | **9.3** | | **8.4** | | **7.9** | | **9.4** | | **7.7** | | **6.1** | | **6.4** | |
| (a) Annual Money Growth (last 5 yrs.) | 9.2 | (4.1) | 8.7 | (6.7) | 7.5 | (12.7) | 9.7 | (1.5) | 6.9 | (15.4) | 6.6 | (17.1) | 5.2 | (24.2) |
| (b) Inflation Variability (last 5 yrs.) | 9.6 | (1.0) | 7.8 | (5.6) | 8.8 | (3.0) | 9.4 | (1.5) | 7.3 | (6.6) | 6.9 | (7.8) | 7.9 | (5.3) |
| (c) Recent Inflation Rate | 9.1 | (4.5) | 8.7 | (6.4) | 7.3 | (13.3) | 9.0 | (5.3) | 9.0 | (5.3) | 4.7 | (26.3) | 6.2 | (19.0) |
| **IV. Freedom to Use Alternative Currencies** | **7.0** | | **10.0** | | **8.0** | | **5.0** | | **10.0** | | **9.9** | | **9.8** | |
| (a) Ownership of Foreign Currency | 10.0 | | 10.0 | | 10.0 | | 10.0 | | 10.0 | | 10.0 | | 10.0 | |
| (b) Black Market Exchange Rates (Prem.) | 4.0 | (30.0) | 10.0 | (0.0) | 6.0 | (20.0) | 0.0 | (65.0) | 10.0 | (0.0) | 9.8 | (1.0) | 9.6 | (2.0) |
| **V. Legal Structure and Property Rights** | | | | | **2.5** | | **3.1** | | **3.5** | | **5.3** | | **4.8** | |
| (a) Private Ownership Rights | | | | | 2.8 | | 2.2 | | 3.2 | | 5.5 | | 4.4 | |
| (b) Viability of Contracts | | | | | 3.0 | | 4.0 | | 4.0 | | 3.7 | | 3.1 | |
| (c) Rule of Law | | | | | 1.7 | | 3.1 | | 3.3 | | 7.0 | | 7.0 | |
| **VI. International Exchange** | **5.5** | | **6.2** | | **4.0** | | | | **5.8** | | **7.4** | | | |
| (a) Taxes on International Trade | | | | | | | | | | | | | | |
| i. Taxes as a Percentage of Exports and Imports | 5.7 | (6.4) | 6.5 | (5.3) | 5.5 | (6.7) | | | | | | | | |
| ii. Mean Tariff Rate | | | | | 1.8 | (41.0) | | | 6.0 | (20.0) | 8.0 | (10.1) | | |
| iii. Standard Deviation of Tariff Rates | | | | | | | | | | | 7.4 | (6.5) | | |
| (b) Non-tariff Regulatory Trade Barriers | | | | | | | | | | | | | | |
| i. Non-tariff Trade Restraints (% of trade covered) | | | | | | | | | | | | | | |
| ii. Size of Trade Sector (% of GDP) | 4.9 | (62.0) | 5.4 | (70.4) | 5.9 | (80.3) | 3.5 | (54.2) | 5.2 | (76.1) | 6.0 | (91.3) | 6.3 | (96.7) |
| **VII. Freedom of Exchange in Financial Markets** | | | | | **3.7** | | **4.8** | | **4.8** | | **5.7** | | **7.4** | |
| (a) Ownership of Banks | | | | | | | | | | | | | | |
| (b) Extension of Credit | 8.9 | (90.3) | 8.5 | (86.6) | 8.0 | (81.9) | 7.1 | (74.0) | 7.3 | (75.3) | 8.4 | (85.9) | 9.8 | (97.9) |
| (c) Avoidance of Negative Interest Rates | | | | | 4.0 | | 8.0 | | 8.0 | | 4.0 | | 8.0 | |
| (d) Capital Transactions with Foreigners | 2.0 | | 2.0 | | 0.0 | | 0.0 | | 0.0 | | 5.0 | | 5.0 | |

# Hong Kong

| | 1970 | 1975 | 1980 | 1985 | 1990 | 1995 | 1997 |
|---|---|---|---|---|---|---|---|
| **Summary Ratings** | 9.4 | 9.3 | 9.6 | 9.3 | 9.3 | 9.8 | 9.4 |
| **Rank** | 1 | 1 | 1 | 2 | 1 | 1 | 1 |

| Components of Economic Freedom | 1970 | | 1975 | | 1980 | | 1985 | | 1990 | | 1995 | | 1997 | |
|---|---|---|---|---|---|---|---|---|---|---|---|---|---|---|
| **I. Size of Government** | **9.0** | | **9.4** | | **9.5** | | **9.4** | | **9.3** | | **9.2** | | **9.2** | |
| (a) Government Consumption (% of Total) | 9.0 | (9.9) | 9.0 | (9.9) | 9.1 | (9.3) | 8.9 | (10.6) | 8.7 | (11.6) | 8.5 | (12.7) | 8.6 | (12.4) |
| (b) Transfers and Subsidies (% of GDP) | | | 9.8 | (1.1) | 10.0 | (0.6) | 9.9 | (0.9) | 9.9 | (0.9) | 9.8 | (1.1) | 9.8 | (1.1) |
| **II. Structure of the Economy and Use of Markets** | **10.0** | | **10.0** | | **10.0** | | **9.6** | | **9.7** | | **9.7** | | **9.7** | |
| (a) Government Enterprises | 10.0 | (9.1) | 10.0 | (16.4) | 10.0 | (16.5) | 10.0 | (17.9) | 10.0 | (13.2) | 10.0 | (14.0) | 10.0 | |
| (b) Price Controls | | | | | | | | | 10.0 | | 9.0 | | 9.0 | |
| (c) Top Marginal Tax Rate | 10.0 | (15) | 10.0 | (15) | 10.0 | (15) | 9.0 | (25) | 9.0 | (25) | 10.0 | (20) | 10.0 | (20) |
| (d) Conscription | 10.0 | | 10.0 | | 10.0 | | 10.0 | | 10.0 | | 10.0 | | 10.0 | |
| **III. Monetary Policy and Price Stability** | **8.3** | | **8.9** | | **8.0** | | **9.1** | | **8.7** | | **9.1** | | **9.2** | |
| (a) Annual Money Growth (last 5 yrs.) | | | 8.9 | (5.5) | 9.0 | (4.8) | 9.5 | (2.6) | 8.4 | (8.2) | 8.8 | (6.1) | 9.7 | (1.6) |
| (b) Inflation Variability (last 5 yrs.) | 8.3 | (4.4) | 8.7 | (3.3) | 8.0 | (5.0) | 9.0 | (2.6) | 8.9 | (2.9) | 9.0 | (2.6) | 9.2 | (2.0) |
| (c) Recent Inflation Rate | 8.3 | (8.6) | 9.1 | (4.6) | 7.0 | (15.0) | 8.9 | (5.7) | 8.9 | (5.7) | 9.5 | (2.6) | 8.8 | (5.8) |
| **IV. Freedom to Use Alternative Currencies** | **10.0** | | **10.0** | | **10.0** | | **10.0** | | **10.0** | | **10.0** | | **10.0** | |
| (a) Ownership of Foreign Currency | 10.0 | | 10.0 | | 10.0 | | 10.0 | | 10.0 | | 10.0 | | 10.0 | |
| (b) Black Market Exchange Rates (Prem.) | 10.0 | (0.0) | 10.0 | (0.0) | 10.0 | (0.0) | 10.0 | (0.0) | 10.0 | (0.0) | 10.0 | (0.0) | 10.0 | (0.0) |
| **V. Legal Structure and Property Rights** | **8.5** | | **7.4** | | **9.6** | | **7.3** | | **7.4** | | **10.0** | | **7.9** | |
| (a) Private Ownership Rights | 9.1 | | 7.6 | | 9.4 | | 6.1 | | 6.6 | | 10.0 | | 10.0 | |
| (b) Viability of Contracts | 7.8 | | 7.2 | | 9.4 | | 7.6 | | 8.8 | | 10.0 | | 6.6 | |
| (c) Rule of Law | | | | | 10.0 | | 8.2 | | 6.7 | | 10.0 | | 7.0 | |
| **VI. International Exchange** | **9.9** | | **9.6** | | **9.7** | | **9.8** | | **9.9** | | **9.9** | | **10.0** | |
| (a) Taxes on International Trade | | | | | | | | | | | | | | |
| i. Taxes as a Percentage of Exports and Imports | 10.0 | (0.0) | 9.5 | (0.7) | 9.7 | (0.5) | 9.6 | (0.6) | 9.7 | (0.4) | 9.8 | (0.3) | | |
| ii. Mean Tariff Rate | | | 10.0 | (0.0) | 10.0 | (0.0) | 10.0 | (0.0) | 10.0 | (0.0) | 10.0 | (0.0) | 10.0 | (0.0) |
| iii. Standard Deviation of Tariff Rates | | | | | | | | | 10.0 | (0.0) | 10.0 | (0.0) | 10.0 | (0.0) |
| (b) Non-tariff Regulatory Trade Barriers | | | | | | | | | | | | | | |
| i. Non-tariff Trade Restraints (% of trade covered) | | | | | | | 9.7 | (3.4) | 10.0 | (0.5) | 10.0 | (0.5) | | |
| ii. Size of Trade Sector (% of GDP) | 9.8 | (181.5) | 8.4 | (163.7) | 8.9 | (180.6) | 9.8 | (208.6) | 10.0 | (260.1) | 10.0 | (302.9) | 10.0 | (265.4) |
| **VII. Freedom of Exchange in Financial Markets** | | | **10.0** | | **10.0** | | **10.0** | | **10.0** | | **9.9** | | **9.9** | |
| (a) Ownership of Banks | 10.0 | (100) | 10.0 | (100) | 10.0 | (100) | 10.0 | (100) | 10.0 | (100) | 10.0 | (100) | 10.0 | (100) |
| (b) Extension of Credit | | | | | | | | | 9.8 | (98.1) | 9.6 | (96.7) | 9.3 | (94.0) |
| (c) Avoidance of Negative Interest Rates | | | 10.0 | | 10.0 | | 10.0 | | 10.0 | | 10.0 | | 10.0 | |
| (d) Capital Transactions with Foreigners | 5.0 | | 10.0 | | 10.0 | | 10.0 | | 10.0 | | 10.0 | | 10.0 | |

# HUNGARY

| | 1970 | 1975 | 1980 | 1985 | 1990 | 1995 | 1997 |
|---|---|---|---|---|---|---|---|
| **Summary Ratings** | | | 4.8 | 4.8 | 4.9 | 6.8 | 7.4 |
| **Rank** | | | 67 | 69 | 71 | 49 | 42 |

| Components of Economic Freedom | 1970 | | 1975 | | 1980 | | 1985 | | 1990 | | 1995 | | 1997 | |
|---|---|---|---|---|---|---|---|---|---|---|---|---|---|---|
| **I. Size of Government** | **8.1** | | **8.1** | | **8.2** | | **4.7** | | **5.2** | | **5.8** | | **6.6** | |
| (a) Government Consumption (% of Total) | 8.1 | (15.1) | 8.1 | (15.0) | 8.2 | (14.4) | 8.3 | (13.9) | 8.1 | (14.7) | 8.2 | (14.2) | 8.3 | (14.0) |
| (b) Transfers and Subsidies (% of GDP) | | | | | | | 1.1 | (33.3) | 2.3 | (28.7) | 3.3 | (25.0) | 4.9 | (19.0) |
| **II. Structure of the Economy and Use of Markets** | | | | | | | | | **2.8** | | **4.9** | | **4.9** | |
| (a) Government Enterprises | 0.0 | (93.7) | 0.0 | (93.8) | 0.0 | (92.6) | 0.0 | (83.5) | 0.0 | (68.5) | 4.0 | | 4.0 | |
| (b) Price Controls | | | | | | | | | 6.0 | | 7.0 | | 7.0 | |
| (c) Top Marginal Tax Rate | | | | | | | | | 3.0 | (50) | 4.0 | (44) | 4.0 | (42) |
| (d) Conscription | 0.0 | | 0.0 | | 0.0 | | 0.0 | | 1.0 | | 3.0 | | 3.0 | |
| **III. Monetary Policy and Price Stability** | **9.2** | | **9.1** | | **8.6** | | **9.1** | | **7.5** | | **6.4** | | **7.4** | |
| (a) Annual Money Growth (last 5 yrs.) | | | | | 8.3 | (8.7) | 8.7 | (6.7) | 6.9 | (15.5) | 6.9 | (15.7) | 7.0 | (14.8) |
| (b) Inflation Variability (last 5 yrs.) | 9.3 | (1.8) | 9.0 | (2.5) | 8.9 | (2.8) | 9.8 | (0.5) | 6.9 | (7.8) | 7.6 | (5.9) | 8.9 | (2.9) |
| (c) Recent Inflation Rate | 9.0 | (4.9) | 9.1 | (4.4) | 8.8 | (6.0) | 8.8 | (5.9) | 8.8 | (5.9) | 4.7 | (26.7) | 6.3 | (18.5) |
| **IV. Freedom to Use Alternative Currencies** | **0.0** | | **0.0** | | **0.0** | | **0.0** | | **2.8** | | **7.5** | | **10.0** | |
| (a) Ownership of Foreign Currency | 0.0 | | 0.0 | | 0.0 | | 0.0 | | 0.0 | | 5.0 | | 10.0 | |
| (b) Black Market Exchange Rates (Prem.) | 0.0 | (342.0) | 0.0 | (317.0) | 0.0 | (244.0) | 0.0 | (210.0) | 5.6 | (22.0) | 10.0 | (0.0) | 10.0 | (0.0) |
| **V. Legal Structure and Property Rights** | | | | | | | **7.2** | | **7.8** | | **9.5** | | **10.0** | |
| (a) Private Ownership Rights | | | | | | | 7.4 | | 8.6 | | 10.0 | | 10.0 | |
| (b) Viability of Contracts | | | | | | | 6.1 | | 6.4 | | 8.4 | | 10.0 | |
| (c) Rule of Law | | | | | | | 8.2 | | 8.3 | | 10.0 | | 10.0 | |
| **VI. International Exchange** | | | | | **7.1** | | **7.6** | | **6.0** | | **7.0** | | **6.4** | |
| (a) Taxes on International Trade | | | | | | | | | | | | | | |
| i. Taxes as a Percentage of Exports and Imports | | | | | 6.7 | (5.0) | 7.5 | (3.7) | 6.7 | (5.0) | 5.8 | (6.3) | 8.8 | (1.8) |
| ii. Mean Tariff Rate | | | | | | | | | | | 7.8 | (11.0) | 7.1 | (14.4) |
| iii. Standard Deviation of Tariff Rates | | | | | | | | | 5.6 | (11.0) | 6.1 | (9.7) | 3.2 | (16.9) |
| (b) Non-tariff Regulatory Trade Barriers | | | | | | | | | | | | | | |
| i. Non-tariff Trade Restraints (% of trade covered) | | | | | | | | | | | 9.0 | (9.7) | | |
| ii. Size of Trade Sector (% of GDP) | 7.3 | (62.6) | 9.9 | (90.4) | 8.2 | (80.3) | 7.9 | (82.3) | 5.3 | (59.7) | 6.3 | (75.8) | 6.5 | (79.4) |
| **VII. Freedom of Exchange in Financial Markets** | | | | | **2.3** | | **1.3** | | **3.0** | | **5.8** | | **6.2** | |
| (a) Ownership of Banks | 0.0 | (0-10) | 0.0 | (0-10) | 0.0 | (0-10) | 0.0 | (0-10) | 2.0 | (12) | 8.0 | (80) | 8.0 | (91) |
| (b) Extension of Credit | | | | | 4.1 | (46.8) | 4.8 | (53.2) | 4.7 | (52.0) | 3.9 | (45.5) | 3.3 | (39.7) |
| (c) Avoidance of Negative Interest Rates | | | | | 6.0 | | | | 6.0 | | 6.0 | | 8.0 | |
| (d) Capital Transactions with Foreigners | 0.0 | | 0.0 | | 0.0 | | 0.0 | | 0.0 | | 5.0 | | 5.0 | |

# ICELAND

| | 1970 | 1975 | 1980 | 1985 | 1990 | 1995 | 1997 |
|---|---|---|---|---|---|---|---|
| **Summary Ratings** | 6.4 | 4.4 | 5.5 | 5.7 | 7.5 | 8.1 | 8.0 |
| **Rank** | 29 | 61 | 44 | 44 | 22 | 16 | 25 |

| Components of Economic Freedom | 1970 | | 1975 | | 1980 | | 1985 | | 1990 | | 1995 | | 1997 | |
|---|---|---|---|---|---|---|---|---|---|---|---|---|---|---|
| **I. Size of Government** | **7.7** | | **7.1** | | **7.0** | | **6.9** | | **6.9** | | **6.9** | | **7.0** | |
| (a) Government Consumption (% of Total) | 7.7 | (17.3) | 6.8 | (21.9) | 6.8 | (22.2) | 6.9 | (21.5) | 6.4 | (23.9) | 6.1 | (25.6) | 6.2 | (25.3) |
| (b) Transfers and Subsidies (% of GDP) | | | 7.4 | (9.9) | 7.2 | (10.6) | 6.9 | (11.7) | 7.4 | (10.1) | 7.7 | (9.1) | 7.8 | (8.7) |
| **II. Structure of the Economy and Use of Markets** | | | | | **5.3** | | **5.6** | | **6.4** | | **6.2** | | **6.2** | |
| (a) Government Enterprises | 8.0 | (20.2) | 8.0 | (17.6) | 8.0 | (15.3) | 8.0 | (16.1) | 7.0 | (22.2) | 7.0 | (24.8) | 7.0 | |
| (b) Price Controls | | | | | | | | | 6.0 | | 6.0 | | 6.0 | |
| (c) Top Marginal Tax Rate | | | | | 0.0 | (63) | 1.0 | (56) | 5.0 | (40) | 4.0 | (47) | 4.0 | (42) |
| (d) Conscription | | | 10.0 | | 10.0 | | 10.0 | | 10.0 | | 10.0 | | 10.0 | |
| **III. Monetary Policy and Price Stability** | **7.6** | | **4.0** | | **3.1** | | **2.7** | | **5.7** | | **9.1** | | **9.3** | |
| (a) Annual Money Growth (last 5 yrs.) | 8.5 | (7.4) | 5.0 | (24.8) | 2.6 | (37.1) | 1.6 | (41.8) | 4.6 | (26.9) | 8.5 | (7.3) | 8.4 | (8.2) |
| (b) Inflation Variability (last 5 yrs.) | 7.6 | (6.1) | 5.5 | (11.2) | 6.9 | (7.7) | 2.8 | (18.0) | 8.8 | (3.0) | 9.2 | (2.1) | 9.9 | (0.3) |
| (c) Recent Inflation Rate | 6.7 | (16.4) | 1.6 | (41.9) | 0.0 | (52.5) | 3.7 | (31.3) | 3.7 | (31.3) | 9.5 | (2.8) | 9.7 | (1.8) |
| **IV. Freedom to Use Alternative Currencies** | **4.5** | | **0.0** | | **4.1** | | **3.4** | | **10.0** | | **10.0** | | **10.0** | |
| (a) Ownership of Foreign Currency | 0.0 | | 0.0 | | 0.0 | | 0.0 | | 10.0 | | 10.0 | | 10.0 | |
| (b) Black Market Exchange Rates (Prem.) | 9.0 | (5.0) | 0.0 | (106.0) | 8.2 | (9.0) | 6.8 | (16.0) | 10.0 | (0.0) | 10.0 | (0.0) | 10.0 | (0.0) |
| **V. Legal Structure and Property Rights** | **9.1** | | **7.5** | | **8.1** | | **8.7** | | **10.0** | | **10.0** | | **10.0** | |
| (a) Private Ownership Rights | 8.3 | | 5.3 | | 5.8 | | 8.7 | | 10.0 | | 10.0 | | 10.0 | |
| (b) Viability of Contracts | 9.9 | | 9.7 | | 8.6 | | 7.6 | | 10.0 | | 10.0 | | 10.0 | |
| (c) Rule of Law | | | | | 10.0 | | 10.0 | | 10.0 | | 10.0 | | 10.0 | |
| **VI. International Exchange** | **3.8** | | **4.4** | | **6.3** | | **7.2** | | **7.6** | | **8.2** | | **7.6** | |
| (a) Taxes on International Trade | | | | | | | | | | | | | | |
| i. Taxes as a Percentage of Exports and Imports | 3.3 | (10.0) | 4.6 | (8.1) | 5.7 | (6.5) | 6.9 | (4.6) | 7.3 | (4.0) | 9.5 | (0.7) | 9.7 | (0.5) |
| ii. Mean Tariff Rate | | | | | 8.1 | (9.6) | 8.7 | (6.7) | 9.2 | (3.8) | 9.3 | (3.7) | 9.3 | (3.7) |
| iii. Standard Deviation of Tariff Rates | | | | | | | | | 7.0 | (7.5) | 7.1 | (7.3) | 4.8 | (13.0) |
| (b) Non-tariff Regulatory Trade Barriers | | | | | | | | | | | | | | |
| i. Non-tariff Trade Restraints (% of trade covered) | | | | | | | | | 8.9 | (10.9) | 9.9 | (1.4) | 9.3 | (6.7) |
| ii. Size of Trade Sector (% of GDP) | 5.1 | (86.8) | 3.9 | (73.7) | 3.2 | (69.8) | 3.8 | (80.6) | 2.1 | (67.0) | 1.7 | (67.5) | 1.9 | (71.5) |
| **VII. Freedom of Exchange in Financial Markets** | | | **3.6** | | **4.1** | | **4.1** | | **4.9** | | **6.3** | | **6.4** | |
| (a) Ownership of Banks | | | 2.0 | (23) | 2.0 | (23) | 2.0 | (26) | 2.0 | (28) | 2.0 | (27) | 2.0 | (28) |
| (b) Extension of Credit | 9.1 | (92.0) | 9.4 | (94.8) | 9.6 | (96.0) | 9.7 | (96.8) | 8.7 | (88.2) | 9.4 | (94.1) | 9.6 | (96.4) |
| (c) Avoidance of Negative Interest Rates | | | 2.0 | | 4.0 | | 4.0 | | 8.0 | | 10.0 | | 10.0 | |
| (d) Capital Transactions with Foreigners | 0.0 | | 2.0 | | 2.0 | | 2.0 | | 2.0 | | 5.0 | | 5.0 | |

# INDIA

| | 1970 | 1975 | 1980 | 1985 | 1990 | 1995 | 1997 |
|---|---|---|---|---|---|---|---|
| **Summary Ratings** | 4.0 | 3.6 | 4.3 | 4.1 | 4.1 | 5.0 | 5.8 |
| **Rank** | 51 | 71 | 77 | 87 | 93 | 93 | 86 |

| Components of Economic Freedom | 1970 | | 1975 | | 1980 | | 1985 | | 1990 | | 1995 | | 1997 | |
|---|---|---|---|---|---|---|---|---|---|---|---|---|---|---|
| **I. Size of Government** | **8.9** | | **8.9** | | **8.7** | | **8.3** | | **8.2** | | **8.3** | | **8.0** | |
| (a) Government Consumption (% of Total) | 8.9 | (10.5) | 8.8 | (11.4) | 8.7 | (11.7) | 8.2 | (14.1) | 8.0 | (15.7) | 8.1 | (15.2) | 8.0 | (15.2) |
| (b) Transfers and Subsidies (% of GDP) | | | 9.1 | (3.8) | 8.7 | (5.4) | 8.4 | (6.5) | 8.4 | (6.5) | 8.5 | (6.0) | | |
| **II. Structure of the Economy and Use of Markets** | **2.3** | | **1.3** | | **1.7** | | **1.3** | | **2.4** | | **4.1** | | **3.5** | |
| (a) Government Enterprises | 2.0 | (38.4) | 0.0 | (41.0) | 0.0 | (46.7) | 0.0 | (49.5) | 0.0 | (42.3) | 2.0 | (36.6) | 2.0 | |
| (b) Price Controls | | | | | | | | | 3.0 | | 4.0 | | 2.0 | |
| (c) Top Marginal Tax Rate | 0.0 | (85) | 0.0 | (77) | 1.0 | (60) | 0.0 | (62) | 2.0 | (53) | 5.0 | (40) | 5.0 | (40) |
| (d) Conscription | 10.0 | | 10.0 | | 10.0 | | 10.0 | | 10.0 | | 10.0 | | 10.0 | |
| **III. Monetary Policy and Price Stability** | **8.9** | | **8.4** | | **8.1** | | **8.6** | | **8.6** | | **8.4** | | **8.7** | |
| (a) Annual Money Growth (last 5 yrs.) | 8.9 | (5.4) | 8.2 | (8.9) | 8.4 | (7.9) | 7.8 | (10.8) | 8.0 | (9.8) | 7.7 | (11.4) | 7.9 | (10.6) |
| (b) Inflation Variability (last 5 yrs.) | 8.2 | (4.6) | 7.1 | (7.2) | 8.1 | (4.8) | 9.6 | (1.1) | 9.4 | (1.5) | 9.1 | (2.3) | 9.3 | (1.7) |
| (c) Recent Inflation Rate | 9.7 | (1.7) | 9.7 | (-1.4) | 7.7 | (11.5) | 8.5 | (7.5) | 8.5 | (7.5) | 8.4 | (8.2) | 8.9 | (5.5) |
| **IV. Freedom to Use Alternative Currencies** | **0.0** | | **4.1** | | **4.5** | | **3.6** | | **4.0** | | **4.2** | | **7.0** | |
| (a) Ownership of Foreign Currency | 0.0 | | 0.0 | | 0.0 | | 0.0 | | 0.0 | | 0.0 | | 5.0 | |
| (b) Black Market Exchange Rates (Prem.) | 0.0 | (67.0) | 8.2 | (9.0) | 9.0 | (5.0) | 7.2 | (14.0) | 8.0 | (10.0) | 8.4 | (8.0) | 9.0 | (5.0) |
| **V. Legal Structure and Property Rights** | **3.2** | | **2.5** | | **5.9** | | **5.3** | | **4.0** | | **7.1** | | **7.6** | |
| (a) Private Ownership Rights | 4.1 | | 1.7 | | 4.6 | | 7.4 | | 7.3 | | 10.0 | | 10.0 | |
| (b) Viability of Contracts | 2.3 | | 3.3 | | 4.9 | | 5.2 | | 2.8 | | 6.8 | | 8.3 | |
| (c) Rule of Law | | | | | 8.3 | | 3.1 | | 1.7 | | 4.1 | | 4.1 | |
| **VI. International Exchange** | | | **0.9** | | **0.7** | | **0.9** | | **1.1** | | **1.7** | | **4.1** | |
| (a) Taxes on International Trade | | | | | | | | | | | | | | |
| i. Taxes as a Percentage of Exports and Imports | | | 0.1 | (14.8) | 0.0 | (15.5) | 0.0 | (24.2) | 0.0 | (20.7) | 1.4 | (13.0) | 3.2 | (10.2) |
| ii. Mean Tariff Rate | | | | | 0.0 | (74.3) | 0.0 | (98.8) | 0.0 | (79.2) | 0.0 | (55.2) | 4.0 | (30.0) |
| iii. Standard Deviation of Tariff Rates | | | | | | | | | 0.0 | (45.2) | 0.6 | (23.6) | 4.4 | (14.0) |
| (b) Non-tariff Regulatory Trade Barriers | | | | | | | | | | | | | | |
| i. Non-tariff Trade Restraints (% of trade covered) | | | | | | | 1.9 | (80.7) | 3.5 | (65.4) | 3.7 | (62.6) | | |
| ii. Size of Trade Sector (% of GDP) | 0.0 | (8.2) | 2.8 | (12.8) | 4.2 | (16.6) | 3.3 | (15.0) | 4.2 | (18.3) | 6.2 | (27.7) | 6.1 | (27.2) |
| **VII. Freedom of Exchange in Financial Markets** | **3.6** | | **2.6** | | **3.5** | | **3.6** | | **3.5** | | **3.9** | | **3.8** | |
| (a) Ownership of Banks | 0.0 | (0-10) | 0.0 | (0-10) | 0.0 | (0-10) | 0.0 | (0-10) | 0.0 | (5-10) | 2.0 | (10-15) | 2.0 | (10-15) |
| (b) Extension of Credit | 7.7 | (79.1) | 7.8 | (79.7) | 7.4 | (76.6) | 7.6 | (78.3) | 7.1 | (73.9) | 6.4 | (67.8) | 6.1 | (64.4) |
| (c) Avoidance of Negative Interest Rates | 8.0 | | 4.0 | | 8.0 | | 8.0 | | 8.0 | | 8.0 | | 8.0 | |
| (d) Capital Transactions with Foreigners | 0.0 | | 0.0 | | 0.0 | | 0.0 | | 0.0 | | 0.0 | | 0.0 | |

# INDONESIA

| | 1970 | 1975 | 1980 | 1985 | 1990 | 1995 | 1997 |
|---|---|---|---|---|---|---|---|
| **Summary Ratings** | 4.8 | 5.0 | 5.2 | 5.9 | 6.8 | 7.3 | 7.2 |
| **Rank** | 44 | 47 | 53 | 40 | 32 | 43 | 49 |

| Components of Economic Freedom | 1970 | | 1975 | | 1980 | | 1985 | | 1990 | | 1995 | | 1997 | |
|---|---|---|---|---|---|---|---|---|---|---|---|---|---|---|
| **I. Size of Government** | **9.3** | | **9.2** | | **8.5** | | **8.6** | | **9.0** | | **9.3** | | **9.4** | |
| (a) Government Consumption (% of Total) | 9.1 | (9.3) | 8.6 | (12.2) | 7.8 | (16.7) | 7.8 | (16.4) | 8.4 | (13.0) | 8.8 | (11.3) | 9.0 | (10.0) |
| (b) Transfers and Subsidies (% of GDP) | 9.4 | (2.7) | 9.7 | (1.5) | 9.2 | (3.3) | 9.5 | (2.5) | 9.6 | (2.0) | 9.9 | (0.9) | 9.7 | (1.6) |
| **II. Structure of the Economy and Use of Markets** | | | **3.9** | | **2.5** | | **3.6** | | **5.1** | | **4.0** | | **4.0** | |
| (a) Government Enterprises | 4.0 | (40.4) | 4.0 | (39.4) | 2.0 | (49.5) | 2.0 | (45.8) | 4.0 | (32.1) | 4.0 | (33.9) | 4.0 | |
| (b) Price Controls | | | | | | | | | 6.0 | | 2.0 | | 2.0 | |
| (c) Top Marginal Tax Rate | | | 4.0 | (48) | 3.0 | (50) | 7.0 | (35) | 7.0 | (35) | 8.0 | (30) | 8.0 | (30) |
| (d) Conscription | 3.0 | | 3.0 | | 3.0 | | 0.0 | | 0.0 | | 0.0 | | 0.0 | |
| **III. Monetary Policy and Price Stability** | **2.5** | | **5.0** | | **5.0** | | **8.7** | | **8.2** | | **8.7** | | **8.2** | |
| (a) Annual Money Growth (last 5 yrs.) | 0.0 | (143.9) | 3.6 | (32.0) | 5.2 | (24.1) | 8.3 | (8.3) | 7.5 | (12.3) | 8.6 | (7.2) | 7.5 | (12.5) |
| (b) Inflation Variability (last 5 yrs.) | 0.0 | (449.9) | 3.6 | (16.1) | 6.1 | (9.8) | 8.6 | (3.5) | 7.9 | (5.4) | 9.4 | (1.5) | 9.4 | (1.4) |
| (c) Recent Inflation Rate | 7.3 | (13.6) | 7.8 | (11.2) | 3.8 | (31.0) | 9.1 | (4.3) | 9.1 | (4.3) | 8.0 | (9.9) | 7.6 | (12.0) |
| **IV. Freedom to Use Alternative Currencies** | **8.3** | | **9.3** | | **9.8** | | **9.3** | | **10.0** | | **10.0** | | **9.9** | |
| (a) Ownership of Foreign Currency | 10.0 | | 10.0 | | 10.0 | | 10.0 | | 10.0 | | 10.0 | | 10.0 | |
| (b) Black Market Exchange Rates (Prem.) | 6.6 | (17.0) | 8.6 | (7.0) | 9.6 | (2.0) | 8.6 | (7.0) | 10.0 | (0.0) | 10.0 | (0.0) | 9.8 | (1.0) |
| **V. Legal Structure and Property Rights** | **3.8** | | **3.4** | | **3.1** | | **4.2** | | **5.5** | | **7.6** | | **7.6** | |
| (a) Private Ownership Rights | 4.5 | | 3.5 | | 4.6 | | 6.1 | | 6.6 | | 10.0 | | 10.0 | |
| (b) Viability of Contracts' | 3.1 | | 3.3 | | 3.0 | | 3.4 | | 6.4 | | 8.4 | | 8.3 | |
| (c) Rule of Law | | | | | 1.7 | | 3.1 | | 3.3 | | 4.1 | | 4.1 | |
| **VI. International Exchange** | **5.5** | | **5.4** | | **6.7** | | **5.8** | | **6.7** | | **7.1** | | **6.9** | |
| (a) Taxes on International Trade | | | | | | | | | | | | | | |
| i. Taxes as a Percentage of Exports and Imports | 5.4 | (6.9) | 7.3 | (4.0) | 8.1 | (2.9) | 8.9 | (1.6) | 8.3 | (2.5) | 8.6 | (2.1) | 9.3 | (1.0) |
| ii. Mean Tariff Rate | | | 2.3 | (38.5) | 4.2 | (29.0) | 6.4 | (18.1) | 5.9 | (20.3) | 6.6 | (17.0) | 7.4 | (13.2) |
| iii. Standard Deviation of Tariff Rates | | | | | | | | | 3.3 | (16.7) | 3.6 | (16.1) | 3.2 | (17.0) |
| (b) Non-tariff Regulatory Trade Barriers | | | | | | | | | | | | | | |
| i. Non-tariff Trade Restraints (% of trade covered) | | | | | | | 0.5 | (94.7) | 9.1 | (9.4) | 9.7 | (2.7) | | |
| ii. Size of Trade Sector (% of GDP) | 5.8 | (28.4) | 8.7 | (45.0) | 10.0 | (54.4) | 7.7 | (43.5) | 8.4 | (49.9) | 8.2 | (51.7) | 8.8 | (56.4) |
| **VII. Freedom of Exchange in Financial Markets** | **0.6** | | **0.6** | | **2.0** | | **3.1** | | **4.9** | | **5.8** | | **5.8** | |
| (a) Ownership of Banks | 0.0 | (0-10) | 0.0 | (0-10) | 0.0 | (0-10) | 2.0 | (10-15) | 2.0 | (15-25) | 5.0 | (40-60) | 5.0 | (40-60) |
| (b) Extension of Credit | | | | | 7.3 | (75.2) | 7.3 | (75.7) | 9.2 | (92.4) | 9.3 | (93.9) | 9.3 | (93.5) |
| (c) Avoidance of Negative Interest Rates | 2.0 | | 2.0 | | 2.0 | | 4.0 | | 10.0 | | 10.0 | | 10.0 | |
| (d) Capital Transactions with Foreigners | 0.0 | | 0.0 | | 0.0 | | 0.0 | | 0.0 | | 0.0 | | 0.0 | |

# IRAN

| | 1970 | 1975 | 1980 | 1985 | 1990 | 1995 | 1997 |
|---|---|---|---|---|---|---|---|
| **Summary Ratings** | 6.2 | 6.2 | 3.4 | 3.4 | 4.3 | 3.9 | 5.0 |
| **Rank** | 34 | 25 | 97 | 98 | 89 | 112 | 99 |

| Components of Economic Freedom | 1970 | | 1975 | | 1980 | | 1985 | | 1990 | | 1995 | | 1997 | |
|---|---|---|---|---|---|---|---|---|---|---|---|---|---|---|
| **I. Size of Government** | **9.0** | | **6.0** | | **6.9** | | **8.3** | | **8.5** | | **8.3** | | **8.5** | |
| (a) Government Consumption (% of Total) | | | 4.2 | (35.9) | 5.6 | (28.3) | 7.2 | (19.6) | 8.0 | (15.2) | 7.3 | (19.2) | 7.5 | (17.9) |
| (b) Transfers and Subsidies (% of GDP) | 9.0 | (4.3) | 7.7 | (8.9) | 8.2 | (7.0) | 9.3 | (3.0) | 8.9 | (4.4) | 9.3 | (3.1) | 9.4 | (2.7) |
| **II. Structure of the Economy and Use of Markets** | | | **5.0** | | | | **1.0** | | **1.3** | | **2.3** | | **2.3** | |
| (a) Government Enterprises | 4.0 | | 4.0 | | 2.0 | (47.6) | 2.0 | (40.0) | 2.0 | (42.2) | 2.0 | (39.1) | 2.0 | |
| (b) Price Controls | | | | | | | | | 2.0 | | 2.0 | | 2.0 | |
| (c) Top Marginal Tax Rate | | | 8.0 | (40) | | | 0.0 | (90) | 0.0 | (75) | 4.0 | (54) | 4.0 | (54) |
| (d) Conscription | 0.0 | | 0.0 | | 3.0 | | 0.0 | | 0.0 | | 0.0 | | 0.0 | |
| **III. Monetary Policy and Price Stability** | **9.6** | | **7.3** | | **5.9** | | **7.5** | | **8.2** | | **4.7** | | **6.9** | |
| (a) Annual Money Growth (last 5 yrs.) | 9.6 | (1.8) | 4.7 | (26.6) | 4.6 | (26.8) | 5.9 | (20.3) | 6.9 | (15.3) | 4.7 | (26.4) | 4.7 | (26.5) |
| (b) Inflation Variability (last 5 yrs.) | 9.6 | (1.1) | 8.5 | (3.8) | 7.7 | (5.9) | 7.4 | (6.5) | 8.7 | (3.2) | 7.3 | (6.7) | 9.4 | (1.5) |
| (c) Recent Inflation Rate | 9.7 | (1.7) | 8.8 | (5.8) | 5.3 | (23.4) | 9.1 | (4.7) | 9.1 | (4.7) | 2.1 | (39.5) | 6.6 | (17.2) |
| **IV. Freedom to Use Alternative Currencies** | **7.0** | | **7.3** | | **5.0** | | **5.0** | | **5.0** | | **0.0** | | **2.5** | |
| (a) Ownership of Foreign Currency | 5.0 | | 5.0 | | 10.0 | | 10.0 | | 10.0 | | 0.0 | | 5.0 | |
| (b) Black Market Exchange Rates (Prem.) | 9.0 | (5.0) | 9.6 | (2.0) | 0.0 | (164.0) | 0.0 | (533.0) | 0.0 | (2197.0) | 0.0 | (115.0) | 0.0 | (60.0) |
| **V. Legal Structure and Property Rights** | **4.6** | | **3.7** | | **0.5** | | **1.5** | | **2.3** | | **5.9** | | **7.5** | |
| (a) Private Ownership Rights | 4.9 | | 4.5 | | 0.0 | | 0.0 | | 1.2 | | 5.5 | | 7.2 | |
| (b) Viability of Contracts | 4.3 | | 2.8 | | 0.0 | | 1.6 | | 4.0 | | 5.2 | | 8.3 | |
| (c) Rule of Law | | | | | 1.7 | | 3.1 | | 1.7 | | 7.0 | | 7.0 | |
| **VI. International Exchange** | **3.5** | | **8.3** | | **3.2** | | **2.7** | | **5.6** | | **5.1** | | **4.8** | |
| (a) Taxes on International Trade | | | | | | | | | | | | | | |
| i. Taxes as a Percentage of Exports and Imports | 2.4 | (11.4) | 7.6 | (3.6) | 0.0 | (17.0) | 0.5 | (14.2) | 5.1 | (7.3) | 8.6 | (2.1) | 5.2 | (7.3) |
| ii. Mean Tariff Rate | | | | | 5.9 | (20.7) | 5.9 | (20.7) | 5.9 | (20.7) | 5.9 | (20.7) | | |
| iii. Standard Deviation of Tariff Rates | | | | | | | | | | | | | | |
| (b) Non-tariff Regulatory Trade Barriers | | | | | | | | | | | | | | |
| i. Non-tariff Trade Restraints (% of trade covered) | | | | | | | | | | | 0.1 | (99.3) | | |
| ii. Size of Trade Sector (% of GDP) | 6.2 | (40.5) | 10.0 | (76.0) | 4.1 | (29.7) | 0.0 | (16.0) | 6.0 | (45.5) | 4.6 | (36.4) | 3.9 | (32.7) |
| **VII. Freedom of Exchange in Financial Markets** | | | | | **1.7** | | **1.5** | | **1.8** | | **2.0** | | **4.0** | |
| (a) Ownership of Banks | | | | | 0.0 | (0-5) | 0.0 | (0-5) | 0.0 | (0) | 0.0 | (0-5) | 0.0 | (0-5) |
| (b) Extension of Credit | 9.7 | (97.2) | 8.2 | (83.3) | 7.8 | (80.2) | 6.9 | (71.8) | 8.5 | (86.6) | 9.4 | (94.7) | 9.6 | (96.7) |
| (c) Avoidance of Negative Interest Rates | | | | | 0.0 | | 0.0 | | 0.0 | | 0.0 | | 8.0 | |
| (d) Capital Transactions with Foreigners | 5.0 | | 5.0 | | 0.0 | | 0.0 | | 0.0 | | 0.0 | | 0.0 | |

# IRELAND

| | 1970 | 1975 | 1980 | 1985 | 1990 | 1995 | 1997 |
|---|---|---|---|---|---|---|---|
| **Summary Ratings** | 6.8 | 6.2 | 6.6 | 6.7 | 7.3 | 8.6 | 8.7 |
| **Rank** | 22 | 25 | 21 | 26 | 28 | 6 | 6 |

| Components of Economic Freedom | 1970 | | 1975 | | 1980 | | 1985 | | 1990 | | 1995 | | 1997 | |
|---|---|---|---|---|---|---|---|---|---|---|---|---|---|---|
| **I. Size of Government** | **7.2** | | **6.0** | | **6.1** | | **5.8** | | **6.3** | | **6.0** | | **6.0** | |
| (a) Government Consumption (% of Total) | 7.8 | (16.5) | 6.9 | (21.3) | 6.8 | (22.0) | 6.7 | (22.5) | 7.1 | (20.3) | 6.9 | (21.5) | 7.0 | (21.1) |
| (b) Transfers and Subsidies (% of GDP) | 6.5 | (13.2) | 5.1 | (18.3) | 5.4 | (17.5) | 4.9 | (19.3) | 5.4 | (17.3) | 5.1 | (18.5) | 5.0 | (18.8) |
| **II. Structure of the Economy and Use of Markets** | | | **4.3** | | **5.1** | | **4.8** | | **6.7** | | **7.6** | | **7.9** | |
| (a) Government Enterprises | 6.0 | (27.3) | 6.0 | (30.0) | 7.0 | (24.6) | 7.0 | (24.7) | 10.0 | (11.1) | 10.0 | (14.3) | 10.0 | (14.2) |
| (b) Price Controls | | | | | | | | | 7.0 | | 8.0 | | 9.0 | |
| (c) Top Marginal Tax Rate | | | 0.0 | (80) | 1.0 | (60) | 0.0 | (65) | 1.0 | (58) | 3.0 | (48) | 3.0 | (48) |
| (d) Conscription | | | 10.0 | | 10.0 | | 10.0 | | 10.0 | | 10.0 | | 10.0 | |
| **III. Monetary Policy and Price Stability** | **8.8** | | **7.5** | | **7.7** | | **8.8** | | **9.0** | | **9.5** | | **9.3** | |
| (a) Annual Money Growth (last 5 yrs.) | 9.5 | (2.6) | 8.4 | (7.8) | 7.4 | (12.9) | 9.5 | (2.8) | 9.1 | (4.3) | 9.1 | (4.6) | 8.7 | (6.5) |
| (b) Inflation Variability (last 5 yrs.) | 8.9 | (2.7) | 8.1 | (4.7) | 8.6 | (3.5) | 8.1 | (4.8) | 9.0 | (2.6) | 9.5 | (1.3) | 9.5 | (1.4) |
| (c) Recent Inflation Rate | 8.1 | (9.7) | 6.0 | (20.1) | 7.1 | (14.7) | 9.0 | (5.2) | 9.0 | (5.2) | 9.9 | (0.4) | 9.6 | (1.8) |
| **IV. Freedom to Use Alternative Currencies** | **5.0** | | **5.0** | | **5.0** | | **4.7** | | **4.9** | | **10.0** | | **10.0** | |
| (a) Ownership of Foreign Currency | 0.0 | | 0.0 | | 0.0 | | 0.0 | | 0.0 | | 10.0 | | 10.0 | |
| (b) Black Market Exchange Rates (Prem.) | 10.0 | (0.0) | 10.0 | (0.0) | 10.0 | (0.0) | 9.4 | (3.0) | 9.8 | (1.0) | 10.0 | (0.0) | 10.0 | (0.0) |
| **V. Legal Structure and Property Rights** | **9.3** | | **7.7** | | **7.8** | | **7.7** | | **9.1** | | **10.0** | | **10.0** | |
| (a) Private Ownership Rights | 10.0 | | 7.3 | | 8.2 | | 8.7 | | 10.0 | | 10.0 | | 10.0 | |
| (b) Viability of Contracts | 8.6 | | 8.1 | | 6.8 | | 7.6 | | 8.8 | | 10.0 | | 10.0 | |
| (c) Rule of Law | | | | | 8.3 | | 6.6 | | 8.3 | | 10.0 | | 10.0 | |
| **VI. International Exchange** | **5.6** | | **7.3** | | **8.2** | | **8.4** | | **8.0** | | **8.4** | | **8.8** | |
| (a) Taxes on International Trade | | | | | | | | | | | | | | |
| i. Taxes as a Percentage of Exports and Imports | 5.4 | (6.9) | 6.8 | (4.8) | 7.7 | (3.5) | 8.0 | (3.0) | 8.0 | (3.0) | 8.8 | (1.8) | 9.7 | (0.5) |
| ii. Mean Tariff Rate | | | 8.1 | (9.4) | 8.2 | (8.8) | 8.5 | (7.5) | 8.5 | (7.4) | 8.7 | (6.7) | 8.6 | (6.9) |
| iii. Standard Deviation of Tariff Rates | | | | | | | | | 7.1 | (7.2) | 7.6 | (5.9) | 7.6 | (6.0) |
| (b) Non-tariff Regulatory Trade Barriers | | | | | | | | | | | | | | |
| i. Non-tariff Trade Restraints (% of trade covered) | | | | | 9.2 | (8.2) | 9.0 | (9.7) | 8.9 | (10.9) | 9.1 | (9.0) | 9.3 | (6.7) |
| ii. Size of Trade Sector (% of GDP) | 6.1 | (78.9) | 6.4 | (88.0) | 7.5 | (108.4) | 7.5 | (114.3) | 6.8 | (111.3) | 7.7 | (134.1) | 8.7 | (155.1) |
| **VII. Freedom of Exchange in Financial Markets** | **6.0** | | **5.8** | | **6.3** | | **7.1** | | **7.3** | | **8.2** | | **8.3** | |
| (a) Ownership of Banks | 8.0 | | 8.0 | (95) | 8.0 | (91) | 8.0 | (87) | 8.0 | (90) | 8.0 | (93) | 8.0 | (93) |
| (b) Extension of Credit | 7.1 | | 6.3 | | 6.2 | (65.9) | 5.4 | (58.4) | 6.1 | (64.9) | 6.7 | (70.5) | 6.9 | (72.0) |
| (c) Avoidance of Negative Interest Rates | 4.0 | | 4.0 | | 6.0 | | 10.0 | | 10.0 | | 10.0 | | 10.0 | |
| (d) Capital Transactions with Foreigners | 5.0 | | 5.0 | | 5.0 | | 5.0 | | 5.0 | | 8.0 | | 8.0 | |

# ISRAEL

| | 1970 | 1975 | 1980 | 1985 | 1990 | 1995 | 1997 |
|---|---|---|---|---|---|---|---|
| **Summary Ratings** | 4.8 | 4.4 | 4.0 | 4.4 | 4.8 | 6.3 | 6.5 |
| **Rank** | 44 | 61 | 86 | 79 | 77 | 60 | 66 |

| Components of Economic Freedom | 1970 | | 1975 | | 1980 | | 1985 | | 1990 | | 1995 | | 1997 | |
|---|---|---|---|---|---|---|---|---|---|---|---|---|---|---|
| **I. Size of Government** | **5.6** | | **4.2** | | **3.7** | | **4.3** | | **5.2** | | **5.0** | | **4.7** | |
| (a) Government Consumption (% of Total) | 4.0 | (37.3) | 3.0 | (42.3) | 2.9 | (43.2) | 3.8 | (38.5) | 4.8 | (32.9) | 4.9 | (32.4) | 4.9 | (32.2) |
| (b) Transfers and Subsidies (% of GDP) | 7.2 | (10.8) | 5.3 | (17.7) | 4.5 | (20.8) | 4.8 | (19.7) | 5.6 | (16.7) | 5.1 | (18.6) | 4.5 | (20.8) |
| **II. Structure of the Economy and Use of Markets** | | | | | **1.4** | | **2.1** | | **1.7** | | **3.3** | | **3.3** | |
| (a) Government Enterprises | 2.0 | | 2.0 | | 2.0 | | 2.0 | | 2.0 | | 2.0 | | 2.0 | |
| (b) Price Controls | | | | | | | | | 0.0 | | 5.0 | | 5.0 | |
| (c) Top Marginal Tax Rate | | | | | 1.0 | (66) | 3.0 | (60) | 4.0 | (51) | 4.0 | (50) | 4.0 | (50) |
| (d) Conscription | 0.0 | | 0.0 | | 0.0 | | 0.0 | | 0.0 | | 0.0 | | 0.0 | |
| **III. Monetary Policy and Price Stability** | **8.5** | | **5.1** | | **0.7** | | **0.0** | | **2.2** | | **8.1** | | **8.4** | |
| (a) Annual Money Growth (last 5 yrs.) | 9.3 | (3.4) | 6.4 | (18.0) | 2.0 | (40.0) | 0.0 | (169.3) | 1.5 | (42.6) | 7.3 | (13.5) | 7.7 | (11.4) |
| (b) Inflation Variability (last 5 yrs.) | 8.1 | (4.9) | 5.9 | (10.2) | 0.0 | (37.4) | 0.0 | (103.7) | 5.3 | (11.7) | 8.6 | (3.5) | 9.4 | (1.6) |
| (c) Recent Inflation Rate | 8.1 | (9.6) | 3.0 | (35.2) | 0.0 | (134.7) | 0.0 | (260.0) | 0.0 | (260.0) | 8.3 | (8.4) | 8.2 | (9.0) |
| **IV. Freedom to Use Alternative Currencies** | **2.0** | | **2.5** | | **7.4** | | **6.8** | | **7.1** | | **7.5** | | **7.4** | |
| (a) Ownership of Foreign Currency | 0.0 | | 5.0 | | 5.0 | | 5.0 | | 5.0 | | 5.0 | | 5.0 | |
| (b) Black Market Exchange Rates (Prem.) | 4.0 | (30.0) | 0.0 | (60.0) | 9.8 | (1.0) | 8.6 | (7.0) | 9.2 | (4.0) | 10.0 | (0.0) | 9.8 | (1.0) |
| **V. Legal Structure and Property Rights** | **7.8** | | **8.0** | | **5.3** | | **7.3** | | **5.2** | | **8.5** | | **8.5** | |
| (a) Private Ownership Rights | 7.4 | | 7.0 | | 6.4 | | 7.4 | | 7.3 | | 10.0 | | 10.0 | |
| (b) Viability of Contracts | 8.2 | | 9.0 | | 7.5 | | 6.4 | | 6.4 | | 8.4 | | 8.3 | |
| (c) Rule of Law | | | | | 1.7 | | 8.2 | | 1.7 | | 7.0 | | 7.0 | |
| **VI. International Exchange** | **4.3** | | **4.8** | | **6.4** | | **7.3** | | **7.8** | | **7.4** | | **8.2** | |
| (a) Taxes on International Trade | | | | | | | | | | | | | | |
| i. Taxes as a Percentage of Exports and Imports | 4.1 | (8.9) | 4.7 | (8.0) | 6.6 | (5.1) | 8.1 | (2.9) | 9.4 | (0.9) | 9.8 | (0.2) | 9.8 | (0.2) |
| ii. Mean Tariff Rate | | | | | | | | | | | 8.3 | (8.3) | | |
| iii. Standard Deviation of Tariff Rates | | | | | | | | | | | 5.7 | (10.8) | | |
| (b) Non-tariff Regulatory Trade Barriers | | | | | | | | | | | | | | |
| i. Non-tariff Trade Restraints (% of trade covered) | | | | | | | | | | | | | | |
| ii. Size of Trade Sector (% of GDP) | 4.8 | (70.0) | 5.1 | (76.5) | 5.7 | (90.8) | 5.2 | (86.3) | 3.7 | (69.1) | 3.5 | (69.1) | 3.9 | (75.9) |
| **VII. Freedom of Exchange in Financial Markets** | **2.3** | | **2.2** | | **1.5** | | **1.1** | | **3.1** | | **4.2** | | **4.9** | |
| (a) Ownership of Banks | 0.0 | (0-5) | 0.0 | (0-5) | 0.0 | (0-5) | 0.0 | (0-10) | 0.0 | (0-10) | 0.0 | (0-10) | 0.0 | (0-10) |
| (b) Extension of Credit | 5.5 | (59.3) | 5.4 | (58.4) | 4.7 | (52.4) | 2.7 | (34.3) | 4.9 | (54.2) | 7.9 | (81.3) | 9.1 | (91.5) |
| (c) Avoidance of Negative Interest Rates | | | | | 0.0 | | 0.0 | | 6.0 | | 8.0 | | 10.0 | |
| (d) Capital Transactions with Foreigners | 2.0 | | 2.0 | | 2.0 | | 2.0 | | 2.0 | | 2.0 | | 2.0 | |

# ITALY

| | 1970 | 1975 | 1980 | 1985 | 1990 | 1995 | 1997 |
|---|---|---|---|---|---|---|---|
| **Summary Ratings** | 6.8 | 5.5 | 5.5 | 6.0 | 7.4 | 7.5 | 7.9 |
| **Rank** | 22 | 42 | 44 | 36 | 24 | 40 | 31 |

| Components of Economic Freedom | 1970 | | 1975 | | 1980 | | 1985 | | 1990 | | 1995 | | 1997 | |
|---|---|---|---|---|---|---|---|---|---|---|---|---|---|---|
| **I. Size of Government** | **6.7** | | **6.4** | | **5.8** | | **4.6** | | **4.9** | | **4.7** | | **5.7** | |
| (a) Government Consumption (% of Total) | 7.5 | (18.3) | 7.4 | (18.8) | 7.2 | (19.7) | 6.9 | (21.4) | 6.7 | (22.3) | 7.0 | (20.7) | 7.0 | (21.0) |
| (b) Transfers and Subsidies (% of GDP) | 5.9 | (15.6) | 5.4 | (17.5) | 4.4 | (20.9) | 2.4 | (28.5) | 3.1 | (25.8) | 2.3 | (28.7) | 4.4 | (21.0) |
| **II. Structure of the Economy and Use of Markets** | | | **3.8** | | **2.1** | | **2.1** | | **3.5** | | **4.2** | | **4.2** | |
| (a) Government Enterprises | 4.0 | | 4.0 | (30.4) | 4.0 | (25.9) | 4.0 | (33.2) | 4.0 | (30.3) | 6.0 | (28.3) | 6.0 | |
| (b) Price Controls | | | | | | | | | 5.0 | | 5.0 | | 5.0 | |
| (c) Top Marginal Tax Rate | | | 5.0 | (48) | 0.0 | (72) | 0.0 | (81) | 1.0 | (66) | 1.0 | (67) | 1.0 | (67.2) |
| (d) Conscription | 0.0 | | 0.0 | | 1.0 | | 1.0 | | 3.0 | | 3.0 | | 3.0 | |
| **III. Monetary Policy and Price Stability** | **8.4** | | **7.3** | | **7.1** | | **8.3** | | **8.9** | | **9.3** | | **9.5** | |
| (a) Annual Money Growth (last 5 yrs.) | 7.4 | (12.8) | 7.5 | (12.7) | 6.5 | (17.7) | 8.1 | (9.7) | 8.8 | (6.3) | 9.5 | (2.5) | 9.5 | (2.7) |
| (b) Inflation Variability (last 5 yrs.) | 9.3 | (1.8) | 7.8 | (5.6) | 9.0 | (2.4) | 8.5 | (3.7) | 9.7 | (0.7) | 9.4 | (1.4) | 9.6 | (0.9) |
| (c) Recent Inflation Rate | 8.6 | (6.9) | 6.8 | (16.1) | 5.8 | (20.9) | 8.2 | (9.0) | 8.2 | (9.0) | 9.0 | (5.1) | 9.5 | (2.6) |
| **IV. Freedom to Use Alternative Currencies** | **4.8** | | **4.1** | | **5.0** | | **5.0** | | **10.0** | | **10.0** | | **10.0** | |
| (a) Ownership of Foreign Currency | 0.0 | | 0.0 | | 0.0 | | 0.0 | | 10.0 | | 10.0 | | 10.0 | |
| (b) Black Market Exchange Rates (Prem.) | 9.6 | (2.0) | 8.2 | (9.0) | 10.0 | (0.0) | 10.0 | (0.0) | 10.0 | (0.0) | 10.0 | (0.0) | 10.0 | (0.0) |
| **V. Legal Structure and Property Rights** | **6.6** | | **3.7** | | **5.4** | | **8.1** | | **9.5** | | **8.5** | | **9.4** | |
| (a) Private Ownership Rights | 7.0 | | 3.8 | | 4.3 | | 7.4 | | 10.0 | | 10.0 | | 10.0 | |
| (b) Viability of Contracts | 6.2 | | 3.6 | | 3.7 | | 8.8 | | 10.0 | | 8.4 | | 8.3 | |
| (c) Rule of Law | | | | | 8.3 | | 8.2 | | 8.3 | | 7.0 | | 10.0 | |
| **VI. International Exchange** | **8.5** | | **8.3** | | **8.4** | | **8.5** | | **8.2** | | **8.5** | | **8.4** | |
| (a) Taxes on International Trade | | | | | | | | | | | | | | |
| i. Taxes as a Percentage of Exports and Imports | 9.9 | (0.2) | 9.8 | (0.3) | 9.7 | (0.4) | 9.8 | (0.3) | 9.8 | (0.3) | 9.8 | (0.3) | 9.8 | (0.3) |
| ii. Mean Tariff Rate | | | 7.8 | (11.0) | 8.2 | (8.8) | 8.5 | (7.5) | 8.5 | (7.4) | 8.7 | (6.7) | 8.6 | (6.9) |
| iii. Standard Deviation of Tariff Rates | | | | | | | | | 7.1 | (7.2) | 7.6 | (5.9) | 7.6 | (6.0) |
| (b) Non-tariff Regulatory Trade Barriers | | | | | | | | | | | | | | |
| i. Non-tariff Trade Restraints (% of trade covered) | | | | | 8.3 | (17.2) | 8.2 | (18.2) | 8.9 | (10.9) | 9.1 | (9.0) | 9.3 | (6.7) |
| ii. Size of Trade Sector (% of GDP) | 4.8 | (32.9) | 5.7 | (41.3) | 6.1 | (46.7) | 5.6 | (46.1) | 4.5 | (40.0) | 5.4 | (50.9) | 4.8 | (46.3) |
| **VII. Freedom of Exchange in Financial Markets** | **6.3** | | **5.5** | | **4.9** | | **5.3** | | **6.3** | | **7.3** | | **7.8** | |
| (a) Ownership of Banks | 5.0 | (40-75) | 5.0 | (40-75) | 5.0 | (40-75) | 5.0 | (40-75) | 5.0 | (62) | 5.0 | (60-75) | 5.0 | (60-75) |
| (b) Extension of Credit | 7.5 | (77.9) | 6.2 | (66.0) | 5.6 | (60.5) | 5.2 | (57.2) | 5.3 | (57.9) | 6.2 | (65.3) | 6.2 | (65.5) |
| (c) Avoidance of Negative Interest Rates | 8.0 | | 6.0 | | 4.0 | | 6.0 | | 10.0 | | 10.0 | | 10.0 | |
| (d) Capital Transactions with Foreigners | 5.0 | | 5.0 | | 5.0 | | 5.0 | | 5.0 | | 8.0 | | 10.0 | |

# JAMAICA

| | 1970 | 1975 | 1980 | 1985 | 1990 | 1995 | 1997 |
|---|---|---|---|---|---|---|---|
| **Summary Ratings** | | 5.0 | 4.1 | 5.1 | 5.7 | 7.3 | 7.4 |
| **Rank** | | 47 | 79 | 62 | 52 | 43 | 42 |

| Components of Economic Freedom | 1970 | | 1975 | | 1980 | | 1985 | | 1990 | | 1995 | | 1997 | |
|---|---|---|---|---|---|---|---|---|---|---|---|---|---|---|
| **I. Size of Government** | **7.9** | | **7.5** | | **6.4** | | **8.8** | | **8.5** | | **8.3** | | **6.7** | |
| (a) Government Consumption (% of Total) | 7.9 | (16.1) | 6.8 | (21.7) | 6.4 | (24.1) | 7.6 | (17.4) | 7.5 | (18.4) | 7.5 | (18.3) | 6.7 | (22.7) |
| (b) Transfers and Subsidies (% of GDP) | | | 8.2 | (7.0) | | | 10.0 | (0.5) | 9.6 | (2.0) | 9.1 | (3.9) | | |
| **II. Structure of the Economy and Use of Markets** | | | **3.1** | | **2.3** | | **3.7** | | **5.9** | | **6.2** | | **6.2** | |
| (a) Government Enterprises | 4.0 | (34.4) | 2.0 | (45.6) | 2.0 | (46.5) | 4.0 | (13.4) | 6.0 | (21.3) | 6.0 | | 6.0 | |
| (b) Price Controls | | | | | | | | | 4.0 | | 4.0 | | 4.0 | |
| (c) Top Marginal Tax Rate | 0.0 | (75) | 2.0 | (60) | 0.0 | (80) | 1.0 | (58) | 7.0 | (33) | 8.0 | (27) | 8.0 | (27) |
| (d) Conscription | | | 10.0 | | 10.0 | | 10.0 | | 10.0 | | 10.0 | | 10.0 | |
| **III. Monetary Policy and Price Stability** | **8.7** | | **5.8** | | **6.9** | | **5.3** | | **6.1** | | **3.5** | | **6.9** | |
| (a) Annual Money Growth (last 5 yrs.) | 8.0 | (9.9) | 6.6 | (17.1) | 6.4 | (18.1) | 6.4 | (17.8) | 6.2 | (19.0) | 0.8 | (45.9) | 6.2 | (19.2) |
| (b) Inflation Variability (last 5 yrs.) | 9.2 | (1.9) | 4.9 | (12.8) | 7.9 | (5.3) | 5.6 | (11.0) | 8.2 | (4.5) | 5.3 | (11.7) | 6.7 | (8.2) |
| (c) Recent Inflation Rate | 8.9 | (5.6) | 5.8 | (20.8) | 6.3 | (18.3) | 3.9 | (30.7) | 3.9 | (30.7) | 4.4 | (27.9) | 7.8 | (11.2) |
| **IV. Freedom to Use Alternative Currencies** | **8.8** | | **2.8** | | **0.0** | | **3.1** | | **2.3** | | **9.3** | | **8.5** | |
| (a) Ownership of Foreign Currency | | | 0.0 | | 0.0 | | 0.0 | | 0.0 | | 10.0 | | 10.0 | |
| (b) Black Market Exchange Rates (Prem.) | 8.8 | (6.0) | 5.6 | (22.0) | 0.0 | (61.0) | 6.2 | (19.0) | 4.6 | (27.0) | 8.6 | (7.0) | 7.0 | (15.0) |
| **V. Legal Structure and Property Rights** | | | | | **3.2** | | **3.9** | | **4.6** | | **8.0** | | **8.5** | |
| (a) Private Ownership Rights | | | | | 4.2 | | 3.5 | | 5.3 | | 10.0 | | 10.0 | |
| (b) Viability of Contracts | | | | | 3.7 | | 5.2 | | 5.2 | | 6.8 | | 8.3 | |
| (c) Rule of Law | | | | | 1.7 | | 3.1 | | 3.3 | | 7.0 | | 7.0 | |
| **VI. International Exchange** | | | **6.5** | | **7.6** | | **7.5** | | **6.2** | | **6.9** | | **6.7** | |
| (a) Taxes on International Trade | | | | | | | | | | | | | | |
| i. Taxes as a Percentage of Exports and Imports | | | 7.3 | (4.0) | 9.4 | (0.9) | 8.9 | (1.7) | | | | | | |
| ii. Mean Tariff Rate | | | | | 6.7 | (16.5) | 6.6 | (17.0) | 6.6 | (17.0) | 7.2 | (14.0) | 7.2 | (14.0) |
| iii. Standard Deviation of Tariff Rates | | | | | | | | | | | 5.0 | (12.5) | | |
| (b) Non-tariff Regulatory Trade Barriers | | | | | | | | | | | | | | |
| i. Non-tariff Trade Restraints (% of trade covered) | | | | | | | | | | | 9.3 | (6.6) | | |
| ii. Size of Trade Sector (% of GDP) | 4.0 | (70.6) | 4.5 | (80.9) | 5.4 | (102.1) | 6.1 | (121.6) | 5.1 | (108.0) | 6.1 | (135.8) | 5.5 | (123.3) |
| **VII. Freedom of Exchange in Financial Markets** | | | | | **3.7** | | **4.1** | | **6.9** | | **7.8** | | **7.7** | |
| (a) Ownership of Banks | | | | | | | 5.0 | (40) | 10.0 | (95-100) | 10.0 | (95-100) | 10.0 | (95-100) |
| (b) Extension of Credit | 7.9 | (81.4) | 7.8 | (80.2) | 5.7 | (61.2) | 5.5 | (59.8) | 8.0 | (81.6) | 7.0 | (72.8) | 6.4 | (67.9) |
| (c) Avoidance of Negative Interest Rates | | | | | 4.0 | | 4.0 | | 8.0 | | 6.0 | | 6.0 | |
| (d) Capital Transactions with Foreigners | 2.0 | | 2.0 | | 2.0 | | 2.0 | | 2.0 | | 8.0 | | 8.0 | |

# JAPAN

| | 1970 | 1975 | 1980 | 1985 | 1990 | 1995 | 1997 |
|---|---|---|---|---|---|---|---|
| **Summary Ratings** | 7.3 | 7.0 | 7.4 | 7.7 | 8.3 | 8.2 | 8.3 |
| **Rank** | 16 | 14 | 11 | 12 | 7 | 12 | 14 |

| Components of Economic Freedom | 1970 | | 1975 | | 1980 | | 1985 | | 1990 | | 1995 | | 1997 | |
|---|---|---|---|---|---|---|---|---|---|---|---|---|---|---|
| **I. Size of Government** | **9.1** | | **8.2** | | **7.9** | | **7.7** | | **7.7** | | **7.5** | | **8.3** | |
| (a) Government Consumption (% of Total) | 8.5 | (12.5) | 8.1 | (14.9) | 8.2 | (14.3) | 8.3 | (14.0) | 8.4 | (13.5) | 8.3 | (14.0) | 8.3 | (13.9) |
| (b) Transfers and Subsidies (% of GDP) | 9.7 | (1.6) | 8.3 | (6.7) | 7.6 | (9.2) | 7.2 | (10.9) | 7.0 | (11.5) | 6.8 | (12.2) | | |
| **II. Structure of the Economy and Use of Markets** | | | **5.6** | | **5.3** | | **5.6** | | **6.0** | | **5.0** | | **5.0** | |
| (a) Government Enterprises | 8.0 | (12.7) | 8.0 | (15.6) | 8.0 | (19.6) | 8.0 | (17.9) | 8.0 | (20.4) | 6.0 | (28.5) | 6.0 | (26.5) |
| (b) Price Controls | | | | | | | | | 6.0 | | 5.0 | | 5.0 | |
| (c) Top Marginal Tax Rate | | | 1.0 | (68) | 0.0 | (75) | 1.0 | (70) | 2.0 | (65) | 2.0 | (65) | 2.0 | (65) |
| (d) Conscription | 10.0 | | 10.0 | | 10.0 | | 10.0 | | 10.0 | | 10.0 | | 10.0 | |
| **III. Monetary Policy and Price Stability** | **9.1** | | **8.0** | | **9.2** | | **9.7** | | **9.6** | | **9.5** | | **9.5** | |
| (a) Annual Money Growth (last 5 yrs.) | 8.9 | (5.3) | 7.9 | (10.5) | 9.5 | (2.4) | 9.8 | (1.2) | 9.6 | (2.1) | 9.1 | (4.5) | 8.9 | (5.7) |
| (b) Inflation Variability (last 5 yrs.) | 9.7 | (0.7) | 7.6 | (5.9) | 9.3 | (1.8) | 9.7 | (0.9) | 9.7 | (0.8) | 9.5 | (1.2) | 9.8 | (0.5) |
| (c) Recent Inflation Rate | 8.7 | (6.5) | 8.6 | (7.2) | 8.9 | (5.4) | 9.6 | (2.1) | 9.6 | (2.1) | 9.9 | (-0.6) | 9.9 | (0.6) |
| **IV. Freedom to Use Alternative Currencies** | **4.9** | | **7.5** | | **7.5** | | **7.5** | | **10.0** | | **10.0** | | **10.0** | |
| (a) Ownership of Foreign Currency | 0.0 | | 5.0 | | 5.0 | | 5.0 | | 10.0 | | 10.0 | | 10.0 | |
| (b) Black Market Exchange Rates (Prem.) | 9.8 | (1.0) | 10.0 | (0.0) | 10.0 | (0.0) | 10.0 | (0.0) | 10.0 | (0.0) | 10.0 | (0.0) | 10.0 | (0.0) |
| **V. Legal Structure and Property Rights** | **9.1** | | **7.1** | | **8.3** | | **8.6** | | **9.5** | | **10.0** | | **10.0** | |
| (a) Private Ownership Rights | 9.6 | | 7.0 | | 8.8 | | 8.7 | | 10.0 | | 10.0 | | 10.0 | |
| (b) Viability of Contracts | 8.6 | | 7.2 | | 6.2 | | 8.8 | | 10.0 | | 10.0 | | 10.0 | |
| (c) Rule of Law | | | | | 10.0 | | 8.2 | | 8.3 | | 10.0 | | 10.0 | |
| **VI. International Exchange** | **7.0** | | **7.9** | | **8.0** | | **8.1** | | **7.9** | | **7.6** | | **7.9** | |
| (a) Taxes on International Trade | | | | | | | | | | | | | | |
| i. Taxes as a Percentage of Exports and Imports | 8.1 | (2.8) | 9.1 | (1.3) | 9.4 | (0.9) | 9.5 | (0.8) | 9.4 | (0.9) | 8.9 | (1.6) | 9.0 | (1.5) |
| ii. Mean Tariff Rate | | | 7.8 | (11.0) | 8.1 | (9.5) | 8.7 | (6.7) | 8.6 | (6.9) | 8.7 | (6.3) | 8.8 | (6.0) |
| iii. Standard Deviation of Tariff Rates | | | | | | | | | 6.7 | (8.3) | 6.6 | (8.4) | 6.8 | (8.0) |
| (b) Non-tariff Regulatory Trade Barriers | | | | | | | | | | | | | | |
| i. Non-tariff Trade Restraints (% of trade covered) | | | | | 7.6 | (24.4) | 7.6 | (24.3) | 9.1 | (8.6) | 9.2 | (8.1) | 9.3 | (7.4) |
| ii. Size of Trade Sector (% of GDP) | 4.2 | (20.3) | 5.1 | (25.6) | 5.4 | (28.3) | 4.5 | (25.5) | 2.8 | (20.6) | 0.8 | (17.3) | 2.2 | (21.0) |
| **VII. Freedom of Exchange in Financial Markets** | **5.7** | | **5.6** | | **6.1** | | **7.0** | | **7.8** | | **7.8** | | **7.9** | |
| (a) Ownership of Banks | 8.0 | (82) | 8.0 | (77) | 5.0 | (71) | 5.0 | (69) | 5.0 | (74) | 5.0 | (66) | 5.0 | (60-70) |
| (b) Extension of Credit | 9.4 | (94.5) | 9.1 | (91.8) | 8.3 | (84.4) | 8.5 | (86.4) | 8.8 | (89.0) | 8.8 | (89.1) | 8.8 | (89.5) |
| (c) Avoidance of Negative Interest Rates | 4.0 | | 4.0 | | 10.0 | | 10.0 | | 10.0 | | 10.0 | | 10.0 | |
| (d) Capital Transactions with Foreigners | 2.0 | | 2.0 | | 2.0 | | 5.0 | | 8.0 | | 8.0 | | 8.0 | |

# JORDAN

| | 1970 | 1975 | 1980 | 1985 | 1990 | 1995 | 1997 |
|---|---|---|---|---|---|---|---|
| **Summary Ratings** | | 5.6 | 5.6 | 6.1 | 4.9 | 6.1 | 6.1 |
| **Rank** | | 38 | 41 | 34 | 71 | 67 | 78 |

| Components of Economic Freedom | 1970 | | 1975 | | 1980 | | 1985 | | 1990 | | 1995 | | 1997 | |
|---|---|---|---|---|---|---|---|---|---|---|---|---|---|---|
| **I. Size of Government** | | | **5.4** | | **7.2** | | **7.7** | | **7.7** | | **7.6** | | **7.6** | |
| (a) Government Consumption (% of Total) | | | 5.4 | (29.6) | 5.9 | (26.8) | 6.6 | (22.9) | 6.2 | (25.1) | 5.8 | (27.4) | 5.9 | (26.6) |
| (b) Transfers and Subsidies (% of GDP) | | | | | 8.4 | (6.3) | 8.7 | (5.1) | 9.1 | (3.7) | 9.4 | (2.7) | 9.2 | (3.4) |
| **II. Structure of the Economy and Use of Markets** | | | | | | | | | **2.8** | | **2.1** | | **2.1** | |
| (a) Government Enterprises | 0.0 | (82.2) | 0.0 | (83.3) | 0.0 | (53.1) | 0.0 | (52.7) | 0.0 | | 0.0 | | 0.0 | |
| (b) Price Controls | | | | | | | | | 2.0 | | 2.0 | | 2.0 | |
| (c) Top Marginal Tax Rate | | | | | | | | | 5.0 | (45) | | | | |
| (d) Conscription | 0.0 | | 10.0 | | 10.0 | | 10.0 | | 10.0 | | 10.0 | | 10.0 | |
| **III. Monetary Policy and Price Stability** | | | **7.5** | | **7.4** | | **8.8** | | **8.2** | | **9.5** | | **9.5** | |
| (a) Annual Money Growth (last 5 yrs.) | | | 7.0 | (14.9) | 5.9 | (20.7) | 9.5 | (-2.5) | 8.2 | (9.0) | 9.8 | (1.0) | 9.3 | (-3.4) |
| (b) Inflation Variability (last 5 yrs.) | | | 8.0 | (4.9) | 6.6 | (8.4) | 7.1 | (7.3) | 6.7 | (8.1) | 9.5 | (1.2) | 9.8 | (0.5) |
| (c) Recent Inflation Rate | 8.8 | (5.9) | 7.6 | (12.2) | 9.8 | (1.1) | 9.7 | (-1.5) | 9.7 | (-1.5) | 9.3 | (3.4) | 9.5 | (2.7) |
| **IV. Freedom to Use Alternative Currencies** | **4.4** | | **4.9** | | **7.5** | | **7.2** | | **3.9** | | **4.9** | | **4.9** | |
| (a) Ownership of Foreign Currency | 0.0 | | 0.0 | | 5.0 | | 5.0 | | 0.0 | | 0.0 | | 0.0 | |
| (b) Black Market Exchange Rates (Prem.) | 8.8 | (6.0) | 9.8 | (1.0) | 10.0 | (0.0) | 9.4 | (3.0) | 7.8 | (11.0) | 9.8 | (1.0) | 9.8 | (1.0) |
| **V. Legal Structure and Property Rights** | | | | | **1.9** | | **3.1** | | **3.2** | | **7.2** | | **7.0** | |
| (a) Private Ownership Rights | | | | | 1.6 | | 3.5 | | 4.6 | | 7.7 | | 10.0 | |
| (b) Viability of Contracts | | | | | 2.4 | | 2.8 | | 1.6 | | 6.8 | | 6.6 | |
| (c) Rule of Law | | | | | 1.7 | | 3.1 | | 3.3 | | 7.0 | | 4.1 | |
| **VI. International Exchange** | | | **6.0** | | **6.1** | | **6.7** | | **5.9** | | **7.4** | | **6.7** | |
| (a) Taxes on International Trade | | | | | | | | | | | | | | |
| i. Taxes as a Percentage of Exports and Imports | | | 5.5 | (6.8) | 5.3 | (7.1) | 5.9 | (6.1) | 6.7 | (5.0) | 6.2 | (5.7) | 6.3 | (5.5) |
| ii. Mean Tariff Rate | | | | | | | 7.2 | (13.8) | | | | | | |
| iii. Standard Deviation of Tariff Rates | | | | | | | | | 2.6 | (18.5) | | | | |
| (b) Non-tariff Regulatory Trade Barriers | | | | | | | | | | | | | | |
| i. Non-tariff Trade Restraints (% of trade covered) | | | | | | | | | 7.4 | (25.6) | 8.7 | (12.9) | | |
| ii. Size of Trade Sector (% of GDP) | 2.0 | (44.6) | 7.5 | (110.8) | 8.1 | (124.1) | 7.2 | (113.1) | 9.5 | (154.6) | 7.6 | (126.2) | 7.5 | (125.1) |
| **VII. Freedom of Exchange in Financial Markets** | | | **4.8** | | **5.0** | | **4.8** | | **4.6** | | **5.3** | | **6.4** | |
| (a) Ownership of Banks | | | 5.0 | (40-75) | 5.0 | (40-75) | 5.0 | (40-75) | 5.0 | (40-75) | 5.0 | (40-75) | 5.0 | (40-75) |
| (b) Extension of Credit | 9.2 | (93.0) | 8.1 | (82.5) | 8.9 | (90.1) | 8.2 | (83.9) | 8.0 | (81.5) | 9.2 | (93.0) | 9.5 | (95.6) |
| (c) Avoidance of Negative Interest Rates | | | | | | | | | 4.0 | | 6.0 | | 10.0 | |
| (d) Capital Transactions with Foreigners | 2.0 | | 2.0 | | 2.0 | | 2.0 | | 2.0 | | 2.0 | | 2.0 | |

# KENYA

| | 1970 | 1975 | 1980 | 1985 | 1990 | 1995 | 1997 |
|---|---|---|---|---|---|---|---|
| **Summary Ratings** | 5.0 | 4.8 | 4.8 | 5.1 | 5.1 | 6.2 | 6.8 |
| **Rank** | 43 | 53 | 67 | 62 | 64 | 64 | 57 |

| Components of Economic Freedom | 1970 | | 1975 | | 1980 | | 1985 | | 1990 | | 1995 | | 1997 | |
|---|---|---|---|---|---|---|---|---|---|---|---|---|---|---|
| **I. Size of Government** | **8.3** | | **8.2** | | **7.9** | | **7.7** | | **8.0** | | **8.6** | | **7.3** | |
| (a) Government Consumption (% of Total) | 6.9 | (21.3) | 6.9 | (21.2) | 6.4 | (24.2) | 6.6 | (23.3) | 6.6 | (23.1) | 7.6 | (17.6) | 7.3 | (19.1) |
| (b) Transfers and Subsidies (% of GDP) | 9.7 | (1.6) | 9.4 | (2.7) | 9.5 | (2.3) | 8.9 | (4.7) | 9.4 | (2.8) | 9.6 | (1.9) | | |
| **II. Structure of the Economy and Use of Markets** | **3.3** | | **2.3** | | **2.7** | | **2.3** | | **3.0** | | **3.6** | | **5.3** | |
| (a) Government Enterprises | 4.0 | (30.5) | 2.0 | (43.6) | 2.0 | (46.4) | 2.0 | (40.5) | 2.0 | (44.5) | 2.0 | (50.5) | 2.0 | |
| (b) Price Controls | | | | | | | | | 2.0 | | 4.0 | | 6.0 | |
| (c) Top Marginal Tax Rate | 0.0 | (70) | 0.0 | (70) | 1.0 | (65) | 0.0 | (65) | 3.0 | (50) | 3.0 | (50) | 7.0 | (35) |
| (d) Conscription | 10.0 | | 10.0 | | 10.0 | | 10.0 | | 10.0 | | 10.0 | | 10.0 | |
| **III. Monetary Policy and Price Stability** | **7.9** | | **7.6** | | **8.1** | | **9.0** | | **8.4** | | **7.2** | | **7.5** | |
| (a) Annual Money Growth (last 5 yrs.) | 9.1 | (4.8) | 8.9 | (5.5) | 8.5 | (7.3) | 9.1 | (4.5) | 7.5 | (12.3) | 6.7 | (16.7) | 7.7 | (11.4) |
| (b) Inflation Variability (last 5 yrs.) | 7.7 | (5.6) | 6.4 | (9.0) | 7.5 | (6.2) | 9.5 | (1.3) | 9.4 | (1.4) | 7.3 | (6.7) | 7.0 | (7.5) |
| (c) Recent Inflation Rate | 6.9 | (15.3) | 7.6 | (11.8) | 8.1 | (9.6) | 8.4 | (8.2) | 8.4 | (8.2) | 7.7 | (11.3) | 7.7 | (11.6) |
| **IV. Freedom to Use Alternative Currencies** | **1.9** | | **4.2** | | **4.0** | | **4.8** | | **4.4** | | **7.3** | | **9.4** | |
| (a) Ownership of Foreign Currency | 0.0 | | 0.0 | | 0.0 | | 0.0 | | 0.0 | | 5.0 | | 10.0 | |
| (b) Black Market Exchange Rates (Prem.) | 3.8 | (31.0) | 8.4 | (8.0) | 8.0 | (10.0) | 9.6 | (2.0) | 8.8 | (6.0) | 9.6 | (2.0) | 8.8 | (6.0) |
| **V. Legal Structure and Property Rights** | **4.0** | | **3.6** | | **4.7** | | **5.5** | | **5.1** | | **5.7** | | **5.4** | |
| (a) Private Ownership Rights | 4.9 | | 3.5 | | 5.2 | | 4.8 | | 3.2 | | 7.7 | | 7.2 | |
| (b) Viability of Contracts | 3.1 | | 3.7 | | 5.6 | | 5.2 | | 4.0 | | 5.2 | | 4.8 | |
| (c) Rule of Law | | | | | 3.3 | | 6.6 | | 8.3 | | 4.1 | | 4.1 | |
| **VI. International Exchange** | **6.6** | | **6.7** | | **4.2** | | **3.8** | | **3.7** | | **6.0** | | **6.4** | |
| (a) Taxes on International Trade | | | | | | | | | | | | | | |
| i. Taxes as a Percentage of Exports and Imports | 6.3 | (5.6) | 6.3 | (5.5) | 5.9 | (6.1) | 5.1 | (7.4) | 5.8 | (6.3) | 6.3 | (5.6) | 6.2 | (5.7) |
| ii. Mean Tariff Rate | | | | | 1.9 | (40.3) | 2.2 | (39.2) | 1.3 | (43.7) | 3.2 | (34.0) | | |
| iii. Standard Deviation of Tariff Rates | | | | | | | | | 1.4 | (21.6) | 4.7 | (13.3) | | |
| (b) Non-tariff Regulatory Trade Barriers | | | | | | | | | | | | | | |
| i. Non-tariff Trade Restraints (% of trade covered) | | | | | 3.3 | (67.3) | 3.3 | (67.3) | 6.2 | (37.8) | 10.0 | (0.2) | | |
| ii. Size of Trade Sector (% of GDP) | 7.4 | (60.5) | 7.6 | (64.3) | 7.6 | (67.0) | 5.7 | (51.7) | 6.2 | (57.6) | 7.6 | (73.0) | 6.8 | (66.2) |
| **VII. Freedom of Exchange in Financial Markets** | **4.9** | | **3.1** | | **4.3** | | **4.7** | | **5.2** | | **6.0** | | **7.0** | |
| (a) Ownership of Banks | | | 2.0 | (10-40) | 2.0 | (10-40) | 2.0 | (39) | 5.0 | (40-75) | 5.0 | (40-75) | 5.0 | (40-75) |
| (b) Extension of Credit | 7.7 | (79.1) | 7.6 | (77.9) | 8.4 | (85.1) | 7.8 | (80.5) | 6.7 | (69.8) | 7.0 | (73.2) | 6.9 | (72.1) |
| (c) Avoidance of Negative Interest Rates | 8.0 | | 4.0 | | 8.0 | | 10.0 | | 10.0 | | 4.0 | | 8.0 | |
| (d) Capital Transactions with Foreigners | 0.0 | | 0.0 | | 0.0 | | 0.0 | | 0.0 | | 8.0 | | 8.0 | |

# KUWAIT

| | 1970 | 1975 | 1980 | 1985 | 1990 | 1995 | 1997 |
|---|---|---|---|---|---|---|---|
| **Summary Ratings** | | | 5.1 | 7.1 | 5.8 | 7.1 | 7.5 |
| **Rank** | | | 56 | 17 | 50 | 47 | 39 |

| Components of Economic Freedom | 1970 | | 1975 | | 1980 | | 1985 | | 1990 | | 1995 | | 1997 | |
|---|---|---|---|---|---|---|---|---|---|---|---|---|---|---|
| **I. Size of Government** | **6.1** | | **4.6** | | **5.9** | | **5.0** | | **5.4** | | **5.1** | | **6.0** | |
| (a) Government Consumption (% of Total) | 6.1 | (26.0) | 4.6 | (33.7) | 5.9 | (26.6) | 5.0 | (31.9) | 3.4 | (40.6) | 2.7 | (44.4) | 4.0 | (37.0) |
| (b) Transfers and Subsidies (% of GDP) | | | | | | | | | 7.5 | (9.8) | 7.5 | (9.7) | 7.9 | (8.2) |
| **II. Structure of the Economy and Use of Markets** | | | | | | | | | | | **4.4** | | **5.8** | |
| (a) Government Enterprises | | | 2.0 | | 2.0 | (43.5) | 0.0 | (61.3) | 2.0 | (46.0) | 4.0 | (21.8) | 4.0 | |
| (b) Price Controls | | | | | | | | | | | 6.0 | | 6.0 | |
| (c) Top Marginal Tax Rate | | | | | | | | | | | | | 10.0 | (0) |
| (d) Conscription | | | 1.0 | | 1.0 | | 1.0 | | 0.0 | | 0.0 | | 0.0 | |
| **III. Monetary Policy and Price Stability** | **9.8** | | **5.2** | | **3.2** | | **8.1** | | **7.1** | | **8.8** | | **9.0** | |
| (a) Annual Money Growth (last 5 yrs.) | | | 5.5 | (22.3) | 5.9 | (20.5) | 8.2 | (9.0) | 8.6 | (7.0) | 10.0 | (-0.2) | 9.4 | (-2.8) |
| (b) Inflation Variability (last 5 yrs.) | 9.7 | (0.7) | 0.0 | (61.7) | 2.1 | (19.8) | 7.0 | (7.4) | 4.6 | (13.6) | 7.5 | (6.2) | 7.5 | (6.2) |
| (c) Recent Inflation Rate | 9.9 | (0.6) | 9.9 | (-0.6) | 1.5 | (42.6) | 9.0 | (4.9) | 8.0 | (9.8) | 8.7 | (6.3) | 9.9 | (0.7) |
| **IV. Freedom to Use Alternative Currencies** | **10.0** | | **10.0** | | **10.0** | | **10.0** | | **10.0** | | **10.0** | | **10.0** | |
| (a) Ownership of Foreign Currency | 10.0 | | 10.0 | | 10.0 | | 10.0 | | | | 10.0 | | 10.0 | |
| (b) Black Market Exchange Rates (Prem.) | 10.0 | (0.0) | 10.0 | (0.0) | 10.0 | (0.0) | 10.0 | (0.0) | 10.0 | (0.0) | 10.0 | (0.0) | 10.0 | (0.0) |
| **V. Legal Structure and Property Rights** | | | | | **1.1** | | **5.6** | | **2.6** | | **8.5** | | **8.8** | |
| (a) Private Ownership Rights | | | | | 1.0 | | 4.8 | | 1.9 | | 10.0 | | 10.0 | |
| (b) Viability of Contracts | | | | | 1.1 | | 4.0 | | 3.4 | | 8.4 | | 6.6 | |
| (c) Rule of Law | | | | | | | 8.2 | | 2.5 | | 7.0 | | 10.0 | |
| **VI. International Exchange** | | | | | | | **8.0** | | **8.0** | | **8.0** | | **7.7** | |
| (a) Taxes on International Trade | | | | | | | | | | | | | | |
| i. Taxes as a Percentage of Exports and Imports | | | | | | | | | 9.2 | (1.2) | 9.4 | (0.9) | 9.4 | (1.0) |
| ii. Mean Tariff Rate | | | | | | | 9.2 | (4.0) | | | | | | |
| iii. Standard Deviation of Tariff Rates | | | | | | | | | | | | | | |
| (b) Non-tariff Regulatory Trade Barriers | | | | | | | | | | | | | | |
| i. Non-tariff Trade Restraints (% of trade covered) | | | | | | | | | | | | | | |
| ii. Size of Trade Sector (% of GDP) | 4.3 | (83.9) | 5.5 | (106.5) | 5.8 | (112.6) | 4.8 | (96.4) | 5.0 | (103.0) | 4.4 | (103.8) | 3.3 | (87.4) |
| **VII. Freedom of Exchange in Financial Markets** | | | **5.3** | | **5.3** | | **6.0** | | **2.5** | | **4.8** | | **5.2** | |
| (a) Ownership of Banks | | | 5.0 | (40-75) | 5.0 | (40-75) | 5.0 | (40-75) | 5.0 | (40-75) | 5.0 | (40-75) | 5.0 | (40-75) |
| (b) Extension of Credit | 10.0 | (99.9) | 9.9 | (98.8) | 9.8 | (98.2) | 7.8 | (79.7) | 0.1 | (10.9) | 2.2 | (29.7) | 4.2 | (47.5) |
| (c) Avoidance of Negative Interest Rates | | | | | | | 10.0 | | | | 10.0 | | 10.0 | |
| (d) Capital Transactions with Foreigners | 2.0 | | 2.0 | | 2.0 | | 2.0 | | 2.0 | | 2.0 | | 2.0 | |

# LATVIA

| | 1970 | 1975 | 1980 | 1985 | 1990 | 1995 | 1997 |
|---|---|---|---|---|---|---|---|
| **Summary Ratings** | | | | | | 5.7 | 6.7 |
| **Rank** | | | | | | 77 | 60 |

| Components of Economic Freedom | 1970 | | 1975 | | 1980 | | 1985 | | 1990 | | 1995 | | 1997 | |
|---|---|---|---|---|---|---|---|---|---|---|---|---|---|---|
| **I. Size of Government** | | | | | | | | | **8.3** | | **5.6** | | **5.7** | |
| (a) Government Consumption (% of Total) | | | | | | | | | 8.3 | (14.0) | 6.0 | (26.2) | 6.1 | (25.7) |
| (b) Transfers and Subsidies (% of GDP) | | | | | | | | | | | 5.2 | (18.2) | 5.3 | (17.7) |
| **II. Structure of the Economy and Use of Markets** | | | | | | | | | | | **3.8** | | **5.8** | |
| (a) Government Enterprises | | | | | | | | | | | 0.0 | | 4.0 | |
| (b) Price Controls | | | | | | | | | 0.0 | | 6.0 | | 6.0 | |
| (c) Top Marginal Tax Rate | | | | | | | | | | | 7.0 | (35) | 9.0 | (25) |
| (d) Conscription | | | | | | | | | 0.0 | | 1.0 | | 3.0 | |
| **III. Monetary Policy and Price Stability** | | | | | | | | | **7.1** | | **2.3** | | **5.3** | |
| (a) Annual Money Growth (last 5 yrs.) | | | | | | | | | | | 0.1 | (49.5) | 6.3 | (18.5) |
| (b) Inflation Variability (last 5 yrs.) | | | | | | | 8.9 | (2.7) | 7.4 | (6.4) | 0.0 | (365.3) | 0.7 | (23.4) |
| (c) Recent Inflation Rate | | | | | | | | | 6.9 | (15.7) | 6.8 | (16.0) | 8.7 | (6.5) |
| **IV. Freedom to Use Alternative Currencies** | | | | | | | | | **2.5** | | **7.3** | | **7.3** | |
| (a) Ownership of Foreign Currency | | | | | | | | | 5.0 | | 5.0 | | 5.0 | |
| (b) Black Market Exchange Rates (Prem.) | | | | | | | | | 0.0 | (1969.0) | 9.6 | (2.0) | 9.6 | (2.0) |
| **V. Legal Structure and Property Rights** | | | | | | | | | | | | | **7.2** | |
| (a) Private Ownership Rights | | | | | | | | | | | | | 8.6 | |
| (b) Viability of Contracts | | | | | | | | | | | | | 7.4 | |
| (c) Rule of Law | | | | | | | | | | | | | 5.5 | |
| **VI. International Exchange** | | | | | | | | | | | **8.2** | | **7.8** | |
| (a) Taxes on International Trade | | | | | | | | | | | | | | |
| i. Taxes as a Percentage of Exports and Imports | | | | | | | | | | | 9.4 | (0.9) | 9.6 | (0.5) |
| ii. Mean Tariff Rate | | | | | | | | | | | | | 8.8 | (6.0) |
| iii. Standard Deviation of Tariff Rates | | | | | | | | | | | | | 5.7 | (10.7) |
| (b) Non-tariff Regulatory Trade Barriers | | | | | | | | | | | | | | |
| i. Non-tariff Trade Restraints (% of trade covered) | | | | | | | | | | | | | | |
| ii. Size of Trade Sector (% of GDP) | | | | | | | | | 5.6 | (96.7) | 5.1 | (96.1) | 5.7 | (111.1) |
| **VII. Freedom of Exchange in Financial Markets** | | | | | | | | | | | **5.1** | | **7.0** | |
| (a) Ownership of Banks | | | | | | | | | | | | | | |
| (b) Extension of Credit | | | | | | | | | | | 4.9 | (53.9) | 6.7 | (70.5) |
| (c) Avoidance of Negative Interest Rates | | | | | | | | | | | 2.0 | | 6.0 | |
| (d) Capital Transactions with Foreigners | | | | | | | | | 0.0 | | 8.0 | | 8.0 | |

# LITHUANIA

| | 1970 | 1975 | 1980 | 1985 | 1990 | 1995 | 1997 |
|---|---|---|---|---|---|---|---|
| **Summary Ratings** | | | | | | 5.7 | 6.6 |
| **Rank** | | | | | | 77 | 62 |

| Components of Economic Freedom | 1970 | 1975 | 1980 | 1985 | 1990 | | 1995 | | 1997 | |
|---|---|---|---|---|---|---|---|---|---|---|
| **I. Size of Government** | | | | | **6.2** | | **7.0** | | **7.0** | |
| (a) Government Consumption (% of Total) | | | | | 6.2 | (25.2) | 6.7 | (22.6) | 6.7 | (22.6) |
| (b) Transfers and Subsidies (% of GDP) | | | | | | | 7.3 | (10.4) | 7.3 | (10.3) |
| **II. Structure of the Economy and Use of Markets** | | | | | | | **3.4** | | **4.7** | |
| (a) Government Enterprises | | | | | | | 0.0 | | 4.0 | |
| (b) Price Controls | | | | | 0.0 | | 4.0 | | 4.0 | |
| (c) Top Marginal Tax Rate | | | | | | | 7.0 | (35) | 7.0 | (33) |
| (d) Conscription | | | | | 0.0 | | 3.0 | | 3.0 | |
| **III. Monetary Policy and Price Stability** | | | | | | | **0.8** | | **3.8** | |
| (a) Annual Money Growth (last 5 yrs.) | | | | | | | 0.0 | (53.0) | 4.3 | (28.6) |
| (b) Inflation Variability (last 5 yrs.) | | | | | | | 0.0 | (329.2) | 0.0 | (109.6) |
| (c) Recent Inflation Rate | | | | | 10.0 | (-0.2) | 2.4 | (38.1) | 7.0 | (14.9) |
| **IV. Freedom to Use Alternative Currencies** | | | | | **2.5** | | **7.5** | | **7.5** | |
| (a) Ownership of Foreign Currency | | | | | 5.0 | | 5.0 | | 5.0 | |
| (b) Black Market Exchange Rates (Prem.) | | | | | 0.0 | (1969.0) | 10.0 | (0.0) | 10.0 | (0.0) |
| **V. Legal Structure and Property Rights** | | | | | | | | | **7.2** | |
| (a) Private Ownership Rights | | | | | | | | | 8.6 | |
| (b) Viability of Contracts | | | | | | | | | 7.4 | |
| (c) Rule of Law | | | | | | | | | 5.5 | |
| **VI. International Exchange** | | | | | | | **8.2** | | **8.1** | |
| (a) Taxes on International Trade | | | | | | | | | | |
| i. Taxes as a Percentage of Exports and Imports | | | | | | | 9.5 | (0.7) | 9.6 | (0.6) |
| ii. Mean Tariff Rate | | | | | | | 9.1 | (4.5) | 9.1 | (4.6) |
| iii. Standard Deviation of Tariff Rates | | | | | | | 6.4 | (9.0) | 6.3 | (9.2) |
| (b) Non-tariff Regulatory Trade Barriers | | | | | | | | | | |
| i. Non-tariff Trade Restraints (% of trade covered) | | | | | | | | | | |
| ii. Size of Trade Sector (% of GDP) | | | | | 7.2 | (117.2) | 6.8 | (119.1) | 6.5 | (114.6) |
| **VII. Freedom of Exchange in Financial Markets** | | | | | | | **5.2** | | **6.8** | |
| (a) Ownership of Banks | | | | | 0.0 | (0) | 5.0 | (40-75) | 5.0 | (40-75) |
| (b) Extension of Credit | | | | | | | 8.1 | (83.1) | 6.1 | (65.1) |
| (c) Avoidance of Negative Interest Rates | | | | | | | 0.0 | | 8.0 | |
| (d) Capital Transactions with Foreigners | | | | | 0.0 | | 8.0 | | 8.0 | |

# LUXEMBOURG

| | 1970 | 1975 | 1980 | 1985 | 1990 | 1995 | 1997 |
|---|---|---|---|---|---|---|---|
| **Summary Ratings** | 9.1 | 8.8 | 9.0 | 9.4 | 8.3 | 8.4 | 8.5 |
| **Rank** | 3 | 2 | 2 | 1 | 7 | 9 | 9 |

| Components of Economic Freedom | 1970 | | 1975 | | 1980 | | 1985 | | 1990 | | 1995 | | 1997 | |
|---|---|---|---|---|---|---|---|---|---|---|---|---|---|---|
| **I. Size of Government** | **6.8** | | **7.8** | | **7.6** | | **7.7** | | **5.2** | | **5.3** | | **5.1** | |
| (a) Government Consumption (% of Total) | 8.3 | (13.6) | 7.8 | (16.4) | 7.6 | (17.8) | 7.7 | (16.9) | 7.6 | (17.8) | 7.3 | (19.4) | 7.2 | (19.8) |
| (b) Transfers and Subsidies (% of GDP) | 5.3 | (17.8) | | | | | | | 2.9 | (26.6) | 3.3 | (25.2) | 3.1 | (26.0) |
| **II. Structure of the Economy and Use of Markets** | | | | | | | | | **4.4** | | **5.9** | | **6.6** | |
| (a) Government Enterprises | 7.0 | | 7.0 | | 7.0 | (22.0) | 8.0 | (18.2) | 8.0 | (19.2) | 8.0 | | 8.0 | |
| (b) Price Controls | | | | | | | | | 2.0 | | 5.0 | | 7.0 | |
| (c) Top Marginal Tax Rate | | | | | | | | | 1.0 | (56) | 3.0 | (50) | 3.0 | (52.5) |
| (d) Conscription | 10.0 | | 10.0 | | 10.0 | | 10.0 | | 10.0 | | 10.0 | | 10.0 | |
| **III. Monetary Policy and Price Stability** | **7.5** | | **8.5** | | **8.5** | | **9.4** | | **9.1** | | **9.4** | | **9.4** | |
| (a) Annual Money Growth (last 5 yrs.) | | | | | 8.6 | (7.0) | 9.8 | (0.8) | 8.4 | (7.8) | 9.1 | (4.6) | 9.3 | (3.5) |
| (b) Inflation Variability (last 5 yrs.) | 8.0 | (4.9) | 7.2 | (7.1) | 8.6 | (3.6) | 8.9 | (2.7) | 9.5 | (1.2) | 9.2 | (1.9) | 9.2 | (2.1) |
| (c) Recent Inflation Rate | 7.0 | (15.1) | 9.8 | (-0.9) | 8.4 | (7.9) | 9.4 | (3.0) | 9.3 | (3.4) | 9.9 | (0.7) | 9.7 | (1.4) |
| **IV. Freedom to Use Alternative Currencies** | **10.0** | | **10.0** | | **10.0** | | **10.0** | | **10.0** | | **10.0** | | **10.0** | |
| (a) Ownership of Foreign Currency | 10.0 | | 10.0 | | 10.0 | | 10.0 | | 10.0 | | 10.0 | | 10.0 | |
| (b) Black Market Exchange Rates (Prem.) | 10.0 | (0.0) | 10.0 | (0.0) | 10.0 | (0.0) | 10.0 | (0.0) | 10.0 | (0.0) | 10.0 | (0.0) | 10.0 | (0.0) |
| **V. Legal Structure and Property Rights** | **9.9** | | **8.4** | | **8.6** | | **10.0** | | **10.0** | | **10.0** | | **10.0** | |
| (a) Private Ownership Rights | 10.0 | | 10.0 | | 8.6 | | 10.0 | | 10.0 | | 10.0 | | 10.0 | |
| (b) Viability of Contracts | 9.9 | | 6.7 | | 7.2 | | 10.0 | | 10.0 | | 10.0 | | 10.0 | |
| (c) Rule of Law | | | | | 10.0 | | 10.0 | | 10.0 | | 10.0 | | 10.0 | |
| **VI. International Exchange** | **9.1** | | **7.9** | | **8.7** | | **8.8** | | **8.4** | | **8.5** | | **8.5** | |
| (a) Taxes on International Trade | | | | | | | | | | | | | | |
| i. Taxes as a Percentage of Exports and Imports | 9.9 | (0.1) | | | 9.9 | (0.1) | 9.9 | (0.1) | 9.9 | (0.1) | 9.9 | (0.1) | 9.9 | (0.1) |
| ii. Mean Tariff Rate | | | 8.1 | (9.4) | 8.2 | (8.8) | 8.5 | (7.5) | 8.5 | (7.4) | 8.7 | (6.7) | 8.6 | (6.9) |
| iii. Standard Deviation of Tariff Rates | | | | | | | | | 7.1 | (7.2) | 7.6 | (5.9) | 7.6 | (6.0) |
| (b) Non-tariff Regulatory Trade Barriers | | | | | | | | | | | | | | |
| i. Non-tariff Trade Restraints (% of trade covered) | | | | | 8.7 | (12.6) | 8.6 | (14.3) | 8.9 | (10.9) | 9.1 | (9.0) | 9.3 | (6.7) |
| ii. Size of Trade Sector (% of GDP) | 7.1 | (162.0) | 7.3 | (177.7) | 6.8 | (174.9) | 7.6 | (208.6) | 6.6 | (194.3) | 5.6 | (172.3) | 5.5 | (170.9) |
| **VII. Freedom of Exchange in Financial Markets** | **10.0** | | **10.0** | | **10.0** | | **10.0** | | **10.0** | | **9.1** | | **9.2** | |
| (a) Ownership of Banks | 10.0 | (95-100) | 10.0 | (95-100) | 10.0 | (95-100) | 10.0 | (95-100) | 10.0 | (95-100) | 10.0 | (95-100) | 10.0 | (95-100) |
| (b) Extension of Credit | | | | | | | | | | | 5.9 | (62.7) | 6.3 | (67.0) |
| (c) Avoidance of Negative Interest Rates | 10.0 | | 10.0 | | 10.0 | | 10.0 | | 10.0 | | 10.0 | | 10.0 | |
| (d) Capital Transactions with Foreigners | 10.0 | | 10.0 | | 10.0 | | 10.0 | | 10.0 | | 10.0 | | 10.0 | |

# MADAGASCAR

| | 1970 | 1975 | 1980 | 1985 | 1990 | 1995 | 1997 |
|---|---|---|---|---|---|---|---|
| **Summary Ratings** | 5.6 | 4.1 | 4.1 | 4.4 | 3.8 | 3.9 | 3.9 |
| **Rank** | 37 | 65 | 79 | 79 | 99 | 112 | 119 |

| Components of Economic Freedom | 1970 | | 1975 | | 1980 | | 1985 | | 1990 | | 1995 | | 1997 | |
|---|---|---|---|---|---|---|---|---|---|---|---|---|---|---|
| **I. Size of Government** | **8.6** | | **8.8** | | **8.6** | | **9.0** | | **9.5** | | **9.7** | | **9.6** | |
| (a) Government Consumption (% of Total) | 8.2 | (14.2) | 8.8 | (11.2) | 8.6 | (11.9) | 9.0 | (9.9) | 9.3 | (8.5) | 9.6 | (6.9) | 9.5 | (7.4) |
| (b) Transfers and Subsidies (% of GDP) | 9.0 | (4.2) | | | | | | | 9.8 | (1.4) | 9.8 | (1.1) | 9.8 | (1.3) |
| **II. Structure of the Economy and Use of Markets** | | | | | | | | | **0.1** | | **0.1** | | **0.1** | |
| (a) Government Enterprises | 0.0 | (70.3) | 0.0 | (59.2) | 0.0 | (65.4) | 0.0 | (79.9) | 0.0 | | 0.0 | | 0.0 | |
| (b) Price Controls | | | | | | | | | 0.0 | | 0.0 | | 0.0 | |
| (c) Top Marginal Tax Rate | | | | | | | | | | | | | | |
| (d) Conscription | 0.0 | | | | 1.0 | | 1.0 | | 1.0 | | 1.0 | | 1.0 | |
| **III. Monetary Policy and Price Stability** | **8.8** | | **8.3** | | **7.6** | | **7.6** | | **7.3** | | **3.3** | | **6.0** | |
| (a) Annual Money Growth (last 5 yrs.) | 8.9 | (5.4) | 8.8 | (5.8) | 6.8 | (15.9) | 8.1 | (9.7) | 6.3 | (18.7) | 5.0 | (25.1) | 5.5 | (22.4) |
| (b) Inflation Variability (last 5 yrs.) | 9.0 | (2.5) | 7.0 | (7.5) | 8.9 | (2.8) | 6.9 | (7.8) | 8.1 | (4.8) | 4.0 | (14.9) | 3.8 | (15.4) |
| (c) Recent Inflation Rate | 8.6 | (6.9) | 9.1 | (4.7) | 7.0 | (15.0) | 7.9 | (10.4) | 7.7 | (11.5) | 1.0 | (45.2) | 8.5 | (7.4) |
| **IV. Freedom to Use Alternative Currencies** | **9.6** | | **2.7** | | **0.0** | | **4.1** | | **4.3** | | **4.8** | | **3.3** | |
| (a) Ownership of Foreign Currency | | | 0.0 | | 0.0 | | 0.0 | | 0.0 | | 0.0 | | 0.0 | |
| (b) Black Market Exchange Rates (Prem.) | 9.6 | (2.0) | 5.4 | (23.0) | 0.0 | (51.0) | 8.2 | (9.0) | 8.6 | (7.0) | 9.6 | (2.0) | 6.6 | (17.0) |
| **V. Legal Structure and Property Rights** | | | | | | | **3.4** | | **2.5** | | **2.5** | | **2.2** | |
| (a) Private Ownership Rights | | | | | | | 2.2 | | 1.9 | | 0.9 | | 0.0 | |
| (b) Viability of Contracts | | | | | | | 1.6 | | 2.2 | | 0.0 | | 0.0 | |
| (c) Rule of Law | | | | | | | 6.6 | | 3.5 | | 7.0 | | 7.0 | |
| **VI. International Exchange** | **1.5** | | **1.9** | | **4.2** | | **2.5** | | **4.2** | | **5.8** | | **3.7** | |
| (a) Taxes on International Trade | | | | | | | | | | | | | | |
| i. Taxes as a Percentage of Exports and Imports | 0.0 | (15.1) | 0.8 | (13.8) | 4.3 | (8.5) | | | 0.7 | (14.0) | 4.3 | (8.5) | 3.4 | (10.0) |
| ii. Mean Tariff Rate | | | | | 3.7 | (31.5) | 0.8 | (46.0) | 2.8 | (36.0) | 4.0 | (30.0) | | |
| iii. Standard Deviation of Tariff Rates | | | | | | | | | | | | | | |
| (b) Non-tariff Regulatory Trade Barriers | | | | | | | | | | | | | | |
| i. Non-tariff Trade Restraints (% of trade covered) | | | | | 4.3 | (56.7) | 4.3 | (56.7) | 9.8 | (1.7) | 9.8 | (1.7) | | |
| ii. Size of Trade Sector (% of GDP) | 5.4 | (40.7) | 4.7 | (36.7) | 5.3 | (43.1) | 3.0 | (30.6) | 4.9 | (43.6) | 6.1 | (54.8) | 4.6 | (42.3) |
| **VII. Freedom of Exchange in Financial Markets** | **2.7** | | **2.4** | | **2.6** | | **2.7** | | **1.9** | | **2.4** | | **4.3** | |
| (a) Ownership of Banks | 0.0 | (0) | 0.0 | (0) | 0.0 | (0) | 0.0 | (0) | 0.0 | (0-10) | 2.0 | (10-40) | 2.0 | (10-40) |
| (b) Extension of Credit | 9.4 | (94.9) | 8.6 | (87.4) | 9.2 | (92.6) | 9.7 | (97.4) | 9.2 | (92.5) | 8.9 | (89.9) | 8.2 | (83.5) |
| (c) Avoidance of Negative Interest Rates | | | | | | | | | 0.0 | | 0.0 | | 6.0 | |
| (d) Capital Transactions with Foreigners | 0.0 | | 0.0 | | 0.0 | | 0.0 | | 0.0 | | 0.0 | | 2.0 | |

# MALAWI

| | 1970 | 1975 | 1980 | 1985 | 1990 | 1995 | 1997 |
|---|---|---|---|---|---|---|---|
| **Summary Ratings** | | 5.0 | 3.9 | 4.4 | 4.7 | 4.1 | 4.6 |
| **Rank** | | 47 | 89 | 79 | 79 | 109 | 107 |

| Components of Economic Freedom | 1970 | | 1975 | | 1980 | | 1985 | | 1990 | | 1995 | | 1997 | |
|---|---|---|---|---|---|---|---|---|---|---|---|---|---|---|
| **I. Size of Government** | **8.6** | | **8.8** | | **8.2** | | **8.3** | | **8.6** | | **7.2** | | **8.5** | |
| (a) Government Consumption (% of Total) | 7.5 | (18.3) | 7.7 | (17.0) | 6.9 | (21.6) | 7.1 | (20.3) | 7.6 | (17.4) | 7.2 | (19.8) | 8.5 | (12.9) |
| (b) Transfers and Subsidies (% of GDP) | 9.6 | (1.8) | 9.9 | (1.0) | 9.6 | (2.0) | 9.5 | (2.3) | 9.5 | (2.4) | | | | |
| **II. Structure of the Economy and Use of Markets** | | | **2.3** | | **2.8** | | **2.5** | | **1.6** | | **4.0** | | **3.5** | |
| (a) Government Enterprises | 6.0 | (17.2) | 2.0 | (44.5) | 0.0 | (69.3) | 0.0 | (71.9) | 0.0 | (45.3) | 0.0 | (75.7) | 0.0 | |
| (b) Price Controls | | | | | | | | | 0.0 | | 4.0 | | 4.0 | |
| (c) Top Marginal Tax Rate | | | 0.0 | (69) | 4.0 | (45) | 3.0 | (50) | 3.0 | (50) | 7.0 | (35) | 5.0 | (38) |
| (d) Conscription | | | 10.0 | | 10.0 | | 10.0 | | 10.0 | | 10.0 | | 10.0 | |
| **III. Monetary Policy and Price Stability** | **8.4** | | **8.0** | | **8.1** | | **8.5** | | **7.0** | | **1.1** | | **3.8** | |
| (a) Annual Money Growth (last 5 yrs.) | 8.6 | (6.8) | 7.7 | (11.5) | 9.9 | (-0.5) | 8.4 | (8.0) | 5.7 | (21.4) | 3.4 | (33.2) | 4.1 | (29.6) |
| (b) Inflation Variability (last 5 yrs.) | 8.4 | (4.0) | 7.8 | (5.5) | 7.6 | (5.9) | 8.9 | (2.7) | 7.3 | (6.6) | 0.0 | (28.5) | 0.0 | (26.9) |
| (c) Recent Inflation Rate | 8.2 | (8.8) | 8.4 | (8.2) | 6.8 | (15.8) | 8.2 | (8.9) | 7.8 | (10.9) | 0.0 | (90.4) | 7.3 | (13.4) |
| **IV. Freedom to Use Alternative Currencies** | **3.4** | | **2.2** | | **0.2** | | **2.0** | | **3.6** | | **4.9** | | **3.4** | |
| (a) Ownership of Foreign Currency | 0.0 | | 0.0 | | 0.0 | | 0.0 | | 0.0 | | 0.0 | | 0.0 | |
| (b) Black Market Exchange Rates (Prem.) | 6.8 | (16.0) | 4.4 | (28.0) | 0.4 | (48.0) | 4.0 | (30.0) | 7.2 | (14.0) | 9.8 | (1.0) | 6.8 | (16.0) |
| **V. Legal Structure and Property Rights** | | | | | **3.6** | | **4.0** | | **4.6** | | **4.4** | | **6.0** | |
| (a) Private Ownership Rights | | | | | 5.2 | | 4.8 | | 5.9 | | 5.5 | | 7.2 | |
| (b) Viability of Contracts | | | | | 3.7 | | 4.0 | | 4.6 | | 3.7 | | 6.6 | |
| (c) Rule of Law | | | | | 1.7 | | 3.1 | | 3.3 | | 4.1 | | 4.1 | |
| **VI. International Exchange** | **6.3** | | **7.2** | | **3.4** | | **4.0** | | **4.9** | | **3.9** | | **4.8** | |
| (a) Taxes on International Trade | | | | | | | | | | | | | | |
| i. Taxes as a Percentage of Exports and Imports | 6.6 | (5.1) | 7.5 | (3.8) | 5.6 | (6.6) | 4.1 | (8.8) | 6.2 | (5.7) | 6.2 | (5.7) | 4.6 | (8.1) |
| ii. Mean Tariff Rate | | | | | | | 6.7 | (16.7) | 7.0 | (15.2) | 3.8 | (30.8) | 4.9 | (25.3) |
| iii. Standard Deviation of Tariff Rates | | | | | | | | | | | 3.8 | (15.5) | 5.4 | (11.6) |
| (b) Non-tariff Regulatory Trade Barriers | | | | | | | | | | | | | | |
| i. Non-tariff Trade Restraints (% of trade covered) | | | | | 0.0 | (100.0) | 0.4 | (96.1) | 0.9 | (91.3) | 0.9 | (91.3) | | |
| ii. Size of Trade Sector (% of GDP) | 5.6 | (63.4) | 6.3 | (75.0) | 5.2 | (63.6) | 4.1 | (54.1) | 4.3 | (57.9) | 5.3 | (72.7) | 3.8 | (56.8) |
| **VII. Freedom of Exchange in Financial Markets** | | | **3.2** | | **3.7** | | **4.2** | | **4.2** | | **3.1** | | **2.8** | |
| (a) Ownership of Banks | | | 2.0 | (10-40) | 2.0 | (10-40) | 2.0 | (10-40) | 2.0 | (10-40) | 2.0 | (10-40) | 2.0 | (10-40) |
| (b) Extension of Credit | 8.4 | (85.5) | 6.4 | (67.2) | 7.7 | (79.4) | 5.5 | (59.5) | 7.8 | (80.4) | 5.0 | (54.6) | 3.3 | (39.8) |
| (c) Avoidance of Negative Interest Rates | | | | | 4.0 | | 8.0 | | 6.0 | | 4.0 | | 4.0 | |
| (d) Capital Transactions with Foreigners | 2.0 | | 2.0 | | 2.0 | | 2.0 | | 2.0 | | 2.0 | | 2.0 | |

# MALAYSIA

| | 1970 | 1975 | 1980 | 1985 | 1990 | 1995 | 1997 |
|---|---|---|---|---|---|---|---|
| **Summary Ratings** | 6.5 | 6.4 | 7.1 | 7.3 | 7.7 | 7.6 | 7.5 |
| **Rank** | 27 | 21 | 13 | 16 | 15 | 38 | 39 |

| Components of Economic Freedom | 1970 | | 1975 | | 1980 | | 1985 | | 1990 | | 1995 | | 1997 | |
|---|---|---|---|---|---|---|---|---|---|---|---|---|---|---|
| **I. Size of Government** | **7.5** | | **7.4** | | **7.6** | | **7.9** | | **8.2** | | **8.0** | | **8.1** | |
| (a) Government Consumption (% of Total) | 6.9 | (21.4) | 6.4 | (23.9) | 6.3 | (24.6) | 6.7 | (22.7) | 7.0 | (21.0) | 7.0 | (20.9) | 7.2 | (19.8) |
| (b) Transfers and Subsidies (% of GDP) | 8.1 | (7.3) | 8.4 | (6.4) | 8.8 | (4.8) | 9.2 | (3.6) | 9.5 | (2.4) | 9.0 | (4.0) | 9.0 | (4.1) |
| **II. Structure of the Economy and Use of Markets** | | | **4.8** | | **4.0** | | **5.5** | | **5.4** | | **5.3** | | **5.5** | |
| (a) Government Enterprises | 4.0 | (32.3) | 4.0 | (32.9) | 4.0 | (35.5) | 4.0 | (50.1) | 4.0 | (35.8) | 4.0 | (34.1) | 4.0 | |
| (b) Price Controls | | | | | | | | | 5.0 | | 4.0 | | 4.0 | |
| (c) Top Marginal Tax Rate | | | 4.0 | (50) | 2.0 | (60) | 6.0 | (45) | 6.0 | (45) | 7.0 | (32) | 8.0 | (30) |
| (d) Conscription | 10.0 | | 10.0 | | 10.0 | | 10.0 | | 10.0 | | 10.0 | | 10.0 | |
| **III. Monetary Policy and Price Stability** | **9.3** | | **8.1** | | **8.5** | | **9.5** | | **8.7** | | **8.6** | | **8.9** | |
| (a) Annual Money Growth (last 5 yrs.) | 9.3 | (-3.7) | 8.1 | (9.4) | 8.1 | (9.7) | 9.8 | (0.9) | 8.7 | (6.5) | 7.5 | (12.4) | 7.9 | (10.4) |
| (b) Inflation Variability (last 5 yrs.) | 8.8 | (2.9) | 6.7 | (8.3) | 8.8 | (3.1) | 8.9 | (2.6) | 7.9 | (5.2) | 9.4 | (1.5) | 9.5 | (1.2) |
| (c) Recent Inflation Rate | 9.9 | (-0.4) | 9.4 | (-3.1) | 8.6 | (6.9) | 9.7 | (-1.5) | 9.4 | (3.0) | 9.0 | (5.0) | 9.4 | (2.9) |
| **IV. Freedom to Use Alternative Currencies** | **4.9** | | **7.5** | | **10.0** | | **7.5** | | **10.0** | | **10.0** | | **9.7** | |
| (a) Ownership of Foreign Currency | 0.0 | | 5.0 | | 10.0 | | 5.0 | | 10.0 | | 10.0 | | 10.0 | |
| (b) Black Market Exchange Rates (Prem.) | 9.8 | (1.0) | 10.0 | (0.0) | 10.0 | (0.0) | 10.0 | (0.0) | 10.0 | (0.0) | 10.0 | (0.0) | 9.4 | (3.0) |
| **V. Legal Structure and Property Rights** | **6.2** | | **5.3** | | **7.3** | | **6.7** | | **7.7** | | **7.2** | | **7.5** | |
| (a) Private Ownership Rights | 6.5 | | 4.8 | | 8.4 | | 6.1 | | 6.6 | | 7.7 | | 7.2 | |
| (b) Viability of Contracts | 5.8 | | 5.8 | | 6.8 | | 5.8 | | 8.2 | | 6.8 | | 8.3 | |
| (c) Rule of Law | | | | | 6.7 | | 8.2 | | 8.3 | | 7.0 | | 7.0 | |
| **VI. International Exchange** | **5.9** | | **7.0** | | **7.0** | | **7.9** | | **7.6** | | **7.8** | | **6.9** | |
| (a) Taxes on International Trade | | | | | | | | | | | | | | |
| i. Taxes as a Percentage of Exports and Imports | 4.7 | (8.0) | 5.3 | (7.0) | 4.9 | (7.7) | 6.2 | (5.7) | 7.9 | (3.2) | 8.9 | (1.6) | 8.9 | (1.6) |
| ii. Mean Tariff Rate | | | 7.6 | (12.0) | 7.9 | (10.6) | 7.3 | (13.6) | 7.4 | (13.0) | 7.4 | (12.8) | 8.2 | (9.1) |
| iii. Standard Deviation of Tariff Rates | | | | | | | | | 5.0 | (12.5) | 4.4 | (14.0) | 2.2 | (19.4) |
| (b) Non-tariff Regulatory Trade Barriers | | | | | | | | | | | | | | |
| i. Non-tariff Trade Restraints (% of trade covered) | | | | | | | 9.6 | (3.7) | 9.7 | (2.8) | 9.8 | (2.1) | | |
| ii. Size of Trade Sector (% of GDP) | 9.1 | (79.9) | 9.5 | (86.8) | 10.0 | (112.6) | 10.0 | (104.7) | 10.0 | (150.6) | 10.0 | (194.4) | 10.0 | (187.1) |
| **VII. Freedom of Exchange in Financial Markets** | **6.4** | | **5.9** | | **5.8** | | **6.8** | | **6.9** | | **7.0** | | **6.9** | |
| (a) Ownership of Banks | 5.0 | (40-75) | 5.0 | (40-75) | 5.0 | (40-75) | 5.0 | (40-75) | 5.0 | (40-75) | 5.0 | (40-75) | 5.0 | (40-75) |
| (b) Extension of Credit | 9.9 | (98.7) | 8.0 | (82.2) | 7.7 | (78.9) | 7.8 | (80.3) | 8.3 | (84.3) | 8.5 | (86.6) | 8.3 | (84.5) |
| (c) Avoidance of Negative Interest Rates | | | | | 6.0 | | 10.0 | | 10.0 | | 10.0 | | 10.0 | |
| (d) Capital Transactions with Foreigners | 5.0 | | 5.0 | | 5.0 | | 5.0 | | 5.0 | | 5.0 | | 5.0 | |

# MALI

| | 1970 | 1975 | 1980 | 1985 | 1990 | 1995 | 1997 |
|---|---|---|---|---|---|---|---|
| **Summary Ratings** | | 4.8 | 5.3 | 5.3 | 5.0 | 5.1 | 4.7 |
| **Rank** | | 53 | 50 | 55 | 67 | 91 | 103 |

| Components of Economic Freedom | 1970 | | 1975 | | 1980 | | 1985 | | 1990 | | 1995 | | 1997 | |
|---|---|---|---|---|---|---|---|---|---|---|---|---|---|---|
| **I. Size of Government** | **8.8** | | **9.3** | | **9.2** | | **9.2** | | **9.1** | | **8.6** | | **8.3** | |
| (a) Government Consumption (% of Total) | 8.8 | (11.0) | 9.0 | (9.8) | 9.0 | (10.2) | 8.9 | (10.4) | 8.2 | (14.4) | 8.6 | (12.4) | 8.3 | (13.8) |
| (b) Transfers and Subsidies (% of GDP) | | | 9.5 | (2.3) | 9.5 | (2.3) | 9.5 | (2.3) | 10.0 | (0.6) | | | | |
| **II. Structure of the Economy and Use of Markets** | | | | | | | | | **1.7** | | **3.5** | | **3.5** | |
| (a) Government Enterprises | 6.0 | (10.7) | 6.0 | (16.8) | 4.0 | (21.4) | 4.0 | (22.4) | 4.0 | | 4.0 | | 4.0 | |
| (b) Price Controls | | | | | | | | | 0.0 | | 4.0 | | 4.0 | |
| (c) Top Marginal Tax Rate | | | | | | | | | | | | | | |
| (d) Conscription | | | 10.0 | | 10.0 | | 0.0 | | 0.0 | | 0.0 | | 0.0 | |
| **III. Monetary Policy and Price Stability** | **8.3** | | **6.5** | | **7.9** | | **8.6** | | **9.3** | | **6.8** | | **7.3** | |
| (a) Annual Money Growth (last 5 yrs.) | 9.1 | (4.3) | 7.0 | (15.3) | 8.1 | (9.3) | 7.7 | (11.4) | 9.0 | (-5.0) | 7.7 | (11.6) | 6.9 | (15.3) |
| (b) Inflation Variability (last 5 yrs.) | 6.9 | (7.8) | 7.2 | (7.1) | 8.8 | (2.9) | 8.3 | (4.3) | 9.4 | (1.6) | 5.2 | (12.0) | 5.4 | (11.6) |
| (c) Recent Inflation Rate | 8.8 | (6.1) | 5.4 | (23.0) | 6.7 | (16.3) | 9.7 | (1.3) | 9.5 | (2.7) | 7.5 | (12.5) | 9.6 | (1.8) |
| **IV. Freedom to Use Alternative Currencies** | **4.7** | | **4.3** | | **4.5** | | **4.9** | | **4.6** | | **4.9** | | **4.8** | |
| (a) Ownership of Foreign Currency | 0.0 | | 0.0 | | 0.0 | | 0.0 | | 0.0 | | 0.0 | | 0.0 | |
| (b) Black Market Exchange Rates (Prem.) | 9.4 | (3.0) | 8.6 | (7.0) | 9.0 | (5.0) | 9.8 | (1.0) | 9.2 | (4.0) | 9.8 | (1.0) | 9.6 | (2.0) |
| **V. Legal Structure and Property Rights** | | | | | **3.2** | | **2.3** | | **2.4** | | **2.2** | | **2.2** | |
| (a) Private Ownership Rights | | | | | 2.8 | | 2.2 | | 1.9 | | 0.0 | | 0.0 | |
| (b) Viability of Contracts | | | | | 1.1 | | 1.6 | | 2.2 | | 0.0 | | 0.0 | |
| (c) Rule of Law | | | | | 5.8 | | 3.1 | | 3.3 | | 7.0 | | 7.0 | |
| **VI. International Exchange** | | | **1.9** | | **5.0** | | **4.9** | | **5.4** | | **7.0** | | | |
| (a) Taxes on International Trade | | | | | | | | | | | | | | |
| i. Taxes as a Percentage of Exports and Imports | | | 0.6 | (14.1) | 7.5 | (3.8) | 6.7 | (5.0) | 6.9 | (4.6) | 6.8 | (4.8) | | |
| ii. Mean Tariff Rate | | | | | 3.0 | (35.0) | 3.0 | (35.0) | 5.0 | (25.0) | 3.0 | (35.0) | | |
| iii. Standard Deviation of Tariff Rates | | | | | | | | | | | 9.0 | (2.4) | | |
| (b) Non-tariff Regulatory Trade Barriers | | | | | | | | | | | | | | |
| i. Non-tariff Trade Restraints (% of trade covered) | | | | | 4.2 | (58.0) | 4.2 | (58.0) | 4.2 | (58.0) | 9.9 | (1.0) | | |
| ii. Size of Trade Sector (% of GDP) | 4.2 | (32.5) | 5.2 | (41.3) | 5.9 | (49.4) | 7.4 | (64.6) | 5.5 | (49.7) | 6.3 | (59.9) | 6.1 | (58.6) |
| **VII. Freedom of Exchange in Financial Markets** | | | **4.2** | | **4.2** | | **4.6** | | **5.1** | | **4.4** | | **4.5** | |
| (a) Ownership of Banks | | | 2.0 | (10-40) | 2.0 | (10-40) | 2.0 | (10-40) | 2.0 | (10-40) | 2.0 | (10-40) | 2.0 | (10-40) |
| (b) Extension of Credit | 8.6 | (87.0) | 9.8 | (97.7) | 9.9 | (98.7) | 9.7 | (96.9) | 9.5 | (95.6) | 8.6 | (87.0) | 8.9 | (90.3) |
| (c) Avoidance of Negative Interest Rates | | | | | 4.0 | | 6.0 | | 8.0 | | 6.0 | | 6.0 | |
| (d) Capital Transactions with Foreigners | 2.0 | | 2.0 | | 2.0 | | 2.0 | | 2.0 | | 2.0 | | 2.0 | |

# MALTA

| | 1970 | 1975 | 1980 | 1985 | 1990 | 1995 | 1997 |
|---|---|---|---|---|---|---|---|
| **Summary Ratings** | 6.2 | 5.6 | 5.2 | 5.1 | 5.2 | 6.5 | 6.3 |
| **Rank** | 34 | 38 | 53 | 62 | 60 | 56 | 70 |

| Components of Economic Freedom | 1970 | | 1975 | | 1980 | | 1985 | | 1990 | | 1995 | | 1997 | |
|---|---|---|---|---|---|---|---|---|---|---|---|---|---|---|
| **I. Size of Government** | **6.8** | | **6.6** | | **7.0** | | **6.5** | | **6.3** | | **6.4** | | **5.9** | |
| (a) Government Consumption (% of Total) | 7.2 | (19.9) | 7.1 | (20.4) | 7.2 | (20.0) | 7.1 | (20.2) | 6.8 | (21.9) | 6.2 | (25.1) | 6.3 | (24.7) |
| (b) Transfers and Subsidies (% of GDP) | 6.5 | (13.3) | 6.1 | (14.7) | 6.8 | (12.2) | 5.9 | (15.7) | 5.9 | (15.6) | 6.5 | (13.4) | 5.6 | (16.8) |
| **II. Structure of the Economy and Use of Markets** | | | | | **3.3** | | **4.3** | | **2.8** | | **5.3** | | **5.3** | |
| (a) Government Enterprises | 4.0 | (36.5) | 2.0 | (46.3) | 4.0 | (28.6) | 6.0 | (20.0) | 6.0 | (28.8) | 6.0 | | 6.0 | |
| (b) Price Controls | | | | | | | | | 0.0 | | 2.0 | | 2.0 | |
| (c) Top Marginal Tax Rate | | | | | 0.0 | (65) | 0.0 | (65) | 0.0 | (65) | 7.0 | (35) | 7.0 | (35) |
| (d) Conscription | | | | | 10.0 | | 10.0 | | 10.0 | | 10.0 | | 10.0 | |
| **III. Monetary Policy and Price Stability** | **9.1** | | **8.9** | | **8.4** | | **9.4** | | **9.7** | | **9.5** | | **9.5** | |
| (a) Annual Money Growth (last 5 yrs.) | 8.9 | (5.7) | 8.6 | (7.1) | 8.9 | (5.5) | 9.6 | (-2.1) | 10.0 | (-0.2) | 9.9 | (-0.4) | 9.6 | (-1.9) |
| (b) Inflation Variability (last 5 yrs.) | 8.9 | (2.7) | 9.1 | (2.3) | 8.8 | (3.0) | 8.8 | (3.1) | 9.7 | (0.6) | 9.6 | (0.9) | 9.5 | (1.2) |
| (c) Recent Inflation Rate | 9.5 | (2.7) | 8.9 | (5.4) | 7.5 | (12.4) | 9.9 | (0.6) | 9.4 | (3.2) | 8.9 | (5.6) | 9.4 | (3.0) |
| **IV. Freedom to Use Alternative Currencies** | **9.4** | | **4.5** | | **3.8** | | **4.3** | | **4.8** | | **4.6** | | **4.7** | |
| (a) Ownership of Foreign Currency | | | 0.0 | | 0.0 | | 0.0 | | 0.0 | | 0.0 | | 0.0 | |
| (b) Black Market Exchange Rates (Prem.) | 9.4 | (3.0) | 9.0 | (5.0) | 7.6 | (12.0) | 8.6 | (7.0) | 9.6 | (2.0) | 9.2 | (4.0) | 9.4 | (3.0) |
| **V. Legal Structure and Property Rights** | | | | | | | **3.5** | | **4.8** | | **9.5** | | **10.0** | |
| (a) Private Ownership Rights | | | | | | | 3.5 | | 5.9 | | 10.0 | | 10.0 | |
| (b) Viability of Contracts | | | | | | | 4.0 | | 5.2 | | 8.4 | | 10.0 | |
| (c) Rule of Law | | | | | | | 3.1 | | 3.3 | | 10.0 | | 10.0 | |
| **VI. International Exchange** | **4.7** | | **6.5** | | **6.3** | | **6.2** | | **6.1** | | **6.4** | | **5.1** | |
| (a) Taxes on International Trade | | | | | | | | | | | | | | |
| i. Taxes as a Percentage of Exports and Imports | 4.9 | (7.6) | 6.9 | (4.6) | 6.7 | (4.9) | 7.0 | (4.5) | 6.7 | (4.9) | 7.1 | (4.4) | 5.5 | (6.7) |
| ii. Mean Tariff Rate | | | | | | | | | | | | | | |
| iii. Standard Deviation of Tariff Rates | | | | | | | | | | | | | | |
| (b) Non-tariff Regulatory Trade Barriers | | | | | | | | | | | | | | |
| i. Non-tariff Trade Restraints (% of trade covered) | | | | | | | | | | | | | | |
| ii. Size of Trade Sector (% of GDP) | 3.9 | (129.3) | 5.3 | (179.1) | 5.3 | (187.4) | 4.1 | (160.9) | 4.5 | (184.1) | 4.7 | (201.4) | 3.8 | (177.9) |
| **VII. Freedom of Exchange in Financial Markets** | **3.1** | | **3.2** | | **4.0** | | **3.9** | | **3.8** | | **4.8** | | **4.7** | |
| (a) Ownership of Banks | 0.0 | (0-10) | 0.0 | (0-10) | 0.0 | (0-10) | 0.0 | (0) | 0.0 | (0) | 0.0 | (0-10) | 0.0 | (0-10) |
| (b) Extension of Credit | 8.3 | (84.8) | 8.8 | (89.4) | 9.4 | (94.4) | 9.1 | (91.6) | 8.3 | (84.2) | 8.5 | (86.4) | 7.8 | (80.3) |
| (c) Avoidance of Negative Interest Rates | | | | | 6.0 | | 6.0 | | 6.0 | | 10.0 | | 10.0 | |
| (d) Capital Transactions with Foreigners | 2.0 | | 2.0 | | 2.0 | | 2.0 | | 2.0 | | 2.0 | | 2.0 | |

# MAURITIUS

| | 1970 | 1975 | 1980 | 1985 | 1990 | 1995 | 1997 |
|---|---|---|---|---|---|---|---|
| **Summary Ratings** | | 4.6 | 4.7 | 6.4 | 6.0 | 7.9 | 7.6 |
| **Rank** | | 57 | 70 | 27 | 43 | 23 | 36 |

| Components of Economic Freedom | 1970 | | 1975 | | 1980 | | 1985 | | 1990 | | 1995 | | 1997 | |
|---|---|---|---|---|---|---|---|---|---|---|---|---|---|---|
| **I. Size of Government** | **8.6** | | **8.2** | | **8.2** | | **8.4** | | **8.5** | | **8.4** | | **8.3** | |
| (a) Government Consumption (% of Total) | 8.0 | (15.2) | 8.0 | (15.2) | 7.9 | (15.7) | 8.1 | (14.7) | 8.0 | (15.4) | 7.9 | (15.7) | 8.0 | (15.7) |
| (b) Transfers and Subsidies (% of GDP) | 9.3 | (3.2) | 8.3 | (6.6) | 8.4 | (6.5) | 8.7 | (5.2) | 9.0 | (4.2) | 8.9 | (4.4) | 8.6 | (5.8) |
| **II. Structure of the Economy and Use of Markets** | | | | | **5.4** | | **6.9** | | **5.9** | | **6.2** | | **6.9** | |
| (a) Government Enterprises | 4.0 | (32.2) | 6.0 | (18.8) | 6.0 | (33.6) | 6.0 | (31.6) | 6.0 | (30.8) | 6.0 | (32.0) | 6.0 | |
| (b) Price Controls | | | | | | | | | 4.0 | | 4.0 | | 6.0 | |
| (c) Top Marginal Tax Rate | | | | | 3.0 | (50) | 7.0 | (35) | 7.0 | (35) | 8.0 | (30) | 8.0 | (30) |
| (d) Conscription | | | 10.0 | | 10.0 | | 10.0 | | 10.0 | | 10.0 | | 10.0 | |
| **III. Monetary Policy and Price Stability** | **9.6** | | **4.9** | | **6.4** | | **9.2** | | **8.0** | | **9.2** | | **9.3** | |
| (a) Annual Money Growth (last 5 yrs.) | 9.8 | (1.1) | 3.8 | (30.9) | 8.9 | (5.7) | 9.7 | (-1.4) | 6.7 | (16.3) | 9.0 | (5.3) | 9.5 | (2.7) |
| (b) Inflation Variability (last 5 yrs.) | 9.2 | (2.0) | 1.9 | (20.2) | 5.8 | (10.5) | 9.5 | (1.1) | 9.4 | (1.6) | 9.5 | (1.4) | 9.6 | (1.1) |
| (c) Recent Inflation Rate | 9.7 | (1.6) | 8.9 | (5.3) | 4.7 | (26.6) | 8.4 | (8.2) | 8.0 | (10.1) | 9.1 | (4.7) | 8.8 | (5.9) |
| **IV. Freedom to Use Alternative Currencies** | **0.0** | | **0.3** | | **1.0** | | **4.9** | | **4.2** | | **10.0** | | **9.9** | |
| (a) Ownership of Foreign Currency | | | 0.0 | | 0.0 | | 0.0 | | 0.0 | | 10.0 | | 10.0 | |
| (b) Black Market Exchange Rates (Prem.) | 0.0 | (55.0) | 0.6 | (47.0) | 2.0 | (40.0) | 9.8 | (1.0) | 8.4 | (8.0) | 10.0 | (0.0) | 9.8 | (1.0) |
| **V. Legal Structure and Property Rights** | | | | | | | **6.5** | | **6.4** | | **8.0** | | **7.6** | |
| (a) Private Ownership Rights | | | | | | | 6.1 | | 5.9 | | 10.0 | | 10.0 | |
| (b) Viability of Contracts | | | | | | | 5.2 | | 5.2 | | 6.8 | | 8.3 | |
| (c) Rule of Law | | | | | | | 8.2 | | 8.3 | | 7.0 | | 4.1 | |
| **VI. International Exchange** | **5.3** | | **5.3** | | **3.6** | | **3.9** | | **4.0** | | **5.7** | | **3.8** | |
| (a) Taxes on International Trade | | | | | | | | | | | | | | |
| i. Taxes as a Percentage of Exports and Imports | 5.6 | (6.6) | 5.3 | (7.1) | 3.6 | (9.6) | 3.6 | (9.6) | 4.9 | (7.6) | 5.8 | (6.3) | 6.7 | (5.0) |
| ii. Mean Tariff Rate | | | | | 3.0 | (34.9) | 3.0 | (34.9) | 4.5 | (27.6) | 5.3 | (23.4) | 4.2 | (29.1) |
| iii. Standard Deviation of Tariff Rates | | | | | | | | | 0.0 | (91.5) | | | 0.0 | (26.2) |
| (b) Non-tariff Regulatory Trade Barriers | | | | | | | | | | | | | | |
| i. Non-tariff Trade Restraints (% of trade covered) | | | | | 3.5 | (65.0) | 5.0 | (50.0) | 6.5 | (35.2) | 6.5 | (35.2) | | |
| ii. Size of Trade Sector (% of GDP) | 4.4 | (85.1) | 5.6 | (112.3) | 5.3 | (112.6) | 4.8 | (108.9) | 5.8 | (137.7) | 4.8 | (121.9) | 5.1 | (130.9) |
| **VII. Freedom of Exchange in Financial Markets** | | | **5.1** | | **5.3** | | **6.7** | | **6.5** | | **8.7** | | **8.8** | |
| (a) Ownership of Banks | | | 8.0 | (75-90) | 8.0 | (75-90) | 8.0 | (75-90) | 10.0 | (90-100) | 10.0 | (90-100) | 10.0 | (90-100) |
| (b) Extension of Credit | 7.9 | (80.7) | 5.5 | (59.0) | 6.2 | (65.5) | 7.1 | (74.1) | 6.0 | (63.7) | 6.6 | (69.0) | 6.9 | (71.6) |
| (c) Avoidance of Negative Interest Rates | | | | | | | 10.0 | | 8.0 | | 10.0 | | 8.0 | |
| (d) Capital Transactions with Foreigners | 2.0 | | 2.0 | | 2.0 | | 2.0 | | 2.0 | | 8.0 | | 10.0 | |

# MEXICO

| | 1970 | 1975 | 1980 | 1985 | 1990 | 1995 | 1997 |
|---|---|---|---|---|---|---|---|
| **Summary Ratings** | 7.0 | 5.7 | 4.9 | 4.5 | 6.4 | 7.4 | 7.7 |
| **Rank** | 19 | 37 | 63 | 76 | 38 | 42 | 35 |

| Components of Economic Freedom | 1970 | | 1975 | | 1980 | | 1985 | | 1990 | | 1995 | | 1997 | |
|---|---|---|---|---|---|---|---|---|---|---|---|---|---|---|
| **I. Size of Government** | **9.4** | | **8.9** | | **8.7** | | **8.6** | | **9.1** | | **8.2** | | **8.4** | |
| (a) Government Consumption (% of Total) | 9.3 | (8.2) | 8.7 | (11.7) | 8.4 | (13.4) | 8.5 | (12.5) | 8.9 | (10.8) | 8.4 | (13.5) | 8.8 | (11.3) |
| (b) Transfers and Subsidies (% of GDP) | 9.5 | (2.2) | 9.0 | (4.1) | 8.9 | (4.4) | 8.7 | (5.4) | 9.4 | (2.7) | 8.1 | (7.5) | 8.1 | (7.5) |
| **II. Structure of the Economy and Use of Markets** | | | **3.5** | | **3.1** | | **3.1** | | **3.5** | | **5.8** | | **6.5** | |
| (a) Government Enterprises | 4.0 | (33.3) | 2.0 | (40.2) | 2.0 | (43.5) | 2.0 | (38.0) | 4.0 | (23.2) | 6.0 | (19.6) | 6.0 | |
| (b) Price Controls | | | | | | | | | 0.0 | | 5.0 | | 7.0 | |
| (c) Top Marginal Tax Rate | | | 5.0 | (47) | 4.0 | (55) | 4.0 | (55) | 7.0 | (40) | 7.0 | (35) | 7.0 | (35) |
| (d) Conscription | 5.0 | | 5.0 | | 5.0 | | 5.0 | | 5.0 | | 5.0 | | 5.0 | |
| **III. Monetary Policy and Price Stability** | **8.8** | | **7.4** | | **6.5** | | **1.0** | | **1.5** | | **4.4** | | **6.3** | |
| (a) Annual Money Growth (last 5 yrs.) | 8.9 | (5.5) | 7.7 | (11.5) | 5.1 | (24.7) | 1.1 | (44.3) | 0.0 | (67.4) | 5.1 | (24.4) | 7.2 | (14.2) |
| (b) Inflation Variability (last 5 yrs.) | 9.2 | (2.0) | 8.2 | (4.5) | 9.1 | (2.3) | 1.9 | (20.3) | 0.0 | (43.9) | 5.6 | (11.0) | 5.4 | (11.5) |
| (c) Recent Inflation Rate | 8.2 | (9.0) | 6.4 | (17.9) | 5.4 | (22.8) | 0.0 | (54.0) | 4.4 | (28.1) | 2.4 | (37.9) | 6.2 | (19.0) |
| **IV. Freedom to Use Alternative Currencies** | **10.0** | | **10.0** | | **5.0** | | **7.5** | | **10.0** | | **10.0** | | **9.9** | |
| (a) Ownership of Foreign Currency | 10.0 | | 10.0 | | 10.0 | | 10.0 | | 10.0 | | 10.0 | | 10.0 | |
| (b) Black Market Exchange Rates (Prem.) | 10.0 | (0.0) | 10.0 | (0.0) | 0.0 | (92.0) | 5.0 | (25.0) | 10.0 | (0.0) | 10.0 | (0.0) | 9.8 | (1.0) |
| **V. Legal Structure and Property Rights** | **5.2** | | **4.7** | | **6.4** | | **4.8** | | **7.3** | | **7.2** | | **8.5** | |
| (a) Private Ownership Rights | 4.9 | | 4.1 | | 7.6 | | 3.5 | | 7.3 | | 7.7 | | 10.0 | |
| (b) Viability of Contracts | 5.4 | | 5.4 | | 4.9 | | 2.8 | | 6.4 | | 6.8 | | 8.3 | |
| (c) Rule of Law | | | | | 6.7 | | 8.2 | | 8.3 | | 7.0 | | 7.0 | |
| **VI. International Exchange** | **3.6** | | **3.4** | | **1.6** | | **4.4** | | **7.7** | | **8.3** | | **7.9** | |
| (a) Taxes on International Trade | | | | | | | | | | | | | | |
| i. Taxes as a Percentage of Exports and Imports | 4.8 | (7.8) | 4.7 | (7.9) | 0.0 | (17.6) | 8.3 | (2.6) | 8.7 | (2.0) | 9.5 | (0.7) | 9.4 | (1.0) |
| ii. Mean Tariff Rate | | | | | 3.8 | (30.9) | 4.0 | (30.0) | 7.8 | (11.1) | 7.5 | (12.6) | 7.4 | (13.1) |
| iii. Standard Deviation of Tariff Rates | | | | | | | | | 7.2 | (7.0) | 7.8 | (5.4) | 5.8 | (10.6) |
| (b) Non-tariff Regulatory Trade Barriers | | | | | | | | | | | | | | |
| i. Non-tariff Trade Restraints (% of trade covered) | | | | | 0.0 | (100.0) | 0.8 | (92.2) | 8.1 | (18.6) | 8.3 | (17.4) | 9.3 | (6.9) |
| ii. Size of Trade Sector (% of GDP) | 0.7 | (15.4) | 0.0 | (14.7) | 3.4 | (23.7) | 3.7 | (25.9) | 5.6 | (38.3) | 8.2 | (58.8) | 8.2 | (60.5) |
| **VII. Freedom of Exchange in Financial Markets** | | | **4.1** | | **4.6** | | **2.0** | | **4.5** | | **7.2** | | **6.2** | |
| (a) Ownership of Banks | | | 8.0 | (90) | 8.0 | (90) | 0.0 | (0) | 0.0 | (0) | 8.0 | (90) | 8.0 | (90) |
| (b) Extension of Credit | 4.1 | (47.2) | 1.9 | (26.7) | 4.3 | (48.7) | 2.3 | (30.8) | 5.5 | (59.5) | 8.1 | (83.2) | 5.6 | (60.5) |
| (c) Avoidance of Negative Interest Rates | | | | | 4.0 | | 4.0 | | 8.0 | | 8.0 | | 6.0 | |
| (d) Capital Transactions with Foreigners | 2.0 | | 2.0 | | 2.0 | | 2.0 | | 5.0 | | 5.0 | | 5.0 | |

# MOROCCO

| | 1970 | 1975 | 1980 | 1985 | 1990 | 1995 | 1997 |
|---|---|---|---|---|---|---|---|
| **Summary Ratings** | 5.5 | 4.9 | 4.0 | 4.8 | 4.6 | 5.9 | 6.0 |
| **Rank** | 40 | 51 | 86 | 69 | 81 | 74 | 82 |

| Components of Economic Freedom | 1970 | | 1975 | | 1980 | | 1985 | | 1990 | | 1995 | | 1997 | |
|---|---|---|---|---|---|---|---|---|---|---|---|---|---|---|
| **I. Size of Government** | **8.3** | | **7.9** | | **8.0** | | **8.1** | | **8.4** | | **8.2** | | **7.0** | |
| (a) Government Consumption (% of Total) | 8.3 | (14.1) | 7.3 | (19.0) | 6.9 | (21.3) | 7.3 | (19.4) | 7.3 | (19.2) | 7.2 | (19.6) | 7.0 | (20.7) |
| (b) Transfers and Subsidies (% of GDP) | | | 8.5 | (6.0) | 9.0 | (4.1) | 8.9 | (4.6) | 9.5 | (2.3) | 9.1 | (3.9) | | |
| **II. Structure of the Economy and Use of Markets** | | | **3.1** | | **0.9** | | **0.1** | | **0.1** | | **2.2** | | **2.4** | |
| (a) Government Enterprises | 2.0 | (40.3) | 0.0 | (47.3) | 0.0 | (52.5) | 0.0 | | 0.0 | (41.8) | 0.0 | (55.8) | 0.0 | |
| (b) Price Controls | | | | | | | | | 0.0 | | 4.0 | | 4.0 | |
| (c) Top Marginal Tax Rate | | | 8.0 | (39) | 2.0 | (64) | 0.0 | (87) | 0.0 | (87) | 3.0 | (46) | 4.0 | (44) |
| (d) Conscription | 1.0 | | 1.0 | | 1.0 | | 1.0 | | 1.0 | | 1.0 | | 1.0 | |
| **III. Monetary Policy and Price Stability** | **9.2** | | **7.9** | | **8.2** | | **9.0** | | **8.4** | | **8.8** | | **9.3** | |
| (a) Annual Money Growth (last 5 yrs.) | 9.4 | (3.1) | 7.2 | (13.9) | 8.2 | (9.0) | 9.0 | (4.9) | 7.2 | (13.8) | 8.8 | (5.8) | 9.2 | (3.9) |
| (b) Inflation Variability (last 5 yrs.) | 9.0 | (2.4) | 6.7 | (8.4) | 8.2 | (4.5) | 9.6 | (0.9) | 9.1 | (2.4) | 9.1 | (2.2) | 9.0 | (2.5) |
| (c) Recent Inflation Rate | 9.3 | (3.5) | 9.7 | (1.5) | 8.1 | (9.5) | 8.3 | (8.4) | 8.9 | (5.7) | 8.4 | (8.0) | 9.6 | (2.0) |
| **IV. Freedom to Use Alternative Currencies** | **3.9** | | **4.7** | | **4.9** | | **4.3** | | **3.7** | | **4.9** | | **4.8** | |
| (a) Ownership of Foreign Currency | 0.0 | | 0.0 | | 0.0 | | 0.0 | | 0.0 | | 0.0 | | 0.0 | |
| (b) Black Market Exchange Rates (Prem.) | 7.8 | (11.0) | 9.4 | (3.0) | 9.8 | (1.0) | 8.6 | (7.0) | 7.4 | (13.0) | 9.8 | (1.0) | 9.6 | (2.0) |
| **V. Legal Structure and Property Rights** | **3.2** | | **2.5** | | **1.8** | | **3.6** | | **4.0** | | **8.1** | | **8.5** | |
| (a) Private Ownership Rights | 3.6 | | 3.0 | | 1.3 | | 4.8 | | 4.6 | | 7.7 | | 7.2 | |
| (b) Viability of Contracts | 2.7 | | 1.9 | | 2.4 | | 2.8 | | 4.0 | | 6.8 | | 8.3 | |
| (c) Rule of Law | | | | | 1.7 | | 3.1 | | 3.3 | | 10.0 | | 10.0 | |
| **VI. International Exchange** | **5.4** | | **5.4** | | **2.7** | | **6.0** | | **5.0** | | **5.3** | | | |
| (a) Taxes on International Trade | | | | | | | | | | | | | | |
| i. Taxes as a Percentage of Exports and Imports | 5.7 | (6.5) | 5.0 | (7.5) | 2.9 | (10.7) | 5.7 | (6.4) | 4.3 | (8.6) | 5.5 | (6.8) | | |
| ii. Mean Tariff Rate | | | | | 0.0 | (54.0) | 5.3 | (23.5) | 5.3 | (23.5) | 5.4 | (22.8) | | |
| iii. Standard Deviation of Tariff Rates | | | | | | | | | | | 4.7 | (13.2) | | |
| (b) Non-tariff Regulatory Trade Barriers | | | | | | | | | | | | | | |
| i. Non-tariff Trade Restraints (% of trade covered) | | | | | 5.0 | (50.1) | 7.2 | (27.6) | | | | | | |
| ii. Size of Trade Sector (% of GDP) | 4.7 | (39.2) | 6.5 | (55.8) | 5.0 | (45.3) | 6.3 | (59.7) | 5.9 | (59.0) | 5.9 | (61.3) | 5.2 | (55.0) |
| **VII. Freedom of Exchange in Financial Markets** | | | | | **4.2** | | **4.5** | | **4.9** | | **5.1** | | **5.1** | |
| (a) Ownership of Banks | 5.0 | (40-75) | 5.0 | (40-75) | 5.0 | (40-75) | 5.0 | (40-75) | 5.0 | (40-75) | 5.0 | (40-75) | 5.0 | (40-75) |
| (b) Extension of Credit | | | | | 6.0 | (63.7) | 5.2 | (57.1) | 4.7 | (52.5) | 5.7 | (61.5) | 6.0 | (63.5) |
| (c) Avoidance of Negative Interest Rates | | | | | | | 6.0 | | 8.0 | | 8.0 | | 8.0 | |
| (d) Capital Transactions with Foreigners | 0.0 | | 2.0 | | 2.0 | | 2.0 | | 2.0 | | 2.0 | | 2.0 | |

# MYANMAR

| | 1970 | 1975 | 1980 | 1985 | 1990 | 1995 | 1997 |
|---|---|---|---|---|---|---|---|
| Summary Ratings | | | 2.4 | 2.1 | 1.3 | 1.6 | 2.1 |
| Rank | | | 105 | 109 | 115 | 122 | 123 |

| Components of Economic Freedom | 1970 | | 1975 | | 1980 | | 1985 | | 1990 | | 1995 | | 1997 | |
|---|---|---|---|---|---|---|---|---|---|---|---|---|---|---|
| **I. Size of Government** | | | | | | | | | | | | | | |
| (a) Government Consumption (% of Total) | | | | | | | | | | | | | | |
| (b) Transfers and Subsidies (% of GDP) | | | | | | | | | | | | | | |
| **II. Structure of the Economy and Use of Markets** | | | | | | | | | **2.0** | | **2.0** | | **2.0** | |
| (a) Government Enterprises | 2.0 | | 2.0 | | 2.0 | | 2.0 | | 2.0 | (45.0) | 2.0 | | 2.0 | |
| (b) Price Controls | | | | | | | | | 0.0 | | 0.0 | | 0.0 | |
| (c) Top Marginal Tax Rate | | | | | | | | | | | | | | |
| (d) Conscription | 0.0 | | 10.0 | | 10.0 | | 10.0 | | 10.0 | | 10.0 | | 10.0 | |
| **III. Monetary Policy and Price Stability** | **8.8** | | **4.9** | | **9.1** | | **9.6** | | **5.2** | | **5.8** | | **6.0** | |
| (a) Annual Money Growth (last 5 yrs.) | 9.1 | (-4.3) | 6.4 | (17.9) | 8.9 | (5.6) | 9.5 | (2.3) | 6.0 | (20.2) | 3.8 | (30.9) | 4.8 | (26.2) |
| (b) Inflation Variability (last 5 yrs.) | 7.6 | (6.0) | 1.5 | (21.2) | 8.6 | (3.5) | 9.6 | (1.0) | 3.2 | (17.1) | 7.6 | (6.0) | 7.6 | (6.0) |
| (c) Recent Inflation Rate | 9.7 | (-1.4) | 6.7 | (16.5) | 9.8 | (1.2) | 9.7 | (1.6) | 6.3 | (18.5) | 6.1 | (19.4) | 5.6 | (22.0) |
| **IV. Freedom to Use Alternative Currencies** | **0.0** | | **0.0** | | **0.0** | | **0.0** | | **0.0** | | **0.0** | | **0.0** | |
| (a) Ownership of Foreign Currency | 0.0 | | 0.0 | | 0.0 | | 0.0 | | 0.0 | | 0.0 | | 0.0 | |
| (b) Black Market Exchange Rates (Prem.) | 0.0 | (261.0) | 0.0 | (235.0) | 0.0 | (459.0) | 0.0 | (341.0) | 0.0 | (1134.0) | 0.0 | (1864.0) | 0.0 | (2604.0) |
| **V. Legal Structure and Property Rights** | | | | | **5.0** | | **4.0** | | **2.2** | | **3.5** | | **6.3** | |
| (a) Private Ownership Rights | | | | | 3.4 | | 4.8 | | 3.2 | | 3.2 | | 7.2 | |
| (b) Viability of Contracts | | | | | 3.7 | | 4.0 | | 0.0 | | 0.5 | | 4.8 | |
| (c) Rule of Law | | | | | 8.3 | | 3.1 | | 3.3 | | 7.0 | | 7.0 | |
| **VI. International Exchange** | **1.7** | | **0.0** | | **0.8** | | **0.0** | | **0.0** | | **0.0** | | **0.0** | |
| (a) Taxes on International Trade | | | | | | | | | | | | | | |
| i. Taxes as a Percentage of Exports and Imports | 2.4 | (11.4) | 0.0 | (19.3) | 0.5 | (14.2) | 0.0 | (17.6) | 0.0 | (25.9) | 0.0 | (31.8) | 0.0 | (46.5) |
| ii. Mean Tariff Rate | | | | | | | | | | | | | | |
| iii. Standard Deviation of Tariff Rates | | | | | | | | | | | | | | |
| (b) Non-tariff Regulatory Trade Barriers | | | | | | | | | | | | | | |
| i. Non-tariff Trade Restraints (% of trade covered) | | | | | | | | | | | | | | |
| ii. Size of Trade Sector (% of GDP) | 0.0 | (14.0) | 0.0 | (12.0) | 1.4 | (22.0) | 0.0 | (13.2) | 0.0 | (7.5) | 0.0 | (2.6) | 0.0 | (1.8) |
| **VII. Freedom of Exchange in Financial Markets** | **1.2** | | **0.5** | | **0.1** | | **0.0** | | **0.0** | | **0.0** | | **0.0** | |
| (a) Ownership of Banks | 0.0 | (0-10) | 0.0 | (0-10) | 0.0 | (0-10) | 0.0 | (0-10) | 0.0 | (0-10) | 0.0 | (0-10) | 0.0 | (0-10) |
| (b) Extension of Credit | 4.4 | (49.4) | 1.9 | (27.1) | 0.4 | (14.0) | 0.0 | (6.1) | | | | | | |
| (c) Avoidance of Negative Interest Rates | | | | | 0.0 | | 0.0 | | 0.0 | | 0.0 | | 0.0 | |
| (d) Capital Transactions with Foreigners | 0.0 | | 0.0 | | 0.0 | | 0.0 | | 0.0 | | 0.0 | | 0.0 | |

# NAMIBIA

| | 1970 | 1975 | 1980 | 1985 | 1990 | 1995 | 1997 |
|---|---|---|---|---|---|---|---|
| **Summary Ratings** | | | | | 5.2 | 5.3 | 6.4 |
| **Rank** | | | | | 60 | 86 | 68 |

| Components of Economic Freedom | 1970 | 1975 | 1980 | | 1985 | | 1990 | | 1995 | | 1997 | |
|---|---|---|---|---|---|---|---|---|---|---|---|---|
| **I. Size of Government** | | | **5.6** | | **4.3** | | **6.8** | | **4.2** | | **4.1** | |
| (a) Government Consumption (% of Total) | | | 5.6 | (28.4) | 4.3 | (35.6) | 4.4 | (34.9) | 4.2 | (36.3) | 4.1 | (36.4) |
| (b) Transfers and Subsidies (% of GDP) | | | | | | | 9.3 | (3.2) | | | | |
| **II. Structure of the Economy and Use of Markets** | | | | | | | | | | | **5.9** | |
| (a) Government Enterprises | | | | | | | | | | | | |
| (b) Price Controls | | | | | | | 2.0 | | 4.0 | | 4.0 | |
| (c) Top Marginal Tax Rate | | | | | | | | | | | 7.0 | (35) |
| (d) Conscription | | | | | | | 10.0 | | 10.0 | | 10.0 | |
| **III. Monetary Policy and Price Stability** | | | | | **6.0** | | **8.2** | | **7.6** | | **7.7** | |
| (a) Annual Money Growth (last 5 yrs.) | | | | | | | | | 5.8 | (20.9) | 5.9 | (20.7) |
| (b) Inflation Variability (last 5 yrs.) | | | | | 7.0 | (7.6) | 8.0 | (5.0) | 8.3 | (4.2) | 9.0 | (2.6) |
| (c) Recent Inflation Rate | | | | | 5.0 | (24.8) | 8.3 | (8.3) | 8.6 | (7.2) | 8.3 | (8.3) |
| **IV. Freedom to Use Alternative Currencies** | | | | | **2.5** | | **4.7** | | **5.0** | | **5.0** | |
| (a) Ownership of Foreign Currency | | | | | 0.0 | | 0.0 | | 0.0 | | 0.0 | |
| (b) Black Market Exchange Rates (Prem.) | | | | | 5.0 | (25.0) | 9.4 | (3.0) | 10.0 | (0.0) | 10.0 | (0.0) |
| **V. Legal Structure and Property Rights** | | | | | | | **2.2** | | **5.5** | | **8.8** | |
| (a) Private Ownership Rights | | | | | | | 0.0 | | 3.2 | | 10.0 | |
| (b) Viability of Contracts | | | | | | | 3.4 | | 3.7 | | 6.6 | |
| (c) Rule of Law | | | | | | | 3.3 | | 10.0 | | 10.0 | |
| **VI. International Exchange** | | | | | | | **5.7** | | **4.2** | | **6.9** | |
| (a) Taxes on International Trade | | | | | | | | | | | | |
| i. Taxes as a Percentage of Exports and Imports | | | | | | | 5.1 | (7.3) | 4.3 | (8.6) | | |
| ii. Mean Tariff Rate | | | | | | | | | 6.1 | (19.7) | 8.2 | (8.8) |
| iii. Standard Deviation of Tariff Rates | | | | | | | | | 1.2 | (21.9) | 5.6 | (11.0) |
| (b) Non-tariff Regulatory Trade Barriers | | | | | | | | | | | | |
| i. Non-tariff Trade Restraints (% of trade covered) | | | | | | | | | | | | |
| ii. Size of Trade Sector (% of GDP) | | | 10.0 | (143.2) | 7.4 | (109.8) | 7.1 | (108.7) | 6.8 | (109.1) | 6.6 | (107.1) |
| **VII. Freedom of Exchange in Financial Markets** | | | | | | | **5.5** | | **6.1** | | **6.0** | |
| (a) Ownership of Banks | | | | | | | | | | | | |
| (b) Extension of Credit | | | | | | | 9.3 | (93.6) | 9.1 | (91.8) | 8.7 | (88.5) |
| (c) Avoidance of Negative Interest Rates | | | | | | | 6.0 | | 8.0 | | 8.0 | |
| (d) Capital Transactions with Foreigners | | | | | | | 2.0 | | 2.0 | | 2.0 | |

# NEPAL

| | 1970 | 1975 | 1980 | 1985 | 1990 | 1995 | 1997 |
|---|---|---|---|---|---|---|---|
| Summary Ratings | | | 5.4 | 5.4 | 4.9 | 5.2 | 5.3 |
| Rank | | | 48 | 52 | 71 | 87 | 94 |

| Components of Economic Freedom | 1970 | | 1975 | | 1980 | | 1985 | | 1990 | | 1995 | | 1997 | |
|---|---|---|---|---|---|---|---|---|---|---|---|---|---|---|
| **I. Size of Government** | | | **9.3** | | **9.5** | | **8.8** | | **9.1** | | **8.9** | | **9.0** | |
| (a) Government Consumption (% of Total) | | | 9.3 | (8.4) | 9.5 | (7.5) | 8.8 | (10.8) | 9.1 | (9.4) | 8.9 | (10.6) | 9.0 | (10.1) |
| (b) Transfers and Subsidies (% of GDP) | | | | | | | | | | | | | | |
| **II. Structure of the Economy and Use of Markets** | | | | | | | | | **2.9** | | **2.9** | | **2.9** | |
| (a) Government Enterprises | 2.0 | (49.0) | 4.0 | (32.5) | 4.0 | (37.3) | 2.0 | (45.8) | 2.0 | (43.2) | 2.0 | | 2.0 | |
| (b) Price Controls | | | | | | | | | 2.0 | | 2.0 | | 2.0 | |
| (c) Top Marginal Tax Rate | | | | | | | | | | | | | | |
| (d) Conscription | | | 10.0 | | 10.0 | | 10.0 | | 10.0 | | 10.0 | | 10.0 | |
| **III. Monetary Policy and Price Stability** | **8.3** | | **5.9** | | **7.8** | | **8.2** | | **8.1** | | **8.0** | | **8.7** | |
| (a) Annual Money Growth (last 5 yrs.) | 8.9 | (5.3) | 7.7 | (11.6) | 7.1 | (14.4) | 7.8 | (10.8) | 6.9 | (15.7) | 7.2 | (13.9) | 8.3 | (8.4) |
| (b) Inflation Variability (last 5 yrs.) | 7.2 | (7.0) | 5.5 | (11.3) | 7.9 | (5.4) | 9.1 | (2.2) | 9.5 | (1.3) | 8.2 | (4.6) | 9.4 | (1.4) |
| (c) Recent Inflation Rate | 8.6 | (7.1) | 4.5 | (27.5) | 8.5 | (7.6) | 7.7 | (11.4) | 7.9 | (10.7) | 8.7 | (6.3) | 8.3 | (8.5) |
| **IV. Freedom to Use Alternative Currencies** | **0.0** | | **1.0** | | **5.0** | | **3.9** | | **3.4** | | **3.1** | | **2.8** | |
| (a) Ownership of Foreign Currency | 0.0 | | 0.0 | | 0.0 | | 0.0 | | 0.0 | | 0.0 | | 0.0 | |
| (b) Black Market Exchange Rates (Prem.) | 0.0 | (55.0) | 2.0 | (40.0) | 10.0 | (0.0) | 7.8 | (11.0) | 6.8 | (16.0) | 6.2 | (19.0) | 5.6 | (22.0) |
| **V. Legal Structure and Property Rights** | | | | | | | | | | | | | | |
| (a) Private Ownership Rights | | | | | | | | | | | | | | |
| (b) Viability of Contracts | | | | | | | | | | | | | | |
| (c) Rule of Law | | | | | | | | | | | | | | |
| **VI. International Exchange** | **0.4** | | **3.1** | | **4.6** | | **5.8** | | **4.4** | | **6.5** | | **6.6** | |
| (a) Taxes on International Trade | | | | | | | | | | | | | | |
| i. Taxes as a Percentage of Exports and Imports | 0.6 | (14.1) | 4.1 | (8.9) | 4.3 | (8.6) | 4.9 | (7.7) | 4.1 | (8.8) | 6.5 | (5.3) | 6.9 | (4.7) |
| ii. Mean Tariff Rate | | | | | 5.6 | (22.1) | 5.5 | (22.6) | 5.5 | (22.6) | 6.8 | (16.1) | | |
| iii. Standard Deviation of Tariff Rates | | | | | | | | | | | 3.6 | (15.9) | | |
| (b) Non-tariff Regulatory Trade Barriers | | | | | | | | | | | | | | |
| i. Non-tariff Trade Restraints (% of trade covered) | | | | | | | 8.9 | (10.7) | | | 9.9 | (0.7) | | |
| ii. Size of Trade Sector (% of GDP) | 0.0 | (13.2) | 0.5 | (22.3) | 2.7 | (30.3) | 2.7 | (31.5) | 2.4 | (31.6) | 5.8 | (58.8) | 5.9 | (59.6) |
| **VII. Freedom of Exchange in Financial Markets** | | | | | **2.7** | | **2.5** | | **3.8** | | **3.7** | | **3.8** | |
| (a) Ownership of Banks | 0.0 | (0-10) | 0.0 | (0-10) | 0.0 | (0-10) | 0.0 | (0-10) | 0.0 | (0-10) | 0.0 | (0-10) | 0.0 | (0-10) |
| (b) Extension of Credit | | | | | 5.6 | (59.9) | 5.0 | (55.2) | 6.3 | (66.7) | 8.4 | (85.4) | 8.5 | (86.4) |
| (c) Avoidance of Negative Interest Rates | | | | | 6.0 | | 6.0 | | 10.0 | | 8.0 | | 8.0 | |
| (d) Capital Transactions with Foreigners | 0.0 | | 0.0 | | 0.0 | | 0.0 | | 0.0 | | 0.0 | | 0.0 | |

# NETHERLANDS

| | 1970 | 1975 | 1980 | 1985 | 1990 | 1995 | 1997 |
|---|---|---|---|---|---|---|---|
| **Summary Ratings** | 8.6 | 7.4 | 7.8 | 7.8 | 8.1 | 8.4 | 8.5 |
| **Rank** | 5 | 12 | 8 | 10 | 10 | 9 | 9 |

| Components of Economic Freedom | 1970 | | 1975 | | 1980 | | 1985 | | 1990 | | 1995 | | 1997 | |
|---|---|---|---|---|---|---|---|---|---|---|---|---|---|---|
| **I. Size of Government** | **6.1** | | **5.0** | | **4.4** | | **4.3** | | **4.8** | | **4.7** | | **5.1** | |
| (a) Government Consumption (% of Total) | 7.1 | (20.3) | 6.7 | (22.2) | 6.8 | (22.2) | 7.0 | (21.0) | 7.2 | (19.9) | 7.3 | (19.3) | 7.3 | (19.0) |
| (b) Transfers and Subsidies (% of GDP) | 5.0 | (18.7) | 3.2 | (25.6) | 2.1 | (29.4) | 1.5 | (31.6) | 2.3 | (28.7) | 2.0 | (29.7) | 2.8 | (27.0) |
| **II. Structure of the Economy and Use of Markets** | | | **3.8** | | **3.6** | | **3.1** | | **4.4** | | **5.1** | | **6.0** | |
| (a) Government Enterprises | 4.0 | (33.7) | 4.0 | (33.6) | 7.0 | (22.9) | 6.0 | (28.0) | 6.0 | (25.0) | 6.0 | | 6.0 | |
| (b) Price Controls | | | | | | | | | 7.0 | | 7.0 | | 8.0 | |
| (c) Top Marginal Tax Rate | | | 5.0 | (46) | 0.0 | (72) | 0.0 | (72) | 0.0 | (72) | 2.0 | (60) | 2.0 | (60) |
| (d) Conscription | 0.0 | | 0.0 | | 1.0 | | 1.0 | | 1.0 | | 3.0 | | 10.0 | |
| **III. Monetary Policy and Price Stability** | **9.2** | | **8.7** | | **9.2** | | **9.3** | | **9.4** | | **9.6** | | **9.4** | |
| (a) Annual Money Growth (last 5 yrs.) | 9.2 | (3.8) | 8.3 | (8.5) | 9.2 | (3.9) | 9.0 | (4.8) | 9.2 | (4.2) | 9.1 | (4.3) | 8.7 | (6.3) |
| (b) Inflation Variability (last 5 yrs.) | 9.6 | (1.0) | 9.7 | (0.7) | 9.3 | (1.6) | 9.3 | (1.8) | 9.6 | (1.0) | 9.9 | (0.4) | 9.9 | (0.4) |
| (c) Recent Inflation Rate | 8.8 | (6.2) | 8.0 | (10.2) | 8.9 | (5.5) | 9.6 | (1.8) | 9.5 | (2.3) | 9.7 | (1.6) | 9.6 | (1.9) |
| **IV. Freedom to Use Alternative Currencies** | **10.0** | | **10.0** | | **10.0** | | **10.0** | | **10.0** | | **10.0** | | **10.0** | |
| (a) Ownership of Foreign Currency | 10.0 | | 10.0 | | 10.0 | | 10.0 | | 10.0 | | 10.0 | | 10.0 | |
| (b) Black Market Exchange Rates (Prem.) | 10.0 | (0.0) | 10.0 | (0.0) | 10.0 | (0.0) | 10.0 | (0.0) | 10.0 | (0.0) | 10.0 | (0.0) | 10.0 | (0.0) |
| **V. Legal Structure and Property Rights** | **10.0** | | **8.1** | | **9.0** | | **9.6** | | **9.6** | | **10.0** | | **10.0** | |
| (a) Private Ownership Rights | 10.0 | | 7.3 | | 7.6 | | 10.0 | | 10.0 | | 10.0 | | 10.0 | |
| (b) Viability of Contracts | 10.0 | | 9.0 | | 9.4 | | 8.8 | | 8.8 | | 10.0 | | 10.0 | |
| (c) Rule of Law | | | | | 10.0 | | 10.0 | | 10.0 | | 10.0 | | 10.0 | |
| **VI. International Exchange** | **8.8** | | **8.6** | | **8.7** | | **8.8** | | **8.5** | | **8.6** | | **8.6** | |
| (a) Taxes on International Trade | | | | | | | | | | | | | | |
| i. Taxes as a Percentage of Exports and Imports | 8.9 | (1.7) | 9.1 | (1.3) | 9.7 | (0.4) | 9.7 | (0.4) | 9.7 | (0.5) | 9.7 | (0.5) | 9.7 | (0.5) |
| ii. Mean Tariff Rate | | | 8.1 | (9.4) | 8.2 | (8.8) | 8.5 | (7.5) | 8.5 | (7.4) | 8.7 | (6.7) | 8.6 | (6.9) |
| iii. Standard Deviation of Tariff Rates | | | | | | | | | 7.1 | (7.2) | 7.6 | (5.9) | 7.6 | (6.0) |
| (b) Non-tariff Regulatory Trade Barriers | | | | | | | | | | | | | | |
| i. Non-tariff Trade Restraints (% of trade covered) | | | | | 8.0 | (19.9) | 7.9 | (21.4) | 8.9 | (10.9) | 9.1 | (9.0) | 9.3 | (6.7) |
| ii. Size of Trade Sector (% of GDP) | 8.5 | (88.7) | 8.4 | (93.6) | 8.7 | (102.7) | 9.3 | (116.8) | 7.8 | (103.7) | 7.1 | (100.2) | 7.2 | (104.0) |
| **VII. Freedom of Exchange in Financial Markets** | **7.1** | | **7.1** | | **9.1** | | **8.4** | | **8.9** | | **9.6** | | **9.6** | |
| (a) Ownership of Banks | 10.0 | (95-100) | 10.0 | (95-100) | 10.0 | (95-100) | 8.0 | (82) | 10.0 | (95-100) | 10.0 | (95-100) | 10.0 | (95-100) |
| (b) Extension of Credit | 6.4 | (67.2) | 7.5 | (77.6) | 8.1 | (83.2) | 7.5 | (77.6) | 7.5 | (77.7) | 8.1 | (82.4) | 8.3 | (84.9) |
| (c) Avoidance of Negative Interest Rates | 10.0 | | 6.0 | | 10.0 | | 10.0 | | 10.0 | | 10.0 | | 10.0 | |
| (d) Capital Transactions with Foreigners | 2.0 | | 5.0 | | 8.0 | | 8.0 | | 8.0 | | 10.0 | | 10.0 | |

# NEW ZEALAND

| | 1970 | 1975 | 1980 | 1985 | 1990 | 1995 | 1997 |
|---|---|---|---|---|---|---|---|
| **Summary Ratings** | 7.0 | 6.0 | 6.4 | 6.2 | 8.1 | 9.1 | 9.1 |
| **Rank** | 19 | 32 | 24 | 32 | 10 | 3 | 3 |

| Components of Economic Freedom | 1970 | | 1975 | | 1980 | | 1985 | | 1990 | | 1995 | | 1997 | |
|---|---|---|---|---|---|---|---|---|---|---|---|---|---|---|
| **I. Size of Government** | **7.7** | | **5.9** | | **5.4** | | **5.8** | | **4.8** | | **7.0** | | **7.1** | |
| (a) Government Consumption (% of Total) | 7.7 | (17.1) | 7.2 | (19.6) | 6.7 | (22.6) | 7.0 | (20.9) | 6.9 | (21.2) | 7.4 | (18.9) | 7.4 | (18.8) |
| (b) Transfers and Subsidies (% of GDP) | | | 4.6 | (20.2) | 4.2 | (21.9) | 4.5 | (20.6) | 2.6 | (27.5) | 6.6 | (12.8) | 6.8 | (12.4) |
| **II. Structure of the Economy and Use of Markets** | | | **4.4** | | **4.0** | | **3.3** | | **7.9** | | **9.2** | | **9.2** | |
| (a) Government Enterprises | 4.0 | (33.9) | 4.0 | (34.0) | 4.0 | (35.0) | 4.0 | (31.0) | 7.0 | (23.9) | 10.0 | (13.3) | 10.0 | (11.7) |
| (b) Price Controls | | | | | | | | | 9.0 | | 10.0 | | 10.0 | |
| (c) Top Marginal Tax Rate | | | 3.0 | (60) | 2.0 | (61.5) | 0.0 | (66) | 7.0 | (33) | 7.0 | (33) | 7.0 | (33) |
| (d) Conscription | 10.0 | | 10.0 | | 10.0 | | 10.0 | | 10.0 | | 10.0 | | 10.0 | |
| **III. Monetary Policy and Price Stability** | **8.3** | | **7.7** | | **8.3** | | **8.0** | | **6.4** | | **9.5** | | **9.6** | |
| (a) Annual Money Growth (last 5 yrs.) | 9.7 | (-1.8) | 7.6 | (12.2) | 8.9 | (5.6) | 8.3 | (8.5) | 1.8 | (40.9) | 9.1 | (4.7) | 9.3 | (3.5) |
| (b) Inflation Variability (last 5 yrs.) | 7.8 | (5.6) | 8.5 | (3.7) | 9.2 | (2.0) | 8.7 | (3.3) | 7.8 | (5.4) | 9.9 | (0.3) | 9.6 | (1.0) |
| (c) Recent Inflation Rate | 7.3 | (13.3) | 7.2 | (14.1) | 6.9 | (15.4) | 7.2 | (14.2) | 9.5 | (2.7) | 9.5 | (2.3) | 9.9 | (-0.5) |
| **IV. Freedom to Use Alternative Currencies** | **3.9** | | **4.5** | | **5.0** | | **4.6** | | **10.0** | | **10.0** | | **10.0** | |
| (a) Ownership of Foreign Currency | 0.0 | | 0.0 | | 0.0 | | 0.0 | | 10.0 | | 10.0 | | 10.0 | |
| (b) Black Market Exchange Rates (Prem.) | 7.8 | (11.0) | 9.0 | (5.0) | 10.0 | (0.0) | 9.2 | (4.0) | 10.0 | (0.0) | 10.0 | (0.0) | 10.0 | (0.0) |
| **V. Legal Structure and Property Rights** | **9.3** | | **7.2** | | **9.1** | | **8.7** | | **9.6** | | **10.0** | | **10.0** | |
| (a) Private Ownership Rights | 9.6 | | 5.5 | | 9.2 | | 8.7 | | 10.0 | | 10.0 | | 10.0 | |
| (b) Viability of Contracts | 9.1 | | 9.0 | | 8.1 | | 7.6 | | 8.8 | | 10.0 | | 10.0 | |
| (c) Rule of Law | | | | | 10.0 | | 10.0 | | 10.0 | | 10.0 | | 10.0 | |
| **VI. International Exchange** | **7.3** | | **7.0** | | **7.0** | | **7.2** | | **6.8** | | **7.9** | | **8.3** | |
| (a) Taxes on International Trade | | | | | | | | | | | | | | |
| i. Taxes as a Percentage of Exports and Imports | 8.2 | (2.7) | 8.4 | (2.4) | 8.3 | (2.5) | 8.7 | (2.0) | 8.9 | (1.7) | 9.1 | (1.4) | 8.9 | (1.6) |
| ii. Mean Tariff Rate | | | 6.2 | (18.9) | 7.4 | (13.0) | 6.8 | (16.0) | 7.1 | (14.5) | 8.3 | (8.5) | 8.9 | (5.4) |
| iii. Standard Deviation of Tariff Rates | | | | | | | | | 3.7 | (15.7) | 5.8 | (10.4) | 7.2 | (7.1) |
| (b) Non-tariff Regulatory Trade Barriers | | | | | | | | | | | | | | |
| i. Non-tariff Trade Restraints (% of trade covered) | | | | | 5.4 | (46.4) | 6.8 | (32.4) | 8.9 | (11.5) | 10.0 | (0.2) | 10.0 | (0.2) |
| ii. Size of Trade Sector (% of GDP) | 5.1 | (48.3) | 5.5 | (54.9) | 5.8 | (62.1) | 5.7 | (64.6) | 4.5 | (54.7) | 4.6 | (58.7) | 4.3 | (56.6) |
| **VII. Freedom of Exchange in Financial Markets** | **5.8** | | **5.6** | | **5.7** | | **6.1** | | **9.7** | | **9.9** | | **9.4** | |
| (a) Ownership of Banks | 5.0 | (40-75) | 5.0 | (40-75) | 5.0 | (40-75) | 5.0 | (40-75) | 10.0 | (95-100) | 10.0 | (95-100) | 10.0 | (95-100) |
| (b) Extension of Credit | 7.7 | (79.6) | 7.1 | (73.6) | 7.3 | (75.3) | 6.6 | (69.0) | 8.6 | (87.6) | 9.5 | (95.7) | 9.7 | (97.5) |
| (c) Avoidance of Negative Interest Rates | | | | | 6.0 | | 8.0 | | 10.0 | | 10.0 | | 10.0 | |
| (d) Capital Transactions with Foreigners | 5.0 | | 5.0 | | 5.0 | | 5.0 | | 10.0 | | 10.0 | | 8.0 | |

# NICARAGUA

| | 1970 | 1975 | 1980 | 1985 | 1990 | 1995 | 1997 |
|---|---|---|---|---|---|---|---|
| **Summary Ratings** | | 7.6 | 3.7 | 2.0 | 2.9 | 5.7 | 6.9 |
| **Rank** | | 10 | 91 | 110 | 107 | 77 | 56 |

| Components of Economic Freedom | 1970 | | 1975 | | 1980 | | 1985 | | 1990 | | 1995 | | 1997 | |
|---|---|---|---|---|---|---|---|---|---|---|---|---|---|---|
| **I. Size of Government** | **8.8** | | **9.2** | | **8.2** | | **5.7** | | **5.6** | | **8.5** | | **8.4** | |
| (a) Government Consumption (% of Total) | 8.8 | (11.0) | 9.0 | (10.3) | 7.3 | (19.3) | 3.0 | (42.6) | 3.0 | (42.6) | 8.5 | (12.7) | 8.4 | (13.3) |
| (b) Transfers and Subsidies (% of GDP) | | | 9.5 | (2.4) | 9.0 | (4.1) | 8.4 | (6.2) | 8.3 | (6.8) | 8.5 | (6.0) | | |
| **II. Structure of the Economy and Use of Markets** | | | **7.4** | | **2.5** | | **1.9** | | **0.0** | | **4.2** | | **4.2** | |
| (a) Government Enterprises | 4.0 | (31.5) | 6.0 | (29.8) | 0.0 | (71.9) | 0.0 | | 0.0 | (52.1) | 0.0 | (66.5) | 0.0 | |
| (b) Price Controls | | | | | | | | | 0.0 | | 4.0 | | 4.0 | |
| (c) Top Marginal Tax Rate | | | 10.0 | (21) | 5.0 | (50) | 5.0 | (50) | | | 8.0 | (30) | 8.0 | (30) |
| (d) Conscription | 3.0 | | 5.0 | | 5.0 | | 0.0 | | 0.0 | | 10.0 | | 10.0 | |
| **III. Monetary Policy and Price Stability** | **9.2** | | **7.9** | | **4.0** | | **0.0** | | **0.0** | | **2.7** | | **6.7** | |
| (a) Annual Money Growth (last 5 yrs.) | 8.8 | (5.9) | 7.5 | (12.3) | 4.7 | (26.7) | 0.0 | (69.6) | 0.0 | (2072.1) | 0.0 | (89.1) | 5.5 | (22.5) |
| (b) Inflation Variability (last 5 yrs.) | 8.9 | (2.7) | 7.6 | (6.0) | 4.6 | (13.6) | 0.0 | (60.1) | 0.0 | (4792.5) | 0.0 | (1852.1) | 6.1 | (9.7) |
| (c) Recent Inflation Rate | 9.8 | (-1.1) | 8.7 | (6.8) | 2.7 | (36.6) | 0.0 | (168.1) | 0.0 | (5012.7) | 8.0 | (9.8) | 8.6 | (-7.1) |
| **IV. Freedom to Use Alternative Currencies** | **8.1** | | **7.9** | | **5.0** | | **0.0** | | **4.0** | | **6.7** | | **9.9** | |
| (a) Ownership of Foreign Currency | 10.0 | | 10.0 | | 10.0 | | 0.0 | | 0.0 | | 5.0 | | 10.0 | |
| (b) Black Market Exchange Rates (Prem.) | 6.2 | (19.0) | 5.8 | (21.0) | 0.0 | (91.0) | 0.0 | (382.0) | 8.0 | (10.0) | 8.4 | (8.0) | 9.8 | (1.0) |
| **V. Legal Structure and Property Rights** | | | | | **1.9** | | **2.2** | | **3.2** | | **5.0** | | **5.4** | |
| (a) Private Ownership Rights | | | | | 2.3 | | 0.9 | | 4.6 | | 5.5 | | 7.2 | |
| (b) Viability of Contracts | | | | | 1.8 | | 2.8 | | 1.6 | | 5.2 | | 4.8 | |
| (c) Rule of Law | | | | | 1.7 | | 3.1 | | 3.3 | | 4.1 | | 4.1 | |
| **VI. International Exchange** | **6.2** | | **6.2** | | **2.5** | | **3.4** | | **5.8** | | **5.6** | | | |
| (a) Taxes on International Trade | | | | | | | | | | | | | | |
| i. Taxes as a Percentage of Exports and Imports | 7.0 | (4.5) | 6.7 | (4.9) | 4.2 | (8.7) | 5.1 | (7.4) | 7.1 | (4.3) | 6.1 | (5.9) | | |
| ii. Mean Tariff Rate | | | | | 0.0 | (54.0) | 0.0 | (54.0) | 5.0 | (24.8) | 7.9 | (10.7) | | |
| iii. Standard Deviation of Tariff Rates | | | | | | | | | | | 2.9 | (17.8) | | |
| (b) Non-tariff Regulatory Trade Barriers | | | | | | | | | | | | | | |
| i. Non-tariff Trade Restraints (% of trade covered) | | | | | | | 7.2 | (27.8) | | | | | | |
| ii. Size of Trade Sector (% of GDP) | 4.1 | (55.3) | 4.9 | (65.7) | 4.8 | (67.5) | 0.0 | (36.6) | 4.7 | (71.4) | 5.7 | (90.9) | 7.5 | (121.0) |
| **VII. Freedom of Exchange in Financial Markets** | | | | | | | **1.1** | | **0.8** | | **6.8** | | **7.3** | |
| (a) Ownership of Banks | | | | | | | | | | | | | | |
| (b) Extension of Credit | | | | | | | 3.8 | (44.0) | 2.8 | (35.4) | 10.0 | (99.8) | 9.3 | (93.6) |
| (c) Avoidance of Negative Interest Rates | | | | | 0.0 | | 0.0 | | 0.0 | | 6.0 | | 8.0 | |
| (d) Capital Transactions with Foreigners | 5.0 | | 5.0 | | 0.0 | | 0.0 | | 0.0 | | 5.0 | | 5.0 | |

# NIGER

| | 1970 | 1975 | 1980 | 1985 | 1990 | 1995 | 1997 |
|---|---|---|---|---|---|---|---|
| **Summary Ratings** | | 5.5 | 5.1 | 5.0 | 4.4 | 4.6 | 4.8 |
| **Rank** | | 42 | 56 | 66 | 84 | 100 | 102 |

| Components of Economic Freedom | 1970 | | 1975 | | 1980 | | 1985 | | 1990 | | 1995 | | 1997 | |
|---|---|---|---|---|---|---|---|---|---|---|---|---|---|---|
| **I. Size of Government** | **9.2** | | **8.8** | | **9.0** | | **8.8** | | **8.3** | | **8.2** | | **8.2** | |
| (a) Government Consumption (% of Total) | 9.2 | (8.9) | 8.8 | (11.1) | 8.6 | (12.1) | 8.8 | (10.9) | 8.3 | (14.1) | 8.2 | (14.1) | 8.2 | (14.2) |
| (b) Transfers and Subsidies (% of GDP) | | | | | 9.5 | (2.5) | | | | | | | | |
| **II. Structure of the Economy and Use of Markets** | | | | | | | | | **0.0** | | **3.5** | | **3.5** | |
| (a) Government Enterprises | 4.0 | (36.8) | 4.0 | | 4.0 | (33.5) | 4.0 | (29.4) | 0.0 | (76.5) | 4.0 | | 4.0 | |
| (b) Price Controls | | | | | | | | | 0.0 | | 4.0 | | 4.0 | |
| (c) Top Marginal Tax Rate | | | | | | | | | | | | | | |
| (d) Conscription | | | 10.0 | | | | 0.0 | | 0.0 | | 0.0 | | 0.0 | |
| **III. Monetary Policy and Price Stability** | **8.6** | | **6.4** | | **6.2** | | **8.5** | | **9.5** | | **7.6** | | **8.1** | |
| (a) Annual Money Growth (last 5 yrs.) | 9.4 | (2.8) | 6.1 | (19.5) | 5.0 | (25.0) | 9.3 | (3.3) | 9.9 | (-0.6) | 9.3 | (3.5) | 9.8 | (-1.2) |
| (b) Inflation Variability (last 5 yrs.) | 7.8 | (5.6) | 4.2 | (14.6) | 7.9 | (5.4) | 7.4 | (6.6) | 8.9 | (2.9) | 4.6 | (13.4) | 5.2 | (11.9) |
| (c) Recent Inflation Rate | 8.6 | (7.1) | 8.7 | (-6.4) | 5.8 | (20.8) | 8.8 | (-5.9) | 9.7 | (-1.6) | 8.9 | (5.4) | 9.4 | (3.1) |
| **IV. Freedom to Use Alternative Currencies** | **4.8** | | **4.8** | | **4.8** | | **4.9** | | **4.6** | | **4.9** | | **4.8** | |
| (a) Ownership of Foreign Currency | 0.0 | | 0.0 | | 0.0 | | 0.0 | | 0.0 | | 0.0 | | 0.0 | |
| (b) Black Market Exchange Rates (Prem.) | 9.6 | (2.0) | 9.6 | (2.0) | 9.6 | (2.0) | 9.8 | (1.0) | 9.2 | (4.0) | 9.8 | (1.0) | 9.6 | (2.0) |
| **V. Legal Structure and Property Rights** | | | | | **4.2** | | **4.6** | | **4.9** | | **0.7** | | **2.6** | |
| (a) Private Ownership Rights | | | | | 4.0 | | 3.5 | | 3.2 | | 0.0 | | 4.4 | |
| (b) Viability of Contracts | | | | | 2.8 | | 4.0 | | 3.4 | | 2.1 | | 3.1 | |
| (c) Rule of Law | | | | | 5.8 | | 6.6 | | 8.3 | | 0.0 | | 0.0 | |
| **VI. International Exchange** | | | **5.6** | | **5.1** | | **3.0** | | **2.6** | | **5.3** | | | |
| (a) Taxes on International Trade | | | | | | | | | | | | | | |
| i. Taxes as a Percentage of Exports and Imports | | | 5.5 | (6.7) | 4.4 | (8.4) | 3.7 | (9.5) | 3.5 | (9.8) | 2.8 | (10.8) | | |
| ii. Mean Tariff Rate | | | | | | | | | | | | | | |
| iii. Standard Deviation of Tariff Rates | | | | | | | | | | | | | | |
| (b) Non-tariff Regulatory Trade Barriers | | | | | | | | | | | | | | |
| i. Non-tariff Trade Restraints (% of trade covered) | | | | | | | 1.0 | (90.0) | 1.0 | (90.0) | 9.1 | (9.0) | | |
| ii. Size of Trade Sector (% of GDP) | 2.9 | (28.9) | 5.9 | (50.2) | 7.1 | (62.9) | 5.6 | (51.1) | 3.7 | (38.0) | 3.8 | (39.7) | 4.7 | (47.6) |
| **VII. Freedom of Exchange in Financial Markets** | | | **3.2** | | **2.9** | | **3.0** | | **4.2** | | **4.4** | | **4.2** | |
| (a) Ownership of Banks | | | 2.0 | (10-40) | 2.0 | (10-40) | 2.0 | (10-40) | 2.0 | (10-40) | 5.0 | (40-75) | 5.0 | (40-75) |
| (b) Extension of Credit | 9.5 | (95.5) | 8.9 | (89.7) | 8.8 | (89.0) | 8.0 | (82.3) | 8.2 | (83.7) | 7.5 | (77.2) | 6.5 | (68.0) |
| (c) Avoidance of Negative Interest Rates | | | | | 2.0 | | | | 8.0 | | 6.0 | | 6.0 | |
| (d) Capital Transactions with Foreigners | 0.0 | | 0.0 | | 0.0 | | 0.0 | | 0.0 | | 0.0 | | 0.0 | |

# NIGERIA

| | 1970 | 1975 | 1980 | 1985 | 1990 | 1995 | 1997 |
|---|---|---|---|---|---|---|---|
| **Summary Ratings** | 4.0 | 3.8 | 3.1 | 3.6 | 3.6 | 3.4 | 4.7 |
| **Rank** | 51 | 69 | 101 | 95 | 104 | 119 | 103 |

| Components of Economic Freedom | 1970 | | 1975 | | 1980 | | 1985 | | 1990 | | 1995 | | 1997 | |
|---|---|---|---|---|---|---|---|---|---|---|---|---|---|---|
| **I. Size of Government** | **9.5** | | **8.6** | | **7.6** | | **8.9** | | **6.9** | | **8.3** | | **8.8** | |
| (a) Government Consumption (% of Total) | 9.1 | (9.3) | 7.9 | (15.9) | 7.6 | (17.6) | 8.0 | (15.5) | 6.9 | (21.4) | 8.3 | (13.6) | 8.8 | (10.9) |
| (b) Transfers and Subsidies (% of GDP) | 9.9 | (0.8) | 9.4 | (2.8) | | | 9.8 | (1.3) | | | | | | |
| **II. Structure of the Economy and Use of Markets** | | | **3.3** | | **1.3** | | **2.5** | | **1.4** | | **2.6** | | **4.5** | |
| (a) Government Enterprises | 8.0 | (14.6) | 4.0 | (30.7) | 0.0 | (50.9) | 0.0 | (49.8) | 0.0 | (88.1) | 0.0 | | 0.0 | |
| (b) Price Controls | | | | | | | | | 0.0 | | 0.0 | | 4.0 | |
| (c) Top Marginal Tax Rate | | | 0.0 | (75) | 0.0 | (70) | 3.0 | (55) | 2.0 | (55) | 7.0 | (35) | 9.0 | (25) |
| (d) Conscription | 10.0 | | 10.0 | | 10.0 | | 10.0 | | 10.0 | | 10.0 | | 10.0 | |
| **III. Monetary Policy and Price Stability** | **3.4** | | **4.5** | | **7.3** | | **8.4** | | **5.5** | | **1.1** | | **5.5** | |
| (a) Annual Money Growth (last 5 yrs.) | 8.0 | (10.0) | 4.8 | (25.9) | 4.9 | (25.5) | 8.6 | (7.1) | 6.0 | (20.1) | 2.2 | (38.9) | 5.2 | (24.2) |
| (b) Inflation Variability (last 5 yrs.) | 2.1 | (19.8) | 3.5 | (16.3) | 9.4 | (1.4) | 7.4 | (6.5) | 1.9 | (20.2) | 1.1 | (22.4) | 3.3 | (16.7) |
| (c) Recent Inflation Rate | 0.0 | (51.3) | 5.3 | (23.5) | 7.5 | (12.4) | 9.3 | (3.7) | 8.6 | (7.2) | 0.0 | (55.8) | 8.0 | (10.2) |
| **IV. Freedom to Use Alternative Currencies** | **0.0** | | **0.7** | | **0.0** | | **0.0** | | **2.7** | | **0.0** | | **2.5** | |
| (a) Ownership of Foreign Currency | 0.0 | | 0.0 | | 0.0 | | 0.0 | | 0.0 | | 0.0 | | 5.0 | |
| (b) Black Market Exchange Rates (Prem.) | 0.0 | (62.0) | 1.4 | (43.0) | 0.0 | (72.0) | 0.0 | (270.0) | 5.4 | (23.0) | 0.0 | (286.0) | 0.0 | (271.0) |
| **V. Legal Structure and Property Rights** | **3.5** | | **3.5** | | **2.8** | | **1.5** | | **3.0** | | **4.5** | | **5.4** | |
| (a) Private Ownership Rights | 2.8 | | 3.5 | | 3.6 | | 2.2 | | 3.2 | | 3.2 | | 4.4 | |
| (b) Viability of Contracts | 4.3 | | 3.6 | | 3.0 | | 1.0 | | 4.0 | | 3.7 | | 4.8 | |
| (c) Rule of Law | | | | | 1.7 | | 1.4 | | 1.7 | | 7.0 | | 7.0 | |
| **VI. International Exchange** | **4.6** | | **5.8** | | **4.4** | | **5.4** | | **5.2** | | **3.9** | | | |
| (a) Taxes on International Trade | | | | | | | | | | | | | | |
| i. Taxes as a Percentage of Exports and Imports | 5.6 | (6.6) | 5.6 | (6.6) | 4.3 | (8.5) | 6.6 | (5.1) | 7.3 | (4.0) | | | | |
| ii. Mean Tariff Rate | | | | | 3.5 | (32.6) | 2.6 | (37.0) | 3.1 | (34.3) | 3.4 | (32.8) | | |
| iii. Standard Deviation of Tariff Rates | | | | | | | | | 0.0 | (30.8) | 0.0 | (25.0) | | |
| (b) Non-tariff Regulatory Trade Barriers | | | | | | | | | | | | | | |
| i. Non-tariff Trade Restraints (% of trade covered) | | | | | | | 8.3 | (17.0) | 9.1 | (8.7) | 9.1 | (8.8) | | |
| ii. Size of Trade Sector (% of GDP) | 2.2 | (19.6) | 6.5 | (41.2) | 7.3 | (48.6) | 4.0 | (28.5) | 10.0 | (72.2) | 3.8 | (30.1) | 3.3 | (28.2) |
| **VII. Freedom of Exchange in Financial Markets** | | | **1.3** | | **1.3** | | **1.9** | | **2.3** | | **3.2** | | **3.0** | |
| (a) Ownership of Banks | | | 2.0 | (10-20) | 2.0 | (10-40) | 2.0 | (10-40) | 2.0 | (10-40) | 5.0 | (40-75) | 5.0 | (40-75) |
| (b) Extension of Credit | | | | | | | | | 8.5 | (86.8) | 8.6 | (87.0) | 7.6 | (78.0) |
| (c) Avoidance of Negative Interest Rates | 2.0 | | 2.0 | | 2.0 | | 4.0 | | 0.0 | | 0.0 | | 0.0 | |
| (d) Capital Transactions with Foreigners | 0.0 | | 0.0 | | 0.0 | | 0.0 | | 0.0 | | 0.0 | | 0.0 | |

# NORWAY

| | 1970 | 1975 | 1980 | 1985 | 1990 | 1995 | 1997 |
|---|---|---|---|---|---|---|---|
| **Summary Ratings** | 7.0 | 6.1 | 6.2 | 6.8 | 7.7 | 8.1 | 8.1 |
| **Rank** | 19 | 30 | 28 | 24 | 15 | 16 | 22 |

| Components of Economic Freedom | 1970 | | 1975 | | 1980 | | 1985 | | 1990 | | 1995 | | 1997 | |
|---|---|---|---|---|---|---|---|---|---|---|---|---|---|---|
| **I. Size of Government** | **5.5** | | **5.1** | | **4.8** | | **5.0** | | **4.0** | | **4.8** | | **5.1** | |
| (a) Government Consumption (% of Total) | 6.4 | (24.0) | 5.9 | (27.1) | 5.6 | (28.6) | 5.8 | (27.5) | 5.4 | (29.6) | 5.4 | (29.8) | 5.3 | (29.8) |
| (b) Transfers and Subsidies (% of GDP) | 4.5 | (20.6) | 4.4 | (21.0) | 4.1 | (22.1) | 4.3 | (21.4) | 2.7 | (27.3) | 4.2 | (21.8) | 4.8 | (19.5) |
| **II. Structure of the Economy and Use of Markets** | | | **2.1** | | **2.1** | | **2.5** | | **3.8** | | **5.2** | | **5.5** | |
| (a) Government Enterprises | 4.0 | (31.7) | 4.0 | (30.5) | 4.0 | (35.9) | 4.0 | (34.2) | 4.0 | (37.4) | 4.0 | (43.1) | 4.0 | |
| (b) Price Controls | | | | | | | | | 5.0 | | 7.0 | | 8.0 | |
| (c) Top Marginal Tax Rate | | | 0.0 | (74) | 0.0 | (75) | 1.0 | (64) | 3.0 | (54) | 5.0 | (42) | 5.0 | (41.7) |
| (d) Conscription | 1.0 | | 1.0 | | 1.0 | | 1.0 | | 1.0 | | 3.0 | | 3.0 | |
| **III. Monetary Policy and Price Stability** | **8.3** | | **8.4** | | **8.7** | | **8.4** | | **8.3** | | **9.2** | | **9.5** | |
| (a) Annual Money Growth (last 5 yrs.) | 8.8 | (6.0) | 8.0 | (10.2) | 9.7 | (1.5) | 7.5 | (12.7) | 6.6 | (16.8) | 8.8 | (5.9) | 9.6 | (2.2) |
| (b) Inflation Variability (last 5 yrs.) | 8.6 | (3.6) | 9.2 | (2.1) | 8.9 | (2.6) | 8.9 | (2.8) | 8.9 | (2.7) | 9.4 | (1.4) | 9.4 | (1.4) |
| (c) Recent Inflation Rate | 7.4 | (12.8) | 8.0 | (10.0) | 7.4 | (13.1) | 9.0 | (5.2) | 9.2 | (3.9) | 9.4 | (3.1) | 9.4 | (2.8) |
| **IV. Freedom to Use Alternative Currencies** | **5.0** | | **4.9** | | **4.7** | | **5.0** | | **10.0** | | **10.0** | | **10.0** | |
| (a) Ownership of Foreign Currency | 0.0 | | 0.0 | | 0.0 | | 0.0 | | 10.0 | | 10.0 | | 10.0 | |
| (b) Black Market Exchange Rates (Prem.) | 10.0 | (0.0) | 9.8 | (1.0) | 9.4 | (3.0) | 10.0 | (0.0) | 10.0 | (0.0) | 10.0 | (0.0) | 10.0 | (0.0) |
| **V. Legal Structure and Property Rights** | **9.5** | | **7.6** | | **8.3** | | **9.5** | | **9.8** | | **10.0** | | **10.0** | |
| (a) Private Ownership Rights | 9.1 | | 5.9 | | 6.4 | | 9.4 | | 10.0 | | 10.0 | | 10.0 | |
| (b) Viability of Contracts | 9.9 | | 9.4 | | 8.7 | | 9.1 | | 9.4 | | 10.0 | | 10.0 | |
| (c) Rule of Law | | | | | 10.0 | | 10.0 | | 10.0 | | 10.0 | | 10.0 | |
| **VI. International Exchange** | **8.4** | | **8.6** | | **8.8** | | **8.8** | | **8.4** | | **8.0** | | **7.7** | |
| (a) Taxes on International Trade | | | | | | | | | | | | | | |
| i. Taxes as a Percentage of Exports and Imports | 8.9 | (1.6) | 9.7 | (0.5) | 9.8 | (0.3) | 9.8 | (0.3) | 9.8 | (0.3) | 9.7 | (0.4) | 9.8 | (0.3) |
| ii. Mean Tariff Rate | | | 8.3 | (8.5) | 8.8 | (6.2) | 8.9 | (5.7) | 8.9 | (5.7) | 8.8 | (5.9) | 8.8 | (6.1) |
| iii. Standard Deviation of Tariff Rates | | | | | | | | | 7.2 | (6.9) | 5.7 | (10.7) | 3.8 | (15.5) |
| (b) Non-tariff Regulatory Trade Barriers | | | | | | | | | | | | | | |
| i. Non-tariff Trade Restraints (% of trade covered) | | | | | 8.5 | (15.2) | 8.6 | (14.2) | 8.9 | (10.9) | 9.1 | (9.0) | 9.7 | (3.0) |
| ii. Size of Trade Sector (% of GDP) | 7.0 | (74.1) | 7.0 | (78.8) | 6.7 | (80.3) | 6.1 | (78.7) | 5.5 | (74.7) | 4.8 | (70.0) | 5.1 | (75.5) |
| **VII. Freedom of Exchange in Financial Markets** | **5.4** | | **5.9** | | **5.8** | | **7.8** | | **8.3** | | **8.5** | | **8.5** | |
| (a) Ownership of Banks | 10.0 | (95-100) | 10.0 | (95-100) | 10.0 | (95-100) | 10.0 | (95-100) | 8.0 | (75-95) | 8.0 | (75-95) | 8.0 | (75-95) |
| (b) Extension of Credit | 6.3 | (67.1) | 5.7 | (61.5) | 5.1 | (55.5) | 6.0 | (63.8) | 7.3 | (75.2) | 7.9 | (81.1) | 8.2 | (83.9) |
| (c) Avoidance of Negative Interest Rates | | | | | 6.0 | | 10.0 | | 10.0 | | 10.0 | | 10.0 | |
| (d) Capital Transactions with Foreigners | 0.0 | | 2.0 | | 2.0 | | 5.0 | | 8.0 | | 8.0 | | 8.0 | |

# OMAN

| | 1970 | 1975 | 1980 | 1985 | 1990 | 1995 | 1997 |
|---|---|---|---|---|---|---|---|
| **Summary Ratings** | | | 6.6 | 7.5 | 6.8 | 7.7 | 7.6 |
| **Rank** | | | 21 | 13 | 32 | 34 | 36 |

| Components of Economic Freedom | 1970 | | 1975 | | 1980 | | 1985 | | 1990 | | 1995 | | 1997 | |
|---|---|---|---|---|---|---|---|---|---|---|---|---|---|---|
| **I. Size of Government** | **6.4** | | **4.8** | | **5.8** | | **5.9** | | **4.7** | | **7.0** | | **7.2** | |
| (a) Government Consumption (% of Total) | 3.5 | (39.8) | 0.0 | (66.6) | 2.1 | (47.4) | 2.5 | (45.5) | 0.0 | (58.8) | 4.2 | (36.0) | 4.6 | (33.9) |
| (b) Transfers and Subsidies (% of GDP) | 9.3 | (3.2) | 9.7 | (1.7) | 9.6 | (2.0) | 9.3 | (3.1) | 9.3 | (2.9) | 9.8 | (1.3) | 9.8 | (1.4) |
| **II. Structure of the Economy and Use of Markets** | | | **6.1** | | **6.1** | | **6.1** | | **5.4** | | **5.4** | | **5.4** | |
| (a) Government Enterprises | 0.0 | (65.9) | 2.0 | (43.7) | 2.0 | (58.8) | 2.0 | | 2.0 | | 2.0 | | 2.0 | |
| (b) Price Controls | | | | | | | | | 4.0 | | 4.0 | | 4.0 | |
| (c) Top Marginal Tax Rate | | | 10.0 | (0) | 10.0 | (0) | 10.0 | (0) | 10.0 | (0) | 10.0 | (0) | 10.0 | (0) |
| (d) Conscription | | | 10.0 | | 10.0 | | 10.0 | | 10.0 | | 10.0 | | 10.0 | |
| **III. Monetary Policy and Price Stability** | **8.2** | | **4.8** | | **3.3** | | **8.9** | | **6.7** | | **8.9** | | **8.5** | |
| (a) Annual Money Growth (last 5 yrs.) | | | 4.6 | (27.1) | 7.8 | (11.1) | 8.8 | (6.1) | 8.9 | (-5.4) | 9.9 | (-0.6) | 8.9 | (-5.6) |
| (b) Inflation Variability (last 5 yrs.) | 7.6 | (6.1) | 0.0 | (75.6) | 2.2 | (19.4) | 8.1 | (4.8) | 4.5 | (13.7) | 7.6 | (6.1) | 8.1 | (4.7) |
| (c) Recent Inflation Rate | 8.8 | (-6.2) | 9.5 | (2.4) | 0.0 | (51.1) | 9.9 | (-0.5) | 6.7 | (16.6) | 9.3 | (3.7) | 8.6 | (7.2) |
| **IV. Freedom to Use Alternative Currencies** | | | **10.0** | | **10.0** | | **10.0** | | **10.0** | | **10.0** | | **10.0** | |
| (a) Ownership of Foreign Currency | | | 10.0 | | 10.0 | | 10.0 | | 10.0 | | 10.0 | | 10.0 | |
| (b) Black Market Exchange Rates (Prem.) | | | 10.0 | (0.0) | 10.0 | (0.0) | 10.0 | (0.0) | 10.0 | (0.0) | 10.0 | (0.0) | 10.0 | (0.0) |
| **V. Legal Structure and Property Rights** | | | | | | | **6.0** | | **5.3** | | **7.7** | | **7.5** | |
| (a) Private Ownership Rights | | | | | | | 4.8 | | 4.6 | | 7.7 | | 7.2 | |
| (b) Viability of Contracts | | | | | | | 5.2 | | 4.6 | | 8.4 | | 8.3 | |
| (c) Rule of Law | | | | | | | 8.2 | | 6.7 | | 7.0 | | 7.0 | |
| **VI. International Exchange** | **8.5** | | | | | | **8.6** | | **8.1** | | **7.8** | | **8.0** | |
| (a) Taxes on International Trade | | | | | | | | | | | | | | |
| i. Taxes as a Percentage of Exports and Imports | 9.5 | (0.8) | | | | | 9.1 | (1.4) | 9.3 | (1.0) | 9.3 | (1.1) | 9.4 | (0.9) |
| ii. Mean Tariff Rate | | | | | | | 9.4 | (3.0) | | | 8.9 | (5.7) | | |
| iii. Standard Deviation of Tariff Rates | | | | | | | | | | | 6.3 | (9.2) | | |
| (b) Non-tariff Regulatory Trade Barriers | | | | | | | | | | | | | | |
| i. Non-tariff Trade Restraints (% of trade covered) | | | | | | | | | | | | | | |
| ii. Size of Trade Sector (% of GDP) | 6.2 | (93.4) | 7.5 | (118.2) | 6.3 | (100.3) | 5.3 | (87.0) | 4.9 | (83.3) | 4.6 | (79.7) | 4.4 | (78.4) |
| **VII. Freedom of Exchange in Financial Markets** | | | | | **6.3** | | **7.1** | | **7.1** | | **7.1** | | **7.1** | |
| (a) Ownership of Banks | | | 5.0 | (40-75) | 8.0 | (75-95) | 8.0 | (75-90) | 8.0 | (75-95) | 8.0 | (75-95) | 8.0 | (75-95) |
| (b) Extension of Credit | | | | | 9.8 | (97.8) | 9.0 | (91.1) | 9.3 | (93.4) | 9.3 | (93.5) | 9.3 | (93.2) |
| (c) Avoidance of Negative Interest Rates | | | | | | | 10.0 | | 10.0 | | 10.0 | | 10.0 | |
| (d) Capital Transactions with Foreigners | 2.0 | | 2.0 | | 2.0 | | 2.0 | | 2.0 | | 2.0 | | 2.0 | |

# PAKISTAN

| | 1970 | 1975 | 1980 | 1985 | 1990 | 1995 | 1997 |
|---|---|---|---|---|---|---|---|
| **Summary Ratings** | 3.6 | 2.9 | 3.5 | 4.2 | 4.4 | 5.6 | 5.6 |
| **Rank** | 55 | 79 | 94 | 85 | 84 | 81 | 88 |

| Components of Economic Freedom | 1970 | | 1975 | | 1980 | | 1985 | | 1990 | | 1995 | | 1997 | |
|---|---|---|---|---|---|---|---|---|---|---|---|---|---|---|
| **I. Size of Government** | **9.4** | | **9.1** | | **9.2** | | **9.2** | | **8.3** | | **8.9** | | **8.3** | |
| (a) Government Consumption (% of Total) | 8.8 | (11.1) | 8.8 | (11.2) | 8.9 | (10.8) | 8.5 | (12.9) | 7.6 | (17.5) | 8.3 | (13.8) | 8.3 | (13.7) |
| (b) Transfers and Subsidies (% of GDP) | 10.0 | (0.0) | 9.3 | (3.0) | 9.5 | (2.2) | 9.9 | (0.7) | 8.9 | (4.4) | 9.4 | (2.7) | | |
| **II. Structure of the Economy and Use of Markets** | | | **0.4** | | **2.1** | | **1.7** | | **3.4** | | **3.9** | | **4.6** | |
| (a) Government Enterprises | 0.0 | (49.0) | 0.0 | (65.4) | 0.0 | (65.3) | 0.0 | (53.9) | 2.0 | (49.4) | 2.0 | (46.8) | 2.0 | |
| (b) Price Controls | | | | | | | | | | | 4.0 | | 4.0 | |
| (c) Top Marginal Tax Rate | | | 1.0 | (61) | 2.0 | (55) | 1.0 | (60) | 3.0 | (50) | 4.0 | (45) | 7.0 | (35) |
| (d) Conscription | 10.0 | | 0.0 | | 10.0 | | 10.0 | | 10.0 | | 10.0 | | 10.0 | |
| **III. Monetary Policy and Price Stability** | **9.2** | | **6.7** | | **8.1** | | **8.9** | | **8.6** | | **8.2** | | **8.4** | |
| (a) Annual Money Growth (last 5 yrs.) | 9.6 | (2.0) | 8.5 | (7.7) | 6.7 | (16.4) | 8.7 | (6.6) | 8.1 | (9.4) | 8.3 | (8.7) | 8.2 | (9.0) |
| (b) Inflation Variability (last 5 yrs.) | 9.0 | (2.6) | 6.6 | (8.5) | 9.3 | (1.7) | 9.1 | (2.3) | 9.0 | (2.4) | 9.2 | (2.0) | 9.3 | (1.9) |
| (c) Recent Inflation Rate | 9.1 | (4.3) | 5.2 | (24.0) | 8.2 | (9.1) | 9.1 | (4.5) | 8.7 | (6.5) | 7.2 | (13.8) | 7.7 | (11.4) |
| **IV. Freedom to Use Alternative Currencies** | **0.0** | | **3.3** | | **2.3** | | **4.6** | | **6.1** | | **7.2** | | **4.5** | |
| (a) Ownership of Foreign Currency | 0.0 | | 0.0 | | 0.0 | | 0.0 | | 5.0 | | 5.0 | | 0.0 | |
| (b) Black Market Exchange Rates (Prem.) | 0.0 | (134.0) | 6.6 | (17.0) | 4.6 | (27.0) | 9.2 | (4.0) | 7.2 | (14.0) | 9.4 | (3.0) | 9.0 | (5.0) |
| **V. Legal Structure and Property Rights** | **1.9** | | **0.8** | | **2.3** | | **3.5** | | **2.4** | | **6.6** | | **7.0** | |
| (a) Private Ownership Rights | 1.4 | | 0.6 | | 2.2 | | 3.5 | | 2.6 | | 7.7 | | 10.0 | |
| (b) Viability of Contracts | 2.3 | | 1.0 | | 3.0 | | 4.0 | | 2.8 | | 5.2 | | 6.6 | |
| (c) Rule of Law | | | | | 1.7 | | 3.1 | | 1.7 | | 7.0 | | 4.1 | |
| **VI. International Exchange** | **1.1** | | **1.5** | | **0.9** | | **1.1** | | **1.9** | | **3.3** | | **5.0** | |
| (a) Taxes on International Trade | | | | | | | | | | | | | | |
| i. Taxes as a Percentage of Exports and Imports | 0.3 | (14.5) | 0.0 | (15.3) | 0.0 | (15.3) | 0.2 | (14.7) | 0.0 | (16.5) | 4.1 | (8.9) | 4.8 | (7.7) |
| ii. Mean Tariff Rate | | | | | 0.0 | (77.6) | 0.0 | (78.0) | 0.0 | (58.8) | 0.0 | (61.1) | | |
| iii. Standard Deviation of Tariff Rates | | | | | | | | | 0.0 | (34.0) | 1.2 | (21.9) | | |
| (b) Non-tariff Regulatory Trade Barriers | | | | | | | | | | | | | | |
| i. Non-tariff Trade Restraints (% of trade covered) | | | | | | | 1.7 | (83.1) | 7.5 | (25.4) | 8.6 | (14.5) | | |
| ii. Size of Trade Sector (% of GDP) | 3.2 | (22.4) | 5.3 | (33.1) | 5.6 | (36.6) | 5.0 | (34.0) | 5.0 | (35.0) | 4.9 | (35.8) | 5.2 | (39.1) |
| **VII. Freedom of Exchange in Financial Markets** | **4.1** | | **2.0** | | **3.4** | | **4.1** | | **3.5** | | **3.3** | | **3.2** | |
| (a) Ownership of Banks | 0.0 | (0-10) | 0.0 | (0) | 0.0 | (0) | 0.0 | (0) | 0.0 | (0) | 0.0 | (0) | 0.0 | (0) |
| (b) Extension of Credit | 7.4 | (76.8) | 6.7 | (70.0) | 6.5 | (68.6) | 7.7 | (79.2) | 6.9 | (72.2) | 6.0 | (63.9) | 5.7 | (60.8) |
| (c) Avoidance of Negative Interest Rates | 8.0 | | 0.0 | | 6.0 | | 8.0 | | 6.0 | | 6.0 | | 6.0 | |
| (d) Capital Transactions with Foreigners | 2.0 | | 2.0 | | 2.0 | | 2.0 | | 2.0 | | 2.0 | | 2.0 | |

# PANAMA

| | 1970 | 1975 | 1980 | 1985 | 1990 | 1995 | 1997 |
|---|---|---|---|---|---|---|---|
| **Summary Ratings** | | 7.7 | 6.7 | 7.0 | 6.9 | 8.1 | 8.3 |
| **Rank** | | 7 | 20 | 19 | 30 | 16 | 14 |

| Components of Economic Freedom | 1970 | | 1975 | | 1980 | | 1985 | | 1990 | | 1995 | | 1997 | |
|---|---|---|---|---|---|---|---|---|---|---|---|---|---|---|
| **I. Size of Government** | | | **7.6** | | **7.2** | | **7.5** | | **7.3** | | **7.5** | | **7.4** | |
| (a) Government Consumption (% of Total) | | | 6.2 | (25.4) | 5.7 | (28.2) | 6.1 | (25.8) | 6.4 | (24.2) | 6.7 | (22.5) | 6.6 | (23.2) |
| (b) Transfers and Subsidies (% of GDP) | | | 9.1 | (3.8) | 8.8 | (4.9) | 8.8 | (4.8) | 8.1 | (7.4) | 8.3 | (6.7) | 8.3 | (6.8) |
| **II. Structure of the Economy and Use of Markets** | | | **4.8** | | **4.4** | | **4.4** | | **4.3** | | **6.4** | | **6.4** | |
| (a) Government Enterprises | 6.0 | (26.7) | 4.0 | (42.9) | 4.0 | (39.9) | 4.0 | (31.4) | 6.0 | (22.1) | 6.0 | (16.1) | 6.0 | |
| (b) Price Controls | | | | | | | | | 2.0 | | 4.0 | | 4.0 | |
| (c) Top Marginal Tax Rate | | | 4.0 | (52) | 3.0 | (56) | 3.0 | (56) | 3.0 | (56) | 9.0 | (30) | 9.0 | (30) |
| (d) Conscription | | | 10.0 | | 10.0 | | 10.0 | | 10.0 | | 10.0 | | 10.0 | |
| **III. Monetary Policy and Price Stability** | **9.5** | | **8.5** | | **5.6** | | **9.6** | | **9.8** | | **9.0** | | **9.2** | |
| (a) Annual Money Growth (last 5 yrs.) | 9.1 | (4.7) | 8.9 | (5.4) | 8.0 | (10.0) | 9.9 | (0.6) | 10.0 | (-0.3) | 7.8 | (11.1) | 8.3 | (8.5) |
| (b) Inflation Variability (last 5 yrs.) | 9.7 | (0.7) | 8.7 | (3.2) | 5.6 | (11.0) | 9.0 | (2.4) | 9.5 | (1.2) | 9.3 | (1.9) | 9.5 | (1.3) |
| (c) Recent Inflation Rate | 9.8 | (1.1) | 8.0 | (10.3) | 3.3 | (33.7) | 9.8 | (0.8) | 9.9 | (0.6) | 9.9 | (0.5) | 9.7 | (1.3) |
| **IV. Freedom to Use Alternative Currencies** | **10.0** | | **10.0** | | **10.0** | | **10.0** | | **10.0** | | **10.0** | | **10.0** | |
| (a) Ownership of Foreign Currency | 10.0 | | 10.0 | | 10.0 | | 10.0 | | 10.0 | | 10.0 | | 10.0 | |
| (b) Black Market Exchange Rates (Prem.) | 10.0 | (0.0) | 10.0 | (0.0) | 10.0 | (0.0) | 10.0 | (0.0) | 10.0 | (0.0) | 10.0 | (0.0) | 10.0 | (0.0) |
| **V. Legal Structure and Property Rights** | | | | | **2.7** | | **3.5** | | **3.3** | | **6.6** | | **6.9** | |
| (a) Private Ownership Rights | | | | | 4.0 | | 3.5 | | 3.9 | | 7.7 | | 7.2 | |
| (b) Viability of Contracts | | | | | 2.4 | | 4.0 | | 2.8 | | 5.2 | | 6.6 | |
| (c) Rule of Law | | | | | 1.7 | | 3.1 | | 3.3 | | 7.0 | | 7.0 | |
| **VI. International Exchange** | **6.5** | | **7.5** | | **8.5** | | **7.4** | | **6.0** | | **7.7** | | **8.8** | |
| (a) Taxes on International Trade | | | | | | | | | | | | | | |
| i. Taxes as a Percentage of Exports and Imports | 6.9 | (4.7) | 7.9 | (3.2) | 7.9 | (3.1) | 7.3 | (4.1) | 8.8 | (1.8) | 9.1 | (1.4) | | |
| ii. Mean Tariff Rate | | | | | | | | | 2.0 | (40.0) | 5.6 | (22.0) | 8.3 | (8.3) |
| iii. Standard Deviation of Tariff Rates | | | | | | | | | | | | | | |
| (b) Non-tariff Regulatory Trade Barriers | | | | | | | | | | | | | | |
| i. Non-tariff Trade Restraints (% of trade covered) | | | | | | | | | | | | | | |
| ii. Size of Trade Sector (% of GDP) | 5.5 | (79.3) | 6.7 | (101.3) | 10.0 | (186.9) | 7.7 | (128.2) | 9.5 | (165.4) | 10.0 | (198.8) | 10.0 | (185.3) |
| **VII. Freedom of Exchange in Financial Markets** | | | **8.1** | | **8.2** | | **8.1** | | **8.8** | | **9.4** | | **9.4** | |
| (a) Ownership of Banks | | | 8.0 | (75-90) | 8.0 | (75-90) | 8.0 | (75-90) | 8.0 | (75-95) | 8.0 | (80-95) | 8.0 | (80-95) |
| (b) Extension of Credit | 9.7 | (97.3) | 8.3 | (84.4) | 8.8 | (89.4) | 8.5 | (86.6) | 9.3 | (93.4) | 9.9 | (98.9) | 9.9 | (99.0) |
| (c) Avoidance of Negative Interest Rates | | | | | | | | | 10.0 | | 10.0 | | 10.0 | |
| (d) Capital Transactions with Foreigners | 8.0 | | 8.0 | | 8.0 | | 8.0 | | 8.0 | | 10.0 | | 10.0 | |

# Papua New Guinea

| | 1970 | 1975 | 1980 | 1985 | 1990 | 1995 | 1997 |
|---|---|---|---|---|---|---|---|
| **Summary Ratings** | | 4.6 | 4.9 | 6.3 | 6.0 | 5.9 | 5.6 |
| **Rank** | | 57 | 63 | 30 | 43 | 74 | 88 |

| Components of Economic Freedom | 1970 | | 1975 | | 1980 | | 1985 | | 1990 | | 1995 | | 1997 | |
|---|---|---|---|---|---|---|---|---|---|---|---|---|---|---|
| **I. Size of Government** | **4.9** | | **3.8** | | **5.7** | | **7.8** | | **7.2** | | **7.2** | | **4.5** | |
| (a) Government Consumption (% of Total) | 4.9 | (32.1) | 3.8 | (38.5) | 5.7 | (28.1) | 6.1 | (25.9) | 5.4 | (29.6) | 7.2 | (19.6) | 4.5 | (34.2) |
| (b) Transfers and Subsidies (% of GDP) | | | | | | | 9.5 | (2.5) | 9.1 | (3.8) | | | | |
| **II. Structure of the Economy and Use of Markets** | | | | | | | | | | | | | | |
| (a) Government Enterprises | | | | | | | | | | | | | | |
| (b) Price Controls | | | | | | | | | | | | | | |
| (c) Top Marginal Tax Rate | | | | | | | | | 4.0 | (45) | | | 7.0 | (35) |
| (d) Conscription | | | | | 10.0 | | 10.0 | | 10.0 | | 10.0 | | 10.0 | |
| **III. Monetary Policy and Price Stability** | **9.2** | | **8.5** | | **8.3** | | **8.8** | | **8.8** | | **7.1** | | **8.0** | |
| (a) Annual Money Growth (last 5 yrs.) | | | | | 9.3 | (3.5) | 9.5 | (2.7) | 8.8 | (5.8) | 7.8 | (10.9) | 7.0 | (14.8) |
| (b) Inflation Variability (last 5 yrs.) | 9.4 | (1.4) | 7.5 | (6.2) | 6.9 | (7.6) | 7.2 | (6.9) | 8.4 | (4.0) | 7.5 | (6.2) | 7.4 | (6.4) |
| (c) Recent Inflation Rate | 8.9 | (5.7) | 9.5 | (2.3) | 8.6 | (7.1) | 9.7 | (1.6) | 9.2 | (4.1) | 6.1 | (19.7) | 9.5 | (2.4) |
| **IV. Freedom to Use Alternative Currencies** | | | **0.0** | | **0.0** | | **4.6** | | **4.3** | | **4.3** | | **4.8** | |
| (a) Ownership of Foreign Currency | | | 0.0 | | 0.0 | | 0.0 | | 0.0 | | 0.0 | | 0.0 | |
| (b) Black Market Exchange Rates (Prem.) | | | | | | | 9.2 | (4.0) | 8.6 | (7.0) | 8.6 | (7.0) | 9.6 | (2.0) |
| **V. Legal Structure and Property Rights** | | | | | | | **6.8** | | **6.2** | | **5.9** | | **7.3** | |
| (a) Private Ownership Rights | | | | | | | 6.1 | | 5.9 | | 5.5 | | 10.0 | |
| (b) Viability of Contracts | | | | | | | 7.6 | | 4.6 | | 5.2 | | 4.8 | |
| (c) Rule of Law | | | | | | | 6.6 | | 8.3 | | 7.0 | | 7.0 | |
| **VI. International Exchange** | | | **7.6** | | **7.8** | | **7.3** | | **6.9** | | **6.6** | | **4.6** | |
| (a) Taxes on International Trade | | | | | | | | | | | | | | |
| i. Taxes as a Percentage of Exports and Imports | | | 7.7 | (3.4) | 7.8 | (3.3) | 6.1 | (5.9) | 5.3 | (7.1) | 6.0 | (6.0) | | |
| ii. Mean Tariff Rate | | | | | | | 8.6 | (7.0) | 8.6 | (7.0) | | | 5.9 | (20.7) |
| iii. Standard Deviation of Tariff Rates | | | | | | | | | | | 7.0 | (7.5) | 2.4 | (19.1) |
| (b) Non-tariff Regulatory Trade Barriers | | | | | | | | | | | | | | |
| i. Non-tariff Trade Restraints (% of trade covered) | | | | | | | | | | | | | | |
| ii. Size of Trade Sector (% of GDP) | 6.3 | (72.4) | 7.1 | (86.1) | 7.6 | (96.5) | 7.1 | (94.6) | 6.4 | (89.6) | 7.1 | (102.8) | 6.9 | (101.4) |
| **VII. Freedom of Exchange in Financial Markets** | | | **4.2** | | **3.9** | | **4.2** | | **4.3** | | **5.1** | | **5.0** | |
| (a) Ownership of Banks | | | 5.0 | (40-60) | 5.0 | (40-60) | 5.0 | (40-60) | 5.0 | (40-60) | 5.0 | (45-55) | 5.0 | (45-55) |
| (b) Extension of Credit | | | 8.4 | (85.3) | 7.5 | (77.4) | 8.6 | (87.5) | 8.7 | (88.6) | 5.9 | (62.8) | 5.3 | (57.9) |
| (c) Avoidance of Negative Interest Rates | | | | | | | | | | | 8.0 | | 8.0 | |
| (d) Capital Transactions with Foreigners | 0.0 | | 0.0 | | 0.0 | | 0.0 | | 0.0 | | 2.0 | | 2.0 | |

# PARAGUAY

| | 1970 | 1975 | 1980 | 1985 | 1990 | 1995 | 1997 |
|---|---|---|---|---|---|---|---|
| **Summary Ratings** | | | 6.2 | 6.0 | 6.3 | 7.8 | 7.6 |
| **Rank** | | | 28 | 36 | 40 | 29 | 36 |

| Components of Economic Freedom | 1970 | | 1975 | | 1980 | | 1985 | | 1990 | | 1995 | | 1997 | |
|---|---|---|---|---|---|---|---|---|---|---|---|---|---|---|
| **I. Size of Government** | **9.3** | | **9.5** | | **9.5** | | **9.5** | | **9.6** | | **9.0** | | **7.9** | |
| (a) Government Consumption (% of Total) | 8.9 | (10.4) | 9.4 | (7.7) | 9.5 | (7.4) | 9.4 | (7.9) | 9.5 | (7.4) | 8.8 | (11.2) | 7.9 | (15.8) |
| (b) Transfers and Subsidies (% of GDP) | 9.7 | (1.6) | 9.6 | (2.0) | 9.6 | (2.0) | 9.6 | (2.1) | 9.6 | (1.8) | 9.3 | (3.0) | | |
| **II. Structure of the Economy and Use of Markets** | | | | | | | **6.0** | | **5.6** | | **6.8** | | **6.8** | |
| (a) Government Enterprises | 8.0 | (13.1) | 8.0 | (10.4) | 8.0 | (13.7) | 6.0 | (26.3) | 7.0 | (24.0) | 7.0 | (23.9) | 7.0 | |
| (b) Price Controls | | | | | | | | | 4.0 | | 6.0 | | 6.0 | |
| (c) Top Marginal Tax Rate | | | | | | | 8.0 | (30) | 8.0 | (30) | 10.0 | (0) | 10.0 | (0) |
| (d) Conscription | 0.0 | | 0.0 | | 1.0 | | 0.0 | | 0.0 | | 0.0 | | 0.0 | |
| **III. Monetary Policy and Price Stability** | **9.3** | | **7.6** | | **6.9** | | **6.7** | | **4.9** | | **7.1** | | **8.0** | |
| (a) Annual Money Growth (last 5 yrs.) | 9.2 | (4.0) | 7.2 | (14.0) | 6.1 | (19.6) | 8.3 | (8.7) | 3.6 | (32.1) | 5.6 | (22.2) | 7.5 | (12.4) |
| (b) Inflation Variability (last 5 yrs.) | 9.1 | (2.2) | 7.0 | (7.5) | 7.9 | (5.2) | 6.8 | (7.9) | 8.6 | (3.6) | 8.3 | (4.3) | 8.1 | (4.9) |
| (c) Recent Inflation Rate | 9.6 | (1.9) | 8.7 | (6.6) | 6.7 | (16.7) | 5.0 | (25.2) | 2.7 | (36.3) | 7.4 | (13.0) | 8.4 | (8.0) |
| **IV. Freedom to Use Alternative Currencies** | **8.3** | | **8.7** | | **9.3** | | **5.0** | | **7.4** | | **8.7** | | **8.9** | |
| (a) Ownership of Foreign Currency | 10.0 | | 10.0 | | 10.0 | | 10.0 | | 10.0 | | 10.0 | | 10.0 | |
| (b) Black Market Exchange Rates (Prem.) | 6.6 | (17.0) | 7.4 | (13.0) | 8.6 | (7.0) | 0.0 | (213.0) | 4.8 | (26.0) | 7.4 | (13.0) | 7.8 | (11.0) |
| **V. Legal Structure and Property Rights** | | | | | **4.3** | | **4.8** | | **5.3** | | **6.0** | | **5.6** | |
| (a) Private Ownership Rights | | | | | 5.4 | | 4.8 | | 5.9 | | 5.5 | | 4.4 | |
| (b) Viability of Contracts | | | | | 5.6 | | 6.4 | | 6.4 | | 8.4 | | 8.3 | |
| (c) Rule of Law | | | | | 1.7 | | 3.1 | | 3.3 | | 4.1 | | 4.1 | |
| **VI. International Exchange** | **2.9** | | **3.5** | | **3.1** | | **5.4** | | **6.5** | | **7.9** | | **7.0** | |
| (a) Taxes on International Trade | | | | | | | | | | | | | | |
| i. Taxes as a Percentage of Exports and Imports | 3.3 | (10.1) | 4.1 | (8.8) | 6.0 | (6.0) | 8.5 | (2.2) | 7.8 | (3.3) | 8.6 | (2.1) | | |
| ii. Mean Tariff Rate | | | | | 0.0 | (71.0) | 0.0 | (71.7) | 6.8 | (16.0) | 8.1 | (9.3) | 8.1 | (9.6) |
| iii. Standard Deviation of Tariff Rates | | | | | | | | | 4.9 | (12.7) | 7.2 | (6.9) | 7.3 | (6.7) |
| (b) Non-tariff Regulatory Trade Barriers | | | | | | | | | | | | | | |
| i. Non-tariff Trade Restraints (% of trade covered) | | | | | | | 9.0 | (9.9) | | | 9.8 | (1.8) | | |
| ii. Size of Trade Sector (% of GDP) | 2.1 | (31.0) | 2.0 | (31.9) | 4.0 | (44.0) | 4.3 | (48.4) | 6.3 | (72.7) | 3.7 | (47.8) | 3.5 | (46.5) |
| **VII. Freedom of Exchange in Financial Markets** | | | | | | | | | **5.4** | | **9.2** | | **9.2** | |
| (a) Ownership of Banks | | | | | | | | | | | | | | |
| (b) Extension of Credit | | | | | | | | | 9.9 | (99.4) | 9.7 | (97.5) | 9.6 | (96.0) |
| (c) Avoidance of Negative Interest Rates | | | | | | | | | 2.0 | | 8.0 | | 8.0 | |
| (d) Capital Transactions with Foreigners | 5.0 | | 5.0 | | 5.0 | | 5.0 | | 5.0 | | 10.0 | | 10.0 | |

# PERU

| | 1970 | 1975 | 1980 | 1985 | 1990 | 1995 | 1997 |
|---|---|---|---|---|---|---|---|
| **Summary Ratings** | 4.7 | 3.5 | 3.4 | 2.3 | 3.7 | 7.5 | 7.9 |
| **Rank** | 46 | 72 | 97 | 108 | 102 | 40 | 31 |

| Components of Economic Freedom | 1970 | | 1975 | | 1980 | | 1985 | | 1990 | | 1995 | | 1997 | |
|---|---|---|---|---|---|---|---|---|---|---|---|---|---|---|
| **I. Size of Government** | **8.8** | | **8.9** | | **8.8** | | **9.1** | | **9.1** | | **9.0** | | **8.7** | |
| (a) Government Consumption (% of Total) | 8.1 | (14.7) | 8.2 | (14.3) | 8.0 | (15.3) | 8.5 | (12.7) | 8.9 | (10.5) | 9.0 | (10.2) | 8.1 | (14.8) |
| (b) Transfers and Subsidies (% of GDP) | 9.5 | (2.3) | 9.6 | (1.9) | 9.6 | (1.9) | 9.6 | (1.8) | 9.3 | (3.0) | 9.1 | (3.9) | 9.3 | (3.3) |
| **II. Structure of the Economy and Use of Markets** | | | **3.5** | | **2.7** | | **2.0** | | **3.6** | | **6.6** | | **7.3** | |
| (a) Government Enterprises | 6.0 | (24.3) | 4.0 | (36.8) | 4.0 | (28.1) | 4.0 | (42.7) | 6.0 | (19.0) | 8.0 | (17.9) | 8.0 | |
| (b) Price Controls | | | | | | | | | 2.0 | | 6.0 | | 8.0 | |
| (c) Top Marginal Tax Rate | | | 4.0 | (51) | 2.0 | (65) | 0.0 | (65) | 4.0 | (45) | 8.0 | (30) | 8.0 | (30) |
| (d) Conscription | 0.0 | | 0.0 | | 0.0 | | 0.0 | | 0.0 | | 0.0 | | 0.0 | |
| **III. Monetary Policy and Price Stability** | **7.7** | | **6.4** | | **1.7** | | **0.0** | | **0.0** | | **2.6** | | **5.0** | |
| (a) Annual Money Growth (last 5 yrs.) | 6.6 | (16.9) | 6.3 | (18.6) | 2.2 | (39.1) | 0.0 | (98.5) | 0.0 | (690.3) | 0.0 | (58.2) | 2.3 | (38.4) |
| (b) Inflation Variability (last 5 yrs.) | 8.5 | (3.7) | 7.7 | (5.9) | 3.1 | (17.3) | 0.0 | (37.9) | 0.0 | (2341.4) | 0.0 | (127.5) | 4.4 | (14.1) |
| (c) Recent Inflation Rate | 8.1 | (9.3) | 5.4 | (23.2) | 0.0 | (65.9) | 0.0 | (167.8) | 0.0 | (6134.8) | 7.6 | (12.2) | 8.3 | (8.4) |
| **IV. Freedom to Use Alternative Currencies** | **3.6** | | **0.0** | | **3.2** | | **0.0** | | **5.9** | | **10.0** | | **10.0** | |
| (a) Ownership of Foreign Currency | 0.0 | | 0.0 | | 0.0 | | 0.0 | | 5.0 | | 10.0 | | 10.0 | |
| (b) Black Market Exchange Rates (Prem.) | 7.2 | (14.0) | 0.0 | (56.0) | 6.4 | (18.0) | 0.0 | (51.0) | 6.8 | (16.0) | 10.0 | (0.0) | 10.0 | (0.0) |
| **V. Legal Structure and Property Rights** | **1.7** | | **1.4** | | **3.9** | | **1.2** | | **2.6** | | **8.0** | | **7.9** | |
| (a) Private Ownership Rights | 0.3 | | 0.0 | | 4.0 | | 1.6 | | 3.2 | | 10.0 | | 10.0 | |
| (b) Viability of Contracts | 3.1 | | 2.8 | | 4.3 | | 0.7 | | 2.8 | | 6.8 | | 6.6 | |
| (c) Rule of Law | | | | | 3.3 | | 1.4 | | 1.7 | | 7.0 | | 7.0 | |
| **VI. International Exchange** | **4.1** | | **3.7** | | **2.0** | | **2.6** | | **3.3** | | **7.1** | | **7.0** | |
| (a) Taxes on International Trade | | | | | | | | | | | | | | |
| i. Taxes as a Percentage of Exports and Imports | 4.1 | (8.9) | 3.7 | (9.5) | 2.9 | (10.6) | 4.5 | (8.3) | 7.4 | (3.9) | 6.3 | (5.5) | 6.9 | (4.6) |
| ii. Mean Tariff Rate | | | | | 0.0 | (57.0) | 0.0 | (64.0) | 2.8 | (36.0) | 6.5 | (17.6) | 7.3 | (13.3) |
| iii. Standard Deviation of Tariff Rates | | | | | | | 1.2 | (22.0) | 0.0 | (25.0) | 8.2 | (4.4) | 8.8 | (2.9) |
| (b) Non-tariff Regulatory Trade Barriers | | | | | | | | | | | | | | |
| i. Non-tariff Trade Restraints (% of trade covered) | | | | | | | 4.7 | (53.4) | 4.4 | (55.7) | 10.0 | (0.0) | | |
| ii. Size of Trade Sector (% of GDP) | 4.3 | (33.9) | 3.9 | (32.8) | 5.0 | (41.8) | 4.5 | (39.4) | 0.3 | (23.6) | 1.5 | (28.1) | 1.6 | (29.4) |
| **VII. Freedom of Exchange in Financial Markets** | | | | | **2.3** | | **2.2** | | **1.8** | | **7.7** | | **8.3** | |
| (a) Ownership of Banks | | | | | | | | | | | | | | |
| (b) Extension of Credit | 5.1 | (56.1) | 3.4 | (40.3) | 5.4 | (58.9) | 4.9 | (54.3) | 3.6 | (42.1) | 9.3 | (93.8) | 9.2 | (92.4) |
| (c) Avoidance of Negative Interest Rates | | | | | 0.0 | | 0.0 | | 0.0 | | 6.0 | | 8.0 | |
| (d) Capital Transactions with Foreigners | 0.0 | | 2.0 | | 2.0 | | 2.0 | | 2.0 | | 8.0 | | 8.0 | |

# PHILIPPINES

| | 1970 | 1975 | 1980 | 1985 | 1990 | 1995 | 1997 |
|---|---|---|---|---|---|---|---|
| **Summary Ratings** | 5.1 | 4.9 | 5.1 | 4.9 | 5.6 | 7.7 | 7.9 |
| **Rank** | 41 | 51 | 56 | 67 | 55 | 34 | 31 |

| Components of Economic Freedom | 1970 | | 1975 | | 1980 | | 1985 | | 1990 | | 1995 | | 1997 | |
|---|---|---|---|---|---|---|---|---|---|---|---|---|---|---|
| **I. Size of Government** | **9.3** | | **9.0** | | **9.2** | | **9.6** | | **9.2** | | **9.2** | | **8.1** | |
| (a) Government Consumption (% of Total) | 8.6 | (12.3) | 8.1 | (14.7) | 8.6 | (12.4) | 9.1 | (9.4) | 8.6 | (12.4) | 8.4 | (13.3) | 8.1 | (15.1) |
| (b) Transfers and Subsidies (% of GDP) | 10.0 | (0.4) | 9.9 | (0.8) | 9.8 | (1.1) | 10.0 | (0.2) | 9.9 | (0.9) | 9.9 | (0.7) | | |
| **II. Structure of the Economy and Use of Markets** | | | **4.5** | | **3.7** | | **5.6** | | **5.9** | | **6.3** | | **6.9** | |
| (a) Government Enterprises | 7.0 | (17.1) | 6.0 | (21.4) | 6.0 | (27.4) | 8.0 | (19.5) | 8.0 | (18.2) | 8.0 | (20.6) | 8.0 | |
| (b) Price Controls | | | | | | | | | 2.0 | | 3.0 | | 5.0 | |
| (c) Top Marginal Tax Rate | | | 3.0 | (56) | 1.0 | (70) | 1.0 | (60) | 7.0 | (35) | 7.0 | (35) | 7.0 | (35) |
| (d) Conscription | 3.0 | | 3.0 | | 3.0 | | 10.0 | | 10.0 | | 10.0 | | 10.0 | |
| **III. Monetary Policy and Price Stability** | **9.0** | | **7.3** | | **7.9** | | **6.1** | | **5.3** | | **8.2** | | **8.5** | |
| (a) Annual Money Growth (last 5 yrs.) | 8.9 | (5.7) | 7.2 | (13.9) | 7.8 | (11.0) | 8.4 | (7.9) | 0.0 | (118.7) | 7.5 | (12.5) | 7.2 | (14.0) |
| (b) Inflation Variability (last 5 yrs.) | 9.6 | (1.0) | 6.4 | (9.1) | 8.8 | (2.9) | 3.5 | (16.4) | 8.7 | (3.3) | 8.6 | (3.5) | 9.5 | (1.3) |
| (c) Recent Inflation Rate | 8.4 | (7.9) | 8.1 | (9.3) | 7.2 | (14.3) | 6.5 | (17.6) | 7.4 | (13.0) | 8.5 | (7.6) | 8.8 | (6.1) |
| **IV. Freedom to Use Alternative Currencies** | **0.0** | | **3.7** | | **4.7** | | **4.3** | | **4.3** | | **10.0** | | **9.5** | |
| (a) Ownership of Foreign Currency | 0.0 | | 0.0 | | 0.0 | | 0.0 | | 0.0 | | 10.0 | | 10.0 | |
| (b) Black Market Exchange Rates (Prem.) | 0.0 | (73.0) | 7.4 | (13.0) | 9.4 | (3.0) | 8.6 | (7.0) | 8.6 | (7.0) | 10.0 | (0.0) | 9.0 | (5.0) |
| **V. Legal Structure and Property Rights** | **4.4** | | **4.4** | | **3.0** | | **1.7** | | **2.5** | | **6.3** | | **7.6** | |
| (a) Private Ownership Rights | 4.9 | | 3.8 | | 3.6 | | 2.2 | | 1.9 | | 7.7 | | 10.0 | |
| (b) Viability of Contracts | 3.9 | | 4.9 | | 3.7 | | 1.6 | | 4.0 | | 6.8 | | 8.3 | |
| (c) Rule of Law | | | | | 1.7 | | 1.4 | | 1.7 | | 4.1 | | 4.1 | |
| **VI. International Exchange** | **5.5** | | **2.2** | | **4.6** | | **4.5** | | **6.5** | | **7.1** | | **7.4** | |
| (a) Taxes on International Trade | | | | | | | | | | | | | | |
| i. Taxes as a Percentage of Exports and Imports | 4.7 | (7.9) | 1.1 | (13.4) | 5.5 | (6.8) | 5.9 | (6.2) | 5.6 | (6.6) | 5.7 | (6.4) | 7.6 | (3.6) |
| ii. Mean Tariff Rate | | | 1.2 | (44.0) | 2.4 | (38.0) | 4.5 | (27.6) | 5.1 | (24.3) | 4.5 | (27.6) | 6.4 | (18.2) |
| iii. Standard Deviation of Tariff Rates | | | | | | | | | 6.3 | (9.2) | 8.0 | (4.9) | | |
| (b) Non-tariff Regulatory Trade Barriers | | | | | | | | | | | | | | |
| i. Non-tariff Trade Restraints (% of trade covered) | | | | | | | 1.7 | (83.0) | 8.5 | (15.0) | 9.5 | (5.0) | | |
| ii. Size of Trade Sector (% of GDP) | 7.3 | (42.6) | 7.9 | (48.1) | 8.2 | (52.0) | 6.9 | (45.9) | 8.8 | (60.8) | 10.0 | (80.5) | 10.0 | (101.9) |
| **VII. Freedom of Exchange in Financial Markets** | | | **5.5** | | **5.2** | | **4.4** | | **6.1** | | **7.5** | | **7.6** | |
| (a) Ownership of Banks | | | 5.0 | (40-75) | 5.0 | (40-75) | 5.0 | (70-75) | 8.0 | (88) | 8.0 | (90) | 8.0 | (90) |
| (b) Extension of Credit | 5.9 | (62.9) | 7.6 | (78.6) | 6.4 | (67.8) | 7.2 | (75.0) | 6.8 | (70.9) | 7.4 | (76.2) | 7.4 | (76.7) |
| (c) Avoidance of Negative Interest Rates | | | 8.0 | | 8.0 | | 4.0 | | 8.0 | | 10.0 | | 10.0 | |
| (d) Capital Transactions with Foreigners | 0.0 | | 2.0 | | 2.0 | | 2.0 | | 2.0 | | 5.0 | | 5.0 | |

# POLAND

| | 1970 | 1975 | 1980 | 1985 | 1990 | 1995 | 1997 |
|---|---|---|---|---|---|---|---|
| Summary Ratings | | | | 3.5 | 4.0 | 6.4 | 6.0 |
| Rank | | | | 96 | 95 | 57 | 82 |

| Components of Economic Freedom | 1970 | | 1975 | | 1980 | | 1985 | | 1990 | | 1995 | | 1997 | |
|---|---|---|---|---|---|---|---|---|---|---|---|---|---|---|
| **I. Size of Government** | | | **8.0** | | **8.6** | | **5.6** | | **4.1** | | **5.0** | | **5.3** | |
| (a) Government Consumption (% of Total) | | | 8.0 | (15.6) | 8.6 | (12.1) | 8.5 | (13.0) | 5.6 | (28.7) | 6.6 | (23.0) | 6.9 | (21.6) |
| (b) Transfers and Subsidies (% of GDP) | | | | | | | 2.7 | (27.4) | 2.7 | (27.4) | 3.5 | (24.4) | 3.7 | (23.5) |
| **II. Structure of the Economy and Use of Markets** | | | | | | | | | **0.9** | | **4.1** | | **3.4** | |
| (a) Government Enterprises | 0.0 | (40.7) | 0.0 | | 0.0 | | 0.0 | | 0.0 | (80.2) | 2.0 | (58.0) | 2.0 | |
| (b) Price Controls | | | | | | | | | 2.0 | | 7.0 | | 5.0 | |
| (c) Top Marginal Tax Rate | | | | | | | | | | | 4.0 | (45) | 4.0 | (44) |
| (d) Conscription | 0.0 | | 0.0 | | 0.0 | | 0.0 | | 0.0 | | 1.0 | | 1.0 | |
| **III. Monetary Policy and Price Stability** | | | **9.3** | | **8.6** | | **4.3** | | **0.0** | | **4.7** | | **6.0** | |
| (a) Annual Money Growth (last 5 yrs.) | | | | | | | 5.9 | (20.5) | 0.0 | (110.4) | 3.8 | (30.9) | 3.5 | (32.7) |
| (b) Inflation Variability (last 5 yrs.) | | | 9.0 | (2.4) | 9.2 | (2.0) | 0.0 | (37.4) | 0.0 | (167.6) | 5.9 | (10.2) | 7.5 | (6.3) |
| (c) Recent Inflation Rate | | | 9.5 | (2.4) | 8.0 | (9.8) | 6.8 | (15.8) | 0.0 | (435.7) | 4.4 | (28.2) | 7.1 | (14.8) |
| **IV. Freedom to Use Alternative Currencies** | **2.5** | | **2.5** | | **2.5** | | **2.5** | | **9.1** | | **10.0** | | **7.5** | |
| (a) Ownership of Foreign Currency | 5.0 | | 5.0 | | 5.0 | | 5.0 | | 10.0 | | 10.0 | | 5.0 | |
| (b) Black Market Exchange Rates (Prem.) | 0.0 | (3150.0) | 0.0 | (3786.0) | 0.0 | (298.0) | 0.0 | (301.0) | 8.2 | (9.0) | 10.0 | (0.0) | 10.0 | (0.0) |
| **V. Legal Structure and Property Rights** | | | | | | | **4.0** | | **6.0** | | **9.5** | | **9.0** | |
| (a) Private Ownership Rights | | | | | | | 3.5 | | 7.3 | | 10.0 | | 10.0 | |
| (b) Viability of Contracts | | | | | | | 2.2 | | 4.0 | | 8.4 | | 10.0 | |
| (c) Rule of Law | | | | | | | 6.6 | | 6.7 | | 10.0 | | 7.0 | |
| **VI. International Exchange** | | | | | | | **5.5** | | **6.6** | | **6.2** | | **5.0** | |
| (a) Taxes on International Trade | | | | | | | | | | | | | | |
| i. Taxes as a Percentage of Exports and Imports | | | | | | | 4.3 | (8.6) | 6.0 | (6.0) | 5.7 | (6.4) | 8.1 | (2.9) |
| ii. Mean Tariff Rate | | | | | | | 7.3 | (13.6) | 7.7 | (11.7) | 6.3 | (18.4) | 6.5 | (17.6) |
| iii. Standard Deviation of Tariff Rates | | | | | | | | | 6.4 | (8.9) | 6.9 | (7.8) | 0.0 | (27.5) |
| (b) Non-tariff Regulatory Trade Barriers | | | | | | | | | | | | | | |
| i. Non-tariff Trade Restraints (% of trade covered) | | | | | | | | | | | | | | |
| ii. Size of Trade Sector (% of GDP) | | | | | 7.3 | (59.2) | 3.9 | (35.1) | 5.5 | (50.2) | 5.2 | (50.5) | 5.8 | (57.9) |
| **VII. Freedom of Exchange in Financial Markets** | | | | | **0.0** | | **0.0** | | **0.1** | | **4.0** | | **5.1** | |
| (a) Ownership of Banks | 0.0 | (0-10) | 0.0 | (10) | 0.0 | (0-10) | 0.0 | (0-10) | 0.0 | (0-10) | 2.0 | (10-20) | 2.0 | (20-40) |
| (b) Extension of Credit | | | | | 0.0 | (4.8) | 0.0 | (7.6) | 0.3 | (13.1) | 3.1 | (38.1) | 3.7 | (43.3) |
| (c) Avoidance of Negative Interest Rates | | | | | | | | | 0.0 | | 6.0 | | 10.0 | |
| (d) Capital Transactions with Foreigners | 0.0 | | 0.0 | | 0.0 | | 0.0 | | 0.0 | | 5.0 | | 5.0 | |

# PORTUGAL

| | 1970 | 1975 | 1980 | 1985 | 1990 | 1995 | 1997 |
|---|---|---|---|---|---|---|---|
| **Summary Ratings** | 5.6 | 3.4 | 5.6 | 5.7 | 6.4 | 7.8 | 8.0 |
| **Rank** | 37 | 73 | 41 | 44 | 38 | 29 | 25 |

| Components of Economic Freedom | 1970 | | 1975 | | 1980 | | 1985 | | 1990 | | 1995 | | 1997 | |
|---|---|---|---|---|---|---|---|---|---|---|---|---|---|---|
| **I. Size of Government** | **7.8** | | **7.1** | | **6.7** | | **6.2** | | **6.6** | | **6.7** | | **6.8** | |
| (a) Government Consumption (% of Total) | 7.8 | (16.4) | 8.0 | (15.3) | 7.8 | (16.8) | 7.6 | (17.6) | 7.2 | (19.8) | 6.9 | (21.4) | 6.8 | (21.8) |
| (b) Transfers and Subsidies (% of GDP) | | | 6.2 | (14.6) | 5.7 | (16.3) | 4.8 | (19.5) | 5.9 | (15.5) | 6.5 | (13.4) | | |
| **II. Structure of the Economy and Use of Markets** | **2.1** | | **1.0** | | **1.0** | | **2.0** | | **3.9** | | **5.2** | | **5.5** | |
| (a) Government Enterprises | 2.0 | (41.8) | 2.0 | (39.7) | 2.0 | (42.2) | 4.0 | (30.5) | 4.0 | (29.9) | 6.0 | (23.2) | 6.0 | |
| (b) Price Controls | | | | | | | | | 4.0 | | 5.0 | | 6.0 | |
| (c) Top Marginal Tax Rate | 3.0 | (58) | 0.0 | (82) | 0.0 | (84) | 0.0 | (69) | 5.0 | (40) | 5.0 | (40) | 5.0 | (40) |
| (d) Conscription | 0.0 | | 0.0 | | 0.0 | | 0.0 | | 0.0 | | 3.0 | | 3.0 | |
| **III. Monetary Policy and Price Stability** | **9.5** | | **7.4** | | **7.4** | | **7.4** | | **7.6** | | **8.7** | | **9.1** | |
| (a) Annual Money Growth (last 5 yrs.) | 9.7 | (1.5) | 7.5 | (12.4) | 7.6 | (11.9) | 7.6 | (12.2) | 6.8 | (16.0) | 8.3 | (8.7) | 8.5 | (7.4) |
| (b) Inflation Variability (last 5 yrs.) | 9.1 | (2.1) | 7.9 | (5.2) | 8.7 | (3.3) | 8.9 | (2.6) | 8.5 | (3.7) | 9.0 | (2.6) | 9.3 | (1.7) |
| (c) Recent Inflation Rate | 9.6 | (2.0) | 6.8 | (16.2) | 5.8 | (20.9) | 5.7 | (21.7) | 7.4 | (12.8) | 9.0 | (5.2) | 9.5 | (2.6) |
| **IV. Freedom to Use Alternative Currencies** | **5.0** | | **0.8** | | **4.8** | | **4.8** | | **4.7** | | **10.0** | | **10.0** | |
| (a) Ownership of Foreign Currency | 0.0 | | 0.0 | | 0.0 | | 0.0 | | 0.0 | | 10.0 | | 10.0 | |
| (b) Black Market Exchange Rates (Prem.) | 10.0 | (0.0) | 1.6 | (42.0) | 9.6 | (2.0) | 9.6 | (2.0) | 9.4 | (3.0) | 10.0 | (0.0) | 10.0 | (0.0) |
| **V. Legal Structure and Property Rights** | **6.3** | | **0.9** | | **9.2** | | **7.1** | | **9.1** | | **9.5** | | **9.0** | |
| (a) Private Ownership Rights | 8.3 | | 0.3 | | 9.0 | | 5.5 | | 10.0 | | 10.0 | | 10.0 | |
| (b) Viability of Contracts | 4.3 | | 1.5 | | 8.7 | | 7.6 | | 8.8 | | 8.4 | | 10.0 | |
| (c) Rule of Law | | | | | 10.0 | | 8.2 | | 8.3 | | 10.0 | | 7.0 | |
| **VI. International Exchange** | **7.0** | | **6.2** | | **7.7** | | **8.3** | | **8.0** | | **8.4** | | **8.4** | |
| (a) Taxes on International Trade | | | | | | | | | | | | | | |
| i. Taxes as a Percentage of Exports and Imports | 7.9 | (3.2) | 6.9 | (4.6) | 8.6 | (2.1) | 9.2 | (1.2) | 9.1 | (1.3) | 9.8 | (0.3) | 9.7 | (0.5) |
| ii. Mean Tariff Rate | | | | | | | | | 8.5 | (7.4) | 8.7 | (6.7) | 8.6 | (6.9) |
| iii. Standard Deviation of Tariff Rates | | | | | | | | | 7.1 | (7.2) | 7.6 | (5.9) | 7.6 | (6.0) |
| (b) Non-tariff Regulatory Trade Barriers | | | | | | | | | | | | | | |
| i. Non-tariff Trade Restraints (% of trade covered) | | | | | | | | | 8.1 | (19.1) | 8.7 | (13.4) | 9.3 | (6.7) |
| ii. Size of Trade Sector (% of GDP) | 4.9 | (50.2) | 4.3 | (48.2) | 5.5 | (63.0) | 5.8 | (71.5) | 5.8 | (76.2) | 5.2 | (73.9) | 4.4 | (63.6) |
| **VII. Freedom of Exchange in Financial Markets** | **3.4** | | **2.7** | | **2.9** | | **4.2** | | **5.0** | | **6.3** | | **7.5** | |
| (a) Ownership of Banks | 0.0 | (0-10) | 0.0 | (0-10) | 0.0 | (5-10) | 0.0 | (0-10) | 2.0 | (15) | 2.0 | (20-40) | 5.0 | (40-60) |
| (b) Extension of Credit | 9.4 | (94.6) | 6.9 | (72.0) | 6.3 | (66.7) | 5.9 | (62.8) | 5.4 | (58.8) | 5.4 | (58.2) | 6.9 | (72.3) |
| (c) Avoidance of Negative Interest Rates | | | | | 4.0 | | 10.0 | | 8.0 | | 10.0 | | 10.0 | |
| (d) Capital Transactions with Foreigners | 2.0 | | 2.0 | | 2.0 | | 2.0 | | 5.0 | | 8.0 | | 8.0 | |

# ROMANIA

| | 1970 | 1975 | 1980 | 1985 | 1990 | 1995 | 1997 |
|---|---|---|---|---|---|---|---|
| Summary Ratings | | | | 3.5 | 4.2 | 4.5 | 4.6 |
| Rank | | | | 96 | 91 | 103 | 107 |

| Components of Economic Freedom | 1970 | | 1975 | | 1980 | | 1985 | | 1990 | | 1995 | | 1997 | |
|---|---|---|---|---|---|---|---|---|---|---|---|---|---|---|
| **I. Size of Government** | | | | | **7.8** | | **8.8** | | **6.4** | | **7.0** | | **7.4** | |
| (a) Government Consumption (% of Total) | | | | | 9.4 | (8.0) | 9.6 | (6.5) | 7.7 | (16.8) | 7.7 | (16.8) | 8.7 | (11.8) |
| (b) Transfers and Subsidies (% of GDP) | | | | | 6.3 | (14.1) | 8.0 | (7.9) | 5.1 | (18.6) | 6.2 | (14.6) | 6.2 | (14.4) |
| **II. Structure of the Economy and Use of Markets** | | | | | | | | | **0.0** | | **2.3** | | **2.3** | |
| (a) Government Enterprises | 0.0 | | 0.0 | | 0.0 | | 0.0 | | 0.0 | | 0.0 | (54.0) | 0.0 | |
| (b) Price Controls | | | | | | | | | 0.0 | | 6.0 | | 6.0 | |
| (c) Top Marginal Tax Rate | | | | | | | | | | | 1.0 | (60) | 1.0 | (60) |
| (d) Conscription | 0.0 | | 0.0 | | 1.0 | | 0.0 | | 0.0 | | 1.0 | | 1.0 | |
| **III. Monetary Policy and Price Stability** | | | | | **8.8** | | **9.3** | | **7.8** | | **1.0** | | **0.0** | |
| (a) Annual Money Growth (last 5 yrs.) | | | | | 7.8 | (11.2) | 9.8 | (1.2) | 8.3 | (8.7) | 0.0 | (97.9) | 0.0 | (78.7) |
| (b) Inflation Variability (last 5 yrs.) | | | 9.8 | (0.4) | 8.8 | (3.1) | 8.1 | (4.7) | 7.9 | (5.3) | 0.0 | (68.3) | 0.0 | (71.3) |
| (c) Recent Inflation Rate | | | | | 9.9 | (0.6) | 9.9 | (0.4) | 7.3 | (13.7) | 2.9 | (35.3) | 0.0 | (146.7) |
| **IV. Freedom to Use Alternative Currencies** | **0.0** | | **0.0** | | **0.0** | | **0.0** | | **2.5** | | **4.7** | | **4.4** | |
| (a) Ownership of Foreign Currency | 0.0 | | 0.0 | | 0.0 | | 0.0 | | 5.0 | | 0.0 | | 0.0 | |
| (b) Black Market Exchange Rates (Prem.) | 0.0 | (521.0) | 0.0 | (596.0) | 0.0 | (628.0) | 0.0 | (1246.0) | 0.0 | (416.0) | 9.4 | (3.0) | 8.8 | (6.0) |
| **V. Legal Structure and Property Rights** | | | | | | | **3.4** | | **6.0** | | **6.6** | | **8.5** | |
| (a) Private Ownership Rights | | | | | | | 4.8 | | 5.9 | | 7.7 | | 10.0 | |
| (b) Viability of Contracts | | | | | | | 2.2 | | 4.0 | | 5.2 | | 8.3 | |
| (c) Rule of Law | | | | | | | 3.1 | | 8.3 | | 7.0 | | 7.0 | |
| **VI. International Exchange** | | | | | | | | | **8.1** | | **7.7** | | **7.0** | |
| (a) Taxes on International Trade | | | | | | | | | | | | | | |
| i. Taxes as a Percentage of Exports and Imports | | | | | | | | | 9.7 | (0.4) | 8.2 | (2.7) | 8.2 | (2.6) |
| ii. Mean Tariff Rate | | | | | | | | | | | 6.2 | (18.8) | 6.2 | (18.8) |
| iii. Standard Deviation of Tariff Rates | | | | | | | | | | | | | | |
| (b) Non-tariff Regulatory Trade Barriers | | | | | | | | | | | | | | |
| i. Non-tariff Trade Restraints (% of trade covered) | | | | | | | | | | | 10.0 | (0.0) | | |
| ii. Size of Trade Sector (% of GDP) | | | | | 8.3 | (75.3) | 4.2 | (41.6) | 4.0 | (42.9) | 5.4 | (59.4) | 5.9 | (66.5) |
| **VII. Freedom of Exchange in Financial Markets** | **0.0** | | **0.0** | | **0.0** | | **0.0** | | **0.0** | | **1.1** | | **1.4** | |
| (a) Ownership of Banks | 0.0 | (0) | 0.0 | (0) | 0.0 | (0) | 0.0 | (0) | 0.0 | (0) | 2.0 | (10-40) | 0.0 | (0-10) |
| (b) Extension of Credit | 0.0 | (0.0) | 0.0 | (0.0) | 0.0 | (0.0) | 0.0 | (0.0) | 0.0 | (0.0) | 0.0 | (0.1) | 4.1 | (47.0) |
| (c) Avoidance of Negative Interest Rates | | | | | | | | | 0.0 | | 0.0 | | 0.0 | |
| (d) Capital Transactions with Foreigners | 0.0 | | 0.0 | | 0.0 | | 0.0 | | 0.0 | | 2.0 | | 2.0 | |

# RUSSIA

| | 1970 | 1975 | 1980 | 1985 | 1990 | 1995 | 1997 |
|---|---|---|---|---|---|---|---|
| **Summary Ratings** | | 1.8 | 1.8 | 1.8 | 1.7 | 5.0 | 5.4 |
| **Rank** | | 83 | 107 | 111 | 114 | 93 | 93 |

| Components of Economic Freedom | 1970 | | 1975 | | 1980 | | 1985 | | 1990 | | 1995 | | 1997 | |
|---|---|---|---|---|---|---|---|---|---|---|---|---|---|---|
| **I. Size of Government** | | | **3.5** | | **3.7** | | **3.5** | | **3.7** | | **6.9** | | **6.5** | |
| (a) Government Consumption (% of Total) | | | 5.0 | (31.5) | 5.4 | (29.7) | 5.1 | (31.0) | 5.3 | (29.8) | 5.8 | (27.3) | 5.5 | (28.8) |
| (b) Transfers and Subsidies (% of GDP) | | | 2.0 | (30.0) | 2.0 | (30.0) | 2.0 | (30.0) | 2.0 | (30.0) | 7.9 | (8.2) | 7.4 | (10.0) |
| **II. Structure of the Economy and Use of Markets** | | | **0.0** | | **0.0** | | **0.0** | | **0.0** | | **2.8** | | **3.5** | |
| (a) Government Enterprises | 0.0 | | 0.0 | | 0.0 | | 0.0 | | 0.0 | (90.0) | 2.0 | (45.0) | 4.0 | (35.0) |
| (b) Price Controls | | | | | | | | | 0.0 | | 5.0 | | 5.0 | |
| (c) Top Marginal Tax Rate | | | 0.0 | (100) | 0.0 | (100) | 0.0 | (100) | 0.0 | (80) | 2.0 | (54) | 2.0 | (54) |
| (d) Conscription | 0.0 | | 0.0 | | 0.0 | | 0.0 | | 0.0 | | 0.0 | | 0.0 | |
| **III. Monetary Policy and Price Stability** | | | **8.9** | | **8.6** | | **8.7** | | **7.9** | | **0.0** | | **2.3** | |
| (a) Annual Money Growth (last 5 yrs.) | | | 8.3 | (8.3) | 7.9 | (10.6) | 8.1 | (9.6) | 8.1 | (9.7) | 0.0 | (401.4) | 0.0 | (141.9) |
| (b) Inflation Variability (last 5 yrs.) | | | 9.6 | (1.1) | 9.3 | (1.8) | 9.4 | (1.4) | 8.9 | (2.7) | 0.0 | (522.9) | 0.0 | (318.6) |
| (c) Recent Inflation Rate | | | | | | | 8.5 | (7.3) | 6.8 | (15.9) | 0.0 | (170.7) | 6.7 | (16.6) |
| **IV. Freedom to Use Alternative Currencies** | **0.0** | | **0.0** | | **0.0** | | **0.0** | | **0.0** | | **7.5** | | **7.5** | |
| (a) Ownership of Foreign Currency | 0.0 | | 0.0 | | 0.0 | | 0.0 | | 0.0 | | 5.0 | | 5.0 | |
| (b) Black Market Exchange Rates (Prem.) | 0.0 | (606.0) | 0.0 | (391.0) | 0.0 | (359.0) | 0.0 | (637.0) | 0.0 | (1969.0) | 10.0 | (0.0) | 10.0 | (0.0) |
| **V. Legal Structure and Property Rights** | | | | | | | | | | | | | **5.4** | |
| (a) Private Ownership Rights | | | | | | | | | | | | | 7.2 | |
| (b) Viability of Contracts | | | | | | | | | | | | | 4.8 | |
| (c) Rule of Law | | | | | | | | | | | | | 4.1 | |
| **VI. International Exchange** | | | | | | | | | | | **6.9** | | **7.1** | |
| (a) Taxes on International Trade | | | | | | | | | | | | | | |
| i. Taxes as a Percentage of Exports and Imports | | | | | | | | | | | 7.1 | (4.4) | 6.6 | (5.1) |
| ii. Mean Tariff Rate | | | | | | | | | | | 7.7 | (11.5) | 7.5 | (12.7) |
| iii. Standard Deviation of Tariff Rates | | | | | | | | | | | 5.0 | (12.4) | 6.7 | (8.3) |
| (b) Non-tariff Regulatory Trade Barriers | | | | | | | | | | | | | | |
| i. Non-tariff Trade Restraints (% of trade covered) | | | | | | | | | | | | | | |
| ii. Size of Trade Sector (% of GDP) | | | | | | | | | 7.2 | (36.1) | 9.5 | (50.4) | 8.1 | (44.5) |
| **VII. Freedom of Exchange in Financial Markets** | | | **0.0** | | **0.0** | | **0.0** | | **0.0** | | **4.0** | | **4.5** | |
| (a) Ownership of Banks | 0.0 | (0) | 0.0 | (0) | 0.0 | (0) | 0.0 | (0) | 0.0 | (0) | 2.0 | (32) | 2.0 | (22) |
| (b) Extension of Credit | | | | | | | | | 0.0 | (5.0) | 4.5 | (50.4) | 4.4 | (50.0) |
| (c) Avoidance of Negative Interest Rates | | | 0.0 | | 0.0 | | 0.0 | | 0.0 | | 8.0 | | 10.0 | |
| (d) Capital Transactions with Foreigners | 0.0 | | 0.0 | | 0.0 | | 0.0 | | 0.0 | | 2.0 | | 2.0 | |

# RWANDA

| | 1970 | 1975 | 1980 | 1985 | 1990 | 1995 | 1997 |
|---|---|---|---|---|---|---|---|
| **Summary Ratings** | | 2.1 | 3.7 | | 3.9 | 3.9 | 3.7 |
| **Rank** | | 82 | 91 | | 96 | 112 | 120 |

| Components of Economic Freedom | 1970 | | 1975 | | 1980 | | 1985 | | 1990 | | 1995 | | 1997 | |
|---|---|---|---|---|---|---|---|---|---|---|---|---|---|---|
| **I. Size of Government** | **9.2** | | **8.8** | | **9.2** | | **8.6** | | **9.0** | | **9.5** | | **9.3** | |
| (a) Government Consumption (% of Total) | 9.2 | (9.0) | 7.6 | (17.6) | 8.4 | (13.0) | 8.6 | (12.3) | 8.9 | (10.8) | 9.4 | (8.0) | 9.3 | (8.3) |
| (b) Transfers and Subsidies (% of GDP) | | | 10.0 | (0.6) | 9.9 | (0.8) | | | 9.2 | (3.5) | 9.5 | (2.2) | | |
| **II. Structure of the Economy and Use of Markets** | | | | | | | | | **2.9** | | **2.9** | | **2.0** | |
| (a) Government Enterprises | 6.0 | | 6.0 | (16.9) | 4.0 | (39.4) | 4.0 | (42.4) | 4.0 | | 4.0 | | 2.0 | |
| (b) Price Controls | | | | | | | | | 0.0 | | 0.0 | | 0.0 | |
| (c) Top Marginal Tax Rate | | | | | | | | | | | | | | |
| (d) Conscription | | | 10.0 | | 10.0 | | 10.0 | | 10.0 | | 10.0 | | 10.0 | |
| **III. Monetary Policy and Price Stability** | **6.0** | | **2.5** | | **8.2** | | **8.9** | | **8.2** | | **2.9** | | **5.2** | |
| (a) Annual Money Growth (last 5 yrs.) | 7.9 | (10.5) | 7.3 | (13.4) | 7.1 | (14.5) | 9.5 | (-2.4) | 9.9 | (0.8) | 5.4 | (22.9) | 5.7 | (21.8) |
| (b) Inflation Variability (last 5 yrs.) | 2.0 | (20.0) | 0.0 | (33.5) | 8.0 | (5.0) | 8.0 | (5.1) | 7.3 | (6.7) | 3.3 | (16.8) | 3.5 | (16.2) |
| (c) Recent Inflation Rate | 8.0 | (9.9) | 0.0 | (88.0) | 9.4 | (3.1) | 9.1 | (4.6) | 7.3 | (13.5) | 0.0 | (54.2) | 6.3 | (18.6) |
| **IV. Freedom to Use Alternative Currencies** | **2.4** | | **0.5** | | **0.0** | | **0.1** | | **2.2** | | **7.2** | | **2.5** | |
| (a) Ownership of Foreign Currency | | | 0.0 | | 0.0 | | 0.0 | | 0.0 | | 5.0 | | 5.0 | |
| (b) Black Market Exchange Rates (Prem.) | 2.4 | (38.0) | 1.0 | (45.0) | 0.0 | (67.0) | 0.2 | (49.0) | 4.4 | (28.0) | 9.4 | (3.0) | 0.0 | (61.0) |
| **V. Legal Structure and Property Rights** | | | | | | | | | | | | | | |
| (a) Private Ownership Rights | | | | | | | | | | | | | | |
| (b) Viability of Contracts | | | | | | | | | | | | | | |
| (c) Rule of Law | | | | | | | | | | | | | | |
| **VI. International Exchange** | | | **0.0** | | **1.3** | | | | **0.6** | | **1.0** | | | |
| (a) Taxes on International Trade | | | | | | | | | | | | | | |
| i. Taxes as a Percentage of Exports and Imports | | | 0.0 | (16.5) | 1.1 | (13.3) | | | 0.5 | (14.2) | 0.3 | (14.6) | | |
| ii. Mean Tariff Rate | | | | | | | | | | | 3.0 | (34.8) | | |
| iii. Standard Deviation of Tariff Rates | | | | | | | | | | | 0.0 | (33.1) | | |
| (b) Non-tariff Regulatory Trade Barriers | | | | | | | | | | | | | | |
| i. Non-tariff Trade Restraints (% of trade covered) | | | | | 1.0 | (90.0) | 1.0 | (90.0) | 1.0 | (90.0) | 1.0 | (90.0) | | |
| ii. Size of Trade Sector (% of GDP) | 0.0 | (26.7) | 0.0 | (26.9) | 2.2 | (40.8) | 0.0 | (30.7) | 0.0 | (19.6) | 0.0 | (35.7) | 0.0 | (28.8) |
| **VII. Freedom of Exchange in Financial Markets** | **1.4** | | **1.3** | | **3.4** | | **3.6** | | **3.8** | | **1.8** | | **1.9** | |
| (a) Ownership of Banks | 0.0 | (0) | 0.0 | (0) | 0.0 | (0) | 0.0 | (0-10) | 0.0 | (0-10) | 0.0 | (0-10) | 0.0 | (0-10) |
| (b) Extension of Credit | 5.0 | (54.8) | 4.5 | (50.2) | 8.9 | (90.2) | 7.5 | (77.8) | 6.1 | (64.8) | 8.4 | (85.4) | 8.8 | (89.0) |
| (c) Avoidance of Negative Interest Rates | | | | | 6.0 | | 8.0 | | 10.0 | | 0.0 | | 0.0 | |
| (d) Capital Transactions with Foreigners | 0.0 | | 0.0 | | 0.0 | | 0.0 | | 0.0 | | 0.0 | | 0.0 | |

# SENEGAL

| | 1970 | 1975 | 1980 | 1985 | 1990 | 1995 | 1997 |
|---|---|---|---|---|---|---|---|
| **Summary Ratings** | | | 5.0 | 4.9 | 5.0 | 4.2 | 4.7 |
| **Rank** | | | 61 | 67 | 67 | 108 | 103 |

| Components of Economic Freedom | 1970 | | 1975 | | 1980 | | 1985 | | 1990 | | 1995 | | 1997 | |
|---|---|---|---|---|---|---|---|---|---|---|---|---|---|---|
| **I. Size of Government** | **8.1** | | **8.7** | | **8.1** | | **7.8** | | **7.9** | | **8.3** | | **8.7** | |
| (a) Government Consumption (% of Total) | 8.1 | (14.9) | 8.0 | (15.5) | 7.3 | (19.3) | 7.8 | (16.3) | 7.9 | (16.1) | 8.3 | (13.9) | 8.7 | (11.7) |
| (b) Transfers and Subsidies (% of GDP) | | | 9.4 | (2.6) | 9.0 | (4.2) | | | | | | | | |
| **II. Structure of the Economy and Use of Markets** | | | | | | | **2.3** | | **3.0** | | **2.6** | | **3.3** | |
| (a) Government Enterprises | 6.0 | (22.3) | 4.0 | (33.9) | 4.0 | (36.7) | 4.0 | (36.2) | 6.0 | (30.1) | 6.0 | | 6.0 | |
| (b) Price Controls | | | | | | | | | 0.0 | | 2.0 | | 4.0 | |
| (c) Top Marginal Tax Rate | | | | | | | 1.0 | (65) | 4.0 | (48) | 0.0 | (64) | 0.0 | (64) |
| (d) Conscription | 0.0 | | 0.0 | | 0.0 | | 0.0 | | 0.0 | | 0.0 | | 0.0 | |
| **III. Monetary Policy and Price Stability** | **9.4** | | **7.6** | | **8.1** | | **8.8** | | **9.5** | | **7.7** | | **8.0** | |
| (a) Annual Money Growth (last 5 yrs.) | 9.7 | (1.7) | 7.1 | (14.8) | 7.8 | (11.2) | 9.0 | (5.0) | 9.6 | (-2.0) | 8.6 | (6.9) | 8.6 | (7.0) |
| (b) Inflation Variability (last 5 yrs.) | 9.0 | (2.6) | 8.0 | (5.1) | 8.9 | (2.6) | 9.4 | (1.6) | 9.0 | (2.5) | 5.7 | (10.9) | 5.9 | (10.4) |
| (c) Recent Inflation Rate | 9.6 | (2.0) | 7.7 | (11.6) | 7.7 | (11.5) | 8.1 | (9.3) | 9.8 | (1.2) | 8.8 | (5.9) | 9.5 | (2.5) |
| **IV. Freedom to Use Alternative Currencies** | **4.8** | | **4.8** | | **4.8** | | **4.9** | | **4.6** | | **4.9** | | **4.8** | |
| (a) Ownership of Foreign Currency | 0.0 | | 0.0 | | 0.0 | | 0.0 | | 0.0 | | 0.0 | | 0.0 | |
| (b) Black Market Exchange Rates (Prem.) | 9.6 | (2.0) | 9.6 | (2.0) | 9.6 | (2.0) | 9.8 | (1.0) | 9.2 | (4.0) | 9.8 | (1.0) | 9.6 | (2.0) |
| **V. Legal Structure and Property Rights** | | | | | **3.6** | | **4.0** | | **4.0** | | **1.0** | | **2.7** | |
| (a) Private Ownership Rights | | | | | 4.6 | | 4.8 | | 4.6 | | 0.9 | | 0.0 | |
| (b) Viability of Contracts | | | | | 4.3 | | 4.0 | | 4.0 | | 2.1 | | 1.4 | |
| (c) Rule of Law | | | | | 1.7 | | 3.1 | | 3.3 | | 0.0 | | 7.0 | |
| **VI. International Exchange** | | | **4.9** | | **3.4** | | **4.5** | | **4.3** | | **4.4** | | **4.3** | |
| (a) Taxes on International Trade | | | | | | | | | | | | | | |
| i. Taxes as a Percentage of Exports and Imports | | | 4.2 | (8.7) | 2.4 | (11.4) | 4.5 | (8.3) | 2.1 | (11.8) | 1.3 | (13.0) | 0.6 | (14.1) |
| ii. Mean Tariff Rate | | | | | | | 2.2 | (39.0) | 3.0 | (35.0) | 3.2 | (34.2) | 7.4 | (12.8) |
| iii. Standard Deviation of Tariff Rates | | | | | | | | | | | | | | |
| (b) Non-tariff Regulatory Trade Barriers | | | | | | | | | | | | | | |
| i. Non-tariff Trade Restraints (% of trade covered) | | | | | | | 7.0 | (30.0) | 8.5 | (15.0) | 9.3 | (7.2) | | |
| ii. Size of Trade Sector (% of GDP) | 5.4 | (59.4) | 6.8 | (78.4) | 6.1 | (72.3) | 5.7 | (70.6) | 4.5 | (58.9) | 5.1 | (68.6) | 5.1 | (70.7) |
| **VII. Freedom of Exchange in Financial Markets** | | | | | **4.5** | | **4.0** | | **4.5** | | **3.3** | | **3.7** | |
| (a) Ownership of Banks | | | 2.0 | (10-40) | 2.0 | (10-40) | 2.0 | (10-40) | 2.0 | (10-40) | 2.0 | (10-40) | 2.0 | (10-40) |
| (b) Extension of Credit | | | | | 9.3 | (93.6) | 9.5 | (95.6) | 9.6 | (95.9) | 8.4 | (85.2) | 7.7 | (79.6) |
| (c) Avoidance of Negative Interest Rates | | | | | 8.0 | | 6.0 | | 8.0 | | 4.0 | | 6.0 | |
| (d) Capital Transactions with Foreigners | 0.0 | | 0.0 | | 0.0 | | 0.0 | | 0.0 | | 0.0 | | 0.0 | |

# Sierra Leone

| | 1970 | 1975 | 1980 | 1985 | 1990 | 1995 | 1997 |
|---|---|---|---|---|---|---|---|
| **Summary Ratings** | | 3.9 | 4.1 | 3.0 | 2.9 | 3.7 | 3.2 |
| **Rank** | | 66 | 79 | 103 | 107 | 116 | 121 |

| Components of Economic Freedom | 1970 | | 1975 | | 1980 | | 1985 | | 1990 | | 1995 | | 1997 | |
|---|---|---|---|---|---|---|---|---|---|---|---|---|---|---|
| **I. Size of Government** | | | **9.2** | | **9.3** | | **9.6** | | **9.2** | | **8.6** | | **9.2** | |
| (a) Government Consumption (% of Total) | | | 8.7 | (11.8) | 9.3 | (8.4) | 9.2 | (8.9) | 8.7 | (11.8) | 8.3 | (13.8) | 9.2 | (9.0) |
| (b) Transfers and Subsidies (% of GDP) | | | 9.7 | (1.6) | | | 10.0 | (0.6) | 9.7 | (1.6) | 9.0 | (4.3) | | |
| **II. Structure of the Economy and Use of Markets** | | | | | | | | | **2.1** | | **3.9** | | **3.9** | |
| (a) Government Enterprises | 6.0 | (14.0) | 4.0 | (33.3) | 2.0 | (61.6) | 0.0 | (81.4) | 0.0 | | 0.0 | | 0.0 | |
| (b) Price Controls | | | | | | | | | 2.0 | | 6.0 | | 6.0 | |
| (c) Top Marginal Tax Rate | | | | | | | | | | | | | | |
| (d) Conscription | | | 10.0 | | 10.0 | | 10.0 | | 10.0 | | 10.0 | | 10.0 | |
| **III. Monetary Policy and Price Stability** | **9.3** | | **7.5** | | **7.8** | | **0.5** | | **0.0** | | **2.5** | | **6.4** | |
| (a) Annual Money Growth (last 5 yrs.) | 9.7 | (1.7) | 7.5 | (12.6) | 6.4 | (18.1) | 1.6 | (41.8) | 0.0 | (73.0) | 4.0 | (29.9) | 5.0 | (25.1) |
| (b) Inflation Variability (last 5 yrs.) | 8.8 | (3.1) | 7.2 | (6.9) | 8.9 | (2.8) | 0.0 | (26.1) | 0.0 | (29.2) | 0.0 | (26.1) | 7.7 | (5.8) |
| (c) Recent Inflation Rate | 9.5 | (-2.7) | 7.8 | (11.0) | 8.0 | (9.9) | 0.0 | (85.1) | 0.0 | (89.2) | 3.3 | (33.5) | 6.7 | (16.8) |
| **IV. Freedom to Use Alternative Currencies** | **9.6** | | **0.0** | | **0.0** | | **0.0** | | **0.0** | | **7.3** | | **2.5** | |
| (a) Ownership of Foreign Currency | | | 0.0 | | 0.0 | | 0.0 | | 0.0 | | 5.0 | | 5.0 | |
| (b) Black Market Exchange Rates (Prem.) | 9.6 | (2.0) | 0.0 | (53.0) | 0.0 | (62.0) | 0.0 | (206.0) | 0.0 | (165.0) | 9.6 | (2.0) | 0.0 | (86.0) |
| **V. Legal Structure and Property Rights** | | | | | | | **5.1** | | **4.7** | | **0.0** | | **2.2** | |
| (a) Private Ownership Rights | | | | | | | 4.8 | | 3.2 | | 0.0 | | 0.0 | |
| (b) Viability of Contracts | | | | | | | 4.0 | | 2.8 | | 0.0 | | 0.0 | |
| (c) Rule of Law | | | | | | | 6.6 | | 8.3 | | 0.0 | | 7.0 | |
| **VI. International Exchange** | | | **3.4** | | **3.4** | | **2.9** | | **3.0** | | **3.0** | | **0.0** | |
| (a) Taxes on International Trade | | | | | | | | | | | | | | |
| i. Taxes as a Percentage of Exports and Imports | | | 3.1 | (10.4) | 1.1 | (13.3) | 2.1 | (11.9) | 6.0 | (6.0) | 4.9 | (7.7) | 0.0 | (15.3) |
| ii. Mean Tariff Rate | | | | | 4.8 | (25.8) | 4.8 | (25.8) | | | 4.8 | (25.8) | | |
| iii. Standard Deviation of Tariff Rates | | | | | | | | | | | | | | |
| (b) Non-tariff Regulatory Trade Barriers | | | | | | | | | | | | | | |
| i. Non-tariff Trade Restraints (% of trade covered) | | | | | | | 0.0 | (100.0) | 0.0 | (100.0) | 0.0 | (100.0) | | |
| ii. Size of Trade Sector (% of GDP) | 4.7 | (61.9) | 4.4 | (61.5) | 5.0 | (73.1) | 6.4 | (96.9) | 1.9 | (49.1) | 0.0 | (38.8) | 0.1 | (42.6) |
| **VII. Freedom of Exchange in Financial Markets** | | | **2.5** | | **3.2** | | **0.9** | | **1.9** | | **2.2** | | **2.0** | |
| (a) Ownership of Banks | | | 2.0 | (10-40) | 2.0 | (10-40) | 2.0 | (10-40) | 2.0 | (10-40) | 2.0 | (10-40) | 2.0 | (10-40) |
| (b) Extension of Credit | 7.7 | (79.2) | 6.3 | (66.7) | 5.6 | (60.1) | 1.6 | (24.0) | 6.5 | (68.1) | 5.3 | (57.5) | 4.7 | (52.0) |
| (c) Avoidance of Negative Interest Rates | | | | | 6.0 | | 0.0 | | 0.0 | | 2.0 | | 2.0 | |
| (d) Capital Transactions with Foreigners | 0.0 | | 0.0 | | 0.0 | | 0.0 | | 0.0 | | 0.0 | | 0.0 | |

# SINGAPORE

| | 1970 | 1975 | 1980 | 1985 | 1990 | 1995 | 1997 |
|---|---|---|---|---|---|---|---|
| **Summary Ratings** | 7.7 | 7.6 | 8.0 | 8.4 | 9.1 | 9.4 | 9.4 |
| **Rank** | 13 | 10 | 5 | 5 | 2 | 2 | 1 |

| Components of Economic Freedom | 1970 | | 1975 | | 1980 | | 1985 | | 1990 | | 1995 | | 1997 | |
|---|---|---|---|---|---|---|---|---|---|---|---|---|---|---|
| **I. Size of Government** | **8.9** | | **8.9** | | **8.9** | | **8.0** | | **8.5** | | **8.7** | | **8.6** | |
| (a) Government Consumption (% of Total) | 8.1 | (15.0) | 8.1 | (14.9) | 7.9 | (15.9) | 6.4 | (24.0) | 7.5 | (18.1) | 7.8 | (16.5) | 7.4 | (18.8) |
| (b) Transfers and Subsidies (% of GDP) | 9.6 | (1.8) | 9.8 | (1.4) | 9.8 | (1.1) | 9.6 | (1.8) | 9.4 | (2.6) | 9.6 | (1.8) | 9.8 | (1.4) |
| **II. Structure of the Economy and Use of Markets** | **5.4** | | **4.9** | | **4.9** | | **6.0** | | **7.5** | | **7.5** | | **7.5** | |
| (a) Government Enterprises | 8.0 | (19.4) | 7.0 | (25.0) | 7.0 | (24.2) | 6.0 | (34.7) | 8.0 | (18.6) | 8.0 | | 8.0 | |
| (b) Price Controls | | | | | | | | | 8.0 | | 8.0 | | 8.0 | |
| (c) Top Marginal Tax Rate | 4.0 | (55) | 4.0 | (55) | 4.0 | (55) | 8.0 | (40) | 9.0 | (33) | 9.0 | (30) | 9.0 | (28) |
| (d) Conscription | 0.0 | | 0.0 | | 0.0 | | 0.0 | | 0.0 | | 0.0 | | 0.0 | |
| **III. Monetary Policy and Price Stability** | **9.7** | | **8.8** | | **8.5** | | **9.5** | | **9.0** | | **9.5** | | **9.7** | |
| (a) Annual Money Growth (last 5 yrs.) | 9.3 | (3.3) | 9.0 | (5.2) | 9.4 | (3.3) | 9.9 | (0.3) | 9.1 | (4.4) | 9.6 | (2.2) | 9.9 | (-0.5) |
| (b) Inflation Variability (last 5 yrs.) | 9.8 | (0.5) | 7.9 | (5.2) | 8.6 | (3.6) | 8.9 | (2.8) | 8.9 | (2.7) | 9.4 | (1.5) | 9.4 | (1.6) |
| (c) Recent Inflation Rate | 9.8 | (0.9) | 9.6 | (2.2) | 7.7 | (11.5) | 9.8 | (-1.1) | 9.0 | (4.9) | 9.5 | (2.7) | 9.7 | (1.5) |
| **IV. Freedom to Use Alternative Currencies** | **4.9** | | **5.0** | | **5.0** | | **7.5** | | **10.0** | | **10.0** | | **10.0** | |
| (a) Ownership of Foreign Currency | 0.0 | | 0.0 | | 0.0 | | 5.0 | | 10.0 | | 10.0 | | 10.0 | |
| (b) Black Market Exchange Rates (Prem.) | 9.8 | (1.0) | 10.0 | (0.0) | 10.0 | (0.0) | 10.0 | (0.0) | 10.0 | (0.0) | 10.0 | (0.0) | 10.0 | (0.0) |
| **V. Legal Structure and Property Rights** | **8.5** | | **7.4** | | **8.9** | | **8.2** | | **8.8** | | **10.0** | | **10.0** | |
| (a) Private Ownership Rights | 9.1 | | 7.6 | | 9.4 | | 8.7 | | 8.6 | | 10.0 | | 10.0 | |
| (b) Viability of Contracts | 7.8 | | 7.2 | | 7.5 | | 7.6 | | 9.4 | | 10.0 | | 10.0 | |
| (c) Rule of Law | | | | | 10.0 | | 8.2 | | 8.3 | | 10.0 | | 10.0 | |
| **VI. International Exchange** | **9.5** | | **9.7** | | **9.8** | | **9.5** | | **9.8** | | **9.7** | | **9.9** | |
| (a) Taxes on International Trade | | | | | | | | | | | | | | |
| i. Taxes as a Percentage of Exports and Imports | 9.3 | (1.0) | 9.5 | (0.7) | 9.7 | (0.5) | 9.8 | (0.3) | 9.9 | (0.2) | 9.9 | (0.1) | | |
| ii. Mean Tariff Rate | | | | | 9.9 | (0.3) | 9.9 | (0.3) | 9.9 | (0.4) | 9.9 | (0.4) | 9.9 | (0.4) |
| iii. Standard Deviation of Tariff Rates | | | | | | | | | 9.3 | (1.8) | 8.9 | (2.7) | | |
| (b) Non-tariff Regulatory Trade Barriers | | | | | | | | | | | | | | |
| i. Non-tariff Trade Restraints (% of trade covered) | | | | | | | 8.5 | (14.7) | 9.9 | (1.0) | 10.0 | (0.3) | | |
| ii. Size of Trade Sector (% of GDP) | 10.0 | (231.6) | 10.0 | (302.5) | 10.0 | (439.6) | 10.0 | (338.5) | 10.0 | (386.4) | 10.0 | (355.6) | 10.0 | |
| **VII. Freedom of Exchange in Financial Markets** | | | **8.9** | | **9.2** | | **9.8** | | **9.7** | | **9.7** | | **9.7** | |
| (a) Ownership of Banks | | | 10.0 | (95-100) | 10.0 | (95-100) | 10.0 | (100) | 10.0 | (95-100) | 10.0 | (95-100) | 10.0 | (95-100) |
| (b) Extension of Credit | 7.7 | (79.5) | 8.5 | (86.7) | 8.8 | (89.0) | 8.9 | (89.9) | 8.6 | (87.6) | 8.6 | (87.5) | 8.7 | (88.4) |
| (c) Avoidance of Negative Interest Rates | | | | | 10.0 | | 10.0 | | 10.0 | | 10.0 | | 10.0 | |
| (d) Capital Transactions with Foreigners | 5.0 | | 8.0 | | 8.0 | | 10.0 | | 10.0 | | 10.0 | | 10.0 | |

# SLOVAKIA

| | 1970 | 1975 | 1980 | 1985 | 1990 | 1995 | 1997 |
|---|---|---|---|---|---|---|---|
| **Summary Ratings** | | | | | 3.9 | 6.2 | 6.1 |
| **Rank** | | | | | 96 | 64 | 78 |

| Components of Economic Freedom | 1970 | | 1975 | | 1980 | | 1985 | | 1990 | | 1995 | | 1997 | |
|---|---|---|---|---|---|---|---|---|---|---|---|---|---|---|
| **I. Size of Government** | | | **5.9** | | **5.8** | | **5.3** | | **2.7** | | **5.5** | | **4.8** | |
| (a) Government Consumption (% of Total) | | | 5.9 | (26.6) | 5.8 | (27.3) | 5.3 | (30.1) | 5.3 | (29.9) | 5.5 | (29.2) | 4.8 | (32.7) |
| (b) Transfers and Subsidies (% of GDP) | | | | | | | | | 0.0 | (37.2) | | | | |
| **II. Structure of the Economy and Use of Markets** | | | | | | | | | **1.0** | | **2.4** | | **2.6** | |
| (a) Government Enterprises | 0.0 | | 0.0 | | 0.0 | | 0.0 | | 0.0 | | 0.0 | (75.1) | 0.0 | |
| (b) Price Controls | | | | | | | | | 0.0 | | 4.0 | | 4.0 | |
| (c) Top Marginal Tax Rate | | | | | | | | | 4.0 | (55) | 4.0 | (42) | 4.0 | (42) |
| (d) Conscription | 0.0 | | 0.0 | | 0.0 | | 0.0 | | 0.0 | | 1.0 | | 3.0 | |
| **III. Monetary Policy and Price Stability** | | | | | | | **9.4** | | **8.8** | | **7.3** | | **8.6** | |
| (a) Annual Money Growth (last 5 yrs.) | | | | | | | 9.4 | (3.0) | 9.9 | (0.4) | 7.3 | (13.4) | 8.8 | (6.1) |
| (b) Inflation Variability (last 5 yrs.) | | | | | | | 9.1 | (2.2) | 8.4 | (4.0) | 6.4 | (9.0) | 8.4 | (4.1) |
| (c) Recent Inflation Rate | | | 9.9 | (0.7) | 9.4 | (2.9) | 9.7 | (1.7) | 8.1 | (9.5) | 8.1 | (9.7) | 8.7 | (6.7) |
| **IV. Freedom to Use Alternative Currencies** | **0.0** | | **0.0** | | **0.0** | | **0.0** | | **0.0** | | **7.5** | | **6.4** | |
| (a) Ownership of Foreign Currency | 0.0 | | 0.0 | | 0.0 | | 0.0 | | 0.0 | | 5.0 | | 5.0 | |
| (b) Black Market Exchange Rates (Prem.) | 0.0 | (525.0) | 0.0 | (359.0) | 0.0 | (387.0) | 0.0 | (423.0) | 0.0 | (61.0) | 10.0 | (0.0) | 7.8 | (11.0) |
| **V. Legal Structure and Property Rights** | | | | | | | **7.3** | | **7.8** | | **7.6** | | **6.3** | |
| (a) Private Ownership Rights | | | | | | | 7.4 | | 8.6 | | 7.7 | | 7.2 | |
| (b) Viability of Contracts | | | | | | | 6.4 | | 6.4 | | 5.2 | | 4.8 | |
| (c) Rule of Law | | | | | | | 8.2 | | 8.3 | | 10.0 | | 7.0 | |
| **VI. International Exchange** | | | | | | | | | | | **8.7** | | **8.8** | |
| (a) Taxes on International Trade | | | | | | | | | | | | | | |
| i. Taxes as a Percentage of Exports and Imports | | | | | | | | | 7.3 | (4.0) | | | | |
| ii. Mean Tariff Rate | | | | | | | | | | | 8.8 | (6.1) | 9.0 | (4.8) |
| iii. Standard Deviation of Tariff Rates | | | | | | | | | | | | | | |
| (b) Non-tariff Regulatory Trade Barriers | | | | | | | | | | | | | | |
| i. Non-tariff Trade Restraints (% of trade covered) | | | | | | | | | | | | | | |
| ii. Size of Trade Sector (% of GDP) | | | | | | | | | | | 8.6 | (124.7) | 8.1 | (119.9) |
| **VII. Freedom of Exchange in Financial Markets** | | | | | | | | | | | **4.3** | | **5.3** | |
| (a) Ownership of Banks | 0.0 | (0) | 0.0 | (0) | 0.0 | (0) | 0.0 | (0) | 0.0 | (0) | 5.0 | (40-75) | 2.0 | (10-20) |
| (b) Extension of Credit | | | | | | | | | | | 4.4 | (50.0) | 4.4 | (49.8) |
| (c) Avoidance of Negative Interest Rates | | | | | | | | | | | 6.0 | | 10.0 | |
| (d) Capital Transactions with Foreigners | 0.0 | | 0.0 | | 0.0 | | 0.0 | | 0.0 | | 2.0 | | 5.0 | |

# SLOVENIA

| | 1970 | 1975 | 1980 | 1985 | 1990 | 1995 | 1997 |
|---|---|---|---|---|---|---|---|
| **Summary Ratings** | | | | | | 5.6 | 6.3 |
| **Rank** | | | | | | 81 | 70 |

| Components of Economic Freedom | 1970 | | 1975 | | 1980 | | 1985 | | 1990 | | 1995 | | 1997 | |
|---|---|---|---|---|---|---|---|---|---|---|---|---|---|---|
| **I. Size of Government** | | | | | | | | | **6.1** | | **3.6** | | **3.6** | |
| (a) Government Consumption (% of Total) | | | | | | | | | 6.1 | (25.9) | 6.1 | (25.8) | 6.0 | (26.5) |
| (b) Transfers and Subsidies (% of GDP) | | | | | | | | | | | 1.1 | (33.2) | 1.3 | (32.5) |
| **II. Structure of the Economy and Use of Markets** | | | | | | | | | | | **3.0** | | **3.0** | |
| (a) Government Enterprises | | | | | | | | | | | 0.0 | (75.1) | 0.0 | |
| (b) Price Controls | | | | | | | | | | | 6.0 | | 6.0 | |
| (c) Top Marginal Tax Rate | | | | | | | | | | | | | 3.0 | (50) |
| (d) Conscription | | | | | | | | | | | 3.0 | | 3.0 | |
| **III. Monetary Policy and Price Stability** | | | | | | | | | | | **2.5** | | **6.4** | |
| (a) Annual Money Growth (last 5 yrs.) | | | | | | | | | | | 0.0 | (57.5) | 4.6 | (26.9) |
| (b) Inflation Variability (last 5 yrs.) | | | | | | | | | | | 0.0 | (79.6) | 6.5 | (8.8) |
| (c) Recent Inflation Rate | | | | | | | | | | | 7.5 | (12.6) | 8.2 | (9.1) |
| **IV. Freedom to Use Alternative Currencies** | | | | | | | | | **2.5** | | **7.5** | | **7.5** | |
| (a) Ownership of Foreign Currency | | | | | | | | | 5.0 | | 5.0 | | 5.0 | |
| (b) Black Market Exchange Rates (Prem.) | | | | | | | | | 0.0 | (106.0) | 10.0 | (0.0) | 10.0 | (0.0) |
| **V. Legal Structure and Property Rights** | | | | | | | | | | | **8.5** | | **8.2** | |
| (a) Private Ownership Rights | | | | | | | | | | | 8.9 | | 8.6 | |
| (b) Viability of Contracts | | | | | | | | | | | 6.8 | | 7.4 | |
| (c) Rule of Law | | | | | | | | | | | 10.0 | | 8.6 | |
| **VI. International Exchange** | | | | | | | | | | | | | **8.2** | |
| (a) Taxes on International Trade | | | | | | | | | | | | | | |
| i. Taxes as a Percentage of Exports and Imports | | | | | | | | | | | | | | |
| ii. Mean Tariff Rate | | | | | | | | | | | | | 7.9 | (10.6) |
| iii. Standard Deviation of Tariff Rates | | | | | | | | | | | | | | |
| (b) Non-tariff Regulatory Trade Barriers | | | | | | | | | | | | | | |
| i. Non-tariff Trade Restraints (% of trade covered) | | | | | | | | | | | | | 9.8 | (2.0) |
| ii. Size of Trade Sector (% of GDP) | | | | | | | | | | | 5.8 | (109.6) | 5.8 | (110.9) |
| **VII. Freedom of Exchange in Financial Markets** | | | | | | | | | | | **6.0** | | **6.0** | |
| (a) Ownership of Banks | | | | | | | | | | | 5.0 | (40-75) | 5.0 | (50-60) |
| (b) Extension of Credit | | | | | | | | | | | 6.1 | (65.0) | 6.5 | (68.1) |
| (c) Avoidance of Negative Interest Rates | | | | | | | | | | | 8.0 | | 8.0 | |
| (d) Capital Transactions with Foreigners | 0.0 | | 0.0 | | 0.0 | | 0.0 | | 0.0 | | 5.0 | | 5.0 | |

# SOMALIA

| | 1970 | 1975 | 1980 | 1985 | 1990 | 1995 | 1997 |
|---|---|---|---|---|---|---|---|
| **Summary Ratings** | | | | 3.3 | | | |
| **Rank** | | | | 99 | | | |

| Components of Economic Freedom | 1970 | | 1975 | | 1980 | | 1985 | | 1990 | | 1995 | | 1997 | |
|---|---|---|---|---|---|---|---|---|---|---|---|---|---|---|
| **I. Size of Government** | **8.8** | | **6.8** | | **8.3** | | **8.3** | | | | | | | |
| (a) Government Consumption (% of Total) | 8.8 | (11.0) | 6.8 | (22.1) | 8.3 | (13.8) | 8.3 | (13.9) | | | | | | |
| (b) Transfers and Subsidies (% of GDP) | | | | | | | | | | | | | | |
| **II. Structure of the Economy and Use of Markets** | | | | | | | | | **1.0** | | | | | |
| (a) Government Enterprises | | | 2.0 | | 2.0 | | 2.0 | | 2.0 | | | | | |
| (b) Price Controls | | | | | | | | | 0.0 | | | | | |
| (c) Top Marginal Tax Rate | | | | | | | | | | | | | | |
| (d) Conscription | 10.0 | | 10.0 | | 10.0 | | 0.0 | | 1.0 | | 10.0 | | 10.0 | |
| **III. Monetary Policy and Price Stability** | **8.6** | | **7.3** | | **1.7** | | **3.9** | | **0.0** | | | | | |
| (a) Annual Money Growth (last 5 yrs.) | 7.4 | (13.1) | 7.3 | (13.4) | 5.2 | (24.1) | 4.9 | (25.7) | 0.0 | (90.7) | | | | |
| (b) Inflation Variability (last 5 yrs.) | 8.7 | (3.3) | 8.0 | (5.0) | 0.0 | (35.2) | 2.7 | (18.3) | 0.0 | (67.4) | | | | |
| (c) Recent Inflation Rate | 9.9 | (0.7) | 6.6 | (16.9) | 0.0 | (100.9) | 4.1 | (29.6) | 0.0 | (215.5) | | | | |
| **IV. Freedom to Use Alternative Currencies** | **6.2** | | **2.2** | | **0.9** | | **0.0** | | **0.0** | | **0.0** | | **2.5** | |
| (a) Ownership of Foreign Currency | | | 0.0 | | 0.0 | | 0.0 | | 0.0 | | 0.0 | | 5.0 | |
| (b) Black Market Exchange Rates (Prem.) | 6.2 | (19.0) | 4.4 | (28.0) | 1.8 | (41.0) | 0.0 | (147.0) | 0.0 | (200.0) | 0.0 | (545.0) | 0.0 | (200.0) |
| **V. Legal Structure and Property Rights** | | | | | | | **3.9** | | **1.4** | | **0.0** | | **0.0** | |
| (a) Private Ownership Rights | | | | | | | 0.9 | | 0.5 | | 0.0 | | 0.0 | |
| (b) Viability of Contracts | | | | | | | 2.8 | | 0.4 | | 0.0 | | 0.0 | |
| (c) Rule of Law | | | | | | | 8.2 | | 3.3 | | 0.0 | | 0.0 | |
| **VI. International Exchange** | | | **1.5** | | **3.1** | | **1.9** | | | | | | | |
| (a) Taxes on International Trade | | | | | | | | | | | | | | |
| i. Taxes as a Percentage of Exports and Imports | | | 0.7 | (14.0) | 3.0 | (10.5) | | | | | | | | |
| ii. Mean Tariff Rate | | | | | | | 4.0 | (30.0) | | | | | | |
| iii. Standard Deviation of Tariff Rates | | | | | | | | | | | | | | |
| (b) Non-tariff Regulatory Trade Barriers | | | | | | | | | | | | | | |
| i. Non-tariff Trade Restraints (% of trade covered) | | | | | 0.0 | (100.0) | 0.0 | (100.0) | 0.0 | (100.0) | 0.0 | (100.0) | | |
| ii. Size of Trade Sector (% of GDP) | **1.5** | **(28.3)** | **3.7** | **(39.3)** | **10.0** | **(121.7)** | **0.0** | **(25.6)** | **4.1** | **(47.5)** | | | | |
| **VII. Freedom of Exchange in Financial Markets** | | | | | | | | | | | | | | |
| (a) Ownership of Banks | | | | | | | | | | | | | | |
| (b) Extension of Credit | | | | | | | | | | | | | | |
| (c) Avoidance of Negative Interest Rates | | | 4.0 | | 0.0 | | 0.0 | | 0.0 | | 0.0 | | 0.0 | |
| (d) Capital Transactions with Foreigners | 0.0 | | 0.0 | | 0.0 | | 0.0 | | 0.0 | | 0.0 | | 0.0 | |

# SOUTH AFRICA

| | 1970 | 1975 | 1980 | 1985 | 1990 | 1995 | 1997 |
|---|---|---|---|---|---|---|---|
| **Summary Ratings** | 7.6 | 6.2 | 6.0 | 5.6 | 5.9 | 6.6 | 7.3 |
| **Rank** | 14 | 25 | 32 | 47 | 48 | 54 | 47 |

| Components of Economic Freedom | 1970 | | 1975 | | 1980 | | 1985 | | 1990 | | 1995 | | 1997 | |
|---|---|---|---|---|---|---|---|---|---|---|---|---|---|---|
| **I. Size of Government** | **8.6** | | **8.2** | | **8.1** | | **7.6** | | **7.5** | | **7.5** | | **7.5** | |
| (a) Government Consumption (% of Total) | 7.8 | (16.6) | 7.2 | (19.6) | 7.0 | (20.9) | 6.3 | (24.4) | 6.3 | (24.8) | 6.3 | (24.7) | 6.1 | (25.7) |
| (b) Transfers and Subsidies (% of GDP) | 9.3 | (3.0) | 9.2 | (3.4) | 9.3 | (3.2) | 8.8 | (4.8) | 8.8 | (4.8) | 8.7 | (5.3) | 8.8 | (4.9) |
| **II. Structure of the Economy and Use of Markets** | | | **1.8** | | **1.7** | | **2.5** | | **3.9** | | **5.9** | | **5.9** | |
| (a) Government Enterprises | 2.0 | (43.3) | 2.0 | (48.2) | 2.0 | (50.9) | 2.0 | (42.2) | 4.0 | (34.2) | 6.0 | (26.2) | 6.0 | |
| (b) Price Controls | | | | | | | | | 4.0 | | 6.0 | | 6.0 | |
| (c) Top Marginal Tax Rate | | | 1.0 | (66) | 2.0 | (60) | 4.0 | (50) | 5.0 | (45) | 4.0 | (43) | 4.0 | (45) |
| (d) Conscription | 3.0 | | 3.0 | | 0.0 | | 0.0 | | 0.0 | | 10.0 | | 10.0 | |
| **III. Monetary Policy and Price Stability** | **9.4** | | **8.2** | | **7.0** | | **7.1** | | **7.7** | | **8.1** | | **8.1** | |
| (a) Annual Money Growth (last 5 yrs.) | 9.4 | (2.9) | 8.2 | (8.9) | 7.8 | (11.0) | 6.3 | (18.6) | 6.5 | (17.3) | 6.8 | (16.0) | 6.4 | (18.1) |
| (b) Inflation Variability (last 5 yrs.) | 9.5 | (1.2) | 8.5 | (3.8) | 8.1 | (4.7) | 8.5 | (3.7) | 9.5 | (1.3) | 9.3 | (1.8) | 9.6 | (0.9) |
| (c) Recent Inflation Rate | 9.4 | (3.0) | 7.8 | (10.9) | 5.2 | (24.1) | 6.4 | (18.1) | 7.0 | (15.1) | 8.2 | (8.8) | 8.4 | (7.8) |
| **IV. Freedom to Use Alternative Currencies** | **4.5** | | **4.4** | | **4.4** | | **2.5** | | **4.7** | | **5.0** | | **6.2** | |
| (a) Ownership of Foreign Currency | 0.0 | | 0.0 | | 0.0 | | 0.0 | | 0.0 | | 0.0 | | 2.5 | |
| (b) Black Market Exchange Rates (Prem.) | 9.0 | (5.0) | 8.8 | (6.0) | 8.8 | (6.0) | 5.0 | (25.0) | 9.4 | (3.0) | 10.0 | (0.0) | 9.8 | (1.0) |
| **V. Legal Structure and Property Rights** | **8.9** | | **6.5** | | **6.6** | | **5.2** | | **3.8** | | **6.8** | | **8.5** | |
| (a) Private Ownership Rights | 8.7 | | 6.2 | | 7.0 | | 6.1 | | 3.2 | | 7.7 | | 10.0 | |
| (b) Viability of Contracts | 9.1 | | 6.7 | | 6.2 | | 6.4 | | 6.4 | | 8.4 | | 8.3 | |
| (c) Rule of Law | | | | | | | 3.1 | | 1.7 | | 4.1 | | 7.0 | |
| **VI. International Exchange** | **8.1** | | **8.5** | | **8.6** | | **7.6** | | **7.2** | | **6.1** | | **7.7** | |
| (a) Taxes on International Trade | | | | | | | | | | | | | | |
| i. Taxes as a Percentage of Exports and Imports | 8.7 | (2.0) | 8.7 | (2.0) | 9.2 | (1.2) | 9.1 | (1.4) | 8.5 | (2.2) | 9.3 | (1.0) | 9.9 | (0.1) |
| ii. Mean Tariff Rate | | | | | 8.1 | (9.4) | 8.8 | (6.0) | 7.8 | (11.0) | 6.1 | (19.7) | 8.2 | (8.8) |
| iii. Standard Deviation of Tariff Rates | | | | | | | | | 5.5 | (11.3) | 1.2 | (21.9) | 5.6 | (11.0) |
| (b) Non-tariff Regulatory Trade Barriers | | | | | | | | | | | | | | |
| i. Non-tariff Trade Restraints (% of trade covered) | | | | | | | 4.5 | (55.0) | 7.7 | (22.9) | 8.5 | (15.0) | | |
| ii. Size of Trade Sector (% of GDP) | 6.8 | (47.6) | 7.9 | (58.6) | 8.3 | (63.6) | 6.9 | (55.4) | 5.3 | (45.2) | 5.6 | (49.5) | 6.0 | (54.4) |
| **VII. Freedom of Exchange in Financial Markets** | **6.6** | | **6.7** | | **6.0** | | **7.2** | | **7.2** | | **7.7** | | **7.7** | |
| (a) Ownership of Banks | 10.0 | (100) | 10.0 | (100) | 10.0 | (100) | 10.0 | (100) | 10.0 | (100) | 10.0 | (100) | 10.0 | (100) |
| (b) Extension of Credit | 8.3 | (84.6) | 8.3 | (84.7) | 8.3 | (84.2) | 9.2 | (92.4) | 9.1 | (92.1) | 9.2 | (92.9) | 9.1 | (92.2) |
| (c) Avoidance of Negative Interest Rates | | | | | 4.0 | | 8.0 | | 8.0 | | 10.0 | | 10.0 | |
| (d) Capital Transactions with Foreigners | 2.0 | | 2.0 | | 2.0 | | 2.0 | | 2.0 | | 2.0 | | 2.0 | |

# SOUTH KOREA

| | 1970 | 1975 | 1980 | 1985 | 1990 | 1995 | 1997 |
|---|---|---|---|---|---|---|---|
| **Summary Ratings** | 6.3 | 5.6 | 5.7 | 6.0 | 6.6 | 7.7 | 7.3 |
| **Rank** | 32 | 38 | 38 | 36 | 35 | 34 | 47 |

| Components of Economic Freedom | 1970 | | 1975 | | 1980 | | 1985 | | 1990 | | 1995 | | 1997 | |
|---|---|---|---|---|---|---|---|---|---|---|---|---|---|---|
| **I. Size of Government** | **9.3** | | **9.0** | | **8.8** | | **8.8** | | **8.6** | | **8.6** | | **8.4** | |
| (a) Government Consumption (% of Total) | 8.8 | (11.2) | 8.4 | (13.5) | 8.0 | (15.2) | 8.1 | (14.7) | 7.9 | (15.9) | 7.9 | (16.2) | 7.7 | (17.2) |
| (b) Transfers and Subsidies (% of GDP) | 9.9 | (1.0) | 9.6 | (2.0) | 9.6 | (2.0) | 9.5 | (2.2) | 9.3 | (2.9) | 9.3 | (2.9) | 9.1 | (3.7) |
| **II. Structure of the Economy and Use of Markets** | | | **4.2** | | **3.4** | | **4.2** | | **3.0** | | **3.2** | | **3.5** | |
| (a) Government Enterprises | 6.0 | (25.3) | 7.0 | (21.1) | 7.0 | (22.6) | 7.0 | (25.4) | 7.0 | (19.2) | 6.0 | (25.5) | 6.0 | |
| (b) Price Controls | | | | | | | | | 0.0 | | 0.0 | | 0.0 | |
| (c) Top Marginal Tax Rate | | | 2.0 | (63) | 0.0 | (89) | 2.0 | (65) | 3.0 | (60) | 5.0 | (48) | 6.0 | (44) |
| (d) Conscription | 0.0 | | 0.0 | | 0.0 | | 0.0 | | 0.0 | | 0.0 | | 0.0 | |
| **III. Monetary Policy and Price Stability** | **6.6** | | **5.9** | | **6.7** | | **8.6** | | **8.6** | | **8.7** | | **9.6** | |
| (a) Annual Money Growth (last 5 yrs.) | 4.4 | (28.1) | 5.7 | (21.6) | 6.2 | (18.8) | 8.6 | (7.1) | 8.6 | (7.0) | 7.8 | (10.8) | 9.9 | (-0.4) |
| (b) Inflation Variability (last 5 yrs.) | 9.3 | (1.8) | 7.3 | (6.8) | 8.8 | (3.0) | 8.0 | (4.9) | 9.2 | (1.9) | 9.3 | (1.9) | 9.5 | (1.3) |
| (c) Recent Inflation Rate | 6.2 | (19.1) | 4.8 | (26.0) | 5.0 | (24.9) | 9.1 | (4.6) | 8.0 | (9.9) | 8.9 | (5.6) | 9.5 | (2.4) |
| **IV. Freedom to Use Alternative Currencies** | **3.0** | | **4.8** | | **3.9** | | **3.9** | | **4.9** | | **10.0** | | **9.8** | |
| (a) Ownership of Foreign Currency | 0.0 | | 0.0 | | 0.0 | | 0.0 | | 0.0 | | 10.0 | | 10.0 | |
| (b) Black Market Exchange Rates (Prem.) | 6.0 | (20.0) | 9.6 | (2.0) | 7.8 | (11.0) | 7.8 | (11.0) | 9.8 | (1.0) | 10.0 | (0.0) | 9.6 | (2.0) |
| **V. Legal Structure and Property Rights** | **6.0** | | **4.7** | | **6.8** | | **5.0** | | **7.2** | | **9.0** | | **8.1** | |
| (a) Private Ownership Rights | 6.5 | | 5.2 | | 6.6 | | 6.1 | | 8.6 | | 10.0 | | 10.0 | |
| (b) Viability of Contracts | 5.4 | | 4.2 | | 5.6 | | 6.4 | | 9.4 | | 10.0 | | 10.0 | |
| (c) Rule of Law | | | | | 8.3 | | 2.3 | | 3.3 | | 7.0 | | 4.1 | |
| **VI. International Exchange** | **7.3** | | **7.8** | | **6.9** | | **6.7** | | **7.5** | | **7.7** | | **5.8** | |
| (a) Taxes on International Trade | | | | | | | | | | | | | | |
| i. Taxes as a Percentage of Exports and Imports | 8.3 | (2.5) | 7.9 | (3.1) | 7.3 | (4.1) | 7.6 | (3.6) | 7.7 | (3.4) | 8.7 | (2.0) | 8.8 | (1.8) |
| ii. Mean Tariff Rate | | | | | 5.9 | (20.4) | 5.4 | (23.0) | 7.3 | (13.3) | 7.7 | (11.5) | 7.9 | (10.6) |
| iii. Standard Deviation of Tariff Rates | | | | | | | | | 7.3 | (6.7) | 7.4 | (6.6) | 0.0 | (27.0) |
| (b) Non-tariff Regulatory Trade Barriers | | | | | | | | | | | | | | |
| i. Non-tariff Trade Restraints (% of trade covered) | | | | | | | 7.2 | (27.7) | 8.3 | (16.7) | | | | |
| ii. Size of Trade Sector (% of GDP) | 4.6 | (37.3) | 7.6 | (64.1) | 8.3 | (74.3) | 7.1 | (66.9) | 6.0 | (60.1) | 6.4 | (67.2) | 7.1 | (77.0) |
| **VII. Freedom of Exchange in Financial Markets** | | | **3.9** | | **4.3** | | **6.3** | | **7.2** | | **7.2** | | **7.2** | |
| (a) Ownership of Banks | | | 5.0 | (68) | 5.0 | (63) | 5.0 | (59) | 5.0 | (58) | 5.0 | (58) | 5.0 | (62) |
| (b) Extension of Credit | 10.0 | (99.5) | 9.7 | (97.1) | 9.3 | (93.9) | 9.2 | (93.1) | 9.4 | (94.8) | 9.7 | (97.4) | 9.8 | (97.9) |
| (c) Avoidance of Negative Interest Rates | | | 2.0 | | 4.0 | | 10.0 | | 10.0 | | 10.0 | | 10.0 | |
| (d) Capital Transactions with Foreigners | 0.0 | | 0.0 | | 0.0 | | 2.0 | | 5.0 | | 5.0 | | 5.0 | |

# SPAIN

| | 1970 | 1975 | 1980 | 1985 | 1990 | 1995 | 1997 |
|---|---|---|---|---|---|---|---|
| **Summary Ratings** | 6.5 | 5.9 | 6.2 | 6.3 | 7.0 | 7.9 | 8.2 |
| **Rank** | 27 | 33 | 28 | 30 | 29 | 23 | 18 |

| Components of Economic Freedom | 1970 | | 1975 | | 1980 | | 1985 | | 1990 | | 1995 | | 1997 | |
|---|---|---|---|---|---|---|---|---|---|---|---|---|---|---|
| **I. Size of Government** | **8.4** | | **7.9** | | **7.3** | | **6.5** | | **6.5** | | **6.0** | | **7.0** | |
| (a) Government Consumption (% of Total) | 8.5 | (12.8) | 8.3 | (13.9) | 7.8 | (16.5) | 7.4 | (18.7) | 7.2 | (20.0) | 6.9 | (21.2) | 7.0 | (21.0) |
| (b) Transfers and Subsidies (% of GDP) | 8.4 | (6.4) | 7.5 | (9.5) | 6.8 | (12.3) | 5.5 | (16.9) | 5.8 | (16.0) | 5.1 | (18.5) | | |
| **II. Structure of the Economy and Use of Markets** | | | **4.6** | | **2.5** | | **2.5** | | **4.3** | | **3.7** | | **4.3** | |
| (a) Government Enterprises | 6.0 | | 6.0 | (17.3) | 4.0 | (27.1) | 4.0 | (30.2) | 4.0 | (33.5) | 4.0 | | 4.0 | |
| (b) Price Controls | | | | | | | | | 6.0 | | 5.0 | | 6.0 | |
| (c) Top Marginal Tax Rate | | | 4.0 | (55) | 1.0 | (66) | 1.0 | (66) | 3.0 | (56) | 2.0 | (56) | 3.0 | (56) |
| (d) Conscription | 0.0 | | 1.0 | | 1.0 | | 1.0 | | 3.0 | | 3.0 | | 3.0 | |
| **III. Monetary Policy and Price Stability** | **9.1** | | **7.3** | | **7.8** | | **8.7** | | **8.2** | | **9.4** | | **9.5** | |
| (a) Annual Money Growth (last 5 yrs.) | 9.2 | (4.2) | 6.9 | (15.7) | 7.6 | (12.2) | 8.3 | (8.3) | 6.8 | (16.0) | 9.8 | (1.2) | 9.2 | (3.9) |
| (b) Inflation Variability (last 5 yrs.) | 9.5 | (1.4) | 8.5 | (3.7) | 8.6 | (3.5) | 9.2 | (2.1) | 9.2 | (2.0) | 9.5 | (1.3) | 9.6 | (1.0) |
| (c) Recent Inflation Rate | 8.8 | (5.9) | 6.6 | (16.8) | 7.3 | (13.4) | 8.5 | (7.7) | 8.5 | (7.3) | 9.0 | (4.8) | 9.6 | (2.1) |
| **IV. Freedom to Use Alternative Currencies** | **4.4** | | **4.8** | | **5.0** | | **4.8** | | **4.8** | | **10.0** | | **10.0** | |
| (a) Ownership of Foreign Currency | 0.0 | | 0.0 | | 0.0 | | 0.0 | | 0.0 | | 10.0 | | 10.0 | |
| (b) Black Market Exchange Rates (Prem.) | 8.8 | (6.0) | 9.6 | (2.0) | 10.0 | (0.0) | 9.6 | (2.0) | 9.6 | (2.0) | 10.0 | (0.0) | 10.0 | (0.0) |
| **V. Legal Structure and Property Rights** | **7.0** | | **5.0** | | **6.8** | | **7.0** | | **8.5** | | **9.5** | | **10.0** | |
| (a) Private Ownership Rights | 8.3 | | 5.5 | | 6.1 | | 8.1 | | 10.0 | | 10.0 | | 10.0 | |
| (b) Viability of Contracts | 5.8 | | 4.5 | | 5.9 | | 6.4 | | 8.8 | | 8.4 | | 10.0 | |
| (c) Rule of Law | | | | | 8.3 | | 6.6 | | 6.7 | | 10.0 | | 10.0 | |
| **VI. International Exchange** | **5.0** | | **6.6** | | **7.6** | | **7.8** | | **8.0** | | **8.4** | | **8.5** | |
| (a) Taxes on International Trade | | | | | | | | | | | | | | |
| i. Taxes as a Percentage of Exports and Imports | 5.5 | (6.7) | 5.9 | (6.1) | 8.2 | (2.7) | 8.0 | (3.0) | 9.0 | (1.5) | 9.9 | (0.2) | 9.7 | (0.5) |
| ii. Mean Tariff Rate | | | 8.1 | (9.4) | 8.2 | (8.8) | 8.5 | (7.5) | 8.5 | (7.4) | 8.7 | (6.7) | 8.6 | (6.9) |
| iii. Standard Deviation of Tariff Rates | | | | | | | | | 7.1 | (7.2) | 7.6 | (5.9) | 7.6 | (6.0) |
| (b) Non-tariff Regulatory Trade Barriers | | | | | | | | | | | | | | |
| i. Non-tariff Trade Restraints (% of trade covered) | | | | | | | | | 8.9 | (10.9) | 9.1 | (9.0) | 9.3 | (6.7) |
| ii. Size of Trade Sector (% of GDP) | 3.6 | (27.5) | 3.9 | (30.9) | 4.1 | (33.8) | 5.2 | (43.5) | 4.0 | (37.5) | 4.9 | (46.9) | 5.6 | (54.8) |
| **VII. Freedom of Exchange in Financial Markets** | | | **6.0** | | **6.7** | | **7.4** | | **8.2** | | **8.1** | | **8.2** | |
| (a) Ownership of Banks | | | 8.0 | (80-90) | 8.0 | (80-90) | 8.0 | (92) | 8.0 | (80-95) | 8.0 | (85-95) | 8.0 | (85-95) |
| (b) Extension of Credit | 7.5 | (77.2) | 8.4 | (85.4) | 7.9 | (81.0) | 6.4 | (67.9) | 6.5 | (68.1) | 6.3 | (66.6) | 6.7 | (70.6) |
| (c) Avoidance of Negative Interest Rates | | | | | 6.0 | | 10.0 | | 10.0 | | 10.0 | | 10.0 | |
| (d) Capital Transactions with Foreigners | 2.0 | | 2.0 | | 5.0 | | 5.0 | | 8.0 | | 8.0 | | 8.0 | |

# SRI LANKA

| | 1970 | 1975 | 1980 | 1985 | 1990 | 1995 | 1997 |
|---|---|---|---|---|---|---|---|
| **Summary Ratings** | | | 4.2 | 4.8 | 4.5 | 6.3 | 6.5 |
| **Rank** | | | 78 | 69 | 82 | 60 | 66 |

| Components of Economic Freedom | 1970 | | 1975 | | 1980 | | 1985 | | 1990 | | 1995 | | 1997 | |
|---|---|---|---|---|---|---|---|---|---|---|---|---|---|---|
| **I. Size of Government** | **8.1** | | **8.5** | | **8.5** | | **8.7** | | **8.6** | | **8.4** | | **8.7** | |
| (a) Government Consumption (% of Total) | 8.2 | (14.1) | 9.0 | (10.2) | 9.1 | (9.6) | 8.7 | (11.4) | 8.7 | (11.4) | 8.3 | (13.5) | 8.5 | (12.5) |
| (b) Transfers and Subsidies (% of GDP) | 8.0 | (7.8) | 7.9 | (8.1) | 7.8 | (8.4) | 8.7 | (5.1) | 8.5 | (6.0) | 8.5 | (5.9) | 8.8 | (4.9) |
| **II. Structure of the Economy and Use of Markets** | | | | | **2.3** | | **2.3** | | **4.7** | | **5.3** | | **5.3** | |
| (a) Government Enterprises | 4.0 | (37.0) | 2.0 | (40.5) | 2.0 | (53.5) | 2.0 | (54.3) | 4.0 | (39.2) | 4.0 | | 4.0 | |
| (b) Price Controls | | | | | | | | | 4.0 | | 4.0 | | 4.0 | |
| (c) Top Marginal Tax Rate | | | | | 0.0 | (61) | 0.0 | (61) | | | 7.0 | (35) | 7.0 | (35) |
| (d) Conscription | | | 10.0 | | 10.0 | | 10.0 | | 10.0 | | 10.0 | | 10.0 | |
| **III. Monetary Policy and Price Stability** | **9.0** | | **8.3** | | **6.8** | | **8.3** | | **7.2** | | **8.7** | | **8.9** | |
| (a) Annual Money Growth (last 5 yrs.) | 9.6 | (-1.8) | 9.0 | (4.8) | 5.9 | (20.6) | 8.0 | (9.8) | 7.6 | (12.1) | 8.1 | (9.3) | 8.7 | (6.6) |
| (b) Inflation Variability (last 5 yrs.) | 8.5 | (3.8) | 6.9 | (7.8) | 8.6 | (3.6) | 7.0 | (7.5) | 8.0 | (5.0) | 9.8 | (0.5) | 9.7 | (0.6) |
| (c) Recent Inflation Rate | 9.0 | (5.2) | 8.9 | (5.4) | 6.0 | (20.0) | 9.9 | (0.6) | 5.9 | (20.3) | 8.1 | (9.3) | 8.2 | (9.0) |
| **IV. Freedom to Use Alternative Currencies** | **0.0** | | **0.0** | | **4.1** | | **3.0** | | **2.6** | | **4.8** | | **4.9** | |
| (a) Ownership of Foreign Currency | 0.0 | | 0.0 | | 0.0 | | 0.0 | | 0.0 | | 0.0 | | 0.0 | |
| (b) Black Market Exchange Rates (Prem.) | 0.0 | (104.0) | 0.0 | (92.0) | 8.2 | (9.0) | 6.0 | (20.0) | 5.2 | (24.0) | 9.6 | (2.0) | 9.8 | (1.0) |
| **V. Legal Structure and Property Rights** | | | | | **3.9** | | **3.5** | | **2.1** | | **6.6** | | **7.6** | |
| (a) Private Ownership Rights | | | | | 4.6 | | 4.8 | | 3.2 | | 7.7 | | 10.0 | |
| (b) Viability of Contracts | | | | | 3.7 | | 4.0 | | 2.8 | | 5.2 | | 8.3 | |
| (c) Rule of Law | | | | | 3.3 | | 1.4 | | 0.0 | | 7.0 | | 4.1 | |
| **VI. International Exchange** | **1.9** | | **3.5** | | **2.9** | | **5.1** | | **4.3** | | **5.9** | | **5.8** | |
| (a) Taxes on International Trade | | | | | | | | | | | | | | |
| i. Taxes as a Percentage of Exports and Imports | 0.5 | (14.2) | 2.6 | (11.1) | 2.2 | (11.7) | 2.9 | (10.6) | 4.1 | (8.8) | 7.0 | (4.5) | 7.5 | (3.7) |
| ii. Mean Tariff Rate | | | | | 1.7 | (41.3) | 4.2 | (29.0) | 4.6 | (26.9) | 4.8 | (26.1) | 6.0 | (20.0) |
| iii. Standard Deviation of Tariff Rates | | | | | | | | | 0.0 | (25.5) | 2.8 | (18.1) | 3.8 | (15.4) |
| (b) Non-tariff Regulatory Trade Barriers | | | | | | | | | | | | | | |
| i. Non-tariff Trade Restraints (% of trade covered) | | | | | | | 8.6 | (13.9) | 9.0 | (10.1) | 9.6 | (3.8) | | |
| ii. Size of Trade Sector (% of GDP) | 5.2 | (54.1) | 5.7 | (62.4) | 7.6 | (87.0) | 5.3 | (64.0) | 5.4 | (68.2) | 6.1 | (81.6) | 5.8 | (80.0) |
| **VII. Freedom of Exchange in Financial Markets** | | | | | **3.6** | | **5.0** | | **4.7** | | **6.1** | | **6.0** | |
| (a) Ownership of Banks | | | 5.0 | (40-75) | 5.0 | (40-75) | 5.0 | (40-75) | 5.0 | (40-75) | 5.0 | (40-75) | 5.0 | (40-75) |
| (b) Extension of Credit | | | | | 6.0 | (63.8) | 7.7 | (79.1) | 6.3 | (66.7) | 8.3 | (84.2) | 7.8 | (80.4) |
| (c) Avoidance of Negative Interest Rates | | | | | 4.0 | | 8.0 | | 8.0 | | 10.0 | | 10.0 | |
| (d) Capital Transactions with Foreigners | 0.0 | | 0.0 | | 0.0 | | 0.0 | | 0.0 | | 2.0 | | 2.0 | |

# SWEDEN

| | 1970 | 1975 | 1980 | 1985 | 1990 | 1995 | 1997 |
|---|---|---|---|---|---|---|---|
| **Summary Ratings** | 6.2 | 6.2 | 6.3 | 7.0 | 7.5 | 7.9 | 8.0 |
| **Rank** | 34 | 25 | 25 | 19 | 22 | 23 | 25 |

| Components of Economic Freedom | 1970 | | 1975 | | 1980 | | 1985 | | 1990 | | 1995 | | 1997 | |
|---|---|---|---|---|---|---|---|---|---|---|---|---|---|---|
| **I. Size of Government** | **5.5** | | **4.2** | | **3.8** | | **3.7** | | **3.2** | | **2.8** | | **3.1** | |
| (a) Government Consumption (% of Total) | 5.5 | (29.0) | 5.0 | (31.8) | 4.2 | (36.3) | 4.3 | (35.3) | 4.4 | (34.9) | 4.8 | (33.0) | 4.7 | (33.4) |
| (b) Transfers and Subsidies (% of GDP) | | | 3.3 | (25.0) | 3.4 | (24.7) | 3.1 | (26.0) | 2.0 | (29.9) | 0.8 | (34.1) | 1.4 | (31.9) |
| **II. Structure of the Economy and Use of Markets** | **2.1** | | **2.7** | | **2.4** | | **3.3** | | **4.2** | | **5.2** | | **4.8** | |
| (a) Government Enterprises | 2.0 | (46.2) | 4.0 | (38.1) | 4.0 | (41.2) | 6.0 | (28.0) | 6.0 | (22.8) | 6.0 | (28.3) | 6.0 | |
| (b) Price Controls | | | | | | | | | 6.0 | | 8.0 | | 7.0 | |
| (c) Top Marginal Tax Rate | 2.0 | (61) | 1.0 | (70) | 0.0 | (87) | 0.0 | (80) | 0.0 | (72) | 1.0 | (58) | 1.0 | (57) |
| (d) Conscription | 3.0 | | 3.0 | | 3.0 | | 3.0 | | 3.0 | | 3.0 | | 3.0 | |
| **III. Monetary Policy and Price Stability** | **9.2** | | **8.2** | | **8.4** | | **9.0** | | **8.8** | | **9.4** | | **9.6** | |
| (a) Annual Money Growth (last 5 yrs.) | | | 8.6 | (7.0) | 8.3 | (8.7) | 8.9 | (5.5) | 8.7 | (6.6) | 9.8 | (0.9) | 9.6 | (1.8) |
| (b) Inflation Variability (last 5 yrs.) | 9.4 | (1.5) | 8.8 | (2.9) | 9.4 | (1.5) | 9.5 | (1.3) | 9.4 | (1.4) | 9.1 | (2.2) | 9.6 | (0.9) |
| (c) Recent Inflation Rate | 9.0 | (5.2) | 7.1 | (14.5) | 7.7 | (11.7) | 8.7 | (6.6) | 8.2 | (8.8) | 9.3 | (3.7) | 9.7 | (1.7) |
| **IV. Freedom to Use Alternative Currencies** | **4.5** | | **7.4** | | **7.0** | | **7.4** | | **7.5** | | **10.0** | | **10.0** | |
| (a) Ownership of Foreign Currency | 0.0 | | 5.0 | | 5.0 | | 5.0 | | 5.0 | | 10.0 | | 10.0 | |
| (b) Black Market Exchange Rates (Prem.) | 9.0 | (5.0) | 9.8 | (1.0) | 9.0 | (5.0) | 9.8 | (1.0) | 10.0 | (0.0) | 10.0 | (0.0) | 10.0 | (0.0) |
| **V. Legal Structure and Property Rights** | **8.6** | | **7.2** | | **7.8** | | **8.7** | | **10.0** | | **9.5** | | **10.0** | |
| (a) Private Ownership Rights | 7.4 | | 4.5 | | 5.2 | | 7.4 | | 10.0 | | 10.0 | | 10.0 | |
| (b) Viability of Contracts | 9.9 | | 10.0 | | 8.5 | | 8.8 | | 10.0 | | 8.4 | | 10.0 | |
| (c) Rule of Law | | | | | 10.0 | | 10.0 | | 10.0 | | 10.0 | | 10.0 | |
| **VI. International Exchange** | **8.2** | | **8.4** | | **8.5** | | **9.0** | | **8.7** | | **8.6** | | **8.6** | |
| (a) Taxes on International Trade | | | | | | | | | | | | | | |
| i. Taxes as a Percentage of Exports and Imports | 9.3 | (1.0) | 9.3 | (1.0) | 9.5 | (0.7) | 9.8 | (0.3) | 9.7 | (0.4) | 9.7 | (0.4) | 9.8 | (0.3) |
| ii. Mean Tariff Rate | | | 8.4 | (8.0) | 8.5 | (7.5) | 9.2 | (4.1) | 9.1 | (4.7) | 8.7 | (6.7) | 8.6 | (6.9) |
| iii. Standard Deviation of Tariff Rates | | | | | | | | | 8.1 | (4.8) | 7.6 | (5.9) | 7.6 | (6.0) |
| (b) Non-tariff Regulatory Trade Barriers | | | | | | | | | | | | | | |
| i. Non-tariff Trade Restraints (% of trade covered) | | | | | | | | | 9.6 | (4.5) | 9.7 | (3.4) | 9.3 | (6.7) |
| ii. Size of Trade Sector (% of GDP) | 5.4 | (48.2) | 5.8 | (55.9) | 6.0 | (60.8) | 6.3 | (68.9) | 5.1 | (59.5) | 6.1 | (75.5) | 6.4 | (80.6) |
| **VII. Freedom of Exchange in Financial Markets** | **5.5** | | **5.1** | | **6.0** | | **7.2** | | **8.8** | | **8.5** | | **8.5** | |
| (a) Ownership of Banks | | | 8.0 | (75-90) | 8.0 | (75-90) | 8.0 | (75-90) | 8.0 | (75-90) | 8.0 | (75-90) | 8.0 | (75-90) |
| (b) Extension of Credit | 7.1 | (73.8) | 6.8 | (71.2) | 6.4 | (67.5) | 5.8 | (62.1) | 6.9 | (71.7) | 5.5 | (59.2) | 5.6 | (60.3) |
| (c) Avoidance of Negative Interest Rates | 8.0 | | 4.0 | | 8.0 | | 10.0 | | 10.0 | | 10.0 | | 10.0 | |
| (d) Capital Transactions with Foreigners | 2.0 | | 2.0 | | 2.0 | | 5.0 | | 10.0 | | 10.0 | | 10.0 | |

# SWITZERLAND

| | 1970 | 1975 | 1980 | 1985 | 1990 | 1995 | 1997 |
|---|---|---|---|---|---|---|---|
| **Summary Ratings** | 8.9 | 8.0 | 8.4 | 8.7 | 8.6 | 8.5 | 8.5 |
| **Rank** | 4 | 5 | 4 | 3 | 4 | 8 | 9 |

| Components of Economic Freedom | 1970 | | 1975 | | 1980 | | 1985 | | 1990 | | 1995 | | 1997 | |
|---|---|---|---|---|---|---|---|---|---|---|---|---|---|---|
| **I. Size of Government** | **8.1** | | **7.7** | | **7.1** | | **7.1** | | **6.5** | | **6.1** | | **6.3** | |
| (a) Government Consumption (% of Total) | 8.1 | (15.1) | 7.7 | (17.0) | 7.8 | (16.7) | 7.6 | (17.8) | 7.2 | (19.6) | 7.3 | (19.2) | 7.3 | (19.2) |
| (b) Transfers and Subsidies (% of GDP) | | | | | 6.5 | (13.4) | 6.5 | (13.2) | 5.8 | (16.0) | 5.0 | (18.9) | 5.2 | (18.0) |
| **II. Structure of the Economy and Use of Markets** | | | **7.2** | | **7.2** | | **7.2** | | **7.4** | | **7.1** | | **7.1** | |
| (a) Government Enterprises | 8.0 | | 8.0 | | 8.0 | | 8.0 | | 8.0 | | 8.0 | | 8.0 | |
| (b) Price Controls | | | | | | | | | 7.0 | | 6.0 | | 6.0 | |
| (c) Top Marginal Tax Rate | | | 7.0 | (38-42) | 7.0 | (31-44) | 7.0 | (33-46) | 8.0 | (33-43) | 8.0 | (35-39) | 8.0 | (33-43) |
| (d) Conscription | 5.0 | | 5.0 | | 5.0 | | 5.0 | | 5.0 | | 5.0 | | 5.0 | |
| **III. Monetary Policy and Price Stability** | **9.5** | | **9.1** | | **9.3** | | **9.5** | | **9.6** | | **9.5** | | **9.3** | |
| (a) Annual Money Growth (last 5 yrs.) | 9.7 | (1.4) | 9.3 | (3.4) | 9.0 | (5.1) | 9.8 | (1.0) | 9.9 | (0.6) | 9.5 | (2.3) | 8.2 | (8.9) |
| (b) Inflation Variability (last 5 yrs.) | 9.6 | (0.9) | 9.6 | (1.1) | 9.5 | (1.1) | 9.3 | (1.8) | 9.8 | (0.6) | 9.3 | (1.7) | 9.6 | (1.0) |
| (c) Recent Inflation Rate | 9.1 | (4.7) | 8.6 | (7.1) | 9.5 | (2.7) | 9.5 | (2.4) | 9.1 | (4.3) | 9.8 | (1.1) | 10.0 | (-0.2) |
| **IV. Freedom to Use Alternative Currencies** | **10.0** | | **10.0** | | **10.0** | | **10.0** | | **10.0** | | **10.0** | | **10.0** | |
| (a) Ownership of Foreign Currency | 10.0 | | 10.0 | | 10.0 | | 10.0 | | 10.0 | | 10.0 | | 10.0 | |
| (b) Black Market Exchange Rates (Prem.) | 10.0 | (0.0) | 10.0 | (0.0) | 10.0 | (0.0) | 10.0 | (0.0) | 10.0 | (0.0) | 10.0 | (0.0) | 10.0 | (0.0) |
| **V. Legal Structure and Property Rights** | **10.0** | | **9.3** | | **9.4** | | **10.0** | | **10.0** | | **10.0** | | **9.4** | |
| (a) Private Ownership Rights | 10.0 | | 10.0 | | 9.4 | | 10.0 | | 10.0 | | 10.0 | | 10.0 | |
| (b) Viability of Contracts | 10.0 | | 8.7 | | 8.7 | | 10.0 | | 10.0 | | 10.0 | | 8.3 | |
| (c) Rule of Law | | | | | 10.0 | | 10.0 | | 10.0 | | 10.0 | | 10.0 | |
| **VI. International Exchange** | **7.1** | | **7.8** | | **8.3** | | **8.4** | | **7.8** | | **7.8** | | **8.5** | |
| (a) Taxes on International Trade | | | | | | | | | | | | | | |
| i. Taxes as a Percentage of Exports and Imports | 7.3 | (4.0) | 7.7 | (3.5) | 8.4 | (2.4) | 8.7 | (2.0) | 8.7 | (1.9) | 8.5 | (2.3) | 9.8 | (0.3) |
| ii. Mean Tariff Rate | | | 8.8 | (5.8) | 9.1 | (4.6) | 9.1 | (4.4) | 9.1 | (4.4) | 9.3 | (3.6) | 9.5 | (2.4) |
| iii. Standard Deviation of Tariff Rates | | | | | | | | | 4.8 | (13.0) | 5.4 | (11.6) | 7.0 | (7.4) |
| (b) Non-tariff Regulatory Trade Barriers | | | | | | | | | | | | | | |
| i. Non-tariff Trade Restraints (% of trade covered) | | | | | 8.1 | (19.5) | 8.0 | (19.6) | 9.7 | (2.7) | 9.7 | (2.7) | 9.0 | (9.8) |
| ii. Size of Trade Sector (% of GDP) | 6.5 | (66.5) | 5.5 | (59.4) | 6.5 | (76.2) | 6.2 | (76.9) | 5.5 | (72.0) | 4.7 | (66.1) | 5.2 | (74.9) |
| **VII. Freedom of Exchange in Financial Markets** | | | **5.2** | | **7.4** | | **8.5** | | **8.5** | | **8.5** | | **8.5** | |
| (a) Ownership of Banks | | | 5.0 | (40-75) | 5.0 | (40-75) | 5.0 | (51) | 5.0 | (67) | 5.0 | (40-75) | 5.0 | (40-75) |
| (b) Extension of Credit | 8.7 | (87.8) | 8.8 | (89.1) | 9.0 | (90.6) | 9.2 | (92.4) | 9.4 | (94.5) | 9.2 | (92.3) | 9.2 | (92.3) |
| (c) Avoidance of Negative Interest Rates | | | 6.0 | | 6.0 | | 10.0 | | 10.0 | | 10.0 | | 10.0 | |
| (d) Capital Transactions with Foreigners | 2.0 | | 2.0 | | 10.0 | | 10.0 | | 10.0 | | 10.0 | | 10.0 | |

# SYRIA

| | 1970 | 1975 | 1980 | 1985 | 1990 | 1995 | 1997 |
|---|---|---|---|---|---|---|---|
| **Summary Ratings** | 4.3 | 5.4 | 3.5 | 2.9 | 2.8 | 3.9 | 4.4 |
| **Rank** | 48 | 45 | 94 | 105 | 110 | 112 | 112 |

| Components of Economic Freedom | 1970 | | 1975 | | 1980 | | 1985 | | 1990 | | 1995 | | 1997 | |
|---|---|---|---|---|---|---|---|---|---|---|---|---|---|---|
| **I. Size of Government** | **8.5** | | **7.5** | | **6.7** | | **5.9** | | **7.7** | | **7.9** | | **7.5** | |
| (a) Government Consumption (% of Total) | 7.3 | (19.3) | 6.4 | (24.1) | 6.1 | (25.8) | 5.9 | (26.8) | 7.7 | (17.0) | 7.9 | (15.7) | 7.5 | (17.9) |
| (b) Transfers and Subsidies (% of GDP) | 9.7 | (1.7) | 8.6 | (5.5) | 7.4 | (10.2) | | | | | | | | |
| **II. Structure of the Economy and Use of Markets** | | | | | | | | | **0.0** | | **0.0** | | **0.0** | |
| (a) Government Enterprises | 0.0 | (74.2) | 0.0 | (74.4) | 0.0 | (70.2) | 0.0 | (66.3) | 0.0 | (55.6) | 0.0 | | 0.0 | |
| (b) Price Controls | | | | | | | | | 0.0 | | 0.0 | | 0.0 | |
| (c) Top Marginal Tax Rate | | | | | | | | | | | | | | |
| (d) Conscription | 0.0 | | 0.0 | | 0.0 | | 0.0 | | 0.0 | | 0.0 | | 0.0 | |
| **III. Monetary Policy and Price Stability** | **8.8** | | **6.7** | | **7.3** | | **8.0** | | **7.3** | | **8.5** | | **8.4** | |
| (a) Annual Money Growth (last 5 yrs.) | 8.3 | (8.3) | 6.8 | (16.1) | 6.8 | (15.8) | 6.9 | (15.5) | 7.1 | (14.5) | 8.1 | (9.6) | 8.5 | (7.3) |
| (b) Inflation Variability (last 5 yrs.) | 8.6 | (3.6) | 5.1 | (12.3) | 8.6 | (3.6) | 7.9 | (5.2) | 8.7 | (3.1) | 8.6 | (3.5) | 8.5 | (3.8) |
| (c) Recent Inflation Rate | 9.4 | (3.0) | 8.2 | (8.8) | 6.5 | (17.5) | 9.2 | (4.1) | 6.1 | (19.3) | 8.9 | (5.4) | 8.3 | (8.5) |
| **IV. Freedom to Use Alternative Currencies** | **3.3** | | **9.9** | | **6.5** | | **0.0** | | **0.0** | | **0.0** | | **2.9** | |
| (a) Ownership of Foreign Currency | 0.0 | | 10.0 | | 10.0 | | 0.0 | | 0.0 | | 0.0 | | 0.0 | |
| (b) Black Market Exchange Rates (Prem.) | 6.6 | (17.0) | 9.8 | (1.0) | 3.0 | (35.0) | 0.0 | (251.0) | 0.0 | (301.0) | 0.0 | (301.0) | 5.8 | (21.0) |
| **V. Legal Structure and Property Rights** | | | | | **0.7** | | **2.7** | | **2.6** | | **6.3** | | **6.9** | |
| (a) Private Ownership Rights | | | | | 0.0 | | 2.2 | | 1.9 | | 7.7 | | 7.2 | |
| (b) Viability of Contracts | | | | | 0.5 | | 2.8 | | 2.8 | | 6.8 | | 6.6 | |
| (c) Rule of Law | | | | | 1.7 | | 3.1 | | 3.3 | | 4.1 | | 7.0 | |
| **VI. International Exchange** | **3.7** | | **4.6** | | **3.0** | | **3.7** | | **4.5** | | **6.7** | | **6.9** | |
| (a) Taxes on International Trade | | | | | | | | | | | | | | |
| i. Taxes as a Percentage of Exports and Imports | 3.8 | (9.3) | 4.3 | (8.5) | 5.3 | (7.1) | 6.3 | (5.6) | 8.1 | (2.9) | 7.1 | (4.3) | 7.4 | (3.9) |
| ii. Mean Tariff Rate | | | | | 2.5 | (37.3) | 4.6 | (27.0) | 5.9 | (20.4) | 7.0 | (14.8) | | |
| iii. Standard Deviation of Tariff Rates | | | | | | | | | 0.0 | (27.7) | | | | |
| (b) Non-tariff Regulatory Trade Barriers | | | | | | | | | | | | | | |
| i. Non-tariff Trade Restraints (% of trade covered) | | | | | 0.0 | (100.0) | 0.0 | (100.0) | 3.9 | (61.0) | 6.3 | (36.6) | | |
| ii. Size of Trade Sector (% of GDP) | 3.4 | (38.6) | 5.2 | (55.4) | 4.9 | (53.7) | 2.3 | (37.2) | 4.6 | (55.1) | 5.8 | (71.4) | 5.8 | (71.8) |
| **VII. Freedom of Exchange in Financial Markets** | **0.9** | | **0.1** | | **0.2** | | **0.4** | | **0.3** | | **0.4** | | **0.2** | |
| (a) Ownership of Banks | 0.0 | (0) | 0.0 | (0) | 0.0 | (0) | 0.0 | (0) | 0.0 | (0) | 0.0 | (0) | 0.0 | (0) |
| (b) Extension of Credit | 3.0 | (37.4) | 0.5 | (14.8) | 0.7 | (16.3) | 1.7 | (25.6) | 1.5 | (23.3) | 1.9 | (27.5) | 1.0 | (19.2) |
| (c) Avoidance of Negative Interest Rates | | | | | | | 0.0 | | 0.0 | | 0.0 | | 0.0 | |
| (d) Capital Transactions with Foreigners | 0.0 | | 0.0 | | 0.0 | | 0.0 | | 0.0 | | 0.0 | | 0.0 | |

# TAIWAN

| | 1970 | 1975 | 1980 | 1985 | 1990 | 1995 | 1997 |
|---|---|---|---|---|---|---|---|
| **Summary Ratings** | 6.6 | 6.1 | 6.8 | 7.1 | 7.6 | 7.8 | 7.1 |
| **Rank** | 24 | 30 | 16 | 17 | 19 | 29 | 51 |

| Components of Economic Freedom | 1970 | | 1975 | | 1980 | | 1985 | | 1990 | | 1995 | | 1997 | |
|---|---|---|---|---|---|---|---|---|---|---|---|---|---|---|
| **I. Size of Government** | | | **8.2** | | **8.0** | | **7.8** | | **7.6** | | **7.8** | | **7.3** | |
| (a) Government Consumption (% of Total) | | | 6.8 | (21.7) | 6.5 | (23.6) | 6.4 | (24.0) | 6.4 | (23.9) | 7.1 | (20.3) | 7.3 | (19.3) |
| (b) Transfers and Subsidies (% of GDP) | | | 9.5 | (2.2) | 9.4 | (2.6) | 9.2 | (3.6) | 8.9 | (4.7) | 8.5 | (5.9) | | |
| **II. Structure of the Economy and Use of Markets** | | | **2.1** | | **2.1** | | **2.1** | | **3.9** | | **4.4** | | **3.1** | |
| (a) Government Enterprises | 2.0 | (43.1) | 2.0 | (46.1) | 2.0 | (44.3) | 2.0 | (43.0) | 2.0 | (44.3) | 2.0 | (47.2) | 2.0 | |
| (b) Price Controls | | | | | | | | | 6.0 | | 6.0 | | 2.0 | |
| (c) Top Marginal Tax Rate | | | 3.0 | (60) | 3.0 | (60) | 3.0 | (60) | 5.0 | (50) | 7.0 | (40) | 7.0 | (40) |
| (d) Conscription | 0.0 | | 0.0 | | 0.0 | | 0.0 | | 0.0 | | 0.0 | | 0.0 | |
| **III. Monetary Policy and Price Stability** | **9.0** | | **6.7** | | **7.2** | | **9.1** | | **8.7** | | **9.7** | | **9.9** | |
| (a) Annual Money Growth (last 5 yrs.) | 8.5 | (7.7) | 6.2 | (19.1) | 7.3 | (13.7) | 9.2 | (3.9) | 7.6 | (12.2) | 10.0 | (0.1) | 10.0 | (0.1) |
| (b) Inflation Variability (last 5 yrs.) | 9.2 | (2.0) | 5.0 | (12.6) | 8.3 | (4.3) | 8.1 | (4.8) | 9.5 | (1.3) | 9.8 | (0.4) | 9.9 | (0.3) |
| (c) Recent Inflation Rate | 9.3 | (3.4) | 9.0 | (5.2) | 6.2 | (19.0) | 10.0 | (-0.2) | 9.2 | (4.1) | 9.4 | (3.0) | 10.0 | (0.2) |
| **IV. Freedom to Use Alternative Currencies** | **9.7** | | **9.5** | | **9.9** | | **9.7** | | **10.0** | | **10.0** | | **10.0** | |
| (a) Ownership of Foreign Currency | 10.0 | | 10.0 | | 10.0 | | 10.0 | | 10.0 | | 10.0 | | 10.0 | |
| (b) Black Market Exchange Rates (Prem.) | 9.4 | (3.0) | 9.0 | (5.0) | 9.8 | (1.0) | 9.4 | (3.0) | 10.0 | (0.0) | 10.0 | (0.0) | 10.0 | (0.0) |
| **V. Legal Structure and Property Rights** | **7.5** | | **6.2** | | **8.9** | | **8.2** | | **9.0** | | **9.0** | | **8.1** | |
| (a) Private Ownership Rights | 9.1 | | 5.8 | | 8.6 | | 8.7 | | 8.6 | | 10.0 | | 10.0 | |
| (b) Viability of Contracts | 5.8 | | 6.6 | | 8.1 | | 7.6 | | 10.0 | | 10.0 | | 10.0 | |
| (c) Rule of Law | | | | | 10.0 | | 8.2 | | 8.3 | | 7.0 | | 4.1 | |
| **VI. International Exchange** | **5.7** | | **7.0** | | **8.0** | | **8.1** | | **8.1** | | **8.4** | | | |
| (a) Taxes on International Trade | | | | | | | | | | | | | | |
| i. Taxes as a Percentage of Exports and Imports | 5.7 | (6.4) | 6.8 | (4.8) | 7.6 | (3.6) | 8.1 | (2.8) | 8.6 | (2.1) | 8.9 | (1.7) | | |
| ii. Mean Tariff Rate | | | | | | | | | 8.1 | (9.7) | 8.4 | (8.0) | | |
| iii. Standard Deviation of Tariff Rates | | | | | | | | | | | | | | |
| (b) Non-tariff Regulatory Trade Barriers | | | | | | | | | | | | | | |
| i. Non-tariff Trade Restraints (% of trade covered) | | | | | | | | | | | | | | |
| ii. Size of Trade Sector (% of GDP) | 5.7 | (60.7) | 7.4 | (82.5) | 9.1 | (106.3) | 7.9 | (97.8) | 6.8 | (88.5) | 6.9 | (95.6) | 6.6 | (93.3) |
| **VII. Freedom of Exchange in Financial Markets** | **2.7** | | **4.2** | | **4.1** | | **5.2** | | **6.2** | | **6.1** | | **5.5** | |
| (a) Ownership of Banks | 0.0 | (0-5) | 0.0 | (3) | 0.0 | (10) | 2.0 | (12) | 2.0 | (16) | 2.0 | (15-25) | 2.0 | (15-25) |
| (b) Extension of Credit | 7.1 | (73.9) | 7.8 | (79.7) | 7.5 | (77.8) | 8.0 | (82.2) | 8.5 | (86.2) | 8.3 | (85.0) | | |
| (c) Avoidance of Negative Interest Rates | | | 8.0 | | 8.0 | | 10.0 | | 10.0 | | 10.0 | | 10.0 | |
| (d) Capital Transactions with Foreigners | 2.0 | | 2.0 | | 2.0 | | 2.0 | | 5.0 | | 5.0 | | 5.0 | |

# TANZANIA

| | 1970 | 1975 | 1980 | 1985 | 1990 | 1995 | 1997 |
|---|---|---|---|---|---|---|---|
| **Summary Ratings** | 4.3 | 3.2 | 4.1 | 3.0 | 3.5 | 5.0 | 5.6 |
| **Rank** | 48 | 75 | 79 | 103 | 105 | 93 | 88 |

| Components of Economic Freedom | 1970 | | 1975 | | 1980 | | 1985 | | 1990 | | 1995 | | 1997 | |
|---|---|---|---|---|---|---|---|---|---|---|---|---|---|---|
| **I. Size of Government** | **10.0** | | **8.7** | | **9.1** | | **8.1** | | **7.7** | | **7.9** | | **8.3** | |
| (a) Government Consumption (% of Total) | | | 7.4 | (18.9) | 8.2 | (14.5) | 7.5 | (18.1) | 7.7 | (17.1) | 7.9 | (16.1) | 8.3 | (13.7) |
| (b) Transfers and Subsidies (% of GDP) | 10.0 | (0.2) | 10.0 | (0.1) | 10.0 | (0.0) | 8.7 | (5.2) | | | | | | |
| **II. Structure of the Economy and Use of Markets** | **1.0** | | **1.3** | | | | **0.0** | | **0.8** | | **3.3** | | **3.7** | |
| (a) Government Enterprises | 2.0 | (47.3) | 0.0 | (49.0) | 0.0 | (53.8) | 0.0 | (53.5) | 0.0 | | 0.0 | | 2.0 | |
| (b) Price Controls | | | | | | | | | 0.0 | | 4.0 | | 4.0 | |
| (c) Top Marginal Tax Rate | 0.0 | (70) | 0.0 | (80) | | | 0.0 | (95) | 3.0 | (50) | 8.0 | (30) | 7.0 | (35) |
| (d) Conscription | 0.0 | | 10.0 | | 10.0 | | 0.0 | | 0.0 | | 0.0 | | 0.0 | |
| **III. Monetary Policy and Price Stability** | **9.3** | | **6.5** | | **5.5** | | **6.5** | | **6.1** | | **5.0** | | **6.7** | |
| (a) Annual Money Growth (last 5 yrs.) | | | 7.0 | (15.1) | 5.9 | (20.3) | 7.9 | (10.4) | 4.0 | (30.0) | 4.5 | (27.6) | 6.6 | (17.0) |
| (b) Inflation Variability (last 5 yrs.) | 9.4 | (1.6) | 7.8 | (5.6) | 6.5 | (8.7) | 8.4 | (3.9) | 8.7 | (3.3) | 6.4 | (9.1) | 7.6 | (6.1) |
| (c) Recent Inflation Rate | 9.3 | (3.5) | 4.8 | (26.1) | 4.0 | (30.2) | 3.3 | (33.3) | 5.6 | (21.8) | 4.2 | (28.9) | 6.0 | (19.9) |
| **IV. Freedom to Use Alternative Currencies** | **1.9** | | **0.0** | | **0.0** | | **0.0** | | **0.0** | | **7.4** | | **6.7** | |
| (a) Ownership of Foreign Currency | 0.0 | | 0.0 | | 0.0 | | 0.0 | | 0.0 | | 5.0 | | 5.0 | |
| (b) Black Market Exchange Rates (Prem.) | 3.8 | (31.0) | 0.0 | (203.0) | 0.0 | (224.0) | 0.0 | (259.0) | 0.0 | (78.0) | 9.8 | (1.0) | 8.4 | (8.0) |
| **V. Legal Structure and Property Rights** | | | | | **6.2** | | **6.0** | | **5.5** | | **5.7** | | **6.3** | |
| (a) Private Ownership Rights | | | | | 5.5 | | 4.8 | | 4.6 | | 7.7 | | 7.2 | |
| (b) Viability of Contracts | | | | | 4.9 | | 5.2 | | 5.2 | | 5.2 | | 4.8 | |
| (c) Rule of Law | | | | | 8.3 | | 8.2 | | 6.7 | | 4.1 | | 7.0 | |
| **VI. International Exchange** | **6.0** | | **5.4** | | **4.8** | | **3.0** | | **4.0** | | **4.8** | | **6.3** | |
| (a) Taxes on International Trade | | | | | | | | | | | | | | |
| i. Taxes as a Percentage of Exports and Imports | 5.8 | (6.3) | 5.1 | (7.3) | 4.9 | (7.7) | 5.8 | (6.3) | 5.0 | (7.5) | 4.6 | (8.1) | 9.1 | (1.3) |
| ii. Mean Tariff Rate | | | | | | | 3.6 | (32.0) | 4.1 | (29.7) | 6.1 | (19.5) | 5.7 | (21.6) |
| iii. Standard Deviation of Tariff Rates | | | | | | | | | | | 5.1 | (12.3) | 4.4 | (14.0) |
| (b) Non-tariff Regulatory Trade Barriers | | | | | | | | | | | | | | |
| i. Non-tariff Trade Restraints (% of trade covered) | | | | | | | 0.0 | (100.0) | 2.0 | (79.7) | 2.0 | (79.7) | | |
| ii. Size of Trade Sector (% of GDP) | 6.7 | (52.5) | 6.0 | (49.2) | 4.6 | (39.5) | 0.7 | (23.5) | 5.3 | (48.6) | 6.6 | (62.9) | 6.0 | (57.7) |
| **VII. Freedom of Exchange in Financial Markets** | **1.0** | | **0.1** | | **1.0** | | **0.0** | | **2.4** | | **1.9** | | **2.2** | |
| (a) Ownership of Banks | 0.0 | (0) | 0.0 | (0) | 0.0 | (0) | 0.0 | (0) | 0.0 | (0-5) | 0.0 | (0-5) | 0.0 | (0-5) |
| (b) Extension of Credit | 3.6 | (42.3) | 0.4 | (13.2) | 0.0 | (9.3) | 0.0 | (8.9) | 6.9 | (72.0) | 4.1 | (46.9) | 3.2 | (38.7) |
| (c) Avoidance of Negative Interest Rates | | | | | 4.0 | | 0.0 | | 4.0 | | 4.0 | | 6.0 | |
| (d) Capital Transactions with Foreigners | 0.0 | | 0.0 | | 0.0 | | 0.0 | | 0.0 | | 0.0 | | 0.0 | |

# THAILAND

| | 1970 | 1975 | 1980 | 1985 | 1990 | 1995 | 1997 |
|---|---|---|---|---|---|---|---|
| **Summary Ratings** | 6.4 | 5.6 | 5.8 | 6.1 | 6.8 | 7.6 | 8.2 |
| **Rank** | 29 | 38 | 36 | 34 | 32 | 38 | 18 |

| Components of Economic Freedom | 1970 | | 1975 | | 1980 | | 1985 | | 1990 | | 1995 | | 1997 | |
|---|---|---|---|---|---|---|---|---|---|---|---|---|---|---|
| **I. Size of Government** | **9.1** | | **9.2** | | **8.9** | | **8.7** | | **9.0** | | **8.9** | | **8.9** | |
| (a) Government Consumption (% of Total) | 8.3 | (13.9) | 8.5 | (12.9) | 7.9 | (15.8) | 7.6 | (17.9) | 8.2 | (14.3) | 8.0 | (15.6) | 7.9 | (15.7) |
| (b) Transfers and Subsidies (% of GDP) | 10.0 | (0.5) | 10.0 | (0.6) | 9.9 | (0.7) | 9.8 | (1.2) | 9.9 | (1.0) | 9.8 | (1.1) | 9.8 | (1.2) |
| **II. Structure of the Economy and Use of Markets** | | | **4.1** | | **3.1** | | **2.7** | | **4.6** | | **5.4** | | **6.6** | |
| (a) Government Enterprises | 4.0 | (30.0) | 6.0 | (19.3) | 4.0 | (30.9) | 4.0 | (31.4) | 7.0 | (15.1) | 7.0 | (20.3) | 7.0 | |
| (b) Price Controls | | | | | | | | | 4.0 | | 4.0 | | 5.0 | |
| (c) Top Marginal Tax Rate | | | 3.0 | (60) | 3.0 | (60) | 2.0 | (65) | 4.0 | (55) | 7.0 | (37) | 7.0 | (37) |
| (d) Conscription | 0.0 | | 0.0 | | 0.0 | | 0.0 | | 0.0 | | 0.0 | | 10.0 | |
| **III. Monetary Policy and Price Stability** | **9.1** | | **8.3** | | **8.2** | | **9.3** | | **8.7** | | **9.1** | | **9.3** | |
| (a) Annual Money Growth (last 5 yrs.) | 10.0 | (0.2) | 9.0 | (5.0) | 8.3 | (8.7) | 9.4 | (-3.0) | 8.0 | (10.0) | 8.9 | (5.3) | 9.4 | (3.1) |
| (b) Inflation Variability (last 5 yrs.) | 8.2 | (4.5) | 6.7 | (8.4) | 8.9 | (2.9) | 9.0 | (2.5) | 9.3 | (1.7) | 9.6 | (1.0) | 9.6 | (1.0) |
| (c) Recent Inflation Rate | 9.0 | (-5.0) | 9.3 | (3.5) | 7.5 | (12.7) | 9.6 | (2.2) | 8.8 | (5.8) | 8.8 | (6.0) | 8.9 | (5.4) |
| **IV. Freedom to Use Alternative Currencies** | **5.0** | | **4.8** | | **4.5** | | **4.7** | | **7.5** | | **10.0** | | **10.0** | |
| (a) Ownership of Foreign Currency | 0.0 | | 0.0 | | 0.0 | | 0.0 | | 5.0 | | 10.0 | | 10.0 | |
| (b) Black Market Exchange Rates (Prem.) | 10.0 | (0.0) | 9.6 | (2.0) | 9.0 | (5.0) | 9.4 | (3.0) | 10.0 | (0.0) | 10.0 | (0.0) | 10.0 | (0.0) |
| **V. Legal Structure and Property Rights** | **6.2** | | **5.3** | | **7.0** | | **6.0** | | **7.8** | | **7.2** | | **8.5** | |
| (a) Private Ownership Rights | 6.5 | | 4.8 | | 6.6 | | 4.8 | | 8.0 | | 7.7 | | 10.0 | |
| (b) Viability of Contracts | 5.8 | | 5.8 | | 6.2 | | 5.2 | | 8.8 | | 6.8 | | 8.3 | |
| (c) Rule of Law | | | | | 8.3 | | 8.2 | | 6.7 | | 7.0 | | 7.0 | |
| **VI. International Exchange** | **4.5** | | **4.2** | | **4.9** | | **5.9** | | **4.9** | | **6.0** | | **7.0** | |
| (a) Taxes on International Trade | | | | | | | | | | | | | | |
| i. Taxes as a Percentage of Exports and Imports | 4.4 | (8.4) | 5.3 | (7.0) | 5.4 | (6.9) | 5.7 | (6.5) | 6.4 | (5.4) | 7.7 | (3.5) | 8.4 | (2.3) |
| ii. Mean Tariff Rate | | | 2.6 | (37.0) | 3.5 | (32.3) | 3.8 | (31.2) | 1.8 | (40.8) | 2.8 | (36.0) | 4.5 | (27.6) |
| iii. Standard Deviation of Tariff Rates | | | | | | | | | 1.4 | (21.5) | 3.2 | (16.9) | | |
| (b) Non-tariff Regulatory Trade Barriers | | | | | | | | | | | | | | |
| i. Non-tariff Trade Restraints (% of trade covered) | | | | | | | 8.8 | (12.4) | 9.2 | (8.5) | 9.5 | (5.5) | | |
| ii. Size of Trade Sector (% of GDP) | 4.9 | (34.4) | 5.7 | (41.3) | 7.2 | (54.5) | 6.2 | (49.2) | 9.0 | (75.5) | 10.0 | (89.6) | 10.0 | (93.4) |
| **VII. Freedom of Exchange in Financial Markets** | | | **5.6** | | **5.3** | | **6.8** | | **6.5** | | **7.9** | | **7.9** | |
| (a) Ownership of Banks | | | 8.0 | (75-95) | 8.0 | (75-95) | 8.0 | (75-95) | 8.0 | (80-90) | 8.0 | (90-95) | 8.0 | (90-95) |
| (b) Extension of Credit | 7.4 | (76.7) | 7.2 | (75.0) | 7.8 | (80.1) | 7.7 | (79.5) | 8.6 | (87.7) | 9.1 | (92.2) | 9.2 | (92.5) |
| (c) Avoidance of Negative Interest Rates | | | | | 4.0 | | 10.0 | | 8.0 | | 10.0 | | 10.0 | |
| (d) Capital Transactions with Foreigners | 2.0 | | 2.0 | | 2.0 | | 2.0 | | 2.0 | | 5.0 | | 5.0 | |

# TOGO

| | 1970 | 1975 | 1980 | 1985 | 1990 | 1995 | 1997 |
|---|---|---|---|---|---|---|---|
| **Summary Ratings** | | | 4.4 | 5.9 | 4.9 | 4.7 | 4.6 |
| **Rank** | | | 75 | 40 | 71 | 98 | 107 |

| Components of Economic Freedom | 1970 | | 1975 | | 1980 | | 1985 | | 1990 | | 1995 | | 1997 | |
|---|---|---|---|---|---|---|---|---|---|---|---|---|---|---|
| **I. Size of Government** | **6.9** | | **6.0** | | **5.5** | | **8.9** | | **7.8** | | **8.3** | | **8.7** | |
| (a) Government Consumption (% of Total) | 6.9 | (21.3) | 6.0 | (26.3) | 5.5 | (29.1) | 8.2 | (14.2) | 7.8 | (16.6) | 8.3 | (13.8) | 8.7 | (11.5) |
| (b) Transfers and Subsidies (% of GDP) | | | | | | | 9.5 | (2.4) | | | | | | |
| **II. Structure of the Economy and Use of Markets** | | | | | | | | | **0.0** | | **0.9** | | **0.9** | |
| (a) Government Enterprises | 0.0 | (54.2) | 0.0 | (50.2) | 0.0 | (52.5) | 2.0 | (40.0) | 0.0 | (54.8) | 0.0 | (51.7) | 0.0 | |
| (b) Price Controls | | | | | | | | | 0.0 | | 2.0 | | 2.0 | |
| (c) Top Marginal Tax Rate | | | | | | | | | | | | | | |
| (d) Conscription | | | | | | | 0.0 | | 0.0 | | 0.0 | | 0.0 | |
| **III. Monetary Policy and Price Stability** | **9.1** | | **6.8** | | **6.7** | | **8.7** | | **9.4** | | **6.7** | | **6.7** | |
| (a) Annual Money Growth (last 5 yrs.) | 8.8 | (5.9) | 7.8 | (11.1) | 6.7 | (16.5) | 8.8 | (6.2) | 9.4 | (-2.9) | 7.9 | (10.6) | 7.2 | (14.3) |
| (b) Inflation Variability (last 5 yrs.) | 8.9 | (2.8) | 3.3 | (16.7) | 5.6 | (11.1) | 8.0 | (4.9) | 9.4 | (1.6) | 4.5 | (13.7) | 4.7 | (13.2) |
| (c) Recent Inflation Rate | 9.7 | (-1.6) | 9.1 | (-4.3) | 7.9 | (10.5) | 9.3 | (3.4) | 9.4 | (3.0) | 7.6 | (12.2) | 8.1 | (9.6) |
| **IV. Freedom to Use Alternative Currencies** | 4.8 | | **4.8** | | **4.8** | | **4.9** | | **4.6** | | **4.9** | | **4.8** | |
| (a) Ownership of Foreign Currency | 0.0 | | 0.0 | | 0.0 | | 0.0 | | 0.0 | | 0.0 | | 0.0 | |
| (b) Black Market Exchange Rates (Prem.) | 9.6 | (2.0) | 9.6 | (2.0) | 9.6 | (2.0) | 9.8 | (1.0) | 9.2 | (4.0) | 9.8 | (1.0) | 9.6 | (2.0) |
| **V. Legal Structure and Property Rights** | | | | | **3.0** | | **4.2** | | **4.4** | | **4.8** | | **4.2** | |
| (a) Private Ownership Rights | | | | | 2.8 | | 5.5 | | 5.9 | | 5.5 | | 4.4 | |
| (b) Viability of Contracts | | | | | 3.0 | | 4.0 | | 4.0 | | 2.1 | | 1.4 | |
| (c) Rule of Law | | | | | 3.3 | | 3.1 | | 3.3 | | 7.0 | | 7.0 | |
| **VI. International Exchange** | | | **5.6** | | **3.2** | | **6.1** | | **5.6** | | | | | |
| (a) Taxes on International Trade | | | | | | | | | | | | | | |
| i. Taxes as a Percentage of Exports and Imports | | | 5.2 | (7.2) | 1.7 | (12.4) | 4.3 | (8.6) | 3.9 | (9.2) | | | | |
| ii. Mean Tariff Rate | | | | | | | | | | | | | | |
| iii. Standard Deviation of Tariff Rates | | | | | | | | | | | | | | |
| (b) Non-tariff Regulatory Trade Barriers | | | | | | | | | | | | | | |
| i. Non-tariff Trade Restraints (% of trade covered) | | | | | | | 8.0 | (20.0) | 8.0 | (20.0) | 9.3 | (7.0) | | |
| ii. Size of Trade Sector (% of GDP) | 6.2 | (88.4) | 6.6 | (97.1) | 7.0 | (107.4) | 6.6 | (105.5) | 4.7 | (78.8) | 4.2 | (74.6) | 3.8 | (71.4) |
| **VII. Freedom of Exchange in Financial Markets** | | | | | **4.5** | | **4.6** | | **4.6** | | **4.4** | | **3.9** | |
| (a) Ownership of Banks | | | 2.0 | (10-40) | 2.0 | (10-40) | 2.0 | (10-40) | 2.0 | (10-40) | 2.0 | (10-40) | 2.0 | (10-40) |
| (b) Extension of Credit | | | | | 9.2 | (92.5) | 9.8 | (98.1) | 9.7 | (97.6) | 9.1 | (91.4) | 8.9 | (89.9) |
| (c) Avoidance of Negative Interest Rates | | | | | 8.0 | | 8.0 | | 8.0 | | 8.0 | | 6.0 | |
| (d) Capital Transactions with Foreigners | 0.0 | | 0.0 | | 0.0 | | 0.0 | | 0.0 | | 0.0 | | 0.0 | |

# TRINIDAD & TOBAGO

| | 1970 | 1975 | 1980 | 1985 | 1990 | 1995 | 1997 |
|---|---|---|---|---|---|---|---|
| **Summary Ratings** | | 4.7 | 5.0 | 4.8 | 5.4 | 7.2 | 7.5 |
| **Rank** | | 55 | 61 | 69 | 57 | 45 | 39 |

| Components of Economic Freedom | 1970 | | 1975 | | 1980 | | 1985 | | 1990 | | 1995 | | 1997 | |
|---|---|---|---|---|---|---|---|---|---|---|---|---|---|---|
| **I. Size of Government** | **7.5** | | **6.7** | | **7.8** | | **5.7** | | **7.6** | | **8.1** | | **8.6** | |
| (a) Government Consumption (% of Total) | 7.5 | (17.9) | 6.7 | (22.4) | 7.0 | (20.8) | 5.4 | (29.5) | 7.7 | (16.8) | 7.7 | (17.1) | 8.6 | (11.9) |
| (b) Transfers and Subsidies (% of GDP) | | | | | 8.5 | (6.0) | 6.1 | (14.9) | 7.4 | (10.0) | 8.4 | (6.2) | | |
| **II. Structure of the Economy and Use of Markets** | | | | | | | **3.8** | | **5.3** | | **5.4** | | **5.9** | |
| (a) Government Enterprises | 2.0 | (45.9) | 2.0 | (45.8) | 2.0 | (47.6) | 2.0 | (40.6) | 4.0 | (34.6) | 4.0 | | 4.0 | |
| (b) Price Controls | | | | | | | | | 4.0 | | 6.0 | | 6.0 | |
| (c) Top Marginal Tax Rate | | | | | | | 4.0 | (50) | 7.0 | (35) | 5.0 | (38) | 7.0 | (35) |
| (d) Conscription | | | 10.0 | | 10.0 | | 10.0 | | 10.0 | | 10.0 | | 10.0 | |
| **III. Monetary Policy and Price Stability** | **9.1** | | **5.3** | | **5.4** | | **7.8** | | **8.1** | | **8.0** | | **8.5** | |
| (a) Annual Money Growth (last 5 yrs.) | 10.0 | (0.2) | 6.7 | (16.4) | 5.7 | (21.4) | 8.8 | (5.8) | 9.5 | (2.7) | 8.2 | (9.2) | 8.1 | (9.6) |
| (b) Inflation Variability (last 5 yrs.) | 8.2 | (4.5) | 3.1 | (17.3) | 5.9 | (10.3) | 6.7 | (8.3) | 7.8 | (5.5) | 6.4 | (9.0) | 8.2 | (4.5) |
| (c) Recent Inflation Rate | 9.2 | (4.0) | 6.0 | (20.1) | 4.5 | (27.5) | 8.0 | (10.1) | 6.9 | (15.5) | 9.3 | (3.8) | 9.2 | (4.2) |
| **IV. Freedom to Use Alternative Currencies** | **7.2** | | **0.7** | | **0.1** | | **1.1** | | **1.0** | | **9.7** | | **9.6** | |
| (a) Ownership of Foreign Currency | | | 0.0 | | 0.0 | | 0.0 | | 0.0 | | 10.0 | | 10.0 | |
| (b) Black Market Exchange Rates (Prem.) | 7.2 | (14.0) | 1.4 | (43.0) | 0.2 | (49.0) | 2.2 | (39.0) | 2.0 | (40.0) | 9.4 | (3.0) | 9.2 | (4.0) |
| **V. Legal Structure and Property Rights** | | | | | **6.2** | | **5.1** | | **6.6** | | **5.7** | | **5.4** | |
| (a) Private Ownership Rights | | | | | 5.2 | | 3.5 | | 7.3 | | 7.7 | | 7.2 | |
| (b) Viability of Contracts | | | | | 6.8 | | 5.2 | | 5.8 | | 5.2 | | 4.8 | |
| (c) Rule of Law | | | | | 6.7 | | 6.6 | | 6.7 | | 4.1 | | 4.1 | |
| **VI. International Exchange** | | | **7.0** | | **6.7** | | **5.4** | | **5.5** | | **6.8** | | | |
| (a) Taxes on International Trade | | | | | | | | | | | | | | |
| i. Taxes as a Percentage of Exports and Imports | | | 8.3 | (2.6) | 7.9 | (3.2) | 6.2 | (5.7) | 8.2 | (2.7) | 8.9 | (1.7) | | |
| ii. Mean Tariff Rate | | | | | | | 6.6 | (17.0) | 6.3 | (18.6) | 7.2 | (14.1) | | |
| iii. Standard Deviation of Tariff Rates | | | | | | | | | 3.9 | (15.3) | 4.9 | (12.7) | | |
| (b) Non-tariff Regulatory Trade Barriers | | | | | | | | | | | | | | |
| i. Non-tariff Trade Restraints (% of trade covered) | | | | | | | | | | | 7.7 | (23.4) | | |
| ii. Size of Trade Sector (% of GDP) | 3.9 | (84.4) | 3.8 | (88.2) | 3.6 | (89.4) | 0.1 | (61.0) | 0.9 | (70.9) | 3.0 | (97.1) | 2.7 | (95.0) |
| **VII. Freedom of Exchange in Financial Markets** | | | **4.1** | | **4.2** | | **5.8** | | **5.2** | | **7.4** | | **7.7** | |
| (a) Ownership of Banks | | | 5.0 | (40-75) | 5.0 | (40-75) | 8.0 | (75-90) | 8.0 | (75-90) | 8.0 | (75-90) | 8.0 | (75-90) |
| (b) Extension of Credit | 8.3 | (84.2) | 8.3 | (84.3) | 8.7 | (88.0) | 7.9 | (81.1) | 7.5 | (77.0) | 7.5 | (77.5) | 6.5 | (68.2) |
| (c) Avoidance of Negative Interest Rates | | | | | | | 8.0 | | 6.0 | | 6.0 | | 8.0 | |
| (d) Capital Transactions with Foreigners | 0.0 | | 0.0 | | 0.0 | | 0.0 | | 0.0 | | 8.0 | | 8.0 | |

# TUNISIA

| | 1970 | 1975 | 1980 | 1985 | 1990 | 1995 | 1997 |
|---|---|---|---|---|---|---|---|
| **Summary Ratings** | 4.3 | 4.5 | 4.4 | 4.1 | 5.0 | 6.1 | 6.3 |
| **Rank** | 48 | 59 | 75 | 87 | 67 | 67 | 70 |

| Components of Economic Freedom | 1970 | | 1975 | | 1980 | | 1985 | | 1990 | | 1995 | | 1997 | |
|---|---|---|---|---|---|---|---|---|---|---|---|---|---|---|
| **I. Size of Government** | **8.0** | | **8.4** | | **8.0** | | **7.5** | | **7.4** | | **7.5** | | **7.6** | |
| (a) Government Consumption (% of Total) | 7.0 | (20.7) | 7.2 | (19.8) | 7.3 | (19.0) | 6.7 | (22.5) | 7.1 | (20.5) | 7.0 | (21.1) | 7.0 | (20.7) |
| (b) Transfers and Subsidies (% of GDP) | 9.0 | (4.2) | 9.6 | (1.9) | 8.6 | (5.6) | 8.3 | (6.8) | 7.7 | (9.0) | 8.1 | (7.3) | 8.3 | (6.9) |
| **II. Structure of the Economy and Use of Markets** | | | | | **1.1** | | **1.1** | | **3.0** | | **3.9** | | **3.9** | |
| (a) Government Enterprises | 0.0 | (58.0) | 0.0 | (50.9) | 0.0 | (57.0) | 0.0 | (54.8) | 2.0 | (46.8) | 2.0 | (47.4) | 2.0 | |
| (b) Price Controls | | | | | | | | | 4.0 | | 6.0 | | 6.0 | |
| (c) Top Marginal Tax Rate | | | | | 2.0 | (62) | 2.0 | (62) | | | | | | |
| (d) Conscription | 3.0 | | 3.0 | | 3.0 | | 3.0 | | 3.0 | | 3.0 | | 3.0 | |
| **III. Monetary Policy and Price Stability** | **8.9** | | **7.8** | | **8.2** | | **8.4** | | **9.3** | | **9.3** | | **9.3** | |
| (a) Annual Money Growth (last 5 yrs.) | | | 7.3 | (13.3) | 8.5 | (7.5) | 7.7 | (11.5) | 9.6 | (1.8) | 9.4 | (2.9) | 8.8 | (5.8) |
| (b) Inflation Variability (last 5 yrs.) | 9.2 | (2.1) | 6.9 | (7.8) | 8.6 | (3.4) | 8.3 | (4.4) | 9.2 | (2.0) | 9.6 | (0.9) | 9.9 | (0.3) |
| (c) Recent Inflation Rate | 8.7 | (6.6) | 9.0 | (5.0) | 7.4 | (12.8) | 9.3 | (3.6) | 9.1 | (4.5) | 9.0 | (5.2) | 9.2 | (4.2) |
| **IV. Freedom to Use Alternative Currencies** | **2.0** | | **3.9** | | **3.2** | | **3.8** | | **4.2** | | **4.9** | | **4.7** | |
| (a) Ownership of Foreign Currency | 0.0 | | 0.0 | | 0.0 | | 0.0 | | 0.0 | | 0.0 | | 0.0 | |
| (b) Black Market Exchange Rates (Prem.) | 4.0 | (30.0) | 7.8 | (11.0) | 6.4 | (18.0) | 7.6 | (12.0) | 8.4 | (8.0) | 9.8 | (1.0) | 9.4 | (3.0) |
| **V. Legal Structure and Property Rights** | **3.2** | | **2.5** | | **4.6** | | **3.1** | | **3.3** | | **6.3** | | **8.5** | |
| (a) Private Ownership Rights | 3.6 | | 3.0 | | 2.2 | | 3.5 | | 3.2 | | 7.7 | | 10.0 | |
| (b) Viability of Contracts | 2.7 | | 1.9 | | 3.7 | | 2.8 | | 3.4 | | 6.8 | | 8.3 | |
| (c) Rule of Law | | | | | 8.3 | | 3.1 | | 3.3 | | 4.1 | | 7.0 | |
| **VI. International Exchange** | **3.7** | | **3.6** | | **4.8** | | **3.3** | | **3.3** | | **5.2** | | **4.6** | |
| (a) Taxes on International Trade | | | | | | | | | | | | | | |
| i. Taxes as a Percentage of Exports and Imports | 3.5 | (9.7) | 2.9 | (10.7) | 4.0 | (9.0) | 1.1 | (13.3) | 3.7 | (9.5) | 4.0 | (9.0) | 4.1 | (8.9) |
| ii. Mean Tariff Rate | | | | | 4.7 | (26.4) | 5.2 | (24.0) | 4.5 | (27.5) | 4.5 | (27.5) | 4.5 | (27.6) |
| iii. Standard Deviation of Tariff Rates | | | | | | | | | 0.0 | (37.4) | 5.3 | (11.7) | | |
| (b) Non-tariff Regulatory Trade Barriers | | | | | | | | | | | | | | |
| i. Non-tariff Trade Restraints (% of trade covered) | | | | | | | 2.4 | (76.2) | 3.6 | (63.7) | 6.7 | (32.7) | | |
| ii. Size of Trade Sector (% of GDP) | 4.2 | (46.7) | 5.7 | (64.0) | 7.3 | (85.8) | 5.7 | (70.2) | 7.3 | (94.2) | 6.9 | (93.4) | 6.2 | (86.1) |
| **VII. Freedom of Exchange in Financial Markets** | **3.2** | | **3.3** | | **3.3** | | **3.8** | | **6.5** | | **6.7** | | **6.7** | |
| (a) Ownership of Banks | 2.0 | (10-40) | 2.0 | (10-40) | 2.0 | (10-40) | 2.0 | (35) | 5.0 | (40-60) | 5.0 | (40-60) | 5.0 | (40-60) |
| (b) Extension of Credit | 8.8 | (88.9) | 9.3 | (93.2) | 8.5 | (86.7) | 8.6 | (87.4) | 8.8 | (88.7) | 9.6 | (96.5) | 9.3 | (93.9) |
| (c) Avoidance of Negative Interest Rates | | | | | 4.0 | | 6.0 | | 8.0 | | 8.0 | | 8.0 | |
| (d) Capital Transactions with Foreigners | 0.0 | | 0.0 | | 0.0 | | 0.0 | | 5.0 | | 5.0 | | 5.0 | |

# TURKEY

| | 1970 | 1975 | 1980 | 1985 | 1990 | 1995 | 1997 |
|---|---|---|---|---|---|---|---|
| **Summary Ratings** | 3.0 | 3.3 | 3.3 | 4.5 | 5.1 | 6.3 | 6.6 |
| **Rank** | 57 | 74 | 99 | 76 | 64 | 60 | 62 |

| Components of Economic Freedom | 1970 | | 1975 | | 1980 | | 1985 | | 1990 | | 1995 | | 1997 | |
|---|---|---|---|---|---|---|---|---|---|---|---|---|---|---|
| **I. Size of Government** | **8.6** | | **8.2** | | **8.2** | | **8.0** | | **8.7** | | **8.0** | | **7.3** | |
| (a) Government Consumption (% of Total) | 7.7 | (16.9) | 7.9 | (15.7) | 7.9 | (15.9) | 8.7 | (11.4) | 8.3 | (13.8) | 8.4 | (13.3) | 8.0 | (15.3) |
| (b) Transfers and Subsidies (% of GDP) | 9.5 | (2.4) | 8.5 | (6.0) | 8.5 | (6.0) | 7.3 | (10.4) | 9.1 | (3.9) | 7.7 | (9.1) | 6.6 | (13.0) |
| **II. Structure of the Economy and Use of Markets** | | | **0.4** | | **0.0** | | **0.8** | | **4.4** | | **4.7** | | **5.4** | |
| (a) Government Enterprises | 0.0 | (51.6) | 0.0 | (56.7) | 0.0 | (62.9) | 0.0 | (56.3) | 4.0 | (38.4) | 6.0 | (19.2) | 6.0 | |
| (b) Price Controls | | | | | | | | | 6.0 | | 5.0 | | 7.0 | |
| (c) Top Marginal Tax Rate | | | 1.0 | (68) | 0.0 | (75) | 2.0 | (63) | 4.0 | (50) | 4.0 | (55) | 4.0 | (55) |
| (d) Conscription | 0.0 | | 0.0 | | 0.0 | | 0.0 | | 1.0 | | 1.0 | | 1.0 | |
| **III. Monetary Policy and Price Stability** | **5.5** | | **6.4** | | **0.6** | | **3.1** | | **1.1** | | **0.9** | | **1.6** | |
| (a) Annual Money Growth (last 5 yrs.) | 0.0 | (-64.6) | 5.7 | (21.6) | 1.9 | (40.6) | 3.7 | (31.7) | 0.2 | (49.0) | 0.0 | (61.9) | 0.0 | (77.0) |
| (b) Inflation Variability (last 5 yrs.) | 8.2 | (4.5) | 7.6 | (6.0) | 0.0 | (27.8) | 5.7 | (10.7) | 3.1 | (17.2) | 2.8 | (17.9) | 4.8 | (13.1) |
| (c) Recent Inflation Rate | 8.2 | (8.8) | 5.9 | (20.5) | 0.0 | (85.0) | 0.0 | (52.2) | 0.0 | (58.2) | 0.0 | (87.0) | 0.0 | (81.2) |
| **IV. Freedom to Use Alternative Currencies** | **0.0** | | **3.9** | | **3.4** | | **4.7** | | **9.8** | | **9.8** | | **9.9** | |
| (a) Ownership of Foreign Currency | 0.0 | | 0.0 | | 0.0 | | 0.0 | | 10.0 | | 10.0 | | 10.0 | |
| (b) Black Market Exchange Rates (Prem.) | 0.0 | (55.0) | 7.8 | (11.0) | 6.8 | (16.0) | 9.4 | (3.0) | 9.6 | (2.0) | 9.6 | (2.0) | 9.8 | (1.0) |
| **V. Legal Structure and Property Rights** | **3.8** | | **3.1** | | **5.2** | | **5.6** | | **4.4** | | **6.3** | | **6.0** | |
| (a) Private Ownership Rights | 4.5 | | 2.3 | | 4.0 | | 4.8 | | 5.9 | | 7.7 | | 7.2 | |
| (b) Viability of Contracts | 3.1 | | 3.9 | | 3.7 | | 4.0 | | 4.0 | | 6.8 | | 6.6 | |
| (c) Rule of Law | | | | | 8.3 | | 8.2 | | 3.3 | | 4.1 | | 4.1 | |
| **VI. International Exchange** | **0.0** | | **0.3** | | **2.9** | | **4.6** | | **3.6** | | **6.5** | | **8.3** | |
| (a) Taxes on International Trade | | | | | | | | | | | | | | |
| i. Taxes as a Percentage of Exports and Imports | 0.0 | (16.4) | 0.4 | (14.4) | 5.8 | (6.3) | 8.0 | (3.0) | 8.1 | (2.8) | 9.0 | (1.5) | 9.4 | (0.9) |
| ii. Mean Tariff Rate | | | | | 1.2 | (44.0) | 4.7 | (26.6) | 5.5 | (22.7) | 8.2 | (9.0) | 8.3 | (8.4) |
| iii. Standard Deviation of Tariff Rates | | | | | | | | | 0.0 | (35.7) | 7.7 | (5.7) | | |
| (b) Non-tariff Regulatory Trade Barriers | | | | | | | | | | | | | | |
| i. Non-tariff Trade Restraints (% of trade covered) | | | | | | | 0.3 | (97.2) | 0.4 | (96.4) | 0.4 | (96.4) | | |
| ii. Size of Trade Sector (% of GDP) | 0.0 | (10.3) | 0.0 | (15.0) | 0.0 | (17.1) | 4.5 | (34.8) | 3.5 | (30.9) | 5.2 | (44.2) | 5.7 | (49.0) |
| **VII. Freedom of Exchange in Financial Markets** | | | **3.8** | | **2.9** | | **4.8** | | **3.9** | | **6.2** | | **6.0** | |
| (a) Ownership of Banks | | | 8.0 | (75-90) | 8.0 | (75-90) | 8.0 | (82) | 8.0 | (75-90) | 8.0 | (75-90) | 8.0 | (75-90) |
| (b) Extension of Credit | 5.6 | (60.4) | 5.4 | (58.9) | 3.3 | (39.8) | 3.3 | (39.6) | 5.8 | (62.1) | 7.1 | (73.4) | 6.4 | (67.6) |
| (c) Avoidance of Negative Interest Rates | | | 2.0 | | 0.0 | | 8.0 | | 2.0 | | 8.0 | | 8.0 | |
| (d) Capital Transactions with Foreigners | 0.0 | | 0.0 | | 0.0 | | 0.0 | | 0.0 | | 2.0 | | 2.0 | |

# UGANDA

| | 1970 | 1975 | 1980 | 1985 | 1990 | 1995 | 1997 |
|---|---|---|---|---|---|---|---|
| **Summary Ratings** | | | 2.8 | 2.7 | 2.7 | 4.6 | 6.1 |
| **Rank** | | | 103 | 106 | 111 | 100 | 78 |

| Components of Economic Freedom | 1970 | | 1975 | | 1980 | | 1985 | | 1990 | | 1995 | | 1997 | |
|---|---|---|---|---|---|---|---|---|---|---|---|---|---|---|
| **I. Size of Government** | | | | | | | **8.0** | | **9.5** | | **8.9** | | **8.9** | |
| (a) Government Consumption (% of Total) | | | | | | | 8.0 | (15.5) | 9.5 | (7.5) | 8.9 | (10.5) | 8.9 | (10.7) |
| (b) Transfers and Subsidies (% of GDP) | | | | | | | | | | | | | | |
| **II. Structure of the Economy and Use of Markets** | | | | | | | **2.3** | | **2.3** | | **4.9** | | **5.5** | |
| (a) Government Enterprises | 4.0 | (31.5) | 2.0 | (42.8) | 2.0 | | 2.0 | (26.4) | 2.0 | (47.6) | 2.0 | | 2.0 | |
| (b) Price Controls | | | | | | | | | 0.0 | | 4.0 | | 6.0 | |
| (c) Top Marginal Tax Rate | | | | | | | 0.0 | (70) | 3.0 | (50) | 8.0 | (30) | 8.0 | (30) |
| (d) Conscription | 10.0 | | 10.0 | | 10.0 | | 10.0 | | 10.0 | | 10.0 | | 10.0 | |
| **III. Monetary Policy and Price Stability** | | | **4.7** | | **1.6** | | **0.0** | | **0.4** | | **5.4** | | **7.5** | |
| (a) Annual Money Growth (last 5 yrs.) | | | 5.5 | (22.5) | 3.1 | (34.4) | 0.0 | (76.2) | 0.0 | (410.0) | 3.7 | (31.5) | 7.4 | (12.9) |
| (b) Inflation Variability (last 5 yrs.) | | | 3.8 | (15.5) | 0.0 | (33.8) | 0.0 | (40.8) | 0.0 | (52.4) | 4.4 | (14.1) | 6.3 | (9.3) |
| (c) Recent Inflation Rate | 1.7 | (41.6) | | | | | 0.0 | (120.4) | 1.1 | (44.4) | 8.2 | (9.2) | 8.7 | (6.7) |
| **IV. Freedom to Use Alternative Currencies** | **1.9** | | **0.0** | | **0.0** | | **2.5** | | **1.0** | | **4.7** | | **9.2** | |
| (a) Ownership of Foreign Currency | 0.0 | | 0.0 | | 0.0 | | 0.0 | | 0.0 | | 0.0 | | 10.0 | |
| (b) Black Market Exchange Rates (Prem.) | 3.8 | (31.0) | 0.0 | (390.0) | 0.0 | (360.0) | 5.0 | (25.0) | 2.0 | (40.0) | 9.4 | (3.0) | 8.4 | (8.0) |
| **V. Legal Structure and Property Rights** | | | | | **2.5** | | **2.6** | | **2.1** | | **1.5** | | **4.5** | |
| (a) Private Ownership Rights | | | | | 2.8 | | 3.5 | | 1.9 | | 0.0 | | 4.4 | |
| (b) Viability of Contracts | | | | | 3.0 | | 2.8 | | 2.8 | | 0.5 | | 4.8 | |
| (c) Rule of Law | | | | | 1.7 | | 1.4 | | 1.7 | | 4.1 | | 4.1 | |
| **VI. International Exchange** | | | **0.0** | | **7.2** | | **2.3** | | **2.3** | | **5.9** | | | |
| (a) Taxes on International Trade | | | | | | | | | | | | | | |
| i. Taxes as a Percentage of Exports and Imports | | | 0.0 | (20.4) | 7.9 | (3.1) | 2.3 | (11.6) | 2.8 | (10.8) | 3.2 | (10.2) | | |
| ii. Mean Tariff Rate | | | | | | | 4.0 | (30.0) | 4.0 | (30.1) | 6.6 | (17.1) | | |
| iii. Standard Deviation of Tariff Rates | | | | | | | | | | | 6.4 | (9.1) | | |
| (b) Non-tariff Regulatory Trade Barriers | | | | | | | | | | | | | | |
| i. Non-tariff Trade Restraints (% of trade covered) | | | | | | | 0.1 | (99.0) | 0.1 | (99.0) | 9.5 | (5.0) | | |
| ii. Size of Trade Sector (% of GDP) | 5.5 | (43.5) | 0.0 | (19.6) | 5.3 | (45.5) | 2.1 | (28.7) | 1.1 | (26.6) | 2.4 | (32.4) | 2.7 | (33.9) |
| **VII. Freedom of Exchange in Financial Markets** | | | **2.2** | | **1.7** | | **1.7** | | **2.1** | | **2.9** | | **3.1** | |
| (a) Ownership of Banks | | | 2.0 | (10-40) | 2.0 | (10-40) | 2.0 | (10-40) | 2.0 | (10-40) | 2.0 | (10-40) | 2.0 | (10-40) |
| (b) Extension of Credit | 7.4 | (76.3) | 5.2 | (56.6) | 5.4 | (58.3) | 5.3 | (57.3) | 7.4 | (76.9) | 6.5 | (68.5) | 4.9 | (54.0) |
| (c) Avoidance of Negative Interest Rates | | | | | 0.0 | | 0.0 | | 0.0 | | 4.0 | | 6.0 | |
| (d) Capital Transactions with Foreigners | 0.0 | | 0.0 | | 0.0 | | 0.0 | | 0.0 | | 0.0 | | 0.0 | |

# UKRAINE

| | 1970 | 1975 | 1980 | 1985 | 1990 | 1995 | 1997 |
|---|---|---|---|---|---|---|---|
| **Summary Ratings** | | | | | | 3.1 | 4.5 |
| **Rank** | | | | | | 121 | 110 |

| Components of Economic Freedom | 1970 | 1975 | | 1980 | | 1985 | | 1990 | | 1995 | | 1997 | |
|---|---|---|---|---|---|---|---|---|---|---|---|---|---|
| **I. Size of Government** | | | | **6.4** | | **6.2** | | **6.7** | | **5.7** | | **6.0** | |
| (a) Government Consumption (% of Total) | | | | 6.4 | (24.2) | 6.2 | (25.0) | 6.7 | (22.4) | 5.7 | (27.8) | 6.0 | (26.3) |
| (b) Transfers and Subsidies (% of GDP) | | | | | | | | | | | | | |
| **II. Structure of the Economy and Use of Markets** | | | | | | | | | | **1.8** | | **2.7** | |
| (a) Government Enterprises | | | | | | | | | | 0.0 | | 0.0 | |
| (b) Price Controls | | | | | | | | 0.0 | | 4.0 | | 6.0 | |
| (c) Top Marginal Tax Rate | | | | | | | | | | | | | |
| (d) Conscription | | | | | | | | | | 0.0 | | 0.0 | |
| **III. Monetary Policy and Price Stability** | | | | | | | | | | **0.0** | | **2.2** | |
| (a) Annual Money Growth (last 5 yrs.) | | | | | | | | | | | | 0.0 | (245.9) |
| (b) Inflation Variability (last 5 yrs.) | | | | | | | | | | 0.0 | (1158.3) | 0.0 | (1234.8) |
| (c) Recent Inflation Rate | | | | | | | | 6.7 | (16.3) | 0.0 | (415.5) | 6.6 | (17.2) |
| **IV. Freedom to Use Alternative Currencies** | | **0.0** | | **0.0** | | **0.0** | | **2.5** | | **7.2** | | **7.2** | |
| (a) Ownership of Foreign Currency | | | | | | | | 5.0 | | 5.0 | | 5.0 | |
| (b) Black Market Exchange Rates (Prem.) | | 0.0 | (391.0) | 0.0 | (359.0) | 0.0 | (637.0) | 0.0 | (1969.0) | 9.4 | (3.0) | 9.4 | (3.0) |
| **V. Legal Structure and Property Rights** | | | | | | | | | | | | **5.1** | |
| (a) Private Ownership Rights | | | | | | | | | | | | 7.2 | |
| (b) Viability of Contracts | | | | | | | | | | | | 4.0 | |
| (c) Rule of Law | | | | | | | | | | | | 4.1 | |
| **VI. International Exchange** | | | | | | | | | | | | **7.3** | |
| (a) Taxes on International Trade | | | | | | | | | | | | | |
| i. Taxes as a Percentage of Exports and Imports | | | | | | | | | | | | | |
| ii. Mean Tariff Rate | | | | | | | | | | | | 8.0 | (10.1) |
| iii. Standard Deviation of Tariff Rates | | | | | | | | | | | | 5.6 | (11.0) |
| (b) Non-tariff Regulatory Trade Barriers | | | | | | | | | | | | | |
| i. Non-tariff Trade Restraints (% of trade covered) | | | | | | | | | | | | | |
| ii. Size of Trade Sector (% of GDP) | | | | | | | | 7.0 | (56.3) | 10.0 | (97.3) | 9.5 | (84.8) |
| **VII. Freedom of Exchange in Financial Markets** | | | | | | | | | | **0.7** | | **0.9** | |
| (a) Ownership of Banks | | | | | | | | 0.0 | (0) | 0.0 | (0-10) | 0.0 | (0-10) |
| (b) Extension of Credit | | | | | | | | | | 0.8 | (17.2) | 1.5 | (23.5) |
| (c) Avoidance of Negative Interest Rates | | | | | | | | | | 0.0 | | 0.0 | |
| (d) Capital Transactions with Foreigners | 0.0 | 0.0 | | 0.0 | | 0.0 | | 0.0 | | 2.0 | | 2.0 | |

# UNITED ARAB EMIRATES

| | 1970 | 1975 | 1980 | 1985 | 1990 | 1995 | 1997 |
|---|---|---|---|---|---|---|---|
| **Summary Ratings** | | | 6.1 | 6.9 | 7.6 | | 7.2 |
| **Rank** | | | 31 | 21 | 19 | | 49 |

| Components of Economic Freedom | 1970 | 1975 | | 1980 | | 1985 | | 1990 | | 1995 | | 1997 | |
|---|---|---|---|---|---|---|---|---|---|---|---|---|---|
| **I. Size of Government** | | **4.5** | | **3.7** | | **3.1** | | **7.6** | | **7.9** | | **6.1** | |
| (a) Government Consumption (% of Total) | | 4.5 | (34.4) | 3.7 | (38.7) | 3.1 | (41.8) | 5.3 | (30.1) | 5.9 | (26.8) | 6.1 | (26.0) |
| (b) Transfers and Subsidies (% of GDP) | | | | | | | | 9.8 | (1.2) | 9.9 | (1.0) | | |
| **II. Structure of the Economy and Use of Markets** | | | | | | | | | | | | **8.0** | |
| (a) Government Enterprises | | | | | | | | | | | | 6.0 | |
| (b) Price Controls | | | | | | | | 8.0 | | 8.0 | | 8.0 | |
| (c) Top Marginal Tax Rate | | | | | | | | | | | | 10.0 | (0) |
| (d) Conscription | | | | 3.0 | | 10.0 | | 10.0 | | 10.0 | | 10.0 | |
| **III. Monetary Policy and Price Stability** | | | | **7.2** | | **9.0** | | **9.4** | | | | | |
| (a) Annual Money Growth (last 5 yrs.) | | | | 5.5 | (22.7) | 9.8 | (-0.9) | 9.7 | (1.5) | 7.2 | (13.8) | 8.1 | (9.3) |
| (b) Inflation Variability (last 5 yrs.) | | | | 8.1 | (4.8) | 8.1 | (4.8) | 9.3 | (1.7) | | | | |
| (c) Recent Inflation Rate | | 6.2 | (19.0) | 8.2 | (9.1) | 9.1 | (4.5) | 9.2 | (4.1) | | | | |
| **IV. Freedom to Use Alternative Currencies** | | **10.0** | | **10.0** | | **10.0** | | **10.0** | | **10.0** | | **10.0** | |
| (a) Ownership of Foreign Currency | | 10.0 | | 10.0 | | 10.0 | | 10.0 | | 10.0 | | 10.0 | |
| (b) Black Market Exchange Rates (Prem.) | | 10.0 | (0.0) | 10.0 | (0.0) | 10.0 | (0.0) | 10.0 | (0.0) | 10.0 | (0.0) | 10.0 | (0.0) |
| **V. Legal Structure and Property Rights** | | | | **1.9** | | **4.8** | | **5.4** | | **6.3** | | **6.0** | |
| (a) Private Ownership Rights | | | | 0.8 | | 4.8 | | 4.6 | | 7.7 | | 7.2 | |
| (b) Viability of Contracts | | | | 3.0 | | 1.6 | | 3.4 | | 6.8 | | 6.6 | |
| (c) Rule of Law | | | | 1.7 | | 8.2 | | 8.3 | | 4.1 | | 4.1 | |
| **VI. International Exchange** | | | | | | **8.9** | | **8.9** | | | | | |
| (a) Taxes on International Trade | | | | | | | | | | | | | |
| i. Taxes as a Percentage of Exports and Imports | | | | | | 10.0 | (0.0) | 10.0 | (0.0) | | | | |
| ii. Mean Tariff Rate | | | | | | 9.2 | (4.0) | | | | | | |
| iii. Standard Deviation of Tariff Rates | | | | | | | | | | | | | |
| (b) Non-tariff Regulatory Trade Barriers | | | | | | | | | | | | | |
| i. Non-tariff Trade Restraints (% of trade covered) | | | | | | | | | | | | | |
| ii. Size of Trade Sector (% of GDP) | | 5.5 | (103.2) | 6.4 | (112.4) | 5.0 | (89.7) | 5.9 | (107.3) | 7.7 | (141.8) | 7.6 | (141.5) |
| **VII. Freedom of Exchange in Financial Markets** | | **7.9** | | **7.8** | | **5.6** | | **5.8** | | **5.7** | | **5.8** | |
| (a) Ownership of Banks | | 5.0 | (40-75) | 5.0 | (40-75) | 5.0 | (40-75) | 5.0 | (40-75) | 5.0 | (40-75) | 5.0 | (40-75) |
| (b) Extension of Credit | | 9.0 | (90.8) | 8.6 | (87.0) | 7.1 | (73.4) | 7.8 | (79.7) | 7.5 | (77.2) | 8.0 | (81.6) |
| (c) Avoidance of Negative Interest Rates | | | | | | | | | | | | | |
| (d) Capital Transactions with Foreigners | | 10.0 | | 10.0 | | 5.0 | | 5.0 | | 5.0 | | 5.0 | |

# UNITED KINGDOM

| | 1970 | 1975 | 1980 | 1985 | 1990 | 1995 | 1997 |
|---|---|---|---|---|---|---|---|
| **Summary Ratings** | 6.6 | 5.9 | 6.8 | 8.2 | 8.6 | 8.8 | 8.9 |
| **Rank** | 24 | 33 | 16 | 6 | 4 | 5 | 5 |

| Components of Economic Freedom | 1970 | | 1975 | | 1980 | | 1985 | | 1990 | | 1995 | | 1997 | |
|---|---|---|---|---|---|---|---|---|---|---|---|---|---|---|
| **I. Size of Government** | **6.7** | | **6.0** | | **5.9** | | **5.7** | | **6.2** | | **5.8** | | **5.9** | |
| (a) Government Consumption (% of Total) | 6.7 | (22.6) | 5.9 | (26.6) | 5.9 | (26.6) | 6.1 | (25.9) | 6.3 | (24.6) | 6.2 | (25.2) | 6.3 | (24.9) |
| (b) Transfers and Subsidies (% of GDP) | | | 6.0 | (15.0) | 5.8 | (15.8) | 5.3 | (17.9) | 6.1 | (14.9) | 5.3 | (17.7) | 5.5 | (17.0) |
| **II. Structure of the Economy and Use of Markets** | | | **2.3** | | **3.3** | | **5.0** | | **7.4** | | **7.8** | | **8.0** | |
| (a) Government Enterprises | 2.0 | (43.4) | 2.0 | (41.8) | 4.0 | (29.1) | 6.0 | (23.5) | 8.0 | (15.3) | 8.0 | (16.4) | 8.0 | (14.5) |
| (b) Price Controls | | | | | | | | | 8.0 | | 9.0 | | 9.0 | |
| (c) Top Marginal Tax Rate | | | 0.0 | (83) | 0.0 | (83) | 2.0 | (60) | 5.0 | (40) | 5.0 | (40) | 6.0 | (40) |
| (d) Conscription | 10.0 | | 10.0 | | 10.0 | | 10.0 | | 10.0 | | 10.0 | | 10.0 | |
| **III. Monetary Policy and Price Stability** | **9.0** | | **6.7** | | **7.8** | | **8.5** | | **7.5** | | **9.3** | | **9.1** | |
| (a) Annual Money Growth (last 5 yrs.) | | | 8.0 | (9.8) | 8.0 | (9.9) | 7.8 | (10.9) | 4.3 | (28.7) | 9.0 | (4.9) | 8.1 | (9.6) |
| (b) Inflation Variability (last 5 yrs.) | 9.4 | (1.5) | 7.2 | (7.0) | 9.0 | (2.4) | 9.0 | (2.5) | 9.4 | (1.4) | 9.3 | (1.7) | 9.8 | (0.6) |
| (c) Recent Inflation Rate | 8.5 | (7.3) | 4.7 | (26.3) | 6.2 | (18.8) | 8.8 | (5.9) | 8.7 | (6.4) | 9.5 | (2.4) | 9.5 | (2.7) |
| **IV. Freedom to Use Alternative Currencies** | **5.0** | | **5.0** | | **5.0** | | **10.0** | | **10.0** | | **10.0** | | **10.0** | |
| (a) Ownership of Foreign Currency | 0.0 | | 0.0 | | 0.0 | | 10.0 | | 10.0 | | 10.0 | | 10.0 | |
| (b) Black Market Exchange Rates (Prem.) | 10.0 | (0.0) | 10.0 | (0.0) | 10.0 | (0.0) | 10.0 | (0.0) | 10.0 | (0.0) | 10.0 | (0.0) | 10.0 | (0.0) |
| **V. Legal Structure and Property Rights** | **9.8** | | **7.0** | | **8.2** | | **8.5** | | **9.5** | | **9.5** | | **10.0** | |
| (a) Private Ownership Rights | 9.6 | | 10.0 | | 6.4 | | 8.7 | | 10.0 | | 10.0 | | 10.0 | |
| (b) Viability of Contracts | 10.0 | | 3.9 | | 8.5 | | 10.0 | | 10.0 | | 8.4 | | 10.0 | |
| (c) Rule of Law | | | | | 10.0 | | 6.6 | | 8.3 | | 10.0 | | 10.0 | |
| **VI. International Exchange** | **3.4** | | **8.6** | | **8.6** | | **8.7** | | **8.3** | | **8.5** | | **8.5** | |
| (a) Taxes on International Trade | | | | | | | | | | | | | | |
| i. Taxes as a Percentage of Exports and Imports | 2.1 | (11.9) | 9.5 | (0.7) | 9.5 | (0.7) | 9.6 | (0.6) | 9.6 | (0.6) | 9.6 | (0.6) | 9.7 | (0.5) |
| ii. Mean Tariff Rate | | | 8.1 | (9.4) | 8.2 | (8.8) | 8.5 | (7.5) | 8.5 | (7.4) | 8.7 | (6.7) | 8.6 | (6.9) |
| iii. Standard Deviation of Tariff Rates | | | | | | | | | 7.1 | (7.2) | 7.6 | (5.9) | 7.6 | (6.0) |
| (b) Non-tariff Regulatory Trade Barriers | | | | | | | | | | | | | | |
| i. Non-tariff Trade Restraints (% of trade covered) | | | | | 8.9 | (11.2) | 8.7 | (12.8) | 8.9 | (10.9) | 9.1 | (9.0) | 9.3 | (6.7) |
| ii. Size of Trade Sector (% of GDP) | 6.8 | (45.2) | 7.5 | (53.6) | 6.9 | (52.3) | 7.0 | (56.6) | 5.9 | (51.5) | 6.3 | (57.7) | 6.1 | (57.3) |
| **VII. Freedom of Exchange in Financial Markets** | **6.5** | | **5.7** | | **8.0** | | **9.8** | | **10.0** | | **9.9** | | **10.0** | |
| (a) Ownership of Banks | 10.0 | (100) | 10.0 | (100) | 10.0 | (100) | 10.0 | (100) | 10.0 | (100) | 10.0 | (100) | 10.0 | (100) |
| (b) Extension of Credit | 6.2 | (65.3) | 7.0 | (72.5) | 7.8 | (79.9) | 9.0 | (91.1) | 9.8 | (97.8) | 9.7 | (97.0) | 9.8 | (98.5) |
| (c) Avoidance of Negative Interest Rates | 8.0 | | 4.0 | | 4.0 | | 10.0 | | 10.0 | | 10.0 | | 10.0 | |
| (d) Capital Transactions with Foreigners | 2.0 | | 2.0 | | 10.0 | | 10.0 | | 10.0 | | 10.0 | | 10.0 | |

# United States

| | 1970 | 1975 | 1980 | 1985 | 1990 | 1995 | 1997 |
|---|---|---|---|---|---|---|---|
| **Summary Ratings** | 8.0 | 8.1 | 8.5 | 8.6 | 8.8 | 8.9 | 9.0 |
| **Rank** | 11 | 3 | 3 | 4 | 3 | 4 | 4 |

| Components of Economic Freedom | 1970 | | 1975 | | 1980 | | 1985 | | 1990 | | 1995 | | 1997 | |
|---|---|---|---|---|---|---|---|---|---|---|---|---|---|---|
| **I. Size of Government** | **6.7** | | **6.9** | | **7.1** | | **6.8** | | **6.8** | | **6.8** | | **6.9** | |
| (a) Government Consumption (% of Total) | 6.7 | (22.6) | 6.8 | (22.2) | 6.9 | (21.2) | 6.9 | (21.5) | 7.0 | (20.8) | 7.3 | (19.0) | 7.4 | (18.7) |
| (b) Transfers and Subsidies (% of GDP) | | | 7.1 | (11.1) | 7.2 | (10.9) | 6.7 | (12.5) | 6.7 | (12.7) | 6.3 | (14.0) | 6.4 | (13.8) |
| **II. Structure of the Economy and Use of Markets** | **3.4** | | **4.8** | | **5.3** | | **6.8** | | **7.9** | | **8.3** | | **8.3** | |
| (a) Government Enterprises | 7.0 | (23.8) | 7.0 | (21.7) | 8.0 | (17.2) | 8.0 | (17.3) | 8.0 | (20.0) | 8.0 | (17.1) | 8.0 | (15.5) |
| (b) Price Controls | | | | | | | | | 8.0 | | 9.0 | | 9.0 | |
| (c) Top Marginal Tax Rate | 0.0 | (70-75) | 0.0 | (70-75) | 0.0 | (70-75) | 4.0 | (50-59) | 7.0 | (33-42) | 7.0 | (40-47) | 7.0 | (40-47) |
| (d) Conscription | 0.0 | | 10.0 | | 10.0 | | 10.0 | | 10.0 | | 10.0 | | 10.0 | |
| **III. Monetary Policy and Price Stability** | **9.4** | | **8.9** | | **8.9** | | **9.1** | | **9.4** | | **9.6** | | **9.8** | |
| (a) Annual Money Growth (last 5 yrs.) | 9.7 | (1.5) | 9.4 | (3.1) | 9.0 | (5.1) | 8.9 | (5.5) | 9.4 | (2.9) | 9.3 | (3.3) | 10.0 | (-0.2) |
| (b) Inflation Variability (last 5 yrs.) | 9.6 | (0.9) | 9.3 | (1.7) | 9.5 | (1.2) | 9.0 | (2.4) | 9.7 | (0.7) | 9.7 | (0.6) | 9.5 | (1.2) |
| (c) Recent Inflation Rate | 9.0 | (5.1) | 8.2 | (9.2) | 8.1 | (9.5) | 9.3 | (3.5) | 9.1 | (4.3) | 9.6 | (2.0) | 9.8 | (-0.8) |
| **IV. Freedom to Use Alternative Currencies** | 10.0 | | 10.0 | | 10.0 | | 10.0 | | 10.0 | | 10.0 | | 10.0 | |
| (a) Ownership of Foreign Currency | 10.0 | | 10.0 | | 10.0 | | 10.0 | | 10.0 | | 10.0 | | 10.0 | |
| (b) Black Market Exchange Rates (Prem.) | 10.0 | (0.0) | 10.0 | (0.0) | 10.0 | (0.0) | 10.0 | (0.0) | 10.0 | (0.0) | 10.0 | (0.0) | 10.0 | (0.0) |
| **V. Legal Structure and Property Rights** | **10.0** | | **9.2** | | **9.4** | | **9.6** | | **9.6** | | **9.5** | | **10.0** | |
| (a) Private Ownership Rights | 10.0 | | 9.4 | | 10.0 | | 10.0 | | 10.0 | | 10.0 | | 10.0 | |
| (b) Viability of Contracts | 10.0 | | 9.0 | | 8.1 | | 8.8 | | 8.8 | | 8.4 | | 10.0 | |
| (c) Rule of Law | | | | | 10.0 | | 10.0 | | 10.0 | | 10.0 | | 10.0 | |
| **VI. International Exchange** | **6.5** | | **7.7** | | **8.4** | | **8.0** | | **7.9** | | **8.0** | | **7.8** | |
| (a) Taxes on International Trade | | | | | | | | | | | | | | |
| i. Taxes as a Percentage of Exports and Imports | 8.4 | (2.4) | 9.0 | (1.5) | 9.3 | (1.1) | 8.9 | (1.7) | 9.0 | (1.5) | 9.2 | (1.2) | 9.4 | (0.9) |
| ii. Mean Tariff Rate | | | 7.9 | (10.3) | 8.5 | (7.3) | 8.7 | (6.6) | 8.8 | (6.2) | 8.8 | (5.9) | 9.1 | (4.3) |
| iii. Standard Deviation of Tariff Rates | | | | | | | | | 6.9 | (7.7) | 6.9 | (7.8) | 5.0 | (12.4) |
| (b) Non-tariff Regulatory Trade Barriers | | | | | | | | | | | | | | |
| i. Non-tariff Trade Restraints (% of trade covered) | | | | | 8.9 | (11.4) | 8.3 | (17.3) | 8.3 | (16.6) | 8.3 | (17.0) | 9.2 | (7.7) |
| ii. Size of Trade Sector (% of GDP) | 1.6 | (11.4) | 3.8 | (16.4) | 4.9 | (21.1) | 3.6 | (17.6) | 4.3 | (21.2) | 4.7 | (24.1) | 4.8 | (24.9) |
| **VII. Freedom of Exchange in Financial Markets** | **9.5** | | **9.1** | | **9.7** | | **9.6** | | **9.7** | | **9.7** | | **9.7** | |
| (a) Ownership of Banks | 10.0 | (100) | 10.0 | (100) | 10.0 | (100) | 10.0 | (100) | 10.0 | (100) | 10.0 | (100) | 10.0 | (100) |
| (b) Extension of Credit | 7.8 | (80.0) | 8.1 | (83.1) | 8.4 | (85.4) | 8.2 | (83.9) | 8.8 | (89.2) | 8.7 | (87.8) | 8.6 | (87.7) |
| (c) Avoidance of Negative Interest Rates | 10.0 | | 8.0 | | 10.0 | | 10.0 | | 10.0 | | 10.0 | | 10.0 | |
| (d) Capital Transactions with Foreigners | 10.0 | | 10.0 | | 10.0 | | 10.0 | | 10.0 | | 10.0 | | 10.0 | |

# URUGUAY

| | 1970 | 1975 | 1980 | 1985 | 1990 | 1995 | 1997 |
|---|---|---|---|---|---|---|---|
| **Summary Ratings** | | 6.5 | 6.3 | 6.8 | 6.9 | 7.2 | 7.4 |
| **Rank** | | 19 | 25 | 24 | 30 | 45 | 42 |

| Components of Economic Freedom | 1970 | | 1975 | | 1980 | | 1985 | | 1990 | | 1995 | | 1997 | |
|---|---|---|---|---|---|---|---|---|---|---|---|---|---|---|
| **I. Size of Government** | **7.6** | | **7.4** | | **8.0** | | **7.5** | | **7.3** | | **6.8** | | **6.4** | |
| (a) Government Consumption (% of Total) | 7.7 | (17.0) | 7.8 | (16.6) | 8.2 | (14.1) | 7.6 | (17.4) | 7.8 | (16.8) | 8.2 | (14.5) | 8.0 | (15.6) |
| (b) Transfers and Subsidies (% of GDP) | 7.4 | (10.0) | 6.9 | (11.8) | 7.7 | (9.1) | 7.4 | (10.0) | 6.9 | (12.0) | 5.4 | (17.3) | 4.9 | (19.3) |
| **II. Structure of the Economy and Use of Markets** | | | **6.9** | | **8.0** | | **8.0** | | **6.7** | | **7.4** | | **7.4** | |
| (a) Government Enterprises | 6.0 | (25.9) | 6.0 | (20.9) | 6.0 | (30.1) | 6.0 | (29.3) | 6.0 | (29.9) | 6.0 | (36.8) | 6.0 | |
| (b) Price Controls | | | | | | | | | 4.0 | | 6.0 | | 6.0 | |
| (c) Top Marginal Tax Rate | | | 7.0 | (41) | 10.0 | (0) | 10.0 | (0) | 10.0 | (0) | 10.0 | (0) | 10.0 | (0) |
| (d) Conscription | 10.0 | | 10.0 | | 10.0 | | 10.0 | | 10.0 | | 10.0 | | 10.0 | |
| **III. Monetary Policy and Price Stability** | **3.6** | | **0.0** | | **1.7** | | **1.5** | | **1.6** | | **0.9** | | **5.3** | |
| (a) Annual Money Growth (last 5 yrs.) | 0.7 | (46.5) | 0.0 | (60.5) | 0.0 | (58.2) | 2.6 | (36.9) | 0.0 | (74.7) | 0.0 | (54.3) | 3.9 | (30.6) |
| (b) Inflation Variability (last 5 yrs.) | 0.0 | (40.6) | 0.0 | (32.6) | 5.3 | (11.8) | 1.9 | (20.4) | 5.0 | (12.4) | 1.1 | (22.3) | 5.5 | (11.2) |
| (c) Recent Inflation Rate | 9.9 | (0.7) | 0.0 | (66.0) | 0.0 | (54.8) | 0.0 | (74.0) | 0.0 | (100.4) | 1.6 | (42.0) | 6.5 | (17.7) |
| **IV. Freedom to Use Alternative Currencies** | **9.7** | | **10.0** | | **10.0** | | **10.0** | | **10.0** | | **10.0** | | **10.0** | |
| (a) Ownership of Foreign Currency | 10.0 | | 10.0 | | 10.0 | | 10.0 | | 10.0 | | 10.0 | | 10.0 | |
| (b) Black Market Exchange Rates (Prem.) | 9.4 | (3.0) | 10.0 | (0.0) | 10.0 | (0.0) | 10.0 | (0.0) | 10.0 | (0.0) | 10.0 | (0.0) | 10.0 | (0.0) |
| **V. Legal Structure and Property Rights** | | | | | **5.7** | | **6.0** | | **6.8** | | **7.7** | | **7.5** | |
| (a) Private Ownership Rights | | | | | 4.1 | | 3.5 | | 5.9 | | 7.7 | | 7.2 | |
| (b) Viability of Contracts | | | | | 4.9 | | 6.4 | | 6.4 | | 8.4 | | 8.3 | |
| (c) Rule of Law | | | | | 8.3 | | 8.2 | | 8.3 | | 7.0 | | 7.0 | |
| **VI. International Exchange** | **5.0** | | **6.0** | | **3.1** | | **5.6** | | **6.1** | | **7.5** | | **7.1** | |
| (a) Taxes on International Trade | | | | | | | | | | | | | | |
| i. Taxes as a Percentage of Exports and Imports | 6.9 | (4.7) | 7.7 | (3.4) | 4.1 | (8.9) | 6.1 | (5.8) | 6.3 | (5.6) | 8.2 | (2.7) | 8.3 | (2.5) |
| ii. Mean Tariff Rate | | | | | | | 3.8 | (31.0) | 3.9 | (30.5) | 8.1 | (9.3) | 8.0 | (10.2) |
| iii. Standard Deviation of Tariff Rates | | | | | | | | | 7.6 | (5.9) | 7.2 | (7.1) | 7.2 | (6.9) |
| (b) Non-tariff Regulatory Trade Barriers | | | | | | | | | | | | | | |
| i. Non-tariff Trade Restraints (% of trade covered) | | | | | | | 8.6 | (14.1) | 8.8 | (12.0) | 10.0 | (0.0) | | |
| ii. Size of Trade Sector (% of GDP) | 0.1 | (30.1) | 1.4 | (37.1) | 0.5 | (35.7) | 2.5 | (47.9) | 1.7 | (46.3) | 0.0 | (38.3) | 0.8 | (45.4) |
| **VII. Freedom of Exchange in Financial Markets** | | | | | **7.0** | | **7.7** | | **7.7** | | **7.4** | | **7.4** | |
| (a) Ownership of Banks | | | 5.0 | (40-75) | 5.0 | (40-75) | 5.0 | (40-75) | 5.0 | (40-75) | 5.0 | (40-75) | 5.0 | (40-75) |
| (b) Extension of Credit | | | | | | | 7.7 | (79.0) | 7.7 | (79.1) | 8.6 | (87.1) | 8.6 | (87.0) |
| (c) Avoidance of Negative Interest Rates | | | | | 6.0 | | 8.0 | | 8.0 | | 6.0 | | 6.0 | |
| (d) Capital Transactions with Foreigners | 8.0 | | 8.0 | | 10.0 | | 10.0 | | 10.0 | | 10.0 | | 10.0 | |

# VENEZUELA

| | 1970 | 1975 | 1980 | 1985 | 1990 | 1995 | 1997 |
|---|---|---|---|---|---|---|---|
| **Summary Ratings** | 7.8 | 6.5 | 6.9 | 5.8 | 5.8 | 4.5 | 6.0 |
| **Rank** | 12 | 19 | 15 | 42 | 50 | 103 | 82 |

| Components of Economic Freedom | 1970 | | 1975 | | 1980 | | 1985 | | 1990 | | 1995 | | 1997 | |
|---|---|---|---|---|---|---|---|---|---|---|---|---|---|---|
| **I. Size of Government** | **8.7** | | **8.4** | | **8.6** | | **8.5** | | **8.6** | | **8.8** | | **8.4** | |
| (a) Government Consumption (% of Total) | 7.6 | (17.6) | 7.4 | (19.0) | 7.6 | (17.7) | 8.2 | (14.4) | 8.6 | (11.9) | 9.1 | (9.3) | 9.3 | (8.6) |
| (b) Transfers and Subsidies (% of GDP) | 9.8 | (1.1) | 9.5 | (2.3) | 9.6 | (2.0) | 8.9 | (4.5) | 8.6 | (5.8) | 8.5 | (6.0) | 7.4 | (9.9) |
| **II. Structure of the Economy and Use of Markets** | | | **5.7** | | **3.6** | | **2.8** | | **3.1** | | **1.8** | | **3.7** | |
| (a) Government Enterprises | 7.0 | (21.1) | 4.0 | (33.6) | 2.0 | (45.6) | 0.0 | (50.1) | 0.0 | (62.2) | 0.0 | (59.7) | 2.0 | |
| (b) Price Controls | | | | | | | | | 4.0 | | 0.0 | | 4.0 | |
| (c) Top Marginal Tax Rate | | | 10.0 | (20) | 7.0 | (45) | 7.0 | (45) | 7.0 | (45) | 7.0 | (34) | 7.0 | (34) |
| (d) Conscription | 0.0 | | 0.0 | | 0.0 | | 1.0 | | 0.0 | | 0.0 | | 0.0 | |
| **III. Monetary Policy and Price Stability** | **9.6** | | **5.9** | | **6.4** | | **7.7** | | **2.6** | | **2.2** | | **0.8** | |
| (a) Annual Money Growth (last 5 yrs.) | 9.4 | (3.0) | 4.8 | (26.0) | 7.3 | (13.6) | 7.3 | (13.3) | 6.1 | (19.7) | 2.9 | (35.8) | 0.0 | (69.9) |
| (b) Inflation Variability (last 5 yrs.) | 9.6 | (1.1) | 4.0 | (15.1) | 7.0 | (7.4) | 7.9 | (5.2) | 0.0 | (30.2) | 3.8 | (15.6) | 0.0 | (29.8) |
| (c) Recent Inflation Rate | 9.7 | (1.3) | 9.0 | (5.1) | 4.8 | (26.0) | 7.9 | (10.4) | 1.7 | (41.7) | 0.0 | (51.9) | 2.3 | (38.6) |
| **IV. Freedom to Use Alternative Currencies** | **10.0** | | **10.0** | | **10.0** | | **7.5** | | **10.0** | | **0.8** | | **9.8** | |
| (a) Ownership of Foreign Currency | 10.0 | | 10.0 | | 10.0 | | 10.0 | | 10.0 | | 0.0 | | 10.0 | |
| (b) Black Market Exchange Rates (Prem.) | 10.0 | (0.0) | 10.0 | (0.0) | 10.0 | (0.0) | 5.0 | (25.0) | 10.0 | (0.0) | 1.6 | (42.0) | 9.6 | (2.0) |
| **V. Legal Structure and Property Rights** | **5.1** | | **1.7** | | **6.1** | | **5.1** | | **6.1** | | **5.7** | | **5.4** | |
| (a) Private Ownership Rights | 4.5 | | 2.3 | | 5.8 | | 4.8 | | 5.9 | | 7.7 | | 7.2 | |
| (b) Viability of Contracts | 5.8 | | 1.2 | | 4.3 | | 4.0 | | 5.8 | | 5.2 | | 4.8 | |
| (c) Rule of Law | | | | | 8.3 | | 6.6 | | 6.7 | | 4.1 | | 4.1 | |
| **VI. International Exchange** | **7.1** | | **7.1** | | **7.4** | | **4.2** | | **5.3** | | **7.9** | | **7.4** | |
| (a) Taxes on International Trade | | | | | | | | | | | | | | |
| i. Taxes as a Percentage of Exports and Imports | 8.1 | (2.9) | 7.5 | (3.7) | 8.0 | (3.0) | 3.9 | (9.1) | 8.5 | (2.2) | 7.9 | (3.1) | 7.8 | (3.3) |
| ii. Mean Tariff Rate | | | | | | | 3.4 | (32.9) | 3.9 | (30.6) | 7.3 | (13.4) | 7.6 | (12.0) |
| iii. Standard Deviation of Tariff Rates | | | | | | | | | 0.2 | (24.4) | 8.1 | (4.8) | 7.6 | (6.1) |
| (b) Non-tariff Regulatory Trade Barriers | | | | | | | | | | | | | | |
| i. Non-tariff Trade Restraints (% of trade covered) | | | | | | | 5.6 | (44.1) | 8.8 | (11.9) | 9.8 | (2.4) | | |
| ii. Size of Trade Sector (% of GDP) | 4.6 | (37.8) | 5.9 | (50.8) | 5.7 | (50.6) | 4.3 | (40.8) | 6.2 | (59.6) | 4.8 | (48.3) | 4.8 | (49.6) |
| **VII. Freedom of Exchange in Financial Markets** | | | **7.4** | | **6.5** | | **6.3** | | **4.6** | | **3.9** | | **5.0** | |
| (a) Ownership of Banks | | | 5.0 | (63) | 5.0 | (75) | 8.0 | (95) | 8.0 | (94) | 8.0 | (91) | 8.0 | (92) |
| (b) Extension of Credit | 9.6 | (96.7) | 9.7 | (97.6) | 9.2 | (92.5) | 8.6 | (87.6) | 5.3 | (57.4) | 1.9 | (27.0) | 7.2 | (74.3) |
| (c) Avoidance of Negative Interest Rates | | | | | 4.0 | | 4.0 | | 0.0 | | 0.0 | | 0.0 | |
| (d) Capital Transactions with Foreigners | 8.0 | | 8.0 | | 8.0 | | 5.0 | | 5.0 | | 5.0 | | 5.0 | |

# ZAMBIA

| | 1970 | 1975 | 1980 | 1985 | 1990 | 1995 | 1997 |
|---|---|---|---|---|---|---|---|
| **Summary Ratings** | 4.3 | 4.7 | 3.1 | 2.5 | 4.5 | 5.5 | |
| **Rank** | 63 | 70 | 102 | 113 | 103 | 92 | |

| Components of Economic Freedom | 1970 | | 1975 | | 1980 | | 1985 | | 1990 | | 1995 | | 1997 | |
|---|---|---|---|---|---|---|---|---|---|---|---|---|---|---|
| **I. Size of Government** | **7.4** | | **6.4** | | **6.4** | | **7.4** | | **7.7** | | **8.7** | | **9.2** | |
| (a) Government Consumption (% of Total) | 5.6 | (28.3) | 4.6 | (34.0) | 5.0 | (31.6) | 5.7 | (27.8) | 6.6 | (23.1) | 8.0 | (15.2) | 8.4 | (13.3) |
| (b) Transfers and Subsidies (% of GDP) | 9.1 | (3.8) | 8.2 | (7.0) | 7.8 | (8.7) | 9.0 | (4.2) | 8.9 | (4.5) | 9.4 | (2.6) | 10.0 | (0.0) |
| **II. Structure of the Economy and Use of Markets** | | | **1.3** | | **1.3** | | **1.3** | | **0.9** | | **3.3** | | **3.6** | |
| (a) Government Enterprises | 0.0 | (85.9) | 0.0 | (94.0) | 0.0 | (77.1) | 0.0 | (90.7) | 0.0 | (44.0) | 0.0 | | 0.0 | |
| (b) Price Controls | | | | | | | | | 0.0 | | 2.0 | | 2.0 | |
| (c) Top Marginal Tax Rate | | | 0.0 | (70) | 0.0 | (70) | 0.0 | (80) | 0.0 | (75) | 7.0 | (35) | 8.0 | (30) |
| (d) Conscription | 10.0 | | 10.0 | | 10.0 | | 10.0 | | 10.0 | | 10.0 | | 10.0 | |
| **III. Monetary Policy and Price Stability** | **6.4** | | **6.8** | | **8.1** | | **4.3** | | **0.1** | | **0.9** | | **1.7** | |
| (a) Annual Money Growth (last 5 yrs.) | 6.9 | (15.7) | 7.9 | (10.3) | 8.4 | (8.1) | 6.3 | (18.4) | 0.0 | (58.6) | 0.0 | (77.1) | 0.0 | (64.4) |
| (b) Inflation Variability (last 5 yrs.) | 4.5 | (13.7) | 5.1 | (12.3) | 8.2 | (4.6) | 5.0 | (12.6) | 0.4 | (23.9) | 0.0 | (49.2) | 0.0 | (44.6) |
| (c) Recent Inflation Rate | 7.7 | (-11.4) | 7.2 | (-14.2) | 7.6 | (11.8) | 1.8 | (41.1) | 0.0 | (106.4) | 2.6 | (36.9) | 4.9 | (25.5) |
| **IV. Freedom to Use Alternative Currencies** | **0.0** | | **0.0** | | **0.0** | | **1.2** | | **0.0** | | **4.7** | | **6.8** | |
| (a) Ownership of Foreign Currency | 0.0 | | 0.0 | | 0.0 | | 0.0 | | 0.0 | | 0.0 | | 10.0 | |
| (b) Black Market Exchange Rates (Prem.) | 0.0 | (56.0) | 0.0 | (140.0) | 0.0 | (70.0) | 2.4 | (38.0) | 0.0 | (212.0) | 9.4 | (3.0) | 3.6 | (32.0) |
| **V. Legal Structure and Property Rights** | | | | | **6.0** | | **4.0** | | **2.5** | | **4.1** | | **4.3** | |
| (a) Private Ownership Rights | | | | | 5.4 | | 4.8 | | 4.6 | | 5.5 | | 7.2 | |
| (b) Viability of Contracts | | | | | 4.3 | | 4.0 | | 0.4 | | 0.0 | | 1.4 | |
| (c) Rule of Law | | | | | 8.3 | | 3.1 | | 2.5 | | 7.0 | | 4.1 | |
| **VI. International Exchange** | | | **8.8** | | **8.8** | | **3.7** | | **4.5** | | **6.8** | | **6.9** | |
| (a) Taxes on International Trade | | | | | | | | | | | | | | |
| i. Taxes as a Percentage of Exports and Imports | | | 8.3 | (2.6) | 8.4 | (2.4) | 5.7 | (6.4) | 6.8 | (4.8) | 7.5 | (3.8) | 7.1 | (4.3) |
| ii. Mean Tariff Rate | | | | | | | 3.0 | (34.8) | 4.9 | (25.6) | 4.9 | (25.6) | 7.3 | (13.6) |
| iii. Standard Deviation of Tariff Rates | | | | | | | | | | | 5.8 | (10.6) | 6.3 | (9.3) |
| (b) Non-tariff Regulatory Trade Barriers | | | | | | | | | | | | | | |
| i. Non-tariff Trade Restraints (% of trade covered) | | | | | | | 0.0 | (100.0) | 0.0 | (100.0) | 8.8 | (12.0) | | |
| ii. Size of Trade Sector (% of GDP) | 10.0 | (90.5) | 10.0 | (92.8) | 9.7 | (86.8) | 7.9 | (73.6) | 7.5 | (72.5) | 9.0 | (91.0) | 7.1 | (72.7) |
| **VII. Freedom of Exchange in Financial Markets** | | | **3.5** | | **3.3** | | **1.6** | | **2.1** | | **2.8** | | **5.4** | |
| (a) Ownership of Banks | | | 2.0 | (10-40) | 2.0 | (10-40) | 2.0 | (10-40) | 2.0 | (10-40) | 5.0 | (40-75) | 5.0 | (40-75) |
| (b) Extension of Credit | 7.0 | (73.2) | 6.8 | (71.3) | 5.7 | (61.2) | 2.3 | (31.0) | 4.6 | (51.7) | 4.5 | (50.2) | 5.5 | (59.4) |
| (c) Avoidance of Negative Interest Rates | | | 4.0 | | 4.0 | | 0.0 | | 0.0 | | 0.0 | | 6.0 | |
| (d) Capital Transactions with Foreigners | 2.0 | | 2.0 | | 2.0 | | 2.0 | | 2.0 | | 2.0 | | 5.0 | |

# ZIMBABWE

| | 1970 | 1975 | 1980 | 1985 | 1990 | 1995 | 1997 |
|---|---|---|---|---|---|---|---|
| **Summary Ratings** | | | 4.1 | 4.0 | 4.5 | 5.4 | 5.0 |
| **Rank** | | | 79 | 91 | 82 | 84 | 99 |

| Components of Economic Freedom | 1970 | | 1975 | | 1980 | | 1985 | | 1990 | | 1995 | | 1997 | |
|---|---|---|---|---|---|---|---|---|---|---|---|---|---|---|
| **I. Size of Government** | **8.4** | | **7.9** | | **7.0** | | **6.9** | | **7.5** | | **6.9** | | **7.5** | |
| (a) Government Consumption (% of Total) | 8.4 | (13.5) | 7.9 | (15.8) | 7.0 | (21.1) | 6.3 | (24.6) | 6.5 | (23.6) | 6.9 | (21.6) | 7.5 | (18.3) |
| (b) Transfers and Subsidies (% of GDP) | | | | | 7.0 | (11.4) | 7.4 | (10.0) | 8.4 | (6.2) | | | | |
| **II. Structure of the Economy and Use of Markets** | | | | | **3.0** | | **2.3** | | **1.8** | | **3.9** | | **4.1** | |
| (a) Government Enterprises | 2.0 | (40.1) | 2.0 | (39.3) | 2.0 | (32.5) | 2.0 | (53.6) | 2.0 | | 2.0 | | 2.0 | |
| (b) Price Controls | | | | | | | | | 2.0 | | 4.0 | | 4.0 | |
| (c) Top Marginal Tax Rate | | | | | 5.0 | (45) | 0.0 | (63) | 1.0 | (60) | 4.0 | (45) | 5.0 | (40) |
| (d) Conscription | 3.0 | | 3.0 | | 1.0 | | 10.0 | | 3.0 | | 10.0 | | 10.0 | |
| **III. Monetary Policy and Price Stability** | **7.6** | | **8.5** | | **8.4** | | **8.3** | | **7.5** | | **6.2** | | **5.0** | |
| (a) Annual Money Growth (last 5 yrs.) | | | | | 7.8 | (11.2) | 8.6 | (7.2) | 7.0 | (14.9) | 3.4 | (32.9) | 1.5 | (42.7) |
| (b) Inflation Variability (last 5 yrs.) | 7.5 | (6.2) | 8.9 | (2.7) | 8.7 | (3.1) | 7.7 | (5.8) | 8.4 | (4.1) | 7.3 | (6.8) | 7.7 | (5.7) |
| (c) Recent Inflation Rate | 7.6 | (-12.1) | 8.1 | (9.5) | 8.7 | (6.6) | 8.7 | (6.5) | 7.1 | (14.8) | 7.9 | (10.7) | 5.8 | (21.0) |
| **IV. Freedom to Use Alternative Currencies** | **3.6** | | **0.0** | | **0.0** | | **0.8** | | **3.5** | | **4.9** | | **6.1** | |
| (a) Ownership of Foreign Currency | 0.0 | | 0.0 | | 0.0 | | 0.0 | | 0.0 | | 0.0 | | 5.0 | |
| (b) Black Market Exchange Rates (Prem.) | 7.2 | (14.0) | 0.0 | (54.0) | 0.0 | (84.0) | 1.6 | (42.0) | 7.0 | (15.0) | 9.8 | (1.0) | 7.2 | (14.0) |
| **V. Legal Structure and Property Rights** | | | | | **2.9** | | **3.1** | | **4.0** | | **3.9** | | **3.9** | |
| (a) Private Ownership Rights | | | | | 3.4 | | 2.2 | | 4.6 | | 5.5 | | 4.4 | |
| (b) Viability of Contracts | | | | | 3.7 | | 4.0 | | 4.0 | | 2.1 | | 3.1 | |
| (c) Rule of Law | | | | | 1.7 | | 3.1 | | 3.3 | | 4.1 | | 4.1 | |
| **VI. International Exchange** | | | **8.1** | | **6.1** | | **4.9** | | **4.8** | | **7.4** | | **3.7** | |
| (a) Taxes on International Trade | | | | | | | | | | | | | | |
| i. Taxes as a Percentage of Exports and Imports | | | 8.6 | (2.1) | 8.9 | (1.7) | 4.7 | (8.0) | 3.9 | (9.2) | 5.4 | (6.9) | | |
| ii. Mean Tariff Rate | | | | | 8.0 | (10.0) | 8.3 | (8.7) | 8.0 | (10.1) | 8.2 | (9.2) | 5.1 | (24.3) |
| iii. Standard Deviation of Tariff Rates | | | | | | | | | 5.3 | (11.8) | | | 0.6 | (23.4) |
| (b) Non-tariff Regulatory Trade Barriers | | | | | | | | | | | | | | |
| i. Non-tariff Trade Restraints (% of trade covered) | | | | | 0.5 | (95.0) | 0.5 | (95.0) | 0.6 | (93.6) | 8.0 | (20.0) | | |
| ii. Size of Trade Sector (% of GDP) | | | 6.8 | (60.2) | 6.0 | (55.6) | 5.8 | (55.6) | 6.4 | (63.6) | 8.8 | (91.2) | 7.9 | (82.3) |
| **VII. Freedom of Exchange in Financial Markets** | | | | | **3.6** | | **3.8** | | **4.4** | | **5.2** | | **5.4** | |
| (a) Ownership of Banks | | | 2.0 | (10-40) | 2.0 | (10-40) | 2.0 | (14) | 2.0 | (10-40) | 5.0 | (40-75) | 5.0 | (40-75) |
| (b) Extension of Credit | | | | | 4.8 | (53.5) | 3.3 | (39.5) | 6.3 | (66.5) | 6.5 | (68.6) | 7.2 | (74.6) |
| (c) Avoidance of Negative Interest Rates | | | | | 6.0 | | 8.0 | | 8.0 | | 8.0 | | 8.0 | |
| (d) Capital Transactions with Foreigners | | | | | 2.0 | | 2.0 | | 2.0 | | 2.0 | | 2.0 | |

# Appendix 1
# Area rating Tables, 1970–1997

## AREA I: SIZE OF GOVERNMENT: CONSUMPTION, TRANSFERS, AND SUBSIDIES

| | 1970 | 1975 | 1980 | 1985 | 1990 | 1995 | 1997 |
|---|---|---|---|---|---|---|---|
| **Albania** | NR | NR | 8.3 | 8.4 | 5.0 | 8.1 | 9.1 |
| **Algeria** | 6.9 | 7.1 | 6.4 | 6.3 | 6.7 | 7.3 | 6.8 |
| **Argentina** | 8.4 | 7.8 | 7.6 | 7.7 | 8.5 | 7.9 | 7.8 |
| **Australia** | 7.3 | 7.2 | 7.0 | 6.7 | 7.0 | 6.6 | 6.6 |
| **Austria** | 6.5 | 5.7 | 5.2 | 5.0 | 5.1 | 4.6 | 4.7 |
| **Bahamas** | 9.8 | 8.8 | 8.9 | 8.9 | 8.9 | 8.5 | NR |
| **Bahrain** | NR | NR | 7.7 | 6.4 | 6.4 | 7.2 | 7.1 |
| **Bangladesh** | NR | 10.0 | 10.0 | 10.0 | 10.0 | 9.9 | 9.9 |
| **Barbados** | 8.6 | 8.7 | 8.6 | 8.2 | 8.2 | 8.3 | 6.3 |
| **Belgium** | 6.0 | 4.7 | 5.0 | 4.9 | 5.4 | 5.2 | 7.4 |
| **Belize** | NR | 7.8 | 8.4 | 7.9 | 8.4 | 8.7 | 8.0 |
| **Benin** | 9.0 | 9.1 | 9.3 | 8.0 | 8.7 | 8.5 | 8.7 |
| **Bolivia** | 9.9 | 8.9 | 8.7 | 9.1 | 8.9 | 8.7 | 8.0 |
| **Botswana** | 8.4 | 7.5 | 7.3 | 6.1 | 6.4 | 5.3 | 5.0 |
| **Brazil** | 7.1 | 6.5 | 7.7 | 7.9 | 6.8 | 6.4 | 6.7 |
| **Bulgaria** | NR | NR | 9.1 | 7.0 | 4.6 | 7.1 | 7.6 |
| **Burundi** | 9.0 | 8.8 | 9.2 | 9.3 | 9.0 | 8.9 | 8.8 |
| **Cameroon** | 8.2 | 9.1 | 9.3 | 9.3 | 8.6 | 9.3 | 8.9 |
| **Canada** | 5.8 | 6.6 | 5.9 | 5.6 | 5.7 | 5.5 | 6.0 |
| **C. African Rep.** | 6.8 | 7.8 | 8.3 | 8.0 | 8.1 | 8.3 | 9.0 |
| **Chad** | 6.5 | 6.9 | 6.1 | 8.9 | 9.4 | 9.5 | 9.5 |
| **Chile** | 7.0 | 7.4 | 7.4 | 6.9 | 7.8 | 7.9 | 7.8 |
| **China** | 8.9 | 8.8 | 6.8 | 7.1 | 7.2 | 7.3 | 7.3 |
| **Colombia** | 8.8 | 9.1 | 8.9 | 8.7 | 8.7 | 8.2 | 7.3 |
| **Congo, Dem. R.** | 8.0 | 9.1 | 9.6 | 9.2 | 9.2 | 9.9 | 9.1 |
| **Congo, Rep. Of** | 8.7 | 7.1 | 5.8 | 6.4 | 7.5 | 7.5 | 5.4 |
| **Costa Rica** | 9.0 | 8.3 | 7.7 | 7.6 | 7.7 | 7.4 | 7.9 |
| **Cote d'Ivoire** | 7.3 | 6.8 | 8.0 | 7.3 | 7.4 | 8.1 | 8.1 |
| **Croatia** | NR | NR | NR | NR | NR | 5.3 | 5.2 |
| **Cyprus** | 9.1 | 7.5 | 8.0 | 7.7 | 7.3 | 7.1 | 7.0 |
| **Czech Rep.** | NR | 5.9 | 5.8 | 5.3 | 2.7 | 3.9 | 4.2 |
| **Denmark** | 5.8 | 5.1 | 4.5 | 4.6 | 4.3 | 3.8 | 4.6 |
| **Dominican Rep.** | 9.0 | 9.4 | 9.4 | 9.4 | 9.7 | 9.7 | 9.2 |
| **Ecuador** | 8.5 | 7.5 | 8.0 | 8.6 | 9.1 | 8.8 | 8.1 |
| **Egypt** | 5.8 | 4.5 | 6.4 | 6.7 | 8.0 | 8.2 | 8.6 |
| **El Salvador** | 8.6 | 8.9 | 8.6 | 8.7 | 9.4 | 9.2 | 9.3 |
| **Estonia** | NR | NR | NR | NR | 7.1 | 6.0 | 5.9 |
| **Fiji** | 7.6 | 8.8 | 8.2 | 7.7 | 8.5 | 8.0 | 8.4 |
| **Finland** | 7.1 | 6.4 | 6.2 | 5.8 | 5.7 | 4.7 | 4.9 |
| **France** | 6.1 | 5.2 | 4.8 | 4.6 | 4.9 | 4.5 | 4.3 |
| **Gabon** | 4.4 | 6.9 | 4.7 | 6.6 | 8.4 | 8.0 | 5.9 |
| **Germany** | 6.4 | 5.7 | 5.7 | 5.5 | 5.7 | 5.2 | 5.2 |

| | 1970 | 1975 | 1980 | 1985 | 1990 | 1995 | 1997 |
|---|---|---|---|---|---|---|---|
| Ghana | 8.8 | 8.7 | 9.1 | 9.4 | 9.2 | 8.8 | 8.7 |
| Greece | 9.2 | 8.8 | 8.4 | 6.5 | 6.1 | 6.4 | 6.7 |
| Guatemala | 9.5 | 9.6 | 9.5 | 9.6 | 9.6 | 9.9 | 9.9 |
| Guinea-Bissau | 7.0 | 6.8 | NR | 8.1 | 8.9 | 9.7 | 9.5 |
| Guyana | 6.8 | 5.4 | 5.2 | 6.6 | 7.9 | 7.0 | 6.5 |
| Haiti | 8.9 | 9.1 | 8.8 | 8.4 | 9.4 | 9.6 | 9.6 |
| Honduras | 9.2 | 9.2 | 8.0 | 8.8 | 8.6 | 8.4 | 7.2 |
| Hong Kong | 9.0 | 9.4 | 9.5 | 9.4 | 9.3 | 9.2 | 9.2 |
| Hungary | 8.1 | 8.1 | 8.2 | 4.7 | 5.2 | 5.8 | 6.6 |
| Iceland | 7.7 | 7.1 | 7.0 | 6.9 | 6.9 | 6.9 | 7.0 |
| India | 8.9 | 8.9 | 8.7 | 8.3 | 8.2 | 8.3 | 8.0 |
| Indonesia | 9.3 | 9.2 | 8.5 | 8.6 | 9.0 | 9.3 | 9.4 |
| Iran | 9.0 | 6.0 | 6.9 | 8.3 | 8.5 | 8.3 | 8.5 |
| Ireland | 7.2 | 6.0 | 6.1 | 5.8 | 6.3 | 6.0 | 6.0 |
| Israel | 5.6 | 4.2 | 3.7 | 4.3 | 5.2 | 5.0 | 4.7 |
| Italy | 6.7 | 6.4 | 5.8 | 4.6 | 4.9 | 4.7 | 5.7 |
| Jamaica | 7.9 | 7.5 | 6.4 | 8.8 | 8.5 | 8.3 | 6.7 |
| Japan | 9.1 | 8.2 | 7.9 | 7.7 | 7.7 | 7.5 | 8.3 |
| Jordan | NR | 5.4 | 7.2 | 7.7 | 7.7 | 7.6 | 7.6 |
| Kenya | 8.3 | 8.2 | 7.9 | 7.7 | 8.0 | 8.6 | 7.3 |
| Kuwait | 6.1 | 4.6 | 5.9 | 5.0 | 5.4 | 5.1 | 6.0 |
| Latvia | NR | NR | NR | NR | 8.3 | 5.6 | 5.7 |
| Lithuania | NR | NR | NR | NR | 6.2 | 7.0 | 7.0 |
| Luxembourg | 6.8 | 7.8 | 7.6 | 7.7 | 5.2 | 5.3 | 5.1 |
| Madagascar | 8.6 | 8.8 | 8.6 | 9.0 | 9.5 | 9.7 | 9.6 |
| Malawi | 8.6 | 8.8 | 8.2 | 8.3 | 8.6 | 7.2 | 8.5 |
| Malaysia | 7.5 | 7.4 | 7.6 | 7.9 | 8.2 | 8.0 | 8.1 |
| Mali | 8.8 | 9.3 | 9.2 | 9.2 | 9.1 | 8.6 | 8.3 |
| Malta | 6.8 | 6.6 | 7.0 | 6.5 | 6.3 | 6.4 | 5.9 |
| Mauritius | 8.6 | 8.2 | 8.2 | 8.4 | 8.5 | 8.4 | 8.3 |
| Mexico | 9.4 | 8.9 | 8.7 | 8.6 | 9.1 | 8.2 | 8.4 |
| Morocco | 8.3 | 7.9 | 8.0 | 8.1 | 8.4 | 8.2 | 7.0 |
| Myanmar | NR | NR | NR | NR | NR | NR | NR |
| Namibia | NR | NR | 5.6 | 4.3 | 6.8 | 4.2 | 4.1 |
| Nepal | NR | 9.3 | 9.5 | 8.8 | 9.1 | 8.9 | 9.0 |
| Netherlands | 6.1 | 5.0 | 4.4 | 4.3 | 4.8 | 4.7 | 5.1 |
| New Zealand | 7.7 | 5.9 | 5.4 | 5.8 | 4.8 | 7.0 | 7.1 |
| Nicaragua | 8.8 | 9.2 | 8.2 | 5.7 | 5.6 | 8.5 | 8.4 |
| Niger | 9.2 | 8.8 | 9.0 | 8.8 | 8.3 | 8.2 | 8.2 |
| Nigeria | 9.5 | 8.6 | 7.6 | 8.9 | 6.9 | 8.3 | 8.8 |
| Norway | 5.5 | 5.1 | 4.8 | 5.0 | 4.0 | 4.8 | 5.1 |
| Oman | 6.4 | 4.8 | 5.8 | 5.9 | 4.7 | 7.0 | 7.2 |
| Pakistan | 9.4 | 9.1 | 9.2 | 9.2 | 8.3 | 8.9 | 8.3 |
| Panama | NR | 7.6 | 7.2 | 7.5 | 7.3 | 7.5 | 7.4 |

| | 1970 | 1975 | 1980 | 1985 | 1990 | 1995 | 1997 |
|---|---|---|---|---|---|---|---|
| **Papua New Guinea** | 4.9 | 3.8 | 5.7 | 7.8 | 7.2 | 7.2 | 4.5 |
| **Paraguay** | 9.3 | 9.5 | 9.5 | 9.5 | 9.6 | 9.0 | 7.9 |
| **Peru** | 8.8 | 8.9 | 8.8 | 9.1 | 9.1 | 9.0 | 8.7 |
| **Philippines** | 9.3 | 9.0 | 9.2 | 9.6 | 9.2 | 9.2 | 8.1 |
| **Poland** | NR | 8.0 | 8.6 | 5.6 | 4.1 | 5.0 | 5.3 |
| **Portugal** | 7.8 | 7.1 | 6.7 | 6.2 | 6.6 | 6.7 | 6.8 |
| **Romania** | NR | NR | 7.8 | 8.8 | 6.4 | 7.0 | 7.4 |
| **Russia** | NR | 3.5 | 3.7 | 3.5 | 3.7 | 6.9 | 6.5 |
| **Rwanda** | 9.2 | 8.8 | 9.2 | 8.6 | 9.0 | 9.5 | 9.3 |
| **Senegal** | 8.1 | 8.7 | 8.1 | 7.8 | 7.9 | 8.3 | 8.7 |
| **Sierra Leone** | NR | 9.2 | 9.3 | 9.6 | 9.2 | 8.6 | 9.2 |
| **Singapore** | 8.9 | 8.9 | 8.9 | 8.0 | 8.5 | 8.7 | 8.6 |
| **Slovakia** | NR | 5.9 | 5.8 | 5.3 | 2.7 | 5.5 | 4.8 |
| **Slovenia** | NR | NR | NR | NR | 6.1 | 3.6 | 3.6 |
| **Somalia** | 8.8 | 6.8 | 8.3 | 8.3 | NR | NR | NR |
| **South Africa** | 8.6 | 8.2 | 8.1 | 7.6 | 7.5 | 7.5 | 7.5 |
| **South Korea** | 9.3 | 9.0 | 8.8 | 8.8 | 8.6 | 8.6 | 8.4 |
| **Spain** | 8.4 | 7.9 | 7.3 | 6.5 | 6.5 | 6.0 | 7.0 |
| **Sri Lanka** | 8.1 | 8.5 | 8.5 | 8.7 | 8.6 | 8.4 | 8.7 |
| **Sweden** | 5.5 | 4.2 | 3.8 | 3.7 | 3.2 | 2.8 | 3.1 |
| **Switzerland** | 8.1 | 7.7 | 7.1 | 7.1 | 6.5 | 6.1 | 6.3 |
| **Syria** | 8.5 | 7.5 | 6.7 | 5.9 | 7.7 | 7.9 | 7.5 |
| **Taiwan** | NR | 8.2 | 8.0 | 7.8 | 7.6 | 7.8 | 7.3 |
| **Tanzania** | 10.0 | 8.7 | 9.1 | 8.1 | 7.7 | 7.9 | 8.3 |
| **Thailand** | 9.1 | 9.2 | 8.9 | 8.7 | 9.0 | 8.9 | 8.9 |
| **Togo** | 6.9 | 6.0 | 5.5 | 8.9 | 7.8 | 8.3 | 8.7 |
| **Trinidad & Tobago** | 7.5 | 6.7 | 7.8 | 5.7 | 7.6 | 8.1 | 8.6 |
| **Tunisia** | 8.0 | 8.4 | 8.0 | 7.5 | 7.4 | 7.5 | 7.6 |
| **Turkey** | 8.6 | 8.2 | 8.2 | 8.0 | 8.7 | 8.0 | 7.3 |
| **Uganda** | NR | NR | NR | 8.0 | 9.5 | 8.9 | 8.9 |
| **Ukraine** | NR | NR | 6.4 | 6.2 | 6.7 | 5.7 | 6.0 |
| **United Arab Emirates** | NR | 4.5 | 3.7 | 3.1 | 7.6 | 7.9 | 6.1 |
| **United Kingdom** | 6.7 | 6.0 | 5.9 | 5.7 | 6.2 | 5.8 | 5.9 |
| **United States** | 6.7 | 6.9 | 7.1 | 6.8 | 6.8 | 6.8 | 6.9 |
| **Uruguay** | 7.6 | 7.4 | 8.0 | 7.5 | 7.3 | 6.8 | 6.4 |
| **Venezuela** | 8.7 | 8.4 | 8.6 | 8.5 | 8.6 | 8.8 | 8.4 |
| **Zambia** | 7.4 | 6.4 | 6.4 | 7.4 | 7.7 | 8.7 | 9.2 |
| **Zimbabwe** | 8.4 | 7.9 | 7.0 | 6.9 | 7.5 | 6.9 | 7.5 |

# Area II: Structure of the Economy and Use of Markets–Production and Allocation via Political Mandates Rather Than Private Enterprises and Markets

| | 1970 | 1975 | 1980 | 1985 | 1990 | 1995 | 1997 |
|---|---|---|---|---|---|---|---|
| Albania | NR | NR | NR | NR | 0.0 | 2.1 | 3.0 |
| Algeria | NR | NR | NR | NR | 1.0 | 1.0 | 1.9 |
| Argentina | NR | 3.6 | 4.4 | 2.9 | 3.8 | 8.4 | 9.5 |
| Australia | NR | 5.0 | 5.0 | 5.0 | 5.6 | 6.5 | 6.3 |
| Austria | NR | 3.1 | 2.4 | 2.4 | 3.8 | 4.6 | 4.9 |
| Bahamas | NR | 8.0 | 7.1 | 6.1 | 5.4 | 6.7 | 6.7 |
| Bahrain | NR | 6.1 | 7.1 | 7.1 | 6.0 | 6.0 | 6.0 |
| Bangladesh | NR | NR | 2.7 | 2.7 | NR | 2.0 | 2.0 |
| Barbados | NR | 4.7 | 4.7 | 4.7 | 5.9 | 6.1 | 6.1 |
| Belgium | NR | 4.1 | 3.3 | 3.3 | 3.4 | 4.8 | 4.8 |
| Belize | NR | NR | NR | 4.8 | 2.5 | 4.8 | 4.7 |
| Benin | NR | NR | NR | NR | NR | 1.9 | 1.9 |
| Bolivia | NR | NR | 2.5 | 4.4 | 4.8 | 6.1 | 7.1 |
| Botswana | NR | 2.3 | 2.3 | 3.1 | 4.3 | 5.9 | 6.2 |
| Brazil | 5.0 | 4.2 | 2.9 | 2.7 | 4.5 | 6.2 | 7.2 |
| Bulgaria | NR | NR | NR | NR | 0.0 | 2.2 | 3.3 |
| Burundi | NR | NR | NR | NR | 1.2 | 2.1 | 3.0 |
| Cameroon | NR | NR | NR | 3.1 | 2.4 | 2.2 | 2.2 |
| Canada | 4.3 | 5.0 | 5.0 | 5.0 | 6.5 | 6.2 | 7.5 |
| C. African Rep. | NR | NR | NR | NR | 0.0 | 0.0 | 0.0 |
| Chad | NR | NR | NR | NR | 1.8 | 1.8 | 1.8 |
| Chile | NR | 2.1 | 3.1 | 2.7 | 5.6 | 7.1 | 6.8 |
| China | NR | NR | NR | 2.3 | 1.9 | 2.5 | 3.2 |
| Colombia | NR | 4.2 | 1.7 | 2.9 | 4.7 | 5.1 | 4.5 |
| Congo, Dem. R. | NR | 2.1 | 1.7 | 1.7 | 2.5 | 2.5 | 3.0 |
| Congo, Rep. Of | NR | NR | NR | NR | 1.9 | 1.6 | 1.6 |
| Costa Rica | NR | 6.2 | 5.2 | 4.4 | 7.4 | 7.4 | 8.1 |
| Cote d'Ivoire | NR | NR | 3.2 | 2.5 | 1.4 | 2.5 | 3.0 |
| Croatia | NR | NR | NR | NR | NR | 1.2 | 2.6 |
| Cyprus | NR | NR | 4.3 | 4.3 | 2.6 | 4.3 | 4.3 |
| Czech Rep. | NR | NR | NR | NR | 1.0 | 4.8 | 5.2 |
| Denmark | NR | 3.7 | 3.3 | 3.3 | 4.2 | 5.8 | 6.1 |
| Dominican Rep. | NR | 2.4 | 3.3 | 3.3 | 3.5 | 6.4 | 6.4 |
| Ecuador | NR | 3.8 | 3.8 | 2.7 | 2.8 | 5.2 | 5.2 |
| Egypt | NR | NR | 1.0 | 1.7 | 1.2 | 2.1 | 2.5 |
| El Salvador | NR | NR | 4.5 | 4.1 | 4.5 | 6.6 | 7.6 |
| Estonia | NR | NR | NR | NR | NR | 4.9 | 5.6 |
| Fiji | NR | 4.4 | 3.1 | 3.4 | 4.3 | 5.3 | 5.3 |
| Finland | NR | 4.6 | 4.2 | 4.2 | 4.2 | 5.7 | 5.4 |
| France | NR | 4.2 | 3.5 | 2.7 | 4.3 | 5.3 | 5.5 |

| | 1970 | 1975 | 1980 | 1985 | 1990 | 1995 | 1997 |
|---|---|---|---|---|---|---|---|
| **Gabon** | NR | NR | NR | NR | 2.4 | 3.1 | 2.9 |
| **Germany** | 5.1 | 5.1 | 4.7 | 4.3 | 5.8 | 6.0 | 5.2 |
| **Ghana** | 1.3 | 1.3 | 1.7 | 1.7 | 2.0 | 5.3 | 5.9 |
| **Greece** | NR | 3.5 | 2.1 | 1.4 | 1.7 | 4.2 | 4.6 |
| **Guatemala** | NR | 8.6 | 8.3 | 5.8 | 6.4 | 6.6 | 7.3 |
| **Guinea-Bissau** | NR | NR | NR | NR | 2.1 | 4.8 | 4.8 |
| **Guyana** | NR | NR | NR | NR | NR | NR | 4.0 |
| **Haiti** | NR | NR | NR | NR | 5.8 | 2.9 | NR |
| **Honduras** | NR | 7.7 | 7.3 | 4.8 | 4.6 | 5.9 | 6.2 |
| **Hong Kong** | 10.0 | 10.0 | 10.0 | 9.6 | 9.7 | 9.7 | 9.7 |
| **Hungary** | NR | NR | NR | NR | 2.8 | 4.9 | 4.9 |
| **Iceland** | NR | NR | 5.3 | 5.6 | 6.4 | 6.2 | 6.2 |
| **India** | 2.3 | 1.3 | 1.7 | 1.3 | 2.4 | 4.1 | 3.5 |
| **Indonesia** | NR | 3.9 | 2.5 | 3.6 | 5.1 | 4.0 | 4.0 |
| **Iran** | NR | 5.0 | NR | 1.0 | 1.3 | 2.3 | 2.3 |
| **Ireland** | NR | 4.3 | 5.1 | 4.8 | 6.7 | 7.6 | 7.9 |
| **Israel** | NR | NR | 1.4 | 2.1 | 1.7 | 3.3 | 3.3 |
| **Italy** | NR | 3.8 | 2.1 | 2.1 | 3.5 | 4.2 | 4.2 |
| **Jamaica** | NR | 3.1 | 2.3 | 3.7 | 5.9 | 6.2 | 6.2 |
| **Japan** | NR | 5.6 | 5.3 | 5.6 | 6.0 | 5.0 | 5.0 |
| **Jordan** | NR | NR | NR | NR | 2.8 | 2.1 | 2.1 |
| **Kenya** | 3.3 | 2.3 | 2.7 | 2.3 | 3.0 | 3.6 | 5.3 |
| **Kuwait** | NR | NR | NR | NR | NR | 4.4 | 5.8 |
| **Latvia** | NR | NR | NR | NR | NR | 3.8 | 5.8 |
| **Lithuania** | NR | NR | NR | NR | NR | 3.4 | 4.7 |
| **Luxembourg** | NR | NR | NR | NR | 4.4 | 5.9 | 6.6 |
| **Madagascar** | NR | NR | NR | NR | 0.1 | 0.1 | 0.1 |
| **Malawi** | NR | 2.3 | 2.8 | 2.5 | 1.6 | 4.0 | 3.5 |
| **Malaysia** | NR | 4.8 | 4.0 | 5.5 | 5.4 | 5.3 | 5.5 |
| **Mali** | NR | NR | NR | NR | 1.7 | 3.5 | 3.5 |
| **Malta** | NR | NR | 3.3 | 4.3 | 2.8 | 5.3 | 5.3 |
| **Mauritius** | NR | NR | 5.4 | 6.9 | 5.9 | 6.2 | 6.9 |
| **Mexico** | NR | 3.5 | 3.1 | 3.1 | 3.5 | 5.8 | 6.5 |
| **Morocco** | NR | 3.1 | 0.9 | 0.1 | 0.1 | 2.2 | 2.4 |
| **Myanmar** | NR | NR | NR | NR | 2.0 | 2.0 | 2.0 |
| **Namibia** | NR | NR | NR | NR | NR | NR | 5.9 |
| **Nepal** | NR | NR | NR | NR | 2.9 | 2.9 | 2.9 |
| **Netherlands** | NR | 3.8 | 3.6 | 3.1 | 4.4 | 5.1 | 6.0 |
| **New Zealand** | NR | 4.4 | 4.0 | 3.3 | 7.9 | 9.2 | 9.2 |
| **Nicaragua** | NR | 7.4 | 2.5 | 1.9 | 0.0 | 4.2 | 4.2 |
| **Niger** | NR | NR | NR | NR | 0.0 | 3.5 | 3.5 |
| **Nigeria** | NR | 3.3 | 1.3 | 2.5 | 1.4 | 2.6 | 4.5 |
| **Norway** | NR | 2.1 | 2.1 | 2.5 | 3.8 | 5.2 | 5.5 |
| **Oman** | NR | 6.1 | 6.1 | 6.1 | 5.4 | 5.4 | 5.4 |

| | 1970 | 1975 | 1980 | 1985 | 1990 | 1995 | 1997 |
|---|---|---|---|---|---|---|---|
| **Pakistan** | NR | 0.4 | 2.1 | 1.7 | 3.4 | 3.9 | 4.6 |
| **Panama** | NR | 4.8 | 4.4 | 4.4 | 4.3 | 6.4 | 6.4 |
| **Pap. New Guinea** | NR | NR | NR | NR | NR | NR | NR |
| **Paraguay** | NR | NR | NR | 6.0 | 5.6 | 6.8 | 6.8 |
| **Peru** | NR | 3.5 | 2.7 | 2.0 | 3.6 | 6.6 | 7.3 |
| **Philippines** | NR | 4.5 | 3.7 | 5.6 | 5.9 | 6.3 | 6.9 |
| **Poland** | NR | NR | NR | NR | 0.9 | 4.1 | 3.4 |
| **Portugal** | 2.1 | 1.0 | 1.0 | 2.0 | 3.9 | 5.2 | 5.5 |
| **Romania** | NR | NR | NR | NR | 0.0 | 2.3 | 2.3 |
| **Russia** | NR | 0.0 | 0.0 | 0.0 | 0.0 | 2.8 | 3.5 |
| **Rwanda** | NR | NR | NR | NR | 2.9 | 2.9 | 2.0 |
| **Senegal** | NR | NR | NR | 2.3 | 3.0 | 2.6 | 3.3 |
| **Sierra Leone** | NR | NR | NR | NR | 2.1 | 3.9 | 3.9 |
| **Singapore** | 5.4 | 4.9 | 4.9 | 6.0 | 7.5 | 7.5 | 7.5 |
| **Slovakia** | NR | NR | NR | NR | 1.0 | 2.4 | 2.6 |
| **Slovenia** | NR | NR | NR | NR | NR | 3.0 | 3.0 |
| **Somalia** | NR | NR | NR | NR | 1.0 | NR | NR |
| **South Africa** | NR | 1.8 | 1.7 | 2.5 | 3.9 | 5.9 | 5.9 |
| **South Korea** | NR | 4.2 | 3.4 | 4.2 | 3.0 | 3.2 | 3.5 |
| **Spain** | NR | 4.6 | 2.5 | 2.5 | 4.3 | 3.7 | 4.3 |
| **Sri Lanka** | NR | NR | 2.3 | 2.3 | 4.7 | 5.3 | 5.3 |
| **Sweden** | 2.1 | 2.7 | 2.4 | 3.3 | 4.2 | 5.2 | 4.8 |
| **Switzerland** | NR | 7.2 | 7.2 | 7.2 | 7.4 | 7.1 | 7.1 |
| **Syria** | NR | NR | NR | NR | 0.0 | 0.0 | 0.0 |
| **Taiwan** | NR | 2.1 | 2.1 | 2.1 | 3.9 | 4.4 | 3.1 |
| **Tanzania** | 1.0 | 1.3 | NR | 0.0 | 0.8 | 3.3 | 3.7 |
| **Thailand** | NR | 4.1 | 3.1 | 2.7 | 4.6 | 5.4 | 6.6 |
| **Togo** | NR | NR | NR | NR | 0.0 | 0.9 | 0.9 |
| **Trinidad & Tob.** | NR | NR | NR | 3.8 | 5.3 | 5.4 | 5.9 |
| **Tunisia** | NR | NR | 1.1 | 1.1 | 3.0 | 3.9 | 3.9 |
| **Turkey** | NR | 0.4 | 0.0 | 0.8 | 4.4 | 4.7 | 5.4 |
| **Uganda** | NR | NR | NR | 2.3 | 2.3 | 4.9 | 5.5 |
| **Ukraine** | NR | NR | NR | NR | NR | 1.8 | 2.7 |
| **Unit. Arab Em.** | NR | NR | NR | NR | NR | NR | 8.0 |
| **United Kingdom** | NR | 2.3 | 3.3 | 5.0 | 7.4 | 7.8 | 8.0 |
| **United States** | 3.4 | 4.8 | 5.3 | 6.8 | 7.9 | 8.3 | 8.3 |
| **Uruguay** | NR | 6.9 | 8.0 | 8.0 | 6.7 | 7.4 | 7.4 |
| **Venezuela** | NR | 5.7 | 3.6 | 2.8 | 3.1 | 1.8 | 3.7 |
| **Zambia** | NR | 1.3 | 1.3 | 1.3 | 0.9 | 3.3 | 3.6 |
| **Zimbabwe** | NR | NR | 3.0 | 2.3 | 1.8 | 3.9 | 4.1 |

# Area III: Monetary Policy and Price Stability–Protection of Money as a Store of Value and Medium of Exchange

| | 1970 | 1975 | 1980 | 1985 | 1990 | 1995 | 1997 |
|---|---|---|---|---|---|---|---|
| **Albania** | NR | NR | NR | 9.8 | 9.8 | 2.7 | 2.5 |
| **Algeria** | 8.5 | 6.1 | 6.5 | 8.2 | 6.0 | 5.2 | 7.6 |
| **Argentina** | 6.7 | 0.0 | 0.0 | 0.0 | 0.0 | 4.0 | 8.9 |
| **Australia** | 9.4 | 7.9 | 8.6 | 9.1 | 8.7 | 9.1 | 9.2 |
| **Austria** | 9.5 | 8.9 | 9.5 | 9.5 | 9.4 | 9.3 | 9.5 |
| **Bahamas** | 9.0 | 8.7 | 8.2 | 8.6 | 9.1 | 9.3 | 9.6 |
| **Bahrain** | 9.0 | 7.0 | 7.5 | 8.2 | 8.3 | 9.4 | 9.0 |
| **Bangladesh** | 8.5 | 2.6 | 6.0 | 8.0 | 9.2 | 8.5 | 9.0 |
| **Barbados** | 8.8 | 7.4 | 6.7 | 8.9 | 8.7 | 9.5 | 8.8 |
| **Belgium** | 9.5 | 8.3 | 9.4 | 9.4 | 9.5 | 9.6 | 9.7 |
| **Belize** | 8.7 | 6.6 | 8.3 | 8.8 | 9.1 | 9.5 | 9.6 |
| **Benin** | 9.0 | 6.9 | 8.4 | 8.1 | 9.0 | 6.9 | 7.9 |
| **Bolivia** | 9.2 | 5.1 | 3.5 | 0.0 | 3.1 | 6.8 | 7.9 |
| **Botswana** | 9.6 | 6.6 | 7.1 | 7.0 | 7.4 | 8.8 | 8.2 |
| **Brazil** | 6.2 | 4.8 | 1.7 | 0.0 | 0.0 | 0.0 | 2.8 |
| **Bulgaria** | NR | NR | NR | 9.7 | 5.9 | 0.0 | 0.0 |
| **Burundi** | 8.9 | 7.2 | 6.5 | 8.2 | 8.6 | 7.5 | 6.6 |
| **Cameroon** | 7.7 | 8.6 | 7.2 | 8.5 | 9.4 | 7.8 | 8.5 |
| **Canada** | 9.1 | 8.4 | 8.9 | 8.6 | 9.4 | 9.4 | 9.3 |
| **C. African Rep.** | 8.4 | 7.4 | 6.5 | 5.8 | 9.5 | 6.8 | 7.6 |
| **Chad** | 9.2 | 8.4 | 8.4 | 7.0 | 7.7 | 6.9 | 7.5 |
| **Chile** | 3.4 | 0.0 | 1.4 | 6.0 | 6.3 | 7.6 | 8.4 |
| **China** | 8.7 | 9.8 | 8.2 | 8.0 | 8.6 | 7.0 | 8.6 |
| **Colombia** | 8.1 | 6.7 | 6.0 | 7.0 | 5.9 | 6.6 | 7.0 |
| **Congo, Dem. R.** | 5.1 | 7.5 | 0.5 | 1.6 | 0.0 | 0.0 | 0.0 |
| **Congo, Rep. Of** | 8.7 | 8.8 | 7.1 | 8.1 | 7.8 | 7.7 | 7.5 |
| **Costa Rica** | 8.9 | 6.1 | 7.1 | 3.3 | 7.4 | 6.9 | 7.5 |
| **Cote d'Ivoire** | 9.1 | 7.8 | 6.2 | 8.9 | 9.2 | 6.6 | 6.8 |
| **Croatia** | NR | NR | NR | NR | NR | 2.8 | 3.6 |
| **Cyprus** | NR | 7.9 | 7.6 | 8.9 | 9.4 | 9.6 | 9.6 |
| **Czech Rep.** | NR | NR | NR | 9.4 | 8.8 | 6.3 | 8.1 |
| **Denmark** | 9.0 | 8.2 | 8.9 | 8.6 | 9.2 | 9.6 | 9.5 |
| **Dominican Rep.** | 9.6 | 7.4 | 8.2 | 3.4 | 2.0 | 5.7 | 8.1 |
| **Ecuador** | 8.3 | 6.4 | 7.2 | 5.2 | 1.7 | 4.7 | 5.8 |
| **Egypt** | 9.6 | 7.7 | 6.6 | 8.4 | 7.4 | 8.4 | 9.1 |
| **El Salvador** | 9.3 | 7.9 | 7.0 | 7.3 | 6.7 | 8.2 | 9.0 |
| **Estonia** | NR | NR | NR | 8.8 | 4.2 | 1.4 | 3.4 |
| **Fiji** | 8.6 | 6.3 | 8.0 | 8.7 | 8.4 | 9.3 | 9.2 |
| **Finland** | 9.0 | 7.1 | 8.7 | 8.7 | 9.0 | 7.7 | 9.3 |
| **France** | 9.4 | 8.2 | 8.4 | 8.8 | 9.5 | 9.8 | 9.7 |
| **Gabon** | 9.6 | 4.8 | 5.9 | 8.2 | 7.3 | 7.2 | 6.9 |

| | 1970 | 1975 | 1980 | 1985 | 1990 | 1995 | 1997 |
|---|---|---|---|---|---|---|---|
| **Germany** | 9.3 | 9.1 | 9.2 | 9.5 | 9.0 | 9.4 | 9.5 |
| **Ghana** | 8.9 | 5.2 | 1.5 | 2.4 | 5.4 | 3.6 | 5.4 |
| **Greece** | 9.4 | 7.4 | 7.6 | 7.4 | 7.3 | 8.0 | 8.5 |
| **Guatemala** | 9.4 | 7.4 | 8.1 | 7.4 | 5.5 | 7.2 | 7.8 |
| **Guinea-Bissau** | NR | 8.7 | 8.1 | 2.9 | 1.2 | 1.8 | 3.0 |
| **Guyana** | 9.3 | 5.9 | 7.7 | 6.9 | 2.6 | 4.1 | 8.2 |
| **Haiti** | 9.0 | 7.9 | 6.5 | 8.3 | 7.8 | 5.0 | 7.0 |
| **Honduras** | 9.3 | 8.4 | 7.9 | 9.4 | 7.7 | 6.1 | 6.4 |
| **Hong Kong** | 8.3 | 8.9 | 8.0 | 9.1 | 8.7 | 9.1 | 9.2 |
| **Hungary** | 9.2 | 9.1 | 8.6 | 9.1 | 7.5 | 6.4 | 7.4 |
| **Iceland** | 7.6 | 4.0 | 3.1 | 2.7 | 5.7 | 9.1 | 9.3 |
| **India** | 8.9 | 8.4 | 8.1 | 8.6 | 8.6 | 8.4 | 8.7 |
| **Indonesia** | 2.5 | 5.0 | 5.0 | 8.7 | 8.2 | 8.7 | 8.2 |
| **Iran** | 9.6 | 7.3 | 5.9 | 7.5 | 8.2 | 4.7 | 6.9 |
| **Ireland** | 8.8 | 7.5 | 7.7 | 8.8 | 9.0 | 9.5 | 9.3 |
| **Israel** | 8.5 | 5.1 | 0.7 | 0.0 | 2.2 | 8.1 | 8.4 |
| **Italy** | 8.4 | 7.3 | 7.1 | 8.3 | 8.9 | 9.3 | 9.5 |
| **Jamaica** | 8.7 | 5.8 | 6.9 | 5.3 | 6.1 | 3.5 | 6.9 |
| **Japan** | 9.1 | 8.0 | 9.2 | 9.7 | 9.6 | 9.5 | 9.5 |
| **Jordan** | NR | 7.5 | 7.4 | 8.8 | 8.2 | 9.5 | 9.5 |
| **Kenya** | 7.9 | 7.6 | 8.1 | 9.0 | 8.4 | 7.2 | 7.5 |
| **Kuwait** | 9.8 | 5.2 | 3.2 | 8.1 | 7.1 | 8.8 | 9.0 |
| **Latvia** | NR | NR | NR | NR | 7.1 | 2.3 | 5.3 |
| **Lithuania** | NR | NR | NR | NR | NR | 0.8 | 3.8 |
| **Luxembourg** | 7.5 | 8.5 | 8.5 | 9.4 | 9.1 | 9.4 | 9.4 |
| **Madagascar** | 8.8 | 8.3 | 7.6 | 7.6 | 7.3 | 3.3 | 6.0 |
| **Malawi** | 8.4 | 8.0 | 8.1 | 8.5 | 7.0 | 1.1 | 3.8 |
| **Malaysia** | 9.3 | 8.1 | 8.5 | 9.5 | 8.7 | 8.6 | 8.9 |
| **Mali** | 8.3 | 6.5 | 7.9 | 8.6 | 9.3 | 6.8 | 7.3 |
| **Malta** | 9.1 | 8.9 | 8.4 | 9.4 | 9.7 | 9.5 | 9.5 |
| **Mauritius** | 9.6 | 4.9 | 6.4 | 9.2 | 8.0 | 9.2 | 9.3 |
| **Mexico** | 8.8 | 7.4 | 6.5 | 1.0 | 1.5 | 4.4 | 6.3 |
| **Morocco** | 9.2 | 7.9 | 8.2 | 9.0 | 8.4 | 8.8 | 9.3 |
| **Myanmar** | 8.8 | 4.9 | 9.1 | 9.6 | 5.2 | 5.8 | 6.0 |
| **Namibia** | NR | NR | NR | 6.0 | 8.2 | 7.6 | 7.7 |
| **Nepal** | 8.3 | 5.9 | 7.8 | 8.2 | 8.1 | 8.0 | 8.7 |
| **Netherlands** | 9.2 | 8.7 | 9.2 | 9.3 | 9.4 | 9.6 | 9.4 |
| **New Zealand** | 8.3 | 7.7 | 8.3 | 8.0 | 6.4 | 9.5 | 9.6 |
| **Nicaragua** | 9.2 | 7.9 | 4.0 | 0.0 | 0.0 | 2.7 | 6.7 |
| **Niger** | 8.6 | 6.4 | 6.2 | 8.5 | 9.5 | 7.6 | 8.1 |
| **Nigeria** | 3.4 | 4.5 | 7.3 | 8.4 | 5.5 | 1.1 | 5.5 |
| **Norway** | 8.3 | 8.4 | 8.7 | 8.4 | 8.3 | 9.2 | 9.5 |
| **Oman** | 8.2 | 4.8 | 3.3 | 8.9 | 6.7 | 8.9 | 8.5 |
| **Pakistan** | 9.2 | 6.7 | 8.1 | 8.9 | 8.6 | 8.2 | 8.4 |

| | 1970 | 1975 | 1980 | 1985 | 1990 | 1995 | 1997 |
|---|---|---|---|---|---|---|---|
| **Panama** | 9.5 | 8.5 | 5.6 | 9.6 | 9.8 | 9.0 | 9.2 |
| **Pap. New Guinea** | 9.2 | 8.5 | 8.3 | 8.8 | 8.8 | 7.1 | 8.0 |
| **Paraguay** | 9.3 | 7.6 | 6.9 | 6.7 | 4.9 | 7.1 | 8.0 |
| **Peru** | 7.7 | 6.4 | 1.7 | 0.0 | 0.0 | 2.6 | 5.0 |
| **Philippines** | 9.0 | 7.3 | 7.9 | 6.1 | 5.3 | 8.2 | 8.5 |
| **Poland** | NR | 9.3 | 8.6 | 4.3 | 0.0 | 4.7 | 6.0 |
| **Portugal** | 9.5 | 7.4 | 7.4 | 7.4 | 7.6 | 8.7 | 9.1 |
| **Romania** | NR | NR | 8.8 | 9.3 | 7.8 | 1.0 | 0.0 |
| **Russia** | NR | 8.9 | 8.6 | 8.7 | 7.9 | 0.0 | 2.3 |
| **Rwanda** | 6.0 | 2.5 | 8.2 | 8.9 | 8.2 | 2.9 | 5.2 |
| **Senegal** | 9.4 | 7.6 | 8.1 | 8.8 | 9.5 | 7.7 | 8.0 |
| **Sierra Leone** | 9.3 | 7.5 | 7.8 | 0.5 | 0.0 | 2.5 | 6.4 |
| **Singapore** | 9.7 | 8.8 | 8.5 | 9.5 | 9.0 | 9.5 | 9.7 |
| **Slovakia** | NR | NR | NR | 9.4 | 8.8 | 7.3 | 8.6 |
| **Slovenia** | NR | NR | NR | NR | NR | 2.5 | 6.4 |
| **Somalia** | 8.6 | 7.3 | 1.7 | 3.9 | 0.0 | NR | NR |
| **South Africa** | 9.4 | 8.2 | 7.0 | 7.1 | 7.7 | 8.1 | 8.1 |
| **South Korea** | 6.6 | 5.9 | 6.7 | 8.6 | 8.6 | 8.7 | 9.6 |
| **Spain** | 9.1 | 7.3 | 7.8 | 8.7 | 8.2 | 9.4 | 9.5 |
| **Sri Lanka** | 9.0 | 8.3 | 6.8 | 8.3 | 7.2 | 8.7 | 8.9 |
| **Sweden** | 9.2 | 8.2 | 8.4 | 9.0 | 8.8 | 9.4 | 9.6 |
| **Switzerland** | 9.5 | 9.1 | 9.3 | 9.5 | 9.6 | 9.5 | 9.3 |
| **Syria** | 8.8 | 6.7 | 7.3 | 8.0 | 7.3 | 8.5 | 8.4 |
| **Taiwan** | 9.0 | 6.7 | 7.2 | 9.1 | 8.7 | 9.7 | 9.9 |
| **Tanzania** | 9.3 | 6.5 | 5.5 | 6.5 | 6.1 | 5.0 | 6.7 |
| **Thailand** | 9.1 | 8.3 | 8.2 | 9.3 | 8.7 | 9.1 | 9.3 |
| **Togo** | 9.1 | 6.8 | 6.7 | 8.7 | 9.4 | 6.7 | 6.7 |
| **Trinidad & Tob.** | 9.1 | 5.3 | 5.4 | 7.8 | 8.1 | 8.0 | 8.5 |
| **Tunisia** | 8.9 | 7.8 | 8.2 | 8.4 | 9.3 | 9.3 | 9.3 |
| **Turkey** | 5.5 | 6.4 | 0.6 | 3.1 | 1.1 | 0.9 | 1.6 |
| **Uganda** | NR | 4.7 | 1.6 | 0.0 | 0.4 | 5.4 | 7.5 |
| **Ukraine** | NR | NR | NR | NR | NR | 0.0 | 2.2 |
| **Unit. Arab Em.** | NR | NR | 7.2 | 9.0 | 9.4 | NR | NR |
| **United Kingdom** | 9.0 | 6.7 | 7.8 | 8.5 | 7.5 | 9.3 | 9.1 |
| **United States** | 9.4 | 8.9 | 8.9 | 9.1 | 9.4 | 9.6 | 9.8 |
| **Uruguay** | 3.6 | 0.0 | 1.7 | 1.5 | 1.6 | 0.9 | 5.3 |
| **Venezuela** | 9.6 | 5.9 | 6.4 | 7.7 | 2.6 | 2.2 | 0.8 |
| **Zambia** | 6.4 | 6.8 | 8.1 | 4.3 | 0.1 | 0.9 | 1.7 |
| **Zimbabwe** | 7.6 | 8.5 | 8.4 | 8.3 | 7.5 | 6.2 | 5.0 |

# AREA IV: FREEDOM TO USE ALTERNATIVE CURRENCIES

| | 1970 | 1975 | 1980 | 1985 | 1990 | 1995 | 1997 |
|---|---|---|---|---|---|---|---|
| Albania | 0.0 | 0.0 | 0.0 | 0.0 | 0.0 | 7.5 | 4.6 |
| Algeria | 0.0 | 0.0 | 0.0 | 0.0 | 0.0 | 0.0 | 0.0 |
| Argentina | 10.0 | 5.0 | 9.9 | 6.0 | 10.0 | 10.0 | 10.0 |
| Australia | 10.0 | 9.9 | 9.9 | 10.0 | 10.0 | 10.0 | 10.0 |
| Austria | 7.5 | 7.5 | 7.5 | 7.5 | 10.0 | 10.0 | 10.0 |
| Bahamas | 7.2 | 3.6 | 3.0 | 3.9 | 3.7 | 4.8 | 4.6 |
| Bahrain | NR | 10.0 | 10.0 | 10.0 | 10.0 | 10.0 | 10.0 |
| Bangladesh | NR | 0.0 | 0.0 | 0.0 | 0.0 | 2.2 | 3.2 |
| Barbados | NR | 3.0 | 3.9 | 3.9 | 4.0 | 4.7 | 4.9 |
| Belgium | 10.0 | 10.0 | 10.0 | 10.0 | 10.0 | 10.0 | 10.0 |
| Belize | NR | 3.6 | 1.6 | 0.0 | 2.5 | 4.7 | 4.6 |
| Benin | 4.8 | 4.8 | 4.8 | 4.9 | 4.6 | 4.9 | 4.8 |
| Bolivia | 6.1 | 9.5 | 7.8 | 4.1 | 9.7 | 9.9 | 9.9 |
| Botswana | NR | 0.6 | 4.0 | 2.8 | 4.3 | 7.3 | 7.3 |
| Brazil | 6.1 | 0.1 | 3.2 | 0.1 | 4.0 | 4.7 | 4.9 |
| Bulgaria | 0.0 | 0.0 | 0.0 | 0.0 | 0.0 | 7.0 | 7.1 |
| Burundi | 5.4 | 0.4 | 0.5 | 2.5 | 4.4 | 0.6 | 4.3 |
| Cameroon | 4.8 | 4.8 | 4.8 | 4.9 | 4.6 | 4.9 | 4.8 |
| Canada | 10.0 | 10.0 | 10.0 | 10.0 | 10.0 | 10.0 | 10.0 |
| C. African Rep. | 4.8 | 4.8 | 4.8 | 4.9 | 4.6 | 4.9 | 4.8 |
| Chad | 4.8 | 4.8 | 4.8 | 4.9 | 4.6 | 4.9 | 4.8 |
| Chile | 5.1 | 4.5 | 6.9 | 7.8 | 10.0 | 9.8 | 9.6 |
| China | 1.0 | 2.6 | 2.5 | 3.9 | 2.5 | 6.8 | 6.8 |
| Colombia | 3.9 | 2.1 | 3.4 | 6.6 | 3.3 | 4.3 | 3.6 |
| Congo, Dem. R. | 8.1 | 0.0 | 0.0 | 4.4 | 3.0 | 4.6 | 7.0 |
| Congo, Rep. Of | 4.8 | 4.8 | 4.8 | 4.9 | 4.6 | 4.9 | 4.8 |
| Costa Rica | 10.0 | 9.2 | 5.0 | 7.6 | 10.0 | 10.0 | 10.0 |
| Cote d'Ivoire | 4.8 | 4.8 | 4.8 | 4.9 | 4.6 | 4.9 | 4.8 |
| Croatia | NR | NR | NR | NR | 2.5 | 6.7 | 5.2 |
| Cyprus | 4.9 | 4.4 | 4.6 | 4.9 | 4.5 | 4.5 | 5.0 |
| Czech Rep. | 0.0 | 0.0 | 0.0 | 0.0 | 0.0 | 7.5 | 7.5 |
| Denmark | 5.0 | 4.9 | 4.8 | 5.0 | 10.0 | 10.0 | 10.0 |
| Dominican Rep. | 2.8 | 2.2 | 3.8 | 6.1 | 0.0 | 4.8 | 7.1 |
| Ecuador | 2.8 | 9.5 | 8.7 | 5.2 | 10.0 | 8.8 | 9.5 |
| Egypt | 0.0 | 4.9 | 9.1 | 5.0 | 5.0 | 7.2 | 7.5 |
| El Salvador | 3.2 | 3.0 | 0.0 | 0.0 | 2.6 | 9.9 | 9.7 |
| Estonia | NR | NR | NR | NR | 2.5 | 7.5 | 7.5 |
| Fiji | 4.8 | 3.3 | 3.2 | 4.2 | 4.6 | 4.9 | 4.7 |
| Finland | 7.5 | 7.4 | 7.4 | 7.5 | 10.0 | 10.0 | 10.0 |
| France | 4.8 | 5.0 | 4.7 | 4.6 | 10.0 | 10.0 | 10.0 |
| Gabon | 4.8 | 4.8 | 4.8 | 4.9 | 4.6 | 4.9 | 4.8 |
| Germany | 10.0 | 10.0 | 10.0 | 10.0 | 10.0 | 10.0 | 10.0 |

| | 1970 | 1975 | 1980 | 1985 | 1990 | 1995 | 1997 |
|---|---|---|---|---|---|---|---|
| Ghana | 0.0 | 0.0 | 0.0 | 0.0 | 4.3 | 7.3 | 7.4 |
| Greece | 7.3 | 7.2 | 6.8 | 5.0 | 7.2 | 7.5 | 10.0 |
| Guatemala | 4.1 | 6.5 | 9.0 | 5.0 | 10.0 | 10.0 | 9.9 |
| Guinea-Bissau | NR | 0.0 | 0.0 | 2.1 | 4.1 | 4.8 | 1.8 |
| Guyana | 8.2 | 0.0 | 0.0 | 0.0 | 4.1 | 7.1 | 7.0 |
| Haiti | 10.0 | 7.5 | 8.0 | 5.0 | 5.0 | 5.3 | 6.9 |
| Honduras | 7.0 | 10.0 | 8.0 | 5.0 | 10.0 | 9.9 | 9.8 |
| Hong Kong | 10.0 | 10.0 | 10.0 | 10.0 | 10.0 | 10.0 | 10.0 |
| Hungary | 0.0 | 0.0 | 0.0 | 0.0 | 2.8 | 7.5 | 10.0 |
| Iceland | 4.5 | 0.0 | 4.1 | 3.4 | 10.0 | 10.0 | 10.0 |
| India | 0.0 | 4.1 | 4.5 | 3.6 | 4.0 | 4.2 | 7.0 |
| Indonesia | 8.3 | 9.3 | 9.8 | 9.3 | 10.0 | 10.0 | 9.9 |
| Iran | 7.0 | 7.3 | 5.0 | 5.0 | 5.0 | 0.0 | 2.5 |
| Ireland | 5.0 | 5.0 | 5.0 | 4.7 | 4.9 | 10.0 | 10.0 |
| Israel | 2.0 | 2.5 | 7.4 | 6.8 | 7.1 | 7.5 | 7.4 |
| Italy | 4.8 | 4.1 | 5.0 | 5.0 | 10.0 | 10.0 | 10.0 |
| Jamaica | 8.8 | 2.8 | 0.0 | 3.1 | 2.3 | 9.3 | 8.5 |
| Japan | 4.9 | 7.5 | 7.5 | 7.5 | 10.0 | 10.0 | 10.0 |
| Jordan | 4.4 | 4.9 | 7.5 | 7.2 | 3.9 | 4.9 | 4.9 |
| Kenya | 1.9 | 4.2 | 4.0 | 4.8 | 4.4 | 7.3 | 9.4 |
| Kuwait | 10.0 | 10.0 | 10.0 | 10.0 | 10.0 | 10.0 | 10.0 |
| Latvia | NR | NR | NR | NR | 2.5 | 7.3 | 7.3 |
| Lithuania | NR | NR | NR | NR | 2.5 | 7.5 | 7.5 |
| Luxembourg | 10.0 | 10.0 | 10.0 | 10.0 | 10.0 | 10.0 | 10.0 |
| Madagascar | 9.6 | 2.7 | 0.0 | 4.1 | 4.3 | 4.8 | 3.3 |
| Malawi | 3.4 | 2.2 | 0.2 | 2.0 | 3.6 | 4.9 | 3.4 |
| Malaysia | 4.9 | 7.5 | 10.0 | 7.5 | 10.0 | 10.0 | 9.7 |
| Mali | 4.7 | 4.3 | 4.5 | 4.9 | 4.6 | 4.9 | 4.8 |
| Malta | 9.4 | 4.5 | 3.8 | 4.3 | 4.8 | 4.6 | 4.7 |
| Mauritius | 0.0 | 0.3 | 1.0 | 4.9 | 4.2 | 10.0 | 9.9 |
| Mexico | 10.0 | 10.0 | 5.0 | 7.5 | 10.0 | 10.0 | 9.9 |
| Morocco | 3.9 | 4.7 | 4.9 | 4.3 | 3.7 | 4.9 | 4.8 |
| Myanmar | 0.0 | 0.0 | 0.0 | 0.0 | 0.0 | 0.0 | 0.0 |
| Namibia | NR | NR | NR | 2.5 | 4.7 | 5.0 | 5.0 |
| Nepal | 0.0 | 1.0 | 5.0 | 3.9 | 3.4 | 3.1 | 2.8 |
| Netherlands | 10.0 | 10.0 | 10.0 | 10.0 | 10.0 | 10.0 | 10.0 |
| New Zealand | 3.9 | 4.5 | 5.0 | 4.6 | 10.0 | 10.0 | 10.0 |
| Nicaragua | 8.1 | 7.9 | 5.0 | 0.0 | 4.0 | 6.7 | 9.9 |
| Niger | 4.8 | 4.8 | 4.8 | 4.9 | 4.6 | 4.9 | 4.8 |
| Nigeria | 0.0 | 0.7 | 0.0 | 0.0 | 2.7 | 0.0 | 2.5 |
| Norway | 5.0 | 4.9 | 4.7 | 5.0 | 10.0 | 10.0 | 10.0 |
| Oman | NR | 10.0 | 10.0 | 10.0 | 10.0 | 10.0 | 10.0 |
| Pakistan | 0.0 | 3.3 | 2.3 | 4.6 | 6.1 | 7.2 | 4.5 |
| Panama | 10.0 | 10.0 | 10.0 | 10.0 | 10.0 | 10.0 | 10.0 |

| | 1970 | 1975 | 1980 | 1985 | 1990 | 1995 | 1997 |
|---|---|---|---|---|---|---|---|
| **Pap. New Guinea** | NR | 0.0 | 0.0 | 4.6 | 4.3 | 4.3 | 4.8 |
| **Paraguay** | 8.3 | 8.7 | 9.3 | 5.0 | 7.4 | 8.7 | 8.9 |
| **Peru** | 3.6 | 0.0 | 3.2 | 0.0 | 5.9 | 10.0 | 10.0 |
| **Philippines** | 0.0 | 3.7 | 4.7 | 4.3 | 4.3 | 10.0 | 9.5 |
| **Poland** | 2.5 | 2.5 | 2.5 | 2.5 | 9.1 | 10.0 | 7.5 |
| **Portugal** | 5.0 | 0.8 | 4.8 | 4.8 | 4.7 | 10.0 | 10.0 |
| **Romania** | 0.0 | 0.0 | 0.0 | 0.0 | 2.5 | 4.7 | 4.4 |
| **Russia** | 0.0 | 0.0 | 0.0 | 0.0 | 0.0 | 7.5 | 7.5 |
| **Rwanda** | 2.4 | 0.5 | 0.0 | 0.1 | 2.2 | 7.2 | 2.5 |
| **Senegal** | 4.8 | 4.8 | 4.8 | 4.9 | 4.6 | 4.9 | 4.8 |
| **Sierra Leone** | 9.6 | 0.0 | 0.0 | 0.0 | 0.0 | 7.3 | 2.5 |
| **Singapore** | 4.9 | 5.0 | 5.0 | 7.5 | 10.0 | 10.0 | 10.0 |
| **Slovakia** | 0.0 | 0.0 | 0.0 | 0.0 | 0.0 | 7.5 | 6.4 |
| **Slovenia** | NR | NR | NR | NR | 2.5 | 7.5 | 7.5 |
| **Somalia** | 6.2 | 2.2 | 0.9 | 0.0 | 0.0 | 0.0 | 2.5 |
| **South Africa** | 4.5 | 4.4 | 4.4 | 2.5 | 4.7 | 5.0 | 6.2 |
| **South Korea** | 3.0 | 4.8 | 3.9 | 3.9 | 4.9 | 10.0 | 9.8 |
| **Spain** | 4.4 | 4.8 | 5.0 | 4.8 | 4.8 | 10.0 | 10.0 |
| **Sri Lanka** | 0.0 | 0.0 | 4.1 | 3.0 | 2.6 | 4.8 | 4.9 |
| **Sweden** | 4.5 | 7.4 | 7.0 | 7.4 | 7.5 | 10.0 | 10.0 |
| **Switzerland** | 10.0 | 10.0 | 10.0 | 10.0 | 10.0 | 10.0 | 10.0 |
| **Syria** | 3.3 | 9.9 | 6.5 | 0.0 | 0.0 | 0.0 | 2.9 |
| **Taiwan** | 9.7 | 9.5 | 9.9 | 9.7 | 10.0 | 10.0 | 10.0 |
| **Tanzania** | 1.9 | 0.0 | 0.0 | 0.0 | 0.0 | 7.4 | 6.7 |
| **Thailand** | 5.0 | 4.8 | 4.5 | 4.7 | 7.5 | 10.0 | 10.0 |
| **Togo** | 4.8 | 4.8 | 4.8 | 4.9 | 4.6 | 4.9 | 4.8 |
| **Trinidad & Tob.** | 7.2 | 0.7 | 0.1 | 1.1 | 1.0 | 9.7 | 9.6 |
| **Tunisia** | 2.0 | 3.9 | 3.2 | 3.8 | 4.2 | 4.9 | 4.7 |
| **Turkey** | 0.0 | 3.9 | 3.4 | 4.7 | 9.8 | 9.8 | 9.9 |
| **Uganda** | 1.9 | 0.0 | 0.0 | 2.5 | 1.0 | 4.7 | 9.2 |
| **Ukraine** | NR | 0.0 | 0.0 | 0.0 | 2.5 | 7.2 | 7.2 |
| **Unit. Arab Em.** | NR | 10.0 | 10.0 | 10.0 | 10.0 | 10.0 | 10.0 |
| **United Kingdom** | 5.0 | 5.0 | 5.0 | 10.0 | 10.0 | 10.0 | 10.0 |
| **United States** | 10.0 | 10.0 | 10.0 | 10.0 | 10.0 | 10.0 | 10.0 |
| **Uruguay** | 9.7 | 10.0 | 10.0 | 10.0 | 10.0 | 10.0 | 10.0 |
| **Venezuela** | 10.0 | 10.0 | 10.0 | 7.5 | 10.0 | 0.8 | 9.8 |
| **Zambia** | 0.0 | 0.0 | 0.0 | 1.2 | 0.0 | 4.7 | 6.8 |
| **Zimbabwe** | 3.6 | 0.0 | 0.0 | 0.8 | 3.5 | 4.9 | 6.1 |

## AREA V: LEGAL STRUCTURE AND PROPERTY RIGHTS–SECURITY OF PROPERTY RIGHTS AND VIABILITY OF CONTRACTS

| | 1970 | 1975 | 1980 | 1985 | 1990 | 1995 | 1997 |
|---|---|---|---|---|---|---|---|
| Albania | NR | NR | NR | 6.3 | 5.9 | 8.0 | 2.5 |
| Algeria | 3.2 | 2.5 | 3.4 | 3.7 | 3.5 | 7.4 | 8.5 |
| Argentina | 4.2 | 1.2 | 4.5 | 3.2 | 5.2 | 8.0 | 8.5 |
| Australia | 9.3 | 7.2 | 8.0 | 8.7 | 8.9 | 10.0 | 10.0 |
| Austria | NR | NR | 9.3 | 9.1 | 10.0 | 10.0 | 10.0 |
| Bahamas | NR | NR | NR | 6.8 | 6.7 | 6.3 | 6.6 |
| Bahrain | NR | NR | NR | 5.9 | 5.9 | 8.5 | 8.5 |
| Bangladesh | NR | NR | 1.9 | 2.2 | 1.7 | 5.3 | 6.9 |
| Barbados | NR | NR | NR | 6.8 | 6.7 | 6.3 | 6.6 |
| Belgium | 9.9 | 8.6 | 8.6 | 9.1 | 10.0 | 9.5 | 9.0 |
| Belize | NR | NR | NR | NR | NR | NR | NR |
| Benin | NR | NR | 4.2 | 4.1 | 4.3 | 3.6 | 3.6 |
| Bolivia | NR | NR | 1.7 | 0.5 | 3.4 | 7.2 | 6.9 |
| Botswana | NR | NR | NR | 6.5 | 6.4 | 8.0 | 7.6 |
| Brazil | 6.2 | 5.6 | 6.0 | 5.6 | 6.4 | 8.0 | 7.9 |
| Bulgaria | NR | NR | NR | 7.6 | 7.4 | 7.2 | 4.8 |
| Burundi | NR | NR | 4.2 | 4.1 | 4.3 | 3.6 | 3.6 |
| Cameroon | NR | NR | 5.7 | 6.0 | 6.0 | 5.9 | 5.4 |
| Canada | 9.9 | 8.2 | 8.4 | 9.1 | 9.6 | 9.5 | 9.4 |
| C. African Rep. | NR | NR | 4.2 | 4.1 | 4.3 | 3.6 | 3.6 |
| Chad | NR | NR | 4.2 | 4.1 | 4.3 | 3.6 | 3.6 |
| Chile | 0.0 | 2.9 | 6.5 | 4.9 | 7.0 | 8.5 | 8.5 |
| China | NR | NR | NR | 6.5 | 5.6 | 8.5 | 8.5 |
| Colombia | 2.5 | 3.2 | 4.5 | 4.3 | 3.9 | 5.8 | 3.5 |
| Congo, Dem. R. | NR | NR | 1.9 | 2.2 | 2.1 | 0.0 | 0.0 |
| Congo, Rep. Of | NR | NR | 4.2 | 2.9 | 2.6 | 4.8 | 4.8 |
| Costa Rica | NR | NR | 4.5 | 5.1 | 5.3 | 6.3 | 6.0 |
| Cote d'Ivoire | NR | NR | NR | 6.4 | 5.1 | 4.5 | 3.8 |
| Croatia | NR | NR | NR | NR | NR | NR | NR |
| Cyprus | NR | NR | NR | 4.4 | 7.3 | 8.5 | 9.0 |
| Czech Rep. | NR | NR | NR | 7.3 | 7.8 | 9.5 | 10.0 |
| Denmark | 9.7 | 8.2 | 8.4 | 9.1 | 9.6 | 10.0 | 10.0 |
| Dominican Rep. | NR | NR | 5.4 | 3.9 | 4.5 | 5.2 | 4.8 |
| Ecuador | 2.5 | 3.8 | 6.4 | 3.9 | 5.1 | 5.5 | 5.1 |
| Egypt | 0.3 | 3.4 | 2.5 | 5.2 | 3.5 | 7.6 | 7.6 |
| El Salvador | NR | NR | 1.9 | 1.7 | 1.7 | 7.2 | 6.9 |
| Estonia | NR | NR | NR | NR | NR | NR | 7.2 |
| Fiji | NR | NR | NR | NR | NR | NR | NR |
| Finland | 9.1 | 7.5 | 8.1 | 9.1 | 9.6 | 10.0 | 10.0 |
| France | 8.5 | 5.9 | 6.7 | 8.3 | 9.1 | 10.0 | 9.0 |
| Gabon | NR | NR | 3.6 | 4.8 | 5.7 | 7.2 | 6.9 |

| | 1970 | 1975 | 1980 | 1985 | 1990 | 1995 | 1997 |
|---|---|---|---|---|---|---|---|
| **Germany** | 9.9 | 8.5 | 8.6 | 8.8 | 10.0 | 10.0 | 10.0 |
| **Ghana** | NR | NR | 3.0 | 2.4 | 6.0 | 6.6 | 6.9 |
| **Greece** | 5.7 | 5.6 | 5.5 | 5.6 | 7.7 | 7.6 | 7.5 |
| **Guatemala** | NR | NR | 2.1 | 2.1 | 2.5 | 5.3 | 4.8 |
| **Guinea-Bissau** | NR | NR | NR | 1.7 | 2.6 | 0.2 | 0.0 |
| **Guyana** | NR | NR | 1.9 | 2.2 | 3.5 | 6.3 | 7.0 |
| **Haiti** | NR | NR | 1.9 | 2.8 | 0.8 | 2.7 | 4.2 |
| **Honduras** | NR | NR | 2.5 | 3.1 | 3.5 | 5.3 | 4.8 |
| **Hong Kong** | 8.5 | 7.4 | 9.6 | 7.3 | 7.4 | 10.0 | 7.9 |
| **Hungary** | NR | NR | NR | 7.2 | 7.8 | 9.5 | 10.0 |
| **Iceland** | 9.1 | 7.5 | 8.1 | 8.7 | 10.0 | 10.0 | 10.0 |
| **India** | 3.2 | 2.5 | 5.9 | 5.3 | 4.0 | 7.1 | 7.6 |
| **Indonesia** | 3.8 | 3.4 | 3.1 | 4.2 | 5.5 | 7.6 | 7.6 |
| **Iran** | 4.6 | 3.7 | 0.5 | 1.5 | 2.3 | 5.9 | 7.5 |
| **Ireland** | 9.3 | 7.7 | 7.8 | 7.7 | 9.1 | 10.0 | 10.0 |
| **Israel** | 7.8 | 8.0 | 5.3 | 7.3 | 5.2 | 8.5 | 8.5 |
| **Italy** | 6.6 | 3.7 | 5.4 | 8.1 | 9.5 | 8.5 | 9.4 |
| **Jamaica** | NR | NR | 3.2 | 3.9 | 4.6 | 8.0 | 8.5 |
| **Japan** | 9.1 | 7.1 | 8.3 | 8.6 | 9.5 | 10.0 | 10.0 |
| **Jordan** | NR | NR | 1.9 | 3.1 | 3.2 | 7.2 | 7.0 |
| **Kenya** | 4.0 | 3.6 | 4.7 | 5.5 | 5.1 | 5.7 | 5.4 |
| **Kuwait** | NR | NR | 1.1 | 5.6 | 2.6 | 8.5 | 8.8 |
| **Latvia** | NR | NR | NR | NR | NR | NR | 7.2 |
| **Lithuania** | NR | NR | NR | NR | NR | NR | 7.2 |
| **Luxembourg** | 9.9 | 8.4 | 8.6 | 10.0 | 10.0 | 10.0 | 10.0 |
| **Madagascar** | NR | NR | NR | 3.4 | 2.5 | 2.5 | 2.2 |
| **Malawi** | NR | NR | 3.6 | 4.0 | 4.6 | 4.4 | 6.0 |
| **Malaysia** | 6.2 | 5.3 | 7.3 | 6.7 | 7.7 | 7.2 | 7.5 |
| **Mali** | NR | NR | 3.2 | 2.3 | 2.4 | 2.2 | 2.2 |
| **Malta** | NR | NR | NR | 3.5 | 4.8 | 9.5 | 10.0 |
| **Mauritius** | NR | NR | NR | 6.5 | 6.4 | 8.0 | 7.6 |
| **Mexico** | 5.2 | 4.7 | 6.4 | 4.8 | 7.3 | 7.2 | 8.5 |
| **Morocco** | 3.2 | 2.5 | 1.8 | 3.6 | 4.0 | 8.1 | 8.5 |
| **Myanmar** | NR | NR | 5.0 | 4.0 | 2.2 | 3.5 | 6.3 |
| **Namibia** | NR | NR | NR | NR | 2.2 | 5.5 | 8.8 |
| **Nepal** | NR | NR | NR | NR | NR | NR | NR |
| **Netherlands** | 10.0 | 8.1 | 9.0 | 9.6 | 9.6 | 10.0 | 10.0 |
| **New Zealand** | 9.3 | 7.2 | 9.1 | 8.7 | 9.6 | 10.0 | 10.0 |
| **Nicaragua** | NR | NR | 1.9 | 2.2 | 3.2 | 5.0 | 5.4 |
| **Niger** | NR | NR | 4.2 | 4.6 | 4.9 | 0.7 | 2.6 |
| **Nigeria** | 3.5 | 3.5 | 2.8 | 1.5 | 3.0 | 4.5 | 5.4 |
| **Norway** | 9.5 | 7.6 | 8.3 | 9.5 | 9.8 | 10.0 | 10.0 |
| **Oman** | NR | NR | NR | 6.0 | 5.3 | 7.7 | 7.5 |
| **Pakistan** | 1.9 | 0.8 | 2.3 | 3.5 | 2.4 | 6.6 | 7.0 |

| | 1970 | 1975 | 1980 | 1985 | 1990 | 1995 | 1997 |
|---|---|---|---|---|---|---|---|
| **Panama** | NR | NR | 2.7 | 3.5 | 3.3 | 6.6 | 6.9 |
| **Pap. New Guinea** | NR | NR | NR | 6.8 | 6.2 | 5.9 | 7.3 |
| **Paraguay** | NR | NR | 4.3 | 4.8 | 5.3 | 6.0 | 5.6 |
| **Peru** | 1.7 | 1.4 | 3.9 | 1.2 | 2.6 | 8.0 | 7.9 |
| **Philippines** | 4.4 | 4.4 | 3.0 | 1.7 | 2.5 | 6.3 | 7.6 |
| **Poland** | NR | NR | NR | 4.0 | 6.0 | 9.5 | 9.0 |
| **Portugal** | 6.3 | 0.9 | 9.2 | 7.1 | 9.1 | 9.5 | 9.0 |
| **Romania** | NR | NR | NR | 3.4 | 6.0 | 6.6 | 8.5 |
| **Russia** | NR | NR | NR | NR | NR | NR | 5.4 |
| **Rwanda** | NR | NR | NR | NR | NR | NR | NR |
| **Senegal** | NR | NR | 3.6 | 4.0 | 4.0 | 1.0 | 2.7 |
| **Sierra Leone** | NR | NR | NR | 5.1 | 4.7 | 0.0 | 2.2 |
| **Singapore** | 8.5 | 7.4 | 8.9 | 8.2 | 8.8 | 10.0 | 10.0 |
| **Slovakia** | NR | NR | NR | 7.3 | 7.8 | 7.6 | 6.3 |
| **Slovenia** | NR | NR | NR | NR | NR | 8.5 | 8.2 |
| **Somalia** | NR | NR | NR | 3.9 | 1.4 | 0.0 | 0.0 |
| **South Africa** | 8.9 | 6.5 | 6.6 | 5.2 | 3.8 | 6.8 | 8.5 |
| **South Korea** | 6.0 | 4.7 | 6.8 | 5.0 | 7.2 | 9.0 | 8.1 |
| **Spain** | 7.0 | 5.0 | 6.8 | 7.0 | 8.5 | 9.5 | 10.0 |
| **Sri Lanka** | NR | NR | 3.9 | 3.5 | 2.1 | 6.6 | 7.6 |
| **Sweden** | 8.6 | 7.2 | 7.8 | 8.7 | 10.0 | 9.5 | 10.0 |
| **Switzerland** | 10.0 | 9.3 | 9.4 | 10.0 | 10.0 | 10.0 | 9.4 |
| **Syria** | NR | NR | 0.7 | 2.7 | 2.6 | 6.3 | 6.9 |
| **Taiwan** | 7.5 | 6.2 | 8.9 | 8.2 | 9.0 | 9.0 | 8.1 |
| **Tanzania** | NR | NR | 6.2 | 6.0 | 5.5 | 5.7 | 6.3 |
| **Thailand** | 6.2 | 5.3 | 7.0 | 6.0 | 7.8 | 7.2 | 8.5 |
| **Togo** | NR | NR | 3.0 | 4.2 | 4.4 | 4.8 | 4.2 |
| **Trinidad & Tob.** | NR | NR | 6.2 | 5.1 | 6.6 | 5.7 | 5.4 |
| **Tunisia** | 3.2 | 2.5 | 4.6 | 3.1 | 3.3 | 6.3 | 8.5 |
| **Turkey** | 3.8 | 3.1 | 5.2 | 5.6 | 4.4 | 6.3 | 6.0 |
| **Uganda** | NR | NR | 2.5 | 2.6 | 2.1 | 1.5 | 4.5 |
| **Ukraine** | NR | NR | NR | NR | NR | NR | 5.1 |
| **Unit. Arab Em.** | NR | NR | 1.9 | 4.8 | 5.4 | 6.3 | 6.0 |
| **United Kingdom** | 9.8 | 7.0 | 8.2 | 8.5 | 9.5 | 9.5 | 10.0 |
| **United States** | 10.0 | 9.2 | 9.4 | 9.6 | 9.6 | 9.5 | 10.0 |
| **Uruguay** | NR | NR | 5.7 | 6.0 | 6.8 | 7.7 | 7.5 |
| **Venezuela** | 5.1 | 1.7 | 6.1 | 5.1 | 6.1 | 5.7 | 5.4 |
| **Zambia** | NR | NR | 6.0 | 4.0 | 2.5 | 4.1 | 4.3 |
| **Zimbabwe** | NR | NR | 2.9 | 3.1 | 4.0 | 3.9 | 3.9 |

## AREA VI: INTERNATIONAL EXCHANGE: FREEDOM TO TRADE WITH FOREIGNERS

| | 1970 | 1975 | 1980 | 1985 | 1990 | 1995 | 1997 |
|---|---|---|---|---|---|---|---|
| **Albania** | NR | NR | NR | NR | NR | 4.2 | 5.8 |
| **Algeria** | NR | NR | 7.8 | 4.7 | 3.6 | 5.0 | 4.7 |
| **Argentina** | NR | 0.6 | 3.4 | 3.7 | 3.9 | 7.3 | 6.6 |
| **Australia** | 7.0 | 6.6 | 7.1 | 7.3 | 6.9 | 8.0 | 8.4 |
| **Austria** | 7.8 | 7.6 | 8.3 | 8.5 | 8.2 | 8.7 | 8.5 |
| **Bahamas** | NR | 4.6 | 4.4 | 5.3 | 3.4 | 3.0 | NR |
| **Bahrain** | NR | NR | NR | 8.6 | 8.4 | 8.0 | 8.0 |
| **Bangladesh** | NR | 3.4 | 0.8 | 1.6 | 1.5 | 0.7 | NR |
| **Barbados** | 5.8 | 5.6 | 6.3 | 6.3 | 5.5 | 5.8 | NR |
| **Belgium** | 9.5 | 9.0 | 9.0 | 9.1 | 8.7 | 8.8 | 8.6 |
| **Belize** | NR | NR | 4.2 | 4.5 | 3.1 | 2.6 | 4.7 |
| **Benin** | NR | 4.0 | 2.2 | 2.1 | NR | NR | NR |
| **Bolivia** | 3.6 | 4.9 | 3.3 | 5.8 | 7.8 | 8.6 | 8.3 |
| **Botswana** | NR | 4.3 | 3.2 | 6.8 | 7.6 | 6.9 | 5.6 |
| **Brazil** | 4.7 | 5.6 | 3.5 | 3.4 | 5.2 | 7.4 | 6.2 |
| **Bulgaria** | NR | NR | NR | 6.6 | 7.9 | 6.5 | 7.7 |
| **Burundi** | NR | 1.3 | 0.4 | 1.0 | 1.1 | 3.9 | 2.9 |
| **Cameroon** | NR | 2.2 | 4.0 | 5.6 | 6.4 | 6.1 | NR |
| **Canada** | 8.2 | 7.6 | 8.2 | 8.6 | 8.2 | 8.7 | 8.5 |
| **C. African Rep.** | NR | NR | 3.8 | 3.9 | 3.0 | 5.8 | NR |
| **Chad** | NR | 4.7 | NR | NR | 7.1 | 8.2 | NR |
| **Chile** | 4.1 | 4.7 | 8.5 | 7.0 | 8.2 | 8.3 | 8.0 |
| **China** | NR | NR | 3.2 | 4.8 | 4.4 | 5.4 | 7.2 |
| **Colombia** | 4.5 | 4.7 | 4.0 | 3.5 | 4.6 | 7.6 | 7.0 |
| **Congo, Dem. R.** | 1.4 | 0.9 | 3.2 | 4.0 | 4.0 | 4.0 | NR |
| **Congo, Rep. Of** | NR | 6.7 | 7.8 | 4.3 | 5.1 | 7.0 | NR |
| **Costa Rica** | 6.4 | 5.6 | 4.9 | 3.5 | 6.4 | 7.6 | 7.9 |
| **Cote d'Ivoire** | NR | NR | 4.3 | 4.8 | 4.1 | 6.3 | 8.8 |
| **Croatia** | NR | NR | NR | NR | NR | 6.7 | 7.0 |
| **Cyprus** | 5.5 | 6.6 | 6.5 | 6.3 | 5.3 | 6.9 | NR |
| **Czech Rep.** | NR | NR | NR | NR | NR | 8.6 | 8.7 |
| **Denmark** | 7.6 | 8.1 | 8.5 | 8.6 | 8.1 | 8.3 | 8.3 |
| **Dominican Rep.** | 0.7 | 1.2 | 3.3 | 5.1 | 4.6 | 5.6 | 6.6 |
| **Ecuador** | 1.0 | 4.5 | 5.1 | 4.1 | 3.5 | 6.6 | 7.1 |
| **Egypt** | NR | 2.5 | 2.3 | 3.6 | 3.9 | 3.8 | NR |
| **El Salvador** | 3.5 | 5.5 | 3.3 | 4.4 | 5.7 | 7.2 | 7.0 |
| **Estonia** | NR | NR | NR | NR | NR | 9.5 | 9.2 |
| **Fiji** | NR | 5.4 | 5.9 | 4.7 | 5.9 | 6.2 | 6.4 |
| **Finland** | 7.9 | 7.6 | 8.5 | 8.6 | 7.7 | 8.4 | 8.4 |
| **France** | 8.3 | 8.3 | 8.5 | 8.5 | 8.3 | 8.4 | 8.5 |
| **Gabon** | 4.3 | 4.9 | 3.6 | 6.1 | 6.0 | 7.1 | NR |
| **Germany** | 8.5 | 8.4 | 8.7 | 8.8 | 8.4 | 8.4 | 8.5 |

| | 1970 | 1975 | 1980 | 1985 | 1990 | 1995 | 1997 |
|---|---|---|---|---|---|---|---|
| **Ghana** | 1.3 | 1.0 | 0.0 | 2.6 | 5.7 | 6.7 | NR |
| **Greece** | 4.9 | 7.1 | 7.5 | 8.0 | 8.0 | 8.2 | 8.1 |
| **Guatemala** | 4.9 | 5.5 | 3.3 | 3.9 | 5.1 | 7.3 | 6.0 |
| **Guinea-Bissau** | NR | NR | NR | NR | NR | NR | NR |
| **Guyana** | NR | NR | NR | 6.5 | NR | NR | NR |
| **Haiti** | NR | 3.0 | 3.8 | 5.8 | 4.3 | NR | NR |
| **Honduras** | 5.5 | 6.2 | 4.0 | NR | 5.8 | 7.4 | NR |
| **Hong Kong** | 9.9 | 9.6 | 9.7 | 9.8 | 9.9 | 9.9 | 10.0 |
| **Hungary** | NR | NR | 7.1 | 7.6 | 6.0 | 7.0 | 6.4 |
| **Iceland** | 3.8 | 4.4 | 6.3 | 7.2 | 7.6 | 8.2 | 7.6 |
| **India** | NR | 0.9 | 0.7 | 0.9 | 1.1 | 1.7 | 4.1 |
| **Indonesia** | 5.5 | 5.4 | 6.7 | 5.8 | 6.7 | 7.1 | 6.9 |
| **Iran** | 3.5 | 8.3 | 3.2 | 2.7 | 5.6 | 5.1 | 4.8 |
| **Ireland** | 5.6 | 7.3 | 8.2 | 8.4 | 8.0 | 8.4 | 8.8 |
| **Israel** | 4.3 | 4.8 | 6.4 | 7.3 | 7.8 | 7.4 | 8.2 |
| **Italy** | 8.5 | 8.3 | 8.4 | 8.5 | 8.2 | 8.5 | 8.4 |
| **Jamaica** | NR | 6.5 | 7.6 | 7.5 | 6.2 | 6.9 | 6.7 |
| **Japan** | 7.0 | 7.9 | 8.0 | 8.1 | 7.9 | 7.6 | 7.9 |
| **Jordan** | NR | 6.0 | 6.1 | 6.7 | 5.9 | 7.4 | 6.7 |
| **Kenya** | 6.6 | 6.7 | 4.2 | 3.8 | 3.7 | 6.0 | 6.4 |
| **Kuwait** | NR | NR | NR | 8.0 | 8.0 | 8.0 | 7.7 |
| **Latvia** | NR | NR | NR | NR | NR | 8.2 | 7.8 |
| **Lithuania** | NR | NR | NR | NR | NR | 8.2 | 8.1 |
| **Luxembourg** | 9.1 | 7.9 | 8.7 | 8.8 | 8.4 | 8.5 | 8.5 |
| **Madagascar** | 1.5 | 1.9 | 4.2 | 2.5 | 4.2 | 5.8 | 3.7 |
| **Malawi** | 6.3 | 7.2 | 3.4 | 4.0 | 4.9 | 3.9 | 4.8 |
| **Malaysia** | 5.9 | 7.0 | 7.0 | 7.9 | 7.6 | 7.8 | 6.9 |
| **Mali** | NR | 1.9 | 5.0 | 4.9 | 5.4 | 7.0 | NR |
| **Malta** | 4.7 | 6.5 | 6.3 | 6.2 | 6.1 | 6.4 | 5.1 |
| **Mauritius** | 5.3 | 5.3 | 3.6 | 3.9 | 4.0 | 5.7 | 3.8 |
| **Mexico** | 3.6 | 3.4 | 1.6 | 4.4 | 7.7 | 8.3 | 7.9 |
| **Morocco** | 5.4 | 5.4 | 2.7 | 6.0 | 5.0 | 5.3 | NR |
| **Myanmar** | 1.7 | 0.0 | 0.8 | 0.0 | 0.0 | 0.0 | 0.0 |
| **Namibia** | NR | NR | NR | NR | 5.7 | 4.2 | 6.9 |
| **Nepal** | 0.4 | 3.1 | 4.6 | 5.8 | 4.4 | 6.5 | 6.6 |
| **Netherlands** | 8.8 | 8.6 | 8.7 | 8.8 | 8.5 | 8.6 | 8.6 |
| **New Zealand** | 7.3 | 7.0 | 7.0 | 7.2 | 6.8 | 7.9 | 8.3 |
| **Nicaragua** | 6.2 | 6.2 | 2.5 | 3.4 | 5.8 | 5.6 | NR |
| **Niger** | NR | 5.6 | 5.1 | 3.0 | 2.6 | 5.3 | NR |
| **Nigeria** | 4.6 | 5.8 | 4.4 | 5.4 | 5.2 | 3.9 | NR |
| **Norway** | 8.4 | 8.6 | 8.8 | 8.8 | 8.4 | 8.0 | 7.7 |
| **Oman** | 8.5 | NR | NR | 8.6 | 8.1 | 7.8 | 8.0 |
| **Pakistan** | 1.1 | 1.5 | 0.9 | 1.1 | 1.9 | 3.3 | 5.0 |
| **Panama** | 6.5 | 7.5 | 8.5 | 7.4 | 6.0 | 7.7 | 8.8 |

| | 1970 | 1975 | 1980 | 1985 | 1990 | 1995 | 1997 |
|---|---|---|---|---|---|---|---|
| **Pap. New Guinea** | NR | 7.6 | 7.8 | 7.3 | 6.9 | 6.6 | 4.6 |
| **Paraguay** | 2.9 | 3.5 | 3.1 | 5.4 | 6.5 | 7.9 | 7.0 |
| **Peru** | 4.1 | 3.7 | 2.0 | 2.6 | 3.3 | 7.1 | 7.0 |
| **Philippines** | 5.5 | 2.2 | 4.6 | 4.5 | 6.5 | 7.1 | 7.4 |
| **Poland** | NR | NR | NR | 5.5 | 6.6 | 6.2 | 5.0 |
| **Portugal** | 7.0 | 6.2 | 7.7 | 8.3 | 8.0 | 8.4 | 8.4 |
| **Romania** | NR | NR | NR | NR | 8.1 | 7.7 | 7.0 |
| **Russia** | NR | NR | NR | NR | NR | 6.9 | 7.1 |
| **Rwanda** | NR | 0.0 | 1.3 | NR | 0.6 | 1.0 | NR |
| **Senegal** | NR | 4.9 | 3.4 | 4.5 | 4.3 | 4.4 | 4.3 |
| **Sierra Leone** | NR | 3.4 | 3.4 | 2.9 | 3.0 | 3.0 | 0.0 |
| **Singapore** | 9.5 | 9.7 | 9.8 | 9.5 | 9.8 | 9.7 | 9.9 |
| **Slovakia** | NR | NR | NR | NR | NR | 8.7 | 8.8 |
| **Slovenia** | NR | NR | NR | NR | NR | NR | 8.2 |
| **Somalia** | NR | 1.5 | 3.1 | 1.9 | NR | NR | NR |
| **South Africa** | 8.1 | 8.5 | 8.6 | 7.6 | 7.2 | 6.1 | 7.7 |
| **South Korea** | 7.3 | 7.8 | 6.9 | 6.7 | 7.5 | 7.7 | 5.8 |
| **Spain** | 5.0 | 6.6 | 7.6 | 7.8 | 8.0 | 8.4 | 8.5 |
| **Sri Lanka** | 1.9 | 3.5 | 2.9 | 5.1 | 4.3 | 5.9 | 5.8 |
| **Sweden** | 8.2 | 8.4 | 8.5 | 9.0 | 8.7 | 8.6 | 8.6 |
| **Switzerland** | 7.1 | 7.8 | 8.3 | 8.4 | 7.8 | 7.8 | 8.5 |
| **Syria** | 3.7 | 4.6 | 3.0 | 3.7 | 4.5 | 6.7 | 6.9 |
| **Taiwan** | 5.7 | 7.0 | 8.0 | 8.1 | 8.1 | 8.4 | NR |
| **Tanzania** | 6.0 | 5.4 | 4.8 | 3.0 | 4.0 | 4.8 | 6.3 |
| **Thailand** | 4.5 | 4.2 | 4.9 | 5.9 | 4.9 | 6.0 | 7.0 |
| **Togo** | NR | 5.6 | 3.2 | 6.1 | 5.6 | NR | NR |
| **Trinidad & Tob.** | NR | 7.0 | 6.7 | 5.4 | 5.5 | 6.8 | NR |
| **Tunisia** | 3.7 | 3.6 | 4.8 | 3.3 | 3.3 | 5.2 | 4.6 |
| **Turkey** | 0.0 | 0.3 | 2.9 | 4.6 | 3.6 | 6.5 | 8.3 |
| **Uganda** | NR | 0.0 | 7.2 | 2.3 | 2.3 | 5.9 | NR |
| **Ukraine** | NR | NR | NR | NR | NR | NR | 7.3 |
| **Unit. Arab Em.** | NR | NR | NR | 8.9 | 8.9 | NR | NR |
| **United Kingdom** | 3.4 | 8.6 | 8.6 | 8.7 | 8.3 | 8.5 | 8.5 |
| **United States** | 6.5 | 7.7 | 8.4 | 8.0 | 7.9 | 8.0 | 7.8 |
| **Uruguay** | 5.0 | 6.0 | 3.1 | 5.6 | 6.1 | 7.5 | 7.1 |
| **Venezuela** | 7.1 | 7.1 | 7.4 | 4.2 | 5.3 | 7.9 | 7.4 |
| **Zambia** | NR | 8.8 | 8.8 | 3.7 | 4.5 | 6.8 | 6.9 |
| **Zimbabwe** | NR | 8.1 | 6.1 | 4.9 | 4.8 | 7.4 | 3.7 |

## AREA VII: FREEDOM OF EXCHANGE IN CAPITAL AND FINANCIAL MARKETS

| | 1970 | 1975 | 1980 | 1985 | 1990 | 1995 | 1997 |
|---|---|---|---|---|---|---|---|
| **Albania** | NR | NR | NR | NR | 0.0 | 2.6 | 3.1 |
| **Algeria** | NR | NR | NR | NR | 0.3 | 0.7 | 0.7 |
| **Argentina** | 5.0 | 4.7 | 3.1 | 2.9 | 2.6 | 8.1 | 8.1 |
| **Australia** | 6.3 | 5.0 | 6.6 | 7.6 | 9.2 | 9.3 | 9.3 |
| **Austria** | 5.6 | 5.0 | 5.5 | 6.0 | 6.7 | 7.0 | 7.6 |
| **Bahamas** | 6.2 | 6.3 | 6.3 | 6.9 | 6.8 | 6.9 | 6.9 |
| **Bahrain** | NR | 6.4 | 6.2 | 6.0 | 6.7 | 6.5 | 7.0 |
| **Bangladesh** | NR | 0.6 | 2.3 | 2.8 | 3.9 | 3.5 | 3.5 |
| **Barbados** | NR | 5.1 | 5.2 | 6.1 | 6.0 | 6.0 | 5.9 |
| **Belgium** | 10.0 | 8.7 | 10.0 | 10.0 | 8.7 | 8.6 | 8.7 |
| **Belize** | NR | NR | 6.9 | 6.7 | 8.2 | 8.3 | 7.9 |
| **Benin** | 2.7 | 2.8 | 3.6 | 4.0 | 4.3 | 4.5 | 4.6 |
| **Bolivia** | NR | NR | 2.0 | NR | 7.3 | 7.5 | 8.3 |
| **Botswana** | NR | NR | 5.8 | 6.9 | 5.5 | 6.0 | 6.6 |
| **Brazil** | 4.6 | 4.6 | 3.7 | 2.4 | 2.7 | 3.1 | 4.5 |
| **Bulgaria** | NR | NR | NR | NR | 1.0 | 4.3 | 4.8 |
| **Burundi** | 1.8 | 1.7 | 1.9 | 2.7 | 2.1 | 1.3 | 2.9 |
| **Cameroon** | NR | NR | 1.9 | 1.9 | 3.5 | 2.7 | 3.2 |
| **Canada** | 8.8 | 8.1 | 9.3 | 9.3 | 9.3 | 9.1 | 9.2 |
| **C. African Rep.** | NR | NR | NR | 2.5 | 4.4 | 3.3 | 3.4 |
| **Chad** | NR | NR | NR | 3.2 | 3.2 | 2.2 | 2.5 |
| **Chile** | NR | 3.5 | 5.9 | 6.5 | 6.6 | 8.1 | 8.0 |
| **China** | NR | NR | 0.0 | 0.7 | 1.7 | 3.0 | 3.0 |
| **Colombia** | NR | NR | 5.3 | 5.3 | 5.9 | 7.2 | 7.1 |
| **Congo, Dem. R.** | 2.6 | 2.8 | 3.1 | 3.4 | 2.3 | 2.5 | 0.7 |
| **Congo, Rep. Of** | NR | NR | 1.9 | 2.5 | 3.7 | 1.8 | 2.9 |
| **Costa Rica** | 8.0 | 6.7 | 6.0 | 7.3 | 7.6 | 8.7 | 9.1 |
| **Cote d'Ivoire** | NR | NR | 4.6 | 5.0 | 4.4 | 4.6 | 5.1 |
| **Croatia** | NR | NR | NR | NR | NR | 2.7 | 4.0 |
| **Cyprus** | 5.3 | 6.1 | 5.1 | 6.0 | 6.4 | 6.5 | 6.4 |
| **Czech Rep.** | NR | NR | NR | NR | NR | 5.5 | 5.4 |
| **Denmark** | 8.0 | 8.0 | 8.2 | 7.9 | 8.0 | 8.5 | 9.0 |
| **Dominican Rep.** | NR | NR | 5.6 | 5.4 | 4.9 | 7.1 | 7.8 |
| **Ecuador** | NR | NR | 4.4 | 3.1 | 4.7 | 7.0 | 8.1 |
| **Egypt** | NR | NR | 2.8 | 3.7 | 3.6 | 6.0 | 5.7 |
| **El Salvador** | NR | NR | NR | 6.1 | 6.1 | 8.0 | 9.2 |
| **Estonia** | NR | NR | NR | NR | NR | 5.1 | 6.8 |
| **Fiji** | NR | 3.3 | 4.8 | 5.4 | 4.3 | 4.8 | 4.7 |
| **Finland** | NR | 6.4 | 6.8 | 7.3 | 7.3 | 8.7 | 8.7 |
| **France** | 6.7 | 7.2 | 7.0 | 7.0 | 7.9 | 8.3 | 8.2 |
| **Gabon** | NR | NR | 1.9 | 2.5 | 3.8 | 3.3 | 4.0 |
| **Germany** | 7.7 | 7.1 | 7.6 | 8.1 | 8.2 | 8.1 | 8.1 |

| | 1970 | 1975 | 1980 | 1985 | 1990 | 1995 | 1997 |
|---|---|---|---|---|---|---|---|
| Ghana | NR | 1.8 | 1.1 | 1.6 | 2.6 | 4.2 | 4.4 |
| Greece | 3.9 | 2.9 | 3.4 | 3.4 | 4.6 | 5.6 | 6.4 |
| Guatemala | 6.3 | 6.9 | 7.5 | 7.5 | 7.5 | 8.2 | 7.6 |
| Guinea-Bissau | NR | NR | NR | NR | 4.0 | 4.4 | 6.1 |
| Guyana | NR | NR | NR | NR | NR | 4.8 | 5.2 |
| Haiti | NR | NR | NR | NR | 2.9 | 3.6 | 5.0 |
| Honduras | NR | NR | 3.7 | 4.8 | 4.8 | 5.7 | 7.4 |
| Hong Kong | NR | 10.0 | 10.0 | 10.0 | 10.0 | 9.9 | 9.9 |
| Hungary | NR | NR | 2.3 | 1.3 | 3.0 | 5.8 | 6.2 |
| Iceland | NR | 3.6 | 4.1 | 4.1 | 4.9 | 6.3 | 6.4 |
| India | 3.6 | 2.6 | 3.5 | 3.6 | 3.5 | 3.9 | 3.8 |
| Indonesia | 0.6 | 0.6 | 2.0 | 3.1 | 4.9 | 5.8 | 5.8 |
| Iran | NR | NR | 1.7 | 1.5 | 1.8 | 2.0 | 4.0 |
| Ireland | 6.0 | 5.8 | 6.3 | 7.1 | 7.3 | 8.2 | 8.3 |
| Israel | 2.3 | 2.2 | 1.5 | 1.1 | 3.1 | 4.2 | 4.9 |
| Italy | 6.3 | 5.5 | 4.9 | 5.3 | 6.3 | 7.3 | 7.8 |
| Jamaica | NR | NR | 3.7 | 4.1 | 6.9 | 7.8 | 7.7 |
| Japan | 5.7 | 5.6 | 6.1 | 7.0 | 7.8 | 7.8 | 7.9 |
| Jordan | NR | 4.8 | 5.0 | 4.8 | 4.6 | 5.3 | 6.4 |
| Kenya | 4.9 | 3.1 | 4.3 | 4.7 | 5.2 | 6.0 | 7.0 |
| Kuwait | NR | 5.3 | 5.3 | 6.0 | 2.5 | 4.8 | 5.2 |
| Latvia | NR | NR | NR | NR | NR | 5.1 | 7.0 |
| Lithuania | NR | NR | NR | NR | NR | 5.2 | 6.8 |
| Luxembourg | 10.0 | 10.0 | 10.0 | 10.0 | 10.0 | 9.1 | 9.2 |
| Madagascar | 2.7 | 2.4 | 2.6 | 2.7 | 1.9 | 2.4 | 4.3 |
| Malawi | NR | 3.2 | 3.7 | 4.2 | 4.2 | 3.1 | 2.8 |
| Malaysia | 6.4 | 5.9 | 5.8 | 6.8 | 6.9 | 7.0 | 6.9 |
| Mali | NR | 4.2 | 4.2 | 4.6 | 5.1 | 4.4 | 4.5 |
| Malta | 3.1 | 3.2 | 4.0 | 3.9 | 3.8 | 4.8 | 4.7 |
| Mauritius | NR | 5.1 | 5.3 | 6.7 | 6.5 | 8.7 | 8.8 |
| Mexico | NR | 4.1 | 4.6 | 2.0 | 4.5 | 7.2 | 6.2 |
| Morocco | NR | NR | 4.2 | 4.5 | 4.9 | 5.1 | 5.1 |
| Myanmar | 1.2 | 0.5 | 0.1 | 0.0 | 0.0 | 0.0 | 0.0 |
| Namibia | NR | NR | NR | NR | 5.5 | 6.1 | 6.0 |
| Nepal | NR | NR | 2.7 | 2.5 | 3.8 | 3.7 | 3.8 |
| Netherlands | 7.1 | 7.1 | 9.1 | 8.4 | 8.9 | 9.6 | 9.6 |
| New Zealand | 5.8 | 5.6 | 5.7 | 6.1 | 9.7 | 9.9 | 9.4 |
| Nicaragua | NR | NR | NR | 1.1 | 0.8 | 6.8 | 7.3 |
| Niger | NR | 3.2 | 2.9 | 3.0 | 4.2 | 4.4 | 4.2 |
| Nigeria | NR | 1.3 | 1.3 | 1.9 | 2.3 | 3.2 | 3.0 |
| Norway | 5.4 | 5.9 | 5.8 | 7.8 | 8.3 | 8.5 | 8.5 |
| Oman | NR | NR | 6.3 | 7.1 | 7.1 | 7.1 | 7.1 |
| Pakistan | 4.1 | 2.0 | 3.4 | 4.1 | 3.5 | 3.3 | 3.2 |
| Panama | NR | 8.1 | 8.2 | 8.1 | 8.8 | 9.4 | 9.4 |

| | 1970 | 1975 | 1980 | 1985 | 1990 | 1995 | 1997 |
|---|---|---|---|---|---|---|---|
| Pap. New Guinea | NR | 4.2 | 3.9 | 4.2 | 4.3 | 5.1 | 5.0 |
| Paraguay | NR | NR | NR | NR | 5.4 | 9.2 | 9.2 |
| Peru | NR | NR | 2.3 | 2.2 | 1.8 | 7.7 | 8.3 |
| Philippines | NR | 5.5 | 5.2 | 4.4 | 6.1 | 7.5 | 7.6 |
| Poland | NR | NR | 0.0 | 0.0 | 0.1 | 4.0 | 5.1 |
| Portugal | 3.4 | 2.7 | 2.9 | 4.2 | 5.0 | 6.3 | 7.5 |
| Romania | 0.0 | 0.0 | 0.0 | 0.0 | 0.0 | 1.1 | 1.4 |
| Russia | NR | 0.0 | 0.0 | 0.0 | 0.0 | 4.0 | 4.5 |
| Rwanda | 1.4 | 1.3 | 3.4 | 3.6 | 3.8 | 1.8 | 1.9 |
| Senegal | NR | NR | 4.5 | 4.0 | 4.5 | 3.3 | 3.7 |
| Sierra Leone | NR | 2.5 | 3.2 | 0.9 | 1.9 | 2.2 | 2.0 |
| Singapore | NR | 8.9 | 9.2 | 9.8 | 9.7 | 9.7 | 9.7 |
| Slovakia | NR | NR | NR | NR | NR | 4.3 | 5.3 |
| Slovenia | NR | NR | NR | NR | NR | 6.0 | 6.0 |
| Somalia | NR | NR | NR | NR | NR | NR | NR |
| South Africa | 6.6 | 6.7 | 6.0 | 7.2 | 7.2 | 7.7 | 7.7 |
| South Korea | NR | 3.9 | 4.3 | 6.3 | 7.2 | 7.2 | 7.2 |
| Spain | NR | 6.0 | 6.7 | 7.4 | 8.2 | 8.1 | 8.2 |
| Sri Lanka | NR | NR | 3.6 | 5.0 | 4.7 | 6.1 | 6.0 |
| Sweden | 5.5 | 5.1 | 6.0 | 7.2 | 8.8 | 8.5 | 8.5 |
| Switzerland | NR | 5.2 | 7.4 | 8.5 | 8.5 | 8.5 | 8.5 |
| Syria | 0.9 | 0.1 | 0.2 | 0.4 | 0.3 | 0.4 | 0.2 |
| Taiwan | 2.7 | 4.2 | 4.1 | 5.2 | 6.2 | 6.1 | 5.5 |
| Tanzania | 1.0 | 0.1 | 1.0 | 0.0 | 2.4 | 1.9 | 2.2 |
| Thailand | NR | 5.6 | 5.3 | 6.8 | 6.5 | 7.9 | 7.9 |
| Togo | NR | NR | 4.5 | 4.6 | 4.6 | 4.4 | 3.9 |
| Trinidad & Tob. | NR | 4.1 | 4.2 | 5.8 | 5.2 | 7.4 | 7.7 |
| Tunisia | 3.2 | 3.3 | 3.3 | 3.8 | 6.5 | 6.7 | 6.7 |
| Turkey | NR | 3.8 | 2.9 | 4.8 | 3.9 | 6.2 | 6.0 |
| Uganda | NR | 2.2 | 1.7 | 1.7 | 2.1 | 2.9 | 3.1 |
| Ukraine | NR | NR | NR | NR | NR | 0.7 | 0.9 |
| Unit. Arab Em. | NR | 7.9 | 7.8 | 5.6 | 5.8 | 5.7 | 5.8 |
| United Kingdom | 6.5 | 5.7 | 8.0 | 9.8 | 10.0 | 9.9 | 10.0 |
| United States | 9.5 | 9.1 | 9.7 | 9.6 | 9.7 | 9.7 | 9.7 |
| Uruguay | NR | NR | 7.0 | 7.7 | 7.7 | 7.4 | 7.4 |
| Venezuela | NR | 7.4 | 6.5 | 6.3 | 4.6 | 3.9 | 5.0 |
| Zambia | NR | 3.5 | 3.3 | 1.6 | 2.1 | 2.8 | 5.4 |
| Zimbabwe | NR | NR | 3.6 | 3.8 | 4.4 | 5.2 | 5.4 |

# Appendix 2
# Explanatory Notes and Data Sources

**Component**

**I-A** The rating for this component is equal to: $(V_{max} - V_i) / (V_{max} - V_{min})$ multiplied by 10. The $V_i$ is the country's actual government consumption as a proportion of total consumption, while the $V_{max}$ and $V_{min}$ represent the maximum and minimum values for this component during the 1990 base year for the countries included in our analysis. Countries with a larger proportion of government expenditures received lower ratings. If the ratio of a country's government consumption to total consumption is close to the minimum value of this ratio during the 1990 base year, the country's rating will be close to 10. In contrast, if this ratio is close to the highest value during the base year, the rating will be close to zero.

Sources World Bank, *1997 World Development Indicators CD-Rom* and International Monetary Fund, *International Financial Statistics* (various issues). The 1997 figures were primarily from the latter publication.

**I-B** The rating for this component is equal to: $(V_{max} - V_i) / (V_{max} - V_{min})$ multiplied by 10. The $V_i$ is the country's ratio of transfers and subsidies to GDP, while the $V_{max}$ and $V_{min}$ represent the maximum and minimum values of this component during the 1990 base year. The formula will generate lower ratings for countries with larger transfer sectors. When the size of a country's transfer sector approaches that of the country with the largest transfer sector during the base year, the rating of the country will approach zero.

Sources World Bank, *1997 World Development Indicators CD-Rom*; International Monetary Fund, *International Financial Statistics* (various issues); International Monetary Fund, *Government Finance Statistics Yearbook* (various years); and Inter-American Development Bank, *Economic and Social Progress in Latin America, 1994.*

**II-A** Data on the number, composition, and share of output supplied by State-Operated Enterprises (SOEs) and government investment as a share of total investment were used to construct the zero-to-10 ratings. Countries with more government enterprise and government investment received lower ratings. When there were few SOEs and government investment was generally less than 15 percent of total investment, countries were given a rating of 10. When there were few SOEs other than those involved in industries where economies of scale reduce the effectiveness of competition (e.g., power generation) and government investment was between 15 and 20 percent of the total, countries received a rating of 8. When there were, again, few SOEs other than those involved in energy and other such industries and government investment was between about 20 and 25 percent of the total, countries were rated at 7. When SOEs were present in the energy, transportation, and communication sectors of the economy and government investment was between about 25 and 30 percent of the total, countries were assigned a rating of 6. When a substantial number of SOEs operated in many sectors, including manufacturing, and government investment was generally between 30 and 40 percent of the total, countries received a rating of 4. When numerous SOEs operated in many sectors, including retail sales, and government investment was between about 40 and 50 percent of the total, countries were rated at 2. A rating of zero was assigned when the economy was dominated by SOEs and government investment exceeded 50 percent of the total.

Sources World Bank Policy Research Report, *Bureaucrats in Business* (1995); Rexford A. Ahene and Bernard S. Katz, eds., *Privatization and Investment in Sub-Saharan Africa* (1992); Manuel Sanchez and Rossana Corona, eds., *Privatization in Latin America* (1993); Iliya Harik and Denis J. Sullivan, eds., *Privatization and Liberalization in the Middle East* (1992); OECD, *Economic Surveys* (various issues); and L. Bouten and M. Sumlinski, *Trends in Private Investment in Developing Countries: Statistics for 1970–1995.*

**II-B** The more widespread the use of price controls, the lower the rating. The survey data of the International Institute for Management Development (IMD), *World Competitiveness Report,* 1990 and 1997, were used to rate the 46 countries (mostly developed economies) covered by this report. For other countries, the Price Waterhouse series, *Doing Business in ...* and other sources were used to categorize countries. Countries were given a rating of 10 if no price controls or marketing boards were present. When price controls were limited to industries where economies of scale may reduce the effectiveness of competition (e.g., power generation), a country was given a rating of 8. When price controls were applied in only a few other industries, such as agriculture, a country was given a rating of 6. When price controls were levied on energy, agriculture, and many other stable products that are widely purchased by households, a rating of 4 was given. When price controls applied to a significant number of products in both agriculture and manufacturing, the rating was 2. A rating of zero was given when there was widespread use of price controls throughout various sectors of the economy.

Sources IMD, *World Competitiveness Report* (various issues); Price Waterhouse, *Doing Business in ...* publication series; World Bank, *Adjustment in Africa: Reforms, Results, and the Road Ahead* (1994); and US State Department, *Country Reports on Economic Policy and Trade Practices* (various years).

**II-C** Data on the top marginal tax rates and the income thresholds at which they take effect were used to construct a rating grid. Countries with higher marginal tax rates that take effect at lower income thresholds received lower ratings. The income threshold data were converted from local currency to 1982/1984 US dollars (using beginning-of-year exchange rates and the US Consumer Price Index). See *Economic Freedom of the World: 1997 Annual Report,* page 265, for the precise relationship between a country's rating and its top marginal tax and income threshold.

Source Price Waterhouse, *Individual Taxes: A Worldwide Summary* (various issues).

**II-D** Data on the use and duration of military conscription were used to construct rating intervals. Countries with longer conscription periods received lower ratings. A rating of 10 was assigned to countries without military conscription. When length of conscription was six months or less, countries were given a rating of 5. When length of conscription was more than six months but not more than 12 months, countries were rated at 3. When length of conscription was more than 12 months but not more than 18 months, countries were assigned a rating of 1. When conscription periods exceeded 18 months, countries were rated zero.

Source International Institute for Strategic Studies, *The Military Balance* (various issues).

**III-A** The M1 money supply figures were used to measure the growth rate of the money supply. The rating is equal to: $(V_{max} - V_i) / (V_{max} - V_{min})$ multiplied by 10. $V_i$ represents the average annual growth rate of the money supply during the last five years adjusted for the growth of real GDP during the previous 10 years. The values for $V_{min}$ and $V_{max}$ were set at zero and 50 percent, respectively. Therefore, if the adjusted growth rate of the money supply during the last five years was zero, indicating that money growth was equal to the long-term growth of real output, the formula generates a rating of 10. Ratings decline as the adjusted money supply growth differs from zero. When the adjusted annual money growth is equal to (or greater than) 50 percent, a rating of zero results.

Sources World Bank, *1997 World Development Indicators CD-Rom*, with updates from International Monetary Fund, *International Financial Statistics* (various issues).

**III-B** The GDP deflator was used as the measure of inflation. When these data were unavailable, the Consumer Price Index was used. The following formula was used to determine the zero-to-10 scale rating for each country: $(V_{max} - V_i) / (V_{max} - V_{min})$ multiplied by 10. $V_i$ represents the country's standard deviation of the annual rate of inflation during the last five years. The values for $V_{min}$ and $V_{max}$ were set at zero and 25 percent, respectively. This procedure will allocate the highest ratings to the countries with least variation in the annual rate of inflation. A perfect 10 results when there is no variation in the rate of inflation over the five-year period. Ratings will decline toward zero as the standard deviation of the inflation rate approaches 25 percent annually.

Sources World Bank, *1997 World Development Indicators CD-Rom*, with updates from International Monetary Fund, *International Financial Statistics* (various issues).

**III-C** The zero-to-10 country ratings were derived by the following formula: $(V_{max} - V_i) / (V_{max} - V_{min})$ multiplied by 10. $V_i$ represents the rate of inflation during the most recent year. The values for $V_{min}$ and $V_{max}$ were set at zero and 50 percent, respectively. The lower the rate of inflation, the higher the rating. Countries that achieve perfect price stability earn a rating of 10. As the inflation rate moves toward a 50 percent annual rate, the rating for this component moves toward zero. A zero rating is assigned to all countries with an inflation rate of 50 percent or more.

Source World Bank, *1997 World Development Indicators CD-Rom*, with updates from International Monetary Fund, *International Financial Statistics* (various issues).

**IV-A** When foreign currency bank accounts were permissible without restrictions both domestically and abroad, the rating was 10; when these accounts were restricted, the rating was zero. If foreign currency bank accounts were permissible domestically but not abroad (or vice versa), the rating was 5.

Sources Currency Data and Intelligence, Inc., *World Currency Yearbook* (various issues) and International Monetary Fund, *Annual Report on Exchange Arrangements and Exchange Restrictions* (various issues).

**IV-B** The formula used to calculate the zero-to-10 ratings for this component was: $(V_{max} - V_i) / (V_{max} - V_{min})$ multiplied by 10. $V_i$ is the country's black-market exchange rate premium. The values for $V_{min}$ and $V_{max}$ were set at zero and 50 percent, respectively. This formula will allocate a rating of 10 to countries without a black-market exchange rate; i.e., those with a domestic currency that is fully convertible without restrictions. When exchange rate controls are present and a black market exists, the ratings will decline toward zero as the black market premium increases toward 50 percent. A zero rating is given when the black market premium is equal to, or greater than, 50 percent.

Sources Currency Data and Intelligence, Inc., *World Currency Yearbook* (various issues of the yearbook and the monthly report supplement) and International Monetary Fund, *International Financial Statistics* (various issues).

**V-A** Countries with less risk of confiscation received higher ratings. The data from 1980 to 1997 on the risk of expropriation are from PRS Group, *International Country Risk Guide* (various issues). The 1980 data are actually for 1982, the initial year of the International Country Risk Guide (ICRG) data source. The 1970 and 1975 data are from Business Environment Risk Intelligence (BERI). The ICRG did not provide ratings for Barbados, Benin, Burundi, Central African Republic, Chad, Estonia, Latvia, Lithuania, Mauritius, Slovenia and Ukraine. We rated these countries based on the ratings for similar countries (in parentheses): for Barbados (Bahamas), Mauritius (Botwsana), Estonia, Latvia, and Lithuania (Poland and Russia), Slovenia (Czech Republic and Slovakia), Ukraine (Bulgaria and Russia), Benin, Burundi, Central African Republic, and Chad (Cameroon, Republic of Congo, Gabon, Mali, and Niger).

While the original rating scale for the ICRG data was zero-to-10, BERI data were on a one-to-four scale. We used regression analysis from the two sources during the initial overlapping year 1982 to merge the two data sets and place the 1970 and 1975 ratings on a scale comparable to that used for the other years. The following regression equation was used to convert the 1970 and 1975 BERI ratings to a scale comparable with that of ICRG: 1982 ICRG Rating $= a + b$ (1982 BERI Rating). The coefficient values for $a$ and $b$ were 0.086 and 2.9, respectively. The t-ratio for the estimated value of $b$ was 4.70 and the R2 for the equation was 0.43.

Because the ICRG ratings inexplicably increase from the mid-1990s to the late 1990s, all ratings were adjusted using the maximum and minimum procedure used in other components in order to make the component consistent over time. The following formula was used to place the figures on a zero-to-10 scale: $(V_i - V_{min})/(V_{max} - V_{min})$ multiplied by 10. $V_i$ is the country's actual value for the component. $V_{max}$ and $V_{min}$ were set at 10 and 2 standard deviations below the average, respectively.

Source PRS Group, *International Country Risk Guide* (various issues).

**V-B** Countries where there is less risk that the government will unilaterally cancel contracts received higher ratings. The data from 1980 to 1997 on the risk of contract repudiation are from PRS Group, *International Country Risk Guide* (various issues). The 1980 data are actually for 1982, the initial year of the International Country Risk Guide (ICRG) data source. The 1970 and 1975 data are from Business Environment Risk Intelligence (BERI). The ICRG did not provide ratings for Barbados, Benin, Burundi, Central African Republic, Chad, Estonia, Latvia, Lithuania, Mauritius, Slovenia and Ukraine. We rated these countries based on the ratings for similar countries (in parentheses): for Barbados (Bahamas), Mauritius (Botwsana), Estonia, Latvia, and Lithuania (Poland and Russia), Slovenia (Czech Republic and Slovakia), Ukraine (Bulgaria and Russia), Benin, Burundi, Central African Republic, and Chad (Cameroon, Republic of Congo, Gabon, Mali, and Niger).

While the original rating scale for the ICRG data was zero-to-10, BERI data were on a one-to-four scale. We used regression analysis from the two sources during the initial overlapping year 1982 to merge the two data sets and place the 1970 and 1975 ratings on a scale comparable to that for the other years. The following regression was used to convert the 1970 and 1975 BERI ratings to a scale comparable with that of ICRG: 1982 ICRG Rating = $a + b$ (1982 BERI Rating). The coefficient values for $a$ and $b$ were –0.164 and 2.96, respectively. The t-ratio for the estimated value of $b$ was 6.73 and the R2 for the equation was 0.62.

Because the ICRG ratings inexplicably increase from the mid-1990s to late 1990s, all ratings were adjusted using the maximum and minimum procedure used in other components in order to make the component consistent over time. The following formula was used to place the figures on a zero-to-10 scale: $(V_i - V_{min})/(V_{max} - V_{min})$ multiplied by 10. $V_i$ is the country's actual value for the component. $V_{max}$ and $V_{min}$ were set at 10 and 2 standard deviations below the average, respectively.

Source PRS Group, *International Country Risk Guide* (various issues).

**V-C** Countries with legal institutions that were more supportive of rule of law received higher ratings. The data from 1980 to 1997 on the rule of law are from PRS Group, *International Country Risk Guide* (various issues). The 1980 data are actually for 1982, the initial year of the International Country Risk Guide (ICRG) data source. The ICRG did not provide ratings for Barbados, Benin, Burundi, Central African Republic, Chad, Estonia, Latvia, Lithuania, Mauritius, Slovenia and Ukraine. We rated these countries based on the ratings for similar countries (in parentheses): for Barbados (Bahamas), Mauritius (Botwsana), Estonia, Latvia, and Lithuania (Poland and Russia), Slovenia (Czech Republic and Slovakia), Ukraine (Bulgaria and Russia), Benin, Burundi, Central African Republic, and Chad (Cameroon, Republic of Congo, Gabon, Mali, and Niger).

Because the ICRG ratings inexplicably increase from the mid-1990s to late 1990s, all ratings were adjusted using the maximum and minimum procedure used in other components in order to make the component consistent over time. The following formula was used to place the figures on a zero-to-10 scale: $(V_i - V_{min})/(V_{max} - V_{min})$ multiplied by 10. $V_i$ is the country's actual value for the component. $V_{max}$ and $V_{min}$ were set at 10 and 2 standard deviations below the average, respectively.

Source PRS Group, *International Country Risk Guide* (various issues).

**VI-A (i)** The formula used to calculate the ratings for this component was: $(V_{max} - V_i) / (V_{max} - V_{min})$ multiplied by 10. $V_i$ represents the revenue derived from taxes on international trade as a share of the trade sector. The values for $V_{min}$ and $V_{max}$ were set at zero and 15 percent, respectively. This formula leads to lower ratings as the average tax rate on international trade increases. Countries with no specific taxes on international trade earn a perfect 10. As the revenues from these taxes rise toward 15 percent of international trade, ratings decline toward zero. (Note that except for two or three extreme observations, the revenues from taxes on international trade as a share of the trade sector are within the zero to 15 percent range.)

Sources International Monetary Fund, *Government Finance Statistics Yearbook* (various issues) and International Monetary Fund, *International Financial Statistics* (various issues).

**VI-A (ii)** The formula used to calculate the zero-to-10 rating for each country was: $(V_{max} - V_i) / (V_{max} - V_{min})$ multiplied by 10. $V_i$ represents the country's mean tariff rate. The values for $V_{min}$ and $V_{max}$ were set at zero and 50 percent, respectively. This formula will allocate a rating of 10 to countries that do not impose tariffs. As the mean tariff rate increases, countries are assigned lower ratings. The rating will decline toward zero as the mean tariff rate approaches 50 percent. (Note that except for two or three extreme observations, all countries have mean tariff rates within this zero to 50 percent range.)

Sources OECD, *Indicators of Tariff and Non-tariff Trade Barriers* (1996); World Bank, *1997 World Development Indicators CD-Rom*; J. Michael Finger, Merlinda D. Ingco, and Ulrich Reincke, *Statistics on Tariff Concessions Given and Received* (1996); Judith M. Dean, Seema Desai, and James Riedel, *Trade Policy Reform in Developing Countries since 1985: A Review of the Evidence* (1994); GATT, *The Tokyo Round of Multilateral Trade Negotiations, Vol. II: Supplementary Report* (1979); UNCTAD, *Revitalizing Development, Growth and International Trade: Assessment and Policy Options* (1987); R. Erzan and K. Kuwahara, The Profile of Protection in Developing Countries, *UNCTAD Review* 1 (1) (1989): 29–49; and Inter-American Development Bank (data supplied to the authors).

**VI-A (iii)** Compared to a uniform tariff, wide variation in tariff rates exerts a more restrictive impact on trade, and therefore on economic freedom. Thus, countries with greater variation in their tariff rates should be given lower ratings. The formula used to calculate the zero-to-10 ratings for this component was: $(V_{max} - V_i) / (V_{max} - V_{min})$ multiplied by 10. $V_i$ represents the standard deviation of the country's tariff rates. The values for $V_{min}$ and $V_{max}$ were set at zero and 25 percent, respectively. This formula will allocate a rating of 10 to countries that impose a uniform tariff. As the standard deviation of tariff rates increases toward 25 percent, ratings decline toward zero. (Note that except a few very extreme observations, the standard deviations of the tariff rates for the countries in our study fall within this zero to 25 percent range.)

Sources OECD, *Indicators of Tariff and Non-tariff Trade Barriers* (1996); World Bank, *1997 World Development Indicators CD-Rom*; Jang-Wha Lee and Phillip Swagel, *Trade Barriers and Trade Flows across Countries and Industries*, NBER Working Paper Series No. 4799 (1994); and Inter-American Development Bank (data supplied to the authors).

**VI-B (i)** The formula used to calculate the ratings for this component was: $(V_{max} - V_i) / (V_{max} - V_{min})$ multiplied by 10. $V_i$ indicates the share of the trade sector covered by non-tariff restrictions. During the 1990 base year, this figure ranged from a low of zero to a high of 100 percent. Thus, the values for $V_{min}$ and $V_{max}$ were set at zero and 100 percent, respectively. This formula will allocate a rating of 10 to countries that do not impose non-tariff trade barriers. Ratings will decline toward zero as the share of the trade sector covered by restrictions increases toward 100 percent. Thus, countries with larger percentages of trade subject to non-tariff restraints receive lower ratings.

Sources UNCTAD, *Directory of Import Regimes: Part 1* (1994); World Bank, *1997 World Development Indicators CD-Rom*; Sam Laird and Alexander Yeats, *Quantitative Methods for Trade Barrier Analysis* (1990); OECD, *Indicators of Tariff and Non-tariff Trade Barriers* (1996); and World Bank, *Adjustment in Africa: Reforms, Results, and the Road Ahead* (1994).

**VI-B (ii)** Regression analysis was used to derive an expected size of the trade sector based on the country's population, geographic size, and locational characteristics. The actual size of the trade sector was then compared with the expected size for the country. If the actual size of the trade sector is greater than expected, this figure will be positive. If it is less than expected, the number will be negative. The percent change of the negative numbers was adjusted to make it symmetrical with the percent change of the positive numbers. The following formula was used to place the figures on a zero-to-10 scale: $(V_i - V_{min}) / (V_{max} - V_{min})$ multiplied by 10. $V_i$ is the country's actual value for the component. $V_{max}$ and $V_{min}$ were set at 100 percent and minus 50 percent, respectively. (Note that minus 50 percent is symmetrical with positive 100 percent.) This procedure allocates higher ratings to countries with large trade sectors compared to what would be expected, given their population, geographic size, and location. On the other hand, countries with small trade sectors relative to the expected size receive lower ratings.

Sources World Bank, *1997 World Development Indicators CD-Rom*; International Monetary Fund, *International Financial Statistics* (various issues); and Central Intelligence Agency, *1997 World Factbook*.

**VII-A** Data on the percentage of bank deposits held in privately owned banks were used to construct rating intervals. Countries with larger shares of privately held deposits received higher ratings. When privately held deposits totaled between 95 and 100 percent, countries were given a rating of 10. When private deposits constituted between 75 and 95 percent of the total, a rating of 8 was assigned. When private deposits were between 40 and 75 percent of the total, the rating was 5. When private deposits totaled between 10 and 40 percent, countries received a rating of 2. A zero rating was assigned when private deposits were 10 percent or less of the total.

Sources Euromoney Publications, *The Telrate Bank Register* (various editions); World Bank, *Adjustment in Africa: Reforms, Results, and the Road Ahead* (1994); Price Waterhouse, *Doing Business in ...* publication series; H.T. Patrick and Y.C. Park, eds., *The Financial Development of Japan, Korea, and Taiwan: Growth, Repression, and Liberalization* (1994); D.C. Cole and B.F. Slade, *Building a Modern Financial System: The Indonesian Experience* (1996); and information supplied by member institutes of the Economic Freedom Network.

**VII-B** For this component, higher values are indicative of greater economic freedom. Thus, the formula used to derive the country ratings for this component was $(V_i - V_{min}) / (V_{max} - V_{min})$ multiplied by 10. $V_i$ is the share of the country's total domestic credit allocated to the private sector. $V_{max}$ is the maximum value and $V_{min}$ the minimum value for the figure during the 1990 base year. Respectively, these figures were 99.9 percent and 10.0 percent. The formula allocates higher ratings as the share of credit extended to the private sector increases. A country's rating will be close to 10 when the private sector's share of domestic credit is near the base-year maximum (99.9 percent). A rating near zero results when the private sector's share of credit is close to the base-year minimum (10.0 percent).

Sources International Monetary Fund, *International Financial Statistics* (the 1997 yearbook and June 1998 monthly supplement) and *Statistical Yearbook of the Republic of China* (1996).

**VII-C** Data on credit-market controls and regulations were used to construct rating intervals. Countries with interest rates determined by the market, stable monetary policy, and positive real deposit and lending rates received higher ratings. When interest rates were determined primarily by market forces and the real rates were positive, countries were given a rating of 10. When interest rates were primarily market-determined but the real rates were sometimes slightly negative (less than 5%) or the differential between the deposit and lending rates was large (8% or more), countries received a rating of 8. When the real deposit or lending rate was persistently negative by a single-digit amount or the differential between them was regulated by the government, countries were rated at 6. When the deposit and lending rates were fixed by the government and the real rates were often negative by single-digit amounts, countries were assigned a rating of 4. When the real deposit or lending rate was persistently negative by a double-digit amount, countries received a rating of 2. A zero rating was assigned when the deposit and lending rates were fixed by the government and real rates were persistently negative by double-digit amounts or hyperinflation had virtually eliminated the credit market.

Source International Monetary Fund, *International Financial Statistics Yearbook* (various issues, as well as the monthly supplements).

**VII-D** Descriptive data on capital-market arrangements were used to place countries into rating categories. Countries with more restrictions on foreign capital transactions received lower ratings. When domestic investments by foreigners and foreign investments by citizens were unrestricted, countries were given a rating of 10. When these investments were restricted only in a few industries (e.g., banking, defence, and telecommunications), countries were assigned a rating of 8. When these investments were permitted but regulatory restrictions slowed the mobility of capital, countries were rated at 5. When either domestic investments by foreigners or foreign investments by citizens required approval from government authorities, countries received a rating of 2. A zero rating was assigned when both domestic investments by foreigners and foreign investments by citizens required government approval.

Sources International Monetary Fund, *Annual Report on Exchange Arrangements and Exchange Restrictions* (various issues) and Price Waterhouse, *Doing Business in . . .* publication series.

# APPENDIX 3
# SELECTED PUBLICATIONS USING RATINGS FROM *ECONOMIC FREEDOM OF THE WORLD*

The following are some of the articles that have used the economic freedom ratings from *Economic Freedom of the World*. In some cases, a brief abstract of the article is provided. Those interested in doing further research using the Economic Freedom index are invited to retrieve the dataset from the website of the Economic Freedom Network, www.freetheworld.com. The most up-to-date information on articles using the index of Economic Freedom can be found at www.freetheworld.com/papers.html.

Ali, Abdiweli M. (1997). Economic Freedom, Democracy and Growth. *Journal of Private Enterprise* 13 (Fall): 1–20.
"This paper takes advantage of newly constructed measures of economic freedom to show the importance of economic freedom on growth. I find that economic freedom is a more robust determinant of growth than political freedom and civil liberty."
Uses summary ratings from *Economic Freedom of the World: 1975–1995* as one variable in a comparison of a number of institutional variables.

Ali, Abdiweli M., and W. Mark Crain (1999). Institutional Distortions, Economic Freedom, and Growth. Draft manuscript (April). James M. Buchanan Center for Political Economy.
This paper examines the robustness of economic freedom as a predictor of growth and investment compared to political rights and civil liberties. It also examines the relation between economic freedom and input price distortions and institutional quality.
Uses summary ratings from *Economic Freedom of the World: 1975–1995* as one of a number of institutional variables.

Ayal, Eliezer B., and Karras Georgios (1998). Components of Economic Freedom and Growth: An Empirical Study. *Journal of Developing Areas* 32 (Spring): 327–38.
The paper uses regression analysis to examine the effect of the components of economic freedom on growth, output and investment and finds that "economic freedom enhances growth both via increasing total factor productivity and via enhancing capital accumulation." It also identifies components that have the highest statistical effects on these variables, with the aim of informing policy makers.
Uses component ratings from *Economic Freedom of the World: 1975–1995* as the main data source for institutional variables.

Berggren, Niclas (1999). Economic Freedom and Equality: Friends or Foes? *Public Choice* 100, 3/4 (September): 203–23.
This paper describes a theoretical model of the relationship between economic freedom and income distribution, and investigates empirical results. The results indicate that "sustained and gradual increases in economic freedom influence equality measures positively ... [but] the absolute

level of economic freedom appears to be negatively related to equality in some cases."
Uses summary ratings from *Economic Freedom of the World: 1975–1995* as the main data source for institutional variables.

Boettke, Peter J. (1999). Why Culture Matters: Economics, Politics and the Imprint of History. Working paper, New York University. Digital document: www.econ.nyu.edu/user/boettke/culture.htm.
This paper, which cites conclusions from *Economic Freedom of the World: 1975–1995*, discusses how culture and history determine whether liberal economic policies will remain in a given country.

Chafuen, Alejandro (1998). Estado y Corrupcion. In Alejandro Chafuen and Eugenio Guzmán, *Corrupción y Gobierno* (Santiago, Chile: Fundación Libertad y Desarrollo): 45–98.
Finds that corruption is negatively related to economic freedom.
*Economic Freedom of the World: 1975–1995* and *Transparency International* are the main data-source for institutional variables.

Dawson, John W. (1998). Institutions, Investment, and Growth: New Cross-Country and Panel Data Evidence. *Economic Inquiry* 36 (October): 603–19.
"This paper outlines the alternative channels through which institutions affect growth, and studies the empirical relationship between institutions, investment, and growth. The empirical results indicate that (i) free-market institutions have a positive effect on growth; (ii) economic freedom affects growth through both a direct effect on total factor productivity and an indirect effect on investment; (iii) political and civil liberties may stimulate investment; (iv) an important interaction exists between freedom and human capital investment; (v) Milton Friedman's conjectures on the relation between political and economic freedom are correct; (vi) promoting economic freedom is an effective policy toward facilitating growth and other types of freedom."
Uses *Economic Freedom of the World: 1975–1995* as the main data source for institutional variables.

De Haan, Jakob, and Clemens L.J. Sierman (1998). Further Evidence on the Relationship between Economic Freedom and Economic Growth. *Public Choice* 95: 363–80.
Primarily investigates the robustness of the index of economic freedom devised by Gerald Scully and D.J. Slottje and determines that the robustness of results depends heavily on how freedom is measured. Finds that some specifications are robust predictors of the growth rate of real per-capita GDP (1980–1992) but few are robust for investment share of GDP.

Empirical analysis on *Economic Freedom of the World: 1975–1995* is limited to correlation with the Scully and Slotjie's index. Suggests further empirical work be done on *Economic Freedom of the World.*

Easton, Steven T., and Michael A. Walker (1997). Income, Growth, and Economic Freedom. *American Economic Review* 87 (2) (May): 328–32.
Finds that economic freedom is an important explanatory variable for steady-state levels of income. The addition of a variable for economic freedom is also shown to increase the explanatory power of a neo-classical growth model.
*Economic Freedom of the World: 1975–1995* is the main data source for institutional variables.

Farr, W. Ken, Richard A. Lord, and J. Larry Wolfenbarger (1998). Economic Freedom, Political Freedom and Economic Well-Being: A Causality Analysis. *Cato Journal* 18 (2) (Fall): 247–62.
The paper uses Granger causality analysis to demonstrate that economic freedom "causes" economic well-being and economic well-being "causes" economic freedom. Additionally, the authors argue that economic well-being causes political freedom but that there is no causation flowing

from political freedom to economic well-being. The paper also finds no evidence of a casual relationship in either direction between economic freedom and political freedom. Indirectly economic freedom causes political freedom through its effect on economic well-being.
*Economic Freedom of the World: 1975–1995* and the Freedom House index of political rights and civil liberties are the main data sources for institutional variables.

Ford, John B., Kiran W. Karande, and Bruce M. Seifert (1998). The Role of Economic Freedom in Explaining the Penetration of Consumer Durables. *Journal of World Business* 33 (1): 69–86.
"The study examines the link between economic freedom (a measure of government intervention) and the penetration of three durable goods (televisions, radios and automobiles) across countries."
Cites conclusions of *Economic Freedom of the World: 1975–1995*; uses other indexes of economic freedom for empirical work.

Goldsmith, Arthur A. (1997). Economic Rights and Government in Developing Countries: Cross-National Evidence on Growth and Development. *Studies in Comparative International Development* 32 (2) (summer): 29–44.
The paper "finds that developing countries that score better in protecting economic rights also tend to grow faster and to score higher in human development. In addition [the paper finds that] economic rights are associated with democratic government and with higher levels of average national income."
Uses summary ratings from *Economic Freedom of the World: 1975–1995* as one of a number of institutional variables.

Grubel, Herbert G. (1998). Economic Freedom and Human Welfare: Some Empirical Findings. *Cato Journal* 18 (2) (Fall): 287–304.
The paper compares economic freedom to income, growth, unemployment in the OECD, the UN Human Development Index, life expectancy, literacy, poverty, and income distribution. It finds that "economic freedom does not have a cost in terms of income levels, income growth, unemployment rates, and human development."
*Economic Freedom of the World: 1997 Annual Report* is the main data source for institutional variables.

Gwartney, James, Randall Holcombe, and Robert Lawson (1998). The Scope of Government and the Wealth of Nations. *Cato Journal* 18 (2) (Fall): 163–90.
The paper examines the effect of the size of government in OECD countries upon economic growth. This paper draws on the authors' Joint Economic Committee Study, *The Size and Functions of Government and Economic Growth.*
Makes reference to the general conclusions regarding economic freedom and income and growth as published in *Economic Freedom of the World: 1975–1995* and *Economic Freedom of the World: 1997 Annual Report.*

Gwartney, James, Robert Lawson and Randall Holcombe (1999). Economic Freedom and the Environment for Economic Growth. *Journal of Institutional and Theoretical Economics* 155 (4): 1–21.
This study examines the relationship between economic freedom and economic growth. The authors find that economic freedom is a "significant determinant of economic growth, even when human and physical capital, and demographics are taken into account." The authors also test for causality. They find that increases in economic freedom lead to higher economic growth but not that higher economic growth leads to higher economic freedom.
Uses summary ratings from *Economic Freedom of the World: 1997 Annual Report* as one of a number of institutional variables.

Hanke, Steve H., and Stephen J.K. Walters (1997). Economic Freedom, Prosperity, and Equality: A Survey. *Cato Journal* 17 (2) (Fall): 117–46.
The article compares several institutional indexes for content and explanatory power: Gerald Scully's studies, The Fraser Institute's *Economic Freedom of the World*, Freedom House's *Economic Freedom Indicators*, The Heritage Foundation's *Indices of Economic Freedom*, The International Institute for Management Development's *World Competitiveness Yearbook 1996*, The World Forum's *Global Competitiveness Report 1996*. Compares liberty and prosperity, equality and foreign policy implications. They find that economic greedom is positively correlated with per-capita GNP.
*Economic Freedom of the World: 1975–1995* is used as one variable in a comparison of a number of institutional variables.

Henderson, David (1998). *The Changing Fortunes of Economic Liberalism.* London: Institute of Economic Affairs.
A comprehensive review of the trends in economic liberalism in the last century. The book covers economic liberalism in thought and practice as well as discussing how the climate of political and popular opinion has both helped and constrained the development of liberal policy. One section uses the *Economic Freedom of the World* to discuss the progress made by countries engaging in economic reform and the appendix discusses the derivation, benefits, and limitations of the *Economic Freedom of the World.*
*Economic Freedom of the World: 1975–1995* is the only quantitative source for institutional variables.

Islam, Sadequil (1996). Economic Freedom, per Capita Income and Economic Growth. *Applied Economics Letters* 3: 595–97.
Examines the effect of economic freedom on income and growth in high-, middle-, and low-income country sets and finds that economic freedom is significant for a sample of all countries but only in some subsets.
Uses the precursor to *Economic Freedom of the World,* Measuring Economic Freedom, by James Gwartney, Walter Block and Robert Lawson, a chapter in Stephen Easton and Michael Walker (eds.), *Rating Global Economic Freedom* (Vancouver: The Fraser Institute, 1992). Measuring Economic Freedom is the main data source for institutional variables.

Johnson, James P., and Tomasz Lenartowicz (1998). Culture, Freedom and Economic Growth: Do Cultural Values Explain Economic Growth? *Journal of World Business* 33 (4): 332–56.
The paper discusses which cultural values are associated with economic freedom, drawing on two international quantitative cultural indexes.
Uses the summary ratings from *Economic Freedom of the World: 1975–1995* as one of a number of institutional variables.

Johnson, Simon, Daniel Kaufmann, and Pablo Zoido-Lobaton (1998). Government in Transition: Regulatory Discretion and the Unofficial Economy. *American Economic Review, Papers and Proceedings* (May): 159–239.
Empirically studies the effect of institutional quality on the share of the unofficial economy in GDP.
Uses the component, Equality of Citizens under the Law and Access of Citizens to a Non-Discriminatory Judiciary, of *Economic Freedom of the World: 1997 Annual Report* as one of a number of institutional variables.

Jordan, Jerry L. (1997). Jobs Creation and Government Policy. *Cato Journal* 16 (3) (Winter): 287–94.
Argues that employment-creating initiatives or job-creation policies hinder the creation of new technology and the process of "creative destruction." Also argues that the role of government

monetary intervention in the economy should be limited to creating stable monetary policy.
Makes reference to the general conclusions of *Economic Freedom of the World: 1975–1995* regarding economic freedom and income and growth.

La Porta, R., L. Lopez-de-Silanes, A. Shleifer, and R. Vishny (1998). The Quality of Government. NBER Working paper no. 6727. Digital document: www.nber.org/papers/w6727.
The paper uses quantitative measures of government performance to determine if countries with different institutional structures have better or worse governments. Historical factors such as legal structures, religion, and ethnolinguistics are used to evaluate economic, political, and cultural theories of institutions and their impact on government intervention, public-sector efficiency, provision of public goods, size of government, and political freedom.
Components of *Economic Freedom of the World: 1975–1995* are used as government performance measures, with several other variables.

Lim, Linda Y.C. (1998). Whose "Model" Failed? Implications of the Asian Economic Crisis. *Washington Quarterly* 21 (3): 25–36.
The paper examines the conflicting interpretations of the role of governments and economic freedom in the success and subsequent crises in Asia.
Cites conclusions of *Economic Freedom of the World: 1975–1995.*

Mbaku , John Mukum, (1998). Constitutional Engineering and the Transition to Democracy in Post-Cold War Africa. *The Independent Review* 2 (4) (Spring): 501–17.
Discusses the constitutional guarantees necessary to secure economic freedom and why such guarantees are important. Focuses specifically on Africa.
Makes reference to the general conclusions of *Economic Freedom of the World: 1975–1995* regarding economic freedom and income and growth.

Mbaku, John Mukum, ed. (1999). *Preparing Africa for the Twenty-First Century: Strategies for Peaceful Coexistence and Sustainable Development.* Aldershot, UK and Brookfield, VT: Ashgage.
Chapter 6, A Balance Sheet of Structural Adjustment in Africa: Towards a Sustainable Development Agenda (John Mukum Mbaku) and chapter 12, Making the State Relevant to African Societies (John Mukum Mbaku) emphasize the constitutional guarantee of economic freedoms as the single most important way both to generate the wealth that Africans need to meet the challenges of the new century and to deal more effectively with the continent's colossal debt.
Makes reference to the general conclusions of *Economic Freedom of the World: 1975–1995* regarding economic freedom and income and growth.

Milhaupt, Curtis (1998). Property Rights in Firms. *Virginia Law Review* 84: 1145–94.
Discusses how differences in property rights and corporate governance systems arise within differing institutional frameworks.
Uses the Property Rights component of *Economic Freedom of the World: 1975–1995* as one of a number of institutional variables in case-study analysis.

Nelson, Michael A., and Ram D. Singh, (1998). Democracy, Economic Freedom, Fiscal Policy and Growth in LDCs: A Fresh Look. *Economic Development and Cultural Change* 46 (4) (July): 677–96.
The study examines the effect of democracy on economic growth after controlling for a number of variables for the size of government and institutions. The study finds that it is not the redistributive policies of democratic governments that hinder development in developing countries but the lack of economic freedom.

Uses the precusor to *Economic Freedom of the World,* Measuring Economic Freedom, by James Gwartney, Walter Block and Robert Lawson, a chapter in Stephen Easton and Michael Walker (eds.), *Rating Global Economic Freedom* (Vancouver: The Fraser Institute, 1992). The summary ratings of Measuring Economic Freedom are used as one variable in a comparison of a number of variables for institutions and the size of government.

Norton, Seth W. (1998). Poverty, Property Rights, and Human Well-being: A Cross-national Study. *Cato Journal* 18 (2) (Fall): 233–45.
The paper compares property rights to indicators of development and determines that the "well-being of the world's poorest inhabitants [is] sensitive to the cross-national specification of property rights." The paper shows that well-specified property rights enhance the well-being of the world's most impoverished.
*Economic Freedom of the World: 1997 Annual Report* and the Heritage Foundation's *Indices of Economic Freedom* are the main data source for institutional variables.

Norton, Seth W. (1998). Property Rights, the Environment, and Economic Well-Being. In Peter J. Hill and Roger E. Meiners (eds.), *Who Owns the Environment* (Rowman & Littlefield): 37–54.
Investigates whether countries with better property rights have better performance on environmental measures.
Uses the summary ratings of *Economic Freedom of the World: 1975–1995* as one of four measures used as proxies for property rights.

Oi, Walter (1999). The Hearty and Cheery State. *Contemporary Economic Policy* 17 (1) (January): 138–46.
Argues that human capital is a consequence of growth, not a cause, and that economic freedom allows the best chance for economic progress.
Makes reference to the general conclusions of *Economic Freedom of the World: 1975–1995* regarding economic freedom and income and growth.

Park, Walter G., and Juan Carlos Ginarte (1997). Intellectual Property Rights and Economic Growth. *Contemporary Economic Policy* 15 (July): 51–61.
The authors have compiled an index of intellectual property rights, and examine its effects on growth and the factors of production (investment, schooling, and R&D). "The paper finds that IPRs affect economic growth indirectly by stimulating the accumulation of factor inputs like R&D and physical capital."
Uses summary ratings of *Economic Freedom of the World: 1975–1995* as a control variable for market institutions in the analysis.

Rose, Andrew (2000). One Money, One Market: Estimating the Effect of Common Currencies on Trade. *Economic Policy* (forthcoming). Digital document: http://haas.berkeley.edu/~arose/Grav.pdf (December 1999).
Investigates the effects of exchange-rate volatility and currency unions on international trade. the author uses the summary ratings to test the sensitivity of his model of trade between nations. Finds a statistically significant relationship between trade among nations and economic freedom.
Uses the summary ratings from *Economic Freedom of the World: 1997Annual Report* as one of a number of variables.

Vamvakidis, Athanasios (1998). Explaining Investment in the WAEMU [West African Economic and Monetary Union]. International Monetary Fund, working paper WP/98/99.
Relates differences in investment as a share of GDP within the West African Economic and Mone-

tary Union to differences in economic freedom using fixed and random-effects models across time. *Economic Freedom of the World: 1975–1995* is the main data source for institutional variables.

Vásquez, Ian (1998). Official Assistance, Economic Freedom, and Policy Change: Is Foreign Aid Like Champagne? *Cato Journal* 18 (2) (Fall): 275–86.
Makes reference to the general conclusions of *Economic Freedom of the World: 1997 Annual Report* regarding economic freedom and income and growth and argues that foreign aid is propping up countries that are not economically free. Mr Vásquez also tests the notion that aid agencies target pro-growth policies. He finds that for the countries where economic freedom declines or does not improve, foreign aid actually increases (19 of 20 cases). As well, in over one-half of these countries GDP per capita declines.
Makes reference to the general conclusions of *Economic Freedom of the World: 1997 Annual Report* regarding economic freedom and income and growth.

Voigt, Stefan (1997). Positive Constitutional Economics: A Survey. *Public Choice* 90: 11–53.
Distinguishes between normative and positive constitutional economics, and between various concepts of the constitution.
Reference to *Economic Freedom of the World: 1975–1995* in a footnote.

Voigt, Stefan (1998). Making Constitutions Work: Conditions for Maintaining the Rule of Law. *Cato Journal* 18 (2) (Fall): 191–208.
Makes reference to the general conclusions of *Economic Freedom of the World: 1975–1995* regarding economic freedom and income and growth and discusses conditions under which the rule of law can be maintained.

Wu, Wenbo, and Otto A. Davis (Forthcoming). Two Freedoms, Economic Growth and Development: An Empirical Study. *Public Choice.*
"The main results are: given economic freedom, the rate of economic growth is independent of political freedom and the level of income; given the level of income, political freedom is independent of economic freedom and the growth rate. The analysis suggests the fundamental effects of economic freedom in fostering economic growth and a high level of income as the condition of a high degree of political freedom." The article also uses principle component analysis to weight the results published in *Economic Freedom of the World.*
*Economic Freedom of the World: 1975–1995* and Freedom House's *Economic Freedom Indicators* on political right and civil liberties are the main data sources for institutional variables.

Wu, Wenbo, and Otto A. Davis (1999). The Two Freedoms in a Growth Model. *Journal of Private Enterprise* 14 (2): 115–43.
The paper develops a theoretical model describing how economic and political freedoms might impact economic growth, then estimates the relative impact of the two on growth in the world as a whole, and for subsets of developing and developed nations.
Summary ratings from *Economic Freedom of the World: 1975–1995* provide a key institutional variable.

Yago Glenn, L. Ramesh, D. Brumbaugh, and J. Barth (1999). *Capital Access Index: Deconstructing Global Financial Architecture: Global Capital Access and Policy Backlash.* Santa Monica, CA: Milken Institute.
The paper focuses on the institutional structures that are involved in capital flows, globalization, and financial crisis. The *Global Capital Access Index* is presented as a means of comparing the financial markets of different countries.
Components of *Economic Freedom of the World: 1975–1995* used in compiling the *Global Capital Index.*

